THE ANTICHRIST
and a Cup of Tea

Tim Cohen

PROPHECY HOUSE, INC.
P.O. Box 461104 · Aurora, CO 80046-1104
www.prophecyhouse.com

To receive Tim Cohen's *Truth in Prophecy* **newsletter,** visit
http://www.prophecyhouse.com/news on the Internet.

Where indicated, Scripture quotations in this book are from the Authorized King James Version of the Bible.

THE ANTICHRIST AND A CUP OF TEA
First edition

Copyright© 1998 by Tim Cohen (TJMH)

March 1998, Prophecy House, Inc.

ISBN 0-9662793-0-1
Bar-code "mark" intentionally omitted from cover.

Library of Congress Catalog Card Number: 98-84509

Printed in the United States of America

Contents

Endorsements

The AntiChrist and a Cup of Tea was originally planned as an appendix to the author's upcoming and much more comprehensive work entitled *Messiah, History, and the Tribulation Period.* Due to significant delays in completing that overall work, however, demand grew from various reviewers of its early drafts, as well as others who heard of them, to publish the material that follows sooner rather than later. Since this material became quite voluminous, easily amounting to a work in its own right, it made sense not to publish it as a large appendix to *Messiah, History, and the Tribulation Period,* but as an entirely separate book. Any endorsements or portions of endorsements cited for *Messiah, History, and the Tribulation Period* below, except where noted, also apply to this book, *The AntiChrist and a Cup of Tea,* inasmuch as they were given when it was still a part of the former:

can see our times.

There are several concepts that were truly impressive to me. I particularly was transfixed by your analysis of Passion Week as a template for understanding the expanse of human history and Daniel's seventieth week. I will ponder your insight and watch as human history and the future unfold. Your book serves to help me understand contemporary times....

— **Ken Klein** • Founder, Ken Klein Ministries, Inc.
Author, *The False Prophet*

Regardless of whether one agrees with all of Tim Cohen's conclusions, his masterpiece work *Messiah, History, and the Tribulation Period,* provides great food for thought. Articulately written, by a Messianic Jew with a deeply personal understanding of Scripture, this provocative book is well researched and thoroughly documented. I commend Tim for the balance maintained in his research and for his non-sensational, scholarly approach....

At the very least, his presentation reaffirms our faith and hope in the risen Christ, while heightening our sense of urgency to share the good news with a lost and dying world. It also causes one to re-examine some popular views on eschatology by bringing together many intricate details and little known facts, and applying them to current world developments....

Challenging, informative, and timely, Tim Cohen's material is must reading!

— **Gary Kah**[1] • Founder, Hope for the World
Author, *En Route To Global Occupation*

....Bible prophecy has once again become an object of major attention on the part of the world and even the church....

....Provocatively titled, this book should become the object of the fascination of many and the even more careful attention of the thoughtful readers of our time. The reader will find many unique interpretations of Holy Scripture in the pages of this book. [Yet]...unique interpretations become the first appearance of what may grow into standing theological positions in the church. ...[No doubt] every reader will be instantly fascinated....

It is a part of the providence of God that the Lord will bring new things to the attention of people.... This certainly will be the case with the reading of this book on the part of many....

....It takes no great capability to note developments *ex post facto* (which is so much the case in our time). Rather, it is of great value to know or even suspect the awful destiny of people and causes in advance. Tim Cohen may well be such a person [with such capability], valuable to the church, both now and in the increasingly provocative days to come. His book is surely destined to affect many an opinion both now and in the future. Prophetic developments are surely upon us and they will be examined with greater clarity by many as a consequence of *The AntiChrist and a Cup of Tea.*

— **David (Dave) Breese** • President, Christian Destiny, Inc.
Author, *Seven Men Who Rule the World from the Grave*

The AntiChrist and a Cup of Tea by Tim Cohen is the most comprehensive study of why Prince Charles could be the AntiChrist. What is more important than the AntiChrist's identity, [however,] is the AntiChrist system that this book uncovers. For the first time, the average person can understand the organizations that are already in place that will allow one man to control the

---

1. Note that Kah gave this endorsement after reading an early draft of *The AntiChrist and a Cup of Tea,* when it was still an appendix to *Messiah, History, and the Tribulation Period.*

world. This book is must reading for those who desire to understand the real power brokers behind the New World Order.

— **Sid Roth** • Author and President, Messianic Vision

THE ANTICHRIST AND A CUP OF TEA by Tim Cohen is a fascinating book that connects the history of the royal family of England to end-time prophecy. The section dealing with the interpretation of the complicated and intricate designs in Prince Charles' Coat of Arms is especially intriguing. Tim was a guest on our ministry for a series of programs and received a tremendous response. History buffs and students of prophecy will enjoy this book.

— **Noah Hutchings** • President, Southwest Radio Church
Author, *Y2K = 666?*

Rarely has a book been so thoroughly researched! The uniqueness of Tim Cohen's work is the way he brings so many facts together that point to a possible candidate for the man the Bible describes as "Antichrist." You may disagree with his conclusion, but you cannot argue with the thoroughness and details of his presentation. The historical "connections" are worth the price of the book alone. May this work prepare us all to be aware of how world events are coming together and fulfilling God's plan, and may it lead those who read it to a personal knowledge and commitment to the true Messiah as our only hope and salvation.

— **David Hocking** • Author and President, Hope for Today

Whenever someone points to a specific individual and suggests that this is indeed the anti-Christ, I start looking for the nearest exit. However, while I am still out with the jury on this one, I have to tell you that this book is one of the most captivating studies on the British Monarchy's leadership involvement with the occult, world wide Freemasonry and the New World Order that you could imagine.

— **Ed Decker** • Founder, Saints Alive in Jesus
Author, *The Dark Side of Freemasonry* and *The God Makers*

[We] have Tim Cohen's provocative new book..., *The AntiChrist and a Cup of Tea*.... Essentially, the entire book presents a fairly solid case for [Prince] Charles as a possible candidate for [the role of the] Anti-christ. It is definitely worth a read!

— **William (Bill) Schnoebelen** • Founder, With One Accord Ministries
Author, *Wicca, Satan's Little White Lie* and *Masonry, Beyond The Light*

....[*Messiah, History, and the Tribulation Period*] is...characterized by broad and vast Biblical knowledge.... I found myself fascinated by your assembling of facts and consequent interpretation.... This fascination certainly extended to your presentation of the future significance of the Prince of Wales. Any reader will...absorb more knowledge than would be the case from nearly every prophetic manuscript he has read....

I recommend the book to students of the Word of God everywhere and particularly those who desire an in-depth knowledge of the prophetic scriptures. ...I would quicken the interest of potential readers by reminding them that Cohen also suggests the possible identification of the anti-Christ. A reading of *Messiah, History, and the Tribulation Period* will be a worthwhile investment of time and intellectual energy.

— **Dave Breese**

...Tim Cohen has written a fascinating and quite amazing integration of the prophetic Scriptures. Its integration of the ages of history and the last days is...unique and new.... The book is detailed and provocative. [*Messiah, History, and the Tribulation Period* is]...a unique contribution to [the study of] prophetic history and eschatology.

— **Daniel Juster** • President, Tikkun Ministries
Author, *Revelation: The Passover Key*

Cohen has written a thought-provoking, riveting, concept concerning the possible identity of the antichrist.... Could this be one of the mysteries Daniel speaks of which will be revealed in the last days? Only time will tell if Cohen's extensive research is correct....

— **Larry Bates** • Founder, Monetary & Economic Review
Author, *The New Economic Disorder*

Mr. Cohen has made an important contribution to the ongoing prophetic debate with *Messiah, History, and the Tribulation Period.* His attempt to integrate the best points of virtually all major schools of prophetic interpretation is, as far as I know, unprecedented in modern times—and he carries it out with remarkable success. Not only that, but just when we thought there was nothing more that could be said about biblical prophecy, Cohen actually manages to plow some interesting new ground on several issues. Whether or not you agree with all of his conclusions, you will find the presentation to be logical, provocative, and thoroughly-researched.

— **Gary Hedrick**[1] • President, The Christian Jew Foundation

Nothing today is as important as the truth of God's plan of redemption and salvation in the Messiah. Cohen has succeeded in not only summarizing very lucidly the many strands of theological Messiology and the Biblical end-times, but he has also given us a new and comprehensive presentation of the subject....

This challenging book fulfills a serious need for a detailed, balanced, informed and sober accounting of prophetic Biblical history. Cohen respectfully provides what I believe to be one of the best windows to glimpse accurately the centrality of the Person and work of Jesus Christ in history and apocalyptic prophecy.

I endorse *Messiah, History, and the Tribulation Period* and know that readers will find here an inspiring and reliable reference work on Christology, Israelology, Biblical Chronology, and Eschatology.... Clearly it is a bold help to the cause of Christ.

— **Rick Drebenstedt** • Pastor and Director, Menorah Ministries

...Tim Cohen's *Messiah, History, and the Tribulation Period*...is...a ground-breaking, major eschatological "gem." ...Cohen's work ventures well beyond ordinary 'Last Days' scenarios and controversies to chart new and illuminating territory, as in his unique harmony of Christ's Crucifixion/Resurrection Week with Scripture's History and Tribulation Weeks. This particular exposition's devotional value alone makes *Messiah, History, and the Tribulation Period* 'meat' doubtless to be profitably chewed on and digested by scholars, clergy and laity alike, for the remainder of this present age and perhaps throughout Eternity.

— **Anton Marco**
Author, *100 Jews Who Met Yeshua and Lived to Tell Others*

1. Please note that Dr. Hedrick has declined either to read or endorse the present work out of a belief that the Church cannot now know the identity of the AntiChrist. Nevertheless, his endorsement of *Messiah, History, and the Tribulation Period* stands.

Preface

In 1956, during the Suez Canal Conflict between Israel and Egypt, my mother and her family fled Egypt as secular Jewish refugees. I was born nine years later, in May 1965. In July 1984, I enrolled in the class of 1988 at the United States Air Force Academy (USAFA), and in November 1986, I received Jesus as my Savior and LORD. When I received Jesus, I was a second-class cadet (junior) at USAFA. Although my experiences at the academy had rarely been what I would call "good," USAFA proved to be the cauldron of affliction from which God would give me the perseverance and strength to proceed with this work. As a born-again Levite or "Jew," I soon realized that my calling in life had little to do with serving in the United States military. My life had been turned upside down.

After reading the entire New Testament, the five books of Moses (Torah), and many of the prophecies in the Old Testament, I found myself increasingly drawn to study the scriptures, to the point where I was unable to concentrate on my studies. One day in early 1987, while walking toward Arnold Hall, my thoughts settled on Revelation 13:18. That was the second day in less than a year that God turned my life upside down. On that day, I prayed for wisdom according to what is written in James 1:5-6 and Revelation 13:18. Within one month of that momentous prayer, a local pastor by the name of Monte Judah invited me to an unusual sabbath meal. While there, Monte showed me his preliminary information on what would become the main subject of this book—Prince Charles of Wales. That information included the prince's English name calculation and a rather poor black and white photocopy of an unofficial version of his heraldic achievement. Through Monte, The LORD challenged me to re-examine what I had been taught to that point concerning eschatology, much of which I subsequently concluded to be false.

I returned to my dorm room at USAFA following that sabbath meal, where I proceeded to tell various classmates

9

that I was going to write a book. At the time, I knew only that the book was to concern biblical prophecy. With that revelation, however, I completely dropped my academic studies, and began the process of voluntarily resigning from the academy. While awaiting a decision from the Secretary of the Air Force, I pursued research on a wide variety of scriptural subjects. This research led almost immediately to a color copy of the official version of the heraldic achievement of the Prince of Wales, which I found in a book on heraldry in the Cadet Library.

In November 1987, my resignation was accepted. Because I resigned in my final year at USAFA, however, I was required to enlist for a period of three years. While training for that enlistment in Texas, I met another man by the name of Steve Klein. Steve spoke of the fact that he and his wife were home-schooling their daughters, to which I made the off-the-cuff remark, "In a little over seven years, you won't have to worry about that." Steve oddly responded, "I hear you," and then invited my room-mate and I to have dinner with his family that evening. When Steve arrived to pick us up, he brought with him a large copy of the official lineage of Queen Elizabeth II. Up to then, I had said nothing to Steve. The lineage later proved to be of great value in preparing this particular work.

Following the war with Iraq in 1990, I left the service. During my period of enlistment, The LORD not only pro-vided me with a condominium, but enabled me to save suf-ficient funds to live for years without work. Over the next three years, I researched the subjects of biblical history and eschatology, and wrote, full-time.

This book, *The AntiChrist and a Cup of Tea,* is merely the first published fruit of ten years of research and writing. As such, it was originally a part of a much larger work still in progress. That work, entitled *Messiah, History, and the Tribulation Period*, is foretold—from my perspective—by a childhood event.

At the age of ten, I enjoyed my only oceangoing fishing trip to date. The night before the "big event," unknown to me, my father and ten other adults—all family members who had prior experience—decided to add some excitement to the event. Each one would contribute $3.00 to a pot, which they decided would be divided in three. The person who caught the first fish would receive $11.00, as would the one who caught the largest and the one who caught the most. Almost from the moment we threw our lines in the next morning, I called to my father for help; something was pulling fiercely on my line, and as a child, I simply lacked the strength to reel it in. With my father's help, however, I was soon staring at a *large* and rare silver salmon. That day, my father caught the most fish, while I caught just one—the first *and* the largest![1]

That event was, if you can receive it, prophetic of my future. From an allegorical standpoint, this book is a part of my childhood silver salmon. May reading it bless you, as writing it has blessed me.

This work is dedicated
to the only God and Savior,
Christ Jesus — יֵשׁוּעַ הַמָּשִׁיחַ.

---

1. At the same time that I was writing this introduction, my father was, unknown to me, publishing his own recollection of this event. As my father recalls, "'Hey Dad,' Tim whispered in my ear, 'isn't this unfair if we know we're going to take their money?' The subject of ten-year-old Tim's concern was a pool my brother and father were creating to add a little spice to our more-or-less annual salmon fishing charter. We were at Ilwaco, Washington, not far north of the mouth of the Columbia River. Eleven of us—all family—would kick in three bucks apiece. One buck each for the one catching the day's biggest salmon, the first salmon, and the most salmon. 'Yep,' I nodded to Tim. 'It's probably unfair.' I smiled and put our six dollars in the pot" (James L. H., "Salmon," *Wild Winds and Other Tails of Growing Up in the Outdoor West* {Washington: Reecer Creek Pub., 1997}, p. 123).

Acknowledgments

The author would like to thank the following individuals for their help, provision of research materials, prayers, and encouragement to persevere in this work: Larry Bates, Chris Beard, Dave Breese, Ray Brubaker, Gisela Chase, David Clarke, John Coleman, John Daniel, Rick Drebenstedt, Mark Ensign, Jodi E., Gary Hansen, David Hocking, James H., Mardie H., Dave Hunt, Roger J., Grant Jeffrey, Monte Judah, Daniel Juster, Gary Kah, Ken Klein, Steve Klein, William Koenig, Larry Kunk, Henry Lamb, Ben Levi, Charlie Osborne, Tom McKenney, Jim Searcy, William Schnoebelen, Sam Schulstad, Fritz Springmeier, Joan Veon, James Wardner, Rob Williams, Dave and Rebecca W.[1]

---

1. Certain individuals and certain last names have been omitted as necessary. To them, the author also extends his thanks.

Introduction

Christians today are often unwilling to debate the possible identity of the AntiChrist, *no matter how compelling the evidence*. Many who are aware of past errors of various prophecy teachers, "scholars," and "authorities," have come to presume that no one can possibly know the Anti-Christ's identity in advance. Others hold this view for what they, until now, have thought were valid theological reasons. These Christians are not the first to ignore, overlook, or misunderstand Revelation 13:18 and other passages related to the AntiChrist. Like many in the past, they have made precisely the opposite mistake of those mentioned above; they have gone to the other extreme of those who have—without proper biblical grounds—made unjustified, speculative, sensational, spurious, and, at times, even outrageous claims concerning the character and identity of the AntiChrist. Those who have erred and those who are mistaken will find *The AntiChrist and a Cup of Tea* to be fundamentally different.

The careful reader will, the author believes, discover that *The AntiChrist and a Cup of Tea* not only presents one of the most thorough treatises on the subject of the Anti-Christ ever written, but it also, without being overly sensationalistic, distinguishes a remarkably well-qualified candidate—*Prince Charles of Wales*—from the plethora of past and present offers.

As a general rule, it is proper that the Church be wary of those who either falsely or mistakenly "claim to be able to identify end-time characters or dates," who instead manage only to discredit Christianity in the eyes of unbelievers. We must point out, however, that the Church is not left without a *clear* means to discern the false from the genuine, something which most Christians, both today and in the past, have unfortunately overlooked. That is, the Apocalypse offers an unmistakable test for *anyone* who would claim to possess a true understanding of the apocalyptic eschatology, a test which, *in the specific context of*

Revelation 13:1-3, is found in Revelation 13:18. Whoever ultimately *passes* that test will differ from others who either sincerely, or for personal gain, daily misinterpret and sensationalize the eschatological scriptures. The study of *biblical* eschatology has been obscured through the centuries by a wide variety of pretenders; in no century has this proven more true than in ours today. Several examples could be cited, not the least of which is the identity of the coming AntiChrist. While many have tried and failed in the past to identify the AntiChrist, the Word of God plainly states that there will be at least one man, and probably others (cf. Dan 2:20-23, 11:32-35, 12:3; Matt 24:15), who, according to Revelation 13:18, shall not only try, but actually *succeed*—"him who has understanding." To the extent that such a man shall have "understanding," so shall he understand the eschatological scriptures in general.

Friend, do not be *unwise*, but wise. Do not rashly assert, contrary to the authority of the written revelation of God (cf. Rev 1:1-3), that such a preordained—even prophesied—call should be abandoned simply because others have gone astray and deceived the body of Christ; for the whole Church has this inspired admonition, "Here is wisdom: <u>Let</u> him who has understanding...." Indeed, may God grant those who are *faithful* to believe the teachings of His written Word real wisdom and understanding, and may he confound those who from *impure* motives insist they have understanding, but deceive and lie.

Many Christians are uncomfortable with the mere suggestion that a *known* individual—especially one like Prince Charles—could be the AntiChrist. The author has even encountered individuals who, as true "newspaper exegetes," would sooner accept a convenient pulpit or media stereotype—regardless of its veracity—than permit themselves to undertake a genuine, biblical consideration or study of the evidence at hand, be it objective or circumstantial.[1] As the scripture says, however, "He who

1. Penny Junor, noting "the trivia and the lies" printed by the media, observes, "The simple fact of the matter was that their readers were more interested in reading about gossip from inside the Palace than about worthy schemes for the inner cities, and if people didn't get it in their usual paper they would change to another" (*Charles* {New York: St. Martin's Press,

answers a matter before he hears it, it is folly and shame to him" (Prov 18:13, AKJV). One pastor, who is heavily involved in the Pensacola "revival," for example, has said, "[Prince] Charles has become an increasingly pathetic figure, and there is no possible way that the Jewish people, or the Muslims, or the Americans (to name just a few ethnic or religious groups) will ever look to him as their world leader." Another pastor, who speaks and teaches as a prophecy "scholar," flatly stated, "Nobody knows who the Antichrist is because he hasn't been revealed yet—maybe a *nephelim*.... To think the people around the world would follow Prince Charles is just ridiculous.... Every born-again believer will know it when the Antichrist has been revealed." Such statements, as this work makes evident, are perhaps *precipitous*.

Friend, there is a side to Prince Charles, as well as to the British monarchy as a whole, that has been carefully hidden from the public and most media—a side that reveals power, influence, fame, and wealth *totally unimagined* by the carefully led and spoon-fed public. It is this side, examined in the context of Bible prophecy, that *The Anti-Christ and a Cup of Tea* addresses. No one who has read this book will ever view the British royal family, or the monarchy's sordid history, in the same propagandized, even brainwashed, light again. As we shall see, the power, influence, fame, and wealth of the British monarchy undergird the entire elitist push for global government, and has done so for centuries. This behind-the-scenes reality has made Prince Charles perhaps *the* central figure among globalists of every sort today. The Prince of Wales, as difficult to fathom as it may be, is literally without peer or serious rival on the globalist stage.

This book is intended for those who will study to show themselves approved, who would sooner accept the Word of God than their own, or another's, predispositions; it is for those who desire *real* wisdom and *genuine* prophetic understanding. If you are in this latter category, then may God bless you and grant you discernment as you proceed.

1987}, p. 222). At best, this is merely a surface explanation.

As you may have already noticed, *The AntiChrist and a Cup of Tea* requires some effort to fully digest. However, if you are like most Christians today, you will find it challenging, thought-provoking, and surprisingly informative. Be a noble Berean (Acts 17:10-12), and you may discover "a word fitly spoken," like "apples of gold in pictures [settings] of silver" (Prov 25:11).

In this book, we will first consider the *modus operandi* of the coming global government, along with the Anti-Christ's probable rise to power in the United Nations Security Council by means of the European Union (chapter 1). Subsequently, we will examine the following:

✓ *who it is* whose royal hegemony over the European Union has already resulted in a request to be its king (chapter 2);

✓ *who it is* whose name calculates to 666 in both English and Hebrew, using the scriptural system (chapter 3);

✓ *who it is* whose lineage places him at the head of the Merovingian dynasty, and asserts descendancy from Israel's King David, Jesus, and Islam's Mohammed, as well as the tribe of Dan and Satan (chapter 4);

✓ *who it is* whose royal ancestors have claimed to sit upon the throne of David for nearly two millennia (chapter 5);

✓ *who it is* whose heraldic achievement is a literal depiction of the satanic imagery associated with the Anti-Christ in both the Old and New Testaments, whose oligarchical powerbase is behind the quest for a New World Order (chapters 6 and 7);

✓ *who it is* whose current power, throne, and "great authority" *literally* derive from the "red dragon" or Satan (chapter 8);

✓ *who it is* whose agenda is specifically geared to address the many ominous and prophetic "signs of the times"—and what those signs are—through "global governance" (chapter 9);

✓ *who it is* whose multifaceted religious, political, and

other ties are apparently set to position him as priest and prophet, not to mention king, to the world's major and minor religions—including apostate Christianity, Judaism, Islam, Hinduism, Buddhism, Zoroastrianism, Wicca, and satanism—and who is a global "mover and shaker" with vast potential wealth (chapter 10);

✓ *who it is* whose media exposure has already exceeded that of every other man in history, who exercises authority over Freemasonry and the Illuminati worldwide, who heads the United World Colleges, who instigated the recent rise in popularity of alternative medicine (good and bad) in the West, who is credited for the success of the watershed 1992 Earth Summit in Rio de Janeiro, who steers the environmental ethics and business agendas for as many as one-hundred or more of the world's largest multinational corporations, who is said to have personally initiated the United Nations' Global Security Programme, and who has already partnered with the World Bank and the United Nations Development Programme in an attempt to achieve a new form of global governance that emphasizes sustainable development and globalist education through public-private (government-business) partnerships worldwide (chapter 11);

✓ *who it is* whose New World Order agenda is reflected in his apparent personal instigation of the entire Mideast "peace process," which to date has resulted in Israel's Oslo I and II accords with the Palestinians as well as a peace treaty between Israel and Jordan (chapter 12);

✓ *who it is* whose life has already been threatened by "terrorists" on several occasions (chapter 13);

✓ *who it is* whose heraldic coat of arms may one day be associated with the image and mark of the beast, and who has already taken an electronic bio-chip implant for personal security (chapter 14); and, finally,

✓ *who it is* whose overall qualifications appear to make him *the first real candidate ever* to fulfill the role of the prophesied AntiChrist (chapter 15).

17

Translations. Issues of translation are important to this work. At times, unfortunately, no currently extant English translation of a passage of scripture is sufficiently accurate or literal to convey a significant point of its underlying Hebrew or Greek text. In such circumstances, it is necessary to turn to the original autographs. Consequently, some of the best and most reliable Hebrew and Greek manuscripts and lexicons were consulted in the course of researching and writing *The AntiChrist and a Cup of Tea*. *Referenced* translations include the Authorized King James Version[1] and Baker's *Interlinear Greek-English New Testament*. No references are made to other published translations. Another work consulted, but not referenced, for example, was Hendrickson's *Interlinear Bible*. All interlinear texts consulted are Strong's coded (see below). In several instances, for the sake of complete accuracy or to bring out some significant point, the author has taken the liberty of offering literal modern-English translations, taken from the Bible's original Hebrew and Greek autographs, as indicated. In an effort to make the original Hebrew and Greek of the Bible more accessible to most readers, *The AntiChrist and a Cup of Tea* employs Strong's reference numbers when examining specific Hebrew and Greek words.[2]

Notice to the "establishment." Although the author is not a "conspiracy theorist" by nature, he has nevertheless taken precautions appropriate to this work. Prior to publication, encrypted electronic copies of this edition of *The*

---

1. Where AKJV or KJV is specified, the use of the King James Version is stressed.
2. Although various scholars dismiss Strong's system, in which most Hebrew and Greek words of the Bible are alphabetized and sequentially numbered, as insufficient and occasionally inaccurate, others find its reference numbers highly useful. Lexical works consulted, most of which are coded to Strong's numbering system, include *The New Englishman's HEBREW CONCORDANCE; The New Englishman's GREEK CONCORDANCE and LEXICON;* William Gesenius' *HEBREW-CHALDEE LEXICON of the OLD TESTAMENT; The New Brown-Driver-Briggs-Gesenius Hebrew-English Lexicon* (Francis Brown, S.R. Driver, and Charles A. Briggs {Massachusetts: Hendrickson Publishers, 1979}); the second edition of the revised *BAG* Greek-English Lexicon (Walter Bauer, William F. Arndt, and F. Wilbur Gingrich, *A Greek-English Lexicon of the New Testament and Other Early Christian Literature,* 2nd ed., rev. F.W. Gingrich and Frederick W. Danker {Illinois: The University of Chicago, 1979}); Joseph Thayer's *GREEK-ENGLISH LEXICON of the NEW TESTAMENT;* James Strong's "A Concise Dictionary of the Words in the Hebrew Bible" and "A Concise Dictionary of the Words in the Greek/New Testament" (*STRONG'S EXHAUSTIVE CONCORDANCE OF THE BIBLE*).

AntiChrist and a Cup of Tea were placed in the hands of trustworthy individuals, around the world, who have the means at their disposal to distribute them widely. *Others* were given the necessary keys to decrypt those copies, which exist in Adobe Acrobat, embedded Novell Envoy, and Internet formats. Should *any* significant harm befall the author (including a serious "accident"), or should the author or his publisher be threatened or subverted, so as to significantly hinder or effectively stop the publication, advertisement, marketing or distribution of *The AntiChrist and a Cup of Tea,* these individuals, who are *not* known to one another, will automatically provide their respective contacts with the necessary keys to decrypt the work for worldwide distribution. Furthermore, the author, who holds the copyright to said work, hereby grants explicit permission to any individual residing in any country where *The AntiChrist and a Cup of Tea* is **banned or disallowed** to **FREELY** copy and distribute said work **solely within that country;** all rights, however, shall remain reserved. Such explicit permission shall be *irrevocable* upon the author's untimely demise or the start of the Great Tribulation, when half of Jerusalem is taken captive.

1

The Footsteps of *the* AntiChrist

The AntiChrist and his denials of God's eternal Truth are explicitly mentioned just four times in the Bible, in only two epistles (1 John 2:18, 2:22, 4:3; 2 John 7). Nevertheless, the biblical identity of the coming AntiChrist is a subject that has fascinated both Christians and non-Christians alike for nearly two millennia. Unfortunately, this fascination has often led to unwarranted speculation. The AntiChrist, when he takes up his role, will not be easy to spot. In fact, apart from the biblical criteria, he will be all but impossible to recognize. To most, he will not be an obviously evil man—at least not initially. Rather, he will live up to the dual meaning of the prefix, "anti," in his New Testament designation. He will be *against* the real Christ while at the same time setting himself *in His place*.[1] To set himself in The Messiah's place, the Anti-Messiah must ultimately be able to convince the unregenerate world that he *is* the "Messiah"—for *all* peoples and *all* religions. As Satan's unorthodox parody of Christ, he will be a counterfeit "Christ," and his disciples and followers, therefore, whatever their religious persuasions, will be counterfeit "Christians."

Although the false prophet is not a major subject of this treatise, some points are relevant. Many have held through the centuries that the false prophet and even the AntiChrist would arise from the Roman Catholic Church. Christians of all backgrounds recognize that while Roman Catholicism has historically advocated a Judeo-Christian morality, it nevertheless remains, in many respects, a pagan religion—a curious mixture of the holy with the profane. According to Revelation 13:11, the false prophet will have "two horns like a lamb," and speak like "a dragon." It seems especially noteworthy, therefore, that Rome's

---

1. For more information, see the section titled "Daniel 9:27 and the Latter Halves of the Weeks" in *Messiah, History, and the Tribulation Period*.

current pope, John Paul II, wears a "two-horned" miter which, around its base, depicts the pope as a lamb wearing the miter. This lamb, *because of the papal miter shown on its head,* actually looks like it has two horns.[1] This same pope, who has "two horns like a lamb," routinely makes statements revealing his intolerance for true Christians, his antichristian ecumenism, and his worship of "Mary" and the dead, which Roman Catholicism euphemistically call "saints." In other words, John Paul II speaks like "a dragon," even the red dragon or Satan (Rev 12:3, 12:9). Given the pope's "Marian devotion" (i.e., worship), it seems only appropriate to note that the author has encountered statements attributed to a Roman Catholic priest and theologian asserting that "Mary" is calling faithful congregants to receive a mark in their hand or forehead for protection from coming catastrophic judgments (cf. Rev 13:16-17). Based upon this and other information, the author agrees with those who have argued that the false prophet, who shall work to exalt the AntiChrist, could readily be Rome's final pope (see Rev 13:11-17, 16:13-14, 19:20; cf. 20:10).[2] Moreover, as we shall see, many of the ancestors of this book's subject—the strongest candidate ever for the role of the AntiChrist—were Roman Catholic. Indeed, the European Union (E.U.) has begun to actively promote Roman Catholicism to the exclusion of true Christianity.[3]

Past suggestions for the identity of the AntiChrist have included Antiochus IV, Caligula, Charlemagne, Mohammed, Napoleon, and Nero. Suggestions in this century, now mostly abandoned, have included Alister Crowley, Francisco Franco, Adolf Hitler, John F. Kennedy, Ayatollah Kohomeini, Benito Mussolini, Yitzhak Rabin, Ronald Reagan, Franklin Delano Roosevelt, and Joseph Stalin. Current suggestions include Yasser Arafat, George Bush, Juan Carlos, Bill Clinton, Louis Farrakhan, Bill Gates, Boutros Boutros Ghali, Mikhail Gorbachev, Al Gore, Otto von

1. Associated Press photograph of the pope in Italy, *The Denver Post,* 29 Sept. 1997, p. 13A.
2. For more information, see the section titled "The History of the Roman Empire and its Modern Thirst for Oil" in *Messiah, History, and the Tribulation Period.*
3. See, for example, Adrian Hilton, *The Principality and Power of Europe* (England: Dorchester House Publications, Box 67, Rickmansworth, Herts WD3 5SJ; 1997).

Habsburg, Saddam Hussein, Henry Kissinger, "Maitreya," Sun Myung Moon, John Paul II, Shimon Peres, Prince Philip, and Maurice Strong. *None* of these suggestions seems truly plausible. Walvoord observes,

> An almost unlimited number of identifications of antichrist to specific historical characters can be found. Among the more prominent are Mohammed, the founder of the Muslim faith; Caligula, a Roman emperor who claimed to be God; and Nero, a popular candidate for the title because of his burning of Rome and persecution of the Jews and Christians. To these can be added almost every prominent ruler of the past, including more modern characters such as Napoleon and Mussolini. In all these historical identifications, there is little more than evidence of being antichristian, but the variety of claims leaves the concept of [*the*] antichrist in considerable confusion.[1]

Indeed, there must be far more than merely antichristian beliefs and activities on the part of a person to justify a consideration of him as *the* AntiChrist. Any individual under serious observation must not only have antichristian beliefs, but also be capable of fulfilling every biblical prophecy related to the AntiChrist, *without exception.* Such a person, for example, must have a name or title that calculates to precisely six-hundred and sixty-six, preferably using a system that was recognized within Judaism — by both believers and unbelievers — when the Apocalypse was first penned (see Rev 13:18). Also, he must be associated in some manner with the imagery of the beast described in Daniel (ch. 7) and the Apocalypse (chs. 12, 13, 17, and 18). Further, he must be a prominent ruler, presumably a prince, of Roman lineage (Dan 9:26-27). Some scholars would even add that he must be a descendent of Israel's tribe of Dan (discussed later).

Besides the biblical "musts" for qualification, there are, in this author's opinion, some prudent "shoulds." Any individual under consideration should have a prominent royal and religious lineage that will be viewed as proof-positive of his claims to world-leadership by all the world's major religions and cults. Also, he should have diverse royal, religious, political, military, and economic connections, as

1. "ANTICHRIST," *The Zondervan Pictorial Encyclopedia of the Bible,* 1976 ed., Vol. 1, p. 179.

well as substantial wealth, to aid in his transition to power. Finally, he should be a man whom the world loves and desires to follow (despite any moral shortcomings he may exhibit), and who appears to be willing and able to cope with global problems and crises (e.g., the environment, religious and ethnic disputes, etc.).

Of course, there are also mistaken criteria. To these lists, for example, many prophecy teachers, "scholars," and "authorities" would add, *incorrectly,* that according to Isaiah 13, Jeremiah 50 to 51, and a host of other Old Testament passages and prophecies, the AntiChrist *must* be of Assyrian and/or Babylonian origin. Others would assert that he will be the King of the North prophesied in Daniel 11 who shall reject the "God of his fathers," meaning The God of Israel, as well as the "desire of women," being a homosexual. However, in their geographical, historical, and scriptural contexts, these prophecies all speak of an individual who shall reside in the "land of the Chaldeans," or what is today modern Iraq, where Saddam Hussein has been rebuilding the ancient capital cities of Nineveh and Babylon. The first capital geographically of the King of the North or the Seleucid dynasty, for example, was *Seleucia* on the Tigris River, or what we now call *Baghdad.*[1] In other words, a man from the region of modern Iraq will fulfill outstanding prophecies concerning the Assyrian, the Babylonian, *and* the King of the North.

Scripturally and historically speaking, the King of the North will *not* reject the "God" of his fathers, implying The God of Israel, but the "gods" (see below) of his fathers, meaning the particular pagan deities to whom his fathers bowed down. Likewise, the King of the North will *not* be a homosexual who wants nothing to do with women. He will *not* reject the "desire of women," meaning women in

---

1. Seleucia (on the Tigris River), the Seleucid dynasty's first capital, was located just a few miles north of Babylon and *barely south of modern Baghdad* (*The Harper ATLAS of the BIBLE,* ed. James B. Pritchard {New York: Harper & Row, Publishers, Inc., 1987}, p. 144). Soon thereafter, a second capital was set up at Syria's Antioch, though Seleucia Pieria (just north of the mouth of the Orontes River in the northeast corner of the Mediterranean Coast), one of nine cities bearing Seleucus' name, was also prominent ("SELEUCIA," Vol. 5, *The Zondervan Pictorial Encyclopedia of the Bible,* 1976 ed., p. 331). Today's Iraq, the capital of which is Baghdad, not only contains the ancient cities of Babylon and Nineveh, but it was the heartland of the Seleucid dynasty, from which arose Antiochus IV Epiphanes.

general, but The Messiah, whom ancient Israel *and* the pagan world acknowledged as both "The Desire of women" (Dan 11:37) *and* "The Desire of all nations" (Hag 2:7)—the promised Seed whom women desired to bear from antiquity (Gen 3:15). In fact, Daniel 11:40-45 depicts the King of the North, or Iraq, in a future conflict with the King of the South, or Egypt, so that the King of the North shall overflow Egypt and overthrow other countries, come against Israel, and then ultimately be destroyed in connection with "news from the east and the north" (cf. Jer 51:33). The King of the North "shall regard neither the gods [Heb., *elohee*] of his fathers nor The Desire of women,[1] nor regard any judge [god; Heb., *eloha*]; for he shall magnify himself above *them* all. But in their place he shall honor a god of fortresses [munitions]; and a god which his fathers did not know he shall honor with gold and silver, with precious stones and pleasant things. Thus he shall act against the strongest fortresses with a foreign god, which he shall acknowledge, *and* advance *its* glory; and he shall cause them to rule over many, and divide the land for profit" (Dan 11:37-39, Heb.; cf. Rev 6:7-8). In their proper contexts, these prophecies all speak of what is now Iraq; they do not speak of the AntiChrist, but of a separate player who shall come upon the world scene during the Tribulation Period.[2] To conclude *on this basis* that

1. In the Zodiac, The Messiah is called "The Desired One" (cf. Hag 2:6-7). For more information, see the section titled "The Gospel and the Zodiac" in *Messiah, History, and the Tribulation Period*.
2. Modern scholars generally overlook the fact that Iraq, the heartland of ancient Assyria and Babylonia, is the historical land of the King of the North, whom the prophet Daniel predicted would conquer much of the Middle East and come against Israel and Mount Zion in the last four years of the Tribulation Period (Dan 11:40-45). Yet Iraq's Saddam Hussein is currently preparing to play the same role in modern history that Babylon's Nebuchadnezzar II played in the destruction of ancient Jerusalem.

   While the Mystery Babylon of the Apocalypse is a global, spiritual Babylon of the last days, possibly with Roman Catholicism at its heart, the Old Testament contains numerous prophecies that apply solely to the role of ancient Babylon (i.e., Babylon in the land of the Chaldeans) *in the Tribulation Period*. The last days, therefore, will see prominent roles for both the ancient Babylon of history under the King of the North and the worldwide, figurative Babylon under the AntiChrist. Unlike other works, this book and the author's forthcoming *Messiah, History, and the Tribulation Period* recognize these distinctions. For a balanced and thorough treatment of the different, but connected roles to be played by the literal Babylon of Iraq and the figurative Babylon of the world in the Tribulation Period, see the chapter titled "The Latter Halves of the Crucifixion, History, and Tribulation Weeks" in *Messiah, History, and the Tribulation Period*.

the AntiChrist will be the King of the North, an apostate Jew or a "Christian" who has rejected the "God" of his fathers, or a homosexual who rejects the "desire of women," is, in all candor, to show some ignorance of the subject matter. As a result of this kind of *isogesis,* many Christians now have misguided expectations concerning the AntiChrist.

We must be more careful in our handling of the Word of God. Our criteria for recognition of the AntiChrist, let alone understanding any other subject of Bible prophecy, must have a sure foundation. At best, the AntiChrist could *theoretically* be of Assyrian *and* Babylonian descent, as well as of Jewish extraction with "Christian" ancestors, but he must also be a prince of Roman lineage who shall come to rule over the modern Roman Empire (cf. Dan 9:27).[1] This makes the AntiChrist a fundamentally different personage from the King of the North; that is, prophecies given concerning the King of the North do not pertain to the AntiChrist.

Friend, have you heard the *footsteps* of the AntiChrist? Is there anyone in the world today who meets all these qualifications? Undoubtedly, many Christians would answer "yes," pointing to someone such as Rome's pope, or the King of Spain, or Gorbachev or Boris Yeltsin, or even overtly wicked men such as Saddam Hussein or Yasser Arafat. The list goes on. Yet, while these individuals are antichristian, none of them meets the required qualifications or "musts," let alone the "shoulds." In fact, with just *one* exception, no human being has ever met more than half of them. Who is that exception? Before answering this question directly, let's first consider the method of the AntiChrist's eventual rise to political power in the light of history, apocalyptic prophecy, and a few current events.

The Roman Empire had its religious, political, military, and economic roots in ancient Babylon, which in turn had

1. Non-futurist methods of apocalyptic interpretation are generally beyond the scope of this particular work. However, for a detailed and reliable examination of the major views (i.e., the idealist or symbolic, preterist or contemporary-historicist, historicist, futurist, preterist-futurist, historicist-futurist, etc.), as well as the first true, *Messiah*-centered harmonization of them, see the concluding chapters titled "Harmonization of the Crucifixion, History, and Tribulation Weeks" and "The Harmony of Weeks" in *Messiah, History, and the Tribulation Period.*

its own in the Tower of Babel. Offering no apologies and showing no shame, the modern European Union has depicted this very tower under construction below an inverted pentagram of twelve stars, a parody of its own counterfeit crown. The E.U.'s purpose, therefore, is to preside over the construction of a final "Babylon project," or the much heralded New World Order. Of course, the Council of Europe began to show its true colors early on, when the president of its Consultative Assembly from 1949 to 1951, Paul-Henri Spaak, proclaimed, "What we want is a man of sufficient stature to hold the allegiance of all people, and to lift us out of the economic morass in which we are sinking. Send us such a man and, be he god or the devil, we will receive him."[1]

In the latter half of the fourth-century A.D., Emperor Valentinian split the Roman Empire into two divisions, as depicted by the two legs in the statue of Nebuchadnezzar's prophetic dream (cf. Dan 2:33), not to mention the two horns of the false prophet (Rev 13:11). The Western Roman Empire retained Rome for its capital and maintained the Roman Catholic Church, whereas the Eastern Roman Empire adopted Constantinople (Byzantium) and formed the Eastern Orthodox Church.

Today, the most powerful country in the West, and perhaps the world, is the United States of America. It also happens to be the home of the United Nations—the embryo of a coming one-world government. The permanent member-states of the United Nations' Security Council currently include Russia, France, China, England, and the United States—the central powers in the Roman Empire over the past several centuries. Even so, the basic East-West division remains, with Russia representing the East

---

1. Hilton, *The Principality and Power of Europe*, pp. 19, 113. The European Union's flag depicts a crown of twelve gold stars against a light blue field. It specifically took this imagery from the woman crowned with twelve stars in Revelation 12. The primary interpretation of that woman, in context, would be that she represents faithful or believing Israel, in which case her crown of stars represent at once the twelve tribes of Israel and the twelve apostles of Christ, to whom the woman gave birth. This is a complex apocalyptic metaphor, one that has important secondary interpretations. However, none of those interpretations may be harmonized with the E.U.'s perversion of the imagery to represent itself. Indeed, the E.U. was more straightforward when it depicted those same stars in the arrangement of an inverted pentagram (ibid., pp. 49-50).

and the United States representing the West. Soon, however, in preparation for a global government under the Anti-Christ, ten horns or kings (representing nations or kingdoms — probably the world's most powerful and/or populous) will arise and supersede these divisions (cf. Dan 7:20*a*, 7:24*a;* Rev 12:3, 13:1, 17:3, 17:7, 17:12). Five will arise from each division (the statue had five toes per foot), being, it would appear, both autocratic and democratic (the feet and toes were a mixture of iron and clay; cf. Dan 2:41-43). This East-West group of ten will, in effect, govern the entire Earth.

Ten horns or kings will therefore constitute the governing body of the final form of the Roman Empire. These kings will be *contemporaries,* so that five shall arise from the East and five from the West. Notice, therefore, that three of the ten kings will be subdued, perhaps in an effort to consolidate power, by an unusual little horn — the Anti-Christ — who shall come in among them as the eleventh (see Dan 7:8, 7:20-21, 7:24-25).[1] Thus, we are told in the Apocalypse that "the beast that was, and is not, is himself also the eighth, and is of the seven..." (Rev 17:11). That is, when counted with the seven contemporary kings who remain in direct power, the AntiChrist will be the eighth, while at the same time, perhaps genealogically, being "of the seven."[2] Nevertheless, the Apocalypse also indicates

1. In speaking of the rise of "the worthless shepherd" over Israel, Zechariah indicated that three other sheperds—presumably Lebanon, Bashan, and Jordan (according to context)—would be "dismissed...in one month" (see Zech 11:1-9, 11:15-17, KJV; cf. Zech 10:2-3; John 10:12-13). This prophecy foreshadows the ultimate "worthless shepherd," or the AntiChrist, who will quickly subdue three of ten kings or "shepherds."

2. Some have observed that according to the *World Book Encyclopedia,* seven emperors of the "Holy Roman Empire" were named Charles. They then note that the prince is a descendant of Charles V, and that the prince will supposedly be Charles VIII. This view is flawed, in that Prince Charles has said that he will one day be known as King Charles III (not VIII). Moreover, by the apostle John's day, the fifth king or kingdom had fallen (Rev 17:10), whereas Charles V was born over a millennium *after* John. The seven kings or *kingdoms* of Revelation 17:10-11, while serving as a prophetic introduction to the seven of ten *contemporary* kings, so that the AntiChrist "is himself also the eighth," as outlined above, are *first of all* the seven *successive* world *kingdoms* of history (preceding the Millennial Kingdom of Christ): "five have fallen" (i.e., Egypt, Babylonia, Assyria, Medo-Persia, and Greece), "one is" (i.e., Rome—from the apostle John's day until now—which constitutes a metamorphosed revival of the ancient Babylonian Empire), and "the other has not yet come, and when he [it] comes, he [it] must continue a short while" (Gk.; cf. Rev 12:12, 13:5). This seventh kingdom, which "has not yet come," will be the global kingdom under the AntiChrist centered at Mystery Babylon, which, although it shall scripturally represent the final form of the Roman Empire in world history (e.g., its ten kings derive from the East-West division of the Roman

that there will yet be *ten* kings, not just seven, under the AntiChrist at the time of Jesus' posttribulational return (Rev 17:12-14). With this in mind, we have no choice but to conclude that the subdued kings will be retained and/or replaced, so that the total number of ten is maintained. If the AntiChrist is to keep his status as the eighth king, however, then these other three would necessarily become his vassals over their respective nations or kingdoms.

This can be a difficult scenario to envision, yet *there is a plausible means by which the AntiChrist's government could without suspicion or significant delay be so formed.* For example, should a *third* nation from the European Union (e.g., Germany), along with four other nations (e.g., Brazil, India, Japan, and Mexico), become a permanent member-state of the U.N. Security Council, as proposed (see below), and should the AntiChrist then arise over the E.U. *as its royal king or head,* the world would *suddenly* have just such a government. That is, the nations would awake one morning only to find that the AntiChrist had automatically acquired (been granted really) sovereignty over three of the ten permanent member-states—England, France, and presumably Germany—governing them, giving him a major or even decisive influence over the other seven. Such a scenario seems most feasible, in the author's opinion, should the AntiChrist be from England, the land that has given the modern world its most widely spoken language—English—and which opposed Nazi Germany and its French collaborators in World War II.[1]

At this point, we would do well, perhaps, to recall the infamous program falsely styled as "The Protocols of the Elders of Zion," which, having been circulated throughout much of this century, states, "Certain members of the seed of David will prepare the Kings and their heirs.... Only the King and the three who stood sponsor for him will know what is coming." Note the phrase "the three who stood sponsor for him." These blasphemous "protocols" appear

---

Empire), shall also be unique. The AntiChrist's global kingdom will, in both a literal and an historical sense, be "of the seven" (e.g., religiously, politically, and militarily).

1. For more information, see the section titled "The History of the Roman Empire and its Modern Thirst for Oil" in *Messiah, History, and the Tribulation Period.*

not to have originated with true Israelites, per se, but with the English-dominated, French-English oligarchical *Priory of Zion.* Consequently, as would be expected from the British monarchy's claims to supposed *Davidic* descent, they purport to plot the establishment of a worldwide "Masonic kingdom" with "an international church" under "the King of the Jews" who "will be the real Pope."[1]

As shown below, globalists have been planning their world government around a future U.N. Security Council consisting of ten permanent member-states. Following Gorbachev's revelation of the fact in 1992, a media blackout ensued. In 1997, however, a number of articles were suddenly released on the issue, indicating that the planned expansion may be just around the corner:

> What he seems to envision is a transition from the system of nation states, inherited from the 18th century, to a more internationalized system that can be more effective in many areas, from controlling nuclear weapons to protecting human rights. He wants a stronger United Nations, with new [permanent] members—including Japan, Germany, Mexico, Brazil and India—added to the Security Council. He wants...to build on trends toward interdependence already set in motion.
>
> Gorbachev said the world's peoples face a turning point in history and need new ways to cope with the challenges, from pollution to economic disparities between rich and poor nations. One way to this end, he added, is to work for greater world integration of "all spheres of human activity," and to do so in the framework of a "democratically organized world community."
>
> Only by moving in this direction, Gorbachev said, can the world hope to control the deadly rivalries that have flared anew among nations and ethnic groups....
>
> [In fact,]...many other political thinkers are embracing similar views. They cite growing world acceptance of treaties on nuclear proliferation and acid rain, and increasing respect for making basic rights globally enforceable....
>
> The former Soviet president is hardly alone in envisioning a strikingly new era of adjustment in the world order. Professor Joseph Nye of Harvard, in the current issue of *Foreign Affairs,* writes that the classic concept of sovereign national states is eroding under "the rapid growth in transnational communications,

1. Michael Baigent, Richard Leigh, and Henry Lincoln, *Holy Blood, Holy Grail* {New York: Dell Publishing, 1983}, pp. 191-195. Please note that the authors of *Holy Blood, Holy Grail* are antichristian, and their works are contrary to God's inspired Word. For more information, see Chapter 4, "Prince of this World—a *Diverse* Lineage."

migration and economic interdependence." This suggests, he adds, that the ideas of "divisible and transferable sovereignty may play an increasing part in a new world order."

....[Nye argues that] Americans should welcome it. Why? Because, says Nye, it promotes stability and security and reduces the risk of nasty surprises.[1]

UNITED NATIONS — A proposal to enlarge the United Nations Security Council from 15 to 24 members by adding five new members with permanent seats and another four serving a two-year term each, was presented Thursday by the chairman of a working group which has been studying council reform for the past three years.

The proposal was drawn up by Razali Ismail, Malaysia's representative, who is also president of this year's General Assembly.

It represents his best attempt to find a compromise on the immensely sensitive issue of the future composition of the organ charged with maintaining international peace and security acceptable to the largest number of United Nations' members.

"The underpinnings of this proposal are based on the need to enhance the representativeness, the credibility, the legitimacy and the authority of the Security Council," Razali told the working group Thursday, saying they would strengthen the council's ability "to deal with issues of peace and security."

The plan calls for the election of two new permanent council members drawn from the industrialized world.

The seats are likely to go to Germany and Japan, both of which are seeking permanent membership in recognition of their economic strength.

The three other new permanent members would be drawn from Africa, Asia and Latin America respectively.[2]

1. Brian Dickinson, Scripps Howard News Service, "Gorbachev envisions warmer post-Cold War world," *Rocky Mountain News,* 11 May 1992, p. 53.

According to Gorbachev, there is an "emerging [international]...awareness of the need for some kind of global government—one in which all members of the world community would take part" (Lindsey, *Planet Earth—2000 A.D.,* p. 57). In establishing his more recent "Gorbachev Foundation USA," he pontificated, "This is the symbol of our irreversible transition from an era of confrontation and militaristic insanity to a New World Order, one that promises dividends for all" (*The Los Angeles Times,* 17 Apr. 1993; see Lindsey, *Planet Earth—2000 A.D.,* p. 61). As the embryo of a world government, to complement a stronger World Court, Gorbachev advocates a greatly strengthened United Nations, one that would possess its own international police force and military structure, incorporating not only the conventional forces of its permanent member-states, but even their nuclear weapons. Such a government, Gorbachev believes, could best serve the cause of peace in our day and have the power necessary to enforce the collective security of the world in the process. Regarding a stronger World Court, we may note the U.N.'s *Genocide Treaty.* Signed even by the United States, this treaty has to date largely been ignored by the U.N. Security Council in the face of true ethnic atrocities and widespread infanticide. In the future, however, it could be used to imprison or execute Christians for a wide variety of "offenses," including opposition to cults, other religions, immorality, and the mark of the beast.

2. The New York Times, "Security Council expansion backed," *The Denver Post,* 21 Mar. 1997,

UNITED NATIONS — The United States will recommend that three permanent seats on the U.N. Security Council be given to developing countries to strengthen their role in global affairs, U.S. officials announced Thursday.

U.S. Ambassador Bill Richardson said the United States also would support permanent membership for Germany and Japan, raising the number of council members from 15 to 20. Currently, 10 of the 15 are chosen by region and serve two-year terms but do not have veto power.

Richardson said a special U.N. committee studying Security Council reform should decide whether the new permanent members would have the same veto power as the United States, Britain, France, Russia and China.

In Washington, State Department spokesman Nicholas Burns said it was up to the developing countries from Asia, Africa and Latin America to decide whether to choose a permanent representative or rotate countries in and out of the seats.

Supporting an enhanced U.N. role for the developing world appeared to be designed at least in part to win their support for Secretary-General Kofi Anan's plan to restructure the U.N. bureaucracy.[1]

India is seeking a permanent seat on the Security Council when the U.N. expands its membership.[2]

UNITED NATIONS — After a crucial push from the United States, the United Nations is about to tackle the tough issue of expanding the 15-member Security Council, the most powerful single agency in the world body.

If the changes go through, Germany, Japan and three or more nations from the developing world will join the United States, Britain, China, France and Russia as permanent members of the council.

The result, supporters say, would be a group more reflective of today's balance of power and more authoritative in its efforts to maintain global law and order....

But the risk is that the power of authoritarian, antidemocratic states within the United Nations would increase and the influence of the United States diminish.

Bill Richardson, the U.S. envoy who has propelled the process forward....views the challenge with characteristic optimism. "We're going all out to get (Germany and Japan) on the Security Council," he told reporters here before launching a 10-nation trip

p. 19A.
1. Robert H. Reid, The Associated Press, "Developing countries posed for U.N. panel," *The Denver Post*, 18 July 1997, p. 23A. Also see "U.S. eyes expanded U.N. council," *Rocky Mountain News*, 18 July 1997, p. 52A.
2. Ved Nanda, "50 years of Indian independence," *The Denver Post*, 15 Aug. 1997, p. 7B.

largely devoted to cultivating support in world capitals for council changes and other U.N. reforms....

While the United Nations is made up of 185 countries, each with an equal vote in the General Assembly, the real seat of power is in the elite membership of the Security Council.

And, to paraphrase George Orwell, in the Security Council, some countries are more equal than others, for the five permanent members are endowed by the U.N. Charter with veto power over any council action.

The U.S. goal is to win agreement on a framework for council expansion by year's end and postpone until later some of the toughest decisions, including which developing countries get to join Germany and Japan as new members and whether any get veto power....

Giving Germany and Japan permanent status, supporters say, would recognize their economic and diplomatic clout. Similarly, adding developing countries would grant recognition to the emerging importance of nations such as South Africa, Egypt, India and the "economic tigers" of Southeast Asia.[1]

---

1. Craig Turner, Los Angeles Times, "U.N. may expand Security Council," *The Denver Post*, 17 Aug. 1997, p. 4A.

2

A Man for Our Times

In *The English Constitution,* Walter Bagehot, a Victo-
rian constitutionalist, made this statement: "All the world
and the glory of it, whatever is most attractive, whatever
is most seductive, has always been offered to the Prince of
Wales of the day, and always will be. It is not rational to
expect the best virtue where temptation is applied in the
most trying form at the frailest time of human life."[1]   At
Buckingham Palace on November 14, 1948, just six
months after the birth of modern Israel, Prince Charles was
born; the following day, he was christened. Then, some
time before July 1992, notwithstanding the fact that the
British monarchy is "the largest constitutional monarchy
remaining in the world, [and]...the highest remaining office
on earth attained by birthright,"[2] the prince, who has
increasing worldwide popularity, began to make his global
aspirations known by declaring, "I want to be King of
Europe!"[3] In March 1995, in a passionate speech to the

1. Anthony Holden, *PRINCE CHARLES* (New York: Atheneum, 1979), p. xxiii. Royalty, 1994, Vol.
   13, No. 2, p. 47.
2. Alan Hamilton, *The Royal 100* (London: Pavilion Books Ltd., 1986), p. 22.
3. Rexella Van Impe, *Jack Van Impe Presents,* KDVR TV Fox 31 (Denver, CO), 14 June 1992.
   Please be aware that while the author possesses a photocopy of a picture of Prince Charles
   having the caption "I want to be King of Europe," the same one shown by Mrs. Van Impe,
   he has thus far been unable to identify the actual publication or article from which it was
   originally taken, as well as its precise date. The following text, however, is found above the
   picture and its caption: "personally made his influence felt throughout the European community, in a way that no other royal has. When, for example, can you remember a speech
   made by the Grand Duke of Luxembourg or King Carl Gustav of Sweden? Prince Charles
   focused his attention beyond Britain's shores long ago. In 1970, when he was 23, he
   chaired the Welsh steering committee for European Conservation Year. That job had the
   two-fold effect of opening his eyes to the conservation problems, not only in Britain, but
   also in the European nations. He has been, in effect, a committed European for two
   decades. His contacts have strengthened over those years. His family's German connections
   have helped Charles understand the nature of Europe's most economically successful nation.
   At the other end of the scale, the friendship he forged with King Juan Carlos of Spain
   (despite the unfortunate row over Gibraltar, which prevented the King from attending Charles's wedding) has given him an [sic]." The prince and Juan Carlos have not only met in the
   past, but vacationed together (Brian Hoey, *Charles & Diana: The Tenth Anniversary*
   {England: Colour Library Books Ltd., 1991}, pp. 142-143, 152-153).
      In the July 11, 1994, broadcast of *Jack Van Impe Presents,* Mrs. Van Impe noted, "Here is

British Council, he further stated, "We must act now to ensure that English—and that, to my way of thinking, means English English—maintains its position as the world language well into the next century."[1] King Farouk once said, "Soon there will be only five kings [in the world]—four in a pack of cards, and the King of England."[2]

Helen Cathcart observed, before the prince had even reached the age of thirty, that heredity had "already caused the personality of Prince Charles to be more assiduously studied and underscored by historians than that of any other young man of our contemporary world.... On his mother's side alone the compound is bewilderingly English,

---

the man who would *like to play* a prominent role in the E.U. and the New World Order; his name is Prince Charles." Jack Van Impe, who categorically asserts, "The AntiChrist will arise out of the European Union," responded, "Prince Charles has put in a request to become the King of the European Union—the head man!" While mistakenly touting the prince as a possibility for the false prophet (if he is anything, he is the AntiChrist), Mr. Van Impe also pointed out that Prince Charles wants to be the king and religious head of, among others, those who adhere to Zoroastrianism (see below), the *old Babylonian religion* (KDVR TV Fox 31, as well as TBN TV 47 and 57 {Denver, CO}). Zoroastrianism, which predicates itself upon the ancient struggle of good against evil, is believed to have originated with Zarathushtra among the Aryans of ancient Persia, whose antichristian religious philosophy may itself be traced back to the "Indo-Iranians," then to the "Indo-Europeans," and finally to the Tower of Babel. The Achaemenid dynasty, which ruled the later Medo-Persian Empire after Babylonia had been conquered under Cyrus the Great, spread Zoroastrianism to Babylonia and elsewhere. The main royal palace of the Achaemenids was Persepolis in Persia. The still later Parthian Empire, so-named after the region of Persia from which it arose, again took up the cause of Zoroastrianism, making it a major world religion by the first century A.D., when the ancient Roman Empire was at its zenith. Under subsequent Muslim persecution, some Zoroastrians left Persia in the tenth century for India, where they became known as the Parsis. While thousands of Zoroastrians remain in Persia, the Parsis now have Zoroastrian communities not only in India, but also in Pakistan, East Africa, Britain (primarily in London), the United States of America (primarily in New York), and Canada (*Eerdmans' Handbook to the World's Religions* {England, 1982; rpt. Michigan: Wm. B. Eerdmans Publishing Co., 1987}, pp. 80-87, 221).

Anthony Holden, in *King Charles III,* offers this speculative, but interesting, fiction concerning Prince Charles' future: "The year is 2015. The new King Charles III, approaching his seventieth birthday, reigns over a proud but tired old Britain.... The monarchy is as popular as ever, thanks to Charles's hard work during the old age of his late mother.... As he enters his thirties[,] William, Prince of Wales,...has high hopes of his new chairmanship of the British Design Council, currently campaigning to ensure that his father's profile appears on the new 'Eurodollar' banknotes soon to be standardized throughout the EEC" ({London: George Weidenfeld & Nicolson Limited, 1988}, p. 203).

1. "Charles: Stop dissin' English," *The Denver Post,* 26 March 1995, p. 2A. Note that since the prince first delivered this speech, the congress of the United States has introduced and passed legislation "to declare English the official language of the United States and limit the federal government from conducting business in foreign tongues" ("Official English bill passes the House," *The Denver Post,* 2 Aug. 1996, p. 22A).
2. As Junor tells it, "King Farouk of Egypt, deposed by a military coup in 1952, once predicted that by the year 2000 there would be only five monarchs left in Europe: the four kings in a pack of cards and the King of England. He could yet be proved right" (p. 259).

Scottish, Welsh, Danish, Germanic, Dutch, French and Russian, with traces of Spanish, Portuguese and other elements sufficient for the Common Market community to view him as a characteristic contemporary synthesis of European man.... Charles may claim to be the most democratic Prince of Wales ever bred."[1] Cathcart, in a somewhat remarkable allusion to the prince's global aspirations, adds, "Chevening lies only twenty-two miles southeast from the heart of London.... [In] Chevening the heir to the throne saw a country house where he could visualise entertaining European and Commonwealth heads of government in his own way, where world leaders of every clime would be able to meet in small groups while enjoying his hospitality, forging new friendships while beneath his roof. It would be entertainment without political or government strings, informal and eventually in a family atmosphere, like the Commonwealth itself.... ....In America, on meeting some ladies who called themselves 'Daughters of the British Empire', as members of an association by that name, he had pressed tender nerves.... 'It would make you more relevant,' he said, 'if you called yourselves "Daughters of the British Commonwealth". And when I come back next, I hope you'll be calling yourselves "Daughters of THE Commonwealth".'"[2] Although Princess Diana had once said of Prince Charles, "He is a doting daddy and does everything perfectly,"[3] the prince has since evidenced different priorities: In 1991, as his son William was undergoing emergency surgery for a near-fatal head wound, "Prince Charles left [the hospital] to go to Covent Garden opera house, where he was host to a party of European Community officials."[4]

Comprised of fifty-three nations and about one-fourth

1. Helen Cathcart, *Prince Charles* (New York: Taplinger Publishing Co., 1977), pp. 1-3. Perhaps more biographies and other biographical material have been written on Prince Charles than *any other contemporary figure,* living or dead, and yet the prince has only *just begun* to make his mark in the annals of history. For more information regarding the prince's lineage, see Chapter 4, "Prince of this World—a *Diverse* Lineage."

2. Cathcart, pp. 158-159. Daughters of the British Empire, which has about 5,000 members nationally, "is comprised of British immigrants, many of whom are war brides, English women who married American servicemen during World War II" (Stacie Oulton, "Denver-area residents pay respects to a princess," *The Denver Post,* 7 Sept. 1997, p. 15A).

3. *Charles & Diana: A Royal Family Album* (New York: Summit Books, 1991), p. 30.

4. "Diana, Her True Story," *Good Housekeeping,* August 1992, p. 178.

of the world's population (cf. Rev 6:8), the Commonwealth of Britain represents all that is *overtly* left of Britain's once globe-encircling empire. Meeting every two years, the Commonwealth remains linked by Britain's language (English), *monarchy, Illuminist Freemasonry*—and cricket. As one writer put it, "Britain still presumes to wield a special sort of global influence."[1] (Actually, she does—and it is by no means benign.) Prince Charles, for example, has observed, "I am sure many people consider that the United Kingdom is in an ideal geographical and historical position to act as an interpreter and mediator between the United States and Europe."[2] From the British monarchy's standpoint, as we shall see, "all roads lead to London." Adrian Hilton states, "It is yet to be decided who will actually *play* Charlemagne in the new empire, but the political leaders—particularly of France and Germany—understand that monetary economics is the instrument of political leadership, and that the wider the currency's domain, the greater the power of those who control it.... The truth is that Britain is at the heart of the world."[3] "Charles," of course, is merely the modern form of "Charlemagne."

Concerning Prince Charles, Jonathan Dimbleby adds, "it is only the very unwise who dismiss him as an anachronism." According to Dimbleby, the prince is "a man for all seasons and for none, a man for his time but not of his time," a man who "rages...at the folly of the world.... Yet...he stands outside the age in which he lives.... If there is always lingering about him an air of sadness, it springs in part from...a sense of the sorrows which he believes the human race is storing up for itself."[4] Mankind, the prince asserts, faces "what could be a final settlement." As Junor puts it, the prince is a "leader of men, a potent force for good and for change."[5]

Whether or not Prince Charles ever becomes King of the European Union or King of England, he could fulfill the

1. Maureen Johnson, "Empire wanes, but Britons keep stiff upper lips," *The Denver Post*, 10 Oct. 1993, p. 21A.
2. Junor, p. 271.
3. Hilton, *The Principality and Power of Europe*, pp. 125, 133.
4. Jonathan Dimbleby, *The Prince of Wales* (Great Britain: Little, Brown & Co., 1994), pp. 404, 565.
5. Junor, pp. 3, 273.

previous chapter's scenario. Consider, for example, the following. Should the E.U. choose to establish its own constitutional monarchy, as Prince Charles appears to have already suggested, the prince need not be accepted as its king to wield control. As it is, Prince Charles performs a wide range of functions on behalf of his mother, Queen Elizabeth II. If the Queen of England—who, as "the world's most traveled woman,"[1] is "universally admired"—were chosen to head such a monarchy rather than her son, the Prince of Wales would nonetheless be the one to exercise that authority. As the queen ages, this reality will only grow. Under such circumstances, Prince Charles could not only gain control of a world government, but he would retain his numerically significant name (and title), "Prince Charles of Wales."[2] In either case, what better way could the E.U., which sees England as an essential but uncertain and somewhat unpredictable partner, strengthen the United Kingdom's commitment to it. Moreover, in a very real sense, the British royal family *is* the royal family of France, Germany, and the other European nations.[3] Prince Philip, the Prince of Wales' father and the Duke of Edinburgh,[4] is fluent in French, German, English, and Greek.[5]

With all this in mind, we should perhaps also observe that the E.U., in its official publication *Europe's Star Choice,* singled out the United Kingdom's flag, or the Union Jack, for sharp criticism due to its failure to represent Wales.[6] Interestingly, the red dragon, or Satan (Rev 12:3, 12:9), is literally the national heraldic symbol of Wales,

1. *Her Majesty The Queen* (Hong Kong: Purnell Books and Intercontinental Book Productions, 1980), p. 36. Before the death of Princess Diana, the queen perhaps had a rival.
2. For more information, see the next chapter, "A Name that Calculates to 666."
3. The British monarchy has particularly strong ancestral ties to France, Germany, and Spain, as well as many other European and non-European nations, through their former and current national monarchies. It is perhaps noteworthy that according to spokespersons for the Priory of Sion (Zion), "in the near future, there would be a dramatic upheaval in France—not a revolution, but a radical change in French institutions that would pave the way for the reinstatement of a monarchy" (Baigent, Leigh, and Lincoln, *Holy Blood, Holy Grail*, p. 225). For more information, see Chapter 4, "Prince of this World—a *Diverse* Lineage."
4. Upon marrying then Princess Elizabeth, England's King George VI made the young Philip Duke of Edinburgh, Earl of Merioneth, and Baron of Greenwich. In 1957, after ten years of service to the realm, Philip's wife, Queen Elizabeth II, made him a prince (Junor, p. 23).
5. Denis Judd, *Prince Philip* (New York: Atheneum, 1981), p. 65.
6. Hilton, *The Principality and Power of Europe*, pp. 50-51.

being central to the Welsh flag. It will take no genius, therefore, to realize that Prince Charles himself could immediately rectify this "unfortunate oversight," since that same Welsh dragon is uniquely integral to his royal heraldic achievement (coat of arms) as the Prince of Wales.[1] Of course, inasmuch as the prince frequently enjoys the media spotlight, there have been both sober, responsible statements and seemingly sensationalistic, irresponsible statements made about him. Herein, a relevant, proper balance in both regards will be presented.[2] Along the latter line, for instance, the *Sun* ran this article:

1. For more information, see Chapter 7's section titled, "The red dragon, or Satan."
2. Certain well-meaning individuals and groups, who have at one time or another spoken to first-hand sources such as the author or Monte Judah, or who have obtained second-, third-, and even fourth-hand information, have begun to make statements and in some cases publish articles showing that Prince Charles may be the AntiChrist. Statements have been made on both radio and television programs, as well as before groups of prophecy buffs, and articles have appeared over the internet and in various ministry newsletters. Unfortunately, the accuracy of these statements and articles has largely been substandard. When dealing with subjects of such gravity, reliability and credibility are imperative.

    Texe Marrs, in his recent book, *Circle of Intrigue,* for example, asserts: "as a prime candidate [for the Inner Circle of the Illuminati and the role of the Antichrist,] we must consider Prince Philip.... Philip, who leads by default due to the stupidity and indiscretions of his son, Prince Charles, oversees Britain's powerful *United Lodge of Freemasonry,* and he presides over the secretive and monarchi[c]al *Order of the Garter.* The Prince is also director of the *World Wildlife Fund"* (p. 70). In point of fact, Prince Philip *does not lead anything* due to "the stupidity and indiscretions of his son," nor does he *directly* oversee the United Grand Lodge of England. Although the prince was offered the position of grand master of this lodge, he declined, allowing it to pass instead to Edward, the Duke of Kent, another Garter knight (Stephen Knight, *The Brotherhood* {London: Harper Collins Publishers, 1983}, pp. 211-212). Moreover, while Prince Philip is now a mason and a companion knight of the Order of the Garter, Queen Elizabeth II and Prince Charles, as the Prince of Wales, are the order's two highest-ranking members. Although Marrs has not documented his sensationalist points, he is, however, at least partially correct in these observations: "certain members of the Illuminati, including Prince Charles and Prince Philip, take part in the rituals and symbols of an odd secret society called the *Order of the Garter.* This Order, with its ceremonial magic, is thought to be a precursor to the coming establishment of the *Circle of the Round Table.* So demented are the leaders of the Illuminati that they fancy themselves to be the modern-day inheritors of the Arthurian legend. Upon the appearance, expected soon, of their great and divine king, or ruler, they would be knights of the Circle of the Round Table, noble and exalted co-rulers of Camelot" (pp. 70, 229). For information on the Illuminati, see Chapter 3, "Prince of this World—a *Diverse* Lineage," as well as the discussion on the Garter in Chapter 7, "The Heraldic Symbols in the Arms and their Interpretations."

    As another example, some have stated that Prince Charles is a vegetarian, and tried to relate this to tribulational events. However, the prince is not a strict vegetarian, inasmuch as he is said to occasionally eat red meat (Hoey, *Charles & Diana: The Tenth Anniversary,* p. 85). According to Diana, Prince Charles "suddenly went all vegetarian and wouldn't kill. His family thought he had gone mad,....but it all came back eventually in his own time. He does that—he has these crazes and then he drops them" ("Diana on the Family," *People* weekly, 20 Oct. 1997, p. 104).

Renowned psychic Sally Montefiore says she has seen "Charlie's angel" several times—and she's absolutely certain that it is watching over Charles.

"Nothing bad can happen to Prince Charles despite the treacherous situations he places himself in," says Sally. "It's almost like he is defying the angel to withdraw its protective shield from around him.

"But the powers of Charlie's angel...[are] extraordinary—and it won't let him down because he has a special destiny. Prince Charles will become King in 1994[1] and lead his nation back to greatness....

"Under his leadership Great Britain will emerge as a true superpower, just as she was 150 years ago."...

...."But the Prince has heard Mrs. Montefiore's claims about Charlie's angel—and he's starting to believe them himself...."

"Charles is not immortal but right now he certainly is immune from death or permanent injury," says psychic Sally....

"Anyone else would have been crippled or killed by the injuries Charles has endured.

"But he will not be harmed because great things await him."[2]

More recently, the popular press has even begun to latch onto "rumors" among Christians that Prince Charles may prove to be the AntiChrist. *Imagine that!* On January 1, 1998, the *Rocky Mountain News,* showing pictures of Prince Charles, Kissinger, Saddam Hussein, Hitler, and King Juan Carlos, observed, "Prince Charles...is the latest world figure to be identified as the antichrist by some believers."[3] Jean Torkelson, in a related article, wrote,

Many today believe the Antichrist has already been born....
Others are naming names.

"Prince Charles is supposed to be the Antichrist, according to the latest rumor," says the Rev. Chuck Wilkes, pastor of Highlands Ranch Community Fellowship....

"Last March was the last big date," says Wilkes. "That's when Prince Charles addressed the European congress, and that day, if you run out the mathematics (according to [those who say that] the Bible [in Daniel 9:27 is referring to the September 1993 Oslo I accord between Israel and the Palestinians]),...was supposed to be the day he revealed himself as the Antichrist [(i.e., the

---

1. So much for the false predictions of another false prophetess! Nevertheless, while 1994 has come and gone, Prince Charles may yet become Europe's king.
2. Ken O'Hara, "Charlie's Angel," *Sun,* 10 March 1992, p. 2.
3. "RECOGNIZE THE ANTICHRIST?," *Rocky Mountain News,* 1 Jan. 1998, p. 5A.

start of the prophesied Great Tribulation)].

"Obviously, that day came and went.".....[1]

What disturbs end-timers is not meeting Jesus, but a predicted enslavement of humanity by satanic forces.

Some end-timers see that happening now. They point to microchip tracking devices, which are being [im]planted in fish and cattle.

Grocery store bar codes are said to contain a secret reference to 666, the biblical mark of the beast.

Some suggest the common Internet prefix "www" refers to the sixth letter in the Hebrew alphabet, another mysterious stamp of 666 upon the world....

Meanwhile, the Roman Catholic Church officially considers the millennium as a time of optimism and hope.

Pope John Paul II has called for a Great Jubilee in 2000, a year to rejoice in the reality of salvation and to be reconciled with one another.[2]

Although much has been written regarding the Anti-Christ's personality and his probable relationship to Rome's papacy, few Christians possess a satisfactory understanding of how such an individual could possibly rise to world prominence. In *GLOBAL PEACE AND THE RISE OF ANTI-CHRIST,* Dave Hunt not only offers relevant historical information, but presents a thought-provoking scenario—one that, although entirely unintentional, points directly, as we shall see, to the Prince of Wales:

> SOMEWHERE, AT THIS VERY MOMENT,...the Antichrist is almost certainly alive—biding his time, awaiting his cue.... Already a mature man, he is probably active in politics, perhaps even an admired world leader.... [He] could be...of great wealth and behind-the-scenes influence, or a sports hero.... Somewhere he is being meticulously groomed....
>
> ....Even so, benevolence, prudence, integrity, and principle mark his circumspect public behavior. Certainly he seems to be no more evil than the accepted norm in today's amoral society. It may be that to this point in his life he is still convinced that his motives are altogether pure and unselfish.
>
> ....The Antichrist is so driven by his dream to rule—yes, perhaps in his own eyes, to *save*—the world, that he will pay any price, even satanic possession, to make his mark in history....

1. For more information, see Chapter 12's sections titled "Is the Church already in Daniel's seventieth 'week'?" and "Identifying the covenant of Daniel 9:27."
2. Jean Torkelson, "Antichrist among us, according to believers," *Rocky Mountain News,* 1 Jan. 1998, p. 20A.

....But Hollywood caricatures play into the hands of the real Antichrist, since no suspicion will rest upon this one whose admirable qualities so well conceal his dark designs....

....He will oppose Christ while pretending to *be* Christ....

....In fact, he will be the closest counterfeit of Christ that Satan can produce. Completely deceived by this brazen masquerade, the world will hail him as its deliverer.

And right there is where the plot thickens. If the Antichrist will indeed pretend to be the Christ, then his followers must be "Christians"!...

The world must be primed both religiously and politically to embrace the Antichrist when he suddenly rises to power. If "Christianity" is to be the official world religion (which must be the case if the Antichrist claims to be Christ), then it must become broad enough to accommodate all of the world's faiths. As for the political climate, the world must be united in the twin causes of global peace and ecological rescue when this man appears....

The mystery of godliness ultimately involves Christ turning men from self to God and indwelling them in preparation for heaven. The mystery of lawlessness ultimately involves Satan turning men from God to self and indwelling them in preparation for hell. Satan's is a gospel of self.... It promises that we each have within ourselves the means of our own salvation.... We are not separated from God by sin; we are alienated from ourselves and our environment through ignorance of who we really are. We imagine ourselves to be weak mortals when in fact we are gods. We do not need a "Savior" external to ourselves, but simply need to learn to tap the infinite potential that lies within. It is the same appealing lie that seduced Eve.[1]

Suddenly secular leaders are declaring that not just religion but "Christianity" is the key to uniting Europe! Why is this so? Since the Antichrist pretends to be Christ, his followers must be "Christians" and his world religion must be a perverted form of "Christianity." Not only the Pope calls for a "spiritually united Europe," but numerous other leaders voice the same novel opinion....

In actual fact, neither the Pope nor Gorbachev has the least sympathy for "born-again" evangelical Christianity,[2] which

1. Dave Hunt, *GLOBAL PEACE AND THE RISE OF ANTICHRIST* (Oregon: Harvest House Publishers, 1990), pp. 5-6, 8-9, 86. *All material from this author is quoted with his permission.*

2. Gorbachev, who believes that Jesus was the "first socialist" and that religion should play a role in social progress, has stated that peace and social harmony in the Middle East "would have to be founded on the spirit of Jesus," in whose footsteps he claims to follow (Allan Shapiro, "A disciple of Jesus, 'the first socialist,'" *The Jerusalem Post,* Int. Ed., 27 June 1992, p. 3). However, throughout his tenure as the Soviet Premiere, far from behaving like a Christian, Gorbachev's greatest concern was to keep Soviet Communism alive, finally liberalizing it, while allowing greater Israeli emigration, only because desperately needed Western aid, capital investment, and trade were conditioned upon such changes. Further, under Gorbachev, the Soviet Union's member-states continued to arm Israel's foes wholeheartedly

John Paul II openly derides and warns his flock against. While encouraging dialogue with Buddhists, Muslims, and Hindus, the Pope warns Catholics "not to be seduced by Protestant fundamentalist sects...."[1] In fact, by "Christianity" both Gorbachev and the Pope mean *Roman Catholicism.* That just happens to have been the official world religion of the Roman Empire—the very religion which must recover that status in preparation for the Antichrist....

The ancient Roman Empire was a pluralistic society.... Any religion was tolerated. There was, however, one exception.... Christians were hated and persecuted and often killed, not because they believed in Christ, but because they believed *only* in Him....

....Tertullian's saying, "The blood of the martyrs is the seed of the church," was all too true. The Emperor Constantine decided that, to unify the Empire, Christians should be given the right to worship as they pleased....

A brilliant military commander, Constantine also understood that there could be no political stability without religious unity. Yet to accomplish that feat would require a union between paganism and Christianity.... The Empire needed an ecumenical religion that would appeal to every citizen in a multicultural society.... Christianity had to undergo a transformation....

Constantine himself exemplified this expediency. He adopted Christ as the new god that had given him victory in the crucial battle at Milvian Bridge in 312 A.D.... Yet, as Caesar, he continued to function as the *Pontifex Maximus* of the Empire's pagan priesthood, known as the Pontifical College. Even as he endowed Christian churches, Constantine continued to support the construction of pagan temples. As a "Christian" Emperor, he

---

(e.g., the PLO, Iran, Iraq, and Syria)—and still do, while Gorbachev himself, like Israel's enemies, equated Zionism with racism ("Gorbachev's visit," *The Jerusalem Post,* Int. Ed., 27 June 1992, p. 8).

Calling environmental destruction "the central issue of our time," deserving "absolute priority above all other problems facing us today," Gorbachev, the "former president of the world's most polluted country," who openly advocates the creation of an "international government" to guard the world's "peace and security," announced his 1993 launching of the *International Green Cross* before an audience of politicians, religious leaders, and scientists at the Global Forum. Through it, Gorbachev hopes to "increase the profile of environmental issues by lobbying world leaders," "prevent environmental disasters," bring about "a new international environmental law," and propose "reform of the United Nations." He states, "We need an ecology of the soul. Without it, all our efforts to save mankind would be pointless. When science and rationality cannot help us, there is only one thing that can save us: our conscience and moral feelings" (Geoffrey Lean, London Observer Service, "Gorbachev launches crusade to save Earth from people," *Rocky Mountain News,* 6 May 1993, p. 36A).

Whatever Gorbachev is, he is not a Christian.

1. According to "Cardinal Joseph Ratzinger, Pope John Paul II's guardian of orthodoxy," "the only valid church community is that in which churches are linked through their bishops to the church in Rome and the pope" ("Vatican warns about straying from Rome," *Rocky Mountain News,* 16 June 1992, p. 4).

automatically became the de facto civil head of the Christian church and seduced her with promises of power. Thus began the destruction of Christianity and the process that created Roman Catholicism as it is today....

"Christianity" became a *means* for nearly everyone. Being a "Christian" was soon essential to anyone who wanted to advance in business, politics, or even the military.... Ecclesiastical posts, from priest to bishop, cardinal, and even Pope, went to the highest bidder....

So the "Christianity" of the Roman Empire, which became known as Roman Catholicism..., was not the same as the biblical Christianity of the early church and of the martyrs. Instead, it was the old paganism of Rome surviving under a thin veneer of Christian terminology and form....

As [the self-declared] head of the church, Constantine claimed two new titles...: *Vicar of Christ and Bishop of Bishops....* *Vicar* comes from the Latin word *vicarius*. The Greek equivalent would be *anti*.... ...Constantine, as Vicar of Christ, was an Antichrist, and so are the Popes, for they bear the same title. Antichrist will be the new Constantine, the head of the...Roman Empire worldwide, while the Pope will be his assistant, the second beast [or false prophet] of Revelation 13....

....It was Constantine who decreed that since Rome was the capital of the Empire, its Bishop should be the ecclesiastical head of the church....

....When the Empire later disintegrated *politically*..., it was held together *religiously* by the all-pervasive presence of the Roman Catholic Church with its ingenious ecumenical blend of paganism and Christianity still headquartered in Rome....

....That the Pope is almost universally recognized as the religious leader of the world [has]...great significance.... Other world leaders are adding their voices to the call by former U.N. Assistant Secretary General [and New Ager] Robert Muller for the Pope to come "to the United Nations [to] speak for all the religions and spiritualities on this planet...." The picture becomes ever clearer and more ominous.[1]

....The heads of state in today's world all recognize that the Pope wields a power which in many ways is even greater than their own. ...Vatican City's citizens are found in great numbers in nearly every country. They constitute an international network that reaches into the inside circles of the world's power centers.... [Much like the Freemasons do for the British monarchy.]

It is not surprising, then, that all the major nations in the world, including the United States, have ambassadors to the Vatican.... When he wanted to make his peace with the West, one of the first moves Gorbachev made was to journey to Rome.... That fact speaks volumes....

1. Hunt, *GLOBAL PEACE AND THE RISE OF ANTICHRIST,* pp. 104-111.

Certainly the rebuilt Babylon in Iraq...does not fit John's description of the *woman*. She is "drunken with the blood of...the martyrs of Jesus" (Revelation 17:6) and "in her was found the blood of prophets and of saints and of all that were slain upon the earth" (Revelation 18:24). Nearly a million martyrs died in the [Roman] Catholic Inquisition in Spain, France, and Holland alone. Yet the phrase "all that were slain upon the earth" indicates again that John is seeing the wickedness and idolatry that came from Babel and culminates in the false church of the last days. It will encompass all religions under the leadership of the Pope in Rome.

That this "last-days" Babylon is described as a *woman* again identifies her as the Roman Catholic Church, for whom a *woman*—"the Virgin Mary"—is the dominant deity....

When asked why they pray to Mary, most [Roman] Catholics will deny that they do so and will insist that they only ask her to intercede.... Yet prayers are addressed *to* Mary for everything from safety to forgiveness of sins and eternal salvation....

No one is more convinced of the authenticity of the Fatima visitations [of "Mary"] than the present Pope. Nor is anyone more devoted to "Mary." John Paul II, who has "dedicated himself and his Pontificate to Our Lady," bears the M for Mary in his coat of arms; his personal motto, embroidered on the inside of his robes in Latin, is *totus tuus sum Maria* (Mary, I'm all yours).... While recovering from the assault upon his life it occurred to him that the assassination attempt on May 13, 1981, had taken place on the anniversary of the Virgin Mary's first appearance, May 13, 1917, at Fatima, Portugal. In a vision she appeared to him to declare that she had spared his life for a special mission he was to fulfill.

John Paul II made a solemn pilgrimage to Fatima on May 13, 1982, where he "prayed before the statue of Our Lady of Fatima. Thousands heard him speak and consecrate the world to Mary as she had requested." On at least three other occasions,...he consecrated the world to our Lady" with "special mention" of the Russian people. She had promised that if the popes and bishops would consecrate the world and Russia to her Immaculate Heart, "...My Immaculate Heart will triumph, Russia will be converted, and there will be peace!"

Such a statement is in the fullest opposition to the clear teaching of the Bible.... Global peace will only be established when Christ returns to reign from Jerusalem.... Yet "Mary" has taken the place of Christ as the one through whom peace will come, and the present Pope and his church support this heresy.[1]

....Since [Roman] Catholicism as it developed beginning with Constantine was paganism disguised as Christianity, it has consistently accommodated itself.... In Haiti, for example, every Voodoo

1. Hunt, *GLOBAL PEACE AND THE RISE OF ANTICHRIST*, pp. 116-117, 120-122, 124-125.

ceremony begins with [Roman] Catholic prayers.... The frightening spiritist cult of Santeria exploding across America is also a blend of African paganism and "Christianity" carried on in the name of [Roman] Catholic saints who front for demons....

[Roman] Catholic retreat centers around the world mix "Christianity" with Hinduism, Buddhism, and all manner of New Age beliefs and practices....

....John Paul II takes a broad-minded view of Buddhism and all other religions. He considers the Tibetan Buddhist Deity Yoga of his good friend the Dalai Lama,[1] along with the prayers of witch doctors, spiritists, and every other "faith," to be generating "profound spiritual energies" that are creating a "new climate of peace."...

Mindful of the mission that "Our Lady" has given him, the current Pope maintains contact with the world's leading religions. He accepts them as worshiping the same God and their prayers as being as effective as those of Christians. Nor has he attempted to convert any of them. He simply wants everyone of every religion to acknowledge him as the moral and spiritual leader of the world.

....Already we are seeing leading Protestants working together with the Roman Catholic Church and adopting its ecumenism. A new spirit of compromise is sweeping the "Christian" church and the entire religious world today....

....In actual fact, the Roman Catholic Church is the most powerful and effective enemy of Christianity in history. Its teachings are masterpieces of deception.

....Yet today's "cult experts" rarely if ever include the Roman Catholic Church on their lists because it is now unacceptably "negative".... Partnership with Rome sets the stage for the rise of Antichrist....

....If the Pope identifies this impostor as the Christ, the obedience of ["faithful" Roman] Catholics is assured. Submission to the Pope is far broader than most people realize....

The Roman Catholic Church, as the sole interpreter of Scripture, seduces its members into embracing a different God, a different Jesus Christ, and a different plan of salvation from that taught in the Bible. Confusion arises because Rome uses biblical terms such as "justification by grace," the "Virgin Birth," the "blood atonement of the cross," and the "Resurrection of Jesus." Yet what Rome means by such language is entirely different from what evangelicals believe and the Bible teaches....

....One's own good deeds, obedience to the Church, and participation in its sacraments must be added to what Christ has done. The Rosary, the Confession to a priest, baptism into the Church, and indulgences earned are also required. And in

---

1. The "Dalai Lama," who is worshiped in Tibet, Hollywood, and elsewhere as "a living god," is considered to be a reincarnation of "the divine Buddha."

addition to Christ's suffering on the cross the individual must also suffer for his own sins in purgatory, where the soul, though cleansed by the blood of Christ, must be more thoroughly "purged." Then there is the endless list of alms, good deeds, and Masses that others must engage in after one is dead in order to obtain his or her release from purgatory and entrance into heaven at last....

...Paul was very explicit: "There be some that...would pervert the gospel of Christ. But though we or an angel from heaven preach any other gospel unto you than that which we have preached unto you, let him be accursed" (Galatians 1:7-9). The Roman Catholic Church, from the Pope down, preaches a far different gospel from that which the apostles preached.... Yet Rome boldly pronounces its own eternal curse upon those who dare to preach Paul's [true] gospel....

....Of course Mormons "name the name of Christ," as do Jehovah's Witnesses, Christian Scientists, and other cultists, occultists, and New Agers—and their "Christ" is a blasphemous counterfeit. So is the "Christ" of Roman Catholicism.[1]

The new Emperor..., the Antichrist, is not yet in position to accomplish the essential Constantinian strategy. In his absence, and in preparation for him, an ecumenical union of all religions is being aggressively pursued....

Indeed, the "engagement of the [Roman] Catholic Church in the ecumenical movement" was significant even before the present Pope took office. This fact may seem to be in conflict with its claims of being the only true and infallible church. However, while damning ex-Catholics and Protestants, [Roman] Catholicism allows for those outside its fold to be saved if ignorant of its claims and sacraments and if they are sincere in their own faith. Thus Mother Teresa and those who work[ed] with her never attempt[ed] to convert to Christ the dying people for whom they care[d]....

The Roman Catholic hierarchy has a long history of leadership in ecumenism. A book could be filled with examples, but a few must suffice. Popes John XXIII and Paul VI joined such notables as the Dalai Lama, Anwar el-Sadat (a Muslim), and [former] U.N. Secretary General U. Thant (a Buddhist), to form The Temple of Understanding, known as the United Nations of World Religions.... [Roman] Catholic Archbishop Angelo Fernandes was for its first eight years the President of the Geneva-based World Conference on Religion and Peace, organized to bring together "a growing network involving all the major religions of the world."...

"His Holiness" the Dalai Lama, who is "God" to most Tibetan Buddhists, has been well-received by Roman Catholic leaders around the world. He...has met five or more times with his good

1. Hunt, *GLOBAL PEACE AND THE RISE OF ANTICHRIST*, pp. 127-130, 136-137, 140-142, 145-146.

48

friend John Paul II. "Both of us have the same aim," says the Dalai Lama....

Encouraging such ecumenism, the Pope has declared that "Christians must work with other religions to secure peace." He has pledged that "the [Roman] Catholic Church intends to 'share in and promote' such ecumenical and inter-religious cooperation."...

....Using his immense prestige and the emotional appeal of global peace, the Pope was able in 1986 to gather the leading figures of 12 world religions together in Assisi, Italy, to pray to whatever "God" each believed in, beseeching these deities to bring peace to the world. To justify honoring the prayers of even witch doctors and fire worshipers, John Paul II told participants that "the challenge of peace...transcends religious differences."[1]

Prince Philip [of Britain] is representative of the growing numbers of nominal "Christians" who are turning back to paganism as a result of their ecological concerns....

....To speak of "spirituality" and "freedom of religion" is popular. To suggest that Jesus Christ as the Savior of sinners is mankind's only hope is not tolerated by those who preach tolerance. All religions must join together in a generic, pagan "spirituality" to rescue the planet....

Ecology and peace are the two great concerns that are sparking the new unity of all religions. Nothing else matters. Doctrinal beliefs are irrelevant....

....Satan's Messiah, with his seemingly unlimited psychic power, will be light-years ahead of any of today's gurus....

Since it is a key factor in establishing world peace, ecumenism will be unstoppable. Those who criticize it on the basis of biblical truth will seem to be small-minded. After all, as **Prince Philip** suggests, it hardly seems practical, when the survival of our species on earth hangs in the balance, to worry about heaven or hell. Environmental concerns and the need for peace at any price clearly take priority.[2]

[During the 1990-91 U.N. conflict with Iraq,] Muslims who protested the presence of "filthy foreigners" upon Islam's holy soil insisted that the Arabs would work out a solution if left to themselves.... In actual fact, had the United States not stepped in immediately Iraq would have taken over Saudi Arabia and a few other countries as well....

Suddenly, thinking Arabs were forced to reevaluate their religion in...that the territory containing the holiest Islamic shrines had to be defended by infidels against Muslims!...

It would be surprising if we did not see as great changes in the Arab world as in the Communist world as the stage is set for the rise of Antichrist.... Even the Bamboo Curtain around China

1. Hunt, *GLOBAL PEACE AND THE RISE OF ANTICHRIST,* pp. 149, 152, 155-156.
2. Hunt, *GLOBAL PEACE AND THE RISE OF ANTICHRIST,* pp. 168-169, 172, 174-176.

must yield as well to worldwide pressures.[1] It is only a matter of time....

Confronted at last by some of the embarrassing questions about Islam, the faith of many Muslims is being shaken. Why did Muhammad with his "new revelation" give his God the same name, Allah, as the chief idol in the *kaaba*, the ancient pagan temple at Mecca? And why, although he destroyed the idols which it housed, did Muhammad retain the *kaaba* itself as a sacred shrine? And why did he keep and continue to revere the Black Stone that had long been worshiped along with the idols in the ancient religious ceremonies of Mecca? And why do Muslims consider the *kaaba* holy and kiss its Black Stone as an important part of their pilgrimage to Mecca?...

Painful though the admission may be, intelligent, thinking Arabs can no longer deny that Islam has been responsible for perpetuating a barbaric medieval mentality....

Unfortunately, the pressure for change is bringing a growing openness to ecumenism that is preparing the Muslim world to embrace the Antichrist....

....It is no longer so difficult to imagine that with a little more preparation Muslims too will be able to embrace and even worship the counterfeit "Christ"—while still professing allegiance to Islam....[2]

Throughout the world and in all ages there have been two general concepts of God: 1) pantheism/naturalism—that the universe itself is God; and 2) supernaturalism—that the Creator is distinct from His creation. Related to these are two more

1. For more information, see Chapter 11's section, titled "Governor of Hong Kong?"
2. Hunt, *GLOBAL PEACE AND THE RISE OF ANTICHRIST,* pp. 227, 229-231.
   Prince Charles, who is slated one day to head the Anglican Protestant Church, has not only sought ecumenical rapprochement with the Vatican and Pope John Paul II, but he has also made extraordinary overtures toward Muslims and Islam. In fact, the prince is perhaps the most popular Westerner in the Muslim world today. Among other deeds, Prince Charles has apparently "converted" to Islam, taking an Arabic title which has caused various Muslims to speculate that he intends to become the head of the Muslim world (for more information, see Chapter 10's sections titled, "A so-called 'Christian' heritage" and "Ties to the New Age Movement, the occult, and false religions").
   Various Islamic nations and other Muslim fundamentalists, as well as fundamentalist Christian organizations, recently joined the Vatican, at the urging of Pope John Paul II, in opposing and denouncing the sexually immoral, pro-infanticide agenda of the September 1994 United Nations' International Conference on Population and Development held in Cairo, Egypt. While the Vatican made overtures even to Iran and Libya, other countries, such as Saudi Arabia, the Sudan, and Lebanon, chose not to attend. As the *Associated Press* put it, "the controversy has made unlikely allies of the Holy See and Muslims" ("Catholics, Mus - lims protest abortions," *Rocky Mountain News,* 2 Sept. 1994, p. 63A). At the fourth U.N. Conference on Women, held in September 1995, the Vatican again collaborated with Islamic nations, including Syria and Iran, "to prevent what both perceived as a challenge to their dogma of purity and ban on extramarital sex" (Uli Schmetzer, "U.N. forum ends in dispute over women's sexual rights," *The Denver Post,* 17 Sept. 1995, p. 18A). The pope has rightly said, "Every family must know how to resist the false sirens of the culture of death" ("Forum to focus on 'empowerment' as well as birth control," *The Denver Post,* 4 Sept. 1994, p. 12A).

opposing views: 1) polytheism—that there are many gods...; and 2) monotheism—that there is only one God.

Antichrist's claims are built upon a pantheistic/polytheistic worldview. If everything is God and there are thus many gods, it then follows that every person is a god whether he realizes it or not.... The Antichrist, having apparently "realized" this inner potential, is in a position to help others to achieve their godhood also. Such is the great lie of the Serpent.

Supernaturalism/monotheism is divided into two rival beliefs: 1) that God is a single being; and 2) that God has always existed in three Persons [or Personalities] who are separate and distinct, yet [eternally united as] one. Only Christians hold the latter view.... Yet it is the only biblical, logical, and philosophically coherent view of God possible.... All other views of God can be accommodated by the [polytheistic] Antichrist—but not the biblical doctrine of the [united] Trinity.

....Just as Israel's misunderstanding of God's triune nature caused her to reject her Messiah, so that same misunderstanding will allow her to be deceived into accepting the Antichrist....[1]

Satan transforms himself "into an angel of light" and inspires his emissaries to masquerade as "the ministers of righteousness".... He prevents his false theology from being unmasked by accusing those who attempt to expose it of being "negative" and "divisive."

The Serpent did not urge Eve to shake her fist at God and denounce Him, nor did he inspire her to practice overtly evil acts. On the contrary, he enticed her with promises of a better "self-image," of being a wiser and better person—of even becoming "like God." What could be wrong with that high ambition? Evil is far more seductive and effective when it is packaged as *good*. If he can encourage expressions of "man's basic goodness" that are high-minded, altruistic, and spiritual, but *without Christ*, Satan is very pleased.[2]

Satan's goal is to pervert the conscience to such an extent that his *lie* is embraced as God's *truth*. Far from desiring to destroy all religion, Satan seeks to be the leader of a *false religion* whose adherents unknowingly worship him. And of course that false religion, as we have seen, must be a perverted form of Christianity....

While raw Satanism is exploding, most people are repelled by it. Satan is most seductive when he masquerades as *God*....

The death, burial, and resurrection of Christ as historic events upon planet Earth make any kind of ecumenical union with the world's religions both impossible and abominable. A dead Buddha or Muhammad has nothing in common with the resurrected

---

1. Hunt, *GLOBAL PEACE AND THE RISE OF ANTICHRIST*, pp. 233-234, 242, 245.
2. As one reviewer noted, "How similar is this to the morals, ideals and values that a great deal of the world's population embraces today?"

Lord Jesus Christ.... Christ alone paid the penalty demanded by the law, which He proved by His resurrection, and He alone can save....

The Antichrist won't even pretend to be Jesus.... On what basis, then, will he claim to be Christ? Almost certainly he will claim to be the latest *reincarnation* of the "Christ Spirit" that was allegedly in Krishna, Rama, Buddha, Jesus, Muhammad, et al [or he will allow others to make that claim on his behalf]....

....Antichrist represents himself, not the God of heaven. Through him "Christianity" becomes the ultimate humanism. The satanic power manifest through Antichrist will be hailed as psychic powers of the mind and thus proof of man's innate Godlike potential....

In contrast to the Antichrist's religion, which exalts self, Christ taught that we must *deny* self and take up the cross to follow Him.[1]

After a honeymoon of peace, love, and brotherhood, the terror of Antichrist's rule will make Hitler's rule seem benevolent. Those who refuse to worship him and submit to the new world order will be summarily executed....

The most fascinating aspect of Hitler's deception was the heavy "Christian" element that was involved—an element that will be absolutely essential under Antichrist. Most of the church in Germany went happily along with the new order. Hitler promised "liberty for all religious denominations," much like the promises now being made in Eastern Europe.

In his March 23, 1933, speech, when he took over as dictator, Hitler praised the Christian faith and promised to respect liberty of conscience....

Thousands of German pastors joined the newly organized "German Christians' Faith Movement," which supported Nazi doctrines and promoted a "Reich Church" that would unite all Protestants under the state. A minority of pastors,...realized at last that Hitler's "Positive Christianity" was in fact anti-Christian....

The "Reich Church," formed under leaders picked by Hitler, was formally recognized by the Reichstag on July 14, 1933. On November 13 a massive rally was held in the Berlin Sportpalast by the "German Christians' Faith Movement." Leaders of the rally proposed abandonment of the Old Testament and revision of the New Testament to fit National Socialism. Resolutions called for "One People, One Reich, One Faith," an oath of allegiance to Hitler to be signed by all pastors, and the exclusion of Jewish Christians by all churches. The Gestapo's reign of terror against followers of Christ began with the arrest of 700 pastors in the fall of 1935.

Always the justification under Hitler, as under Constantine, was ecumenical "unity." We are hearing the same appealing

1. Hunt, *GLOBAL PEACE AND THE RISE OF ANTICHRIST*, pp. 249-250, 252-254.

slogan today....

All the time that he was deliberately moving to destroy Christianity and replace it with his neopagan occultism, Hitler continued to pretend that he was the champion of real Christianity....

We are reminded by the homage afforded to cult leaders that the world remains vulnerable to delusion. The Dalai Lama, for example, is highly honored worldwide.... Yet his public claims are similar to those which will be made by the Antichrist.... He proposes to bring global peace through a heavily demonic Yoga visualization technique.... For this he was awarded the Nobel Peace Prize in 1989! This forerunner of the Antichrist continues to be feted by the Roman Catholic Church, which previously gave Hitler its blessing.

....**It is already a crime punishable under the Genocide Treaty, which was recently signed by the United States, to suggest that any religion is wrong. To be ecumenical and "positive" is required by international law. It is but a small step to Antichrist's harsh rule.**

Today's "Positive Christianity"—which, like Hitler's, dresses occultism in Christian language—has virtually taken over in America and is now being exported into Eastern Europe. Those who promote Positive Thinking, Possibility Thinking, and Positive Confession are among the most influential radio/television preachers.... Any correction is rejected as "negative."[1]

....Many Charismatic leaders are now promoting the idea that the second coming is not the return of our Lord *personally* in His resurrected individual body to earth, but the attainment by His *spiritual body*, the church, to a higher spiritual state evidenced by great signs and wonders....

....And this thesis fits perfectly with the Antichrist's probable claim that he is the reincarnation of the Christ Spirit that was in Jesus—a "higher state of consciousness" into which he promises to lead the world....

....The general effect upon [Charismatic Roman] Catholics of the "baptism in the Spirit" has been to increase their heretical devotion to Mary.... The "spirit" that endorses such delusion will also endorse Antichrist....

On top of her heresies, the Roman Catholic Church consorts with "seducing spirits" such as those that have appeared at Fatima in the form of "Mary" and the *child* "Jesus." These apparitions...have been embraced by every Pope in the past 60 years and thus by hundreds of millions of [Roman] Catholics. Similar appearances have increased around the world.... Always there are "miracles" and "warnings" to the world of coming judgment, with the promise that through the rosary and "Our Lady's" intervention peace can come....

....The message that comes from the "Virgin" is consistent

1. Hunt, *GLOBAL PEACE AND THE RISE OF ANTICHRIST*, pp. 266-268.

with other demonic revelations and is important for the Antichrist: that all religions are basically the same and must come together for peace....

Through his pursuit of the occult and New Age medicine, **Prince Charles**, the next King of England and thus the next head of the Church of England, has concluded that all religions are basically the same. He considers himself to be psychic and believes in guidance from the spirit realm.[1] **The Queen** (also involved in spiritism) and **the Prince** both believe that he, Charles, "is the Chosen One—placed in line for the throne through a divine, preordained plan."[2]

Prince Charles is representative of many other prominent world figures who are also involved in the occult and anticipate the coming of a humanistic one-world religion....

One no longer need travel to a distant place where "Mary" has appeared. Visualization techniques are being taught, from kindergarten to top management seminars, which enable anyone to make contact with "Jesus" or the "Virgin Mary" or "extraterrestrials" or any person from the past or even the future. Through this ancient and powerful method of opening oneself to satanic delusion, demons posing as Jesus are being contacted for "inner healing" and "prayer"....

....It is not difficult to see the day when untold millions of such spirit guides will identify the Antichrist as the Christ and will be believed. What a setup![3]

The "New Age Religion" of the coming "New World Order" is an intoxicating combination of pantheism and polytheism. Pantheists hold that a universal energy flows through, and thus unites, all life. They refer to this impersonal energy as a life- or god-force, and as an oversoul or universal spirit. New Agers alternately speak of it as their "Christ Consciousness," "Cosmic Consciousness," or "Higher Self." As pantheists, New Agers assert that this "energy," which they call "the Christ Energy," may be "channeled" or manipulated to "energize" an individual. An "energized" man or woman, as the teaching goes, not only partakes of the universal "god-force," but may realize his or her own "divine potential" or "godhood." According to pantheists, when an individual dies, he or she merely returns to, or unites with, the universal "force," and does

1. John Dale, *The Prince and the Paranormal: The Psychic Bloodline of the Royal Family* (London: W.H. Allen & Co. Plc, 1986), pp. 14-18.
2. *US*, 14 Jan. 1985, pp. 18-19.
3. Hunt, *GLOBAL PEACE AND THE RISE OF ANTICHRIST*, pp. 270-275, 277-278.

not therefore cease to exist or experience divine judgment. Rather, a deceased person will at some point be reborn in another form—one that hopefully will be more attuned to the cosmic "life-force" and therefore more spiritually evolved. In other words, pantheists are not only natural polytheists, but they promote a kind of individual spiritual evolution through continual reincarnation. New Agers also teach a collective spiritual evolution, believing that when enough human beings have realized their "divine potential," mankind will suddenly take a "quantum spiritual leap" into "godhood" with all the "psychic powers" that it entails.

Many of today's New Age pantheists attempt to redefine and change orthodox Christian terminology and practice to conform with their occult beliefs. Often, these New Age cultists, who call themselves "christs," do not object to being viewed as liberal "Christians."[1] It should come as no surprise, therefore, to one day see the AntiChrist himself claim to be a "Christian." Yet the beliefs of New Agers and other occultists stem from Satan's ancient lie in the Garden of Eden, in which the serpent told the woman that she would not die by disobeying God, but that she would instead retain eternal life and even become "as God [gods], knowing good and evil [calamity, affliction]" (Gen 3:4-5). Gary H. Kah, in *En Route to Global Occupation,* makes these astute observations,

> [Most]...pantheists will automatically support the concept of a one-world government since global unity is essential to the proper flow of the god-force. Humanity will then, presumably, take a "quantum leap" to a higher level of [mystical] existence.... A new age of enlightenment—a New World Order—will be born.
> Pantheism is Satan's religion....
> ....[A] New Ager who has embraced pantheism...may, while in a trance, encounter a spirit which approaches under the guise of being a more highly evolved being....or "ascended master"....
> Those in the fields of philosophy and psychology who have delved into the occult, such as Carl Jung, have had similar experineces—only they refer to these beings as archetypal images or "Ideal Forms." Strict humanists, on the other hand, who do not believe in the existence of a spirit realm, are more commonly

---

1. For more information, see the section titled "The New Age and the spirit of the AntiChrist" in *Messiah, History, and the Tribulation Period.*

approached by beings posing as extraterrestrials....

Through willing or naive vessels who practice occult meditation, Satan is able to orchestrate his worldwide drive for a New World Order. Using secret occult hierarchies, he has systematically advanced his plans....

Tens of thousands of New Agers will appear on the world scene...demanding that a one-world government be established....to deal with existing global problems and to prevent any future catastrophes.... The international media will give full coverage....

....The most convincing arguments will have to do with the environment, global debt, world poverty, and the prevention of war....

The New World Order will appear to come from the bottom up, as something that the people of the world want. It will come in the name of democracy....

The AntiChrist will come to reside over an empowered United Nations or, perhaps, over a newly created global authority....

A World Constitution will be proposed, and a "democratic" World Parliament will be created. World citizens will believe they have a say in matters, not realizing that occult-based secret societies are really the ones in control....

Sovereign nations would [in essence] cease to exist. A single global economic system would be established.... Any real authority would now rest with an international body controlled by Satan himself.

The disputing world religions will become [largely] unified, and...it is not inconceivable that, at some point during his ascent to power, he declares himself to be "the Christ." [He]...might also claim to be the long awaited Messiah to the Jews. To the Buddhists he would be the fifth Buddha; to Moslems, the Imam Mahdi; to Hindus, Krishna. Those [so-called] Christians accepting this lie would unfortunately see in him the fulfillment of the second coming of Christ....

The Christianity represented by the AntiChrist will be a complete counterfeit, saturated with all the pantheistic teachings of eastern mysticism and the ancient mystery religions—the same beliefs held by New Agers and promoted by the secret societies....

The focus will be on elevating self rather than God.... The naive will actually be practicing occultism in the name of Christ, while worshiping the father of lies...

The tragedy is that most people will voluntarily serve this man of lawlessness and his system, seeing him as their savior.... Evil will go forth in the name of goodness....

Christians who...refuse to participate in this system will be seen as obstacles to world peace.[1]

1. Gary H. Kah, *En Route to Global Occupation* (Louisiana: Huntington House Publishers, 1991), pp. 69-70, 73, 75, 146-151.

3

A Name that Calculates to 666

Unlike English, ancient Hebrew and Greek did not use Arabic or Roman numerals to represent numbers. Instead, the characters of the respective alphabets were themselves used. The numbers historically applied to the Hebrew character set, which actually antedate the largely occult Cabala, are today called *cabalic*. With these numbers in mind, recall that the saints are told, "Here is wisdom: Let him who has understanding calculate the number of the beast; for it is the number of a man, and his number *is* 666" (Rev 13:18, Gk.; cf. Gen 7:6; 1 Sam 17:4, 17:7, 17:34-37; 2 Sam 21:19-20; cf. 1 Kin 10:14, 10:24; cf. Gen 7:6; Dan 3:1).

Despite the arguments of some to the contrary, there is no compelling reason, biblically or otherwise, to believe that a correct identification of the AntiChrist through a proper calculation of his name, as spoken of in Revelation 13:18, cannot *precede* the start of the Tribulation Period. In fact, if Prince Charles is the AntiChrist, then this has already been accomplished (see below).[1]

"Prince Charles of Wales," the prince's common name (and title),[2] is of the same form, for example, as "Messiah Jesus of Nazareth."[3] Unlike a manipulated or even contrived name or title (e.g., "Pope Caesar of Rome"), the prince's real-life title not only calculates to six-hundred and sixty-six (666) using the cabalic numbers, but it does so in *more than one language!* This calculation may be

---

1. Such knowledge in no way alters the fact that the general revelation of the AntiChrist—to both believers and apostate Israel—will not itself occur, in the manner spoken of in 2 Thessalonians 2, until just before the midpoint of the Tribulation Period. At that time, the son of perdition will sit in the Temple of God proclaiming his own deity (2 Th 2:3-4, KJV), and the abomination that causes desolation, spoken of by both Daniel and Jesus, will be erected (see Matt 24:4-5, 24:15-26, 24:29; Mark 13:5-6, 13:14-25; cf. 2 Th 2:4-8, Gk.).

2. The prince's full name is "Charles Philip Arthur George."

3. Acts 3:6 and 4:10 literally have "Jesus *The* Christ, The Nazarene" (Gk.), which is equivalent to "Christ Jesus, The Nazarene" (cf. Matt 26:71; Mark 1:24, 10:47, 14:67, 16:6; Luke 4:34, 18:37, 24:19; John 1:45, 18:5-7, 19:19; Acts 2:22, 6:14, 10:38, 22:8, 26:9).

performed in either English or Hebrew through a relatively simple procedure. First, respectively apply the twenty-two cabalic numbers (one for each character in the Hebrew alphabet—see below) to the first twenty-two letters in the English alphabet. Next, because Hebrew has only twenty-two characters, assign the null value (zero) to the last four letters in English (i.e., W, X, Y, and Z). Finally, obtain the sum of the values corresponding to each letter in "PRINCE CHARLES OF WALES" or נסיך צרלס מוילס (*modern* Israeli Hebrew).

The following system, for calculations in English, Hebrew, or Greek, uses the cabalic numbers as just described:[1]

1 →	A	א	(A α)	50 →	N	נ ן	(N ν)	
2 →	B	ב	(B β)	60 →	0	ס	(Ξ ξ)	
3 →	C	ג	(Γ γ)	70 →	P	ע	(O o)	
4 →	D	ד	(Δ δ)	80 →	Q	פ ף	(Π π)	
5 →	E	ה	(E ε)	90 →	R	צ ץ	(*Koppa*)	
6 →	F	ו	(ς)					
7 →	G	ז	(Z ζ)	100 →	S	ק	(P ρ)	
8 →	H	ח	(H η)	200 →	T	ר	(Σ σ)	
9 →	I	ט	(Θ θ)	300 →	U	ש	(T τ)	
				400 →	V	ת	(Y υ)	
10 →	J	י	(I ι)	0 →	W			
20 →	K	כ ך	(K κ)	0 →	X	500 →	Φ φ	
30 →	L	ל	(Λ λ)	0 →	Y	600 →	X χ	
40 →	M	מ ם	(M μ)	0 →	Z	700 →	Ψ ψ	
↳						800 →	Ω ω	
						900 →	*Sampsi*	

In English, 'PRINCE' (70 + 90 + 9 + 50 + 3 + 5) = *227*, 'CHARLES' (3 + 8 + 1 + 90 + 30 + 5 + 100) = *237*, 'OF' (60 + 6) = *66*, and 'WALES' (0 + 1 + 30 + 5 + 100) = *136*. 227 + 237 + 66 + 136 = **666**. In Hebrew, נסיך (50 + 60 + 10 + 20) = *140*, צרלס (90 + 200 + 30 + 60) = *380*, and מוילס (40 + 6 + 10 + 30 + 60) = *146*. 140 + 380 + 146 = **666**.

Three objections in particular might be raised to this system *as it pertains to English*. *First,* it may be argued

1. This system is based upon an original English table from Monte Judah, given in 1987.

that any name calculation should be done using the original Hebrew rather than the English, or some other alphabet.[1] *Second,* the cabalic numbers have been applied sequentially to the English alphabet, rather than phonetically as some might expect. *Third,* the last four letters in the English alphabet are left without numeric values, and are thus assumed to represent zero. However, as shown below, these objections are not entirely sound.

First, it may be counter-argued that the calculation of the AntiChrist's name should be performed in his own native language, thereby eliminating any possible need to transliterate and translate it into a different tongue, which would normally yield only an approximation. (We may also note that English is currently the world's most widely spoken language.) *Second,* a phonetic application of the cabalic numbers to the English alphabet would also be an approximation, just as the transliteration of a word from one language to another yields a word which sounds *approximately* like the original. Given these difficulties, it seems quite reasonable to use the most straightforward application of the cabalic numbers to the English alphabet (i.e., the sequential method) despite the aforementioned objections; such an application precludes all errors of approximation. Further, it must be pointed out that the ancient Greek numbering system was itself historically derived from the Hebrew system in precisely this manner. Yet unlike the unmodified, non-supplemented cabalic numbers used in our English system, the Greek system originally omitted 6 and 90, and added 500, 600, 700, and 800 (after 400). Also, provisions were later made for it to include 6 (final *sigma*) and 90 (arbitrary symbol *Koppa*), as well as incorporate 900 (arbitrary symbol *Sampsi*). *This very system, which the early Church fathers employed to calculate the values of Greek names and other words,[2] is the basis for the number 666 (i.e., χξϛ), uniquely, in the*

1. See, for example, Arnold G. Fruchtenbaum, *The Footsteps of The Messiah* (California: Ariel Press, 1982), p. 173.
2. Irenaeus, Against Heresies, Bk. 5, Ch. 30, Pars. 1 and 3; see *Ante-Nicene Fathers,* ed. Alexander Roberts and James Donaldson (1885-1886; rpt. Massachusetts: Hendrickson Publishers, Inc., 1994), Vol. 1, pp. 558-559.

original Greek text of Revelation 13:18.[1] Therefore, apart from our omission of added numbers (i.e., 500, 600, 700, 800, and 900), the non-phonetic, sequential method used to apply the cabalic numbers to the English alphabet in our system is neither new nor unprecedented; rather, despite possible arguments to the contrary, it is *the* historically, biblically, and theologically accepted method. Indeed, it is also the method recognized by Ladd and others.[2] The authoritative weight of such a calculation in this system, scripturally speaking, is far greater than in any contrived system ever devised, and there are several.[3]

Finally, in the author's opinion, the weight of the evidence presented herein regarding Prince Charles is so great that even if there were no known numbering system whereby his name calculated to 666, one would nonetheless be compelled to conclude that he is plausibly the Anti-Christ. As it is, however, there are at least two languages—Hebrew and English—in which the prince's name calculates to 666, and that on the same numbering system using entirely different combinations of numbers! This would appear to make our "plausibility" a *statistical* certainty.[4] In fact, there is not a known supercomputer on Earth that is even capable of accurately calculating the odds of such a multiple occurrence. Either way, we may be certain that if Prince Charles is the AntiChrist, then there must be such a system, and this system, for lack of one which may seem more palatable, works.

1. The Greek letters assigned to the numbers 600, 60, and 6 are used together in Revelation 13:18 to specify the total number of 666. Other numbers in the Apocalypse are given using actual Greek words, not combinations of specific letters.
2. George Eldon Ladd, *A COMMENTARY on the REVELATION of JOHN* (Michigan: Eerdmans Publishing Co., 1972), p. 186.
3. For typical examples of interesting, but contrived systems, see Church, pp. 240-241.
4. Physicists view an event that is rarer than *one in ten to the fiftieth power* as so improbable as to be impossible. In our case, the odds depict an event that is *far less likely* to occur. In other words, it could only happen by God's sovereign intent.

4

Prince of this World
—a *Diverse* Lineage

Many have concluded that the AntiChrist will require some degree of authority over Jews, "Christians," *and* Muslims to achieve his eventual worldwide dominion. Prince Charles, as documented below, may one day *claim* literal descent from Israel's King David, Jesus the Christ, *and* Islam's Mohammed, not to mention thousands of other historically influential individuals. Further, the "Merovingian" dynasty, as we shall see, appears to be central to such a possibility.

A Merovingian "conspiracy of destiny."   Various researchers and others have come to recognize the fascinating existence of an historical conspiracy to establish a one-world government under a Merovingian descendant. We may begin our account with Merovée, a fifth-century king of the Sicambrians or Germanic Franks (now Germany and France),[1] who worshiped the bear in the form of the Roman *Diana,* who is also known as the Greek *Artemis,* the "virgin-mother goddess" of the wooded hunt and the moon (associated historically with the unicorn).[2] Although

1. According to Baigent, Leigh, and Lincoln, "Between the fifth and seventh centuries the Merovingians ruled large parts of what are now France and Germany. The period of their ascendancy coincides with the period of [England's] King Arthur—a period that constitutes the setting for the romances of the Holy Grail." In the fifth century, the Sicambrian ancestors of the Merovingians "crossed the Rhine and moved en masse into Gaul, establishing themselves in what is now Belgium and northern France, in the vicinity of the Ardennes. A century later this region came to be called the kingdom of Austrasia. And the core of the kingdom of Austrasia was what is now known as Lorraine." The ancestors of the Merovingians may also be traced "to ancient Greece, and specifically to the region known as Arcadia," being "connected with Arcadia's royal house." The Arcadians, who, like the Sicambrian Franks, worshiped the bear, "supposedly migrated up the Danube, then up the Rhine, and established themselves in what is now western Germany" (*Holy Blood, Holy Grail,* pp. 234, 238-239).

2. *Eerdmans' Handbook to the World's Religions,* pp. 393, 400. In the ancient Middle East, *Artemis* was otherwise known as the "Queen of Heaven," or the Babylonian *Ishtar,* the Egyptian *Isis,* the Canaanite *Ashtoreth* (Astarte), *Asherah,* and *Anath,* etc.—all of which originated with Semiramis. For more information, see Chapter 6, "The First Beast and Prince

Merovée's son, Childeric I, practiced witchcraft, his grandson, Clovis I, converted to Roman Catholicism and became the "New Constantine." Some Merovingians claim, however, that Merovée, their forefather, not only had a birthmark in the form of a red cross on his chest, but was a physical descendant of Jesus and Mary the Magdalene. According to this sordid tale, Jesus didn't really die on the cross, but was stolen away from the tomb, only to survive and secretly wed Mary the Magdalene (as well as her presumed sister Martha), with whom he then fathered children. When the Romans temporarily lifted their siege of Jerusalem shortly before its destruction in A.D. 70, Mary the Magdalene fled with her children to France via the Mediterranean Sea, where they eventually married into the royal Frankish family. Viewing themselves as potentially divine, messianic descendants of King David and Jesus, as well as of the Roman emperors, these Merovingians have therefore sought clandestinely to place their offspring upon the thrones of Europe through intermarriage. (Most of Europe's royal families today are supposedly Merovingian in descent.)[1] But that is not all.

Charles' Coat of Arms."

In discussing the pagan priesthood of "Nemi" (i.e., Nimrod), who, as the "dying god-king," is the "King of the Wood," James George Frazer held that "magic is a means of controlling nature and therefore an essential function of kingship," following from a "union of a royal title with priestly duties." According to Frazer, "No class of the community has benefited so much as kings by this belief in the possible incarnation of a god in human form." With this in mind, Frazer speaks of a union in a "sacred grove" of the "oak god," supposedly incarnated in Roman kings, and the "oak-nymph" or "oak-goddess" named "Diana," who, as the "goddess of fertility," is "a divinity of childbirth." The union "must have been intended to quicken the growth of vegetation by homoeopathic magic." The two thus became "King and Queen of the Wood in a solemn marriage, which was intended to make the earth gay with the blossoms of spring and the fruits of autumn, and to gladden the hearts of men and women with healthful offspring;" for "such kings were thought to ensure good weather and the fertility of fields and animals." Nemi, therefore, "embodied the great Aryan god of the oak; and as an oak-god he would mate with the oak-goddess, whether she went by the name of Egeria or Diana" (*The Illustrated Golden Bough*, ed. Mary Douglas {New York: Doubleday & Co., 1978}, pp. 19, 32, 52, 72, 76-78). It seems plausible that Prince Charles, who had studied this particular mythology before his marriage to "Diana" (Cathcart, pp. 74-75, 81), had it in mind when he chose to court her, so that she could dutifully produce "an heir and a spare" and receive the "worship" of the masses. At the princess' funeral, her brother observed, "of all the ironies about Diana, perhaps the greatest is this; that a girl given the name of the ancient goddess of hunting was, in the end, the most hunted person of the modern age" (The Associated Press, "Brother extols Diana's humanity, commitment," *The Denver Post*, 7 Sept. 1997, p. 27A). Going overboard, Elton John eulogized, "Goodbye, England's rose, from a country lost without your soul."

1. J.R. Church, *Guardians of the Grail...and the men who plan to rule the world*, rev. ed. (Okla-

Legend has it that Joseph of Arimathea caught some of the blood of Jesus in the *cup* from which The Lord drank at the Last Supper with His disciples when His side was pierced by a *spear* upon the cross. Due to their contact with Jesus' blood, both the cup and the spear, called the "Spear of Longinus" and the *Spear of Destiny,* have since been associated with certain "magical" powers. The spear, which is said to confer upon its owner the ability to rule the world, but death to anyone who loses it, is currently in the Habsburg Treasure House (a family museum) at Vienna, Austria.[1] But what about the cup? Although some accounts hold that Mary the Magdalene took the *Cup of Destiny,* or the "Holy Grail," with her when she fled to France, others state that Joseph of Arimathea brought it "to England, where he and his offspring became the Guardians of the Grail."[2] It is noteworthy, therefore, that Queen Elizabeth II's lineage, while it shows the genealogies of both the virgin Mary and Jesus' adoptive father Joseph, as found in Luke 3:23c-33 and Matthew 1:3-15, seems to indicate that Merovée, rather than necessarily being a descendant of David through Jesus and Mary the Magdalene, was actually a descendant of David through Anna. Anna is referred to as a "cousin" of Jesus' mother Mary and depicted as a relative, apparently the daughter, of Joseph of Arimathea.[3] (The queen's lineage will later be addressed in detail.)

The Priory of Zion, the Knights Templar, and the Rosicrucians. By 1061, France's Roman Catholic Crusaders had captured Jerusalem. Upon doing so, they set Godfroi de Bouillon, the Merovingian leader of the First Crusade

---

homa: Prophecy Publications, 1991), pp. 12-14, 23, 25, 27, 62, 73, 101.

1. According to Church, Constantine invoked this spear's "serpent powers" to "rise to the throne of the Roman Empire" and afterwards "held it to his breast" while declaring himself to be the "Thirteenth Apostle." Also, later Merovingian kings and emperors are thought to have used it "as a symbol of their power." From the time of Charlemagne, who "founded his whole dynasty on the possession of the Spear," until the fall of the last Habsburg emperor in 1806, "forty-five emperors claimed the Spear of Destiny." More recently, Hitler invaded Austria at the start of World War II to obtain the spear, and committed suicide the day that the American military recovered it in Nuremberg (pp. 44, 54-57, 60, 63-69).

2. Church, pp. 53, 76.

3. In connection with the legend of the Grail, Baigent, Leigh, and Lincoln note that Joseph of Arimathea was supposedly also Perceval's mother's uncle (*Holy Blood, Holy Grail,* p. 290).

and the Duke of Lorraine,[1] who was the grandson of Eustache I and the son of Eustache II, upon the throne; for he claimed Davidic descent.

Later, in either 1090 or 1099, Godfroi founded the Order of Sion (Zion), a secret society.[2] In 1111, 1112, or 1118, Hugues de Payen instituted the Knights Templar (Temple Knights) as a "front organization" for the Order of Zion,[3] and he appointed Godfroi's brother, Baudouin I, as its second grand master (after himself). Subsequently, around 1128, "Saint Bernard, abbot of Clairvaux and the age's [supposed] chief spokesman for Christendom," declared the Temple Knights to be "the epitome and apotheosis of Christian values." The "Church" then officially recognized and incorporated the Temple Knights as "a religious-military order" of "warrior-monks" and "soldier-mystics," and Hugues de Payen received the honorary title of grand master of the Temple Knights.[4] In 1188, the Temple Knights separated from the Order of Zion, which then changed its name to the Priory of Sion (Zion). Also in 1188, the *Priory* of Zion's first grand master, Jean de Gisors, founded the Rosicrucians.[5]

Originally known as the Order of the Poor Knights of Christ and the Temple of Solomon, the Knights Templar, according to tradition, built their quarters upon "the foundations of the ancient temple of Solomon."[6] Initially headquartered in France, however, the Temple Knights, who are thought to have found and plundered some of the hidden treasures of the destroyed Second Temple, adopted the Merovingian birthmark, a red cross, as their symbol. Introduced into England around 1140,[7] and ultimately threatened by the Roman Catholic Church, they found eventual refuge in Scotland, where the French Templars became the Scottish Rite of Freemasonry. The Templars are credited

1. Baigent, Leigh, and Lincoln, *Holy Blood, Holy Grail,* pp. 268-269.
2. Baigent, Leigh, and Lincoln, *Holy Blood, Holy Grail,* p. 111.
3. Baigent, Leigh, and Lincoln, *Holy Blood, Holy Grail,* pp. 86-87.
4. Baigent, Leigh, and Lincoln, *Holy Blood, Holy Grail,* pp. 67, 82, 117.
5. Church, pp. 15-16, 23, 25, 28-29, 86-88. For a brief outline of this historical development with additional details, see Baigent, Leigh, and Lincoln, *Holy Blood, Holy Grail,* pp. 117-118.
6. Baigent, Leigh, and Lincoln, *Holy Blood, Holy Grail,* pp. 66, 118.
7. Charles Boutell, *Boutell's Heraldry,* rev. J.P. Brooke-Little {London: Frederick Warne, 1978; ISBN: 0 7232 2096 4; LCCN: 73-75030}, p. 191.

with having instituted a wealthy and influential "international banking system across Europe." All things considered, the supposed "Protocols of the Elders of Zion," appears not to be a Judaic work, but a modified work of the Priory of Zion,[1] possibly having been altered for public consumption with the complicity of the Illuminati.[2] Nevertheless, with much contrivance, the work was later advanced as proof of a "Jewish conspiracy." As such, it fueled the mass murder of millions of European Jews in this century.[3]

From 1188 to the present day, the Priory of Zion has been the "benefactor" of a struggle for dominance between English and French royalty and nobility. Originally a French-English oligarchical order and secret-society, from which came the Knights Templar and the Rosicrucians, its control came to rest largely with the English side, even while a number of its grand masters resided in France.

Jean de Gisors, the priory's *first* grand master (1188-1220), for example, "was a vassal of the king of England—Henry II, and then Richard I." Note that Henry II was a French Anjou by birth (discussed below). Marie de Saint-Clair, the priory's *second* grand master (1220-1266) and possibly the second wife of Jean de Gisors, "was descended from Henry de Saint-Clair, Baron of Rosslyn in Scotland, who accompanied Godfroi de Bouillon on the First Crusade. Rosslyn itself was situated not far from the Templars' major preceptory in Scotland, and Rosslyn Chapel, built in the fifteenth century, became mantled with Rose-Croix and Freemasonry legends."[4] Today, of course, Scotland is an integral part of the United Kingdom under the English monarchy. The priory's *third* grand master was Guillaume de Gisors (1266-1307).

Edouard de Bar, the priory's *fourth* grand master (1307-1336), "was a grandson of Edward I of England and a nephew of Edward II.... Edouard's daughter married into

---

1. See, for example, Baigent, Leigh, and Lincoln, *Holy Blood, Holy Grail,* pp. 193-195, 294.
2. Note, however, that various apostate Israelites have at times played prominent roles within the Illuminati. For more information, see Chapter 7's section titled, "The Garter."
3. Church, pp. 23-29, 86-87, 167-169. Baigent, Leigh, and Lincoln, *Holy Blood, Holy Grail,* pp. 191-192.
4. Baigent, Leigh, and Lincoln, *Holy Blood, Holy Grail,* pp. 131, 415.

the house of Lorraine.... ...Edouard was grand-nephew of Guillaume's wife, Iolande de Bar."[1] Jeanne de Bar, the priory's *fifth* grand master (1336-1351), was "the elder sister of Edouard" and "a granddaughter of Edward I of England and a niece of Edward II.... Jeanne...seems to have enjoyed extremely cordial relations with the English throne....[and]...to have had similar relations with the king of France." Jean de Saint-Clair, the priory's *sixth* grand master (1351-1366) was not only "descended from the French houses," but "his grandfather was married to Jeanne de Bar's aunt." In other words, he also was a descendant of English royalty.[2] It was during this period, in 1348, that King Edward III founded the Order of the Garter, which, as will be shown later, established itself over the Priory of Zion, the Knights Templar, and the Rosicrucians! In other words, the Order of the Garter became the heart of the ultimate conspiracy for a Luciferic New World Order.[3]

René d'Anjou, the priory's *ninth* grand master (1418-1480), came to hold the titles "count of Bar" and "king of Jerusalem" (see below). René, who "seems to have had a particular preoccupation with the Grail," may have played a key role in the Renaissance. His influence appears to have "prompted Cosimo de' Medici to embark on a series of ambitious projects...destined to transform Western civilization," including the creation of "an academy of Pythagorean and Platonic studies."[4] "Cosimo's academy quickly generated a multitude of similar institutions throughout the Italian peninsula, which became bastions of Western esoteric tradition. And from them the high culture of the Renaissance began to blossom." One of René's daughters "married Henry VI of England and became a prominent figure in the Wars of the Roses." Henry VI also had Anjou blood. Iolande de Bar, another of René d'Anjou's daughters, was the priory's *tenth* grand master (1480-1483).[5]

1. Baigent, Leigh, and Lincoln, *Holy Blood, Holy Grail*, pp. 131, 416.
2. Baigent, Leigh, and Lincoln, *Holy Blood, Holy Grail*, pp. 131, 417.
3. For more information, see Chapter 7's section titled, "The Garter."
4. For more information, see the discussion on the "Platonic ideal" in Chapter 11's section titled, "The United World Colleges."
5. Baigent, Leigh, and Lincoln, *Holy Blood, Holy Grail*, pp. 131, 136, 138-139, 421-422.

Louis de Nevers, the priory's *fifteenth* grand master (1575-1595), "would have functioned in close concert with....[the] treasurer of the military contingent sent by Elizabeth I of England to support the French king. ....In 1582,...Louis was in England, consorting with...John Dee, the foremost English esotericist of his age." Robert Fludd, the priory's *sixteenth* grand master (1595-1637), "inherited John Dee's mantle as England's leading exponent of esoteric thought." Fludd "warmly endorsed" the Rosicrucians, "declaring that the 'highest good' was the 'Magia, Cabala and Alchymia of the Brothers of the Rosy Cross.'" Enjoying the favor of England's King James I and King Charles I, Fludd "was among the conclave of scholars who presided over the translation of the [Authorized] King James Bible."[1] (It appears, then, that despite the claims of some, the AKJV translation was *not* accomplished entirely apart from the influence of heretics and apostates. In fact, it is a noteworthy twist that the British monarchy, which may well prove to have produced *the* AntiChrist, holds a copyright on the translation to this day.) Robert Boyle, the priory's *eighteenth* grand master (1654-1691), "was educated at Eton, where his provost...was closely connected with the Rosicrucian entourage.... ...Boyle was among the first [English] public figures to offer allegiance to the newly restored Stuarts, and Charles II became patron of the Royal Society.... ...Boyle's two closest friends were [Sir] Isaac Newton and John Locke....[who]...shortly after making Boyle's acquaintance, embarked for a lengthy stay in the south of France." Locke "is known to have studied...the history of the legends according to which the Magdalen brought the Holy Grail to Marseilles."[2]

Sir Isaac Newton, the priory's *nineteenth* grand master (1691-1727), who claimed descent from "ancient Scottish nobility," was elected president of the Royal Society in 1703. Newton, who "was militantly, albeit quietly, hostile to the idea of the Trinity" and who "questioned the divinity of Jesus," "more than any other scientist of his age, was steeped in Hermetic texts." "In addition to personally

1. Baigent, Leigh, and Lincoln, *Holy Blood, Holy Grail,* pp. 131, 425-426.
2. Baigent, Leigh, and Lincoln, *Holy Blood, Holy Grail,* pp. 131, 427-428.

annotated copies of the Rosicrucian manifestos, his library included more than a hundred alchemical works." Newton, whose "works reflect interests shared by Masonic figures of the period," was sympathetic to those who "stressed the supremacy of gnosis, or direct knowledge, over faith." Moreover, he befriended "Jean Desaguliers, who was one of the Royal Society's two curators of experiments," and who "became one of the leading figures in the astonishing proliferation of Freemasonry throughout Europe." Desaguliers presided over the masonic initiation of Prince Francois, the Duke of Lorraine. Newton's closest friend, Nicolas Fatio de Duillier, "appears to have worked as a spy, usually against Louis XIV of France."[1]

Charles Radclyffe, the priory's *twentieth* grand master (1727-1746), was, as an illegitimate grandson of King Charles II, created an earl of Derwentwater by King James II. As such, he "devoted much of his life to the Stuart cause." **Charles V de Lorraine**, he priory's *twenty-first* grand master (1746-1780), was probably "exposed...to a Jacobite influence;" for his father "had offered protection and refuge at Bar-le-Duc to the exiled Stuarts." (The Jacobites used three ostrich feathers, derived from the Edward III's son, Edward the Black Prince, as their symbol.[2] In other words, Charles V de Lorraine was at least loosely associated with the Order of the Garter.) Charles was "Austrian field marshal in the eighteenth century, [and] brother-in-law to the Empress Maria Theresa." His court resembled that of René d'Anjou, his ancestor and another prominent Merovingian. Perhaps relevant, Maximilian de Lorraine, the priory's *twenty-second* grand master (1780-1801), "seems to have acted through cultural figures, as well as through certain of his own numerous siblings—Marie Caroline, for instance, who as queen of Naples and Sicily was largely responsible for the spread of Freemasonry in those domains."[3]

Charles Nodier, the priory's *twenty-third* grand master (1801-1844), appears to be the first of the priory's grand

1. Baigent, Leigh, and Lincoln, *Holy Blood, Holy Grail*, pp. 131, 429-431.
2. For more information, see Chapter 7's section titled, "The motto and the heir-apparent's badge."
3. Baigent, Leigh, and Lincoln, *Holy Blood, Holy Grail*, pp. 131, 134, 431-434.

masters lacking "noble blood." Nevertheless, he published a "seditious tract" in London in opposition to Napoleon and claimed involvement in "two separate plots against Napoleon." Victor Hugo, the priory's *twenty-fourth* grand master (1844-1885), whose father "maintained very cordial relations with the conspirators involved in the plot against the [French] emperor," was a "fervent disciple" of Charles Nodier. "Like Newton he was militantly anti-Trinitarian and repudiated Jesus' divinity. [He]...was immersed all his life in esoterica, in Gnostic, Cabalistic, and Hermetic thought.... And he is known to have been connected with a so-called Rose-Croix order." Jean Cocteau, the priory's *twenty-sixth* grand master (1918-?), decorated "such churches as Notre Dame de France in London."[1]

From the above documentation, it seems clear that the Priory of Zion has in fact been more an historical tool of the English monarchy and nobility than of the French. It is of significant interest, therefore, that the Priory of Zion, the Temple Knights, and the Rosicrucians, all of which ultimately derive from the earlier Order of Zion, together gave rise to English and French Freemasonry. Moreover, in 1348, as will be more fully documented later, the Order of the Garter became the major control point from which the English monarchy exercised its global influence.[2]

Recall that Godfroi de Bouillon, a Merovingian crusader, founded the Order of Zion in either 1090 or 1099. Upon Godfroi's death in 1100, Baudouin I (Baldwin I) assumed the title "King of Jerusalem." Following him, Baldwin II, Fulk V (the father of Geoffrey Plantagenet and grandfather of Henry II), Baldwin III, Amalric I, Baldwin IV, Baldwin V, and several others, all of whom were of Merovingian descent, held the title. Eventually it passed to Emperor Charles V de Lorraine, who, as a descendant the Merovingian Hildegarde and the twenty-first grand master of the Priory of Zion, married Eleonore Marie von Habsburg, daughter of Emperor Ferdinand III. The Habsburg (also spelled "Hapsburg") dynasty, which descends separately from Merovée through Alex, the sister of Godfroi and

1. Baigent, Leigh, and Lincoln, *Holy Blood, Holy Grail*, pp. 131, 434-438.
2. For more information, see Chapter 7's section titled, "The Garter."

Baudouin I, has held it ever since. Currently, Otto von Habsburg of Austria, the titular Duke of Lorraine who, under rosier circumstances, "would have been [called] Emperor of Austria, Apostolic King of Hungary and Holy Roman Emperor,"[1] holds the title,[2] while King Juan Carlos of Spain claims it. King Juan likewise descends from Eleonore Marie and Charles V, who, as the grandson of the Spanish Isabella, also ruled Spain as King Charles I.[3]

We may connect the beliefs of the Priory of Zion and its offspring with ancient Zoroastrianism, as well as with the spiritual "enlightenment" represented in the Luciferic "all-seeing eye" of the Illuminati, which is depicted in the capstone at the top of their pyramidal "Great Seal" on the U.S. dollar bill (arguably the world's most important currency). We may also connect them with the modern New Age Movement. Interestingly, from 1188 to 1306, the Priory of Zion supposedly also called itself "Ormus," a name that "figures in Zoroastrian thought and in Gnostic texts, where it is synonymous with the principle of light," although masonic tradition would have us believe that the name derives from an ancient "Egyptian sage and mystic" who conferred a red cross upon his initiates, giving rise to the first Rosicrucians.[4] J.R. Church shows that the Temple Knights seem to believe that their world leader will appear following the alignment of the planets Jupiter, Saturn, Mars, and Mercury, and after a series of major world catastrophes. In 1981 and 1982, at the start of the so-called "Age of Aquarius," Jupiter, Saturn, and Mars conjoined, and in April 1982, Benjamin Creme and the Tara Center announced the supposedly imminent appearance of "Lord Maitreya," their New Age "Christ."[5]

Through his father, Prince Philip, Prince Charles has

---

1. Hilton, *The Principality and Power of Europe*, p. 16. According to Hilton, Otto von Habsburg "has long awaited the emergence of a new order. For any future united Europe, he advocates a strong religious role for the Roman Catholic Church, which he terms 'Europe's ultimate bulwark'" (ibid., p. 35).
2. Baigent, Leigh, and Lincoln, *Holy Blood, Holy Grail*, p. 269.
3. Church, pp. 13, 15-18, 20-22, 62, 86, 93-95, 313-314.
4. Baigent, Leigh, and Lincoln, *Holy Blood, Holy Grail*, pp. 122-123. Note that the Priory of Zion depicted the name "Ormus" as an anagram or acrostic containing the French words for "bear," "gold," and "elm" (ibid., p. 122).
5. Church, pp. 36-49, 165-166.

Charles V de Lorraine as his ancestral uncle, and he descends from the House of Anjou and the Hapsburg dynasty. In this regard, King Juan Carlos of Spain is not unique. Juan Carlos' lineal claim to be the "King of Jerusalem" is the primary reason that some have recently touted him as a possibility for the role of the AntiChrist. However, Prince Charles too could one day make this claim. In fact, when we consider the additional Merovingian lineage of his mother, Queen Elizabeth II, who, unlike both King Juan Carlos and Otto von Habsburg, apparently descends even from *Godfroi de Bouillon* (through Henry the Black of the Guelph Line), it appears that such a claim, based upon essentially the same criteria, would be considerably stronger. Additionally, as Cathcart observes, "Among the unlikely ladies we find Melesende, Queen of Jerusalem, the second wife of one of Prince Charles' Plantagenet forebears."[1]

The Merovingians and the Priory of Zion have long awaited what the *false prophet* Nostradamus referred to as "the Great Monarch," the ultimate "Prince of Lorraine" and "priest-king" *who would work with the pope* to establish a New World Order.[2] Neither *King* Juan Carlos nor Otto von Habsburg is a *prince*. Baigent, Leigh, and Lincoln, baffled by an obscure Priory reference to the Prince of Lorraine's "sacred mission," have incorrectly asserted, "there is no known Prince of Lorraine today, not even a titular one."[3] Should the European Union seek a royal head having a strong Merovingian blood line, even one from the House of Lorraine, which seems plausible from the fact that the union's new currency portrays Charles V,[4] Prince Charles, who has already requested the job, would be an *impeccable* choice. In fact, no stronger candidate exists. This, along with all the other evidence presented herein, should rule out further consideration of King Juan.

Prince Philip's lineage. Robert Lacey remarks, "Philip, Prince of Greece, did not have a drop of Greek blood in his

1. Cathcart, p. 3.
2. Baigent, Leigh, and Lincoln, *Holy Blood, Holy Grail,* pp. 135, 170, 198-199.
3. Baigent, Leigh, and Lincoln, *Holy Blood, Holy Grail,* pp. 224-225.
4. Church, p. 227.

veins, and Princess Elizabeth's governess was right when she compared his ash-blond hair and angular features in July 1939 to those of a Viking. He was in essence a Dane, one of the exports to Greece of the most successful exporting dynasty of modern times, the Danish royal house, usually known to genealogists as the Schleswig Holstein Sonderburg Glucksburgs.... All [of] Philip's sisters had married Germans owning castles and the largest of them all was Schloss Salem, bigger than Buckingham Palace, the home of the Margrave of Baden." Lacey adds, "Apart from eighteen kings of Denmark this family has in recent history also supplied one king to Norway, four to Sweden, six to Greece, seven czars to Russia, and at the same time queen consorts for the Kings of Britain, Germany, and Rumania. So Prince Philip can boast more [recent] blue blood in his veins than Queen Elizabeth II. His ancestry can be traced back to Charlemagne through branches that wind diversely enough to include at one stage Henry Percy,...the legendary Hotspur."[1] Denis Judd adds,

> The Duke of Edinburgh's genealogical background is woven into such a wide and complex tapestry.... Strands come together from such feudal residences as Frederiksborg Castle in Copenhagen, the Greek royal estate of Tatoi, and a Grand Duke's castle in Germany. They can be traced back to the Imperial Russian court at St Petersburg and to the...palaces of the kings and queens of England. Even a cursory glance at Prince Philip's family tree...is enough to show that the "unknown Greek prince" who...came from nowhere to claim the hand of the heiress to the world's proudest and most stable throne had impeccable and impressive royal antecedents....
>
> Like Elizabeth, Philip is a great-great-grandchild of Queen Victoria; like her, he is a descendant of German ruling houses. On his father's side he comes from a Danish royal line that...by 1947, boasted sixteen kings of the House of Oldenburg and three of the House of Glücksburg—and Beck.... Since 1947 there have been two more monarchs, one of them Queen Margrethe II who has

1. Robert Lacey, *Majesty* (New York and London: Harcourt Brace Jovanovich, 1977), pp. 98-99, 102. Lacey adds, "[Philip's British mother] was born a Battenberg.... ...Philip was not born a Mountbatten, since his mother never anglicised her name.... [The] Act of Settlement of 1701....bestowed British nationality and royal status to the Electress Sophia of Hanover and all her descendants. So since he was numbered among these, Prince Philip had technically been a British Royal Highness from the moment of his birth" (ibid., p. 129).

reigned in Denmark.... Six kings of Sweden and seven tsars of Russia grew on the branches of the same tree, not to speak of the Glücksburg women who married into the British royal family....

Equally formidable was the heritage of Philip's mother, Alice of Battenberg and Greece, whose brother...[was] Earl Mountbatten [of Burma]....[1]

Queen Elizabeth II's lineage. According to Anglo-Israelites, the queen descends from King David (and Judah) through Solomon, Josiah, Zedekiah, and a woman named Tea Tephi. The queen's lineage, published in 1977 as "The Illustrious Lineage of The Royal House of Britain," not only concurs, but depicts her household as "The House of David—The Royal Line."[2] Indeed, in November 1985, the then President Ronald Reagan met at the White House with Prince Charles and his wife Diana, whom the president referred to as "Princess David!"[3] Of even greater interest is the fact that in May 1996, Israel's Channel 2 television noted in a widely viewed program that Prince Charles is connected to Israel by his supposed Davidic descent. (The prince is currently very popular in Israel.[4])

Ezekiel tells us that Zedekiah was a "profane, wicked

1. Judd, *Prince Philip*, pp. 23-24. For a more detailed account of Prince Philip's lineage, includ-ing a "royal circle" going back six generations, which also covers Queen Elizabeth II, as well as a Mountbatten family tree going back even further, purporting that the "Mountbattens are a branch of one of the oldest traceable families in Christendom, the House of Brabant," see the covers, and pages 22-30, 65-67, and 247 of the same work.
2. "The Illustrious Lineage of The Royal House of Britain."
   By AVCTORE GV. M. H. MILNER. A.M., S.G.R.Soc, I.V.ADSOC.
   E TYPIS EDD PRIOR R. FOLKARD ET FIL.
   ED. OCTAVA RENOVATA.
   LONDINI: MCMXXIII.
   Published By: The Covenant Publishing Co. Ltd.
   6 Buckingham Gate, London SWiE 6jP
   (First published 1902. This edition 1977.)
3. Alstair Burnet, *In Private—In Public, THE PRINCE AND PRINCESS OF WALES* (New York: Sum-mit Books, 1986), pp. 84-90. Maureen Johnson, "Private thoughts behind royal smile," *The Denver Post*, 2 Nov. 1994, p. 4A.
4. Today's Israeli population, apart from its relatively small number of true Christians, is entirely given to false Judaisms (Reform, Conservative, Orthodox, and Ultra-Orthodox), false religions and Christianities (Islam, Roman Catholicism, etc.), cults (e.g., Masonry), secularism, atheism, and all forms of "New Age" spiritualism and mysticism. Avi and Chaya Mizrachi, for example, observe, "More than 20% of the Israeli population consult with Kabbalistic Rabbis (who use mysticism and the occult) for decisions, or they go to astrologers or use tarot cards" ("Shalom from Israel" {Koinonia; P.O. Box 1491; Libby, MT 59923-1491}, Oct. 1997, p. 1). Further, Israel today accepts sodomy and infanticide, and has little to no respect for The LORD's promises to her forefathers; like Esau before her, she has become willing to sell her birthright for a bowl of soup, if so much. This Israeli apostasy shall serve the AntiChrist's interests, and will soon bring God's swift judgment.

73

prince of Israel" (21:25). Yet Queen Elizabeth II's lineage shows that she not only descends from *David* through **1)** Solomon, Josiah, Zedekiah, and <u>Tea Tephi</u>, but also through **2)** Nathan, Joseph of Arimathea (apparently), <u>Anna</u> (a so-called "cousin" of Jesus' mother Mary), and the House of Tudor (which eventually restored the red dragon to its ancient status as a royal device and supporter); through **3)** Anna, <u>Penardim</u>, Athildis, Clodomir IV, Phara-mond (traditionally, France's first king), Clodion, *Merovée* (Merovic), Childeric I, Clovis I, Roger, etc., Eustache I, Eustache II, *Godfroi de Bouillon* (Godfrey of Bouillon), Henry the Black of the Guelph Line, etc.;[1] as well as through **4)** Penardim, <u>Cadwalladr Frea</u>, etc. (see below). Tea Tephi is represented as having borne the forefathers of the modern British monarchy through King <u>Heremon</u> (Lit., "Eochaidh, the Heremon"), an ancestor of subsequent Irish and Scottish kings.

Herbert W. Armstrong, a cultist, may have been correct when he sought to show that King Heremon's forefathers, and thus the comparatively recent British monarchs, were themselves descendants of Israel's seafaring Danites. In fact, Queen Elizabeth II's lineage also shows that she descends from a man named *Dardanus* through **1)** Tros (Troes) and his descendants (i.e., the House of Troy), and **2)** Heremon and his forefathers. Although Dardanus is rep-resented as descending from Judah (see below), he may have actually arisen from Dan.

Besides through David, Queen Elizabeth II's lineage shows that she descends separately from *Judah* (and pos-sibly *Dan*) through **1)** Zerah, *Dardanus,* <u>Tros</u> (Troes), <u>Priam</u>, the House of Troy, the Sicambrians, and the Franks; through **2)** Tros, the ancient British, and the Byzantine emperors; through **3)** Priam's daughter, the Norse "god of thunder and lightning" *Tror* (*Thor;* cf. Rev 13:11-13), the Norse Line, and the Norse "god" *Odin,* who married

---

1. The queen also descends from the Merovingian Hildegarde. There is no clear indication, however, that while Baudouin I (Baldwin I), Baldwin II, Melisenda (the daughter of Baldwin II and a wife of Fulk V), Baldwin III, Amalric I, Baldwin IV, and Baldwin V are shown on her line-age, she actually descends from any of them. (A more detailed lineage than the one pos-sessed by this author could conceivably show otherwise.) Geoffrey Plantagenet, the father of Henry II, who is in the queen's lineage, was himself the son of Fulk V and his first wife Matilda, not of Melisenda.

Cadwalladr Frea; and through **4)** Heremon, who is represented as a descendant of *Dardanus.*

Cadwalladr Frea and *Odin* are together represented as
the parents of the royalty of **1)** the latter Franks, **2)** the
Anglo-Saxons, **3)** the Saxons, **4)** the Normans, **5)** the
Merovingians, **6)** the French House of Anjou, **7)** the Spanish Line, **8)** the Guelph Line, **9)** the Russian Line, **10)** the
Wettins, and **11)** the Skiolds. All of these royal families,
as supposed descendants of David (through Cadwalladr
Frea) and Judah (through *Odin* and David), are in Queen
Elizabeth II's lineage. Not only does the queen, therefore,
supposedly descend from David and Judah through at least
eleven additional lines, but much of Europe's royalty likewise supposedly descends from David and Judah. Nevertheless, the queen's lineal claims remain by far the most
prodigious.

The day that Jesus was crucified, Wednesday,[1] is
named after the Norse *Odin,* who is otherwise known as
the Anglo-Saxon *Woden* and the German *Wotan,* as well as
the Roman *Mercury* and the Greek *Hermes.* When the
scriptures are considered, it becomes clear from ancient
mythology that *Odin* is none other than Satan himself; for
Odin, by his various names, is identified as the god of war,
thieves, and merchants, and the prince of the power of the
air (i.e., the "wild wind god" who leads the "spirits of the
dead through the air"), who obtained his "wisdom" through
the sacrifice of an eye (cf. the single "all-seeing eye" that
remains) and to whom "victims were hanged on trees in
sacrifice" (cf. Jesus' crucifixion).[2] As shown above, *Odin*
is actually in Queen Elizabeth II's official lineage. That is,
this is what the British monarchy has said about itself.
Odin may have been an historical personage, but in the
context of the queen's lineage, he represents Satan.

Church suggests that the name *Odin* is "a form of the
word Dan." He also argues that the Merovingians, rather
than being actual descendants of Judah and David, are

---

1. For more information, see the chapter titled "Jesus' Fourth-Day Crucifixion and Seventh-Day
Resurrection" in *Messiah, History, and the Tribulation Period.*
2. *Eerdmans' Handbook to the World's Religions,* pp. 119-121, 406, 419, 431. Somewhat in
jest, Holden refers to the British monarchy as "the fount of all wisdom" (*PRINCE CHARLES,*
pp. 312-313).

really descendants of Dan, which, as one of northern Israel's ten tribes, not only "established an idolatrous religion—the worship of the sun and the moon" (derived from the ancient Babylonian religion of Assyria), but may "produce the great usurper, the antichrist." From this, as well as other information, Church speculates that "most of the suffering of Israel down through the centuries has been plotted and perpetrated by ['Gentile' rulers who were themselves descendants of] the lost tribe of Dan."[1]

Henry II, whose parents were Geoffrey Plantagenet and Empress Matilda, was an Anjou by birth (through Fulk V, his grandfather). Henry II married Eleanor of Aquitaine, who bore him Richard I. Eleanor's former husband, Louis VII of France, formed a precedent-setting alliance with the Priory of Zion and the Temple Knights, having personally established ninety-five of the Priory's members in France, some of whom joined the Temple Knights, upon his return to France from the Second Crusade in 1152.[2] Subsequently, Richard I, a homosexual who reigned from 1189 to 1199 and was otherwise known as the "Lionhearted" (*Coeur de Lion*), was the second French Plantagenet (or Angevin) to occupy the English throne. While admitting of England's royal family, "from the Devil we sprang and to the Devil we shall go," he nevertheless defeated Saladin in the Third Crusade in 1191 and "secured a treaty to guarantee Christians safe pilgrimage to Jerusalem."[3] Like Louis VII before him, Richard I maintained an early alliance with the Knights Templar, which, from the times of the crusades to this day, have supposedly provided the British monarchy with "the oldest armed bodyguard in existence." Three members of this bodyguard, comprised of a group of twenty-four knights who are now referred to as "Serjeants-at-Arms," apparently stand-in for the Order of the Garter's twenty-four companion-knights during such functions as the State Opening of Parliament, where they attend the

1. Church, pp. 87, 102, 108-114, 117-129. As Queen Elizabeth II's son, Prince Charles also descends from all these individuals. The underlying significance of his possible Danite ancestry will be examined in the next chapter, "Anglo-Israelism, David's Throne, and the AntiChrist."

2. Baigent, Leigh, and Lincoln, *Holy Blood, Holy Grail,* pp. 118-119.

3. Plantagenet Somerset Fry, *The Kings & Queens of England & Scotland* (London: Dorling Kindersley; New York: Grove Weidenfeld of Grove Press, Inc.; 1990), pp. 22, 37, 42.

British sovereign and escort the royal heralds and pursuivants.[1]

Prince Charles' lineage. All those mentioned above, who are in Prince Philip's and Queen Elizabeth II's lineages, are, of course, in Prince Charles' lineage. Cathcart notes Prince Charles' descent from William the Conqueror, Alfred the Great, Robert the Bruce, Mary the Queen of Scots, the Bowes-Lyons, Charles I, Electress Sophia, a "powerful line of Scandinavian counts and dukes and kings," the Dukes of Normandy and the House of Anjou, the "Anglo-Danish kings to Canute, grandson of Harald Blue-tooth, King of Denmark," King Cole or Ceol, Sweyn Forkbeard, Rollo the Ganger (a cattle thief and pirate who captured the dukedom of Normandy), Vladimir Monomakh the "Great Prince of Kiev," the Battenbergs, as well as "through Henry Tudor—from Llewellyn-ap-Gruffyd, the last native Prince of All Wales." Cathcart also remarks that Prince Charles is related to George Washington, Robert E. Lee, and Alice Liddell, known as Alice in Wonderland. Moreover, the prince is "the most Scottish prince since Charles I and perhaps the most English of princes since Henry VIII."[2] In *PRINCE CHARLES,* Anthony Holden gives the following information regarding the prince's unusually diverse lineage:

> ....The odds against being born to his fate are incalculable....
>
> ....His ancestors include Charlemagne and Genghis Khan,[3] El Cid and George Washington [(through John Smith)], Shakespeare and Count Dracula....
>
> ....As [Sir Iain Moncreiffe]...says, "HRH's [(His Royal Highness's)] breeding is the most important in the world...he is heir to the world's greatest position that is determined solely by heredity...."
>
> **In Prince Charles's veins runs the blood of emperors and kings, Russian boyars, Spanish grandees, noblemen of every European nation**, bishops and judges, knights and squires, and tradesmen.... Prince Charles is a cousin or nephew, in varying

---

1. James and Russell, *At Home with the Royal Family*, pp. 141, 146-147, 206; and Baigent, Leigh, and Lincoln, *Holy Blood, Holy Grail*, p. 121. For more information, see Chapter 7's section titled, "The Garter."
2. Cathcart, pp. 1-4.
3. Aga Khan gave Elizabeth II, then just a princess, a filly as a wedding present (*Her Majesty The Queen*, p. 50).

degrees, of all six wives of Henry VIII;...**he has many descents from the royal houses of Scotland, France, Germany,**[1] **Austria, Denmark, [Greece,]** Sweden, **Norway, Spain**, Portugal, **Russia**, and **the Netherlands**. Many of his ancestors died bloodily, in battle or by the ax....

....Moreover, he descends many times over from Llewellyn the Great, Prince of Wales, and all Welsh kings and princes by way of Hywel Dda back to Cunedda and Old King Coel himself, who reigned...soon after the Romans left Britain....

....Among his celebrated. Viking ancestors were King Sven Forkbeard of Denmark and King Harold Haardrade of Norway, but **he also springs from the ancient "Peace Kings,"** whose vast grave mounds can still be seen at Uppsala in Sweden....

In Russia, he is descended through Czar Nicholas I from both Catherine the Great and Peter the Great. He also has innumerable descents from the Grand Princes of the House of Rurik, who originally founded "all the Russias," among them St. Vladimir of Kiev, who Christianized the Russians....

In what was the Holy Roman Empire, he descends over and over again from Charlemagne and [crusader] Frederick Barbarossa and all the great dynasties, Habsburg and Hohenstaufen, **Guelph** and Hohenzollern, Bavaria and Saxony, Hesse and Baden, Mecklenberg and Wurrttemberg, Brunswick and Anhalt, the Electors Palatine and other Wittelsbachs, plus many of the historic houses such as Hohenlohe and Galen, Moltke and Sickingen, Schwarzenberg and Trauttmansdorff. **Otto the Great and Phillip of Hesse were his direct forefathers. Frederick the Great and the Emperor Charles V were his ancestral uncles**....

In Italy, his forefathers include Dukes of Savoy and the Emperor Frederick II, "Stupor Mundi," and the medieval kings of Sicily, as also the Orsini of Rome (Pope Nicholas III was his ancestral uncle)....

....**The prince's Anglo-Saxon and Danish royal forefathers [and others] sprang from Dark Age kings who incarnated the storm-spirit Woden.... Through the Lusignan crusader kings of Cyprus, titular kings of Jerusalem, Prince Charles descends** a millennium farther back from King Tiridates the Great, the first Christian monarch of all (under whom Armenia was converted in AD 314, before even Rome itself), and thus **from the divine Parthian imperial House of Arsaces (247 BC), which reigned over Persia and Babylonia** and was in its time the mightiest

---

1. In 1917, England's King George V, Prince Charles' great-grandfather, changed his last name from the German *Saxe-Coburg-Gotha* to the more innocuous "Windsor," with his family following suit. Battenberg was then also anglicized to Mountbatten, the name adopted by Prince Philip in 1947 (Junor, p. 22). Queen Elizabeth II's grandchildren, and Princess Anne, are now styled "Mountbatten-Windsor." The British monarchy, therefore, has a comparatively recent German extraction. For the backdrop to these name changes, see Judd, *Prince Philip*, pp. 45-46, 195-197.

dynasty in the ancient world.[1]

Alan Hamilton adds,

He boasts a pedigree that is frightening in its extent. In 1977,...Mr Gerald Paget...produced...*The Lineage and Ancestry of HRH Prince Charles, Prince of Wales*. Mr Paget...traced and enumerated 262,142 ancestors of Prince Charles. It was a slight cheat, for as a result of cousin marriages many of that number are in fact the same person appearing several times; **inbreeding has always been a strong strand in royal pedigrees**. Nevertheless Mr Paget showed that **Prince Charles was in some way descended from just about everybody who was anybody, anywhere, ever.**

Among his more direct forbears are the royal houses of Scotland, France, Germany, Austria, Denmark, [Greece], Sweden, **Norway, Spain**, Portugal, **Russia**, and **the Netherlands**. He can trace a connection to Alfred the Great, Hereward the Wake, William the Conqueror and every English monarch since.... He is descended no fewer than 22 times over from Mary Queen of Scots, and at least once from the Welsh prince Owen Glendower, **the Irish high king Brian Boru**,[2] Robert the Bruce of Scotland, Sven Forkbeard the Viking, Catherine the Great of Russia, Good King Wenceslas of Bohemia, **the emperors Charlemagne and Frederick Barbarossa, Frederick the Great of Prussia, Pope Nicholas II**, and last but far from least among mere commoners, George Washington....

Charles is the twenty-first Prince of Wales, yet strangely only 13 of the previous holders of the title ever became king, and one of those was Edward VIII, who did not stay at his post long enough for his Coronation....[3]

....He himself has said that he will reign as King Charles III,[4] although he would be quite entitled to call himself King Philip, King Arthur II, King George VII, or indeed any other name he cared to choose.[5]

Judd remarks, "Charles Philip Arthur George. Why

1. Holden, *PRINCE CHARLES*, pp. xxv, 330-335.
2. As Fritz Springmeier has documented, the Illuminati is organized around certain leading occult bloodlines, of which the Merovingian lineage is by far the most prominent. Another Illuminati bloodline is the Boru (Kennedy) bloodline.
3. If Prince Charles ever becomes king, even of Europe, he will be the *thirteenth* coronated Prince of Wales.
4. If this is so, it seems unlikely that Prince Charles will succeed his mother to the English throne. King Charles III does *not* calculate to 666 using the scriptural system. For more information, see the preceding chapter, "A Name that Calculates to 666."
5. Hamilton, *The Royal 100,* pp. 17-18. For more information regarding Prince Charles' amazingly diverse lineage, see Appendix B, or pages 222-227, of *King Charles III* by Holden.

those names? Philip was obvious. So was George, on both sides of the family. Arthur has quite often been used by British royalty. But Charles? Was it an unfashionable tribute to the troubled House of Stuart, which had produced Charles I and Charles II? (When the couple's second child was christened Anne it seemed to confirm this theory.)"[1] Actually, Prince Charles has a significant Stuart lineage. We should, however, point out that there are other reasons for the prevalence of certain of the prince's names. Charles, for example, is in reference to Charlemagne; Philip may be in reference to Philip II of France; Arthur is in reference to the legendary King Arthur;[2] and George may be in reference to England's "St. George" or, as we shall see later in this book, France's Merovée.[3] The prince could just as well have been named "Charlemagne Philip Arthur Merovée." Of course, that would have been too telling. When asked why the queen and Prince Philip chose "Charles" as the prince's first name, Buckingham Palace responded that is was for "personal and private reasons."[4]

As the AntiChrist must be, Prince Charles is a prince of Roman ancestry (see Dan 9:26-27). Yet while Holden notes that the prince descends from "crusader kings of Cyprus, titular kings of Jerusalem," he and others curiously neglect to mention the prince's apparent claims to *Davidic* descent as well, not only through the Merovingians, but also through other, non-Merovingian royalty in the lineage of his mother, Queen Elizabeth II. As shown later, the prince also supposedly descends from Mohammed, Islam's false prophet and founder![5]

An "illuminated" lineage. The British monarchy has strong lineal ties to the Illuminati. Fritz Springmeier, who has studied the Illuminati extensively, states,

1. Judd, *Prince Philip,* p. 144.
2. According to Baigent, Leigh, and Lincoln, the name "Arthur" derives from the Welsh word for "bear" (*Holy Blood, Holy Grail,* p. 239).
3. For more information, see Chapter 7's section titled, "The Garter."
4. Junor, p. 21.
5. For more information, see this chapter's later section titled, "Supposed descent from David, Jesus, and Mohammed."

The Illuminati are powerful elite bloodlines of generational satanists who manipulate the world from behind the scenes. Some people have already heard about the Illuminati, but I have been involved for several years in a venture perhaps never before done; I have been extricating members of the Illuminati, or deprogramming them. In doing so, I have taken a topic that was very nebulous and theoretical, that of "the Illuminati," and exposed it in detail, something which remains an ongoing effort. Some of this information specifically involves the British royal family.

The people with whom I have worked, who were members of the Illuminati, can testify full well that the British royal family is part of the Illuminati. In 1995, I combined selected articles that I had written in previous years about these Illuminati bloodlines into the book *The Top 13 Illuminati Bloodlines*. These bloodlines are the Astor, Bundy, Collins, DuPont, Freeman, Li, Onassis, Kennedy, Rockefeller, Rothschild, Russell, Van Duyn, and Merovingian (the 13th bloodline). The British royals are members of the Merovingian dynasty, the 13th and most prominent Illuminati bloodline, the "Holy" bloodline.

Prince Charles is related to the following American Presidents: Washington, Jefferson, Madison, both Harrisons, Tyler, Taylor, and George Bush, as well as Bush's vice-president Dan Quayle. Moreover, the prince is a known descendant of the Kennedy bloodline, and as such, he is a distant relative to John F. Kennedy. Prince Charles is also related to Robert E. Lee and Mrs. Woodrow Wilson, not to mention some others. The British royal family is closely related to the Virginia Tidewater plantation aristocracy, which ran the United States in its first decades. These aristocracy were the Carters, the Lees and Randolphs and the Smiths and Ironmongers who had so much power and wealth in Virginia. And they are Prince Charles' ancestors.

When Prince Charles married Lady Diana Spencer, Illuminati covens and other witchcraft covens in many countries recognized that this was a very important occult marriage. The marriage was observed with great interest by these covens. The media have occasionally made the mistake of telling the public that Prince Charles married a commoner. Lady Diana Spencer's ancestry is not so common.[1] Who are some of Princess Diana's ancestors and kinsmen? They include the following persons: William Vincent Astor, McGeorge Bundy and also Mrs. McGeorge Bundy, Amelia Earhart Putnam (Putnam is of the Collins family), Pierre Samuel DuPont IV, J.D. Rockefeller (I, II, III, and IV) and David Rockefeller, Franklin Delano Roosevelt (and Teddy), Brigham Young (a

---

1. As one columnist put it, "Diana didn't just become a princess; she was carefully chosen for the role. The royal selection process was as cold and prosaic as any thoroughbred auction. At 20, she had the lineage, the upbringing and the docility to appear to meet the requirements for a future Queen of England" (Alessandra Stanley, The New York Times, "Struggle for happiness touched women deeply," *The Denver Post,* 7 Sept. 1997, p. 22A).

81

prominent Mormon of the Merovingian dynasty) and one of his wives Louisa Beeman, Bertrand Arthur William Russell and his fourth wife Edith Finch, John Pierpont Morgan, Henry Cabot Lodge and many other people written about in *The Top 13 Illuminati Bloodlines*.[1] No blood ties between Diana and the Chinese Li Illuminati family, the Turkish Onassis bloodline, or the Reynolds-Dukes Illuminati bloodlines are evident. With such a bloodline, Diana was not supposed to have married a Dodi Fayed, an Egyptian playboy. (Although nothing, of course, has been heard of it in the press, their car accident just happens to have occurred at an important Merovingian ritual site.)[2]

Many Americans couldn't care less about their own genealogy. But bloodlines are very important to the Illuminati. There is no question that the Prince of Wales (who is related to all of Europe's aristocracy including the Russian Romanov family) and his ex-wife Princess Diana are related to some very powerful blue-blood bloodlines. Some of these connections may seem meaningless to the average reader. For example, Prince Charles is related to Genghis Khan, who was a type of the AntiChrist. Genghis Khan's relatives live in Europe and America. Due to having interviewed one of the descendants from this family, I know that most of the family is working for the New World Order, and that it still has a great deal of power. These families connect in unexpected ways too. Genghis Khan married a Jewish (Israelite) woman. Likewise, although the Romanov family dropped out of sight, I know an Illuminati slave (someone under the influence of powerful Illuminati mind-control programming) in Oregon who is a Romanov. Persons with the Romanov name are not ruling countries anymore, but the bloodline still carries occult power within the Illuminati.

There is no way to fully convey to the reader all the hidden connections of these satanic occult bloodlines. It must suffice to say that Prince Charles is well connected with them. The most important occult bloodlines are interwoven. For instance, William II (Prince of Orange) was from the occult Orange lineage, and his wife Mary from the House of Stuart (another occult lineage). Their son William III, therefore, had two strong occult lineages in his veins, making him more powerful in the occult, according to Illuminati thinking, than either of his two parents. As it turns out, this Dutch Freemason William of Orange (William III), who took the British throne in 1688, was a significant part of the Mystery Religions' conspiracy to bring in a New World Order. In fact, many of the important people of the conspiracy trace back to William of Orange. He started the Order of Orange

1. For the genealogical information relating these individuals to Princess Diana, see Gary Royd Roberts and William Adams Reitwiesner, *American Ancestors and Cousins of The Princess of Wales* (Baltimore, Maryland: Genealogical Publications Co.).

2. For more information, see Chapter 10's section titled, "Death of a princess."

patterned after Freemasonry, which is still strong in Ireland. He also got the Scotsman William Paterson to start the mother of all central banks, the Bank of England. The Paterson family still has descendants who are Illuminati. Later, the Bank of England was put under the direction of the Rothschild Illuminati bloodline. Along with this, another Scottish occultist, John Law, started the French central bank in 1716, which he modeled after the Bank of England.

In the book *The Very Rich: A History of Wealth,* by Joseph J. Thorndike, Jr., one reads on page 170, "The British Rothschilds became ardent hunters, famous hosts, and members of the inner circle of the Prince of Wales." If one examines the lives of the British royal family, one will find that they have a lot of contact with the Astors, the Greys, and the Rothschilds, as well as other Illuminati families. Just one example of many to illustrate this is Higham's description of the Prince of Wales' life during the 1930's and '40's, when, as the Duke of Windsor, he married Wallis Warfield Simpson and abdicated his throne and title as King Edward VIII.[1] As the Prince of Wales, Edward was a close friend of Eugene de Rothschild, and spent much time at his Schloss Enzesfeld castle near Vienna. While the prince visited the Rothschilds in 1937, another guest at the castle was Fritz Mandl, a Jewish armament maker who supplied Hitler with weapons. I mention all this because Edward was involved in all kinds of pro-Nazi activity, and was widely viewed as pro-Nazi, and yet here he was visiting with a Jewish Rothschild and a Jewish arms dealer who apparently supplied Hitler with arms. When Louis Rothschild was arrested by the Nazi's, the Duke of Windsor negotiated his release in 1939. Later, on August 15, 1940, Edward sailed with Baron Maurice Rothschild to the Bahamas. And when Wallis Simpson, ultimately styled the Duchess of Windsor, came out of seclusion in December of 1973, it was to attend an Onassis Party in Paris. All these families were above (presided over) World War II.

I have sought to demonstrate that if one understands the hidden occult lineages, history takes on an entirely new shape and meaning. For instance, my co-author Cisco Wheeler, whom I brought out of the Illuminati, is a descendent of President Ulysses Grant. Grant was a descendent of both the Delano and the Collins Illuminati families, being related to Franklin Delano Roosevelt (FDR)! When we start to understand the Illuminati, we not only need to understand their lineages, but also their HIDDEN lineages. These people have large numbers of hidden bastard lineages, through children who themselves are the result of secret satanic ceremonies.[2]

1. Charles Higham, *The Duchess of Windsor* (New York: McGraw-Hill Book Co., 1988).
2. Written correspondence, quoted by permission, from Springmeier. For more information, see the discussion on the Garter in Chapter 7, "The Heraldic Symbols in the Arms and their Interpretations."

Supposed descent from David, Jesus, and Mohammed.
At times, Prince Charles looks, talks, and acts as though he were a Christian, and he certainly seems to have at least a few Christian ancestors. Further, the British monarchy has virtually proclaimed itself to be the legitimate heir to the throne of Israel's King David. The combination of Prince Charles' seemingly Christian veneer with his adherence to Anglo-Israelism could eventually provide him with valuable leverage over both Judaism and Christianity, particularly if he is the AntiChrist. Jesus told unbelieving Israel, "I have come in My Father's name, and you do not receive Me; if another comes in his own name, him you will receive" (John 5:43).

But what about Islam, another major religion? Believe it or not, the prince also supposedly descends from Mohammed. In her book, *Invitation to a Royal Wedding,* Kathryn Spink remarks, "[Prince Charles'] ancestors included such unlikely figures as Mohammed, the Prophet of Islam, and George Washington, the first President of the United States, and he was born to bear a range of titles which are at the very least impressive."[1]

Where presidents of the United States are concerned, consider this somewhat chilling revelation regarding the true reach of the British monarchy: "According to those presidential-race watchers obsessed with blood links to royalty and nobility, Bill Clinton is the blue-blooded winner. 'The presidential candidate with the greatest number of royal genes has always been the victor, without exception, since George Washington,' said Harold Brooks-Baker, director of Burke's Peerage publishing house in London. 'Only the merest drop of royal blood flows in the veins of Sen. Dole,' he added. Both men can trace their ancestry to England's King Henry III, but Clinton's lineage is much more royally rooted, with loose links to Britain's reigning royals, Brooks-Baker said."[2] Like Franklin D. Roosevelt, who was related to the British monarchy and acted on its behalf, Clinton, of course, won the election.

---

1. Kathryn Spink, *Invitation to a Royal Wedding* (England: Colour Library International Ltd., 1981), p. 19.
2. "Royal roots? Clinton gets edge," *The Denver Post,* 29 Oct. 1996, p. 2A.

According to Church, the Priory of Zion is comprised of thousands of nominal (unfaithful) "Protestants, Roman Catholics, Jews, and Moslems."[1] These individuals believe that Jesus didn't really die on the cross, but was stolen away from the tomb and survived. No matter how bizarre, the elements that make up this view are not particularly unique, nor are they repulsive to most non-Christians.[2] In fact, many non-Christians, regardless of their ethnicity, would readily accept such a lie over the truth, which condemns their false religious beliefs and reveals their less than pleasant eternal destiny.

We see, therefore, that Prince Charles, by virtue of his lineage alone, could someday claim for himself royal heirdom to much of the world, including the three major religions that have historically vied for control of Jerusalem (i.e., Judaism, Roman Catholicism, and Islam).[3] Lineage, however, is not the prince's only advantage where such heirdom is concerned; there is, for example, also the British Commonwealth.[4]

1. Church, p. 11.
2. E.g., see Josh McDowell, *The Resurrection Factor* (California: Here's Life Publishers, Inc., 1981), pp. 92-102.
3. For more information, see Chapter 10, "Religious, Political, and Other Ties."
4. For more information, see Chapter 2, "A Man for Our Times."

5

Anglo-Israelism, David's Throne, and the AntiChrist

According to the doctrine of Anglo-Israelism, which the author fully *rejects,* Great Britain and the United States are both significantly populated by the so-called "lost" ten tribes of Israel. Although it is Jesus, not a usurping British monarchy, who truly sits upon David's throne (Isa 9:6-7), the statement at the bottom of Queen Elizabeth II's official Anglo-Israelite lineage nevertheless reads, "David shall never want a Man to sit upon the throne of the house of Israel" (cf. Jer 33:17)! In this vein, on June 2, 1953, with the Knights of the Garter carrying and holding the canopy over her head,[1] Elizabeth II was anointed and crowned at her coronation as "Queen of thy people Israel."[2]

Various Anglo-Israelites, including Prince Charles and his mother, hold that the throne upon which the queen was crowned, the famous Coronation Chair at Westminster Abbey in London, is the rightful throne of Israel's King David. Until recently, they asserted that it had "Jacob's head-stone," on which he rested his head at Bethel, for its base. Legend has it that the prophet Jeremiah took this 336-pound stone, called the *Stone of Destiny,* to Ireland. Used there for a coronation throne, the stone was then brought to Scone (pronounced "skoon") in Scotland, where for a millennium—until 1296—Scottish kings were crowned. Edward I is purported to have subsequently taken the stone by force to England, where it was placed

1. For more information, see the discussion on the Garter in Chapter 7, "The Heraldic Symbols in the Arms and their Interpretations."
2. Both Prince Albert, who became King George VI, and his daughter Elizabeth, who became Queen Elizabeth II, were nearly bypassed for the royal succession due to concerns over the need for "personalities dynamic enough to win back the lustre of the monarchy after abdication" by Edward VIII (Lacey, *Majesty,* pp. 72-74). Cathcart adds, "if he had unexpectedly arrived a week earlier, [before a change to the laws of succession,] Charles would not have been born a Prince at all" (pp. 8-9). It would seem, however, in light of this work, that the queen's son, Prince Charles, has an ignominious destiny to fulfill.

in Westminster Abbey and used, since 1308, for English coronations. Lacey similarly comments, "This statuesque and elaborately carved high-backed oak chair was built by order of King Edward I (reg. 1272-1307, not to be confused with St. Edward, Edward the Confessor, who ruled from 1042 to 1066) to enclose the Stone of Destiny on which Scottish Kings used to sit when they were crowned, and which Edward had stolen from its resting place in the Abbey of Scone in 1296. The stone was said, by legend, to be the pillow on which Jacob slept."[1]

Regarding Elizabeth II's coronation, Lacey records, "Queen Elizabeth II's view of her own function in the summer of 1953 was infused with mysticism.... 'I was glad when they said unto me, We will go into the House of the Lord,' rang out the notes of the opening anthem.... As Handel's setting of 'Zadok the Priest and Nathan the Prophet' carried through the church the text which had been recited at every crowning in England from the coronation of King Edgar the Peaceful in 973, the Queen's jewellery and robes were lifted.... Her ceremonial train made a rich crimson pile.... 'Be thy hands anointed with holy oil, be thy breast anointed with holy oil, be thy head anointed with holy oil,' proclaimed the [apostate] Archbishop of Canterbury, 'as Kings, Priests, and Prophets were anointed.' Enthroned in King Edward's Chair..., Elizabeth II received the elaborate tokens of the responsibility with which she was being invested, the Orb—'remember that the whole world is subject to the power and empire of Christ'[2] —the Sceptre with the Cross, ensign of power and justice, the Rod of Mercy, and also the Royal Ring with a sapphire and ruby cross—'the Wedding Ring of England.'"[3] The Archbishop of Canterbury then placed St. Edward's crown upon Elizabeth II's head, the congregation proudly sang "God Save the Queen" (Britain's National

1. Lacey, *Majesty*, p. 161.
2. The Orb is actually a gold sphere having a Templar or Merovingian cross at its top. For more information, see the discussion on the Garter in Chapter 7, "The Heraldic Symbols in the Arms and their Interpretations."
3. Lacey, *Majesty*, pp. 160-162. For a photograph of Michael Ramsey, former Archbishop of Canterbury, wearing a miter and a crucifix, and holding an opulent Templar cross-tipped staff, see Frazer, page 46. It is reminiscent of the Roman pontiff for its pomp, with a caption comparing "Christian priests and bishops" to "magicians in primitive societies."

Anthem), and the queen took communion.[1]

Nevertheless, some historians have questioned whether Edward I obtained the real Stone of Scone, which may have had a Hebrew inscription, and whether the stone he did obtain is the one that England reluctantly returned to Scotland in November 1996 from Westminster Abbey, which appears to be nothing more than a Scottish "slab of reddish-grey sandstone."[2] The stone is now on display at Edinburgh Castle, Scotland.[3]

Anglo-Israelism received new life in this century through its popularization by the late Herbert W. Armstrong's Worldwide Church of God.[4] As a cornerstone of his theology, Armstrong adopted Anglo-Israelism. Bob Larson comments,

> It was Armstrong's belief in Anglo-Israelism that drew the most theological attention. Though Herbert denied it, his doctrine closely resembled the theory expounded by Canadian Richard Brothers, a psychic visionary who lived in London in the eighteenth century.... Ignoring sound rules of linguistics and hermeneutics, the theory suggests that England ([supposedly the superior] Ephraim) and the Untied States ([supposedly the inferior] Manasseh) are what is left of the so-called Ten Lost Tribes of Israel. Ancient Judah and Israel are believed to [still] be two separate entities.... After the Assyrian captivity, Israel [presumably] migrated northward to eventually become the Anglo-Saxons of British heritage.
>
> Armstrong taught that the promises of God due to his chosen people have been transferred to America and the United Kingdom. He also declared that Queen Elizabeth [II] sits on the throne to which Christ will return. [The]...WCG maintains that the British Coronation Stone of Scone was actually brought to the Emerald Isle by the prophet Jeremiah....
>
> Perhaps the most dangerous Armstrong doctrine is the contention that deity is an attainable goal of man. A recent WCG publication insists "We are to be changed from physical to spiritual [(a denial of the bodily resurrection)]...into the spirit of God.

1. Junor, pp. 27-28.
2. "Palace of Destiny," *Realm,* Sept./Oct. 1994, No. 58, pp. 24, 27.
3. William D. Montalbano, "Scots get the Stone but not at Scone," *The Denver Post,* 16 Nov. 1996, p. 4A. "Royal relic returns to Scottish castle," *The Denver Post,* 22 Nov. 1996, p. 26A.
4. The Worldwide Church of God has *until recently* rejected the biblical doctrine of the Triune Godhead and denied the existence of hell. It has held instead that the believer would ultimately be absorbed spiritually *into* God, thereby becoming a part of God, and that the unbeliever or wicked would be annihilated rather than suffer eternal punishment. Also, it has ardently promotes Anglo-Israelism.

We must be God. Blasphemy? No. Believe it or not, you are a potential omnipotent power. You were born to become God!" Note, the writer doesn't say *a* god. He says *God*. This view, of course, robs Christ of his unique position as eternal God.[1]

Consider also the following brief excerpts from the late Walter Martin's refutation of Anglo-Israelism:

The basic premise of the Anglo-Israelite theory is that...these so-called "lost" tribes are, in reality, the Saxae, or Scythians, who surged westward through Northern Europe and eventually became the ancestors of the Saxons, who later invaded England. The theory maintains that the Anglo-Saxons are the "lost" ten tribes of Israel and are substituted, in Anglo-Israel interpretation and exegesis, for the Israel of the Bible.

In the heyday of the British Empire, when their colonies spanned the globe under Victoria, Anglo-Israelites were in their glory, maintaining that, since the British were the lost tribes and, therefore, inheritors of the covenants and blessings of God, it was obvious that God was honoring His promises and exalting His children in the latter days.

In light of recent history, however, and the loss by Britain of virtually all her colonial possessions, Anglo-Israelites are content to transfer the blessings of the Covenant to the United States, maintaining as they do that Ephraim is Great Britain and Manasseh, the United States. The fact that Ephraim is called "the exalted one" in Scripture and that Manasseh is designated as the inferior of the two, creates both historical and exegetical problems for the Anglo Israelites. This is particularly true because the United States, the inferior (Manasseh), has now far surpassed the allegedly superior Ephraim....

...Anglo-Israelism maintains that Judah represents the Jews who are still under the divine curse and are not to be identified with Israel at all....

Moreover, it should be noted that the Anglo-Israelite theory and the Worldwide Church of God both maintain that the throne of England is the throne of David. In the June 1953 issue of *The Plain Truth* [(a WCG publication)] appears the statement:

Herman L. Hoeh now reveals the astonishing fact that Elizabeth II actually sits on the throne of King David of ISRAEL—that she is a direct descendant, continuing David's dynasty—the VERY THRONE on which Christ shall sit after his return... Elizabeth II was crowned "Queen of thy people Israel." Turning to the article by Hoeh, it clearly states that the throne upon which she was crowned (i.e., the "Stone of Scone," lodged in Westminster

1. Bob Larson, *Larson's New Book of Cults*, rev. (Illinois: Tyndale House Publishers, 1989), pp. 469-471.

Abbey) is really the stone which Jacob used for a pillow, which he took with him when he departed from Bethel, and which later came under the care of Jeremiah the Prophet, who took it with him to England, where it became the Coronation Stone for the British (Davidic) dynasty.

The disturbing scientific fact that the Stone of Scone has been examined and analyzed, and found to be..."...of Scottish origin" does not deaden the enthusiasm of Anglo-Israelites....
The Anglo-Israelites' school of interpretation claims more than 3,000,000 adherents in England, Canada, the British Commonwealth and throughout the world, including the United States. They are found in many already-established denominations in Christian Churches and so do not constitute a separate denomination, preferring to work through all groups, instilling its propaganda....[1]

Martin goes on to quote the following material from pages 37 to 38 of David Baron's, *A Letter to an Inquirer*:

....There is not the least possibility of doubt that many of the settlements of the Diaspora in the time of our Lord, north, south, and west, as well as east..., were made up of those who had never returned to the land of their fathers since the time of the Assyrian and Babylonian exiles, and who were not only descendants of Judah, as Anglo-Israelism ignorantly presupposes, but of all the *twelve tribes scattered abroad* (James 1:1)....
To summarize the state of things in connection with the Hebrew race at the time of Christ, it was briefly this:
I. For some six centuries before, ever since the partial restoration in the days of Cyrus and his successors, the descendants of Abraham were no longer known as divided into tribes but as one people, although up to the time of the destruction of the second temple tribal and family genealogies were for the most part preserved, especially among those who were settled in the land.
II. Part of the nation was in [the land]..., but by far the largest number were scattered far and wide, and formed innumerable communities in many different lands, north and south, east and west. But wherever dispersed and to whatever tribe they may have belonged, they all....anticipated the same future. They had one common center of worship in Jerusalem...and they made pilgrimages thither annually in great numbers at high festivals.
The name of "Jew" and "Israelite" became synonymous terms from about the time of the Captivity....
"That the name 'Jews,'" writes a Continental Bible scholar,

1. Walter Martin, *The Kingdom of the Cults* (Minnesota: Bethany House Publishers, 1985), pp. 307, 309-310. Quoted by permission of CRI.

"became general for all Israelites who were anxious to preserve their theocratic nationality, was the more natural, since the political independence of the ten tribes [from the two] was destroyed."...

Anglo-Israelism teaches that members of the ten tribes are never called "Jews," and that "Jews" are not "Israelites," but both assertions are false....

Now note, Anglo-Israelism tells you to identify the ten tribes with [just two nations]..., but if you are on the line of scripture and true history, you will seek for them "among all nations."...

My last words on this subject must be those of warning and entreaty. Do not think, as so many do, that Anglo-Israelism, even if not true, is only a harmless speculation. **I consider it nothing short of one of the latter-day delusions by which the Evil One seeks to divert the attention of men from things spiritual and eternal....**

And finally, it not only robs the Jewish nation, the true Israel, of many promises in relation to their future by applying [them] to the British race in the present time, but it diverts attention from them as the people in whom is bound up the purpose of God in relation to the nations, and whose receiving again to the heart of God after the long centuries of unbelief, will be as life from the dead to the whole world.[1]

It is evident that the counterfeit theology of Anglo-Israelism lacks any legitimate basis. However, there is an early Church teaching which, if correct, lends substantial support to the contention of Armstrong, some Anglo-Israelites, and others that the British monarchy is related to the tribe of Dan.

Dan and Ephraim are not mentioned in the apocalyptic list of the twelve tribes from which the 144,000 sealed Israelites are to come during the Great Tribulation (see Rev 7:5-8, 14:1-3). While these saints are to be spiritually chaste (Rev 14:4-5, Gk.), Dan and Ephraim led ancient Israel into idolatrous worship, after the manner of the Gentiles, causing Israel to become spiritually defiled (see Judg 17 to 18; 1 Kin 12:26-30; Hos 4:17-19; cf. Deut 29:18-21). Nevertheless, the list alludes to the half-tribe Ephraim through its inclusion of Joseph (cf. Ezek 37:15-19), evidently signifying that those from Ephraim who are in The Son of Joseph (an ancient rabbinic designation for the suffering-Servant Messiah) are eligible.

1. Martin, *The Kingdom of the Cults*, pp. 310, 312-314.

(The half-tribe Manasseh is listed separately from Joseph.) Unlike Ephraim, however, Dan is entirely excluded from the 144,000 sealed Israelites, even though it will inherit its allotted portion of the Land of Israel in the Millennial Kingdom (see Ezek 48:1-2; cf. Josh 19:40-48).[1] While some of northern Israel's Ephraimites apparently repented under Judaea's Hezekiah and Josiah, there is no indication of such repentance among the Danites (see 2 Chr 30:1-11, 30:18-23, 31:1, 34:6-9). Finally, notice that the tribe of Levi, which is omitted from certain Old Testament lists because it has no territorial inheritance in the Land of Israel, is included in the list of the 144,000 sealed Israelites.

Based upon Dan's exclusion from the apocalyptic list, as well as certain Old Testament prophecies and parallels, Irenaeus concluded that the AntiChrist would arise from that tribe,[2] and Hippolytus, observing that both Judah and Dan are called "a lion's whelp" (Gen 49:9; Deut 33:22) and that "the deceiver seeks to liken himself in all things to the Son of God," wrote, "as the Christ springs from the tribe of Judah, so the AntiChrist is to spring from the tribe of Dan."[3] Jacob prophesied, saying, "Dan shall be a red dragon [serpent][4] by The Way [the way], a *horned* serpent

1. A few scholars (e.g., Walvoord) have made the suggestion that Dan is classified with his brother Naphtali who was born to the same mother. Yet no biblical support exists for this position. Indeed, all of Israel's tribes came from just four mothers, and none of them is categorized in such a manner in other lists of the twelve tribes found in the scriptures.
2. Irenaeus, *Against Heresies,* Bk. 5, Ch. 30, Par. 2; see *Ante-Nicene Fathers,* ed. Roberts and Donaldson, Vol. 1, p. 559.
3. Hippolytus, *Treatise on Christ and AntiChrist,* Pars. 6-7 and 14-15; see *Ante-Nicene Fathers,* ed. Roberts and Donaldson, Vol. 5, pp. 206-207.
4. The first Hebrew word translated as "serpent" in Genesis 49:17, which is also found in Genesis 3:1-4 and 3:13-14, Numbers 21:6-9, Deuteronomy 8:15, Job 26:13, Psalms 58:4 and 140:3, Proverbs 23:32, Isaiah 14:29, 27:1, and 65:25, Jeremiah 8:17 and 46:22, Amos 5:19 and 9:3, and Micah 7:17, is Strong's number 5175. In Arabic, this word is used to refer to "the constellation of the serpent or dragon in the northern part of the sky" (William Gesenius, 5175, *HEBREW-CHALDEE LEXICON of the OLD TESTAMENT* {Michigan: Baker Book House Co., 1979}, p. 545). Further, this word is related to another Hebrew word, Strong's number 5153, which refers to the "*red* color of the throat of a serpent [5175, as denom.] when hissing [(cf. Prov 23:31-32)]" (James Strong, 5153, "A Concise Dictionary of the Words in the Hebrew Bible," *STRONG'S EXHAUSTIVE CONCORDANCE OF THE BIBLE* {Tennessee: Abingdon Press, 1986}, p. 102). Therefore, Genesis 49:17, like most of the other verses mentioned above, not only refers to a serpent, but it can also be taken as a reference to a red-colored dragon (i.e., Satan; cf. Num 33:11). In fact, Philo, writing in the first century A.D., not only identified the serpent of Genesis 49:17 as a "dragon," but he also addressed *the* dragon who in the form of a serpent deceived Eve in the Garden of Eden (*On Husbandry* {*Agr.*}, secs. 95-96; see *The Works of PHILO,* trans. C.D. Yonge {Massachusetts: Hendrickson Pub-

[viper] by the path, that bites the horse's heels so that its rider falls backward. I have waited for your Yeshua [Salvation],[1] O LORD!" (Gen 49:17-18, Heb.; cf. Jer 8:16-17, Heb. and KJV). Understood literally, Jacob's prophecy refers to the mortal conflict between the red dragon or Satan, as represented by Dan (cf. Rev 13:2-4), and The Messiah (see Gen 3:15; Rev 12:3-5; cf. Rev 1:18, 20:1-3), who is The Way (John 14:6), as well as the saints in Him (cf. Rev 12:9-17, 20:4), who in the first century were referred to collectively as "the Way" (see Acts 9:2, 19:9, 19:23, 24:14, 24:22, Gk.; cf. 22:4)! We are also told in the pseudepigraphic (Jewish) *Testament of Dan* (found in the *Testaments of the Twelve Patriarchs*) that Dan's prince is Satan (5:6).[2] Ever since the days of Jacob, Israel's twelve tribes have been individually represented by the signs of the twelve houses of the Zodiac. With this in mind, one writer observes, "To Judah was given the insignia of Leo, the Lion, and to Dan was given the insignia of Scorpio, the seed of the serpent."[3] Morris comments, "Dan's bad reputation may be quite old, for this tribe (along with Zebulun) is omitted from the genealogies in the early chapters of 1 Chronicles."[4]

According to Anglo-Israelites, Tea Tephi (a supposed descendent of Solomon) bore the forefathers of today's British monarchy through a man named Heremon, who was himself an ancestor of later Irish kings. Armstrong endeavored to show that these kings, to whom the British monarchy is related, were themselves descendents of the

---

lishers, Inc., 1993}, p. 182). Likewise, the Greek Septuagint renders this Hebrew word as "dragon" in Job 26:13, where it refers to the "apostate dragon," as well as in Isaiah 27:1 and Amos 9:3. Moreover, the creature represented by this word is actually defined as a "dragon" in Isaiah 27:1, so that most English translators not only represent it as such, but some even occasionally render the word itself as "dragon" (e.g., in Job 26:13 or Isaiah 14:29). Finally, the Apocalypse itself explicitly calls this very serpent a "fiery red dragon" (Rev 12:3-4, 12:9; cf. Gen 3:13-15).

1. Targum Jonathan and the Jerusalem Targum both paraphrase the meaning of *Yeshua*—Jesus' Hebrew name—in Genesis 49:18 as "the redemption of the Messiah, the Son of David" (C.F. Keil and F. Delitzsch, "THE FIRST BOOK OF MOSES," Vol. 1 of *Commentary on the Old Testament* {1986; rpt. Massachusetts: Hendrickson Publishers, Inc., 1989}, p. 404).

2. *The Old Testament Pseudepigrapha*, ed. James H. Charlesworth, Vol. 1 (New York: Doubleday, 1983), p. 809. *Ante-Nicene Fathers*, ed. Roberts and Donaldson, Vol. 8, p. 26.

3. Church, pp. 113, 116-117.

4. Leon Morris, *REVELATION*, Tyndale New Testament Commentaries, No. 20 (Michigan: Eerdmans Publishing Company, 1987), pp. 112-113, n. 2.

Danites:

The tribe of Dan occupied two different districts, or provinces, in the Holy Land before the Assyrian captivity. One colony lived on the seacoast. They were principally seamen, and it is recorded Dan abode in ships (Judges 5:17).

When Assyria captured Israel, these Danites struck out in their ships and sailed west through the Mediterranean and, as we shall now note, north to Ireland....

Some historians see a connection between those Danites and the Danoi in Greece and the Tuatha De and Tuatha De Danaan [(meaning "people of the goddess Danu"] of Ireland. *Tuatha De* means "people of God." The name Dunn in the Irish language, for example, means the same as Dan in the Hebrew: judge....

The real ancient history of Ireland is very extensive.... ...Long prior to 700 B.C. a colony of mixed ancestry called "Tuatha De Danaan" arrived in ships, drove out other tribes, and settled there. Later, in the days of David, a colony of Milesians, apparently of the line of Zarah [(presumably Zerah, a descendant of Judah)], arrived in Ireland from the Near East.

Later still, an elderly, white-haired patriarch [(i.e., Jeremiah)], sometimes referred to as a "saint," came to Ireland. With him was the princess daughter of an eastern king [(i.e., Zedekiah)] and a companion called "Simon Brach," spelled in different histories as Breck, Berech, Brach, or Berach. The princess was named Tephi or Tea-Tephi....

This royal party included the son of the king of Ireland [(i.e., Heremon)] who had been in Jerusalem at the time of the [Babylonian] siege. There he had become acquainted with Tea-Tephi. He married her shortly after the city fell. Their young son, now in his late teens, accompanied them to Ireland.

....The son of this...king [Heremon] and the Hebrew princess [Tea Tephi] continued on the throne of Ireland and *this same dynasty continued unbroken* through all the kings of Ireland; was *overturned* and transplanted again in Scotland; again *overturned* and moved to London, England, where *this same dynasty continues today* in the reign of Queen Elizabeth II....

Besides the royal family [of Israel], the prophet [Jeremiah] is thought by some to have brought with them certain remarkable things, including a harp, and a wonderful stone called...[the] "stone of destiny."...

Another strange coincidence—or is it just coincidence?—is that many kings in the history of Ireland and England have been coronated sitting over this stone—including the present queen. The stone rests today in Westminster Abbey in London, and the coronation chair is built over and around it. A sign once beside it labeled [it] "Jacob's pillar-stone" (Gen 28:18)....

In view of the linking together of biblical history, prophecy, and Irish history, can anyone deny that this Hebrew princess was the daughter of King Zedekiah of Judah and therefore heir to the throne of David? That the aged patriarch was in fact Jeremiah, and his companion was Jeremiah's scribe, or secretary, Baruch?[1]

Is it plausible that certain seafaring Danites really did travel to Ireland? Could the tribe of Dan have even been aware of Ireland's existence? It is known that King Solomon traded heavily with the merchants of *Tarshish* (2 Chr 9:21). Regarding *Tarshish,* R.F. Gribble comments,

> [The] ships of Tarshish were symbolic of Mediterranean trade and traders, being well-known in Mediterranean and Red Sea waters, and carrying merchandise of great value.
> The genealogical list of Genesis 10, in connection with 1 Chronicles 1:7, gives an intimation that these special Tarshish ships did business with the Greek isles. Such commerce, carried on in the 6th and 7th centuries B.C., is noted by Herodotus (1.163; 4.152)....
> ....Evidently [Tarshish]...developed trade in minerals (Jer 10:9; Ezek 27:12).... A Phoenician inscription of the 9th cent. B.C., found in 1773 in Sardinia, notes a Tarshish in the island.[2]

In the first century, what now constitutes the United Kingdom—Great Britain and Northern Ireland—was a Roman province, the head of the Roman Empire in the West. Before the Roman Empire, however, today's United Kingdom was known as *Tarshish* (cf. Jonah 1:3).[3] Further, based upon the above mentioned inscription, it appears that *Tarshish* may have established a base on the island of Sardinia, which lies due-west of Rome in the Mediterranean Sea. If so, Dan's merchants could have heard about Ireland's location from the merchants of *Tarshish,* and some of them could have eventually sailed there.

1. H.W. Armstrong, *The United States and Britain in Prophecy* (U.S.A.: Worldwide Church of God, 1986), pp. 98-102.
2. "TARSHISH," *The Zondervan Pictorial Encyclopedia of the Bible,* 1976 ed., Vol. 5, p. 598. For more information , see Chapter 7's section titled, "The royal shield and the arms of the Prin - cipality of Wales."
3. For more information, see the section titled "The Last Four Seals of the Tribulation Week (and the Second Advent)" in *Messiah, History, and the Tribulation Period,* as well as the related note in this work's Chapter 7, "The Heraldic Symbols in the Arms and their Interpretations."

6

The First Beast
and
Prince Charles' Coat of Arms

By the age of *thir-teen,* Charles was granted his own heraldic achievement,[1] or "coat of arms,"[2] and at the age of nineteen, one year before his formal investiture as Prince of Wales (discussed later), he was granted his own

Welsh standard (above).[3] Below, we will examine the symbols found in the prince's official coat of arms,[4] as well as

1. Boutell, *Boutell's Heraldry,* rev. C.W. Scott-Giles and J.P. Brooke-Little (London: Frederick Warne, 1963), pp. 217-218. The design of Prince Charles' heraldic achievement was finalized by 1962 (e.g., see Boutell, plate V).

2. Although we will refer to Prince Charles' full heraldic achievement as his "coat of arms," Boutell correctly observes that this term, while "frequently used as synonymous with achievement, embracing not only the shield but also the crest, supporters (if any) and other accessories," actually applies in a strict sense "only to the heraldic insignia now normally displayed on the shield." According to Boutell, a coat of arms originally consisted of "a coat, or tunic, which a man wore over his armour, and on which were painted or embroidered the same devices as appeared on the wearer's shield" (Boutell, 1978 ed., pp. 21-22). Such a coat or tunic served as a graphic and unmistakable way of identifying an individual in a contest or battle.

3. Holden, *PRINCE CHARLES,* p. 156. Boutell, 1978 ed., p. 258.

4. For a quality color representation of Prince Charles' official heraldic achievement, see Boutell, 1970 or later ed., between pp. 174-177. According to Brooke-Little, "This is the approved design of the arms of the heir-apparent for use by H.R.H. Charles Philip Arthur George, Prince of Wales, Duke of Cornwall and Rothesay, Earl of Chester and Carrick, Baron of Renfrew, Lord of the Isles and Great Steward of Scotland. Worked into the compartment are H.R.H.'s badge as heir-apparent..., the red dragon badge for Wales differenced by a label argent and the arms of the duchy of Cornwall. (This illustration is from an original painting by Mr. Geoffrey Mussett [who is a Herald Painter at the College of Arms].)" For a close unofficial version of the prince's achievement, see *Burke's Guide to the Royal Family,* 1st ed. (London: Burke's Peerage Ltd., 1973), p. 104. The author has been told that this achievement may also be found on page 141 of *Burke's Guide to the British Monarchy,* although he could not verify it. As a knight of the Order of the Garter, the prince's heraldic stall-plate, which contains his actual *graven* achievement, is supposedly displayed in St. George's Chapel along

some unusual variations between it and at least one later, unofficial version.[1] However, before doing so, the words "herald" and "heraldry" should be defined.

A herald may be a messenger who proclaims important news, or a harbinger who gives a sign or an indication of something to come. The heralds of medieval history, for example, communicated challenges and made proclamations at tournaments and battles while recognizing armored combatants by their distinctive insignia, or "devices." These artistic and beastly devices, which were likewise used on seals as a means of personal identification,[2] formed the basis for modern, or institutionalized heraldry. "While still associated with the knightly shield, helm and banner, heraldry was no longer a practical ancillary to the warrior's equipment, but became rather a decorative art.... [The]...heralds began to weave a mystery about their craft, deliberately complicating its nomenclature and language, and introducing unnecessary rules and conventions."[3] The purposes and functions of heraldic arms, designed and produced through the ancient and modern "arts" of heraldry (armory), are not unlike those of heralds. Indeed, those officials whose specialty is heraldry, are called "heralds" (as well as "armorists"). According to *Boutell's Heraldry,*

> In its widest sense, heraldry means all the duties of a herald....
> ....True heraldry does not boast—it aspires. For some, indeed, it possesses a spiritual value.
> In various ways, therefore, heraldry appeals to the mind.... Some [early princes and knights] took a lion or other beast characterizing strength or valour; **some took a religious symbol; and many placed on their shields figures forming a play on their names.** Symbolism of a rudimentary kind was present in early

with all the stall-plates of other Garter knights (except for the sovereign). Likewise, as a knight of both the Order of the Thistle and the Order of the Bath, the prince could have his stall-plate displayed in the chapel of St. Giles church in Edinburgh, Scotland, as well as in Henry VII's Chapel in Westminster Abbey (Boutell, 1978 ed., pp. vi, 194, 196).

1. Unofficial versions of an achievement may reflect an emphasis on the part of the herald that differs from the officially accepted (legal) version of an achievement. In the case of the particular unofficial version of Prince Charles' arms with which this work deals, the deviations suggest some rather interesting points.
2. Boutell, 1978 ed., pp. 176-178.
3. Boutell, 1978 ed., pp. 10-11.

heraldry, and in this respect there is a link between it and the insignia which appeared on the shields and banners in previous periods of history.

At pre-heraldic insignia we need only glance. At all times, and in all parts of the world, men have used symbols to focus ideas and sentiment and express them in visual form. Warriors, and particularly leaders, have been accustomed to display such symbols on shields and standards.... The legions and cohorts of Rome had their insignia....

These insignia of antiquity are [generally] to be regarded as the predecessors and not as the ancestors of medieval heraldry.... [Yet] some of the emblems found in ancient symbolism have survived to take their place as devices in heraldry. For example, **the British tribal emblem of a [red] dragon [which was formerly displayed upon the standards of Roman cohorts] became a supporter of the Royal Arms in Tudor times and is still the badge of Wales**.... In more remote times personal insignia may sometimes have been used to establish identity.... In the 12th century it became purposefully distinctive and consistently hereditary....

A modern herald has defined "true heraldry...as the systematic use of hereditary devices centered on the shield."

....Heralds have [also] drawn on classical and medieval mythology, and on their own creative imaginations, to add a number of monsters and hybrids to the animals of nature.[1]

In heraldry, these monsters and hybrids are called "beasts." Stephen Friar states,

> The vigorous medieval interpretation of beasts, birds, fish, reptiles and chimerical monsters is for many the very quintessence of heraldry.
>
> The magnates of the Middle Ages often possessed one or more distinctive beasts as personal devices, culled from the pages of the bestiaries or from the shadowy traditions of ancestral crusaders. Many of these devices were incorporated into the shield of arms, but a far greater number were adopted as personal badges and were later translated into crests and supporters....
>
> The use of beasts as emblems of authority pre-dates armory [(institutionalized heraldry)] by many centuries.... From the reign of Richard I [the Lionhearted] (1189-99) beasts became increasingly popular as royal devices, and by the fifteenth century the English kings had accumulated a variety of devices as the result of alliance or inheritance. Collectively these, with a number of later additions, are known as the Royal Beasts....[2]

1. Boutell, 1978 ed., pp. 2-4, 81.
2. "Beasts," *A Dictionary of Heraldry,* ed. Stephen Friar (New York: Harmony Books, 1987),

Like heralds, each coat of arms makes certain proclamations about its owner. To some extent, these proclamations may be determined by "reading" the shield and the
devices surrounding it. To read a coat of arms, one should
be familiar with the heraldic terminology used to identify
specific points or locations on, or relative to, an armorial
shield. The shield itself is usually central to the arms. The
upper one-third of the shield is sometimes referred to as
the *Honor* point, the middle one-third as the *Fess* point,
and the lower one-third as the *Nombril* or Navel point.
More frequently, however, a combination of the terms
chief, base (or *ground*), *dexter,* and *sinister* is used. <u>*Chief*</u>
means the *top* of the shield, or the area above it, whereas
<u>*base*</u> and <u>*ground*</u> mean the *bottom* of the shield, or the
area below it. (The area below the shield, at the base of
the coat of arms, is the location of the *Compartment* and a
related *Motto.* The motto, which is usually given in Latin,
expresses an idea, goal, or admonition.) From a frontal
viewpoint, <u>*dexter*</u> means the *left*-hand side of the shield, or
the area to the shield's left, whereas <u>*sinister*</u> means the
right-hand side of the shield, or the area to the shield's
right. The four quadrants, or quarters, of the shield are
specified through combinations of these terms. Chief-
dexter (or dexter-chief), for example, means the top-left
quarter of the shield. As a general rule, armorists (heralds)
read a coat of arms, relative to its central shield, from top
to bottom and left to right.[1]

As we shall see, the coat of arms belonging to Prince
Charles of Wales comprises a literal, graphic representation
of the beast described in Psalm 22:21, Daniel 7:2-24, and
the Apocalypse (e.g., see Rev 12:3, 13:1-4). The Apocalypse describes the dexter beast, the center of the arms,
and the red dragon, whereas the book of Daniel describes
the center of the arms and the sinister beast. Psalm
22:21, on the other hand, describes the dexter and sinister
beasts, as well as the red dragon (see below). Also, there
are descriptions of other parts of the arms elsewhere in the

---

pp. 55-56.
1. "Shields, Points of the," *A Dictionary of Heraldry*, ed. Friar, p. 316. Also see Boutell, 1978
   ed., p. 21.

scriptures.

The dexter beast in Prince Charles' coat of arms, rather than being the "normal" heraldic lion for England, has a body like a leopard for *Germany,* feet like the feet of a bear for *France,* and a mouth like the mouth of a lion for *England*. In other words, it fully represents the Merovingian dynasty, which originated and prospered historically in Germany, France, and England.[1] The sinister beast, a unicorn, faces the dexter beast, stands above the red dragon (see Rev 13:2; cf. 12:3, 12:9), and has eyes like those of a man. This beast is restrained (cf. 2 Th 2:6-7, Gk.) by means of a chain (cf. Ezek 7:23, AKJV). In heraldry, as well as in many New Age circles today, the unicorn is said to represent "the Christ," and in ancient Babylonian artwork, as well as in the book of Daniel, it was portrayed as a beast having a *little horn* (see Dan 7:8, 7:11, 7:20-21, 8:9-11; cf. 8:5-8). Irenaeus, Tertullian, Justinus, and others, likened the horn of the unicorn to the central beam of the cross upon which Jesus was crucified.[2] (The unicorn's horn may also be compared to the spikes that were used to pierce Jesus.) Like certain Renaissance artwork,[3] ancient Babylon's Ishtar Gate incorporates depictions of lions, dragons, and unicorns (or bulls).[4] At His crucifixion, Jesus prayed,

> Many bulls have surrounded Me; strong *bulls* of Bashan have encircled Me. They have opened their mouth at Me as a raging and a roaring lion.... You have brought Me to the dust of death. For dogs have surrounded Me; the assembly of the wicked has enclosed Me. Like a lion, *they pierced* My hands and My feet.... Deliver Me from the sword, My only one from the dog's paw. **Save Me from the lion's mouth and from the horns of the unicorns—the** affliction[5] **of the dragon [sea-monster]!**[6] (Ps

1. For more information, see Chapter 4, "Prince of this World—a *Diverse* Lineage," and Chapter 7's section titled, "The dexter (left-hand) supporter."
2. Odell Shepard, *The Lore of the Unicorn* (New York: Avnel Books, 1982), pp. 80-81.
3. Nancy Hathaway, *The Unicorn* (New York: Avenel Books, 1980), pp. 47, 104-105.
4. *The Thompson CHAIN-REFERENCE BIBLE*, 4th ed., 4334 (Indianapolis, Indiana: B.B. Kirkbride Bible Co., Inc., 1982), p. 318.
5. Strong's no. 6040, עֲנִי or *onee*.
6. Strong's no. 8577, תַן or *tanee*. The translation of this last phrase in Psalm 22:21 (v. 22 in Heb.), "*the* affliction of the dragon [sea monster]," is derived from a concatenation in the Hebrew of two words, Strong's numbers 6040, עֲנִי or *onee*, and 8577, תַנִּין or *taneen*. Strong's no. 8577 is represented with the final *nun* having been dropped or omitted, giv-

22:12-13, 22:15c-16, 22:20-21, Heb.; cf. Ps 22:21, AKJV; Rev 13:1-2)

In 1603, following the death of England's Queen Elizabeth I, Scotland's King James VI assumed England's throne as James I. Upon uniting the crowns of England and Scotland, King James I added Scotland's red lion to England's royal shield of arms and replaced one of

Elizabeth I's two lion supporters (i.e., her sinister supporter) with Scotland's unicorn. Rüdiger R. Beer remarks, "By far the best known unicorn in heraldry is part of the British coat of arms. When England and Scotland united at the beginning of the seventeenth century and James VI of Scotland became James I of the United

---

ing תני or *tanee*. This *nun* may have been dropped inadvertently through a copyist's error, or purposely omitted to create a poetic rhyme with the last word, יחידתי or *y'chee-datee* (tr., "My only one"), of the preceding verse (cf. *onee-tanee*).

In the Masoretic Text, the Hebrew phrase *onee tanee* appears as one word, עניתני or *anee-tanee*. In English, this text is commonly translated as "You have answered [rescued] Me," though some render it simply as "poor," which comes from the same Hebrew word as "afflicted" (cf. the Greek *Codex Sinaiticus*). Along the latter line, the Revised Standard Version (RSV) has "My afflicted soul" (the *New* RSV uses "You have rescued Me"). Yet all these translations are *dubious*. In the case of "You have answered [rescued] Me," *anee-tanee* is alleged to be Strong's number 6030, which in reality bears only a weak resemblance to it, whereas in the other translations, it is viewed as a combination of Strong's number 6041 (for "poor" or "afflicted") and an *inexplicable* or *nonexistent* word (e.g., for "soul"). Further, none of these translations agrees with the immediate context or poetic form of verse 21, a plea for deliverance from *beasts,* and, with the lone exception of the RSV, they ignore verse 24 (v. 25 in Heb.), which clearly addresses an earlier "affliction."

In this author's opinion, therefore, it is best to understand the Hebrew as a concatenation of two words that do exist (i.e., Strong's numbers 6040 and 8577, where the root for 8577 appears to be 8565, תן or *tan*), thereby obtaining "*the* affliction of the dragon [seamonster]." Inasmuch as Jesus' crucifixion upon the cross was typical of the swallowing of Jonah by a "sea monster" (e.g., see Matt 12:40, Gk.), this is a viable translation; moreover, it perfectly fits the immediate context and poetic form of verse 21.

Kingdom, a unicorn replaced one of the pair of lions supporting the shield. The menacing lion and antagonistic unicorn from Psalm 22 thus became fortuitously reunited in heraldry."[1] *Queen Elizabeth II's* coat of arms, as currently displayed in the Garter Throne Room, is shown above.[2] A remarkable graven version of the royal achievement adorns the gates of Buckingham Palace. It displays the dexter lion and the sinister unicorn, each resting upon a base of palm branches that curve around their backsides (perhaps indicating millennial aspirations), as well a "George Pendant" dangling from the central royal shield, over which, in place of the normal helm, there is a lion's head. Moreover, its shield contains the pagan version of the Irish harp, which shows the upper body of a bare-breasted harlot. A photograph of this achievement is shown in *The Illustrated Golden Bough,* with a caption that reads, "In many cultures, the souls of dead kings in particular are thought to migrate into animals, and sometimes living kings may be embodied in them. A trace of this idea survives in European heraldry."[3]

Taken together, the symbols in Prince Charles' coat of arms represent his present and future dominion. It is Interesting, therefore, that the organization of the dexter and sinister beasts in British royal arms, including the prince's, appears to have Babylonian origins. Barbara G. Walker

1. Rüdiger Robert Beer, *Unicorn: Myth and Reality,* trans. Charles M. Stern (New York: Van Nostrand Reinhold Company, 1972), p. 138.
2. As sovereign of the Order of the Garter, Queen Elizabeth II's coat of arms is prominently displayed above her Garter Throne in the Garter Throne Room. For a color photograph of the Garter Throne Room, see page 64 of *Royalty,* Vol. 12, No. 2 (1993). Unlike Prince Charles' coat of arms, the queen's may be readily seen. In fact, her Garter stall-plate, containing her actual *graven* achievement, rather than being displayed in St. George's Chapel along with the stall-plates of other Garter knights, is located above her throne in the British parliament, where she presides annually over the state opening. For a color photograph of the queen's Garter stall-plate, as well as certain other heraldic symbols and badges discussed in this book, see the state opening of parliament shown on page 50 of *Royalty,* Vol. 11, No. 3 (December, 1991). Other color pictures of her arms may be seen, for example, on page 83 of *Debrett's Book of the Royal Wedding* by Hugo Vickers (New York: The Viking Press, 1981); the jacket, inside front cover, and page 96 of *The Royal Family* by Jane Masterson (New York: Crescent Books, 1991); pages 82, 83, and 94 of *Royalty,* Vol. 13, No. 2 (1994). Artistic renditions of the queen's arms may also be found in the various editions of *Boutell's Heraldry,* although the rendition in the 1963 ed. is more accurate than that in later editions (Plate I, facing title page). Likewise, heraldic descriptions of both her arms and Prince Philip's arms may be found on pages 218 or 219-220 of the same work.
3. Frazer, p. 110.

states, "[The unicorn is the classic] symbol of the phallic horse deity, or sacred king incarnate in a horned horse.... A source of the unicorn myth may have been the Babylonian dragon-beast made up of a horselike body...and a flat [single] horned head.... One theory proposes that the unicorn was originally the bull of spring, rearing up and struggling with the lion of summer. Babylonian art showed both animals in profile so the bull appeared to have only one horn. The British coat of arms still has 'the lion and the unicorn' contending in just such a manner."[1]

The pagan lion, dragon, and unicorn symbols were prominent in ancient Babylonia and Assyria, as well as subsequent world empires (e.g., the Medo-Persian, Greek, and Roman empires). Today, however, their greatest applications are to the AntiChrist and his coming worldwide kingdom, with its capital at Mystery Babylon (Rev 17:4-5, 17:18). Inasmuch as the United Kingdom was *Tarshish,* this neo-Babylonian capital will be intimately associated with "Tarshish, and all its young lions" (e.g., see Ezek 38:13; Rev 13:2; cf. Jer 2:14-15, 4:5-7, 5:6).

As will be shown, the mythological unicorn was initially derived from Babylon's spring bull. When considered, this fact should lay to rest the arguments of many modern scholars that the Hebrew word רים, pronounced *re'em* and translated as "unicorn" throughout the Authorized King James Version of the Old Testament, should instead be translated as "wild ox." Given the historical association of the unicorn with the AntiChrist, this matter is significant.

With the lone exception of Deuteronomy 33:17, in which the singular *re'em* must be translated as "wild ox" (due to the fact that Moses ascribed a plural number of horns to it in the original Hebrew), this word may be rendered as "unicorn" (referring to a beast having just one horn) throughout the Hebrew Bible. One could perhaps, however, reasonably argue that the word *re'em* in Numbers 23:22 and 24:8 must also refer to some kind of "wild ox" (since Moses likewise penned Numbers). Nevertheless, besides Psalm 22:21, the following

---

1. Barbara G. Walker, "Unicorn," *The Woman's Encyclopedia of Myths and Secrets* (New York: Harper Collins Publishers, Inc., 1983), pp. 1027-1028.

passages, based upon the original Hebrew text, remain:

> Will the **unicorn** [wild ox] be willing to serve you? Will he bed by your manger? Can you bind the **unicorn** [wild ox] in the furrow with ropes? Or will he plow the valleys behind you? Will you trust him because his strength *is* great? Or will you leave your labor to him? (Job 39:9-11)

> The voice of The LORD breaks the cedars; yes, The LORD splinters the cedars of Lebanon. He makes them also skip like a calf, Lebanon and Sirion like sons of **unicorns**. (Ps 29:5-6)

> "But You, LORD, *are* on high forevermore. For behold, Your enemies, O LORD—for behold, Your enemies shall perish; all the workers of iniquity shall be scattered. But You have exalted like **unicorns** My horn. My eye also has seen *My desire* on My enemies,...on the wicked who rise up against Me." *The* Righteous *One* shall flourish like a palm tree; He shall grow like a cedar in Lebanon. (Ps 92:8-12; cf. Num 23:22, 24:8; 1 Sam 2:10d-e, Heb.; Ps 89:17-29, 132:17-18, Heb.; Zech 14:10, Heb.)

> "For My sword shall be bathed in heaven; indeed, it shall come down on Edom, and on the people of My curse, for judgment." The sword of The LORD is filled with blood, it is made fat with fatness, with the blood of lambs and goats, with the fat of the kidneys of rams. For The LORD has a sacrifice in Bozrah, and a great slaughter in the land of Edom. The **unicorns** shall come down with them, and the young bulls with the mighty bulls; their land shall be soaked with blood, and their dust made fat with fatness. (Isa 34:5-7; cf. Isa 63:1-6; Rev 14:17-20, 19:11-21)

In the third century B.C., when composing the Greek Septuagint, at least seventy of Israel's rabbis (according to rabbinic tradition) together translated the word *re'em* in all of the above passages as *monoceros* (i.e., a beast having one horn projecting from its head). Various scholars have argued that these rabbis, unfamiliar with the beast, mistakenly translated *re'em* as *monoceros*. Yet even Isaiah distinguished the *re'em* from "the young bulls with the mighty bulls" (34:7).

Although the *re'em* spoken of in the scriptures almost certainly *was* a ferocious wild ox, perhaps even the now extinct aurochs, it was the very bull of spring depicted in Babylonian artwork. The significance of this lies not in the fact that the biblical *re'em* was originally a wild ox, but rather in the fact that by the time the Septuagint was produced, this Babylonian bull had long been superseded by its earlier artistic depiction as a unicorn. It seems plausible that the rabbinic translators of the Septuagint had this in mind when they chose to render the Hebrew *re'em* as *monoceros* in Greek (Lat., *unicornis*), the beast that by then had replaced the ancient Babylonian bull in pagan mythology. Consequently, the unicorn is now a symbol that represents both Satan and the AntiChrist. (More will be said on this in the discussion of the sinister unicorn supporter.) Regarding the *re'em* and the lion, Odell Shepard gives this helpful discourse:

> ...[It has been discovered] that *rimu* was the Assyrian name of the gigantic aurochs or *Bos Primigenius*, a species of wild buffalo which became extinct in the sixteenth century. Cuvier, basing his measurement upon remains of the aurochs much smaller than others since discovered, estimated that this animal was twelve feet long and almost seven feet high; its teeth have been found in a cave on Mount Lebanon;...Layard identified the animal with the majestic sculptured bulls of Nineveh. The *Bos Primigenius* now holds the field. Its bulk, speed, and savage ferocity...make it clear why the Hebrews always spoke of the *Re'em* with bated breath....
>
> Before the accession of James I to the throne of England a great variety of "supporters" had been used for the Royal Arms, but a lion had for several generations been one of the two.... On the Royal Arms of Scotland the unicorn had been employed as consistently.... It is often said that the lion and unicorn were chosen as supporters of the British Arms because of the belief in the natural animosity of these two beasts and as a symbol of the reconciliation between England and Scotland.... James kept his Scottish unicorn and he chose the English lion merely because it had been the most persistent supporter of the English Arms before his time. He kept the lion dexter as it had been on Elizabeth [I]'s Arms....
>
> ....It is certain that the presence of the unicorn on the British Royal Arms, reproduced as they are millions of times in every year and scattered throughout the world, has tended to maintain interest in the animal and to develop a curiosity about its tradition....
>
> One recalls in this connection several Biblical references to horns, apparently single....
>
> Thus far we have paid no attention to the total scene...at

Persepolis,[1] in which a beast resembling a powerful lion attacks an apparently one-horned animal.... ...I shall call these animals the lion and the unicorn. The delineation of their conflict was remarkably popular over a great extent of territory and of time. One sees it continually and with only slight variations on cylinder-seals of Babylon[ia] and Assyria, on coins of Mycene, and on *objects d'art* of uncertain origin that were spread through Europe and Asia during the Middle Ages by Scythian traders. The inference is that it had more than a decorative value and was widely recognized as a symbol. But a symbol of what?

Here and there in the unicorn literature of Europe one finds references to a clever ruse employed by the lion in capturing unicorns [via a tree]. [This lion-capture fable]...seems to have been crowded out by the story of the virgin-capture [in which a unicorn (cf. The Messiah) is meekly lured by a virgin (cf. the Church) to his death under a tree (cf. the cross) before a huntsman and his dogs (cf. Satan and those who perpetrated the crucifixion)], yet it may be much older than the Holy Hunt allegory and may have served for ages as a religious symbol in the East....

...Edward Topsell...says of the unicorn: "He is an enemy to Lions, wherefore as soon as ever a Lion seeth a Unicorn, he runneth to a tree for succour, that...he may not only avoid his horn but also destroy him; for the Unicorn in the swiftness of his course runneth against a tree, wherein his sharp horn sticketh fast. Then when the Lion seeth the Unicorn fastened by the horn, without all danger he falleth upon him and killeth him."...

As I have pointed out, the one-horned figures at Persepolis were imitations, both in subject and treatment, of others [found] at Nineveh and Babylon. These in their turn were by no means original, for recent diggings at Ur of the Chaldees have shown...precisely the same conventional treatment of horned animals....

Looking at these objects from the city of Abraham, one realizes that....the pattern or theme of the lion and unicorn conflict can be shown to have endured in art for at least twenty-five hundred years.... Is it possible to make a plausible guess at the meaning these objects had for their makers?... Is it possible that the lion and the unicorn...were solar and lunar emblems?...

That there is some kind of connection between the moon and the unicorn is not a theory but a fact.... On ancient cylinder-seals the crescent moon frequently appears in conjunction with figures of animals which...are represented with single horns. ...The unicorn is commonly, though not always, thought of as white in body; it is an emblem of chastity; it is very swift; according to the best authorities it cannot be taken alive. The animal is most

---

1. Persepolis was the main royal palace of Medo-Persia's Achaemenid dynasty and a major center of Zoroastrianism, which predicates itself upon the ancient struggle of good against evil (*Eerdmans' Handbook to the World's Religions*, p. 82).

readily associated with the new or crescent moon, which might indeed seem to dwellers by the sea to be leading the stars down to the water and to dip its own horn therein before they descend. The crescent moon has been used for ages to represent both celestial motherhood and virginity, whether of Ishtar, Isis, Artemis, [Ashtoreth (Astarte), Asherah, Anath, Diana,] or the Madonna.[1] In all his pictures of the Assumption...Madrid Murillo painted the crescent moon over Mary's head. Old alchemical charts commonly designate the figure of Luna by placing in her right hand a single horn. The ki-lin, or unicorn of China, is commonly represented in bronze, bearing a crescent moon among clouds on his back....

....For is not the [pagan] belief in the moon's power to absorb poisons rising from earth during the darkness closely similar to the belief in the unicorn's water-conning? Does it not recall the vivid picture of the three-legged ass dipping his golden horn into the waters of the firmament and dispelling their corruption?...

If the unicorn [in the lion-capture story] is to represent the moon, then the lion, a common solar emblem, should of course represent the sun, and we have only the tree left to be explained.... Unicorned animals are often found on Assyrian cylinder-seals grouped with a single conventionalized tree in symbolical arrangement. This tree of the cylinder-seals is usually called the Tree of Fortune, but it seems to be ultimately indistinguishable from the Cosmogonic Tree...springing from the nether darkness and holding the earth and heavenly bodies in its branches, familiar in the myths of many peoples.... If the lion and the unicorn are to represent the sun and the moon they will need no less a tree than this as the scene of their encounter.

We are now prepared for a bald statement of the solar-lunar theory concerning the lion-capture [of the unicorn]...: "The Lion-sun flies from the rising Unicorn-moon and hides behind the Tree or Grove of the Underworld; the Moon pursues, and, sinking in her turn, is sun-slain." In other words, just as the lion of our story slips behind the tree to avoid the unicorn's onrush, so the sun goes behind the Tree...; and as the unicorn is caught by the [lodging of its] horn [in the tree] so the moon is held fast during the interlunar period—at which time, many myths assert, the sun eats it up....

Brown also finds significance in the fact that many of these [one-horned] creatures are shown touching or nearly [touching] the symbolic tree with their horns, and that their heads are

---

1. Not only has the unicorn likewise been used to represent the Virgin Mary, but Pope John Paul II and other Roman Catholics are known to have prayed and said the Mass before the "Black Madonna." Located in the shrine of Czestochowa at Jasna Gora, Poland, this demonic image is taken as a depiction of the Virgin Mary holding the Child Jesus.

invariably turned toward this tree.[1]

Before its ancient perversion and corruption, the Zodiac apparently represented the Gospel of Jesus in symbolic form.[2] Could the explanations put forth to date for the combined mythological symbolism of the lion and the unicorn also be corruptions of an original, divine theme? What if the tree whereby the unicorn in the lion-capture fable is slain originally represented the Tree of Life, or Jesus, as well as the cross upon which He was hung? The entire universe is under Jesus' dominion and power, and the stars, planets, moons, etc., rest in His branches (cf. Gen 3:22; Matt 13:31-32; Luke 13:18-19). What if the unicorn pictured Jesus' adversaries—Satan and those in him (e.g., Judas Iscariot and the AntiChrist; see Ps 75:4-5 {KJV}, 75:10*a*)—who in piercing both Jesus and the tree (cross) upon which He hung, became lodged in that tree and were themselves vanquished thereby along with guilt and sin (though certain victories are yet to come)? Besides representing Satan who personifies sin, the unicorn would then also have represented the sins of the redeemed world, Jesus' bride, for whom Jesus was to be pierced. Finally, what if the lion depicted The Lion of the tribe of Judah (see Rev 5:5; cf. Gen 49:8-12; Num 23:24), who, having veiled Himself upon the cross as the Lamb of God (cf. hiding behind the tree), slew Satan in Satan's attempt to slay Him (see Rev 5:6-14)?

As God's Mighty Messenger (Rev 10:1, Gk.), Jesus will shout aloud "with a great voice, as *when* a lion roars," and then "seven thunders" will speak "their voices" (Rev 10:3; cf. Rev 11:19, 16:17-18). Further, He will "roar *over* His enemies" (Isa 42:13, Heb.; see Jer 25:30-38, 50:44; Hos 11:8-12; Joel 3:13-16)! As God's Lion, Jesus will slay the AntiChrist, or Satan's unicorn, ending Satan's dominion.

---

1. Shepard, pp. 44-45, 75-79, 240-244, 247-249.
2. For more information, see Ethelbert W. Bullinger, *The Witness of the Stars* (Michigan: Kregal Publications, 1967); D. James Kennedy, *THE REAL MEANING OF THE ZODIAC* (Florida: Coral Ridge Ministries, 1989); or Troy Lawrence, *The SECRET MESSAGE of the ZODIAC* (California: Here's Life Publishers, Inc., 1990). Also see the section titled "The Gospel and the Zodiac" in *Messiah, History, and the Tribulation Period*.

What about the sun and the moon? In paganism, the sun has long been represented by a lion (cf. Hos 5:13-14), and the moon by a unicorn (cf. Hos 5:7, 5:13). Biblically, however, the sun is a symbol of The Bridegroom, Jesus (see Num 24:17; Ps 19:4-6, Heb.; Isa 62:1; Mal 4:2; Matt 17:2; Rev 1:16, 10:1, 22:16; cf. Ps 89:36), whose glory will be seen upon His saints (e.g., see Judg 5:31, Heb.; Isa 58:10; Matt 13:43; 1 Th 5:5; 2 Pet 1:19; cf. Isa 30:26). Also, the moon is a symbol of Jesus' bride, the saints (e.g., see Ps 89:35-37; Rev 12:1; cf. Gen 37:9-11; Song 6:10; Isa 24:23), who reflect His light in the midst of the darkness of an unregenerate world (cf. Matt 25:5-10; 2 Cor 3:18). Therefore, the sun, representing Messiah Jesus, is associated with the symbol of the lion, whereas the moon, representing His bride, for whom and by whom He was pierced, is associated with the symbol of the unicorn.

Recall that God warned Cain, saying, "If you do well, is there not exaltation? And if you do not do well, Sin is crouching *like a lion* at the door, and his desire is toward you, but you should rule over him" (Gen 4:7, Heb.). Unable to better Him, Satan has always sought to counterfeit the things of God. *The lion and unicorn symbols, besides representing Jesus and His adversaries, respectively, also have counter-applications.* Just as Jesus is The Lion of the Tribe of Judah, Satan too is viewed as a lion (1 Pet 5:8; cf. 2 Tim 4:17). Similarly, just as Satan, in the person of the AntiChrist, is represented as a unicorn, God, in the person of His Son, is represented as The Horn of David (Ps 132:17-18, Heb.; see 1 Sam 2:10*d-e*, Heb.; Ps 75:6-7, 89:19-29, 92:8-12; Luke 1:68-75; cf. Ps 75:10*b*). Having been lured to His death by a virgin under a tree (i.e., the cross), as in the virgin-capture story, Jesus shall yet trample His adversaries beneath His feet; for it is written, "You shall tread upon *the* roaring *lion* and *the* asp, *the* young lion and *the* dragon You shall trample underfoot" (Ps 91:13, Heb.; cf. AKJV).[1] Indeed, as a type of His Son

---

1. According to Shepard, the Talmud records that Adam's first sacrifice was an ox having just one horn on its forehead (p. 45). This would constitute a unique parallel to the sacrifice of The Messiah.

(e.g., see Num 23:21-22, 24:7-8, Heb.; Hos 11:1; Matt 2:14-15), God likens redeemed Israel to a conquering unicorn around the time of Armageddon, stating, "Arise and thresh, *O* daughter of Zion; for I will make your horn iron, and I will make your hooves bronze [brass], and you shall crush [beat in pieces] many peoples" (Mic 4:11-13, Heb.; see Deut 33:26-29; Ps 44:4-5, 89:17-18; Mic 7:8-10; Zech 10:3-5, 10:12; Mal 4:1-3). Further, according to Zechariah 14:10, in which the Hebrew word for *re'em* is generally translated as "raised up" or "rise," Jerusalem itself will be exalted as upon the tip of a unicorn's horn in the Millennial Kingdom (cf. Ps 75:10*b*); that is, she will sit atop *one mountain,* then Earth's highest, which can be likened to the *single horn* of a majestic unicorn.

In The Messiah, who is God's and Judah's Lion, the saints will be victorious in their war against the AntiChrist, Satan's and Britain's counterfeit lion-beast, even though it will cost most of them their physical lives (e.g., see Rev 6:7-11, 12:17, 13:3-17, 15:1-4, 20:4-6). The Horn of David, not the little horn, shall be eternally exalted; for Satan and those in him will be utterly crushed (e.g., see Ps 75, KJV)! It is written,

> How lovely are your tents, *O* Jacob! Your dwellings, *O* Yisra-El!...He shall pour water from His buckets, and His Seed *shall be* in many waters. His King shall be higher than Agag, and His kingdom shall be exalted. God brings Him out of Egypt. He has strength like a wild ox [unicorn]. He shall consume the nations, His enemies. He shall break their bones and pierce *them* with His arrows. He bows down, He lies down as a Lion, and as a Lion, who will rouse Him? Blessed *is* he who blesses You, and cursed *is* he who curses You. (Num 24:5-9, Heb.; cf. 23:21-24)

Unfortunately, if these interpretations are correct, the biblical lion and unicorn symbolism went the way of the Zodiac, having been transformed and incorporated into pagan mythologies. Further, this pagan symbolism has become central to the rise of the AntiChrist. C.W. Scott-Giles and J.P. Brooke-Little, in the somewhat cryptic, occult, and often obscure language of heraldry, summarize the symbols in Prince Charles' arms as follows:

H.R.H. The Prince of Wales bears the Royal Arms differenced by a label of three points argent and with an escutcheon [(small shield)] of the arms of the Principality of Wales ensigned by the Heir Apparent's coronet.... His shield is encircled with the Garter. He also bears the Royal Crest and Supporters, all differenced by a label as in the arms and also by the substitution of his coronet for the crowns in the crest and the supporting lion. His motto is ICH DIEN. His badge as Heir Apparent is, *a plume of three ostrich feathers argent enfiled by a coronet of crosses paty and fleurs-de-lis or, with the motto,* ICH DIEN.... In his full achievement this badge is placed below the shield together with the red dragon of Wales, differenced by a label as in the arms, and the arms of the Duchy of Cornwall: *Sable fifteen bezants,* the shield ensigned with the Heir Apparent's coronet.[1]

Friar adds,

....The badge of the Prince of Wales is *y ddraig goch,* the red dragon, upon a green mount and with a white label of three points about its neck. The so-called Prince of Wales' Feathers' badge, which comprises three white ostrich feathers enfiling a gold coronet...and, on a blue scroll, the motto 'Ich Dien', is the badge of the heir apparent to the English throne....

The Prince of Wales bears the arms of the sovereign differenced by a label of three points argent [(white)] on a shield, crest, and supporters. His crown is similar to that of the Queen but without the arch from front to back. On his shield of arms he bears the arms of the Principality [of Wales] on an inescutcheon ensigned by his crown. His achievement may include the shield of arms of the Duchy of Cornwall *Sable [(Black) with] fifteen Bezants,* and this is usually placed below the principal shield of arms and ensigned by the crown.[2]

It is perhaps interesting to observe at this point that Prince Charles has shown at least a cursory knowledge of, and interest in, heraldry: "While awaiting his posting [to the H.M.S. *Norfolk*] the Prince noted, with an inherited touch of King George VI's interest in heraldry, that the ship's crest was 'a silver ostrich feather with a gold quill ensigned by a gold prince's coronet, the pen piercing a scroll bearing the motto *Ich Dien*'."[3] In the next chapter,

---

1. Boutell, 1978 ed., pp. 218-219. This same heraldic description may be found in editions of Boutell's Heraldry going back to 1963.
2. "Wales, Prince of," *A Dictionary of Heraldry,* ed. Friar, p. 372.
3. Cathcart, p. 128.

we will examine each symbol on Prince Charles' coat of arms. This examination will include the historic origins, heraldic and biblical meanings, and, in several instances, the overall message conveyed.

The *Official* Heraldic Achievement of Prince Charles of Wales*
(as ostensibly described in Daniel and the Apocalypse)

*See the cover of this book for the full-color achievement.

An *Unofficial* Version

7

The Heraldic Symbols in the Arms and their Interpretations

The heart of every heraldic achievement is the shield (e.g., see the center of Prince Charles' arms). Shields, like other unique devices in British arms, may not legally or ethically be imitated for use by others, except as set forth in the laws of the United Kingdom and the British Commonwealth. In this regard, laws governing the use of heraldic devices and other symbols, which are a recognized form of property, are similar worldwide. Consequently, just as no two snowflakes are the same, no two achievements are ever legally identical. James and Russell remark, "Heraldry is basically a picture language developed by knights to make them recognizable in battle. Dressed in armour they all looked identical, so they began to wear sleeveless coats over their armour with obvious symbols on them. Shields bore colours, helmets had crests to show their rank and family. As no two families have the same crest, heraldry became the method of identification and the individual records going back five centuries are still kept up to date by the heralds."[1]

As previously mentioned, there are various later, unofficial versions of Prince Charles' arms that differ somewhat from his official, granted achievement. Immediately below, and in the subsequent discussions on the dexter and sinister supporters, we will compare the official version of the prince's achievement with what may now be the most prevalent rendition among his unofficial versions (both versions appear to be addressed in the scriptures). While examining the devices in Prince Charles' coat of arms, we will proceed from top to bottom, and then from left to

1. James and Russell, *At Home with the Royal Family*, p. 144.

right.

The top of the arms. At the top of Prince Charles' arms, there is a gold "lion" crest. The "lion" itself, which represents the dexter beast, is in a "guardant" posture (i.e., its head faces the observer).[1] It has four claws per foot, like an heraldic bear, as well as a body with leopard's proportions. Like the dexter beast, it has a copy of the heir-apparent's crown upon its head, and the three-horned label of the eldest son (i.e., the prince) is around its neck.

The lion crest in the official version of Prince Charles' coat of arms differs from that in the unofficial version. For example, in the official version, both of the lion's eyes are open, whereas in the unofficial version, the lion looks as if it is winking its right eye (see

Job 15:12-16; Ps 35:17-21; Prov 6:12-19, 10:10; cf. Zech 11:17, KJV).[2] Further, the lion's tail in the unofficial version is substantially longer. In heraldry, the presumed magic of a lion is proportional to the length of its tail.[3] If Prince Charles is the AntiChrist, this, along with the loosed restrainer (discussed later),[4] may symbolize the point of his satanic possession. Finally, with the exception of this beast, and the dexter beast from which it came, all the beasts in Prince Charles'

---

1. A similar crest is found in the arms of the Life Guards, which is the senior regiment of the British Army and one of the two armored regiments of the Royal Household Cavalry (James and Russell, *At Home with the Royal Family*, pp. 123-124). For more information, see this chapter's later section titled, "Related orders and royal guards," as well as the related note in this chapter's section titled, "The dexter (left-hand) supporter."
2. On June 28, 1990, Prince Charles nearly shattered his right arm in a polo fall. Compare this, and the winking of the beast, with Psalm 10:15 and Zechariah 11:17 (KJV).
3. Margaret Young, "Lion," *A Dictionary of Heraldry*, ed. Friar, p. 215.
4. For more information, see this chapter's later section titled, "The sinister (right-hand) supporter."

official arms have protruding tongues. In the unofficial version, however, this beast and the dexter beast also have protruding tongues (see Ps 10:7-9, 12, 52:1-7, 57:4, 64, 73, 120; Isa 54:17, 57:3-4; cf. Job 5:19-23; Jer 9:8; Rev 6:7-8).

There is a second copy of the heir-apparent's gold crown below the lion crest, followed by the silver (white) ermine wreath (or torse), and the silver and gold ermine mantle (or shroud). At the center of these devices, and above the royal shield, is the gold helm. The helm in Prince Charles' arms is that of the British sovereign, though princes of royal blood may also use it.[1]

Notice that the helm has seven curved bars. Interestingly, the word that Daniel used to describe the horns in the fourth beast's head may refer to an object that resembles an elephant's tooth (i.e., a banana-shaped object—like the horn of an ox), a flask (e.g., a test-tube), or a cornet (i.e., a cone-shaped, pointed object).[2] Therefore, it may be applied to these bars. Further, this word is also applicable to the three horns of each eldest-son label (discussed later) and to the horn of the sinister unicorn. Finally, notice that just as each beast on a coat of arms has its own head, so also does the overall coat of arms. That is, *the region near the top of the shield, around the location of the gold helm, is the head of the overall coat of arms* (cf. Dan 2:31-32, 2:35-39, 7:20). This head will be discussed in greater detail later.

A second copy of the eldest-son label lies immediately below the helm, with a third copy of the heir-apparent's crown imposed over its middle horn. Before looking further at this label and the crown imposed over it, let's discuss the royal shield over which both the label and the crown are themselves imposed.

The royal shield and the arms of the Principality of Wales. The royal shield, which is central to Prince Charles'

---

1. Child, *Heraldic Design* (London: G. Bell and Sons, 1965), p. 92.
2. Strong, 7161/7162, "A Concise Dictionary of the Words in the Hebrew Bible," p. 139.

arms, has four quarters. Imposed over these quarters, besides the second eldest-son label and the third heir-apparent crown, we find another quartered shield that represents the arms of the Principality of Wales. This small shield (escutcheon) helps to differentiate Charles' royal shield from a similar design granted to the Prince of Wales of 1890,[1] and it makes Charles' shield essentially identical, apart from unique details of representation, to that of Edward VIII when he was Prince of Wales.[2] The shields of the princes of Wales of 1890 and 1962 are contrasted at right.

In heraldry, the quarters on quartered shields are numbered from left to right and top to bottom as one through four.[3] Quarters one and four on the royal shield contain six lions in guardant postures, each one stretching forth its right-front paw. Called the "lions of England," they represent England and its empire[4] (cf. Ezek 38:13, "the merchants of Tarshish, and all its young lions;" see Ps 35:11-26, 57:3-6, 58; Isa 5:5-7, 5:26-30; cf. 2 Chr 9:16-22; Job 29:17; Jer 2:14-15, 50:17; Nah 2:11-12).[5] In Job 15:25-26, we read, "he stretches

1. For a color representation of these royal shields, see Boutell, plate V, pp. 20-23.
2. Boutell, 1978 ed., p. 221.
3. According to Boutell, "If there are only two coats of arms to be quartered, the more important is placed in the first and fourth quarters, and the other in the second and third.... In the case of three coats of arms, the principal one (normally the paternal coat) is placed in the first quarter and repeated in the fourth, the others being placed in the second and third in order of their importance or acquisition" (1978 ed., p. 136).
4. According to Boutell, there is "no direct evidence as to the insignia of the Norman kings, but there are several indications that a lion was a royal badge long before the emergence of the three lions as the English Royal Arms." By 1198, the royal shield of Richard I, who was otherwise known as the "Lionhearted," contained three passant-guardant lions, referred to collectively as "England." This shield was subsequently borne by all the Plantagenet kings until 1340, when Edward III quartered them with the arms of France, resulting in the six lions since called the "lions of England." Although these lions now occupy the first and fourth quarters of the royal shield, they were originally in the second and third quarters with the lilies (fleurs-de-lis) of France occupying the first and fourth quarters (Boutell, 1978 ed., pp. 206-208, 275).
5. As mentioned earlier, the United Kingdom was *Tarshish*, and it eventually came under

out his hand against God, and acts strong against the Almighty; he rushes at Him with a *bound [stiff]* neck [defiantly], with his thickly bossed [embossed] shields" (Heb.). Representing Scotland, the second quarter contains a red lion holding a sword in its paw, surrounded by a frame bearing the French *fleur-de-lis* (discussed later). The third quarter contains the seven-stringed Irish harp for Ireland, as seen on Ireland's Royal Badge (left).[1] Its design,

Roman jurisdiction. Those who assert that the United Kingdom is not *Tarshish* typically point to the area of Gibraltar, sometimes called "the Rock," as more likely. However, we must point out that Gibraltar was relinquished to Britain by the Treaty of Utrecht at the conclusion of the War of the Spanish Succession in 1713, and Gibraltar's populace remains loyal to Britain. *The debate is entirely academic.* Indeed, Gibraltar is the point from which Prince Charles and Diana embarked upon their honeymoon (Dimbleby, *The Prince of Wales,* pp. 23, 165, 174-175, 292-293; Hoey, *Charles & Diana: The Tenth Anniversary,* p. 69).

Today, the United Kingdom is positioned to become an integral part of the final, world-wide form of the Roman Empire. Therefore, it seems plausible that the phrase "Tarshish, and all its young lions" (Ezek 38:13) is not just a reference to Great Britain, or to the United Kingdom as a whole, but also to England's historical offspring, including the United States of America, Canada, Australia, and New Zealand. The companion phrase, "the merchants of Tarshish" (Ezek 38:13), on the other hand, undoubtedly applies in a somewhat broader sense to the United Kingdom's prominent trading partners, including other members of the European Union. J.R. Church, taking a less restrictive view, comments, "the mother lion will eventually to become Great Britain, whose insignia is a lion. The young lions, then, could include the United States, Canada, Australia, New Zealand, and all the former colonies of Great Britain" (p. 220). Jack Van Impe identifies *Tarshish* as England and the "young lions" as her English-speaking offshoots, whereas Peter Lalonde, borrowing from the others, thinks that "Tarshish" likely refers to Great Britain (*This Week in Bible Prophecy,* TBN TV 57 {Denver, CO}, 1 April 1993). As can be seen from a list of Prince Philip's titles, which are similar to those of Queen Elizabeth II and Prince Charles, the British monarchy practically runs Canada, Australia, and New Zealand (Judd, *Prince Philip,* p. 249). By other means, it now controls the United States.

One of Prince Charles' titles as the Prince of Wales is "Lord of the Isles." Regarding the coming Millennial Kingdom, Psalm 72:10 states, "The kings of Tarshish <u>and of the isles</u> will bring presents; the kings of Sheba and Seba will offer gifts" (see Ps 48:7; cf. Isa 60:9, 66:18-21). In this light, it is noteworthy that Sheba and Dedan (i.e., modern Yemen and Saudi Arabia), which are also mentioned in Ezekiel 38:13, are now located in territory that Great Britain controlled as recently as this, the twentieth century, and that they are associated with Great Britain and its monarchy through British Petroleum. In fact, Great Britain controlled much of the territory of the Middle East prior to the birth of the modern state of Israel in 1948.

1. Boutell, 1978 ed., pp. 215-217. The red lion of Scotland and the Irish harp were both introduced to the royal shield with the accession of the Stuart kings (following the reign of Elizabeth I), before England's union with either of those countries. Later, in connection with the union with Ireland in 1801, the arms of France were omitted (Boutell, 1978 ed., p. 215). Interestingly, this omission took place not long after the Order of the Illuminati was founded (for more information, see this chapter's later discussion on the Order of the Garter). From the reign of George I through that of William IV, the fourth quarter of the royal shield bore the arms of Hanover, which contained the "golden crown of Charlemagne." With the accession in 1837 of Victoria, who did not succeed to the throne of Hanover, that kingdom's arms

which supposedly originates in a Davidic harp brought from Israel (cf. Ps 33:2, 144:9), is not only identical to that of the harp that is being prepared for Israel's next Temple, but also to cave drawings found at Megiddo which may date to shortly after Noah's Flood.[1]

Notice that the dexter beast in Prince Charles' achievement is shown pawing the upper left-hand corner of the harp. *In heraldry, the specific positions of a beast's limbs are both meaningful and intentional* (cf. Prov 6:13). Not only has Britain pawed Ireland since the prince's investiture as Prince of Wales in July 1969, but at Satan's bidding, the beast will persecute and seek to destroy Hebrew Christians (e.g., see Rev 12:1, 12:5-6, 12:13-16), with whom harps are associated (see Rev 14:2-3, 15:2-3).

Imposed over the center of the royal shield, we find Prince Charles' heir-apparent crown, as well as the quartered shield of arms of the Principality of Wales, with each quarter containing one guardant lion.[2] This Welsh shield has *never before* been included in the royal arms, and is derived from Llewelyn ap Gruffydd, a late native Welsh prince.[3] It derives from the native princes of Wales, including Llewellyn the Great, being "quartered gold and red, with four passant [guardant] lions counter-coloured, *i.e.* red on the gold quarters and *vice versa*."[4] Further, it now constitutes Prince Charles'

were removed from the royal shield, which then assumed its present form (Boutell, 1978 ed., pp. 215-217). For color representations of the royal shield in its historical transitions, as well as a brief description of those transitions, see Boutell, plate V, between pp. 20-23.

1. Haim Shapiro, "TREASURES OF THE TEMPLE," *The Jerusalem Post,* Int. Ed., 30 July 1988, p. 9.
2. Boutell, 1978 ed., p. 218.
3. "Wales, Principality of," *A Dictionary of Heraldry,* ed. Friar, p. 373.
4. C.W. Scott-Guiles, *The Romance of Heraldry* (Published by J.M. Dent & Sons; New York: E.P. Dutton & Co., Inc., 1957), p. 74.

standard, which is flown only when he is in Wales.[1]

Besides Scotland's red lion, there are ten lions at the center of Prince Charles' coat of arms (i.e., the six lions of England and the four similar lions of Wales). These ten lions, like the red dragon, have a "passant" heraldic posture (as opposed to a "rampant" posture), in which just the right, front paw is raised. Historically speaking, any lion that was passant-guardant (or even earlier, not rampant) was known as a *lion leopardé*. Thus, we have the heraldic phrase "the lions (leopards) of England."[2] Each of the ten beasts in the center of Prince Charles' coat of arms is a "lion leopardé." However, they are *not* "normal" lion-leopards. In harmony with the dexter beast, they each, like an heraldic bear, have four claws per foot. In other words, they actually represent *lion-leopard-bears*.[3] The same may be said for the red lion of Scotland, which substitutes for the dexter beast on the prince's royal shield. Further, the ten lions represent royal dignitaries. According to the Apocalypse, the AntiChrist will eventually give power to ten kings under his authority for one hour (see Rev 17:12-14; cf. Dan 7:7-8, 7:19-21, 7:24-25; Rev 13:1-9). Also, notice that of these ten lions, only seven have relatively unobscured heads (cf. Rev 12:3, 13:1, 17:3). Finally, excluding either the dexter beast or Scotland's red lion, there are a total of twelve lions in Prince Charles' coat of arms (cf. 1 Kin 10:14-20).

Since 1603, the dexter and sinister supporters in British royal arms, called "royal beasts," have been "the lion for England and the unicorn for Scotland."[4] However, the dexter supporter in Prince Charles' coat of arms is altogether unique in heraldry; it is not the normal lion for England.

1. "Wales, Prince of," *A Dictionary of Heraldry,* ed. Friar, pp. 372-373. According to a royal warrant dated May 21, 1968, the prince's personal flag is "to be flown and used in Wales by His Royal Highness upon all occasions" (Boutell, 1978 ed., p. 258). For a picture of the prince's flying Welsh standard, see Hoey, *Charles & Diana: The Tenth Anniversary,* p. 6.

2. "Leopard," *A Dictionary of Heraldry,* ed. Friar, p. 213.

3. Notice that the four lion-leopards on Prince Charles' standard, shown in the previous chapter, have three claws per foot. Likewise, this section's earlier depictions of the shields of the prince's of Wales of 1890 and 1962 shows all the lion-leopards with three claws per foot, whereas Prince Charles' official heraldic achievement actually has four. For more information, see this chapter's later section titled, "The dexter (left-hand) supporter."

4. Kay W. Holmes, "United Kingdom, Royal Heraldry," *A Dictionary of Heraldry,* ed. Friar, p. 359.

After looking at the eldest-son label, the crown of the heir-apparent, the Garter that encircles the royal shield, and the devices found at the shield's base, we will examine this evil beast.

The label of the eldest son and the crown of the heir-apparent. The eldest-son label and heir-apparent crown are both found five times in the achievement of Prince Charles, in each instance directly associating the given part of the prince's arms with him. Therefore, with the possible exception of the ten lions just discussed and the red lion of Scotland, all the heraldic beasts on Prince Charles' arms pertain specifically to both him and his authority.

The eldest-son label has the appearance of three parallel horns which are, in a manner of speaking, "plucked out by the roots" (i.e., turned upside down). This particular mark of cadency also derives from the Black Prince, being "the distinctive mark of all succeeding Princes of Wales,"[1] and should remain on Prince Charles' arms only while his father is alive.[2] With its current presence in mind, notice that the label on the royal shield is directly below the helm, which contains seven more horns. Recall, therefore, that the region near the top of the shield, around the location of the helm, is the head of the overall coat of arms. In other words, the three horns of this eldest-son label, along with the seven horns in the helm, comprise a total of ten horns that are in the head of the overall coat of arms. Moreover, to the right of this cluster of ten horns "in a head," we find an eleventh horn, or the little horn which has eyes like those of a man (i.e., the unicorn).[3] Regarding the first beast, it is written,

> And another sign appeared in heaven. And, behold, a great, fiery

1. Boutell, 1978 ed., p. 119.
2. The labels of all other members of the British royal family (i.e., all but the eldest son), which are borne on their respective shields of arms, have more than three descending horns. Unlike permanent marks of cadency, the eldest son's label is to be removed from his arms if and when his father dies, so that he becomes the family head. In other words, it normally remains only while his father is living (Boutell, 1978 ed., pp. 117, 131; "Label," *A Dictionary of Heraldry*, ed. Friar, p. 212).
3. For an explanation of this terminology, see the discussion on the sinister supporter.

red dragon having seven heads and ten horns *in a head,*[1] and seven diadems near[2] his heads.... And the great dragon was cast out—the old serpent, called the Devil and Satan, who deceives the whole world—was cast out to the Earth, and his angels were cast out with him. (Rev 12:3 {Gk.}, 12:9 {Gk.}; cf. 20:2)

And I stood upon the sand of the sea. And I saw a beast rise up out of the sea, having seven heads, and ten horns *in a head,* and near its horns *in a head,* ten diadems,[3] and near its heads, names[4] of blasphemy[5] [*a slanderous motto*]. (Rev 13:1, Gk.)

Then one of the seven angels, of those having the seven bowls, came and spoke with me, saying to me, "Come, I will show you the judgment of the great harlot who sits on many waters, with whom the kings of the Earth committed fornication, and those inhabiting the Earth were made drunk with the wine of her fornication." And he carried me away into a desert [wilderness] by The Spirit, and I saw a woman sitting on a red [scarlet, crimson][6] beast, full of names of blasphemy [*a slanderous motto*], having seven heads and ten horns *in a head.* And the woman was arrayed in purple and red [scarlet, crimson], and adorned with gold and precious stone and pearls, having a golden cup in

1. Strong's number 2768, which *literally speaks of "the hair of the head"* (James Strong, 2768, "A Concise Dictionary of the Words in the Greek/New Testament," *STRONG'S EXHAUSTIVE CONCORDANCE OF THE BIBLE* {Tennessee: Abingdon Press, 1986}, p. 54), may be "a projecting extremity in shape like a horn, a point, apex" (Joseph H. Thayer, 2768, *GREEK-ENGLISH LEXICON of the NEW TESTAMENT* {Michigan: Baker Book House, 1977}, p. 344). Like nails and claws, animal horns are made of compressed hair. By implication, therefore, this word (Strong's no. 2768) refers to ten horns which are in a particular head. Moreover, this is perfectly consistent with Daniel 7:20. According to C.F. Keil and F. Delitzsch, "[The] beast must represent not merely the last world-power, but at the same time the last world-ruler....its personal head. The ten horns are to be conceived of as on one of the heads..." ("THE BOOK OF DANIEL," Vol. 9 of *Commentary on the Old Testament* {1986; rpt. Massachusetts: Hendrickson Publishers, Inc., 1989}, p. 277).
2. Strong's number 1909, which, as a preposition, may be translated as "among," "near," "by," "beside," or "below," as well as "on" (Strong, 1909, "A Concise Dictionary of the Words in the Greek/New Testament," p. 39; Thayer, 1909, p. 232).
3. A diadem, according to *The American Heritage Dictionary,* may be a "royal power or dignity." Biblically, it is the crown of a sovereign or royal personage. Given these definitions, consider the ten lions, apart from the red lion of Scotland, at the center of Prince Charles' achievement.
4. Strong's number 3686 refers to a person's distinguishing name, title, or phrase (motto), and its use invokes everything which the name, title, or phrase (motto) covers, to include "rank, authority, interests, pleasure, command, excellences, [and] deeds" (Thayer, 3686, p. 447). Given this definition, consider the Garter motto that surround's the heads of the eleven lions—six for England, four for Wales, and one for Scotland—on the royal shield and the shield of the Principality of Wales.
5. Strong's number 988, which refers to "impious and reproachful speech injurious to the divine majesty," or slander (Thayer, 988, p. 102).
6. The Greek word translated as "red," "scarlet," or "crimson," Strong's number 2847, refers to particular berries which, "when collected and pulverized produce a red which was used in dyeing" (Thayer, 2847, p. 352).

her hand, full of abominations and uncleanness of her fornication. And on her forehead a name *was* written: MYSTERY, BABYLON THE GREAT, THE MOTHER OF THE HARLOTS AND OF THE ABOMINATIONS OF THE EARTH. And I saw the woman drunk with the blood of the saints and with the blood of the witnesses [martyrs] of Jesus. And I marveled, seeing her, with great amazement. But the angel said to me, "Why did you marvel? I will tell you the mystery of the woman, and of the beast which carries her, which has the seven heads and the ten horns *in a head....* Here *is* the mind which has wisdom: The seven heads are seven mountains, where the woman sits on them....[1] And the ten horns which you saw are ten kings who *have* not yet received a kingdom, but *who* receive authority *for* one hour as kings with the beast. These have one mind, and their power and authority they shall cede to the beast. These will make war with The Lamb, and The Lamb will overcome them...." And he said to me, "The waters which you saw, where the harlot sits, are peoples and multitudes, and nations and tongues. And the ten horns which you saw on the beast, these will hate the harlot, and shall make her desolate and naked, and will eat her flesh and burn her down with fire. For God has put it into their hearts to do His mind [will], and to act *in* one mind, and to give their kingdom to the beast, until the words of God are fulfilled. And the woman whom you saw is the great city which has *a* kingdom [kingship] over the kings of the Earth.[2] (Rev 17:1-7, 17:9, 17:12-18, Gk.)

The ten horns described thus far in Prince Charles' arms could well represent the ten horns in the head of the apocalyptic beast. Unlike seven of the ten horns (recall our previous discussion regarding the seven bars in the helm, which forms the head of the overall coat of arms), three are to be "plucked out by

---

1. Rome, which began on the left bank of the Tiber River as a group of seven communities on seven hills, was known among ancient Roman writers as "the city on seven hills."

2. London, through the British Commonwealth (formerly the British Empire), appears to be the *only* city today which has a *literal* kingdom, as well as kingship, over other kings of the Earth. Although Rome has a pope, she does not have a king or a queen. Should the British monarchy be adopted as the monarchy of the European Union, however, so that Prince Charles gains hegemony in the United Nations Security Council in New York, then London—which is currently ruled by a queen (cf. "the mother of harlots")—would effectively have kingship over *all* the kings of the Earth, much as the king of Babylon was "a king of kings" and "ruler over them all" (Dan 2:37-38). Moreover, in partnership with the pope, London (the British monarchy) would rule over Rome.

the roots" (see Dan 7:8, 7:24; cf. the eldest-son label over the shield). Prince Charles' arms do in fact depict such an arrangement (see the above image). Further, the little horn that has eyes like those of a man (i.e., the sinister unicorn—discussed later) is to come up among them (see Dan 7:8, 7:20).

The design of the heir-apparent's crown is based upon the Imperial State Crown (worn by the queen during state functions), which "embodies many historical gems, including the Black Prince's ruby."[1] Other than its lack of bowed arches and an arch from front to back, the heir-apparent's crown is also similar to the St. Edward's Crown (so-called after Edward the Confessor who allegedly believed that he had supernatural healing powers), with which the last forty British monarchs, including the present queen, were coronated: "The St. Edward's Crown...is the official Crown of England and the one with which the Sovereign is usually crowned. Elizabeth II decided she could wear no other.... Then in the Abbey she was crowned with St. Edward's Crown, made in 1661 for Charles II to replace the crown of St. Edward the Confessor destroyed...after the Civil War. This solid gold crown set with pearls and precious stones is most easily identified by its generously bowed arches. On leaving the Abbey modern sovereigns have exchanged this for the Imperial Crown of State whose silver arches are less baroque."[2] The heir-apparent's crown, like that of "St. Edward," has a gold Templar cross and a sphere, called a "mound" or "orb," at its top. While this sphere or globe was formerly "green banded with gold," apparently representing the Earth under Merovingian rule,[3] it is now

1. Timothy B. Benford, *The Royal Family Quiz & Fact Book* (New York: Harper & Row, Publishers, 1987), p. 235. Also see "Coronation, Symbols of," *A Dictionary of Heraldry,* ed. Friar, p. 110.
2. Lacey, *Majesty,* p. 159. "On the day of the ceremony itself Queen Elizabeth II wore Queen Victoria's diadem on her way to the Abbey. This low diamond circlet, originally made for George IV, featured the Cross of St. George and the emblems of the other component parts of the United Kingdom" (ibid., p. 159). One such "emblem" is the *fleur-de-lis.*
3. Lacey notes the "tokens of responsibility" with which British monarch's are invested, including "the Orb—'remember that the whole world is subject to the power and empire of Christ'" (*Majesty,* p. 162). Illustrating some of the intrigue of the Order of the Garter, this

depicted as gold banded with gold.[1]

Crosses on the heir-apparent and state crowns generally have a central pearl. Although gold and silver, respectively, they are identical to the red cross paty of the Temple Knights (right) from which they were derived. The Templar cross, like the modified Templar cross euphemized as "St. George's cross" (discussed below), is often depicted in a circular shield or "roundel." Regarding crosses, Scott-Guiles comments, "Foremost among the emblems of the Holy Wars was, of course, the cross.... Pope Urban II, the

preacher of the First Crusade, decreed this practice.... But when the English adopted St. George as their patron saint they made his red cross their own.... Certain families which have crosses in their shields claim that they signify some ancestor's participation in a crusade."[2] Actually, *St. George*—despite the often *messianic* Arthurian legends concerning a knight by that name—has long been a Garter synonym for *Merovée* (see below).[3]

The French *fleur-de-lis* or lily is interspersed with the Templar crosses on the British royal crowns. Some have suggested that the French lily is actually a derivation of the Judaean lily depicted on an ancient Jewish coin, whereas others think that it came from royal bee of Charlemagne and subsequent French kings (e.g., Merovée's son, Childeric I, who practiced witchcraft and whose grave

---

same royal Orb is depicted in a French drawing dating to around 1615 that depicts Abraham's near-sacrifice of Isaac (Frazer, p. 114). A photograph of Queen Elizabeth II carrying the former royal Orb, which was green banded with gold and about the size of a human head, was taken following her coronation in 1953 (*Her Majesty The Queen*, p. 9). The royal Orb is now gold banded with gold, having a diamond and emerald Templar cross at its top. Interestingly enough, according to Baigent, Leigh, and Lincoln, "Many...[crystal] balls have been found in Merovingian tombs. Their use is unknown" (*Holy Blood, Holy Grail*, caption 29, between pp. 240-241). For more information, see Chapter 8, "The Red Dragon and Prince Charles' Investiture as Prince of Wales."

1. For color representations of these and other crowns, see Boutell, plate XVI, between pp. 178-181.
2. Scott-Guiles, pp. 52-54.
3. For more information, see Chapter 4, "Prince of this World—a Diverse Lineage."

contained 300 such bees).[1]

In addition to the five heir-apparent crowns in Prince Charles' arms, there are two more crowns, one around the neck of the unicorn and the other around the ostrich feathers in the heir-apparent's badge, for a total of seven crowns (otherwise known as coronets or diadems). Recall that the beast has "seven diadems near his heads" (Rev 12:3).

The Garter. England has long had various orders of knights, called knighthoods, of which the most prominent is the Most Noble Order of the Garter. Elizabeth II was installed on April 23, 1948—her birthday and "St. George's Day"—as a "Lady of the Order," and upon becoming queen, as the order's sovereign.[2] King George VI, emphasizing his daughter's "precedence and seniority," installed Prince Philip as a Garter knight eight days after he installed Elizabeth II as a Lady of the Order.[3] Ten years later, on July 26, 1958, the year that the red dragon became the official heraldic symbol of Wales, Prince Charles, as the new Prince of Wales, automatically became a knight of the Order of the Garter, though his formal installation as such did not occur until June 17, 1968.[4] Cathcart, speaking of this event, shows that, like the public generally, she misunderstands the true nature of the Order of the Garter: "But the ceremonies of chivalry are to be taken seriously, with their prayers for steadfastness in the Christian faith. In the procession to the chapel [of St George] there walked such figures of lasting history as Earl Alexander of Tunis, Earl Mountbatten of Burma and Viscount Montgomery of Alamein."[5]

Cathcart adds, "In the Dorset manor of Fordington, villagers roast a sheep on the village green every St George's Day and supposedly send a leg of mutton to Prince Charles

1. Manly P. Hall, *The Secret Teachings of All Ages* (San Francisco: H.S. Crocker Co., Inc., n.d.), p. lxxxvii. Baigent, Leigh, and Lincoln, *Holy Blood, Holy Grail,* captions 30 and 33, between pp. 240-241. For more information, see Chapter 4, "Prince of this World—a *Diverse* Lineage."
2. *Her Majesty The Queen,* p. 12.
3. Judd, *Prince Philip,* pp. 131-132.
4. Holden, *PRINCE CHARLES,* pp. 174, 326.
5. Cathcart, p. 83. Junor, p. 74.

wherever he may be."[1] On this same day, April 23, in an act of apparent Druidic tree-worship, a tree is cut down, decked with "flowers and garlands," and then carried in a procession "accompanied with music and joyful acclamations," with "the chief figure in the procession being the Green George, a young fellow clad from head to foot in green birch branches." The "Green George," or an effigy of him, is then dunked in a river or pond in hopes of bringing forth a year of plentiful rain.[2]

Established in 1348 by King Edward III, a descendant of the French Plantagenets, and his son, Edward the Black Prince, the Order of the Garter is England's (and Europe's) most prestigious and exclusive "Christian" order of chivalry.[3] Originally called "The Order of [the Company of] St. George,"[4] it is the oldest surviving order of chivalry in the world, having absorbed the essential aspects of its few predecessors, including "the Society of St. George in Hungary (1325/6)," "the Order of the Band or Sash in <u>Spain</u> (before 1330)," and, after it was first proposed by the Duke of Normandy in 1344, who later became King John II of <u>France</u>, the Company of the Star (1352). In Garter literature, Edward III is sometimes called "the Founder," and the Order of the Garter is referred to as "the Foundation."[5] John Campbell-Kease asserts,

> Several historians are of the view that at first the 'order' was quite casually formed, perhaps at a tournament [in 1344]—24 knights in two bands of twelve, one under the king, the other under the prince, and only later did it become a permanent institution....
>
> The symbol of the blue garter seems [according to some] to have been suggested by an incident at a ball at Calais in the autumn of 1347, when the young countess of Salisbury, Joan of

1. Cathcart, p. 105.
2. Frazer, pp. 62-63.
3. Benford, p. 100.
4. James and Russell, *At Home with the Royal Family*, p. 36. Laurence R. Taylor, *Indiana Monitor and Freemason's Guide*, 15th ed. (Indiana: Grand Lodge of the State of Indiana, 1993), p. 59, n. 1.
5. Peter J. Begent, *The Most Noble Order of the Garter, Its History and Ceremonial* (Slough: Delworth Printing Ltd., n.d.—1990 or later), p. 2. For a copy of this self-published work, which is copyrighted by the Dean and Cannons of Windsor and illustrates the Order of the Garter and its insignia, write to: St. George's Chapel Bookshop, Ltd.; 8B, The Cloisters; Windsor Castle; Windsor Berks; SL4 1NJ; England.

Kent (later to be Princess of Wales), dropped her garter, which the king picked up and tied round his knee with the now famous words, Honi soit qui mal y pense, 'shame on him who thinks evil of it', and the promise that the garter would become highly honoured. And so it was. The informal creation of the Round Table after the great tournament at Windsor in 1344 was translated, in 1348, into the Order of the Garter—24 young men plus the king and his eldest son....[1]

The armorial bearings (heraldic achievements) of Garter members, both past and present, are emblazoned on their respective stall-plates, and their banners are also hung in the Chapel of St. George at Windsor.[2] Edward III, "inspired by the English legend of King Arthur and the Knights of the Round Table," originally constructed St. George's Chapel in 1350, not to mention St. George's Hall, while making Windsor Castle "one of the most magnificent castles in Europe." In 1472, King Edward IV demolished the original Chapel of St. George and began construction on its famed replacement, which was completed under King Henry VII. His son, King Henry VIII is credited with developing "much of the Order of the Garter ceremony in which the Queen participates annually."[3] Interestingly, Henry VII, who added Welsh blood to the British monarchy, "restored the red dragon to its ancient status as a royal device," and Henry VIII and King Edward VI subsequently used it.[4]

June is a major month for royal ceremonial, to include coronations and parades. It is also significant to pagan worship. June, for example, is the month in which pagans historically mourned the death of Tammuz, the ancient Babylonian perversion of the Zodiac's original symbolic prediction of a future virgin-born Messiah who would suffer, die, and rise from the dead to redeem mankind. June also is the month of Midsummer Eve (the 23rd), when the Druids culled "certain magic plants, whose evanescent virtue can be secured at this mystic season alone." This same eve, now dubbed the "Eve of St. John" for John the

1. John Campbell-Kease, "Garter, The Most Noble Order of the," *A Dictionary of Heraldry*, ed. Friar, p. 160. Also see James and Russell, *At Home with the Royal Family*, pp. 37, 155.
2. Boutell, 1978 ed., pp. 193-194. The royal standard is hung over the queen's pew.
3. James and Russell, *At Home with the Royal Family*, pp. 36-37, 40.
4. For more information, see this chapter's section titled, "The red dragon, or Satan."

Baptizer, "was the day of all days for gathering the wonderful herbs by means of which you could combat fever, cure a host of diseases, and guard yourself against sorcerers and their spells."[1]

Each June, new knights, when required and available, are admitted to the Order of the Garter in an annual ceremony at Garter Chapel—called St. George's Chapel—in Windsor Castle.[2] Prince Charles opines, "I would change nothing. Besides ceremony being a major and important aspect of monarchy, something that has grown and developed over a thousand years in Britain, I happen to enjoy it enormously."[3] According to James and Russell, "every June on the Monday of Ascot week[4] the Queen, as Head of the Order, assembles with twenty-four Companion Knights and walks down the hill from St George's Hall to St George's Chapel for a special service. Each knight wears a dark blue velvet mantle with crimson velvet hood, a black velvet hat with white ostrich plumes, a blue riband with the cross of St George [on a star] plus a gold collar of twenty-six intertwined garters [around roses], one for each of the knights and the Queen and Prince Charles, as 'constituent member of the Order'. Each also wears a dark blue velvet garter [(the queen's is light blue)] embroidered with the motto in gold thread.... [The] Garter ceremony takes place with all the theatrical aplomb of an heraldic festival, and [it]...would not look out of place in a re-make of *The Three Musketeers*."[5]

1. Frazer, pp. 124, 133, 135, 229, 234.
2. Benford, p. 101. *Her Majesty The Queen*, p. 12. For color photographs of the order's annual procession to the chapel, including Queen Elizabeth II wearing her dark blue Garter Mantle (cloak) with the Garter Star and Collar, see *Her Majesty The Queen*, p. 17. For similar photographs of Prince Charles, see *Charles & Diana: A Royal Family Album*, p. 45; and Hoey, *Charles & Diana: The Tenth Anniversary*, p. 115.
3. *Charles & Diana: A Royal Family Album*, p. 44.
4. Apart from royal permission, only royalty, and perhaps the very wealthy, are permitted to attend the annual Ascot races at the Ascot Race Course. These races may serve as a cover for the presence of foreign royals during that week, who attend not just for the races themselves, but to participate in the Order of the Garter ceremony and other meetings.
5. James and Russell, *At Home with the Royal Family*, pp. 37, 155. Apparently standing-in for the Order of the Garter's companion-knights, "twenty-four knights who are Serjeants-at-Arms form the oldest armed bodyguard in existence." During the crusades, these twenty-four knights, *who were Templars,* are "supposed to have formed a bodyguard for King Richard I." Three of the twenty-four Serjeants-at-Arms participate in the State Opening of Parliament, where they attend the sovereign and escort the royal heralds and pursuivants, who, with "a vast knowledge of royal ceremony...assist the Earl Marshal in planning state

What is publicly known of the Garter ceremony evidences the fact that it remains a mixture of the holy with the profane, overseen by unfaithful and apostate "Christians" (e.g., the Bishop of Winchester and the Dean of Windsor). James and Russell observe,

> The whole ceremony [originally] took three days with the sovereign and knights meeting on the first day for a general discussion in a room guarded by Black Rod;[1] day two being the main processional day, Garter Ceremony and state banquet; and the closing day, in contrast to the earlier pomp, being a day of remembrance and prayer, with a requiem mass to end the proceedings.
>
> Just over a century later the College of Arms was founded and the heralds became an intrinsic part of the Garter Ceremony, now presided over by Garter King of Arms....
>
> ....Lacking none of the dignity of bygone days, the ceremony [now] begins in the morning in the Throne Room of Windsor Castle, where the Queen buckles the garter onto the leg of the knight elect in a private ceremony, the knight having first been ritually summoned by Black Rod and the Garter King.
>
> 'To the honour of God Omnipotent,' proclaims the Prelate [(now the Bishop of Winchester)], 'and in Memorial of the Blessed Martyr, Saint George, tie about thy leg, for they Renown, this Most Noble Garter. Wear it as the symbol of the Most Illustrious Order never to be forgotten or laid aside, that hereby thou mayest be admonished to be courageous, and having undertaken a just war, into which thou shalt be engaged, thou mayest stand firm, valiantly fight, courageously and successfully conquer.'
>
> ....After the garter the collar of twenty-six buckled garters in gold surrounding enamelled Tudor roses is placed around the knight's neck by the Queen. The prelate continues:
>
> 'Wear this Collar about thy Neck, adorned with the image of the Blessed Martyr and Soldier of Christ, Saint George, by whose imitation provoked, thou mayest so overpass both prosperous and adverse encounters, that having stoutly vanquished thine enemies, both of body and soul, thou mayest not only receive the praise of this transient Combat, but be crowned with the Palm of Eternal Victory.'
>
> Finally the mantle is placed around the shoulders.

---

ceremonies" and "function in any regal parade...to ensure that everyone is in the right place at the right time, in the right order and dressed correctly" (ibid., pp. 141, 146-147, 206; Baigent, Leigh, and Lincoln, *Holy Blood, Holy Grail,* p. 121).

1. For brief descriptions of the "Gentlemen User of the Black Rod," who "was once responsible for the security of the sovereign" and now "carries a black rod made of ebony in 1883, with a gold sovereign set into the base dated 1904," see James and Russell, *At Home with the Royal Family,* pp. 148, 194.

'You being chosen to be of the Honourable Company of the Most Noble Order of the Garter, shall promise and swear, by the Holy Evangelists, by you here touched, that wittingly or willingly you shall not break any Statutes of the Said Order, or any article in them contained (except in such from which you have received a Dispensation from The Sovereign), the same being agreeable, and not repugnant to the Laws of Almighty God, and the Laws of this realm,...so God help you, and His Holy Word.'

Following this historic but never publicly witnessed ceremony the Queen...leads the way into the Waterloo Chamber for lunch, a simple meal compared to the former banquets of wild boar, duckling, pheasant, rabbit, lobster, quail, pigeon, salmon and crab....

At 2:30 p.m. the public procession starts out from the royal apartments to St George's Chapel; thousands of people apply every year to the Lord Chamberlain's Office to...witness the most historic of all processions. The governor of Windsor Castle heads the Military Knights of Windsor in their red uniforms, followed by the heralds and pursuivants wearing royal crested tabards, then the Knights of the Garter themselves in the full uniform of the Order.... Lastly come the officers of the Order—the Garter King of Arms, the Gentleman Usher of the Black Rod, the Secretary, the Register [(now the Dean of Windsor)] and the Prelate—and the Queen....

In St George's Chapel a simple service takes place, the Garter King of Arms presenting any newly installed knights for a blessing, and the service ending with a prayer: 'God save our gracious Sovereign and all the Companions, living and departed, of the Most Honourable and Noble Order of the Garter.'[1]

Garter "placement." Garter membership now includes Queen Elizabeth II, Prince Charles, Prince Philip, Queen Elizabeth the Queen Mother, Princess Anne, the Duke of Kent,[2] chosen members of *other European and non-European royal families (e.g., the now deceased Japanese Emperor Hirohito),*[3] some of the most powerful *former and*

1. James and Russell, *At Home with the Royal Family,* pp. 155-158. To apply for tickets to attend the procession of the Order of the Garter (for research purposes), write to: The Lord Chamberlain's Office, St James's Palace, London SW1, England (ibid., p. 241).

2. A color picture of the Duke of Kent wearing the Garter Star may be seen in *Majesty* magazine, July 1994, Vol. 15, No. 7, p. 27. The Dukes of Kent and Beaufort sponsored Prince Charles' introduction to the "House of Lords" in 1970 (Cathcart, opposite p. 57).

3. The kings of Norway, Bulgaria, Portugal, Germany, Greece, Belgium, Spain, England, and Denmark, respectively, a number of whom were members of the Order of the Garter, were photographed together, wearing their Garter stars (e.g., the kings of Germany, Greece, England, and it appears Norway, Denmark, and possibly others), at Windsor for the funeral of Edward VII (Lacey, *Majesty,* between pp. 126-127). These same kings of Norway, England, and apparently Denmark were also members of the Committee of 300, whereas some of the other kings mentioned above, besides other royal households (e.g., the Netherlands), had

current world leaders,[1] and a few prestigious public figures. James and Russell state, "The number of knights remains constant although the Queen has the authority to create 'Stranger Knights' if she wishes, a[n] honour offered only to those held in great esteem."[2] Campbell-Kease adds, "Foreign royalty have been appointed as members: 'Stranger Knights and Ladies of the Garter', and they are additional to the twenty-six companion knights. Membership was often used for diplomatic purposes, though today membership of both the Garter and the Thistle is in the personal gift of the sovereign." Garter members are sworn to befriend and defend one another, in both peace and war, throughout the course of their lives: "In 1348 the Black Prince was just eighteen years old, and several other founders not much more.... Thus...the Order of the

---

family representatives who were committee members (John Coleman, *The Committee of 300,* 3rd ed. {Nevada: Joseph Publishing Co., 1994}, pp. 314-315). Their heirs now carry-on in their place. King Haakon of Norway was one of eight "godparents" to the infant Prince Charles (Junor, p. 21; Judd, *Prince Charles,* p. 144). In 1983, King Carl Gustav XVI of Sweden was appointed as a stranger-knight to the Order of the Garter; as such he is supernumerary to it (Begent, p. 14). Anthony Eden, the former Earl of Avon, was also a Garter knight (Begent, p. 1), as were Earl Mountbatten of Burma, Earl Alexander of Tunis, and Viscount Montgomery of Alamein (Cathcart, p. 83; Judd, *Prince Philip,* p. 24).

A color photograph taken in 1971 at Buckingham Palace shows Japanese Emperor Hirohito wearing the Garter Star: "The Emperor is seen wearing the Order of the Garter, which was removed during the Second World War and only restored to him a few months before his visit" (*Her Majesty The Queen,* p. 34). On a visit to Japan in 1970, Prince Charles dined with the late Emperor Hirohito, preparing the way for a 1975 state visit by Queen Elizabeth II and Prince Philip (Cathcart, p. 112). It now appears that the prince was also restoring Hirohito to the Order of the Garter, preparing the way for the emperor's own visit to Buckingham Palace in 1971. Others Garter members are shown in the same photograph, all but Princess Anne wearing their Garter Stars, to include Queen Elizabeth II, Prince Charles, Prince Philip, Princess Anne (who only recently was elevated from the status of "lady" to become a knight-companion of the order), the Duke of Kent, and Queen Elizabeth the Queen Mother (who appears to have also been elevated from her original status as just a lady of the order). Oddly enough, the same photograph also clearly shows Queen Elizabeth II, Prince Charles, Prince Philip, and Emperor Hirohito all wearing the star of another order which is almost certainly Japanese in origin—probably the "Supreme Order of the Chrysanthemum" of which Prince Philip is Grand Cordon (Judd, *Prince Philip,* p. 252). Hirohito's heir has likely since taken his father's place in both orders.

For a color photograph of Prince Charles, Queen Elizabeth the Queen Mother, and the Duke of Kent wearing their Garter insignia "at the service of the Most Noble Order of the Garter in June 1986," see Burnet, *In Private—In Public,* THE PRINCE AND PRINCESS OF WALES, pages 126-127.

1. On June 14, 1954, for example, Queen Elizabeth II installed Winston Churchill as a knight of the Order of the Garter (James and Russell, *At Home with the Royal Family,* p. 156). More recently, the queen likewise installed Margaret Thatcher as such.

2. James and Russell, *At Home with the Royal Family,* p. 37. Note that the Central Chancery "maintains records of the holders of the Orders of Chivalry" (ibid., p. 205).

The AntiChrist and a Cup of Tea

Garter...was a brotherhood..., a fellowship, in which all were equal 'to represent how they ought to be united in all Chances and various Turns of Fortune, co-partners in both Peace and War, assistant to one another in all serious and dangerous Exploits and through the whole Course of their lives to show Fidelity and Friendliness towards one another.'"[1] It is perhaps noteworthy that Queen Elizabeth II, Prince Charles, and Prince Philip are *almost always* photographed wearing their respective Garter Stars, except when wearing suits, regardless of what uniform they have on or how they are otherwise attired. They are also occasionally shown wearing the Garter Collar with its pendant and the blue Garter Riband with its Lesser George.[2]

The Order of the Garter is not only responsible for the creation of the modern Illuminati, as will be shown in the following pages, but it also heads and controls the shadowy "Committee of 300."[3] Not all knights of the Order of

1. Campbell-Kease, "Garter, The Most Noble Order of the," *A Dictionary of Heraldry*, ed. Friar, p. 160.
2. A formal portrait of Queen Elizabeth II and Prince Philip wearing their respective Garter Collars may be seen on page 11 of *Her Majesty The Queen*. The same portrait, taken following the queen's coronation, also shows the queen wearing the Imperial State Crown and the Commonwealth Bracelets, with Prince Philip wearing the Garter Star. A larger portrait of the queen wearing the Garter Collar and State Crown, or a photograph of her wearing the Garter Mantle, Collar, Star, and hat, may be seen on pages 13 and 17, respectively, of the same work. Similar photographs of Prince Charles may be seen on page 126 of Burnet, *In Private—In Public, THE PRINCE AND PRINCESS OF WALES*, and between pages 150-151 of Junor. The Collar and/or Riband are also worn for various official functions, including the State Opening of Parliament and certain funerals (e.g., see *Her Majesty The Queen*, pp. 18-19; *Charles & Diana: The Tenth Anniversary*, pp. 36-37). The insignia of the Order of the Garter will be described in detail later in this section.
3. In Coleman's words, "Queen Elizabeth II....is the head of the Committee of 300." Speaking of the news media, Coleman adds, "These media change artists and news manipulators report directly to the Club of Rome, which, in turn, reports to the Committee of 300, at whose head sits the Queen of England. She rules over a vast network of closely-linked corporations who never pay taxes and are answerable to no one else; who fund their research institutions through foundations whose joint activities have almost total control over our daily lives" (*The Committee of 300*, pp. 22, 102-103). Elsewhere Coleman states, "The Committee of 300 is for the most part under the control of the British monarch, in this case, Queen Elizabeth II" (ibid., p. 239). Coleman, in defense of the existence of the committee, besides tracing its membership, organizations, holdings, and dealings, states, "But there is some proof: Walter Rathenau, a prominent Socialist politician and financial advisor to the Rothschilds..., wrote an article in the WIENER PRESS, which it published on December 24, 1921. In the article, Rathenau made this astonishing comment: 'Only three hundred men, each of whom knows all others, govern the fate of Europe. They select their successors from their own entourage. These men have the means in their hands of putting an end to the form of State which they find unreasonable.'... Further proof that the Committee exists, is found in the vast number of powerful institutions owned and controlled by it...., all of which come under THE MOTHER OF ALL THINK TANKS AND RESEARCH INSTITUTIONS, THE TAVIS-

the Garter, however, are a part of the Committee of 300, whose members are usually chosen from among apostate Anglican Protestants. Loosely speaking, we may think of the Order of the Garter as the board of directors for the British monarchy, which King George VI once described as the "Royal Firm."[1] According to Springmeier, who has both studied the Illuminati extensively and actually depro-grammed and debriefed former members of the order, the Illuminati are organized around the world's thirteen most prominent occult—generational satanic—bloodlines, the thirteenth and most powerful being the Merovingian, or "Holy" bloodline.[2] The Committee of 300 is similarly organized. John Coleman, a former British intelligence ana-lyst and political science officer,[3] states,

> The Committee of 300 has a major bureaucracy at its disposal made up of hundreds of think tanks, and front organizations that run the whole gamut of private business and government leaders....
>
> The Committee of 300, although in existence for more than 150 years,...was always given to issuing orders through other fronts, such as the Royal Institute for International Affairs. When

TOCK INSTITUTE OF HUMAN RELATIONS with its far-flung network of hundreds of branches" (ibid., pp. 108-109). This super-institute is "owned and controlled by the Royal Institute for International Affairs" (ibid., p. 240). Coleman also observes, "The drug trade [worldwide] is controlled by the Committee of 300 from the top down. The drug trade started with the British East India Company and was closely followed by the Dutch East India Company. Both were controlled by a 'Council of 300'" (ibid., p. 141). *All material from this author is quoted with his permission.*

1. Hoey, *Charles & Diana: The Tenth Anniversary,* p. 30.
2. Fritz Springmeier, *The Top 13 Illuminati Bloodlines,* Vol. I (Oregon: 5316 S.E. Lincoln, Port-land, OR 97215; 1995), pp. 228-236. For more information, see Chapter 4, "Prince of this World—a *Diverse* Lineage."
3. According to Coleman, "All the information that I provide in this book comes from years of research, and is backed up by impeccable intelligence sources. Nothing is exaggerated. It is factual and precise, so do not fall into the trap set by the enemy that this material is 'disin-formation.' For the last two decades, I have provided information which has proved to be highly accurate, and which has explained a lot of puzzling events" (*The Committee of 300,* p. 107). Although the author can personally verify the veracity and accuracy of significant aspects of Coleman's work from the author's own research, and can verify much of the rest of Coleman's work from the writings of other authors, the author does not agree with Cole-man on all points, particularly where a number of his clearly biased and scripturally unbal-anced views and statements concerning Israel and Christian fundamentalists are concerned. Moreover, Coleman's work is to be faulted in that it is poorly documented and loosely organized. Nevertheless, if one is willing to look past these shortcomings, one will find a vast amount of particularly incriminating and damning material where the British monarchy is concerned. For this reason, *The Committee of 300* is well worth examining in relation to *The AntiChrist and a Cup of Tea.*

it was decided that a super-body would control European affairs, the RIIA founded the Tavistock Institute, which in turn created NATO....

The Committee is the ultimate secret society made up of an untouchable ruling class, which includes the Queen of England, the Queen of the Netherlands, the Queen of Denmark and the royal families of Europe. These aristocrats decided at the death of Queen Victoria, the matriarch of the Venetian Black Guelphs,[1] that in order to gain world-wide control, it would be necessary for its aristocratic members to "go into business" with the non-aristocratic, but extremely powerful leaders of corporate business on a global scale. And so, the doors to ultimate power were opened to what the Queen of England likes to refer to as "the commoners."[2]

From my days in the [intelligence] field, I know that the heads of foreign governments refer to this all-powerful body as "The Magicians." Stalin coined his own phrase to describe them: "The Dark Forces," and President Eisenhower...referred to it in a colossal understatement as "the military-industrial complex." Stalin kept the USSR heavily armed with conventional and nuclear forces, because he did not trust what he called "the family." His ingrained mistrust and fear of the Committee of 300 proved to be well-founded....

Political and financial control...is exercised through a number of secret societies, most notably, the Scottish Rite of Freemasonry, and perhaps even more importantly, through the Venerable Order of St. John of Jerusalem, an ancient order consisting of the British monarch's hand-picked executives, chosen for their expertise in areas vital to the continued control of the Committee. In my work "The Order of St. John of Jerusalem," published in 1986, I described The Order in the following manner: "...It is therefore not a secret society, except where its [original] purposes have been perverted in the inner councils like the Order of the Garter, which is a prostituted oligarchical creation of the British royal family.... As an example, we find the atheist Lord Peter Carrington, who pretends to be an Anglican Christian, but who is a member of the Order of Osiris and other demonic sects, including Freemasonry, installed as a Knight of the Garter at St. George's Chapel, Windsor Castle, by Her Majesty, Queen Elizabeth II of England, of the Black Nobility Guelphs, also head of the Anglican Church, which she thoroughly despises."...

1. According to Coleman, "The 'Windsors' are in reality of the House of Guelph, one of the Venetian Black Nobility's oldest dynasties" (*The Committee of 300*, p. 321). Recall that Queen Elizabeth II and Prince Charles both descend from *Godfroi de Bouillon* through Henry the Black of the Guelph Line, and that Prince Charles may one day claim the Merovingian crusader title "King of Jerusalem" by virtue of this lineage. For more information, see Chapter 4, "Prince of this World—a *Diverse* Lineage."

2. For concrete examples, see Chapter 11's sections titled, "The World of Business and Finance" and "The United Nations and public-private partnerships."

We have been so brainwashed that we believe the British royal family is just a nice, harmless and colorful institution, and so we fail to realize just how corrupt, and therefore highly dangerous is this institution called the British Monarchy. The Knights of the Order of the Garter are the INNERMOST circle of the most corrupt public servants who have utterly betrayed the trust placed in them by their nation and their people.

The Knights of the Order of the Garter, is Queen Elizabeth's most trusted "privy council."... [The] Knights of the Garter are the inner sanctum, the elite of the elite of Her Majesty's Most Venerable Order of St. John of Jerusalem....

....Like the present royal family, [Lord] Palmerston, [one of the founders of the opium dynasty in China,] like so many of his kind, was not only a Freemason, but also a dedicated follower of Gnosticism. Like the present royal family, Palmerston made a pretense of being a Christian, but was in fact a practicing Satanist. Many satanists became leaders in the hierarchy of the British aristocracy....

....[It] was the power of the Order of the Garter which saved [Japan's] Emperor Hirohitho from most probably being executed as a war criminal. Queen Elizabeth II had maintained a close relationship with the late Emperor Hirohitho (formerly Crown Prince Akihito), and still does with his family....

Every "royal" and [all] so-called European "noble" dynasties past and present, have seats on the Committee of 300, most often by way of nominees. For instance, the Hohenzollern dynasty might be represented by Edward the Duke of Kent; the Braganzas by the Duke of York, and so on. There are just too many of these "royal" families for them all to have direct seats on the Committee of 300.... But the thing to remember is the order of rank; first the royal family members, then dukes, earls, marquises and lords, then finally the "commoners," who usually get the title of "Sir".[1]

---

1. Coleman, *The Committee of 300*, pp. 84-85, 231, 269-271, 322. For lists of most past and present members, institutions, and organizations of the Committee of 300, see pages 311-350 of the same work. Just a few of the more easily recognized names of members, most of whom are on Coleman's list, include Queen Elizabeth II, Prince Charles, Prince Philip, Queen Juliana, Queen Sofia, Queen Margreta, Queen Beatrix, Princess Beatrice of Savoy, Victor Cavendish the Duke of Gloucestor, Edward the Duke of Kent, the Duke of Devonshire, Angus Ogilvie (Ogilvy), Lord Salisbury, Battenburg (family Designate), George Bush, Francois Mitterand, David Rockefeller, who donated the land in New York City on which the Untied Nations' buildings were constructed, Baron Rothschild, Maurice Strong, Cecil Rhodes, Aurelio Peccei, who founded the Club of Rome (from which came the 1957 "Treaty of Rome" that established the European Economic Community, which is now the European Union), John P. Morgan, DuPont, Henry Kissinger, John Forbes, Ted Turner, Earnest Oppenheimer, Aldous Huxley, Alfred P. Sloan, W.E. McClaughlin, Robert Runcie the former Archbishop of Canterbury (a pagan priest who was personally selected by Queen Elizabeth II after having placed the crown upon her head at her coronation), and the now deceased Colonel Mandel House, H.G. Wells, Lloyd George, Arthur Balfour, David *ben* Gurion (modern Israel's first Prime Minister), Chaim Weizmann (modern Israel's first President who has now been superseded by his

The Committee of 300 is a supranational organization whose express purpose, like the Illuminati, is to facilitate the creation of a Luciferic New World Order. This over-arching committee, working through world leaders of virtu-ally all backgrounds and persuasions, the Illuminati, Freemasonry, the intelligence services, all types of organ-ized crime, including global banking,[1] the worldwide drug trade,[2] the media (noted later), and many other agencies,

nephew Ezer Weizmann), Winston Churchill, Louis Mountbatten, Paul Warnke, Cyrus Vance, and George Shultz.

According to Coleman, membership in the Committee of 300, "which has a 150-year his-tory," includes top representatives from the old families of the European Black Nobility, the Illuminati, the Order of St. John of Jerusalem, the Order of Skull and Bones, Lucis Trust, the Vatican, the United Nations (U.N.), the International Monetary Fund (IMF), the Bank of Inter-national Settlements (BIS), NATO, the Central Intelligence Agency (CIA), the Nine Unknown Men, the Club of Rome, the World Wildlife Fund (WWF), Greenpeace, the Sierra Group, Socialist International, Anenherbe-Rosicrucianists, the National and World Council of Churches, the One World Government Church, the Thule Society, "and literally HUNDREDS of other organizations." This membership involves "some of the most brilliant intellects assem-bled to form a completely totalitarianist, absolutely controlled 'new' society" (ibid., pp. 216-218, 237).

1. In discussing the committee's structure, Coleman again notes the Tavistock Institute and then states, "The EAGLE STAR GROUP, which changed its name to the STAR GROUP after the close of the Second World War, is composed of a group of major international companies in overlapping and interfaced areas (1) Insurance, (2) Banking (3) Real Estate (4) Entertainment (5) High Technology.... Banking, while not the mainstay, is vitally important, especially in the areas where banks act as clearing houses and money launderers of drug money. The main 'big name banks' are: The Bank of England, The Federal Reserve Banks, Bank of International Settlements, The World Bank, The Hong Kong and Shanghai Bank, and American Express bank.... Each of these banks is affiliated with and/or controls hundreds of thousands of large and small banks throughout the world. Banks large and small in their thousands are in the Committee of 300 network.... ...Nothing happens on Wall Street that is not controlled by the Bank of England, whose instructions are relayed through the Morgan Bank and then put into action through key brokerage houses, whose top executives are ultimately responsi-ble for carrying out Committee directives" (*The Committee of 300*, pp. 240-241, 246).

2. As quoted earlier, "The drug trade [worldwide] is controlled by the Committee of 300 from the top down. The drug trade started with the British East India Company and was closely followed by the Dutch East India Company. Both were controlled by a 'Council of 300'" (Coleman, *The Committee of 300*, p. 141). To this, Coleman adds, "[The] British Crown, or the Royal Family,...levied a tax on all producers of opium duly registered with the state authority who were sending their opium to China.... Britain has been involved in the China opium trade for more than two centuries. No one is going to be so foolish as to rock the boat when millions upon millions of dollars flow into the bank accounts of the British oligar-chists.... Every British monarch since 1729 has benefited immensely from the drug trade and this holds good for the present occupant of the throne. Their ministers saw to it that wealth flowed into their family coffers.... By the turn of the century,...[their] income from the China opium trade exceeded David Rockefeller's income by SEVERAL BILLION DOLLARS PER ANNUM.... F.S. Turner's book, 'British Opium Policy,' published in 1876, shows how the Brit-ish monarchy and its hangers-on family relatives were deeply involved in the opium trade" (ibid., pp. 152, 155, 161, 183, 200). The British monarchy apparently also controls today's *heroin* trade through Canada, which in turn is controlled by the Canadian Institute for Inter-national Affairs, another child of the London-based Royal Institute for International Affairs (ibid., pp. 253-256). According to Coleman, the worldwide drug trade may be traced from

has vast wealth at its disposal[1] and has literally shaped the course of events in this century, to include fomenting World Wars I and II, and creating the League of Nations and then the United Nations on their ruins. The committee itself is not a monolith; when the British monarchy finds its control or operations threatened, it quickly acts to eliminate the threat, be it internal or external.[2] A more recent example of the committee's tampering was Desert Storm, or the 1991 war against Iraq, which was intentionally misled by the Bush administration to believe that the Untied States would merely blink if Iraq invaded Kuwait in 1990. On the ruins of this *multinational* war, then President George Bush proclaimed the dawning of a "New World Order," publicly floating the committee's goal as a "trial balloon" (see below).[3] Gorbachev—who, upon meeting the

the Tavistock Institute to 1) the British East India Company, 2) the Hong Kong London Council, 3) the Medellin Cartel, and 4) the Cali Cartel (ibid., p. 368).

Coleman is not alone in his assertions concerning the origins of the modern drug trade. It is a known fact that Britain acquired Hong Kong and its surrounding territories as a result of its Opium Wars with China in the last (nineteenth) century. What is perhaps not so well known is that the British monarchy, and Prince Charles in particular, still have very strong "business" ties to Hong Kong. Coleman, John Daniel (author of the *Scarlet and the Beast* trilogy), and others have shown that those ties continue to involve the drug trade. Anyone who pays attention to the news media will recall that the monarchy, through Prince Charles, personally officiated at Britain's recent handover of Hong Kong to communist China, at the start of July 1997. Could this have been more than just the next major international media-blitz for the prince since his extravagant wedding to Diana? One must seriously wonder. For more information, see Chapter 11's section titled, "Governor of Hong Kong?".

1. Besides its wealth from the worldwide drug trade, the British monarchy controls the metal and mineral wealth of South Africa. Coleman states, "The [Arthurian MI6] Round Table was established in South Africa by Cecil Rhodes and funded by the English Rothschild family. Its purpose was to train business leaders loyal to the monarch, who would secure the vast gold and diamond treasures for the British Crown.... By the early 1930s, the British Crown had a stranglehold on the biggest gold and diamond fields ever found in the world. NOW THE COMMITTEE OF 300 HAD AT ITS DISPOSAL BOTH THE VAST FORTUNE COMING FROM THE DRUG TRADE AND THE EQUALLY VAST FORTUNE OF THE MINERAL AND METAL WEALTH OF SOUTH AFRICA. Financial control of the world was complete" (*The Committee of 300*, pp. 207-208). We may trace "the spokes of the drug wheel, including terrorism, production of opium, the gold markets, dirty money laundering and banking, to its central core, the British Crown" (ibid., p. 256). Note that as a Rhodes Scholar, President Clinton is similarly subservient to the British monarchy.

2. One conspiracy-theorist view of the start of World War II, for example, is as follows: Hitler, after having been groomed in Masonry and other areas of the occult, decided that his masonic masters and Masons generally, many of whom were apostate Jews, were a threat to his own "Aryan" aspirations. He therefore determined that the Jews were not just a convenient scapegoat on which to cement his power base, but that both they and the masonic influence in Europe had to be eliminated. Consequently, the British monarchy itself came to feel threatened, and World War II ensued. Is this plausible? *Yes*.

3. Coleman asserts that Bush, "another member of the Committee of 300," acted on behalf of "the Royal Institute for International Affairs (RIIA) who received its mandate from the Com-

pope at the Vatican in December 1989, "realized that the pope had also played a role in what we [communists] came to call the new political thinking,"[1] and who is now clearly associated with the committee *and* Prince Charles[2] — first did so publicly in a 1988 speech before the United Nations' General Assembly. (Of course, Saddam Hussein, who may yet prove to be Daniel's prophesied "King of the North," appears to have been preserved for another day, which the committee mistakenly thinks will be as innocuous as a "Desert Storm II." In fact, that day, may now be on the

---

mittee of 300, also known as the 'Olympians.'" Coleman adds, "the war was fought by American troops to protect the interests of British Petroleum (BP), which is one of the most important companies in the Committee of 300 in which members of Queen Elizabeth's immediate family have a big stake.... ...Britain is in charge of our government.... The plain truth is that the United States has fought in 5 wars this century, for, and on behalf of the infamous Committee of 300" (*The Committee of 300*, pp. 22, 64, 79, 180, 192, 214).

1. Mikhail Gorbachev, "Pope played significant role in changing world," *The Denver Post,* 9 Mar. 1992, p. 7A. This article was reproduced by Gary Kah in *Hope for the World Update,* Fall 1995, p. 6.

2. On October 19, 1994, in what was billed as a "major policy speech" and delivered "to 300 distinguished members of the New York Council on Foreign Relations" (a veiled reference to the U.S. C.F.R.'s master, the supranational Committee of 300, only some of whose members were actually present), Gorbachev "unveiled the final report of the Global Security Project." Called "The Global Security Programme" (non-American English), the report called for "measures to strengthen the authority of the United Nations and regional security institutions." According to the traitorous Senator Alan Cranston, head of the U.S. delegation to the project and Chairman of the Board of the Gorbachev Foundation USA, not to mention a member of the masonic Bohemian Club, "This initiative represents a major step forward in building consensus for the emerging global security system for the coming century, an era where cooperation among nations and peoples must replace our outmoded and dangerous aggressive brinkmanship" ("Mikhail Gorbachev unveils new *Global Security Programme,*" Gorbachev Foundation USA, as reproduced by Gary Kah in *Hope for the World Update,* Fall 1995, pp. 3-4). It is perhaps noteworthy that the effort was strongly supported by the Carnegie Corporation of New York, another Committee of 300 organization (Coleman, *The Committee of 300,* pp. 85-86, 290, 316). In fact, Gorbachev, as President of the Gorbachev Foundation, and at his 1995 State of the World Forum conference in San Francisco, has worked, and continues to work, not just with some of the world's most prominent New Agers, but directly with such Committee of 300 members as George Bush, George Shultz, David Rockefeller, Maurice Strong, Francois Mitterand, and Ted Turner (Kah, "Gorbachev Calls For World Tax...While Wooing Spiritual Leaders," and Samatha Strong, "Gorbachev Forum Highlights World Government," *Hope for the World Update,* Fall 1995, pp. 1-5), all of whom are listed by Coleman (*The Committee of 300,* pp. 312, 317, 319-320). A co-sponsor of Gorbachev's State of the World Forum was The Red Rose Collection, a globalist Rosicrucian organization that promotes New Age ideology (Kah, "World Federalists Call for U.N. Empowerment," ibid., p. 3). Coleman adds, "The Committee of 300 is filled with members of British aristocracy which has corporate interests and associates in every country of the world, including Russia" (ibid., p. 240).

    The punch to the Global Security Programme "unveiled" and trumpeted by Gorbachev, however, is that it was initiated *not* by Gorbachev in 1994, but years earlier at Cambridge University with *Prince Charles'* involvement. See Chapter 11's section titled, "Global Governance, the Global Security Programme, and a possible 'Economic Security Council.'"

horizon.) Just after the ground war against Iraq, in January and March of 1991, Bush asserted,[1]

> We [Americans] can find meaning and reward by serving some higher purpose than ourselves—a shining purpose, the illumination of a thousand points of light....
>
> What is at stake is more than one small country [like Kuwait]; it is a big idea—a New World Order, where diverse nations are drawn together in common cause to achieve the universal aspirations of mankind....
>
> With few exceptions, the world now stands as one.... [For] the first time since World War II, the international community is united. The leadership of the United Nations, once only a hoped-for ideal, is now confirming its founders' vision....
>
> The world can therefore seize this opportunity to fulfill the long-held promise of a New World Order.... Yes, the United States bears a major share of the leadership in this effort. Among the nations of the world, only the United States of America has had both the moral standing and the means to back it up. We are the only nation on this Earth that could assemble the forces of peace.[2]

> "Our commitment to peace in the Middle East does not end with the liberation of Kuwait," Bush said. "The time has come to put an end to the Arab-Israeli conflict."
>
> ....Bush re-emphasized longstanding American policy that Israel must trade territory it seized during Arab-Israeli wars for peace and secure borders.[3]

> ....Bush pledged a "new and vigorous determination" to push a land-for-peace in the Arab-Israeli conflict. He called for finally implementing U.N. Security Council resolutions 242 and 338, which call for Israel to withdraw from occupied territories in exchange for secure borders.[4]

As a member of the Committee of 300, former Prime Minister David *ben* Gurion of Israel, who created the Mossad with the help of MI6, made these remarkable, yet

---

1. This material is excerpted from the author's forthcoming work, *Messiah, History, and the Tribulation Period.*
2. "State of the Union—Bush Seeks to Inspire Support for his Persian Gulf Mission," *Congressional Quarterly,* 2 Feb. 1991, pp. 308-310. Also see Kah, p. 63.
3. Denver Post Wire Services, "Pledge made to maintain Mideast role," *The Denver Post,* 7 Mar. 1991, p. 1A.
4. G.G. LaBelle, The Associated Press, "Baker's peace bid faces battle lines," *The Denver Post,* 9 Mar. 1991, p. 6A. For more information, see Chapter 12, "Prince Charles, the Middle East Peace Talks, and Global Security."

twisted, predictions in 1962: "With the exception of the USSR, as a federated Eurasian state, all other countries will become united in a world alliance, at whose disposal will be an international police force. All armies will be abolished, and there will be no more wars. In Jerusalem, the United Nations will build a shrine to the Prophets to serve the federated union on all continents, as prophesied by Isaiah. Higher education will be the right of every person in the world. A pill to prevent pregnancy will slow down the explosive natural increase in China and India."[1] Indeed, apart from Hebrew Christians, modern Israel is almost entirely apostate, and under Satan's grip.

To be more precise, as Coleman essentially charts it, under the *Committee of 300,* we may place **1)** the royal families of Europe, **2)** British Intelligence or MI6, **3)** the Royal Institute for International Affairs, **4)** the United Nations and its member nations, and **5)** Communism, Fabianism, Zionism (in an effort to control Israel and Jerusalem), Liberalism, Socialism, and Right Wing Parties. Under *British Intelligence,* we may place **1)** the CIA, **2)** the Mossad, and **3)** other intelligence agencies worldwide (detailed below). Under the *Royal Institute for International Affairs (RIIA),* we may place **1)** the Tavistock Institute of Human Relations and **2)** the Executive Arm of the RIIA; **3)** the Rhodes/Milner Group and its Round Table; **4)** Freemasonry and other secret societies, as well as the Nine Unknown Men; **5)** international terrorism; **6)** control of the world's banking, petroleum, mining, insurance, commerce, and industry; and **7)** religious organizations, including the One World Government Church.[2] Under the *Tavistock Institute for Human Relations,* we may place **1)** the Club of Rome, from which came **2)** NATO and today's U.S. military; **3)** the worldwide drug trade, to include the British East India Company, the Hong Kong London Council, the Medellin Cartel, and the Cali Cartel; and **4)** the major institutions, to include the Stanford Research Institute, the Massachusetts Institute of Technology, the Institute for Policy Studies, RAND, the Hudson Institutes, and the

1. Coleman, *The Committee of 300,* pp. xlll-xiv, 235-236.
2. *The Committee of 300,* p. 367.

144

Wharton School of Economics.[1] Under the *Executive Arm of the Royal Institute for International Affairs,* we may place **1)** the various Councils on Foreign Relations (e.g., U.S., Canadian, and Israeli), **2)** the U.S. Trilateral Commission, and **3)** the Bilderbergers. Under the *U.S. Council on Foreign Relations,* we may place control of **1)** the United States Government, which, at least in the United States, involves education, the environment, abortion (the U.S. also promotes infanticide worldwide through "aid" to developing countries), gun control, congress, the senate, and FEMA, as well as **2)** the U.S. media, to include ABC, CBS, NBC, CNN, UPI, the New York Times, the Washington Post, etc.[2] The RIIA works with British Intelligence and its offspring to further **a)** nefarious religious activities, to include so-called Christian publishers promoting one-world government and evolution in education,[3] as well as socialist and humanist ideas such as "tolerance;" **b)** the World Council of Churches and its hierarchy, Liberation Theology, and Socialism; and **c)** secret societies, religious foundations, "church" research groups, the Rockefeller Riverside Church, apostate seminaries and left-wing religious groups, and, finally, schools for indoctrination into one-world government ideas.[4]

Like Queen Elizabeth II and Prince Charles, one of Prince Philip's titles is "Colonel-in-Chief, the Intelligence

1. *The Committee of 300,* p. 368.
2. *The Committee of 300,* p. 369. Note that Ted Turner, owner of CNN, is a recent addition to the Committee of 300 (ibid., pp. 236, 320). Coleman adds, "Going back to RCA, we find that its directorate consists of British-American establishment figures, who feature prominently in other organizations such as: the CFR, NATO, the Club of Rome, the Trilateral Commission, Freemasonry, Skull and Bones, Bilderbergers, Round Table, Milner Group, Cini Foundation, Mont Pelerin Society, and the Jesuits-Aristotle Society.... All three major [U.S.] television networks came as spinoffs from RCA, especially the National Broadcasting Company (NBC), which was closely followed by the American Broadcasting Company (ABC), in 1951. The third big television network was Columbia Broadcasting System (CBS), which like its sister companies, was, and still is, dominated by British intelligence. William Paley was trained in mass brainwashing techniques at the Tavistock Institute prior to being passed as qualified to head CBS. Thus, if we the people of the United States but knew it, all our major television networks are subject to British oversight, and information they provide first goes to London for clearance.... All three major networks are represented on the Committee of 300 and are affiliated with the giant of the mass communications business, Xerox Corporation" (ibid., pp. 248-249).
3. Charles Darwin, the man whose legacy has done so much to harm true Christianity in this century, was a relative of the British royal family; indeed, his remains are buried in Westminster Abbey, the "heart" of Britain's establishment church, to this day.
4. *The Committee of 300,* p. 370.

145

Corps."[1]   According to Coleman, the Committee of 300 "possesses a super-intelligence service that has corrupted the KGB, the Vatican Intelligence, the CIA, the ONI, DGSE, U.S. military intelligence, the State Department intelligence service, and even the most secret of all U.S. intelligence agencies, the Office of National Reconnaissance."[2]   He asserts, "There is no entity the Committee cannot reach and control, and that includes the organized religions of the world. This [committee] then, is the [so-called] all power-ful OLYMPIAN GROUP, whose power base is in London, and the City of London financial center, with its grip on [South Africa's and the world's] minerals, metals and pre-cious gems, [tobacco,] cocaine, [heroin,] opium and phar-maceutical drugs, rentier-financier bankers, cult promoters and founders of rock music. The British Crown is the con-trol point from which all things [related to the creation of a Luciferic New World Order] radiate. As the saying goes, 'They have a finger in every pie.'"[3] Recall, of course, that

1. Judd, *Prince Philip*, p. 249.
2. "The existence of the National Reconnaissance Office (NRO) was known only to a handful of people outside of the Committee of 300, until Truman stumbled upon it quite by accident. Churchill had a hand in setting up the NRO, and he was reportedly livid when Truman [who was controlled through Freemasonry] discovered its existence.... [The NRO] is a creature of the Committee of 300, to whom its reports are routinely sent every few hours" (*The Commit-tee of 300*, p. 237).

    To his earlier statements regarding the committee's Star Group (formerly known as the Eagle Star Group), which controls banking worldwide, as well as Wall Street (ibid., pp. 240-241, 246), Coleman adds, "The English companies controlled by the British royal family are: Eagle Star, Prudential Assurance Company, and the Prudential Insurance Company, which own and control most American insurers, including Allstate Insurance. At the head of the list is Eagle Star, probably the most powerful 'front' for Military Intelligence Department Six (MI6). Eagle Star, although nowhere near as large as Assicurazioni Generale, is perhaps equally important simply because it is owned by members of the Queen of England's family, and as Queen Elizabeth [II] is the titular head of the Committee, Eagle Star is tremendously important. Eagle Star is more than a major 'front' for MI6; it is also a front for major British banks.... It can be said with a great degree of accuracy that the most powerful British oligar-chical families created Eagle Star as a vehicle for 'black operations' against those who oppose Committee of 300 policies" (ibid., p. 244). Coleman elaborates, "As giant-sized as Xerox is, it is dwarfed by the Rank Organization, a London-based conglomerate fully con-trolled by members of Queen Elizabeth's immediate family.... The best proof I can offer of the existence of the Committee of 300, is the Rank Organization, which, in conjunction with Eagle Star IS THE BRITISH CROWN. It is also the black operations center of MI6 (SIS)" (ibid., pp. 250, 253).
3. Coleman, *The Committee of 300*, p. 248. Coleman outlines the aims of the "Olympians," who "believe they are equal in power and stature to the legendary gods of Olympus." These aims include the creation of a New World Order; the elimination of national identities; the destruction of major religions—especially Christianity—through the introduction of new cults and the furtherance of existing ones ("most cults operating in the world today, are the product of British intelligence acting for the oligarchical rulers" of the Committee of 300);

the Order of the Garter is *the* central organ to all this.

Garter symbols. As today's *second-ranking* Garter knight, who is outranked only by his mother the queen, Prince Charles wears the insignia of the order. These insignia include the blue velvet Garter itself, the  gold motto of which is *Honi soit qui mal y pense,* the Collar

---

mass mind control; drastic depopulation through the deaths of about three billion people and a subsequent zero-growth society with abundant "slave labor;" the creation and management of major crises and resulting chaos to maintain and increase control of populations and governments (FEMA—the Federal Emergency Management Agency—in the U.S., exists for this purpose); the legalization of illegal drugs to increase profitability (hence, the Bush and Clinton administrations' so-called "war on drugs" drug-legalization agenda); and to keep the nation of Israel apostate and under masonic hegemony (ibid., pp. 42-47, 230).

With the above objectives in mind, "Britain's MI6 (SAS) promotes a wide variety of kookery such as the New Age, Yogaism, Zenn Bhudism, Witchcraft, Delphic Priesthood of Apollo and hundreds of small 'cults' of all kinds" (ibid., p. 237). Coleman observes that most of today's "Christian" churches "have become little more than social clubs run by the infinitely evil World Council of Churches (WCC), whose beginnings lie not in Moscow but in the City of London.... This body was set up in the 1920s to serve as a vehicle for One World Government policies, and stands as a monument to the long-range planning capabilities of the Committee of 300" (ibid., pp. 289-290; for a chart, see p. 372). (The author does not fully share Coleman's pessimism, and finds his point exaggerated. We must always remember that God is stronger than Satan, and that in Christ, we shall have the final victory.) Coleman adds, "The war on drugs which the Bush administration was allegedly fighting, but which it was not, was for the legalization of ALL types and classes of drugs. Such drugs are not solely a social aberration, but a full-scale attempt to gain control of the minds of the people of this planet.... THIS IS THE PRINCIPAL TASK OF THE COMMITTEE" (ibid., pp. 204-205). "Both prohibition and the distilleries who met the demand for alcohol were creations of the British Crown.... It was an experiment which became the forerunner of today's drug trade, and the lessons learned from the prohibition era are being applied to the soon to be legalized drug trade" (ibid., p. 272).

According to Coleman, "Summarized, the intent and purpose of the Committee of 300 is to bring to pass the following conditions: A One World Government and one-unit monetary system, under permanent non-elected hereditary oligarchists, who self-select from among their numbers, in the form of a feudal system as it was in the Middle Ages. In this One World entity, population will be limited by restrictions on the number of children allowed per family, diseases, wars and famines, until 1 billion people who are useful to the ruling class in areas which will be strictly and clearly defined, will remain as the total population of the world.... Satanism, Luciferianism and Witchcraft, shall be recognized as legitimate One World Government curricula with no private or church schools. All Christian churches have already been subverted [so far as the oligarchists are concerned], and Christianity will become a religion of the past in the One World Government." Of the remaining 1 billion, "500 million will consist of Chinese and Japanese races, selected because they are people who have been regimented for centuries" (ibid., pp. 218-219, 222). Prince Charles, by the way, is *pro*-infanticide.

(from which dangles the George pendant depicting St. George on a white horse slaying a spotted green dragon), the Star, and the blue Riband with its Lesser George. Like the pendent on the Collar, the Lesser George also depicts "Saint" George slaying a spotted dragon.[1] "The Collar [now] consisting of twenty-six red [Tudor] roses each enclosed by the Garter interspersed with twenty-six gold knots and having pendant a representation of St George and the [spotted] Dragon was introduced during the reign of Henry VII, probably shortly before 1500. The Garter Star, a badge which the Companions were to wear upon their coats or cloaks dates from 1626/9. The blue Riband with its Lesser George, a representation of St George slaying the Dragon within the Garter, was first ordered to be worn by Henry VIII."[2] Actually, the twenty-six red roses of the Collar were originally, at the time of Henry VIII, twenty-six roundels of St. George's cross (see below).[3]

The eight-pointed Star of the order, which is made of chipped silver, enamel, and gold, has a central red cross—representative of the emblem of the Merovingian birthmark historically adopted by the Temple Knights and then the Priory of Zion—encircled by the Garter.[4] That is, the Merovingian cross—now euphemistically called the arms of "St. George"—appears as the red quartering device of a white shield surrounded by the Garter, which is imposed over the center of an eight-pointed star. "Companions" and "priests"[5] of the order wear a) the white shield with the Merovingian cross encircled by the Garter, called the Garter Badge of St. George's Cross (companions),[6] or b) a "roundel" similar to it but circular

1. For color representations of the insignia of the Order of the Garter, see Boutell, plate XVII, between pp. 184-187. Note, however, that the depiction of the formerly light blue Garter itself (before George I's reign, but still worn by the present queen) is defective in that rather than being edged with two rows of 169 miniature gold buckles each, as on the actual deep blue Garter in predominant use since George I's reign, it is edged with two gold chains. (The author possesses a color photograph of a deep blue Garter dating to around 1813 in which the buckles are evident. For more information, see the later related note.)
2. Begent, p. 11.
3. Begent, p. 3.
4. For more information, see Chapter 4, "Prince of this World—a *Diverse* Lineage."
5. For more information, see the discussion on the College of St. George in Chapter 10's section titled, "A so-called 'Christian' heritage."
6. For a color picture of Prince Charles' Garter Badge, see Burnet, *In Private—In Public, THE PRINCE AND PRINCESS OF WALES*, p. 127.

(priests), upon the left shoulder of either **a)** the dark blue velvet Garter Mantle (cloak), which has a crimson velvet hood (companions), or **b)** a crimson or murrey (dark purple) robe (priests). Since around 1911, the Sovereign of the Order, unlike the other companions, has worn the Star itself on the left shoulder of the Mantle.[1] Likewise, the "habit" of the Temple Knights, originally a priestly order of apostate Roman Catholic soldiers, "was white with a red cross of eight points worn on the left shoulder."[2] *A version of the Merovingian cross encircled by the Garter, which thus constitutes a roundel, is the central symbol of the Order of the Garter.* As such, it is not only imposed over the center of an eight-pointed silver star to compose the Garter Star,[3] but it is also prominently displayed on the forehead of the black velvet Garter hats worn by Queen Elizabeth II and Prince Charles.[4] The same red cross is likewise hidden in the alternating gold and red quarters of the royal shield, and is similarly surrounded by the Garter.[5]

In other words, the Temple Knights, having been thrust out of France and supposedly the rest of Europe in 1309, being "abolished" by Papal Bull in 1312,[6] had actually become so powerful and influential in Scotland and England that by 1348, if not earlier, the English monarchy had not only joined their cause, but taken up their leadership in the form of the newly constituted Order of the Garter.[7] Indeed, it was the Knights of the Garter who held

---

1. Begent, pp. 1, 9, 13.
2. Boutell, 1978 ed., p. 191.
3. For a color photograph of Prince Charles' Garter Star, see Burnet, *In Private—In Public, THE PRINCE AND PRINCESS OF WALES,* p. 124.
4. *Her Majesty The Queen,* p. 17; and Burnet, *In Private—In Public, THE PRINCE AND PRINCESS OF WALES,* p. 127.
5. A round seal of the English Knights Templar dating to 1303 is comparably encircled by a motto (Baigent, Leigh, and Lincoln, *Holy Blood, Holy Grail,* just above caption 16b, between pp. 240-241).
6. Boutell, 1978 ed., p. 192.
7. The Garter Seal of Henry VII depicts a shield quartered by the Merovingian cross, as on the Garter Star, "marshaled" with the quartered arms of England and France (no doubt taken from the Black Prince's "shield for war"). The modern version of this seal, which is further marshaled with the Irish harp and another device (possibly the red lion of Scotland), now constitutes the badge of the "Garter, Principal King of Arms" (Begent, pp. 9, 17). Similarly, the Merovingian cross is the primary device in the shield of arms belonging to the Garter King of Arms, which is marshaled with a lion of England, the Garter, and a *fleur-de-lis* (lily) for France (Boutell, 1978 ed., pp. 232-233). For more information, see this chapter's later discussion on the Black Prince.

the canopy over Elizabeth II as she was anointed and crowned queen during her 1953 coronation.[1] Furthermore, the modified Templar cross of the Order of the Garter is prominently displayed on the Union Jack and the arms of the British Commonwealth. The Union Jack combines the cross of St. George for England—having a white fringe representing the field of St. George's banner—with the saltires of "St. Andrew" and "St. Patrick" for Scotland and Ireland.[2] Occupying the place of the lions of England on the royal shield, the first and fourth quarters of the Commonwealth's shield each contain the Garter Badge of St. George's Cross. Its second quarter contains the saltire of St. Andrew for Scotland, rather than Scotland's red lion, and the third quarter has a pagan version of a harp, displaying a harlot's breasts, for Ireland (as opposed to the Davidic harp on the royal shield).[3] Likewise, versions of the Garter Badge of St. George's Cross have not only been central to the achievement of the city of London since the middle of the fourteenth century,[4] but also are now flown over Anglican Protestant churches[5] and serve as the symbol of the Red Cross organization, seen throughout the world. In fact, the Merovingian cross is among the most prolific of symbols in British and Commonwealth heraldry.[6] Similarly, since Henry VIII in 1534 took the

1. Begent, p. 1. Previously, Queen Mary wanted to borrow the Duke of Windsor's "diamond-studded Garter Star" for Edward VIII's coronation (Lacey, *Majesty*, p. 85).
2. Boutell, 1978 ed., p. 255. "Except when they bore royal devices, the English standards of the Tudor period always had the cross of St. George at their head" (Boutell, 1978 ed., p. 254). The white ensign of the Royal Navy, which bears the Merovingian cross and shows the union in a canton, is a version of St. George's banner (Boutell, 1978 ed., p. 256). For a picture of Prince Charles and Princess Diana sitting in front of a large Union Jack, see Hoey, *Charles & Diana: The Tenth Anniversary*, p. 96.
3. Boutell, 1978 ed., pp. 213, 215. A crowned lion and a dragon serve as the dexter and sinister supporters in the full achievement of the Commonwealth. With this arrangement in mind, it is not difficult to imagine that the achievement of Prince Charles could one day take the place of the Commonwealth's current arms.
4. Boutell, 1978 ed., p. 235.
5. According to Brooke-Little, the proper banner or flag to be used by Anglican Protestant churches was declared by the Earl Marshal in 1938 as follows: "The Banner or Flag proper to be flown upon any Church within the Provinces of Canterbury and York to be the Cross of St. George and in the first quarter an escutcheon of the Arms of the See in which such Church is ecclesiastically situate" (Boutell, 1978 ed., p. 257).
6. As yet another instance, Jamaica's shield of arms, granted by 1661, consists of the Garter Badge of St. George's Cross charged with five golden pineapples (Boutell, 1978 ed., pp. 243, 245-246). "For visits to other Commonwealth Countries the Queen has adopted a special flag consisting of the arms of the Government of the country in question with the central

inflated and blasphemous title of "Supreme Head on Earth of the Church of England," not only has the English monarch's *coat of arms* or achievement been "prominently displayed in many English churches as tokens of loyalty to the crown and obedience to the sovereign as head of the Church," being required by a statute for "all churches" under Charles II in 1660,[1] but it too has been propagated throughout the Commonwealth.

That is not all, however. A quick search of the Internet, for example, will reveal that there are numerous churches of several denominations besides Anglican Protestant, not to mention other organizations, that are named after "St. George" or have selected "St. George" as their patron "saint." Indeed, like the antichristian "Hiram Abiff" of Freemasonry, "St. George" is said to have died and been resurrected. Since Satan cannot beat Christians, he attempts in a host of ways to co-opt them. To this end, satanic parodies of Christ, preached in a plethora of false gospels, have made the rounds, not just among cultists, but also among ignorant and apostate Christians. Over the centuries, the British monarchy has played a *defining* role in this satanic activity.

The first three degrees of Freemasonry, the Blue Degrees, are common to both the York Rite and the Scottish Rite. These degrees, which are collectively referred to as the Blue Lodge, originated in what is now the United Grand Lodge of England, which is acknowledged by advanced Masons worldwide as the *Mother Lodge* of all Freemasonry.[2] Although few seem to be aware of it, the British monarch, who may serve personally as the grand master of this lodge before *his* coronation as king, installs its grand master, and is, like the Prince of Wales (see below), *over* Freemasonry worldwide.[3] We should not be

motif on her personal flag over all. For example, the Queen's personal flag for use in Jamaica consists of a banner of the [shield of] arms of Jamaica...with the motif from her personal flag in the fess point" (Boutell, 1978 ed., p. 258).

1. John E. Titterton, "Royal Arms in Churches," *A Dictionary of Heraldry*, ed. Friar, p. 288. See Chapter 10's section titled "A so-called 'Christian' Heritage" for more information.

2. The United Grand Lodge of England "has powers to revoke the charter of any Lodge found to be conducting itself in an unworthy, immoral or criminal way." However, "this provision is never implemented" (Knight, *The Brotherhood,* p. 307).

3. The British Monarchy has a long history of deep involvement in Freemasonry. Descriptions

surprised, then, by Elizabeth II's direct oversight of various

of some of the masonic involvement and activities of Queen Elizabeth I (1533-1603), Prince Frederick (1737), King George III (1738-1820), King George IV (1762-1830), Duke Edward Augustus (Duke of Kent, 1767-1820), Augustus Frederick (1813-1843), President George Washington (1797), King Edward VII (1841-1910), Greece's King George I (1845-1913), King George V (1865-1936), Greece's Constantine I (George I's son), Alexander Albert Mountbatten (1st Marquess of Carisbrooke, 1886), Greece's King George II (1890-1947), King George VI (1895-1952), Prince George (Duke of Kent, 1902-1942), King Edward VIII (1936), and Queen Elizabeth II may be found on pages 8-9, 16, 102-105, 107, and 181 in the four volumes of *10,000 Famous Freemasons* by William R. Denslow (1957). Louis Mountbatten was, and Prince Philip is, likewise involved in Freemasonry; their "family name was changed from Battenberg to Mountbatten in 1914 at the outbreak of WW1" (ibid., p. 181). In reading these descriptions, it is interesting to note "Prince of Wales Lodge No. 259, the lodge connected with the royal family" (ibid., p. 181), as well as other "Prince of Wales" lodges, are frequently mentioned, and that a number of the royal personages mentioned above are said to have reached the 33-degree.

"George, Prince of Wales (later George IV and grand master) [was] initiated in 1787, in a special lodge at the Star and Garter, Pall Mall.... He was initiated in a special lodge, Feb. 6, 1787, meeting at the Star and Garter at London.... He served as grand master of the Grand Lodge of England for 23 years, and in 1805 was grand master of the Grand Lodge of Scotland. When he became king, the Duke of Sussex was elected grand master, and the king took the title of grand patron. The Duke of Sussex, his younger brother, was able to bring about a union of the two English [(actually, English and Scottish)] grand lodges in 1813," thus forming the United Grand Lodge of England (ibid., pp. 102-103). On April 28, 1875, Edward VII was elected grand master of the [United] Grand Lodge of England, and, having been installed by the Earl of Caernarvon, served as such until his ascension to the throne in 1901, when he assumed the title, "protector of the craft" (ibid., p. 8). George V, of the "house of Saxe-Coburg-Gotha, which in 1917 changed its name to the house of Windsor," "became grand patron of the three Masonic charities of the Grand Lodge of England" (ibid., p. 103). Before becoming king, Prince Edward of Wales "was a Freemason and supported the application of Ernest Simpson for admission to a masonic lodge.... [He] was told that it was against the masonic law for the husband of his mistress to be admitted. The Prince gave his word that this was not in fact the situation and Ernest Simpson was admitted" (Lacey, *Majesty*, p. 48). As king, Edward VIII became grand master of the United Grand Lodge of England in 1936 (*10,000 Famous Freemasons*, p. 9). Prince George, Duke of Kent, had ascribed the "commoner" Wallis Simpson's enchantment of Edward VIII, who subsequently abdicated the throne to marry her, "to something approaching sorcery" (Lacey, *Majesty*, p. 47). George VI, who was formerly Prince Albert, as king "accepted the rank of past grand master of the [United] Grand Lodge of England, and was ceremonially installed at the Albert Hall in London before an audience of Masons from all parts of the world.... **He** created the precedent of the English sovereign's active participation in Masonic ceremonies, and **personally conducted the installation of three grand masters—the Duke of Kent at Olympia in 1939; the Earl of Harewood in Freemason's Hall in 1943; and the Duke of Devonshire in Albert Hall in 1948.** Only his last illness prevented his installing the Earl of Scarbrough in 1951.... He held the rank of past grand master, and of knight commander of the Temple, was a 33-degree [Mason], and grand inspector general in the Ancient and Accepted Rite of Rose Croix [(meaning, "Red Cross"—of Merovée—and associated with the Rosicrucians)]. Said he of Masonry: 'The world today does require spiritual and moral regeneration. I have no doubt, after many years as a member of our Order, that Freemasonry can play a most important part in this vital need'" (*10,000 Famous Freemasons*, p. 104). **Prince George, Duke of Kent, on "July 19, 1939...was formally installed grand master of the Grand Lodge of England by his brother, King George VI. He was killed, August 25, 1942, in an airplane accident"** (ibid., p. 105). His son Edward, the current Duke of Kent, is the grand master of the United Grand Lodge of England today (Knight, *The Brotherhood*, p. 212), and, like his father before him, remains subservient to the British monarch.

masonic institutions and activities.[1] With these things in mind, note that the Star and *blue* Garter are specifically referred to in the first degree (Entered Apprentice) of the *Blue* Lodge: "The Lamb-skin...is...the badge of a Mason;...[it is] more honorable than the Star and Garter."[2] According to Albert Pike, who wrote Freemasonry's preeminent work *Morals and Dogma*, "Masonry conceals its secrets from all except the adepts and sages, or the elect, and uses false explanations and misinterpretations of its symbols to mislead those who deserve to be misled, to conceal the truth, which it calls light, from them, and to draw them away from it.... The Blue Degrees are but the outer court or portico of the [masonic] Temple. Part of the symbols are displayed there to the Initiate, but he is <u>intentionally misled by false interpretations</u>. It is not intended that he shall understand them; but it is intended that he shall imagine he understands them. Their true explication is reserved for the Adepts, the Princes of Masonry."[3] *The Royal Masonic Cyclopaedia* defines an Adept as "a name given to the Order of the Illuminati."[4] In other words, the Star and Garter are actually considered to be *more* noble, not less, than Freemasonry.[5] Recall, therefore, that the Duke of Kent, who is currently the most powerful Mason in the world by virtue of being the grand

1. Queen Elizabeth II is, among other things, Grand Patroness "of each of the three Royal Masonic Benevolent Institutions conducted by the Grand Lodge of England—one for old people and one each for boys and girls [(e.g., the Royal Masonic Institution for Boys)]" (*10,000 Famous Freemasons*, pp. 16, 181). A picture of Queen Elizabeth II congratulating a 32-degree Mason, Donald M. Dinning, "upon his receiving The Most Excellent Order of the British Empire in a ceremony held at Buckingham Palace...on October 25, 1995," may be seen in the May 1996 *Scottish Rite Journal* (Washington: Southern Jurisdiction USA), Volume CIV, Number 5, page 41. "It is an interesting anomaly that the Queen, as a woman, is banned from entering a masonic temple—yet she is Grand Patroness of the movement. Her two younger sons are already marked down by the elders of Great Queen Street as possible future Grand Masters" (Knight, *The Brotherhood*, p. 215). Of course, the queen also heads the Committee of 300, and "only Freemasons of highest rank had any hope of being selected by the Committee of 300" (Coleman, *The Committee of 300*, p. 191).
2. Taylor, *Indiana Monitor and Freemason's Guide*, pp. 58-59. Also, see Albert G. Mackey, *A Manual of the Lodge* (New York: Clark & Maynard Publishers, 1878), pp. 32-33.
3. Albert Pike, *Morals and Dogma*, pp. 104, 819.
4. Kenneth MacKenzie, *The Royal Masonic Cyclopaedia* (England: The Aquarian Press, 1877), p. 18.
5. The Star of the Order of the Garter is eight-pointed with a central red cross. The last three degrees of the York Rite of Freemasonry are Knight of the Red Cross, Knight of Malta, and Temple Knight. Knight Templar corresponds roughly to the thirty-second degree in the Scottish Rite of Freemasonry.

master of the United Grand Lodge of England, is subservient to the Queen of England and the Prince of Wales through his membership in both the Order of the Garter and the Committee of 300.

Regarding the British monarchy and its participation in the Illuminati and satanism, Springmeier adds,

> Some of what follows may exceed the understanding of the average reader, and will approach the British monarchy from an uncommon angle. This account constitutes an insightful overview of the British royal family and their participation in the Illuminati....
>
> Of great importance in understanding the Illuminati is their mind-control. The Illuminati intentionally create multiple personality disorder (DID) among their people. This means that what the outside world sees is not the whole story. I have firsthand reports from insiders that clearly show that Prince Charles has a hidden satanic side to him. The British royalty, the Swedish royalty, the Dutch, Belgium and Luxembourg royalty, have all been leading secret satanic lives apart from the awareness of the general public. The insider reports that I have received are simply too accurate and numerous to discount. Where's the proof? That is the difficult part; these people are masters of deceit and have all the finances and power they need to pull off long-term programs of secrecy. In fact, it is required of Illuminati members that they do their rituals from memory, and not write down the things that they do in secret.
>
> The British royal family have long been involved with the occult.[1] They have also been actively involved with Freemasonry. In the early history of the Scottish Rite it served as a front for the Stuart cause. The Stuarts/Stewarts have been closely connected with the leadership of both Freemasonry and the Illuminati.[2] Stillson and Hughan's *History of Freemasonry and Concordant Orders* talks about the leadership the Prince of Wales (later King Edward VII) gave to modern English Templarism, and its masonic orders. A host of masonic sources have given the memberships and some of the details of the British Royal family's masonic activities. Queen Elizabeth II, for example, holds the position of Grand Patroness of Freemasonry.[3] Sixty-two Lord Mayors of London have been Masters of the Guildhall Masonic Lodge. This lodge

---

1. For more information, see Chapter 10's section titled, "Ties to the New Age Movement, the occult, and false religions."
2. For more information, see the discussion on the Priory of Zion's grand masters in Chapter 4, "Prince of this World—a *Diverse* Lineage."
3. Knight, *The Brotherhood*, p. 26. Although Springmeier cites Stephen Knight, much of what Knight had to say reflects only a superficial knowledge of the British monarchy's masonic connections, activities, and roles.

has many of the important officials of the City of London, which is the financial capital of not just greater London, but the world. Queen Elizabeth II's coat of arms is one of the 4 coats of arms appearing in the ritual at the crypt inside the Guildhall building to install the lodge's Master.[1]

Ex-Illuminati informants have revealed that the Queen of England *does* participate in the Satanic rituals of the Illuminati. In fact, Great Britain is the mother country of Satanism, and is the center for generational satanism.[2] This is widely known among generational satanists. Obviously then, whoever rules the United Kingdom must tie in powerfully with that satanic power. This explains why Cecil Rhodes and others of the Round Table, like the Rothschilds,[3] wanted to make the world subservient to Great Britain. Note also that the national symbol of Wales is the red dragon (the snake), and for years the chief of Wales was called the dragon. The Gaelic language, which Prince Charles had to learn for his 1969 investiture,[4] is an important language for Satanism, although English and French are also used extensively by the Illuminati; various planning sessions for world dominion, which some ex-Satanists have experienced, were held in French.

The queen also presides over the Knights of the Order of St. John of Jerusalem, the British Protestant part of the Knights of Malta. Interestingly, the masonic reference book *History of Freemasonry and Concordant Orders,* written by a British masonic board of editors and published in London in 1891, states on page 767 that the Knights of St. John are the real lineal descendants of the original Knights of Malta.

Prince Philip plays a role in Freemasonry, having been initiated into Freemasonry on December 5, 1952. There are conflicting claims as to how important the prince's role is in Freemasonry. However, when the Grand Master of the United Grand Lodge of England was named in 1966, Prince Philip had allowed the Queen's cousin, the 30-year old Duke of Kent, to have the position, even though he could have had it.

Prince Charles' private secretary, the Hon. Edward Adeane, son of Lt-Col. the Rt. Hon. Lord Michael Adeane, is a devoted Freemason, but Charles has not publicly joined Freemasonry. The prince has participated in satanic rituals, had Druids at his investiture, etc., but has not publicly made statements which would unequivocally confirm that he is a Freemason.[5] Prince Charles

1. Knight, *The Brotherhood,* pp. 216-218.
2. Brought out in interviews by Fritz Springmeier with numerous ex-witches and ex-satanists.
3. "The Rothschilds have been Freemasons for generations" (Knight, *The Brotherhood,* p. 222).
4. Speaking of the prince's investiture, Junor comments, "His triumph had been the Welsh, a difficult language..., which he had spoken easily and fluently," being "the first English Prince of Wales ever to speak and understand Welsh." The president of Plaid Cymru commented, "His performance was amazing. I have never heard anyone who has taken to Welsh so recently master the language so well" (pp. 78, 88).
5. Actually, Prince Charles has made indirect statements in favor of masonic beliefs, statements

travels all over the world participating in important behind the scenes meetings, and, like Queen Elizabeth II, he is a central member of the Order of the Garter, which is, among other things, an elite group of satanic aristocratic Knights of the Illuminati who control the plans for bringing in the New World Order. The American branch of this is the Society of the Cincinnati. There is also an Irish, Scottish and French counterpart to the Order of the Garter. Charles, who was taught at the important elite school of Gordonstoun, used by the Illuminati,[1] was close to Lord Louis Mountbatten, another major Illuminati figure,[2] until he was assassinated. The prince has rubbed shoulders with the Rothschilds, Juan Carlos, the Pope, Israeli leaders, etc., and he appears to play some type of major role for the Illuminati behind the scenes, besides his public role as the Prince of Wales and the heir-apparent to the throne.

The British royalty have served as important figureheads to British Freemasonry, lending credibility and respectability. British Freemasonry has managed to keep itself free from much of the criticism that the other national masonic groups have brought on themselves. However, much of the credibility of British Freemasonry is undeserved. True, it is what it portrays itself to be to the public for the lower levels. But the lower level Masons, by their dues and activities, are unwittingly supporting an organization

---

which clearly show that his own world-view harmonizes with that of the most occult Masons. For more information, see Chapter 10's section titled, "A so-called 'Christian' heritage."

1. A symbol that may be a precursor to the capstone of the seal of the Illuminati forms the relief over an entrance to the Gordonstoun grounds (see Junor, between pp. 86-87). For more information, see the discussions on Gordonstoun in Chapter 10's section titled, "Ties to the New Age Movement, the occult, and false religions," and in Chapter 11's section titled, "The United World Colleges."

2. Junor notes that Mountbatten "was the man charged with giving India her independence in 1947, and who presided over some of the bloodiest religious massacres in history, that resulted in the partition of the sub-continent into India and Pakistan" (p. 139). He "was a dynamic, tyrannical figure, full of energy and drive and wisdom.... He was a national hero, he had been Supreme Commander in South East Asia during the Second World War, the last Viceroy and first Governor General of India, First Sea Lord, and finally Chief of the Defense Staff. He had spent twenty-three years at the top, he had traveled all over the world.... Charles had been devoted to him ever since he was a small boy.... Obsessed with the concept of the Royal Family, Mountbatten saw it as his role in life to keep it going as a healthy popular institution. He was one of Queen Victoria's great-grandchildren, like George VI.... [When] the name Mountbatten finally became hyphenated to Windsor in 1960 he was a happy man." In determining Prince Charles' future education and his Naval service, it was Mountbatten's recommendation that prevailed (ibid., pp. 62-64). According to the prince, although Mountbatten "could certainly be ruthless with people when the occasion demanded,....people would have followed him into hell, if he had explained the point of such an expedition." (One wonders, "Did he explain it to the prince?") Having planned his own epitaph and funeral, "a blend of military and international, attended by dignitaries from all over the world," in advance, Mountbatten wrote, "His personal leadership, as long ago as 1945, helped to set the line on which the British Empire changed itself into the Commonwealth of sovereign states" (ibid., pp. 143-145).

that is led by satanists at the top.

An example of the subterfuge constantly exercised on the public by Freemasonry is a book purportedly written by a non-Mason entitled *The Unlocked Secret Freemasonry Examined*. The book portrays itself as an unbiased and complete exposé of Free-masonry. It states unequivocally that the masonic order called *Societas Rosicrucian in Anglia* [sic] is only open to Christians and is a "Christian Order." However, Edith Star Miller reprints copies of a number of letters from the chief of the *Societas Rosicrucian in Anglia* (SRIA) which show that the English Grand Masonic Lodge (United Grand Lodge of England), the SRIA, the *Ordo Templi Orientis* or Order of Oriental Templars (also known as the OTO or *Ordo To Ov*), and the German Illuminati are all working together. She briefly explains how she obtained the letters.[1]

Barons, Dukes, Counts, Earls and Knights have been getting involved with the European secret occult societies for centuries. These secret societies are not only being manipulated to serve as fronts for the Illuminati to bring in their New World Order, but also to enrich these Illuminati kingpins through criminal activities. Allow me to give just a brief peek at some of the characters who tie in with the British royal family, who are participating in all this secret activity.

James H. Carey, one of the Rockefeller's Chase Manhattan Bank officers, is also a Knight of the Order of St. John, which Queen Elizabeth II heads. The queen likewise knighted Sir Y.K. Pao, who also sits on the board of Chase Manhattan. Pao is a major figure in the Illuminati Asian drug smuggling.[2]

Another key figure for the British crown is Louis Mortimer Bloomfield, a third Knight of St. John. Bloomfield has been the crown's top secret intelligence man in North America, operating out of Jamaica. He was an intermediary between Winston Churchill and FDR, and was instrumental in merging American and British intelligence operations during World War II. *They have never been unmerged.* Bloomfield was part of the American OSS. As such, he set up a long list of corporations which were used as fronts to invest in Permindex, a "trade organization" hiding one of the Illuminati's most powerful assassination groups. Bloomfield has been instrumental in helping draft UN regulations against hijacking and terrorism. (The fox guards the chickens.)

Eagle Star Insurance Company has been one of the Illuminati's top Canadian financial institutions. N.M. Rothschilds & Sons, Barclay's Bank, Hill Samuel, and Lloyds are all involved with it. MI-6's two top men, Sir Kenneth Keith and Sir Kenneth Strong, were Eagle Star directors. Behind the guise of Great Britain's and Canada's Official Secrets Act, MI-6 has run drugs worldwide for

---

1. Edith Star Miller, *Occult Theocracy,* Appendix IV, pp. 8-35.
2. Sir Y.K. Pao's drug overlord role has been discussed in publications from *Executive Intelligence Review*. See, for example, *Dope, Inc.* (Washington, D.C.: EIR, 1992), pp. 215-218.

the Illuminati.

British MI-6 has been a major vehicle for the Satanic hierarchy working behind the secret veil of Freemasonry to control world events.[1] It is the most secret large intelligence organization in the world.[2]

Finally, it should be noted in this overview, which shows how England is the center for the Illuminati, that the AntiChrist is claimed to have his present-day throne in a London suburb. A number of independent ex-Illuminati sources have described the event of coming before his presence, which is, they say, over-whelming; the immediate reaction of all those coming into his presence is, apparently, to want to worship him. Further, accord-ing to these same sources, he has been on his throne secretly for perhaps a decade and will, someday late in the 1990's, be shown to the world, and enthroned publicly, if Illuminati plans work out, around the year 2000.

In a nutshell, this article has tried to give an overview of how deeply enmeshed the British royal family is within the Illuminati, as well as of the extent of the monarchy's activities at the highest levels of the occult hierarchy. The British royal family is extremely wealthy and extremely powerful, much more so than people imagine. The queen, for a typical example, appoints Canada's Governor-General. Also, there is no question that Prince Charles plays an important role in the World System from behind the scenes.[3]

Further occult ties. Garter knights are now permitted to compass their shields with the Garter, outside of which they may also place the Collar and its pendant.[4] Like the arms of other British royalty since 1837, the deep-blue Garter encircles the royal shield in Prince Charles' arms.[5] There is more to this satanic arrangement than we have so far discussed. As noted earlier, a roundel of the Merovingian cross is hidden on the royal shield with its encircling Garter. What we have not until now pointed out, however, is that the two ends of the Garter are joined and folded in such a way as to give the impression that one end is swallowing the other, like a "serpent swallowing its own tail." As shown below, this is intentional, and has

1. Confidential interviews conducted by Fritz Springmeier.
2. David Wise and Thomas B. Ross, *The Espionage Establishment,* p. 79. British MI-6 is properly known as the British Secret Service, and should not be confused with the U.S. agency by the same name; the U.S. agency performs a different function entirely.
3. Written correspondence, quoted by permission, from Springmeier.
4. Boutell, 1978 ed., p. 193.
5. Boutell, 1978 ed., p. 217.

158

Templar and Rosicrucian origins. Likewise, the Collar's original twenty-six roundels of St. George's cross and its current Tudor roses, each surrounded by the Garter as above, as well as the Garter Star itself, were derived from the earlier symbolism of the Temple Knights and the Rosicrucians: "the god of the Rosicrucians is symbolized by the 'zero': a circle created by the serpent swallowing its own tail. This symbol was superimposed on the [Merovingian, anti-]Christian cross with a sunburst surrounding the circle. The circle also represented the sun, as well as the 'eye' of Osiris, the Egyptian sun-god."[1] The eight-pointed chipped-silver and enamel Garter Star, besides representing the "sunburst surrounding the circle," is similar in design to the "Knights Templar star jewels" of English Freemasonry, which, in place of the central red cross surrounded by the Garter, bear a central cross intertwined with a serpent in front of a brilliant light, a skull and crossbones, a casket, and a dagger lying in what appears to be a pool of blood, all circumferenced by a motto bearing the Latin *Memento Mori,* meaning "death warning."[2] The point, of course, is that all this is directly or indirectly associated with the Garter on Prince Charles' achievement.

We may also note that similar imagery—what appears to be a serpent intertwining a pole intersected by the perpendicular side of a triangle (cf. the central cross intertwined with a serpent) in front of a half-darkened sun representing the Zoroastrian concept of the conflict between good and evil (cf. a brilliant light), and a large, seemingly casket-shaped, black natural magnet (cf. a skull and crossbones, a casket, and a dagger), perhaps intended to act as an hallucinogenic catalyst like a drug—comprises the occult Meditation Room at the United Nations, where "followers of all religions, who visit by the hundreds of thousands each year, may [currently] awaken the 'god within.'"[3] This room, which is designed to look like a pyramid lying on its side with the above three-dimensional

---

1. John Daniel, *Scarlet and the Beast,* Vol. I, 2nd ed. (Texas: Jon Kregel, Inc., 1995), p. 30.
2. For a picture, see Michael Baigent and Richard Leigh, *The Temple and the Lodge* (New York: Arcade Publishing, Inc., 1989), above caption 32, between pp. 194-195.
3. Hunt, *GLOBAL PEACE AND THE RISE OF ANTICHRIST,* p. 275. For a picture of this room, see Church, p. 47, or John Daniel, *Scarlet and the Beast,* Vol. I, 2nd ed., p. 749.

imagery in place of the capstone (i.e., at the front of the room), has just enough seats to accommodate eleven individuals—the AntiChrist and ten kings.[1] Recall that the red lion and ten other lions—*Tarshish* and all its young lions—are represented *within the Garter* on the prince's achievement.[2] Lucis Trust (for "Lucifer Trust") published this advertisement, originally giving the organization's return address as "866 United Nations Plaza," in *Reader's Digest* in October 1982 and again in December 1991: "From the point of Light within the Mind of God, Let light stream forth into the minds of men. Let Light descend on Earth. From the point of Love within the Heart of God, Let love stream forth into the hearts of men. May Christ return to Earth. From the centre where the Will of God is known, Let purpose guide the little wills of men—The purpose which the Masters know and serve. From the centre which we call the race of men, Let the Plan of Love and Light work out, And may it seal the door where evil dwells. Let Light and Love and Power restore the Plan on Earth." According to Lucis Trust, "The Great Invocation belongs to all humanity," and "millions...daily use this prayer to invoke

1. Describing the United Nations' Meditation Room and one related to it in Washington, Church observes, "It...represents a pyramid turned over on its side. The room is very dimly lit. The only source of light comes from a special lens recessed in the ceiling which focuses a beam of light on the altar in the center of the room. The altar is four feet high; it is a dark gray block of crystalline iron ore....the largest of its kind ever mined....described as a lodestone or magnetite. It is strongly magnetic and possesses polarity. On April 24, 1957, the late Dag Hammarskjold, UN Secretary General, described this pagan stone as an altar to universal religion. He said, 'The altar is the symbol of the god of all.' The picture or mural at the front of the room...was painted to open up the wall, to give a feeling of space, of the void—in effect, to extend the room farther out to another dimension. The theme of the mural is infinity.... The circle near the center of the painting represents the All-Seeing Eye. There is a vertical line down the center of the mural with waving lines around it. It is said to represent the tree of life. It may also represent the serpent in the tree. [According to Spenser, 'the]....Meditation Room is constructed in the shape of a wedge....[a] pyramid with the apex cut off.' Another prayer room dedicated to the All-Seeing Eye can be found in the United States Capitol building in Washington, D.C..... The lighting in this Meditation Room is subdued. The concealed light focuses on a white oak altar, similar to the light in the U.N. Meditation Room. There are ten chairs facing the altar, just as there are ten chairs in the United Nations Meditation Room. Ten?... Above the altar in the stained glass window the unfinished pyramid with its capstone containing the All-Seeing Eye is prominently displayed. The New Age Movement, with its roots in the ancient Order of the Knights Templar, has been 'working to set up a universal theocratic state. Already the high priests, the prayers, and the temples of this universal cult are with us'" (pp. 151-153). Church mentions a third meditation room at the Pentagon, which again contains the Luciferic "all-seeing eye" (p. 166).
2. For more information, see this chapter's earlier section titled, "The royal shield and the arms of the Principality of Wales."

peace on earth....for only through humanity can the Plan work out." This blasphemous advertisement, which has non-American English spelling, prominently displays a rose inside a circle.[1] We may note that in 1988, along with a few other men wearing red roses, Prince Charles visited the *Pyramide du Louvre* in Paris, France.[2]

"Organizational" ties to witchcraft. In witchcraft, a coven consists of 13 persons, including a high priest or priestess. Early members—knights, officers, etc.—of the Order of the Garter, which included several of the first heralds of England's *College of Heraldry,* engaged in various covert activities throughout France. Originally established by Edward III for use by the order, and later made an official part of the Royal Household by Richard III's charter in 1484,[3] the College of Heraldry is organized into a *coven* of 13 heralds, including pursuivants (assistant-heralds who aspire to the office of Herald), and is the oldest and most powerful heraldic body in the world.[4] The college's senior heralds (Garter, Clarenceux, and Norroy *and* Ulster) are each styled "King of Heralds" or "King of Arms," with the

1. For pictures of this advertisement, see John Daniel, *Scarlet and the Beast,* Vol. I, 2nd ed., pp. 742-743. An earlier satanic invocation, given by a "spirit guide" to Alice Bailey (the founder of Lucis Trust) in 1940, reads, "Come forth, O Mighty One, The hour of service of the Saving Force has now arrived. Let it be spread abroad, O Mighty One. Let Light and Love and Power and Death Fulfill the purpose of the Coming One" (Brian E. Weiss, "World Goodwill Update," *Hope for the World Update,* Fall 1995, p. 5).
2. *Charles & Diana: A Royal Family Album,* p. 55.
3. Boutell, 1978 ed., p. 262. James and Russell, *At Home with the Royal Family,* p. 144.
4. More specifically, officers of the College of Arms or Heralds' College consist of "three [Herald] Kings of Arms—Garter, Clarenceux, and Norroy *and* Ulster; six Heralds—Lancaster, Somerset, Chester, Richmond, Windsor and York; and four [Herald] Pursuivants—Rouge Dragon, Rouge Croix, Portcullis and Bluemantle," for a total of thirteen heralds. Indicating the importance of the Heralds' College to the Order of the Garter, Rouge Dragon Pursuivant is named for the red dragon of Wales, Rouge Croix Pursuivant is named after the red cross of "St. George," and Bluemantle Pursuivant is named after the dark blue Garter Mantle. "From time to time officers of arms who are not members of the corporation of the College of Arms are appointed by warrant under the [King's or] Queen's sign manual. The duties of these officers, styled 'extras ordinary' [(i.e., extraordinary)], are purely ceremonial.... Frequently such officers are appointed at the time of a coronation and in many cases people so appointed become offer-in ordinary when vacancies occur." Extraordinary *offices* are currently those of Norfolk Herald, Arundel Herald, and Fitzalan Pursuivant. In 1963, for the first time since the end of the fourteenth century, an appointment was also made to the extraordinary office of Wales Herald (Boutell, 1978 ed., p. 263). Extraordinary heralds and pursuivants are not part of the Heralds' College. The thirteen heralds and pursuivants of the College of Arms precede the English monarch in various ceremonies, including the State Opening of Parliament (James and Russell, *At Home with the Royal Family,* pp. 141, 145-146, 197).

most powerful among them being called the "Principal King of Arms." A version of the Garter Badge of St. George's Cross, with a blue (azure) dove placed in each of its four quarters, serves as the arms of the Herald's College.[1] The college's reach extends throughout the British Commonwealth and beyond, to include even the United States.[2] The highest ranking herald in the college, and therefore the world, is the *Garter, Principal King of Arms.* His office as Herald dates to 1415.[3] It was this herald—Anthony Wagner at the time—who created Prince Charles' coat of arms, though the design was clearly not one of his own imagination.[4] Today, as it has been ever since the decline of feudalism, "heralds are found only in the Royal service;" for "more than 500 years ago the Crown assumed the full control of armorial bearings, and has ever since exercised it through Officers of Arms appointed for the purpose."[5]

The high priestess of a coven wears a garter to which

1. Boutell, 1978 ed., pp. 231-233, 260-261.
2. Boutell, 1978 ed., p. 268.
3. Although he is "associated particularly with the Order of the Garter," the Principal King of Arms is "empowered also to exercise a general supervision over the other Herald Kings" (Boutell, 1978 ed., p. 262). James and Russell, *At Home with the Royal Family,* pp. 144, 196.
4. Genealogy plays a major role in the determination and creation of an individual's heraldic achievement. For this reason, the early heralds "inevitably...had to concern themselves with genealogy in connection with cadency and the marshalling of arms" (Boutell, 1978 ed., pp. 261-262; see also pp. 269-270). (The genealogical research of the College of Heraldry is perhaps rivaled only by that of the more recent Mormon cult.) "Since at least 1418, it has been impossible to acquire a legal title to armorial bearings by any other method than inheritance according to the laws of arms, or a grant or confirmation of arms from the duly constituted authorities.... Conjectural descent is inadmissible. A person who bears a device of heraldic appearance invented by himself or an ancestor, and neither granted nor confirmed by the King of Arms, is in fact not armigerous, and the device is not a legal coat of arms." From the fifteenth century to 1686, the laws of arms were periodically enforced by the heralds, through the removal and/or defacement of unlawful arms and other heraldic devices, under the authority of various royal commissions (Boutell, 1978 ed., pp. 262-263, 264). James and Russell make similar points (*At Home with the Royal Family,* p. 146). Nevertheless, the heralds have historically dealt with armorial disputes through the "Court of Chivalry," over which the Constable and Earl Marshal, the Duke of Norfolk, preside. Although the Marshal, "styled Earl Marshal since 1386," ultimately became recognized, since his office is hereditary, as the Officer of State to whom all the heralds were responsible, Scotland's Lyon King of Arms was granted independence from both the Constable and Marshal early on, and, being separate from the College of Arms, receives his office directly from the sovereign. The Lyon King of Arms possesses his own judicial powers and status through the "Court of the Lord Lyon." Today, disputes regarding armorial matters continue to be addressed in the Court of Chivalry and, for Scotland, in the Court of the Lyon King of Arms (Boutell, 1978 ed., pp. 261, 263; see also pp. 231-232). For more information related to the ancient and modern laws of arms, see, for example, Boutell, pp. 261-265.
5. Boutell, 1978 ed., pp. 261, 264.

at least one horseshoe-shaped buckle is attached—one for each coven over which she presides. When two or more covens have "hived off" from a high priestess' coven, she attains the title of "Witch Queen." The Garter of the Order of the Garter is edged with two rows of 169 miniature gold buckles of the type described above, each representing a coven of 13 witches for a total of 169 x 13, or 2,197, witches.[1] That is, it depicts two covens of covens of a coven (2 x 13 covens x 13 covens x 13 witches = 4,394 witches)—one coven of covens of a coven (1 x 13 x 13 x 13 = 2,197) for the sovereign and another for the Prince of Wales. The order's primary membership consists of twenty-six "companion knights," or the sovereign plus twelve knights (13) and the Prince of Wales plus twelve knights (13). Each Garter knight, therefore, is represented as the priest or priestess of a coven of covens (26 x 13 x 13 = 4,394), making each a Witch King or a Witch Queen. The British sovereign, then, is depicted as a Witch King or Witch Queen of Witch Kings and Witch Queens, as is the Prince of Wales. A *witch*—Joan of Kent, the Countess of Salisbury, who later became the Princess of Wales—played a prominent role in Edward III's selection of the Garter as a central symbol of the order.

Interestingly, Prince Charles is the thirteenth Prince of Wales to be formally invested. The prince, despite being over Freemasonry worldwide, was once rumored to have been "secretly initiated into a north London Lodge that practised Black Magic."[2] Moreover, he married *Diana,*

---

1. For a color picture of the deep-blue Garter, as well as the Collar, Star, and Lesser George, see Begent, *The Most Noble Order of the Garter, Its History and Ceremonial,* cover and p. 3.

2. Knight, *The Brotherhood,* p. 5. Knight's information is to be taken with a grain of salt. For example, he wrote that Prince Charles, due to being "a committed (as opposed to nominal) Christian," like his grandmother, refused to "be initiated and take over from the Duke of Kent" on his twenty-first birthday. However, Prince Charles has never been a Christian, let alone a committed one. Nor has his grandmother, the "Queen Mother." Knight, recognizing at least some of the limitations of his own information, admitted, "there was talk that Charles 'was not strictly against Freemasonry', but that he simply had no wish to become involved.... I failed miserably to ascertain more clearly Charles's current thinking on the subject.... Even Sir George Young, former Vice Chief of MI6, told me that the extent of his knowledge about Freemasonry was that 'the Royal Family are all in it'" (ibid., pp. 212-214, 290). Actually, the prince's beliefs perfectly accord with those of masonry (see Chapter 10's section titled, "A so-called 'Christian' heritage). Moreover, whether or not he is a mason is irrelevant. Prince Charles has no great need to fraternize with the masonic rank and file, especially when one considers the fact that he is already over Freemasonry worldwide by virtue of his position within the Order of the Garter.

whose namesake is the patron "goddess" of witchcraft (representing chastity, fertility, the moon, and hunting among other things), "whom all Asia and the world worship" (Acts 19:27; cf. 19:23-36), *on the one day that witches are "sealed" each year*—July 29![1] Indeed, since her death, Diana has literally been "deified" on the Internet, where Wiccan and other pagan prayers (e.g., Buddhist, "Christian," Hindu, Islamic, Jewish, New Age, and Sikh) have been posted not just on her behalf, but *to her!*[2] As if this were not revolting enough, idols of Diana have even begun to join those of Mary in Nativity scenes, and a cult of Diana worship is taking shape to rival that of Roman Catholicism's Mary worship: "But a new figure has joined those in the crib; a large statue of Princess Diana. Italy is not alone in these first stirrings of Diana worship.... At first glance, <u>Diana prophecies</u> appear to be Christian. They promise a spiritual millennium, the working of the Lord's spirit through the world and an overcoming of sorrow—all familiar themes.... Christian fundamentalists may only see Diana as a minor saint, if that, but she may appeal much more strongly as a goddess to the pagan unbelievers who make up the majority of Western society.... Mohammed.... Buddha.... Christianity.... Now,...our society is threatened by science, machines and rationalism. The cult of Diana offers compassion, a war on machines and beauty linked with femininity. Will Diana be our next goddess? We can only guess. But a feminine goddess seems a safe prediction. It may not be Diana; she may be only a John the Baptist coming to announce a new earth. It might be Gaia, the new goddess of the earth worshipped by ecologists, but it will be female.... It may then be a thousand years before we begin to think for ourselves again."[3]

Garter development in history. In 1337, King Edward III commenced a protracted war with France, claiming the right to the French throne through his French mother Isabella, and in 1340, he assumed the title, "King of France."

1. Where the media and the public are concerned, Diana certainly personified such a role.
2. See the page titled "Into the Light" at "http://www.royalnetwork.com/hearts/light.html".
3. Myles Harris, "I predict Diana will be a goddess," *International Express*, U.S. Ed., 16 Dec. 1997, p. 8.

His son, Edward the Black Prince, whose title ostensibly derived from his black heraldic surcoat, later carried the war on in his stead. Concerning this war and the Order of the Garter, Scott-Guiles comments,

> Of the origin of the Most Noble Order we know little. According to its historian, Ashmole, it commemorated an occasion when King Edward [III] had "given forth his own garter as the signal for a battle"....
> So the order may have been intended as a revival of the mythical Round Table.... Even so the symbolism of the Garter itself remains obscure.... Ashmole regarded the Garter as an emblem of "unity in society."
> ....The motto of the Order is a denunciation of those who think ill of some specific project, and not a mere pious invocation of evil upon evil-thinkers in general. "Shame be to him who thinks ill *of it*" was probably directed against anyone who should oppose the King's design on the French crown.... All things considered, it seems highly likely that the Order originally represented the assembly of chivalry to aid King Edward of England to become King Edward of France.[1]

Scott-Guiles' understanding is only partially correct. The Order of the Garter was founded not only as a continuation of the legend of King Arthur's Round Table, with all the mysticism and occultism that entails, but also as the overseer of the inner circles of the Priory of Zion, the Knights Templar, and the Rosicrucians, with the Temple Knights having just been thrust out of France and Europe.[2] Very loosely speaking, where French Freemasonry tends to be atheistic, and was a precursor to Socialism and Communism,[3] English Freemasonry is more spiritualistic, and was a precursor to Capitalism and Fascism.[4] The Order of the Garter, already having had the secret

1. Scott-Guiles, pp. 93-96. Contrary to the Garter motto, the apostle Paul admonished the saints, saying, "See that none render evil for evil unto any *man*" (1 Th 5:15).
2. For more information, see Chapter 4, "Prince of this World—a *Diverse* Lineage."
3. Bruce Lockhart, in *Memoirs of a British Agent*, however, shows that the Bolshevik Revolution was controlled from London (Coleman, *The Committee of 300*, p. 357).
4. According to John Daniel, English Freemasonry currently dominates "Great Britain, Canada, Northeast USA (Eastern Establishment), most oriental countries, Hong Kong, Australia, and South Africa," whereas French Freemasonry dominates "[the] Continent of Europe, southern and Western U.S.A., former U.S.S.R., Pacific Islands, Philippines, Latin and South America, [and] Africa (has recently taken over South Africa) [sic]" (*Scarlet and the Beast*, Vol. I, 2nd ed., pp. 56-57).

advantage of the Priory of Zion, the Templars, and the Rosicrucians, wanted clear control not just of English, but also of French Freemasonry. By the order's reasoning, this would enable it to play the two sides of masonic dominion against one another, as often as necessary, to consolidate its own power structures, such as the more recent Committee of 300, *at the top*—in its own hidden, amoral thrust for world domination *at nearly any price*.[1] Moreover, it would enable the order to experiment with different systems of government on a vast scale, all the while improving the implements of war, in a secondary effort to discover those elements most useful to the final construction of a New World Order, which, it has now been determined, is to constitute a global slave state after the *Platonic ideal*.[2]

It was in this vein that the modern Illuminati began—when Adam Weishaupt, under the apparent indirect influence of the Order of the Garter, infiltrated the masonic lodges of France starting on May 1, 1776.[3] According to Coleman, "the French Revolution was organized and run out of England by Jeremy Bentham and William Petty, the Earl of Shelburne," by means of "the secret Quator Coronati Lodge in London, and the Nine Sister Lodge in Paris."[4] Christians have heard that the Illuminati had certain outward goals, among which were the abolition of oligarchies and governments, the destruction of the major religions, and the elimination of the family unit, patriotism, and private ownership, along with a parallel

1. As mentioned earlier in this section, the world can thank the British monarchy—with its Order of the Garter and Committee of 300—for fomenting World Wars I and II, much of the Arab-Israeli conflict, and more, in this century alone.
2. For more information, see Chapter 11's section titled, "The United World Colleges."
3. The creation of the Illuminati was as much the British Crown's answer to the Declaration of Independence of the United States as it was an attempt to continue the quest for control of France. In fact, through the sublime and covert tools of Freemasonry, the Illuminati, and the Committee of 300, as well as several other secret agencies, the Order of the Garter has gained significant control of far more, including not just France and the United States, where it still "calls the shots," but also the entire British Commonwealth. Moreover, in key respects—such as environmentally and financially—the Order of the Garter controls the machinery of the United Nations, a Committee of 300 creation and stepchild. Should the British monarchy succeed in becoming the monarchy of the European Union, it will undoubtedly seek world hegemony through direct "democratic" control of the United Nations' Security Council. For more information, see Chapter 2, "A Man for Our Times."
4. Coleman, *The Committee of 300*, p. xii.

introduction of communal education for children.[1]   What has perhaps not been realized, however, is that the real agenda of the Illuminati appears not to have been to introduce total societal chaos, as is so commonly believed; rather, it was to eliminate and subdue *all* the British monarchy's potential competition and opposition, while simultaneously aiding its rise to global dominance!

The British monarchy clearly *is* on top.   In fact, the pyramidal seal of the Illuminati had a combined Templar and Garter *precursor,* dating to no later than the early fourteenth century.   In this precursor, the capstone containing a roundel of the "all-seeing eye" of Lucifer was instead shown as a roundel of "St. George's cross"—or, according to the Rosicrucian view, the "eye" of the Egyptian sun-god Osiris, as well as a serpent swallowing its own tail superimposed on the Merovingian cross—with the whole placed over a shield having a serpentine banner (right).[2]   This symbol may be seen today just  above the piscina in the south chapel of the Templar church at Garway, Herefordshire (near the Welsh border)—where, in a foreshadowing of Scottish Rite Freemasonry,[3] it unites a fish for Christianity and a serpent for Satanism beneath its banner.[4]

In 1801, not long after 1776, by an interesting

1. Arno Clemens Gaebelein, *The Conflict of the Ages* (Windward Islands, British West Indies: Pryor N. Russell, 1968), p. 72.
2. The triangular capstone on the seal of the Illuminati also bears a resemblance to the counter-seal of Mary de St. Paul, who, as the granddaughter of Beatrice (Edward I's sister) and John de Dreux (the Duke of Brittany), founded Pembroke College in 1373.   Besides displaying a triangle containing a roundel (like the capstone), this seal has three adjacent roundels which contain the arms of England, France, and De Dreux (Boutell, 1978 ed., pp. 132-133).   The Seal of the Illuminati, which forms the counter-seal of the Great Seal of the United States (as shown on the dollar bill), conforms *precisely* to the design of early *British* seals (Boutell, 1978 ed., pp. 273-274).
3. For more information, see Chapter 4, "Prince of this World—a *Diverse* Lineage," and Chapter 10's section titled, "A so-called 'Christian' heritage."
4. For a picture of this scene, see Baigent, Leigh, and Lincoln, *Holy Blood, Holy Grail,* just below caption 32, between pp. 240-241.   Although these authors seem to have no clue as to the heraldic derivation or meaning of the image, they were helpful enough to show it.   For other information, see Baigent and Leigh, *The Temple and the Lodge,* captions 8-10, between pp. 66-67.

"coincidence," the arms of France were omitted from Britain's royal shield, the convenient occasion being the union with Ireland, though they remain on the badge of the "Garter, Principal King of Arms." In this capacity, the motto of the Garter alludes, historically, to an attempted takeover of France — something that perhaps bears an interesting message for us today. France, like the United Kingdom, is an integral part of the modern European Union. Could it be, therefore, that in the appearance of the Garter on Prince Charles' coat of arms, there is an allusion to the eventual takeover of the E.U. by the AntiChrist, whose intent will appear to be to promote "unity in society"? Should Prince Charles one day gain authority over the E.U., he will have achieved that which Edward III and the Black Prince presumably sought. Today, it appears that the Order of the Garter essentially controls the Illuminati not just in the West, but also in the East through the Committee of 300 and other means.

Garter mimicry of God's heavenly order. Of course, there is more to be said about the Order of the Garter, particularly regarding the composition of its membership, which, as mentioned above, primarily consists of twenty-six "companion knights." These twenty-six knights first-of-all include the sovereign and his (or her) eldest son, the Prince of Wales. Further, when the sovereign or, as has occasionally occurred, the sovereign's eldest son, invests a new knight, two supporting knights are present. Stephen Slater remarks,

> When a new knight is invested, the sovereign presides over the Chapter of the Order in the Throne Room at Windsor Castle.... Knights Elect are presented to the sovereign by Black Rod, Garter King of Arms and two supporting knights. The sovereign personally secures the Garter, places the Riband and Lesser George over the left shoulder, affixes the Star and invests the knight with the Mantle and Collar. At the same time the Admonition is read. This takes the same form as in the time of the Tudors, and possibly earlier. The Admonition upon Putting on the Mantle, for example, is:
>
> > Receive this Robe of heavenly colour, the Livery of this Most

Excellent Order in Augmentation of thine Honour, ennobled with the shield and red Cross of our Lord, by whose power thou mayest safely pierce troops of thine enemies, and be over them ever victorious, and being in this temporal warfare glorious, in egregious and heroic actions, thou mayest obtain eternal and triumphant joy.[1]

Like the true origins of the Order of the Garter, the organization of its membership is thought to be somewhat mysterious. Yet it seems plausible that, among other things, it actually represents a satanic mimicry of God's heavenly organization. We read in the Apocalypse that John saw twenty-four elders in heaven before the throne of The Father and His Son. Similarly, there are twenty-four companion knights in the Garter, in addition to the sovereign and his (or her) eldest son. Also, just as God has appointed two witnesses to prophesy and torment the nations during the Great Tribulation, and then to stand to the left and the right of Jesus in His Kingdom, so also are two supporting knights present at the investiture of a new knight. If these things are so, then they are a sad commentary on what in reality is a satanic (Luciferic), non-Christian order. Considering the order's motto, one cannot help but wonder what "power" President Woodrow Wilson of the United States once had in mind when he remarked, "There is a power, so organized, so subtle, so watchful, so interlocked, so complete, so pervasive that prudent men better not speak above their breath when they speak in condemnation of it."[2]

Related orders and royal guards. Although this section represents a pause in our discussion of Prince Charles' heraldic achievement or coat of arms, its placement is appropriate. Besides the insignia of the Order of the Garter, as well as those of the Order of the Thistle (Scotland's counterpart to the Garter), Prince Charles also wears the insignia of the Order of St. Patrick (Ireland's counterpart to the Garter),[3] and those of the Order of the Bath,

1. Stephen Slater, "Garter, The Most Noble Order of the," *A Dictionary of Heraldry*, ed. Friar, p. 161.
2. Steven Wright, "Environmental Warfare" video (P.O. Box 8426; Clearwater, FL 34618).
3. For a sketch of the Order of St. Patrick's Star, see James and Russell, *At Home with the Royal*

including the badge of its Military Division (see below).[1] The Order of the Thistle, officially founded in 1687 by Scotland's King James VII (or England's King James II), but going back at least a century earlier to James V, consists of just sixteen knights and bears the motto *Nemo Me Impune Lacessit,* meaning "No one Provokes Me with Impunity." The Scottish "Green Rod" serves as the Thistle's counterpart to the Garter's Black Rod. Possibly going back to the ninth century, the Order of the Thistle's roots may actually pre-date the Order of the Garter.[2]

Although Queen Elizabeth II is "Sovereign of the British Orders of Knighthood and Sovereign Head of the Order of St John,"[3] Prince Charles, as the "principal knight" (see below), may be the highest-ranking knight of the Order of the Bath. Based upon the order's heraldic symbolism, it appears either to exist to safeguard the other three British orders—the Order of the Garter, the Order of the Thistle, and the Order of St. Patrick—or to be a super-order of them. If the Order of the Bath is a super-order, and it may not be, the Prince of Wales might, in the final analysis, prove to be the highest-ranking knight of the most elite orders in the world. This may or may not be significant. For purposes of public consumption, all these orders hold their official annual meetings in church chapels.[4]

Like the Order of the Garter, the Order of the Bath has a star, a collar with a pendant, and a robe. An eight-pointed Templar cross not only serves as the enameled white and gold pendant of the Bath Collar, but is also

Family, p. 126. For a color photograph of Prince Charles wearing the St. Patrick Star, see *Her Majesty The Queen,* p. 15.

1. For a color representation of this badge, see Boutell, plate XVIII, between pp. 192-195. For more information on these orders, see Chapter 10's section titled, "A so-called 'Christian' heritage."

2. James and Russell, *At Home with the Royal Family,* pp. 52, 126, 158-159. To apply for tickets to attend the procession of the Order of the Thistle (for research purposes), write to: The Dean of St Giles, St Giles's Cathedral, Edinburgh Scotland (ibid., p. 241). For a color picture of Prince Charles' Thistle Star, see Burnet, *In Private—In Public,* THE PRINCE AND PRINCESS OF WALES, p. 124. For a brief description of the Order of the Thistle, as well as a black-and-white representation of its insignia, see Boutell, 1978 ed., pp. 194-195. Prince Philip also is a Thistle knight and "GBE 1953 (Grand Master of the Order)" (Judd, *Prince Philip,* p. 248).

3. For a list of Queen Elizabeth II's official "titles and distinctions," see James and Russell, *At Home with the Royal Family,* pp. 214-215.

4. See Chapter 10's section titled, "A so-called 'Christian' heritage."

imposed in gold over a silver sunburst to comprise the Bath Star. As the "Great Master"—a blasphemous title similar to "grand master" (cf. Matt 23:10, AKJV)—and Principal Knight Grand Cross of the Order of the Bath, Prince Charles wears the order's insignia over a crimson robe.[1] Attached to a crimson ribbon, the badge of the Bath's Military Division depicts the gold lions of England along with a "conjoined rose, thistle, shamrock, and sceptre," and has a central circlet bearing the motto, *Tria Juncta in Uno* (i.e., "three joined in one"), below which is the Prince of Wales' motto *Ich Dien* (discussed later).[2] This particular combination of the Tudor rose for England, the thistle for Scotland, and the shamrock for Ireland, all sharing a common stem (cf. the scepter above), bears a semblance to the Rosicrucian symbol of the conjoined rose and cross, and is also used as the badge of the United Kingdom.[3] The conjoined rose and cross, interestingly enough, constituted the original cover design of *The New Age Magazine,* now renamed as the *Scottish Rite Journal.*[4]

The Order of the Garter's motto, *Honi Soit Qui Mal y Pense,* is shared by the Life Guards, Blues and Royals (so-named from the Ist Royal Dragoon Guards), Grenadier Guards, and Coldstream Guards. Moreover, the Garter Star serves as the emblem of the Coldstream Guards, who also wear the Tudor Rose on a shoulder as a part of their uniform. The Order of the Thistle's motto, *Nemo Me Impune Lacessit,* is shared by the Scots Guards. Likewise, the Thistle Star serves as the emblem of the Scots Guards. Similarly, the Order of St. Patrick's motto, *Quis Separabit,* meaning "who shall separate," is shared by the Irish Guards, and the St. Patrick Star serves as their emblem. Interestingly, the French Imperial Eagle, surrounded by the Garter, serves as the emblem of the Blues and Royals, and the gold eagle itself remains a part of the Crown Jewels

1. For color photographs of Prince Charles wearing his Bath insignia, see Burnet, *In Private—In Public,* THE PRINCE AND PRINCESS OF WALES, p. 125; and *Charles & Diana: A Royal Family Album,* p. 44.
2. For an outline of the Order of the Bath and its insignia, see Boutell, 1978 ed., p. 196.
3. Boutell, 1978 ed., p. 218. For color representations of the badges of England, Scotland, Ireland, Wales, and the United Kingdom, see Boutell, plate XII, between pages 164-167.
4. For pictures of the original and current cover designs of what is now called the *Scottish Rite Journal,* see John Daniel, *Scarlet and the Beast,* Vol. I, 2nd ed., pp. 746-747.

Collection used in the British monarchy's coronation ceremony.[1] As armored regiments, the Life Guards and the Blues and Royals comprise the Royal Household Cavalry. Similarly, the Grenadier Guards, Coldstream Guards, Scots Guards, Irish Guards, and Welsh Guards comprise the Royal Foot Guards, who perform sentry duty outside Buckingham Palace. Together, the Royal Household Cavalry and the Royal Foot Guards comprise the Royal Household Division.[2] Like the order's themselves, all these regiments are subject to the Prince of Wales.

The base of the coat of arms. At the base of Prince Charles' coat of arms, there is a fourth copy of the heir-apparent's crown, below which is the shield from the arms of the Duke (and Duchy) of Cornwall. This shield is centered upon the Black Prince's *Ich Dien* motto. Above the *Ich,* in the left-hand (dexter) compartment of the base, we find the heir-apparent's badge (which bears the *Ich Dien* motto). Finally, above the *Dien,* in the right-hand (sinister) compartment of the base, there is the red dragon of Wales. As shall become clear, the overall message conveyed at the base is *"Ich,* the Black Prince, *dien* the red dragon," or "I, the Black Prince, serve Satan." After addressing these devices in the given order, we will deal with the two supporters of the royal shield (i.e., the dexter beast and the sinister unicorn).

The arms of the Duke and Duchy of Cornwall. The arms of the Duke and Duchy of Cornwall also belong to Prince Charles, who, besides being the Prince of Wales, is the Duke of Cornwall (see the duke's arms at right). According to Campbell-Kease, the rank of duke is the most senior rank in Britain's peerage. Further, he states, "The word 'duke' is derived from the Latin *dux,* meaning 'leader'. The

---

1. For a color photograph of a set of miniature replicas of the "crown jewels," see *Majesty* magazine, June 1993, Vol. 14, No. 6, p. 2.
2. James and Russell, *At Home with the Royal Family,* pp. 123-127.

rank was introduced in England in 1337, when Edward the Black Prince was made Duke of Cornwall.... The duke (in common with other peers) has certain armorial privileges: he employs a silver helm with gold bars facing the dexter,[1] his coronet of rank ensigns his arms, and he normally has supporters."[2]

Two ostrich feathers adorn the arms of the Duchy of Cornwall, one to the left of the shield and the other to its right. This basic design, to which two Cornish chough[3] supporters were added in June 1968 by a royal warrant, comes from two of the seals of the Black Prince, who set his quartered shield of arms between two ostrich feathers.[4] The shield itself is "surmounted by the coronet of the Heir Apparent" and "shows [fifteen] besants, gold coins brought back by the Crusaders" (whose loyalties were all too often toward the Roman Catholic Church and its heretical clergy, rather than to God).[5] The *Houmout* motto at the base of the arms may mean "magnanimous" (see the later discussion on the Black Prince), "high minded," or "high spirited."[6]

The base of Prince Charles' coat of arms as the Prince of Wales incorporates his arms as the Duke of Cornwall. The flags—burgee and ensign—of the Royal Fowey Yacht Club, as well as the arms of the Cornwall County Council,[7] similarly contain the shield from these arms.

---

1. In the case of Prince Charles, because he is the heir-apparent to the throne, his coat of arms employs the gold sovereign helm.
2. Campbell-Kease, "Duke," *A Dictionary of Heraldry,* ed. Friar, p. 130.
3. The Cornish chough is a black "crow" with red legs and a red bill.
4. Boutell, 1978 ed., pp. 165-166, 219.
5. Burnet, *In Private—In Public, THE PRINCE AND PRINCESS OF WALES,* p. 118.
6. Boutell, 1978 ed., p. 219. For a black-and-white representation of the same duchy arms, see Boutell, 1970 ed. or later, p. 219.
7. Scott-Guiles, p. 71.

The motto and the heir-apparent's badge. The lower left-hand compartment of Prince Charles' coat of arms contains his badge as the heir-apparent to the British throne.[1] Derived from, and possibly first used by, the Black Prince,[2] the badge not only forms the seal on the gold signet ring that Prince Charles wears on the leftmost finger of his left hand, but it is also found imprinted on many British coins. The three elements of the badge are: **1)** three ostrich feathers, **2)** Prince Charles' crown as the heir-apparent (surrounding the feathers), and **3)** the *Ich Dien* motto (taken from the defeated King of Bohemia after the Battle of Crécy).[3]

Like its motto, the badge's three ostrich feathers came from the "shield for peace" in the Black Prince's arms (discussed later).[4] In *The Bestiary of Christ,* Louis Charbonneau-Lassay remarks, "In [ancient] Nubia, Arabia, Persia, Sumeria, Mesopotamia, Assyria, and  Asia Minor, the learned scholars and teachers looked upon the ostrich as one of the birds most favored by various astral influences and as possessing in itself elements of the divine" (cf. Job 39:13-18; Lam 4:3).[5] Ostrich's and heron's feathers now adorn the black velvet hats of Garter knights.

The meaning of *Ich Dien* has been disputed. While Prince Charles understands it to mean "I serve," there are those who believe that *Ich Dien* "is not German but a corruption of the old Welsh *Eich Dyn,* meaning 'Your man'."[6] Scott-Guiles comments, "If *Ich Diene* is German, as is generally supposed (despite Welsh claims), it means 'I serve,' and is thought to refer to the Prince's duty to the

1. For another color representation of this badge, see Boutell, plate XII, between pp. 164-167.
2. "Wales, Prince of," *A Dictionary of Heraldry,* ed. Friar, p. 372. According to Boutell, Edward VI may have been the first to place the Black Prince's group of three ostrich-feather badges within a coronet, "the form in which they are used today" (see 1978 ed., pp. 165-166).
3. Junor, p. 88.
4. Boutell, 1978 ed., pp. 77, 165.
5. Louis Charbonneau-Lassay, *The Bestiary of Christ,* trans. D.M. Dooling (New York: Parabola Books, 1991), p. 275.
6. "Wales, Prince of," *A Dictionary of Heraldry,* ed. Friar, p. 372.

King, his father...: 'The heir, while he is a child, differeth nothing from a servant.'"[1] Prince Charles once said, "I believe it best to confine myself to three basic aims at the start: to show concern for people, to display interest in them as individuals, and to encourage them in a whole host of ways."[2] Holden recalls this comment from the prince regarding his motto: "Of *Ich Dien* ('I serve'), the motto he had inherited from Edward, the Black Prince, he said: 'It means just that. It is the basis of one's job: to serve other people. If you have a sense of duty, and I like to think I have, service means that you give yourself to people, particularly if they want you, and sometimes if they don't.'"[3]

What, therefore, might be the implied message of the heir-apparent's badge? Could it be that Prince Charles, who views himself as a servant of others, whose man he is, will someday proclaim a false, antichristian peace to the world? Holden observes that at Prince Charles' formal investiture as Prince of Wales, the badge's *Ich Dien* motto was "the dominant motif of the day."[4] In fact, the badge itself was prominently displayed on the clear canopy over the prince as the queen placed the coronet on his head.[5]

The red dragon, or Satan. In 1911, the red dragon of Wales was "assigned to the Prince of Wales to place over the royal arms as a central escutcheon [(shield)], to symbolize the Principality."[6] Shortly before his death in February 1952, when Prince Charles was only three years old, King George VI had the red dragon added to his grandson's then future coat of arms. A.C. Fox-Davies recorded, "The red dragon upon a mount vert, which forms a part of the Royal achievement as the badge of Wales, is known as the red dragon of Cadwallader, and in deference to a loudly expressed sentiment on the subject, His Majesty the King has recently added the Welsh dragon differenced by a label

1. Scott-Guiles, pp. 89-91.
2. Holden, *PRINCE CHARLES*, p. 270.
3. Holden, *PRINCE CHARLES*, p. 195.
4. Holden, *PRINCE CHARLES*, p. 181-182.
5. "Memories of the Day," *Majesty* magazine, July 1994, Vol. 15, No. 7, p. 35.
6. "Beasts," *A Dictionary of Heraldry*, ed. Friar, p. 57.

of three points argent [(i.e., the eldest-son label)] as an additional badge to the achievement of His Royal Highness the Prince of Wales. The red dragon was one of the supporters of the Tudor kings, being used by Henry VII, Henry VIII, and Edward VI."[1] Not only is George VI known to have participated in spiritism, psychic healing, and homeopathy,[2] but as the former head of Freemasonry worldwide, he "held the rank of past grand master, and of knight commander of the Temple, was a 33-degree [Mason], and grand inspector general in the Ancient and Accepted Rite of Rose Croix."[3]

Currently, the Royal Badge of Wales consists of the British monarch's crown, the red dragon, and an encircling riband with the motto *Y Ddraig Goch Ddyry Cychwyn,* meaning "The red dragon gives the lead."[4] Calling the 1953 addition of this profane motto "an honourable augmentation," Scott-Giles and Brooke-Little note that the Welsh badge had previously consisted of the red dragon only.[5] He adds, "The Dragon is a monster with a horny head and forked tongue, a scaly back and rolls like armour on chest and belly, bat-like wings, four legs ending in talons, and a pointed tail. It is...rarely displayed. A dragon gules [(red)] occurs in the royal badge for Wales..., and is a common charge in the civic heraldry of the Principality."[6] Fox-Davies similarly comments,

> ....The head of a dragon is like nothing else in heraldry.... It is like nothing else in heaven or on earth. Its neck is covered with scales not unlike those of a fish. All four legs are scaled and have claws, the back is scaled, the tongue is barbed, and the under

1. A.C. Fox-Davies, *Complete Guide to Heraldry* (Nelson Publishers, n.d.), p. 225. For example, Prince Arthur, Henry VII's son, used a version of the Black Prince's ostrich-feather badge in which the feather was held up by a Welsh dragon (Boutell, 1978 ed., p. 166).
2. John Dale, *The Prince and the Paranormal: The Psychic Bloodline of the Royal Family* (London: W.H. Allen & Co. Plc, 1986), pp. 79-82, 89, 96-97, 132, 163, 171-172.
3. Denslow, *10,000 Famous Freemasons,* pp. 104-105. For more information, see the related note in the earlier discussion on the Garter.
4. For a color representation of this badge, see Boutell, plate XII, between pp. 164-167.
5. Boutell, 1978 ed., p. 218.
6. Boutell, 1978 ed., p. 81.

part of the body is likewise scaled, but here, in rolls of a much larger size. Great differences will be found in the shape of the ears, but the wings of the dragon are always represented as the wings of a bat, with the long ribs or bones carried to the base.... The dragon is one of the most artistic of heraldic [beasts]..., and lends itself very readily to the genius of any artist. In nearly all modern representations the tail, like the tongue, will be found ending in a barb....

Whilst we have separate and distinct names for many varieties of dragon-like creatures, other countries in their use of the word "dragon" include the wyvern, basilisk, cockatrice, and other similar creatures [(cf. Job 41; Isa 14:29, 27:1, AKJV)]....[1]

The red dragon in Prince Charles' arms has a third copy of the eldest-son label around its neck, thereby associating it with the prince. In fact, the unique presence of this label around the red dragon's neck actually seems to indicate that at some point the dragon shall *possess* the eldest son, or Prince Charles. According to Friar, this particular dragon came from the Roman Empire:

> *Y ddraig goch*, the red dragon, is the royal badge for Wales and is properly depicted on a grassy mount or on a shield...within a riband ensigned with the Royal Crown and bearing the motto 'Y Ddraig Goch Ddyry Cychwyn' (The red dragon gives the lead). The dragon appears in the arms or as the badge of several old Welsh families, notably the Tudors who, when they ascended the English throne through Henry VII, restored the red dragon to its ancient status as a royal device, together with the white and green liveries worn by Welsh archers who served under the Black Prince in the previous century.
>
> The dragon is believed to have entered British armory through the standards of the Roman cohorts and to have been adopted by the shadowy Celtic warriors of post-Roman Britain, Arthur and Cadwallader among them.[2]

Due to its apparent Roman history, and the fact that it has been incorporated into an image which seems to be identical to, and in all likelihood *is* the beast described in Daniel and the Apocalypse, there can be little doubt that what is now known as the red dragon of Wales is the specific dragon that is identified in Genesis (3:1-4, 3:13-14,

1. Fox-Davies, pp. 224-225.
2. "Wales, Principality of," *A Dictionary of Heraldry,* ed. Friar, p. 373.

49:17, Heb.), the Apocalypse (12:3, 12:9, 20:2), and elsewhere (e.g., Isa 14:29, 27:1, Heb.; Amos 5:19, Heb.; cf. Ps 22:21, Heb.; Rev 13:2) as a symbol of Satan himself. Indeed, the Apocalypse is rich in imagery that early Christians, who were severely persecuted under Rome's satanic yoke, would have understood as direct references to Rome and its evil empire. Therefore, *to the extent that the "red dragon gives the lead," Satan controls Prince Charles*.

The logo of *Peace on Earth* depicts a huge *Welsh* dragon sitting upon and guarding the sphere of the Earth, whereas one of the organization's brochures proclaims, "as we enter what has been described as the Aquarian Age, we are entering a time of cooperation between the spiritual and the material realms, so it is time for us to make peace with the [red] dragon and work in partnership with the wisdom and the power of the earth that the dragon represents."[1] In ancient Babylonia, dragons were similarly worshiped. One writer comments, "The *dragon*, or serpent, was the symbol painted on the great Gate of Ishtar that travelers passed through as they entered ancient Babylon.... The New Age must take particular delight in its portrayal of the dragon as a creature to be loved and taken to heart.... One finds the dragon gracing everything from newsletters to jewelry. There are also crystal dragons as ornaments and idols...."[2] Today, many New Age parents openly promote dragons and serpents, like unicorns, lions, and bears, as good, lovable creatures to their children. Perhaps in that vein, Prince Charles and Princess Diana provided their children "furniture with hand-painted animals from Dragons, a posh London furniture store."[3]

More remains to be said, however, concerning these beasts and their uses in ancient and modern cultures around the world—*over which Prince Charles could have sway merely by virtue of the symbolism in his arms*. Charbonneau-Lassay, for example, notes that "granite lions, crouched and ferocious,...[stand] guard in the company of dragons at the threshold of India's

---

1. Hunt, GLOBAL PEACE AND THE RISE OF ANTICHRIST, pp. 44-45.
2. Texe Marrs, *Mystery Mark of the New Age* (Illinois: Good News Publishers, 1988), p. 115.
3. Bonnie Johnson, "Growing Up Royal," *People Weekly*, 1988, p. 117.

temples...."[1] Regarding China, he adds, "The Chinese see the sacred image of the dragon nearly everywhere.... Among these many dragons, some are good spirits, others are fearsome and maleficent.... The greatest of them all 'is a mysterious, supernatural creature, the reptile-spirit specifically designated in Chinese books as the Dragon above all others.'... The image of the Great Dragon in China is like the symbol of sovereign nobility and divine power...."[2] In this century, largely due to communist China, the red dragon has become loosely associated with Communism (cf. "reds," "the red peril," etc.).

The dexter (left-hand) supporter. *The guardant, dexter supporter in Prince Charles' coat of arms is a beast that has a body like a leopard's body, ferocious feet like those of a bear,[3] and a "mouth like the mouth of a lion."* With the exception of its ferocious red claws,[4] as well as its white fangs and red tongue, this beast is entirely brass (or bronze) in color. The fifth (and last) copy of the prince's heir-apparent crown is upon its head, and a fourth copy of the eldest-son label is around its neck. Due to its guardant posture, this beast's left ear is facing the mouth of the sinister unicorn (see Prov 17:4). It is written,

1. Charbonneau-Lassay, p. 8.
2. Charbonneau-Lassay, p. 414.
3. Typically, heraldic lions have three claws per foot, whereas bears have four or five. For a close unofficial version of Prince Charles' achievement, in which the dexter beast's feet are less exaggerated and perhaps even more bear-like, with the red dragon likewise having four claws per foot, see *Burke's Guide to the Royal Family,* 1st ed. (London: Burke's Peerage Ltd., 1973), p. 104.
4. See the notes on Daniel 7:19 in the later discussion on the sinister unicorn.

> And I stood upon the sand of the sea. And I saw a beast rise up out of the sea.... Now the beast which I saw was like a leopard, his feet were like the feet of a bear, and his mouth like the mouth of a lion. And the dragon gave him his power, his throne, and great authority. (Rev 13:1-2; see Prov 28:15-16; Jer 5:6; Lam 3:10-11; Hos 5:14-15, 13:4-9; Joel 1:6; Amos 5:16-19, Heb.; 1 Pet 5:6-9; cf. Gen 49:17, Heb.; 1 Sam 17:34-37; Ps 22:13, 22:21, Heb.; Jer 4:5-7; Dan 7:2-8, 7:20-25; Rev 12:3)

This beast is said to "rise up out of the sea." As we have seen, Prince Charles' coat of arms represents not only England, but also Scotland, Ireland, and Wales (via the red lion and unicorn, harp, and red dragon, respectively). In other words, it represents the United Kingdom, which in every way—physically, economically, militarily, and religiously—rises "out of the sea." Indeed, it was through its seafaring prowess that Britain built its empire and constituted its Commonwealth. But the AntiChrist will eventually receive worldwide power during the Tribulation Period. It is perhaps noteworthy, therefore, that ships from all the major military powers, including the United Kingdom, have in this century patrolled, as well as exercised influence over, the coastal areas of both Israel and her Arab adversaries from the Mediterranean Sea.

Although it is traditionally supposed to represent England,[1] the dexter beast in Prince Charles' arms is totally unique in history and heraldry. The dexter supporter in the vast majority of current and former coats of arms, including Queen Elizabeth II's (right), has the appearance of a normal lion, with a lion's body and feet. In the few exceptions, this supporter has a lion's mouth and a body with similar proportions to a leopard's. Prince Charles' coat of

1. Boutell, 1978 ed., p. 214.

arms, however, contains the *first* and *only* true heraldic representation of this combination—anywhere ever—with ferocious feet such as those of a bear.[1] The prince's lineage, apart from royal military uniforms,[2] offers perhaps the best explanation for this anomaly. As mentioned earlier, the leopard-like body is for *Germany,* the bear-like feet are for *France,* and the lion-like mouth is for *England*, giving a unique beast that fully represents the Merovingian dynasty, which historically originated and prospered in Germany, France, and England.[3] Through Prince Philip and Queen Elizabeth II, Prince Charles is of German, French, and Russian descent, and his ancestors include rulers of Greece and ancient Persia. The leopard and the bear, besides being associated historically with the Greek and Medo-Persian empires (Dan 7:5-6), are today viewed as representative of Germany and either France or Russia.

Germany, France, and Russia, like England, are major powers within Europe and in the United Nations. But that is not all. We may further assert that these particular nations have for centuries been among the world's most menacing powers. England has been one of the greatest colonial powers the world has ever known (and through her Commonwealth may still be), Russia fomented the Cold War and still threatens the world with nuclear annihilation, and Germany is largely responsible for World Wars I and II. It seems noteworthy that Prince Philip, Prince Charles' father, who was once voted "first choice for a national dictator," and whose "brother-in-law, Prince Christopher of

1. Each June, "for the Queen's Birthday Parade," in the same month as the annual ceremony at Garter Chapel, Prince Charles wears his red uniform as Colonel-in-Chief of the Welsh Guards (cf. the red dragon of Wales), which includes a bearskin (Burnet, *In Private—In Public,* THE PRINCE AND PRINCESS OF WALES, p. 127; *Her Majesty The Queen,* pp. 14-15).
2. Although the royal guards were discussed earlier, more remains to be said regarding their symbols and uniforms. The Royal Household Cavalry, which serves both at Windsor and in Germany, is comprised of the Life Guards, which is the senior regiment of the British Army and bears the royal *lion* as part of its crest, as well as the Blues and Royals. The uniforms of the Royal Household Cavalry, like those of the five regiments of the Royal Foot Guards (i.e., the Grenadier Guards, Coldstream Guards, Scots Guards, Irish Guards, and Welsh Guards), who perform sentry duty outside Buckingham Palace, include *bearskins*. In other words, the royal lion and bearskins are directly associated with the guards of the British monarchy (James and Russell, *At Home with the Royal Family,* pp. 123-127). As we have seen, Prince Charles wears the insignia of a number of these regiments. For more information, see this chapter's earlier section titled, "Related orders and royal guards."
3. For more information, see Chapter 4, "Prince of this World—a *Diverse* Lineage."

181

Hesse, was certainly an active and influential Nazi," has in the past been viewed as a Nazi-sympathizer.[1] France, of course, gave rise to its own menace—Napoleon. In the near future, Gog (Russia), Persia (Iran), and Gomer (Turkey or Germany), in apparent opposition to the United Kingdom's merchants and offspring (i.e., "the merchants of Tarshish, and all its young lions"), may well trigger Armageddon (Ezek 38 to 39).[2] Sraya Shapiro remarks, "devising a millennium in the Middle East with the British Lion looking on benevolently, suggesting practical solutions for the well-being of all concerned," as Winston Churchill envisioned, "would just have been too good to be true."[3]

1. Judd, *Prince Philip*, pp. 14, 66-67, 73, 89. Despite Judd's attempts to gloss over Prince Philip's thinking regarding the Nazis, and his attempts to show the prince's loyalty to World War II Britain (ibid., pp. 89-90), certain statements reveal at the very least the prince's weak moral fiber: "Hitler's march into the Rhineland in 1936 was welcomed by most of the German side of his family but disturbed his British relatives. Where did Philip's loyalties lie? One of his Gordonstoun schoolfellows recalls that he was careful and diplomatic in his comments—'intelligently non-committal' was the phrase used" (ibid., pp. 79-80). Prince Philip's close relations were similarly sympathetic towards the Germans around World War I (ibid., pp. 45-47), and the prince himself had a strong German education. For more information, see the brief discussion on "outcome-based education" (OBE) in Chapter 11's section titled, "The United World Colleges."

2. For more information, see the section titled "The Last Four Seals of the Tribulation Week (and the Second Advent)" in *Messiah, History, and the Tribulation Period*.

3. Sraya Shapiro, "Slouching towards the millennium," *The Jerusalem Post*, Int. Ed., 15 Feb. 1992, p. 23.

   In this author's opinion, Great Britain, next to Rome, Nazi Germany, and Russia, bears perhaps the greatest responsibility for the persecutions, sufferings, and slaughter of Israelites in this century. In the November 1917 Balfour Declaration, Britain's Lloyd George government promised to use its "best endeavors" to establish a "national home for the Jewish people" (i.e., an Israeli state) in the Middle East. The promised homeland was to include not only the territory that Israel now possesses, but also all of modern Jordan. In 1922, Herbert Samuel, then high commissioner for Palestine, and John Shuckburgh, head of the Middle East Department of the Colonial Office, issued a "White Paper," in then Colonial Secretary Winston Churchill's name, that all but revoked the provisions of the Balfour Declaration while suggesting the partitioning of what was to have been the Jewish National Home. Further, the Lloyd George government adopted this new "interpretation" of the Declaration (H.G., "The real author of the Churchill White Paper," *The Jerusalem Post*, Int. Ed., 20 June 1992, p. 11). According to Coleman, Lloyd George and Arthur Balfour were both members of the Committee of 300, as were Israel's first Prime Minister and first President, David *ben* Gurion and Chaim Weizmann (*The Committee of 300*, pp. 235-236, 311, 314, 321).

   Britain's broken promise prevented the establishment of an Israeli state before World War II, greatly reduced the flow of Israelites to the Promised Land, and resulted in the formation of modern Jordan—which was originally intended to be a Palestinian state. Further, it led to another White Paper in 1939 that severely restricted Israelite immigration to the Promised Land ("1922: Britain sets the stage for conflict," *The Jerusalem Post*, Int. Ed., 20 June 1992, p. 11). Consequently, the British Navy forcibly sent many European Israelites who were fleeing Hitler's death camps back to Europe—to their deaths, thereby contributing greatly to the Holocaust. Moreover, it has recently been revealed that "The British [government] knew as early as mid-1941—more than a year earlier than previously acknowledged—that Jews were being systematically slaughtered by the Nazis.... By late

Mythologically, all heraldic beasts have certain attributes. Regarding the bear, Margaret Young remarks, "In the heavily wooded areas of some of the central European countries the bear was a familiar animal, and...it took the place of the lion, in their heraldry, for boldness, courage and majesty."[1] What about lions? Charbonneau-Lassay notes that the lion was adopted "as insignia by the legions of Rome," and that it "shares with numerous animals...the negative role of serving...as an allegorical image for the Antichrist, for Satan."[2] According to Walker, the lion was "usually a symbol of the sun god in Greece and Rome," but it was "more commonly associated with the Goddess in the Middle East and Egypt."[3] Young states,

> **The lions of mythology have magic in their tails.** By sweeping them over their tracks they obliterate their footprints and make their ways unknown. By swinging them over their bodies they render themselves invisible. **Thus the longer the tail, the greater the magic.**
>
> The lion is always alert and sleeps with his eyes open. **It was also believed that the cubs were born dead and remained so for three days, whereupon their father came and breathed into their faces to give them life.** Many other strange beliefs concerning the lion have come down the ages.... **The lion is regarded as the embodiment of courage, strength and nobleness. He is the King of the Beasts, and a fitting symbol of kings and kingdoms.**[4]

1941 'it was perfectly obvious' to the British 'that the Nazis were executing every Jew they could lay their hands on' (Associated Press, "Britain apparently knew about slaughter of Jews," 19 Nov. 1996, *Rocky Mountain News*, p. 23A).

Had the British government kept its word to Israel, as given in 1917, the Nazi Holocaust might not have occurred, and even if it had, the toll on Israelite lives would have been significantly reduced. Surely God will recompense those who are myopic in their view of the Arab-Israeli conflict, who conveniently forget their own blood-stained past while ignoring the Arab and Muslim wickedness toward Israel resulting from it.

1. Young, "Bear," *A Dictionary of Heraldry,* ed. Friar, p. 55.
2. Charbonneau-Lassay, pp. 8, 13.
3. Walker, "Lion," p. 544.
4. Young, "Lion," *A Dictionary of Heraldry,* ed. Friar, pp. 215, 218.

In the official version of Prince Charles' arms, the lower jaw of the dexter beast has a normal shape and all four of the front fangs in its mouth are evident. However, in the unofficial version, the beast appears to have something shaped like a rectangular frame in the lower half of its mouth, virtually concealing its two lower fangs. In other words, it appears to have taken a three-sided, frame-like object into its mouth, over which its sharp tongue protrudes (see Job 20:4-29; Ps 10:2-12, 22:21 {AKJV}, 35:11-26, 50:16-21, 52:1-7, 57:2-4 {KJV}; Isa 5:29-30; cf. Job 29:17; Dan 7:5). The heraldic ostrich has a similar mouth configuration. Regarding its depiction, Scott-Giles and Brooke-Little note that the ostrich is "usually shown with a horseshoe or other metal object in its beak, <u>apparently in exaggerated reference to its digestive powers</u>."[1] Recall that during the Great Tribulation, unregenerate Gentiles will devour Judaea and half of Jerusalem. Finally, notice this beast's bulging eyes (see Ps 73:7).

The sinister (right-hand) supporter. The sinister supporter in Prince Charles' coat of arms is a unicorn that has the fifth (and last) copy of the eldest-son label around its neck. In heraldry, this unicorn represents not only Scotland,[2] but also a counterfeit Christ. Young comments,

> The mystery and magic of the unicorn has been known to all civilizations.... In the world of heraldry it became known as an elegant and beautiful animal, like a horse but with cloven feet, a lion's tail and a goat's beard [(a relatively recent addition)], and a delicate spiraling horn on its forehead. To earlier civilizations it had been known with a different appearance, the flamboyant *ki-lin* of China, and the *kirin* of Japan. In Arabia and Persia it was the *karkardanh*, sometimes a violent and blood-thirsty creature,

1. Boutell, 1978 ed., p. 77.
2. Boutell, 1978 ed., p. 214.

sometimes more graceful. The mount which Alexander the Great tamed and called Bucephalus was said to be a *karkardanh*.

In medieval times the unicorn became the [mythological] symbol of Christ because of its purity and virtue. Besides these qualities it was believed to possess medicinal powers. The horn was an antidote to poison and no animal would drink from a pool until the unicorn had stirred the water with its horn, thus rendering innocuous any poison that a dragon or serpent had deposited therein. Powdered unicorn horn was [allegedly] used as a cure for many ills....[1]

The earliest known depictions of unicorns are those found in the artwork of Mesopotamia. In ancient Chaldean and Babylonian artifacts, unicorns are portrayed as beasts having a single, little horn projecting from their foreheads. The book of Daniel, written while the prophet was in Babylonia, not only represents Alexander the Great as an unstoppable one-horned goat, or *unicorn* (Dan 8:5-8), but in that immediate context, it depicts his most profane successor, Antiochus IV Epiphanes, who was typical of the AntiChrist, as a beast having a single, little horn (Dan 8:9-11). Yet the beast representing the Anti-Christ, besides having such a horn, will also have eyes like those of a man (Dan 7:8, 7:11, 7:20-21). Daniel, in other words, pictures the AntiChrist as a rather exotic unicorn. Johanna Michaelsen remarks,

---

1. Young, "Unicorn," *A Dictionary of Heraldry*, ed. Friar, pp. 353-354. Cf. Ps 75:4-8, NKJV or NAS.

The myth of the unicorn probably originated in ancient Babylon and spread to numerous civilizations around the world, its form and interpretation varying depending on where it found itself [and] in which century. It has...been regarded as a symbol of purity, despite the fact that ancient legends ascribe to it some decidedly impure and unvirginal activities. It is seen as a symbol of opposites, rather like the [Chinese] *yin/yang*.... New Agers have, in fact, adopted the unicorn as one of their major symbols, viewing it as "the spark of divine light in the darkness of matter and evil," and as a symbol of the great world leader whom they expect to bring peace on the earth in the New Age. The Bible identifies this leader as the Antichrist, the little horn that rises in the midst of the ten horns which Daniel saw....[1]

New Agers often uphold unicorns as "spirit guides," telling children that they should have their own "special unicorn" to imagine, call upon, and "love." It is interesting to note in this context that in "Christian" symbolism, the unicorn is sometimes taken to represent the "Virgin Mary."[2] One wonders, then, to whom it is that tens of millions of Roman Catholics are really praying when they call upon the "Virgin Mary." One writer observes,

The *unicorn* is today pictured as a friendly and loving, gentle creature with great appeal to kids. But his origins are occultic. Nimrod, the "Great Hunter" and man-god of Babylon, wore a headdress with a single horn protruding from the front. According to *The Lore of the Unicorn*, the unicorn...was worshiped as sacred in pre-Christian Persepolis.... In ancient China, statues of human heads with a horn were thought to keep demons away from homes.

Odell Shepard...also wrote that the unicorn was a common idol in ancient Babylon and Nineveh where it was used as a charm and a talisman.[3]

Regarding the mythological beliefs of pre-communist China, Charbonneau-Lassay wrote, "it is unicorns that bring human babies to their mothers, and their images are much used luck-bringers in the family." He continues, "In any case, before our era people of almost all countries

1. Johanna Michaelsen, *Like Lambs to the Slaughter* (Oregon: Harvest House Publishers, 1989), p. 221.
2. "Christian Symbols," *A Dictionary of Heraldry*, ed. Friar, p. 91.
3. Marrs, *Mystery Mark of the New Age*, p. 116.

thought of the unicorn, in spite of the elegance of form generally attributed to it, as an invincible and very dangerous animal."[1] Recognizing the unicorn as a symbol of destruction, death, and transformation, Nancy Hathaway writes,

> In the twentieth century the unicorn, after centuries of obsolescence, has emerged in an unexpected guise. Its re-emergence was partially inspired by nineteenth-century investigations into mythology—including such peculiar and wonderful books as *The Unicorn: A Mythological Investigation* by Robert Brown, which approached the unicorn in terms of solar symbolism.... In the beginning of this century, the unicorn began to appear as a symbol of strength. William Butler Yeats, who was fascinated by symbols of all kinds, published a play in 1908 called *The Unicorn from the Stars*. In it the one-horned beast becomes once more a complex and paradoxical symbol:
>
>> *Martin:* There were horses...white horses rushing by, with white shining riders...there was a horse without a rider, and someone caught me up and put me upon him, and we rode away, with the wind, like the wind.... Then I saw the horses we were on had changed to unicorns, and they began trampling the grapes and breaking them.... They tore down the wheat and trampled it on the stones, and then they tore down what was left of the grapes and crushed and bruised and trampled them. I smelt the wine, it was flowing on every side...everything was silent.... I saw a bright many-changing figure...it was holding up a shining vessel...(holds up arms) then the vessel fell and was broken with a great crash...then I saw the unicorns trampling it. They were breaking the world to pieces...when I saw the cracks coming, I shouted for joy! And I heard the command, "Destroy, destroy; destruction is the life-giver; destroy." ...I am to destroy; destruction was the word the messenger spoke.
>> *Father John:* To destroy?
>> *Martin:* To bring again the old disturbed exalted life, the old splendour.
>
> The unicorn here is once again a symbol of transformation, for this unicorn seeks a better world—or a return to a better world—through the purifying, purgative powers of destruction. Its purpose, like that of the Hindu god S[h]iva, is to tear down and to renew....
>   ....Dylan Thomas, in his poem "And death shall have no dominion," refers to "unicorn evils...." The creative powers of the artist and the destructive powers of death are cut from the same cloth as the powers of the unicorn—that is, they are

---

1. Charbonneau-Lassay, pp. 365, 367.

transforming.[1]

Constance Cumbey remarks, "The *Satanic Bible* of Anton Szandor LaVey mentions the name 'Shiva' as a synonym for Lucifer or Satan."[2] Among other things, early Christianity viewed the unicorn as a symbol of Satan and Death (recall the earlier discussion on Psalm 22:21). Beer states,

> At a very early date,...[the unicorn] became an ideograph for Christ, yet it stood also for Death and the Devil; in this last case Asiatic influences were powerfully at work.... Becoming associated with the Virgin through the Son of Man, the unicorn was, further, a symbol of chastity. But because of its boundless strength it also embodied unlimited licentiousness: the horn as aphrodisiac in yet another guise. The contradictory nature of the creature is manifold.... And though the lion symbolizes Christ's sovereignty, the devil, too, roams like a roaring lion....
>
> ....The unicorn was identified by the Church Fathers with everything resisting the domination of Christ and contrary to the Church.... Finally, the Devil himself is represented as a unicorn in patristic works and Coptic incantations....
>
> Pope Gregory the Great called the Prince of Darkness a unicorn....
>
> The so-called Basil version [of *Physiologus*...states]: "The unicorn is evilly inclined toward man. It pursues him, and when it catches him up it pierces him with its horn and devours him." What a contrast that makes to the figure of the Redeemer! The author purported to be Basil in his commentaries pushes this contradiction to its full extent: "Take care then, O Man, to protect thyself from the unicorn, that is to say from the Devil. For he is ill-inclined toward man and skilled in doing him harm. For he stands by the way day and night and by permeating man with his sophistries severs him from God's commandments." Thus the same creature that denotes the Redeemer is also a symbol for his adversary....
>
> The later *Physiologus* of the Waldenses (a twelfth-century Roman Catholic sect) identifies the unicorn with Satan, but the Basilian volume allows an alternative; as we have seen, the unicorn there is concurrently a symbol for Satan and for the Savior.[3]

1. Hathaway, pp. 159-163.
2. Constance Cumbey, *A Planned Deception* (Michigan: Pointe Publishers, Inc., 1985), p. 70.
3. Beer, pp. 9, 24, 50-52.

Eyes like those of a man. Like the dexter beast, the sinister unicorn on Prince Charles' coat of arms is unique.

It not only has a little horn, and brass (or bronze) colored hoofs and nails, but it also has eyes like the eyes of a man. Most unicorns, in history and heraldry, have round horse-like eyes, with no visible eye-whites, including Queen Elizabeth II's (shown at left). Yet in the official version of Prince Charles' coat of arms, the unicorn's one visible eye—its left eye (cf. Zech 11:17, KJV)—is not only similar in shape to a man's eye, but it also has a clearly defined eye-white around its cornea. In the prince's unofficial arms, this eye looks like the eye of a man when the man is viewed from the left side of his face. As a captive prophet in Babylon, Daniel wrote,

> After this I watched in the night visions, and behold, a fourth beast, dreadful and terrifying, and exceedingly strong. And it had huge iron teeth; it devoured and crushed, and *the* residue it trampled with its feet. And it *was* different from all the beasts that *were* before it, and it had ten horns *in its head*. I was considering the horns, and behold, another horn, *a* little *one,* came up among them, before whom three of the first horns were plucked out by the roots [uprooted]. And behold, in this horn, *were* eyes like the eyes of a man, and a mouth speaking great things.... Then I desired to know the truth about the fourth beast, which was different from all of them, exceedingly dreadful, *with* its teeth of iron and its nails [hoofs, claws][1] of brass [bronze, copper,

---

1. This Hebrew-Chaldee word, Strong's number 2953, is used just once more in the Old Testament scriptures, where it refers to the nails of a man (Dan 4:33). However, it may be translated as nails, hoofs, or claws. Besides having a body like a horse, the unicorn in Prince Charles' coat of arms has cloven feet and nails like those of a goat, whereas the feet of the dexter beast have claws.

189

red],[1] *which* devoured, crushed, and *the* residue it trampled with its feet; and about the ten horns that *were* in its head; and about the other *horn* which came up, before whom three fell, even that horn having eyes and a mouth which speaking great things, whose appearance [aspect] was greater [stouter] than his fellows. I was watching; and this *same* horn made war with the saints, and prevailed against them.... ....And he shall be different from the first *ones*, and shall subdue [humble] three kings. And he shall speak words against the Most High, and shall wear-out the saints of the Most High, and shall intend to change times and law. And they shall be given into his hand for a time and times, and half a time. (Dan 7:7-8, 7:19-21, 7:24-25, Heb.; cf. Ps 22:21 {AKJV}, 75:2-7a {KJV}, 144:11; Rev 6:7-8).[2]

1. This Hebrew-Chaldee word, Strong's number 5174, can be translated as "brass," "bronze," "copper," or "red." The possible translation as "red" derives from another Hebrew word, Strong's number 5153, that is directly related to 5174. Strong's number 5153 refers to the "*red* color of the throat of a serpent [5175, as denom.] when hissing" (Strong, 5153, "A Concise Dictionary of the Words in the Hebrew Bible," p. 102).

   Strong's number 5175, which is identical to 5174 (though its pronunciation differs), is used in Arabic to refer to "the constellation of the serpent or dragon in the northern part of the sky" (Gesenius, 5175, p. 545). By implication, therefore, the beast described by Daniel may have bronze- or brass-colored nails or hoofs, or it may have red, serpent- or dragon-colored nails or claws. The unicorn on Prince Charles arms fits the former description, whereas the dexter beast matches the latter (i.e., it's claws are identical in color to the red dragon).

2. Notice that the apocalyptic description of the first beast ascribes multiple heads to it, not just one (see Rev 13:1-3). Further, it is the specific head which is to be wounded of that corporate beast that is to make war against the saints for forty-two months, or three and one-half years (Rev 13:3-8; cf. 11:2-3). In describing this beast, Daniel identifies the little horn that has eyes like those of a man as being the individual who will make war with the saints. Therefore, it appears that this little horn represents the head of the first beast that is to receive the deadly wound. Further, this association clearly implies that the little horn actually protrudes from a particular head on the corporate first beast, and that the given head has eyes like those of a man. Consequently, it should not surprise us to learn that the Hebrew word used in Daniel 7:8 and 7:20 for "horn," Strong's number 7161/7162, most literally refers to a beast that has a single horn which projects from its head (Gesenius, 7161, p. 744). In other words, taken in conjunction with the Apocalypse, Daniel clearly portrays the AntiChrist as a unicorn having human eyes.

A restraining chain. In the original, official version of Prince Charles' coat of arms (used upon cups and plates prepared for his wedding to Diana),[1] a chain, which functions heraldically as a restrainer (cf. 2 Th 2:6-7, Gk.: "the thing restraining....until *it* comes out of *the* way"), holds the unicorn to the

base of the arms (directly above the red dragon). Also, the unicorn's two hind-feet are touching the base. "The verb *restraineth* (*katechó*) quite literally means 'to hold down'...."[2] In conjunction with this, notice that the red dragon is nowhere touching the base's associated rim.

In the later, unofficial version of Prince Charles' arms, the chain is detached from the base, and no longer restrains the unicorn. Further, the unicorn's reared-back countenance looks fierce, and its right-rear hoof is suddenly elevated from the base, evidently lifted against The LORD (see Ps 41:9, Heb.;

cf. Prov 6:13). Not coincidentally, the red dragon's wing-tips, tongue, and front feet are now touching the associated rim (cf. Gen 49:17, Heb.). Interestingly, Jesus quoted Psalm 41:9, which literally speaks of the lifting of a hoof,[3] when referring to Judas Iscariot (see John 13:18), whom he called the "son of perdition" (John 17:12, KJV;

---

1. Spink, p. 60.
2. D. Edmond Hiebert, *The Thessalonian Epistles* (Chicago: Moody Press, 1971), p. 311.
3. Strong's number 6117/6119, translated as "heel" in Psalm 41:9, can also be rendered as "hoof" (e.g., see Gen 49:17; Judg 5:22). Further, Strong's number 6117 can be translated as "restrain."

see Acts 1:15-20; cf. Ps 109). Yet in the context of taking a restrainer "out of *the* way" (see 2 Th 2:6-7, KJV and Gk.; cf. Job 30:10-13), the apostle Paul spoke of the future revelation of another son of perdition (2 Th 2:3-4, KJV).[1] Therefore, this unicorn appears to represent not only "the Christ" in heraldry, but also the biblical son of perdition, the Anti-Christ. Notice, by comparison to the prince's official and unofficial arms, the tame countenance of the unicorn on his mother's arms (left).

The Black Prince and Prince Charles' arms. Finally, as we have seen, a number of the devices in the arms of Prince Charles associate him with Edward the Black Prince,

---

1. Regarding the coming "son of perdition" (2 Th 2:3, KJV), Paul wrote, "And now <u>the thing</u> restraining you know, for him to be revealed at his *own* time; for the mystery of lawlessness is already working, only He [he] is restraining *him* presently, until *it* comes out of *the* way" (2 Th 2:6-7, Gk.). Notice that both a "thing" and a Person (or person) are involved in the process of this restraint (*The Wycliffe Bible Commentary*, ed. Charles F. Pfeiffer and Everett F. Harrison {Chicago: Moody Press, 1962}, p. 1364). In other words, this passage not only speaks of a *thing* restraining the son of perdition (who lifts his hoof against Messiah Jesus and Israel), but also a *Person*, God, or person (e.g., the archangel Michael; cf. Dan 12:1, Heb.) who controls it. Although God may control the restrainer by the power of His Spirit, there is nothing in Paul's statements, explicitly or implicitly, that would allow us to presume that he was in any way referring to the removal of the Spirit-filled Church from the Earth before the completion of the Great Tribulation (Robert H. Gundry, *the church and the tribulation* {Michigan: Zondervan Publishing House, 1973}, pp. 125-128).

   In fact, 2 Thessalonians 2 is entirely posttribulational in nature; for the "gathering together" of the saints to Jesus (2 Th 2:1) at the start of the "Day of The Christ" (2 Th 2:2, Gk.)—which is likewise called the "Day of The Lord of us, Jesus The Christ" (1 Cor 1:8, Gk.), the "Day of The Lord, Jesus" (1 Cor 5:5, KJV; 2 Cor 1:14), etc., or simply the "Day of The Lord [LORD]"—will be *preceded* by both "the apostasy" (i.e., the worldwide falling away from God, His Word, and His Truth by unbelieving Israelites and those who falsely profess to be Christians) and the revelation of "the man of sin, the son of perdition" (2 Th 2:3). However, as discussed in Chapter 3, "A Name that Calculates to 666," the revelation of the son of perdition will not itself occur, in the manner spoken of in 2 Thessalonians 2 (i.e., name calculations and the like excepted), until just before the *midpoint* of the Tribulation Period. Around that time, he will proclaim his deity in the Temple of God (2 Th 2:4), and the abomination that causes desolation, spoken of by both Daniel and Jesus, shall be erected (see Matt 24:4-5, 24:15-26, 24:29; Mark 13:5-6, 13:14-25; cf. 2 Th 2:4-8, Gk.). Further, according to this same passage in 2 Thessalonians, Jesus will return to destroy the impostor "with the brightness of His coming" *after*, not before, he is revealed (see 2 Th 2:8; cf. Matt 24:27-28, 24:30-44; Mark 13:26-33; 1 Th 1:9-10; 2 Th 1:3-10; Rev 1:7, 11:13-19). For more information, see the chapter titled "The Tribulation Period, the Day of The LORD, and God's Wrath" in *Messiah, History, and the Tribulation Period*.

who became a feared military commander throughout Europe following his victory in the Battle of Poitiers in 1356. As a grandson of Isabella of France and Edward II, who was a homosexual satanist, the Black Prince expired one year before his father, King Edward III, having served as the Prince of Wales from 1330 to 1376. To the mind of Froissart, the Black Prince was the "chief flower of chivalry of all the world."[1] The

medallion shown to the right, encircled by the Garter, is supposed to represent the Black Prince before the Judgment Throne of the triune God,[2] in the presence of "Mary." The apparent frog and cat held by what can only be construed as a witch, however, like the prevalence of the occult five-fingered hand, clearly gives away the scene as occult. Notice also the shield held by an angel crowned with a cross, presumably Merovingian, above the Black Prince. Created by Edward III in 1340 to express England's claim upon the French throne,[3] this shield, later known as the Black Prince's "shield for war," depicts the quartered arms of England and France.[4]

Just as the Black Prince wore a black surcoat, which showed his arms, the Garter cap, which Prince Charles wears to Garter services, is, apart from its white feather, black.[5] Interestingly, the so-called *Epistle of Barnabas,* which likely dates to the early second century A.D. (cf.

1. "Black Prince, The," *A Dictionary of Heraldry,* ed. Friar, p. 60.
2. "Christian Symbols," *A Dictionary of Heraldry,* ed. Friar, p. 89.
3. Boutell, 1978 ed., between pp. 22-23 and pp. 119, 130, 165, 207-209.
4. For an outline of this medallion, see Scott-Guiles, p. 95. Edward III's "noble" (gold coin) shows an image of the King bearing this shield and standing in a ship having at its masthead St. George's pennon or flag (Boutell, 1978 ed., p. 278).
5. Burnet, *In Private—In Public, THE PRINCE AND PRINCESS OF WALES,* pp. 126-127.

16:3-5), refers to Satan, in the guise of the AntiChrist, as "the Black One" (4:9, 20:1).[1] Regarding the Black Prince, Scott-Guiles comments,

> Following the example of the three foregoing Edwards, who all adopted badges from their mothers' devices, the Black Prince took these arms as his "shield for peace"..., while his "shield for war" was, of course, the royal coat-of-arms [(i.e., the royal shield)] differenced by a silver label....

> These two shields appear on the sides of his tomb in Canterbury Cathedral. The "shield for peace" is surmounted by a scroll with the motto *Ich Diene*, which also appears on the scrolls pierced by the pens of the feathers....
>
> The "shield for war" is accompanied by the old German word *Houmout*, meaning "Magnanimous," or, as rendered by "Toc H," who have made it their motto, "Hearts High." It has been suggested that those two mottoes should be read in conjunction as "I serve with a high heart."
>
> The effigy of the Black Prince on his tomb...shows him with a surcoat of the Royal Arms. Since the shield with the three feathers is definitely described as his "shield for peace," we may assume that on his peaceful occasions he wore a corresponding surcoat, the ground of which was, of course, black like the field of the shield. His nickname was therefore due to his black heraldic surcoat, and not to any habit of wearing black armour as is popularly supposed....[2]

1. *The Apostolic Fathers,* ed. and rev. Michael W. Holmes, eds. and trans. J.B. Lightfoot and J.R. Harmer, 2nd Ed. (Michigan: Baker Book House, 1992), pp. 283, 323. *Ante-Nicene Fathers,* ed. Roberts and Donaldson, Vol. 1, pp. 139, 149.
2. Scott-Guiles, pp. 89-91. An outline of the Black Prince's shields for war and peace may be found on page 90 of the same work. Also, see Boutell, 1978 ed., p. 77.

8

The Red Dragon and Prince Charles' Investiture as Prince of Wales

In 1958, just as the eagle on the dollar bill is the heraldic symbol of the United States, the red dragon became the official heraldic symbol of the nation of Wales. On July 26 of that year, at the conclusion of the Commonwealth Games in Cardiff, Queen Elizabeth II made her *absent* son, Prince Charles, the Prince of Wales.[1] At that time,

> ....After Prince Philip's opening remarks, they heard the Queen's voice say: "I want to take this opportunity of speaking to all Welsh people, not only in this arena, but wherever they may be.... I intend to create my son Charles Prince of Wales today."
>
> ...36,000 Welsh voices broke into "God Bless the Prince of Wales." When the clamor died down, the Queen's voice continued: "When he is grown up, I will present him to you at Caernarvon...."
>
> In the headmaster's study that afternoon, Charles automatically also became Earl of Chester and Knight Companion of the Most Noble Order of the Garter.... The monarch and the Prince of Wales are the only two ex-officio of the twenty-six Knights of the Garter...; the Prince of Wales's pew, by ancient tradition, is the second in rank (though the first on the left) in St George's Chapel at Windsor, but may not be occupied until he has been formally dubbed and installed by the sovereign. The Queen, perhaps having reflected on her son's reaction at the age of nine years and eight months, did not perform this ceremony (which also entitled him to wear the Garter's resplendent robes and insignia) for another ten years. By that time, June [17,] 1968, it was part of the buildup to his [formal] investiture at Caernarvon and his emergence into full-time public life.[2]

Just over six months later, in February 1959, the queen

1. Holden, *PRINCE CHARLES*, p. 325.
2. Holden, *PRINCE CHARLES*, pp. 119-121, 174.

approved a change to the design of the Welsh Flag. On February 23, the Minister for Welsh Affairs, Henry Brooke, announced, "I now have it in command from the Queen to say that Her Majesty has been pleased to direct that in [the] future only the Red Dragon on a green and white flag and not the flag carrying the augmented Royal Badge shall be flown on Government buildings in Wales and, where appropriate, in London...[but] the augmented Royal Badge will, of course, continue in use for other purposes."[1] Recall that the augmented flag, approved in 1953, bears the profane motto *Y Ddraig Goch Ddyry Cychwyn,* meaning "The red dragon gives the lead."[2]

On July 1, 1969, man first walked on the moon. That morning, before an estimated worldwide television audience of five-hundred million (the largest audience ever before the prince's 1981 marriage ceremony), the investiture of Prince Charles as Prince of Wales took place.[3] Situated at Caernarvon Castle, the "birthplace of the first Prince of Wales," it followed the charter that "created the Black Prince, Edward III's son, Prince of Wales in 1343" (the insignia of which were a coronet, a gold ring, and a silver rod).[4] "The ritual had lain defunct for three hundred years until revived with romantic Celtic enthusiasm by Lloyd George in 1911....for a quasi-religious service mixed with improbable pageantry.... [The] 1911 investiture was little more than an extra ceremonial.... Yet when attending his own first investiture committee, Prince Charles was astonished at the number of people who had come to be involved.... The assembly ranged from Lord Lieutenants to an Archdruid [(i.e., a top satanist)]—even including a woman Catholic Welsh Archbishop.... Slowly, and ultimately with remarkable efficiency, across a sixteen-month task schedule, the whole operation, dragon-like, lumbered forward."[5] For the investiture, both Prince Charles and Prince Philip wore the Garter Collar with its George

1. Boutell, 1978 ed., pp. 258-259.
2. For more information, see the discussion on the red dragon in Chapter 7, "The Heraldic Symbols in the Arms and their Interpretations."
3. Cathcart, p. 93. Junor, pp. 84, 88. See Holden, *PRINCE CHARLES*, photo before p. 163. For more information, see Chapter 10's section titled "Marriage, ascension, and politics."
4. Fry, *The Kings & Queens of England & Scotland,* p. 56.
5. Cathcart, pp. 89, 92-93.

Pendant and the blue Garter Riband with its Lesser George.[1] Upon Prince Charles' arrival at the castle, as if to underscore their apparent ignorance and deplorable scriptural illiteracy, Welsh voices again sang "God Bless the Prince of Wales."[2] Holden summarizes,

> Charles's procession was more splendid than anything he will know again before his own coronation. Flanked by the secretary of state for Wales, the Welsh Herald Extraordinary, and two lords-in-waiting, he was followed by five Welsh peers carrying his insignia. Earl Lloyd George of Dwyfor bore the same silver-gilt sword used by the last Prince of Wales, Lord Heycock the golden rod, Lord Maelor the gold ring embellished with two dragons and an amethyst, Lord Harlech the mantle of purple velvet and ermine, and Lord Ogmore the coronet....
>
> The Queen handed the letters patent to the Home Secretary, James Callaghan.... Almost entirely lacking punctuation,[3] they were something of a mouthful:

>> "Elizabeth the Second, by the Grace of God, of the United Kingdom of Great Britain and Northern Ireland, and of Our other Realms and Territories, Queen, Head of the Commonwealth, Defender of the Faith. **To all Lords, Spiritual and Temporal,** and all other Our Subjects whatsoever to whom these Presents shall come, Greeting. **Know ye that we have made and created, and by these Our Letters Do make and create, our most dear Son Charles Philip Arthur George**, Prince of the United Kingdom of Great Britain and Northern Ireland, Duke of Cornwall and Rothesay, Earl of Carrick, Baron of Renfrew, Lord of the Isles, and Great Steward of Scotland, **Prince of Wales and Earl of Chester**. And to the same, Our most dear Son Charles Philip Arthur George, have given and granted, and by this Our Present Charter, do give, grant, and confirm the name, style, title, dignity and honor of the same Principality and Earldom. And Him, Our most dear Son Charles Philip Arthur George, as he has been accustomed, We do ennoble and invest, with the said Principality and Earldom, by girding him with a Sword, by putting a Coronet on his head and a Gold Ring on his finger, and also by delivering a Gold Rod into his hand, that he may preside there and may direct and defend those parts—To hold to him and his heirs, Kings of the United Kingdom of Great Britain and Northern Ireland and of Our other Realms and

1. For color photographs of the investiture, including Prince Charles' and Prince Philip's attire, see "The 25th Anniversary of the Investiture of the Prince of Wales" and "Memories of the Day," *Majesty* magazine, July 1994, Vol. 15, No. 7, pp. 33, 35, 37, 39. For additional color photographs, see *Her Majesty The Queen*, p. 18. For more information, see Chapter 7's section titled, "The Garter."
2. Holden, *PRINCE CHARLES*, p. 189. Junor, p. 86.
3. The author has taken the liberty of inserting such punctuation.

Territories, Heads of the Commonwealth, for ever...."

As Callaghan struggled on, **the Queen formally invested Charles with the insignia**, and both waited while the Charter was read again in Welsh.... Then came the climax of the ceremony. Kneeling before his mother, the Prince of Wales intoned the oath.... **Placing his hands between the Queen's, he declared: "I, Charles, Prince of Wales, do** become your liege man of life and limb and of earthly **worship**, and faith and truth I will bear unto you to live and die against all manner of folks."[1]

Cathcart similarly remarks, "[Charles was] preceded by the Wales and Chester heralds of arms, by the Secretary of State for Wales and by Garter King of Arms.... In ritual closely based on the Westminster investiture of King Charles I, Prince Charles <u>received from the Queen</u> his ermine mantle in token of leadership, the sword as a symbol of justice, the new-made crown as a token of rank, the ring of Welsh gold in token of duty and the golden verge of pity. Then, to his mother, the Queen, he gave the same pledge of homage given by his father, the strange oath of fealty he had been too young to utter at the Coronation: '<u>I, Charles, Prince of Wales, do...worship</u>, and faith and truth I will bear unto you to live and die against all manner of folks.'"[2] Michèle Brown adds, "Dressed in the [dark] uniform of the Colonel-in-Chief of the newly created Royal Regiment of Wales, Charles appeared bare-headed, flanked by the Secretary of State for Wales, the Wales Herald Extraordinary and two attendant peers. Behind him walked five Welsh peers bearing the insignia of Investiture: the silver-gilt sword, the golden rod signifying authority, the ring, with which the Prince would be married to his country, the mantle of purple silk velvet and ermine, and the coronet. As <u>the Queen invested her son with these insignia</u>, the Letters Patent which created Charles Prince of Wales were read."[3]

The clothing Prince Charles wore that morning, besides his Garter insignia, consisted of a Welsh military uniform

1. Holden, *PRINCE CHARLES*, pp. 191-192.
2. Cathcart, p. 96.
3. Michèle Brown, *PRINCE CHARLES* (New York: Crown Publishers Inc., 1980), pp. 96, 133.

with an ermine-trimmed scarlet surcoat draped over it.[1] Apart from the coronet, the insignia of the investiture included "the ring, formed of two dragons grasping an amethyst; the golden rod or verge of government derived from a shepherd's staff; the sword, with its dragons guarding the crown, [and] the scabbard with the motto *Ich Dien, I Serve*.... As the watchdog of tradition, the Duke of Norfolk [pronounced]....'The heraldic devices are ancient, traditional and correct. There will be no monkeying about.'"[2] Although Prince Charles has not yet entirely fulfilled it, and it may not even pertain to the AntiChrist, the author is nevertheless reminded of the prophecy, "Woe to the idol shepherd that leaveth the flock! the sword shall be upon his arm, and upon his right eye: his arm *shall be* clean dried up [completely withered], and his right eye shall be utterly darkened [blinded]" (Zech 11:17, AKJV; cf. Ps 10:15). Besides the prince's "golden rod" derived from a "shepherd's staff" and his dragon-laden sword, we find parallels to the darkened right eye in his heraldic achievement, as shown earlier,[3] and on June 28, 1990, the prince nearly shattered his right arm in a polo fall.[4]

Trimmed with platinum, the coronet itself was made of gold, containing seventy-five diamonds and twelve emeralds.[5] Cathcart observes, "the designer conceded that there was a hint of the crown of thorns in the interweaving fragile 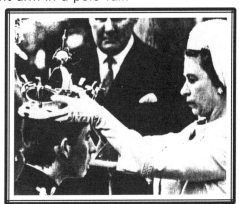 shapes of fleur-de-lys and crosses-patées. But was that

1. Holden, *PRINCE CHARLES*, p. 186.
2. Cathcart, pp. 91, 93. Recall that the Duke of Norfolk is the Earl Marshal over the Court of Chivalry, through which the heralds deal with armorial disputes. Bernard Marmaduke served as the Earl Marshal for this investiture (Junor, p. 85).
3. For more information, see Chapter 7's sections titled, "The top of the arms" and "The sinister (right-hand) supporter."
4. Hoey, *Charles & Diana: The Tenth Anniversary*, pp. 85, 89, 150.
5. Holden, *PRINCE CHARLES*, p. 187. Cathcart, p. 91.

not the humblest of all crowns?"[1] Having been fashioned specifically for Prince Charles, the coronet depicts four gold, diamond-studded Merovingian crosses—one to the North, one to the East, one to the West, and one to the South—as well as four gold *fleur-de-lis* around its circumference. The coronet also bears the gold "mound" or globe, representing the Earth, with a *fifth* gold Merovingian cross above it, at the top-center.[2] A banded gold globe with a cross is similarly depicted at the top-center of the *five* heir-apparent crowns on Prince Charles' coat of arms. (The message seems clear: Prince Charles is to be the prince of this world.) Interestingly, the earliest surviving register of the Order of the Garter (ca. 1534), known as the Black Book from its black velvet cover, contains an illustration of the Order of the Garter's twenty-six companion knights. This illustration shows King Henry VIII seated in the Garter Throne Room surrounded by the remaining twenty-five Garter knights, *five* of whom, including the king, are holding a gold scepter in one hand and a gold globe (mound or "orb") with a gold Merovingian cross at its top-center in the other.[3]

At the center of the investiture, there were three "utility" thrones: "Made of [grey] Welsh slate, those of Prince Philip and Prince Charles were backless, for the benefit of the TV cameras, while the 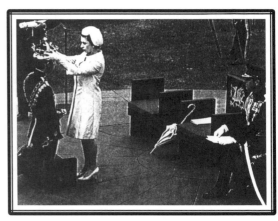 Queen's had a low back for reasons of status rather than

1. Cathcart, p. 91.
2. For relatively clear color photographs of Prince Charles wearing this coronet, see "The 25th Anniversary of the Investiture of the Prince of Wales" and "Memories of the Day," *Majesty* magazine, July 1994, Vol. 15, No. 7, pp. 33, 36.
3. Begent, p. 11.

comfort."[1] *Indeed, the backrest of the queen's throne had the satanic dragon of Wales on it. When she placed the coronet upon her son's head, this dragon was directly behind her and adjacent to Prince Charles' throne.[2]*

Of the AntiChrist, it is written, "And the dragon gave him his power, his throne, and great authority" (Rev 13:2). *As Prince of Wales, Prince Charles receives his power, his throne, and great authority from the red dragon of Wales—"that serpent of old, called the Devil and Satan, who deceives the whole world" (Rev 12:9).* Interestingly, unlike Revelation 12:3, verse 13:2 does not call the apocalyptic dragon "red," and indeed, the

normally red Welsh dragon was depicted in grey on the queen's investiture throne. This is a literal fulfillment of scripture.

Junor, noting that the Earl of Snowdon "created a perfect theatre in the round," comments, "The soaring walls of the castle were emblazoned by tall, white banners bearing red dragons," overlooking "banks of flame-red seats and a carpet of bright green grass in the middle; and at the focal point, beneath a canopy of clear Perspex bearing the Prince of Wales feathers [with his 'Ich Dien' motto]..., stood three thrones of riven Welsh slate on a 28-foot circular slate dais." As Snowdon put it, "You wouldn't be surprised to see them at Stonehenge, would you?" Of the ceremony, Prince Charles affirmed, "Perhaps it's symbolizing 'Ich Dien', if you like, in some way."[3] Notice this arrangement. Prince Charles' motto, meaning "I serve"

1. Holden, *PRINCE CHARLES*, p. 181.
2. For color photographs of the investiture, including the queen's throne and the prince's coronet and other regalia, see pages 35 and 37 of *Majesty* magazine, Vol. 15, No. 7 (July 1994), and page 18 of *Her Majesty The Queen*. For other photographs showing the thrones, see Jeannie Sakol and Caroline Latham, *An Intimate Look at The Lifestyles of Britain's Royal Family, The Royals* (Chicago: Congdon & Weed, Inc., 1987), p. 151; and Brown, *PRINCE CHARLES*, p. 98.
3. Junor, pp. 84-85.

and "your man," stood directly over the central throne bearing the Welsh dragon, which itself was over green grass.[1] As the queen's and indeed the world's "liege man," the arrangement's message was "I serve the red dragon," or "I serve Satan"—essentially the same message conveyed at the base of the prince's coat of arms.[2] Tim Heald recalls, "[The] investiture was a keynote occasion because it was one of the first royal spectaculars which seemed to have been designed almost entirely for television.... After the ceremony,....[there were] little knots of Welsh matrons gathered by the roadside waving flags, usually the Welsh Dragon of Wales, and crying out 'Ooooh, isn't he lovely!'... We all felt that we were in at the beginning of something special that day in Carnarvon Castle."[3] These same flags, depicting the red dragon, were also waved during the ceremony inside the castle.

Ironically, a short Welsh Bible reading followed Prince Charles' investiture, after which the queen presented her son.[4] Junor recounts, "Next there followed a short interdenominational religious service, conducted in both English and Welsh. This, with the participation of Roman Catholic prelates, was one of the most important innovations since Prince Edward's investiture, and although it was not Prince Charles's own doing he has been very much in favour of ecumenical worship ever since. All that was left was for the monarch to present the Prince of Wales to the people.... [It] had been a glorious, colourful, spine-tingling day. But it was not the pageant that had conquered the Welsh.... It was Prince Charles."[5] As "Prince of the Red Dragon," Prince Charles serves Satan, not God. This is especially disturbing when we consider the fact that, contrary to God's Word, his mother currently is, and he is in line to be, the "Supreme Governor" of the Church of England—the Anglican Protestant Church. Junor, and others

1. The red dragon is typically shown standing on a mount of green grass in Welsh heraldry.
2. For more information, see Chapter 7's section titled, "The base of the coat of arms."
3. Tim Heald, "When hope was born," *International Express*, U.S. Ed. No. 132, 29 June - 5 July 1994, p. 34.
4. Holden, *PRINCE CHARLES*, p. 193. A picture of "the Queen leading Prince Charles through the King's Gate to be presented to the people of Wales" may be found on page 39 of the July 1994 issue of *Majesty* magazine (Vol. 15, No. 7). Also see Junor, between pp. 86-87.
5. Junor, p. 89.

like her, could not be more confused in referring to "state ceremonial involving the monarchy" as "the foremost Protestant ceremonies in the land."[1]

Speaking of his 1969 investiture, Prince Charles recalled, "Within the vast ruin of Caernarvon Castle,...<u>my father invested me</u> as Prince of Wales. Upon my head <u>he</u> put a coronet cap as token of principality, and into my hand the gold verge of government, and on the middle finger the gold ring of res-

dragon of Wales

ponsibility. Then leading me by the hand through an archway to one of the towers of the battlements, <u>he</u> presented me to the people of Wales."[2] Either this is a misquotation, or Charles referred to someone other than his mother and Prince Philip as his "father" in connection with his investiture. It was not Prince Philip, who lacks such authority since he is not the British sovereign, but the queen who placed the coronet upon Prince Charles' head; also, it was not Prince Philip, but the queen who led Prince Charles by the hand to present him to the Welsh people! If we accept the above quote as accurate, we must conclude that Prince Charles could only have been referring to some other "father"—that is, the red dragon or Satan.

Cathcart remarks, "Enter a dragon, a dragon in a red coat. Throughout the summer of 1974, Prince Charles told anyone who would listen how much he was looking forward to flying helicopters.... Hence the dragon, the call-sign from Cranwell dredged up in new guise as the Red Dragon of Wales. The Prince approved the scarlet and gold dragon arm-flashes of his training unit with much

---

1. Junor, p. 85.
2. Holden, *PRINCE CHARLES*, p. 176.

pleasure."[1] Along the same lines, we may note that each June, in the same month as the annual ceremony at Garter Chapel, the queen, Prince Charles, and Prince Philip preside over the annual Trooping *the Colour* military parade outside Buckingham Palace, in which all—including Prince Charles who wears his uniform as Colonel-in-Chief of the Welsh Guards—are dressed in bright *red* and have bearskin hats.[2] As knights of the Order of the Garter, the queen, Prince Charles, Prince Philip, etc., also wear the blue Riband with its Lesser George.[3]

Prince Charles and other British royals would like us to believe that they are Christians, yet the apostle Paul warned the saints, saying, "grievous [savage] wolves will come in among you, not sparing the flock" and "from among yourselves men will rise up, speaking the perverted things, to draw away the disciples after themselves" (Acts 20:29-30, Gk.; cf. Matt 22:11-12; Rev 16:15). Similarly, Jesus said, "Then if anyone says to you, 'Look, here is the Christ!,' or 'Here!,' do not believe *it;* for false christs [messiahs] and false prophets shall arise, and will give great signs and wonders, so as to lead astray [deceive], if possible, even the elect. Look, I tell you beforehand" (Matt 24:23-25, Gk.; cf. Mark 13:21-23).

1. Cathcart, p. 147. Opposite page 121, Cathcart shows a black-and-white photograph of the prince wearing such an arm-flash in a Wessex 5 Commando helicopter.
2. For a color photograph of this uniform, see Burnet, *In Private—In Public, THE PRINCE AND PRINCESS OF WALES,* p. 127. The Duke of Kent also is present in red uniform for this ceremony (*Her Majesty The Queen,* pp. 14-15). On other occasions, Prince Charles also wears a predominantly black uniform, with some red, as Colonel of the Welsh Guards (*Charles & Diana: A Royal Family Album,* p. 87).
3. Hoey, *Charles & Diana: The Tenth Anniversary,* p. 36. *Her Majesty The Queen,* pp. 14-15.

9

Signs of the Times
and
the Rise of "Global Governance"

This chapter, which is excerpted from the author's forthcoming book, *Messiah, History, and the Tribulation Period,* constitutes a helpful background to the following chapters. As we shall see, Prince Charles has championed much of the globalist agenda outlined below.

When various Pharisees and Sadducees came to Jesus to tempt Him, wanting Him to show them a sign from Heaven, He replied, "*When* evening arrives, you say, 'Clear weather—for the sky is red;' and at morning, 'Today, *there will be* a storm—for the sky is red, being overcast.' Hypocrites! Indeed, you know *how* to discern the face of the sky, but you cannot *discern* the signs of the times. A wicked and adulterous generation seeks a sign, but no sign shall be given to it, except the sign of Jonah the prophet" (Matt 16:2-4, Gk.; cf. Luke 12:54-56). The Greek word that Jesus used for "hypocrites" most literally means "actors" or "pretenders."[1] Although it may sound unnecessarily insulting, according to Jesus, those who actually claim that they are God's "well-informed" servants, but who are unable or unwilling discern the signs of the times, are in reality "pretenders" or disingenuous.

Among many in today's Church, this is certainly not a popular message. Yet it is central to our time. Though the "Judaeans request a sign, and the Greeks seek after *worldly* wisdom" (1 Cor 1:22, Gk.; cf. Matt 12:38, 16:4; Mark 8:11; Luke 11:29), we, as true Christians, should be able to discern and recognize the signs of the times that precede Jesus' return. Concerning the signs of His coming, and of the completion of the age (Matt 24:3),

1. Strong's no. 5273.

Jesus forewarned His disciples, saying,

See *that* no one misleads you. For many will come in My name, saying, 'I am the Christ [Messiah],' and will deceive many.[1] But you will hear of wars and rumors of wars. See that you are not troubled; it is right for all *these things* to happen, but the completion [end] is not yet. For race [ethnic group] will rise against race [ethnic group], and kingdom against kingdom.[2] And there will be famines[3] and pestilences[4] and earthquakes against places.[5] But all these *things are* a beginning of sorrows [birth-pangs].[6] Then they will deliver you up to tribulation [affliction], and will kill you, and you will be hated by all the nations for My name. And then many will be offended, will betray one another, and will hate one another. And many false prophets will arise and deceive many. And because lawlessness shall be increased, the love of many will grow cold. But the *one* who endures to the completion, that one shall be delivered [protected, rescued, saved]. And this Gospel of the Kingdom will be proclaimed in all the inhabited world, for a testimony to all the nations, and then the completion will have come.... Immediately after the tribulation of those days the sun will be darkened [obscured], and...the stars will fall from the heaven [sky].... (Matt 24:4-14, 24:29, Gk.; cf. Mark 13:4-13, 13:24-25; Luke 21:7-19, 21:25)

As true students of eschatology acknowledge, the above passage best characterizes, and most literally pertains to, the Tribulation Period. In it, Jesus not only

1. Cf. the many cults in which men claim to be God, gods, Christ, and/or christs.
2. Cf. the numerous wars of this century (e.g., WW I, WW II, the Arab-Israeli wars, etc.).
3. Consider the mass starvations in Angola, Ethiopia, Somalia, Sudan, the Ukraine, and elsewhere in this century. For typical documentation, see Hal Lindsey, *Planet Earth—2000 A.D.* (California: Western Front, Ltd., 1994), pp. 93-94, 123-129.
4. Consider the increase in pestilences such as AIDS, various cancers, Cholera, Ebola, Hepatitis, Hanta (e.g., the Four-Corners disease), Legionnaires disease, Malaria, Tuberculosis, etc., not to mention the many horrific biological weapons that may yet be unleashed. For some typical documentation, see Lindsey, *Planet Earth—2000 A.D.*, pp. 103-116.
5. Compare this prophecy with worldwide high-magnitude earthquake data for the past few centuries, and especially the last five decades. Lindsey offers some typical documentation for just the past ten decades (*Planet Earth—2000 A.D.*, pp. 83-85, 89-90, 96-98).
6. Jesus' point here is not that ethnic conflicts and wars, famines, pestilences, and earthquakes, in various places, are peculiar, but that *all these things occurring simultaneously and increasingly,* so that even the world seems ominously aware, will signify the approach of the Tribulation Period, as well as the start of the birth-pangs of the Great Tribulation. Matthew 24:8, like its parallels in Mark and Luke, does not point to the *first half* of the Tribulation Period, but to the Great Tribulation itself (cf. Rev 6:7-8).
   Unlike any time in history past, life on Earth today, even in its waters, could be extinguished virtually overnight. Not only that, but the simultaneous occurrence of *all* the outlined events is now, *for the first time ever,* actually transpiring. Mankind is experiencing a taste of each of the tribulations of which Jesus and the prophets spoke. From a strictly prophetic view, our generation really is unique.

summarized the major events of the first four seals of the Apocalypse (Rev 6:1-8), but He reached forward to the completion of the tribulation under its seventh seal (Rev 6:12b-17).[1] Without belaboring the point, let it be said that every reasonably informed Christian should recognize and understand that many, if not all, of Jesus' last-days predictions have not only historically been, but are even now being, foreshadowed through contemporary happenings. Moreover, the prophetic scriptures, by their repeated use of the birth-pangs metaphor, clearly indicate that such events will occur on an even greater scale, and at an ever increasing frequency and magnitude, as the time of Jesus' return draws near.

These tribulational events, rather than working to prevent the rise and formation of a world government, as some suppose, are actually the particular disturbances that make such a global authority seem truly necessary and justifiable to the minds of secular men and women for the ultimate survival of mankind. In other words, they really serve to accelerate such a government's impending development. Combined with the often exaggerated and occasionally fabricated environmental and ecological claims and other propaganda, not to mention intentionally created and subsequently "managed" crises and societal ills, of various one-worlders (globalists)—who push their insidious, multifaceted agenda on an often ignorant, gullible, and even eager pagan public—such events undoubtedly constitute an effective catalyst for the appearance of the AntiChrist. Coleman, for example, observes, "Today, we find that some of the largest companies, allegedly 'polluting' the earth, are the largest contributors of funds to the environmentalist movement. The big names send forth their message: Prince Philip is one of their heroes, yet his son Prince Charles, owns a million acres of forested land in Wales from which timber is regularly harvested, and in addition, Prince Charles is one of the biggest owners of slum housing in London, where pollution thrives."[2]

1. For information on the sixth and seventh seals, see the chapter titled "The Order of the Seals, Trumpets, and Bowls" in *Messiah, History, and the Tribulation Period.*
2. *The Committee of 300,* p. 192.

As pantheists and polytheists, globalists assert that humanity is "tired of wars and threats of wars;"[1] that "the greatest hope for the survival of life on earth is the establishment of a democratic world government," which alone "can provide the security and authority necessary;" and that "we are on the threshold of a new world order which promises to usher in an era of peace, prosperity, justice and harmony" through "the principle of unity in diversity."[2] Regarding the increasing frequency and violence of earthquakes and volcanic eruptions, which they take as further indications of the need for a world government, they even suggest that we "read all about it in the daily news."[3] While often suppressing unfavorable scientific data and other detrimental information, they emphatically cite the following needs in arguing for the urgent establishment of a world government to take charge of "world affairs" at "this time of extreme global crises":[4]

Wars, ethnic and non-ethnic

(1) to contain and prevent current and future local and regional wars;

(2) to reduce the threat of war generally through the enforcement of world peace and security;

(3) to reduce the growing threat of a nuclear war, including its radioactive fallout and possible subsequent nuclear winter;

    (a) to safely dispose of nuclear and toxic wastes;

(4) to contain the spread of nuclear weapons;

(5) to control and eventually eliminate weapons of mass destruction (nuclear, chemical, and biological);

(6) to disarm national entities and halt the international trade in arms;

1. Kah, *En Route to Global Occupation*, p. 182.
2. Kah, pp. 175 and 210. Compare this "principle" with the phrase *E PLURIBUS UNUM,* meaning "from pluralism, unity," in the heraldic coat of arms of the United States. For more information, see the section titled, "A Place in the Wilderness, Petra, and the United States of America" in *Messiah, History, and the Tribulation Period.*
3. Kah, p. 199.
4. Kah, p. 170.

(7) to prevent international terrorism;

(8) to ensure tolerance of ethnic, religious, racial, political, and cultural differences;

    (a) to enforce a core set of tolerant, non-fundamentalist, beliefs and values, as determined by international consensus, which is conducive to a world government and the maintenance of international peace and security;

(9) to protect human and minority rights, halt rampant rights violations and discrimination (including sexual), and prevent national governments from becoming dictatorial and tyrannical;[1]

(10) to reduce supranational language barriers through the choice of an official world language (e.g., English, the world's foremost language of commerce);

(11) to indoctrinate and initiate people as Luciferic planetary citizens and world patriots for the common good of humanity;[2]

(12) to peacefully settle all supranational problems;

(13) to help the world's numerous refugees;

Famines and radical climate changes

(14) to halt the current decrease in agricultural productivity, which has led to a dwindling world food supply and numerous famines;

(15) to improve world food distribution mechanisms;

(16) to prevent impending universal crop failures, widespread famines and starvations, and a possible mass starvation of hundreds of millions or even billions of people in the near future through

    (a) population control in overpopulated regions

1. Contrary to their serpentine double-talk, globalists are actually planning to achieve their multicultural, internationally interdependent, New World Order through a tyrannical dictatorship that masquerades itself as a benign democracy. For a typical example, see Mikhail Gorbachev's telling statements in the section titled "New York City and the United Nations—the Heart of Political Babylon/Rome" in *Messiah, History, and the Tribulation Period.*
2. Lindsey, *Planet Earth—2000 A.D.,* p. 43.

209

using readily available, highly encouraged, and even mandatory abortion practices and infanticide, as well as various forms of birth control;[1]

(b) the reduction and eventual prevention, for all practical purposes, of the current supranational environmental pollution of the world's air, water, and land resources, which has resulted not only in radical climate changes such as increasingly frequent and destructive floods and hurricanes, but also in atmospheric ozone depletion, acidic rainfall and snowfall, increasing drought conditions, spreading and expanding deserts, soil erosion, and the rapid loss of topsoil and soil fertility; and

(c) reforestation of the Earth and remineralization of its topsoil;

(17) to reduce the wasteful use of land in producing tobacco and satisfying meats (non-vegetarian) diets;

(18) to halt the worldwide use of harmful pesticides;

(19) to prevent mental malfunctioning resulting from malnutrition, which is a threat to civilization;

(20) to prepare for possible mass migrations of people due to unlivable conditions;

Pestilences and drugs

(21) to stop the modern proliferation of virulent, drug-resistant diseases;

(22) to control and eventually eliminate biological weapons;

(23) to improve human welfare and health;

---

1. At the fourth U.N. Conference on Women, which concerned itself largely with "a woman's right to use the birth-control methods of her choice" and lesbian "rights," the female head of the Vatican delegation voiced this dire warning regarding the "Beijing Declaration" (named for the conference's location in China, the child-murdering capital of the world): "This document is obsessed only by the sexual reproductive aspect of women.... It could be turned into a license of coercive population control [as in China] and the practice of the unspeakable crime of abortion" (Uli Schmetzer, "U.N. forum ends in dispute over women's sexual rights," *The Denver Post*, 17 Sept. 1995, p. 18A).

(24) to prevent the use of harmful drugs and alco-
holism, and stop the drug trade;

Earthquakes and volcanic eruptions

(25) to effectively deal with the increasing frequency and magnitude of earthquakes;
(26) to address the increasing frequency and violence of volcanic eruptions, which spread
smoke and dust over wide areas and thus
reduce sunlight reaching the Earth's surface;

The sea and the waves roaring
(see Luke 21:25-26)[1]

(27) to deal with increasingly frequent and destructive floods and hurricanes, and address the
threat of a new ice age or melting polar ice
caps;

Falling Stars
(nuclear war, and comet and asteroid strikes)

(28) to internationalize efforts, such as those of the
United States, to defend against limited nuclear
missile threats;
(29) to internationally coordinate nuclear arsenals,
and possibly create a specific arsenal, to
defend the Earth against limited comet and
asteroid threats;[2]

Other—environmental

(30) to protect dwindling and jeopardized energy
resources such as Mideast oil;
(31) to develop safe (environmentally friendly) and
sustainable energy supplies;
(32) to eliminate pollution and other dangers from
nuclear power plants, and safely dispose of
radioactive waste;
(33) to save the environment and world ecology
from current and impending environmental
crises;

---

1. For some related documentation, see Lindsey, *Planet Earth—2000 A.D.*, pp. 86-91.
2. For more information, see the sections titled "Blood, Fire, and Palm-Trees of Smoke" and "Falling Stars" in *Messiah, History, and the Tribulation Period*.

(34) to avert or minimize extreme global climatic, environmental, ecological, and social catastrophes for everybody;

(35) to halt the current massive deforestation of the world, and reduce forest fires and oceanic pollution, all of which threaten the world's oxygen and fish supplies;

(36) to prevent the extinction and loss of species;

Other—political, economic, and legal

(37) to integrate differing political and economic systems, and overcome national sovereignties to solve supranational problems;

(38) to enforce international law through world courts having mandatory jurisdiction;

(39) to implement and enforce world legislation;

(40) to handle the transition to a new world economic order;

(41) to retire the massive world debt, for which a new global system of finance and credit, including a world currency, is imperative;

(42) to address the inequitable use of natural resources, and plan globally for their wise use and necessary preservation as a common heritage;

(43) to guarantee full employment in the face of widespread poverty, unemployment, and social unrest;

(44) to reduce and eventually eliminate the vast disparities between economies, as well as the primitive lifestyles of many peoples; and

(45) to determine who owns the atmosphere and stratosphere, and facilitate space exploration as a global project.[1]

From the above information, we should realize that those who claim to be enlightened while simultaneously denying or even ridiculing the contemporary existence of

1. Kah, pp. 43, 170-182, 192-200, 210. Also see Lindsey, *Planet Earth—2000 A.D.*, pp. 43-44, 47-48.

eschatologically significant events, whether they be laymen or distinguished seminary professors, are *perhaps* much akin to the *hypocrites* of Jesus' day (see Matt 16:2-4, KJV; cf. Luke 12:54-56), being in reality insufficiently grounded in The Word of God. Indeed, their thinking is not too unlike that of the prophesied scoffers who say, "Where is the promise of His coming? For since the fathers fell asleep, all things remain [continue] as from the beginning of creation" (2 Pet 3:3-4, Gk.). Although Peter forewarned the saints in this very context, saying, "But beloved, do not let this one thing be hidden from you, that with The Lord one day *is* as a thousand years, and a thousand years as one day" (2 Pet 3:8, Gk.; cf. Ps 90:4), these individuals are yet unmindful of the Bible's seven-millennia—or seven-day—chronology, to which the writings of the entire early Church, and ancient Israel, attest. Consequently, they fail to discern that inasmuch as the world is now demonstrably close to the end of the sixth millennium, Jesus' return and the ensuing Sabbath Millennium—the Millennial Kingdom (cf. Heb 4:3-11)—*must* be quite near.[1] This blindness and confusion, for which the *royal-blooded* Charles Darwin is partially to blame, is one of the unwholesome fruits of a replacement theology that has generally rejected Israel in scriptural eschatology in favor of *a supplanting Church* (see Hos 6:1-2; cf. Ps 90:12-17). Moreover, it foreshadows the frog-like spiritual deception that is to engross the world—through Satan, the AntiChrist, and the false prophet—before Christ's return (see Rev 16:13-14); for just as a frog cannot detect a gradual increase in heat, so that it would sooner boil to death in a formerly cool pot of water than leap to safety, the blind cannot see how markedly the present differs from the past, indicating Christ's soon return. They fail to discern the signs of the times.

---

1. For more information, see the chapter titled "A Consistent Biblical Chronology" in *Messiah, History, and the Tribulation Period*.

10

Religious, Political, and Other Ties

Prince Charles' possible claims to leadership of the Jewish and Muslim populations of the world, as well as the final form of the Roman Empire, through his purported lineage, were addressed in Chapter 4, "Prince of this World—a *Diverse* Lineage." Below, we will consider Prince Charles' so-called 'Christian' heritage, his marital infidelity—including Princess Diana's death—and its potential impact upon his future, his political affiliations, aspirations, and privileges, and his ties to the New Age Movement, the occult, and false religions, including Islam. Although this is a *large* chapter, its information is vital.

A so-called 'Christian' heritage.   Although Prince Charles was only nineteen at the time, Dermot Morrah wrote, "No British prince since the Stuarts has cared more sincerely for the things of the mind and the spirit."[1] We may view Morrah's statement as a veiled and somewhat gross reference to King James I, who gave us the Authorized King James Version translation of the Bible.   Prince Charles, of course, has Stuart blood.[2] Of the prince's supposed Christian roots and convictions, Holden notes that Charles opposes racial prejudice and actively campaigns on behalf of the environment, and that he differs from his father in that he is "circumspect, gentle, and kindhearted."[3] In fact, the prince appears to be a bit of a "social worker," endeavoring to help the poor and the disadvantaged.[4] As the "Great Master" (cf. Matt 23:10, AKJV) and Principal Knight Grand Cross of the Order of the Bath, which supposedly ranks third to England's Garter and Scotland's Thistle among British knighthoods and is the

1. Holden, *PRINCE CHARLES,* pp. 250-251.
2. For more information, see Chapter 4, "Prince of this World—a *Diverse* Lineage."
3. Holden, *PRINCE CHARLES,* pp. 18-19, 72.
4. Holden, *PRINCE CHARLES,* pp. 270-282.

"premier meritorious Order of the Crown,"[1] Prince Charles has "vowed 'to defend maidens, widows, and orphans.'"[2] The prince, as Alstair Burnet puts it, "has a list of good causes to support that far outnumber the regiments whose uniform[s] he wears...."[3] Like the Order of the Garter, which meets in St. George's Chapel, knights of both the Order of the Thistle and the Order of the Bath meet in a church's chapel to provide those orders a "Christian" veneer in the eyes of the public, and to cloak their private antichristian and even outright satanic activities. The Order of the Thistle, officially instituted by Scotland's King James VII, who was otherwise known as England's King James II, in 1687, meets in the chapel of St. Giles' Church in Edinburgh, Scotland. Similarly, the Order of the Bath, founded by Henry IV in 1399 and later revived by George I in 1725, has met in King Henry VII's Chapel in Westminster Abbey since 1725.[4]

With "water from the River Jordan," the infant Prince Charles was christened in December 1948.[5] In 1965, at the age of sixteen, he received his Anglican Protestant confirmation, having supposedly had a "keen interest" in Scripture.[6] According to Holden, the Dean of Windsor was "gratified to find the prince unassailed by doubts."[7] His father, Prince Philip, on the other hand, found the "ritualistic Greek Orthodoxy of his childhood, Salem's austere German Protestantism, and the social conventions of established Anglicanism as practiced in the navy and by the royal family all combined to make him cynical of Christianity for some time—agnostic, atheist even. Friends have known him to phone at odd hours to discuss some

1. Conrad Swan, "Bath, The Most Honourable Order of the," *A Dictionary of Heraldry*, ed. Friar, p. 48.
2. Holden, *PRINCE CHARLES*, pp. 216-217.
3. Alstair Burnet, *In Person, THE PRINCE AND PRINCESS OF WALES* (New York: Summit Books, 1985), p. 8.
4. Boutell, 1978 ed., pp. 194, 196; and James and Russell, *At Home with the Royal Family*, p. 52. Similarly, "In 1484 the Kings, Heralds and Pursuivants [of the College of Heraldry], while remaining officers of the Royal Household, were incorporated by Charter,...called 'Coldearber' in the Parish of All Saints the Less in the City of London" (Boutell, 1978 ed., p. 262).
5. Cathcart, p. 11.
6. Holden, *PRINCE CHARLES*, pp. 141-142. Cathcart, p. 37.
7. Holden, *PRINCE CHARLES*, p. 18.

philosophical abstraction, and he can revel in theological arguments with the clerics who are official—and personal—guests of the Queen.... But from his own uncertain spiritual quest came misgivings that Prince Charles should be confirmed as early as sixteen."[1] Prince Philip, as "Master of the Bench of [the] Inner Temple" since 1954, honorary member of the Goat Club and the Danish Dragon Club, and Patron of the Lucifer Golfing Society, clearly remains antichristian.[2]

An outward contrast to Prince Philip, Prince Charles, for his twenty-first birthday, "rose early...to visit the Chapel Royal of St John in the Tower of London in the company of Princess Anne and the Queen Mother to make 'an act of thanksgiving and dedication for his future life'."[3] The prince has observed, "Where Christianity is new it must be much easier to enter into the whole spirit of it whole-heartedly."[4] Junor, evincing the wool pulled over her eyes, commented, "He had been to church regularly throughout his childhood, and...he had been confirmed by the Archbishop of Canterbury, Michael Ramsey, in St George's Chapel, Windsor. One day, as heir to the throne, he would be Head of the Church of England; a belief in God and an acceptance of the teachings of the Church

1. Lacey, *Majesty,* pp. 254-255. Speaking of a Christian veneer, James and Russell add, "One regular but little-known event is the Royal Epiphany Service held on 6 January every year in celebration of the Three Kings' arrival in Bethlehem.... Originally it was the time when the Sovereign gave alms to the poor and needy, and although the ceremony still takes place in the Chapel Royal, the monarch has not been present since...the Hanovarian King George III curtailed many English customs.... The Gentlemen Ushers take the Queen's gifts in procession to the high altar: twenty-five gold sovereigns, frankincense and myrrh carried on silver gilt.... [The]...Queen does not attend the Epiphany Service mainly because it coincides with her winter retreat to Sandringham.... Like the Epiphany Service, the Royal Maundy has a Christian significance, representing as it does the Last Supper.... King George VI only personally attended seven times, but Elizabeth II has personally distributed the Maundy [money] every year of her reign, other than when prevented by pregnancy" (*At Home with the Royal Family,* pp. 151-153). "Ever since the Reformation there have been clergymen in the Royal Household, headed by the Clerk of the Closet, since 1096 the private confessor of the sovereign. There are thirty-six chaplains who are appointed by the Clerk of the Closet.... There are [also] Extra Chaplains, clergymen who have reached the age of 70 and are appointed for their long and distinguished service. There are two Priests in Ordinary who attend services on a rota basis and with the Domestic Chaplain attend to the pastoral care of the Household and Her Majesty's staff" (ibid., p. 195; for details, see pp. 211-213).
2. Judd, *Prince Philip,* pp. 251-252.
3. Cathcart, p. 99. Speaking of the "Queen Mother," Junor notes, "Prince Charles is utterly devoted to his grandmother. It was she who virtually brought him up" (p. 14).
4. Cathcart, p. 65. Junor, p. 57.

were fundamental to his existence. He did, nevertheless, have a genuine faith—one which has remained strong to the present day.... Prince Charles was and still is...an extremely moral and religious man, and fundamentally conservative."[1] (Since the *exceedingly* lewd "Camillagate" conversations between the prince and his mistress, Camilla Parker Bowles, were aired, however, Junor has admitted, "I thought he was better than that.")

Subsequently, on July 29, 1981, Prince Charles and Lady Diana Spencer were married in what appeared to be a generally orthodox Christian wedding, one that was filled with pomp and pageantry.[2] However, like other symbols that may have a dual interpretation—as pagans who favor a Zoroastrian (Babylonian) approach to spirituality, religion, and religious terminology, prefer—the red cross of Merovée, as opposed to the true cross of Christ, was, from the oligarchists' perspective, central to the entire proceeding.[3] In other words, what the British monarchy saw and heard in the ceremony, for example, differs tremendously from what true Christians would have gotten from it. The wedding featured prayers from "representatives of four different churches," including the Roman Catholic Cardinal Hume.[4] A similar ecumenicalism was seen in the earlier wedding of Princess Elizabeth II to Prince Philip, in which Roman Catholic bishops participated.[5] Subsequently, prayers were supposedly a part of the Wales' family routine: "Prince Charles and his wife involve their children in almost everything they do at Highgrove, so before they eat their evening meal together they join...in the nursery for family prayers. This has been the custom since the children were old enough to take part and both parents regard it as an important end to the day and it is something they try never to miss."[6]

Prince Charles, who is slated to one day head the roughly seventy million members of the Anglican

1. Junor, pp. 58, 72.
2. Spink, pp. 6-7, 91-113.
3. Hoey, *Charles & Diana: The Tenth Anniversary,* p. 17.
4. Hoey, *Charles & Diana: The Tenth Anniversary,* p. 64.
5. Judd, *Prince Philip,* p. 131.
6. Hoey, *Charles & Diana: The Tenth Anniversary,* p. 148.

Protestant Church,[1] "is anxious to use his position to encourage rapprochement with Rome."[2] The history of interactions between the Vatican and the British monarchy is filled with twists and turns, as well as alliances at different points. A brief history, as it relates to the prince, follows.

Edward III formed the College of St. George at Windsor Castle in 1348 "as parallel and supportive to his foundation of the Order of the Garter." Yet the Roman pontiff authorized its formation in 1350. Originally, the organization of the college was to include "thirteen Canons, one of whom should be the Warden, a title later changed to Dean, together with thirteen Priest Vicars, later to be Minor Canons, making twenty-six priests in all"—one priest for each of the twenty-six Garter knights. Besides the priests, the college was to include twenty-six bedesmen, now called "military knights." The bedesmen "were to pray daily for the Sovereign and the Knights Companion [of the Order of the Garter] during life and for their souls after death." In other words, the college was to have a coven of 13 priests and a coven of 13 bedesmen for the sovereign and twelve Garter knights, as well as an identical arrangement for the Prince of Wales and twelve Garter knights. Currently, the college consists of the Dean, four Canons, and two Minor Canons, for a total of seven *secular* priests, besides a significant choir. Elizabeth I reduced the number of military knights, who today take part in the ceremonies of the order at St. George's Chapel, to thirteen, leaving just one coven of military knights. Although secular, "[they] have, through the centuries taken part in the religious observances of the Order as well as praying daily for the Sovereign and the Order....: 'God save...all the Companions, living and departed, of the Most Honourable and Noble Order of the Garter.'"[3] This arrangement of covens is in harmony with the Order of the Garter itself.[4] Years later,

1. The Associated Press, "Church of England approves ordination of women priests," *The Denver Post*, 23 Feb. 1994, p. 2A.
2. Holden, *PRINCE CHARLES*, p. 18.
3. Begent, pp. 2, 13. See James and Russell, *At Home with the Royal Family*, pp. 158, 201.
4. For more information, see the discussion on the Garter in Chapter 7, "The Heraldic Symbols in the Arms and their Interpretations."

Pope Leo X gave Henry VIII, who used the red dragon (symbolic of Satan) as a royal device, the title *Fidei Defensor,* or "Defender of the Faith," in connection with Roman Catholicism (see below). Cathcart observes, "At St George's Chapel, Windsor, it was noted that Charles became a frequent communicant."[1]

Following World War II, the British government "recognized the temporal authority claimed by the Pope." It is unlikely that such a recognition could have occurred apart from the approval of the monarchy. More recently, in 1980, Queen Elizabeth II and Prince Philip, dressed entirely in black, visited Pope John Paul II, dressed entirely in white, at the Vatican: "since 1980, the Royal Court of St. James has had a Papal Nuncio (a Vatican ambassador to a foreign court). Relations were improved further when the Queen visited the Pope at the Vatican and willingly wore black in order to be received by him. Perceived by successive popes as a heretic, the Queen would not have been granted an audience unless she had symbolically submitted herself to the radiance of his whiteness. This she did, to the dismay of many Christians back home, and to the insult of those Protestant martyrs who died during the reigns of her forebears."[2] (Notice the *Zoroastrian contrast* between the forces of darkness and those of "light.")

During their "historic visit," in an *unprecedented and remarkably blatant* overture, the queen not only wore her Garter Star and Riband openly, but actually was photographed wearing and fully exposing her light blue Garter just above the elbow on her left arm before the pope. The same photograph also shows, less clearly, Prince Philip wearing and exposing his Garter, just below his left knee.[3] Bear in mind that this was *not* a Garter ceremony. In purposely exposing their garters to the pope, the queen and Prince Philip were, as far as the occult symbolism is concerned, actually holding out the possibility of an

---

1. Cathcart, p. 66.
2. Hilton, *The Principality and Power of Europe,* pp. 52-53.
3. "A Snapshot in Time: An Informal Pictorial History of the Queen's Reign," *Majesty* magazine, Feb. 1992, Vol. 13, No. 2, on p. 12 of special insert between pp. 34-35. Of the Garter, Begent states, "It is worn by the Knights below the left knee and by Ladies above the left elbow" (p. 3). For more information, see Chapter 7's section titled, "The Garter."

alliance between the Order of the Garter and the Vatican (cf. the AntiChrist and the false prophet).   To the author's knowledge, this is the only published photograph of any Garter member actually exposing the Garter, let alone in such a high-level setting.   Clearly, the monarchy wished to send a message.

Since at least the early 1980s, Prince Charles, apparently following the same agenda, has been at the forefront of those advocating rapprochement between the Roman Catholic and Anglican Protestant churches. (Such an occasion, if it were to occur, would no doubt affect other liberal denominations as well.)   In 1982, Pope John Paul II visited Britain, where he participated in an ecumenical service under the authority of Robert Runcie, the Archbishop of Canterbury and a member of the Committee of 300.   The two "knelt together in prayer in an historic act of reconciliation" at Canterbury Cathedral.   "The Prince, as heir apparent and prospective Supreme Governor of the Church of England, sat in the place usually occupied by the sovereign and was later photographed in conversation with the Pope before a brief private audience with him in the Deanery.   The 'Celebration of Faith', as the service had been ecumenically entitled, was a resounding triumph" involving Christians and non-Christians alike.   "This rapprochement reached its culmination when Pope John Paul II visited Britain in 1982, the first Pope to do so since the Reformation. He held joint services with the Archbishop of Canterbury and was received by the Queen.   Since then, there have been further meetings between the Pope and prominent members of the Royal Family, and also between the Pope and the present Archbishop of Canterbury, Dr George Carey. In former times, such a series of happenings would have been unthinkable."[1]   "By 1985, relations between the Vatican and Lambeth Palace were warmer than ever.   In this climate, the Prince wanted to use his visit to Italy to make a further gesture of reconciliation towards Rome....   The Archbishop favoured 'a special service' in St Peter's to celebrate what would have been the first formal act of reconciliation between the papacy and the royal family since

1. Hilton, *The Principality and Power of Europe*, p. 52.

the excommunication of Henry VIII.... Instead, it was agreed that the Prince and Princess should attend the Pope's domestic eucharist in his private chapel. As the Prince would not partake of communion,...only 'the extreme minority' who rejected the Pope's spiritual and ecclesiastical position could dissent.... [The]...Archbishop declared that by attending a private mass in the Vatican, the Prince would be far more effective...in moving the Pope more firmly in favour of ecumenicism.... [The] Prince would cause scandal in Britain only to 'a few on the lunatic fringe.'"[1] Those on the "lunatic fringe," by such a definition, would include true Christians. Nevertheless, it is Runcie, the queen's former pet priest, who is apostate: "The Archbishop of Canterbury, Robert Runcie, has hosted in Canterbury Cathedral the 'Canterbury Festival of Faith and the Environment' featuring 'joint prayer and worship...with Buddhists, Muslims, Baha'is, Jews, Sikhs, and Hindus.'"[2] Moreover, "Runcie...knowingly ordained practising homosexual clergy."[3]

On April 29, 1985, Prince Charles and Princess Diana, each dressed in black, approached the Vatican for their audience with John Paul II, dressed in white (a Zoroastrian contrast).[4] Describing the pope's as "the ultimate presence," the prince had intended to celebrate mass with the pope privately, only to be thwarted at the last moment. While Dimbleby asserts that the queen had not been previously informed of the plan, Junor correctly states, "He was prevented, not by the Queen, as was reported at the time, but by politicians and the church hierarchy."[5] The audience itself, however, proceeded nonetheless. The prince and the pope "talked about unity between the different branches of the Christian faith," the pope noting that "the Anglican Church was in fact closer to the Catholics than the Orthodox at the present time." The prince went on to express his admiration for "the spiritual leadership he so clearly provided in such a difficult and uncertain world."

1. Dimbleby, *The Prince of Wales*, pp. 348-351.
2. Hunt, *GLOBAL PEACE AND THE RISE OF ANTICHRIST*, p. 173.
3. Hilton, *The Principality and Power of Europe*, p. 52.
4. For a photograph of this event, see Hoey, *Charles & Diana: The Tenth Anniversary*, p. 131.
5. Junor, p. 260.

Although Prince Charles did not get to celebrate mass with the pope, an unprecedented gesture from the future head of the Anglican Protestant Church, he nevertheless "asked the Pope to bless them—'which he did very briefly by making the sign of the cross over us.'" The Vatican, for its part, asserted that were it not for "a last-minute cancellation, the Prince would have taken part in an historic act of reconciliation with the Church of Rome." Although various protests were made, such as that of one Christian who noted that Prince Charles had been "ill-advised in spiritual matters by some who have departed from the true teaching of the inspired, infallible and inerrant way of God," the prince wrote a reply denouncing "bigotry and prejudice in all its forms," adding that such attitudes were "the main cause of so much human suffering and misery."[1] Put more mildly, the prince feels that doctrinal disagreement among Christians causes "needless distress."[2] Junor, again showing the wool pulled over her eyes, commented, "Charles is naturally tolerant of other people's views.... It was no surprise, therefore, that he should have wanted to attend a private Mass with the Pope...in 1985—not because of any weakness in his own Anglican faith, but because he believes that by demonstrating religious tolerance himself he might in some way be able to ease the tension between Anglicans and Catholics, especially in Northern Ireland.... [The] Prince was nevertheless bitterly upset and angry. A year later, while staying privately with some Catholic friends,...he accompanied them to a little country church and heard Mass."[3]

Hilton, who starts from the mistaken view that the British monarchy has ever been, and is supposed to be, a truly Christian institution, something which it has *never* been, comments,

> After the Reformation and the adoption of the 39 Articles of

---

1. Dimbleby, *The Prince of Wales,* pp. 347-348, 352-354. While studying at Trinity College, Cambridge, Prince Charles, along with "several of his friends," was "thoroughly inspired" by the apostate "Reverend" Harry Williams, who, as a Fellow of the college, "had written several lively and provocative books including *Objections to Christian Belief and The God I Want*" (Junor, pp. 75-76).
2. Holden, *PRINCE CHARLES,* p. 287.
3. Junor, p. 260.

the Church of England, the Church and State laid their foundations upon the authority of the Bible and a Protestant monarchy.
However, the present Queen, in 1996, appointed an influential
Roman Catholic as her chaplain, and attended Vespers in Westminster Cathedral to celebrate the centenary of the building of
Britain's Roman Catholic centre. Further, Prince Charles, the Heir
to the Throne, is professing an allegiance not to biblical Christianity but to all faiths. The Coronation Oath is clearly being ignored
and undermined through these changes, in a prelude to the
removal of the *Act of Settlement* of 1701, which does not permit
a Roman Catholic, or a monarch married to a Roman Catholic, to
accede to the throne. If this happened, for the first time since the
Glorious Revolution of 1688, Rome would be provided with a vassal monarch with sovereignty over 'Mary's dowry' [(i.e., the
United Kingdom)]. This would inevitably lead to the ascendancy
of Roman traditions over the authority of Scripture which lies at
the heart of Protestantism and the institution of the Monarchy....

....The prospect of the removal of the *Act of Settlement* from
the Statute Books, a change which the Queen and other senior
members of the Royal Family are reported to favour, would be the
crowning glory of the Anglo-Roman Catholic International Commission. The signs are already evident. On the significance of
Prince Charles' bedside rosary, a gift from the Pope, The *Sunday Telegraph* reported: 'How changed is our country. Even 30
years ago, the news that the future Supreme Governor of the
Church of England practised what would have been considered a
Popish superstition would have provoked outrage. A century
before it might have provoked revolution....'

....Lord St John of Fawsley, a devout Roman Catholic...seems
to have become the Queen's personal spokesman. The fact that
the Supreme governor of the Church of England is surrounded by
such influential Roman Catholics highlights the progressive Anglican subjection to the Papacy....

It is curious that with an ecumenical climate in which it is not
supposed to matter which denomination one belongs to, the
recent high-profile conversions to Rome of leading politicians and
members of the Royal Family have enjoyed huge media attention,
as have the conversions of members of the Anglican clergy.[1]

The British monarchy's apparent agenda to "break
down the walls" between Roman Catholicism and not just
Anglican Protestantism, but Christianity generally, has
taken hold of some of Christianity's most prominent

---

1. Hilton, *The Principality and Power of Europe*, pp. 53, 55, 173. Junor adds, "According to the
   Act of Settlement of 1701, which was drawn up to prevent descendants of the [Roman]
   Catholic King James II from returning to the throne, those who inherit the crown are forbid-
   den 'to be reconciled to or hold communion with the See or Church of Rome'" (p. 260).

spokespersons, including such men and women as Charles Colson and Paul and Jan Crouch, who head the Trinity Broadcasting Network (TBN)! Although sincere in their desires and efforts to serve Christ, despite some significant deviations from sound doctrine, they have *unwittingly* allowed themselves to be compromised through their direct association with Queen Elizabeth II and Prince Philip.

Charles (Chuck) Colson, for example—who, like so many professing Christians, confusedly calls the pagan and now-deceased "Mother Teresa," who accepted false beliefs as potentially leading to salvation, a "Christian"—has stated on Christian radio that he received his Templeton Prize for Progress in Religion award money, on behalf of Prison Fellowship, from the hands of Prince Philip at Buckingham Palace! A moving and often tremendous apologist for the faith, Colson was awarded the prize, the monetary value of which "exceeds every other established award, including the Nobel prizes," for having "shown 'extraordinary originality in advancing humankind's understanding of God.'" Named as the recipient of the Templeton Prize in March 1993, just one year later, in March 1994, Colson (a Protestant), along with Richard John Neuhaus (a Roman Catholic), rocked evangelical Christianity with the release of a joint Protestant and Roman Catholic declaration entitled, "Evangelicals and Catholics Together: The Christian Mission in the Third Millennium." Although mostly sound in its statements, the declaration put aside major differences of belief to leave the *general public* with the *intended misperception* that the declaration's "Roman Catholic" participants and signers represented typical Roman Catholic belief, and vice versa, which they do not. The net effect, of course, was to leave the public with the false view that true Christian belief and typical Roman Catholic belief are not really all that far apart, and that the two really should join ranks. Whether or not this is the current understanding of Colson, it is an important goal of the British monarchy, which has been happy to employ his talents in accomplishing it. If and when the pope partners as the false prophet with the AntiChrist, so that one represents Roman Catholicism and the other *supposedly* Protestantism and the Reformation, such public confusion will only harm the Church by tending to leave it in the middle, where *both* Roman Catholicism and apostate Protestantism *may be accepted,* rather than polarizing it squarely on the side of the truth of the Reformation. Hunt, in *A Woman Rides the Beast,* states, "The most significant event in nearly 500 years of church history was revealed as a *fait accompli* on March 29, 1994. On that day leading American evangelicals and [Roman] Catholics signed a joint declaration titled 'Evangelicals and Catholics Together: The Christian Mission in the 3rd Millennium.' The document, in effect, overturned the Reformation and will unquestionably have far-reaching repercussions throughout the Christian world for years to come. This startling development was the culmination of careful planning and negotiations over the previous two years. Each step was continuously monitored and approved by the Vatican."[1] All this, of course, is *not* meant to detract from Colson's eloquent, inspiring, and at times *brilliant* defense of Christianity, including on September 2, 1993, at the University of Chicago, before an ecumenist audience which included "many delegates of the Parliament of the World's Religions."[2]

TBN, on the other hand, has now made famous its own heraldic crest, which, perhaps from ignorance, parodies the opposing lion and unicorn arrangement of the ancient Assyrian and Babylonian religious seals.[3] TBN's unicorn, however, differs markedly from the pagan goat-unicorn of standard heraldry; although its eyes have a human profile, like those of the goat-unicorn on Prince Charles' achievement, and its horn is blended into the crest's mantle, it otherwise looks like a horse.[4] Nevertheless, its arrangement seems to derive from the same source as that of the British monarchy's heraldic achievements. When this

---

1. Dave Hunt, *A Woman Rides the Beast* (Oregon: Harvest House Publishers, 1994), p. 5. For more information, see *A Woman Rides the Beast*.
2. Charles W. Colson, "The Enduring Revolution: 1993 Templeton Address," *SOURCES,* No. 4, p. 2; Colson and Richard John Neuhaus, "Evangelicals & Catholics Together: The Christian Mission in the Third Millennium," *First Things,* May 1994; and "Evangelicals & Catholics Together," 15 June 1994. For these and other materials, contact Prison Fellowship.
3. See Chapter 6, "The First Beast and Prince Charles' Coat of Arms."
4. See Chapter 7's section titled, "The sinister (right-hand) supporter."

author approached Paul Crouch for support in disseminating this work, inasmuch as he heads the world's largest Christian television broadcasting network, he politely but curiously replied, "TBN does not promote materials outside of those that we use for our own ministry purposes."[1] While wondering how it could be that *credibly* revealing the plausible identity of the AntiChrist fails to accord with TBN's "ministry purposes," the author learned that Paul and Jan Crouch, as aired on TBN itself, had recently met with Queen Elizabeth II and Prince Philip to brief them on plans for various future TBN activities!

That the British monarchy sits at the top of a global neo-Babylonian system seems evident. Additional illustrations may be offered. John Daniel, for example, observes,

> In January 1983 the Queen and her consort toured the United States. There seemed to be no apparent reason for her visit, other than the honor bestowed on her by the Bohemian Club....
>
> The Bohemian Club is a West Coast center for the inner elite of Templar Scottish Rite Freemasonry in the United States. Some of its members are Senator Alan Cranston, [former] FBI Director William Webster, [and] former secretaries of state George Shultz and Henry Kissinger.[2]
>
> On February 3, 1983, a five minute segment of the Bohemian Club's extravaganza in honor of Queen Elizabeth was aired on all three television networks. The event began with a view of the Queen sitting slightly high in the middle of the auditorium, as if on top of a pyramid. Two dancers entered the stage wearing huge hats hanging from cables. The cone of the first hat was representative of a walled city with a pyramid, or ziggurat towering in the middle. Obviously, it portrayed ancient Babylon. At the base of the pyramid two doors continuously flapped open and shut displaying inside a large picture of Prince Charles, successor to the British throne, and his wife, Princess Diana.... The cone on the second hat portrayed the city of London, with Big Ben towering in the center. [Then]...a voice bellowed, "Oh Queen, you have

1. Correspondence from Paul F. Crouch, dated December 9, 1997.
2. Senator Alan Cranston has been a lead U.S. participant in the Global Security Programme initiated by Prince Charles, and is Chairman of the Board of the Gorbachev Foundation USA. Shultz and Kissinger, on the other hand, are both prominent members of the Committee of 300. Finally, recall that Prince Charles' *Ich Dien* motto was taken from the defeated King of *Bohemia* by the Black Prince after the Battle of Crécy. For more information, see the related notes in the discussion on the Committee of 300 in the subsection titled "Garter 'placement'" in Chapter 7's discussion on the Garter, as well as Chapter 11's section titled "Global Governance, the Global Security Programme, and a possible 'Economic Security Council.'" Also, see Chapter 7's section titled, "The motto and the heir-apparent's badge."

227

traversed the ages from Babylon to London!" Ever so slightly, and without a smile, Queen Elizabeth nodded as if in agreement to the statement.

That night the Bohemian Club, an arm of Templar Scottish Rite Freemasonry, [apparently] acknowledged London as the seat of Mystery Babylon. Queen Elizabeth accepted that acknowledgment.[1]

As Hilton puts it, "The Vatican recognises that the defeat of Protestantism here would weaken it throughout all Europe." Noting a *Catholic Herald* prediction that the "days of the Anglican Church are numbered, and most of its worshipers will return to the true faith of their distant medieval forebears," he observes,

> It is almost a symbolic fulfillment of that prophecy that the 20 pence coin of the British colony Gibraltar, issued by Parliament and approved by the Queen, bears an engraving of Mary crowned 'Queen of Heaven' and titled 'Our Lady of Europa'. The head of the Queen on the other side is simply titled 'Elizabeth II—Gibraltar', without her usual titles of D.G. REG. F.D.—Queen by the Grace of God, Defender of the Faith. As portentous as such obvious Roman Catholic symbolism is [in connection with Europe's "goddess worship" and Queen Elizabeth II], the British postage stamps issued in 1984 to commemorate the second election to the European Parliament went even further. They depicted a whore riding a beast over seven mounds or waves. Such imagery has startling similarities to passages from the book of *Revelation* which a succession of theologians from Wycliffe to Spurgeon has identified as representing Papal Rome.
>
> Roman Catholic imagery is endemic in Europe, and has been wholeheartedly embraced by the European government. The design of the European flag was inspired by the halo of 12 stars around pictures of the [Black] Madonna [which, the Vatican claims, represents the glorified woman of Revelation 12 rather than a demonic impostor], and appears prominently on the Council of Europe stained-glass window in Strasbourg Cathedral.[2]

Prince Charles' ecumenicalism is not limited to

1. John Daniel, *Scarlet and the Beast*, Vol. II, 1st ed. (Texas: Jon Kregel, Inc., 1994), pp. 25-26.
2. Hilton, *The Principality and Power of Europe*, pp. 48-49. This window shows the "goddess" "holding the 1000-year-old symbol of political unification—the crown of the Holy Roman Empire" (ibid., copyright page). Actually, it is the crown of Charlemagne or "Charles." According to Hilton, "Europe was consecrated to Mary by the Vatican in 1309, and placed under her patronage. The shrine of 'Our Lady of Europa', in Gibraltar, was instituted at the consecration. This shrine is being renovated" (ibid., p. 35).

Protestant Christianity and Roman Catholicism. As an ecumenist and Garter Illuminist who, as heir to the British throne, is *over* Freemasonry worldwide,[1] the prince also embraces the occult, cults, and false religions in general:

> He believes that racial and religious differences, and a lack of understanding of other people's cultures and traditions, are the most explosive issues of the day. They are the cause of tension, bloodshed and misery not just on the streets of Britain but all over the world; and have been for centuries.... In opening the Tenth International Council Meeting of UWC [(United World Colleges)] in 1985 he said, 'It is a great pity that there aren't enough students from the Middle Eastern countries. There aren't enough Moslem students. One of the great problems, it seems to me, is the increasing degree of misunderstanding between the Islamic approach to life and indeed the misunderstanding between different branches of the Islamic faith. To...improve understanding in Britain, where large numbers of Moslems live, the Prince suggested to Sir Richard Attenborough that he should produce a series for Channel 4 television to explain a variety of different religious beliefs. The Prince contributed a foreword....
>
> ....The Prince is unlikely to abandon his ecumenical lead. He sees it not as a failure to uphold the Protestant reformed religion, but as another pragmatic step to meet the needs of modern society.[2]

> The Prince has said he wants to be called "defender of faith" and not "defender of THE faith" when he becomes king.
>
> The move, making him a figurehead for all religions and denominations in Britain, would end a 450-year tradition....
>
> The Prince says: "I happen to believe that the Catholic subjects of the sovereign are as important as Protestants, not to mention the Islamic, Hindu and Zoroastrian."...
>
> One of Charles's friends added: "...What the Prince is saying is not out of step with some senior churchmen.
>
> "What is so wrong about the future head of state defending the faith of his subjects, whatever their faith is?"
>
> Charles, although a regular churchgoer, is a radical thinker who has worked to achieve an understanding and tolerance of a wide variety of religions. He has researched beliefs ranging from Buddhism and Hinduism to Jungism and shown admiration for

---

1. For more information, see the discussion on the Garter in Chapter 7, "The Heraldic Symbols in the Arms and their Interpretations."
2. Junor, pp. 260-261. According to the prince, "Tolerance and patience are what is needed, the simple effort to try to understand the other person's point of view and his idealism, and not to condemn it outright" (ibid., p. 80). For more information, see the next chapter's section titled, "The United World Colleges."

their teachings....

Charles's remarks were welcomed by Roman Catholic leaders and spokesmen for other religions.[1]

This week, in the much-heralded Jonathan Dimbleby programme on his 25 years as the Prince of Wales, broadcast on ITV, Charles rejected the present exclusive association between the monarchy and the Church of England. "I happen to believe," he is quoted as saying, "that the Catholic subjects of the sovereign are as important (as the Protestants), not to mention the Islamic, Hindu and Zoroastrian subjects."...

Charles wishes to...[become], as he puts it, not Defender of the Faith, but Defender of Faith.[2]

Some clergy have attempted to gloss-over the prince's statements. Dimbleby, however, quoting them more fully, lays that falsehood to rest:

...."[Charles] had not only explored Hinduism and Buddhism but remained unwilling to dismiss the idea of reincarnation. He had also decided that it was important to understand Islam and...was drawn towards some of that great religion's guiding tenets; he identified strongly with those who saw in Islam, Judaism and Christianity a common belief in a monotheistic creation which was of greater significance than the doctrinal hostilities which...had pitted each faith against the other.

He was dismayed by the schisms within the Christian communion. In particular, as he had demonstrated so forcibly in his attempt to attend mass in the Pontiff's private chapel during his official visit to Italy in 1985, he was contemptuous of doctrinal and liturgical disputes that divided the Roman from the Anglican Church....

....[All this] had come to form the bedrock of his conviction that salvation springs less from religion than from faith....

His attitudes are not bounded by ecumenicism. Although he has long deplored the schisms within the Christian Church and has been scathing about the exclusive forms of evangelism represented by Protestant sects like the Free Presbyterians.... 'I've always felt that the Catholic subjects of the sovereign are equally as important as the Anglican ones, as the Protestant ones. Likewise, I think that the Islamic subjects or the Hindu subjects or the Zoroastrian subjects [(or the Jewish subjects)] of the sovereign are of equal and vital importance.'...

1. Robert Jobson, "Queen's Rift With Charles," *International Express,* U.S. Ed. No. 132, 29 June - 5 July 1994, pp. 1-2.
2. David Starkey, "If Church and Crown divide," *International Express,* U.S. Ed. No. 132, 29 June - 5 July 1994, p. 8.

To this extent he finds himself at ease walking between and within all those religions in addition to being a practising Christian.... To be Defender of the Faith was for him to be 'Defender of the Divine in existence, the pattern of the Divine which is, I think, in all of us but which, because we are human beings, can be expressed in so many different ways.'...

After the publication of the Prince's interview,...the Archbishop [of Canterbury, George Carey,] allowed himself to be tempted into remarking on BBC Radio that the Prince had 'intended' to say that he wanted to be Defender of the *Christian* Faith.... According to the Archbishop, what the Prince had said 'was perfectly compatible.... As heir, he has to be concerned with every citizen, regardless of creed.... I believe that that is what he intended to say.... What can be changed is the Coronation Service which can reflect the multicultural society in which we live' [by giving prominence to leaders from other faiths].

The Archbishop's minimalist interpretation...was not easy to reconcile with the Prince's words.... [The] Prince amplified his perspective thus:

> I feel, you know, that certainly the great Middle Eastern religions—Judaism, Islam, Christianity, all stemming from the same geographical area—all have a great deal in common. And I think Christianity had a great deal more in common a long time ago than it does now—sadly in my opinion. And I think a lot of that is due to the great schism between the Orthodox Church and the Roman Church before the Reformation produced Protestantism. But I also think there are aspects of Hinduism and Buddhism, again further east, which are attached by very profound threads to Islam, Christianity and Judaism. And when you begin to look at what these religions are saying you find that so much of the wisdom that is represented within these religions coincides. [All the great prophets, all the great thinkers, all those who have achieved an awareness of the aspects of life which lie beneath the surface, all have showed the same understanding of the universe or the nature of God or of the purpose of our existence—and that is why I think it so important to understand the common threads which link us all in one great and important tapestry.]...

....The Archbishop also welcomed the drift of the Prince's comments about the importance of faith in an increasingly secular society.... [The] participation by the leaders of other faiths in his coronation would be an ecumenical gesture that the Prince favoured, but it seemed unlikely to meet the full challenge of the Prince's faith....

....Some advisors believe that....it should be possible to include in the coronation a supplementary declaration affirming the Prince's belief in the divinity of other religions and, in the

231

process, diluting the 'exclusive' character of the Oath...which so disturbs the Prince....

As sovereign, the Prince would have to meet three other legal requirements.... He would have to declare himself to be a faithful Protestant...; that he was in communion with the Church of England...; and that he would 'maintain' the Church of England and the Church of Scotland.... In themselves, none of these three would cause him any anxiety.[1]

In 1521, England's King Henry VIII, whose heraldic arms were supported by the red dragon,[2] published *Assertio Septem Sacramentorum,* "In Defence of the Seven Sacraments" (of Roman Catholicism). As a polemical response to Martin Luther's writings, it upheld Rome's spurious papal authority and called for obedience. Widely debated in Europe, the work was warmly received in Rome, and prompted Pope Leo X to formally confer on Henry VIII the title *Fidei Defensor,* or as since commonly rendered in English, "Defender of the Faith." Henry VIII later abandoned Roman Catholicism, while, in 1534, blasphemously asserting himself to be "the Supreme Head [on Earth] of the Church of England," so that he could divorce and remarry. Although Leo X had not authorized the king to "pass the title to his heirs," the English Parliament chose to do so in 1543 in "The Act of the King's Style," which "declared that the words *Fidei Defensor* were 'united and annexed for ever to the imperial crown'." While the title was originally granted for Henry VIII's defense of the *religion of Rome,* "FD", for *Fidei Defensor,* has since been placed by the head of the reigning monarch on British coinage. Ironically, Westminster Abbey, the "shrine" of Anglicanism, remains "vested in a family of Roman Catholic dukes."[3] In Dimbleby's biographical documentary titled, "Charles: The Private Man, The Public Role," the prince stated, "I personally would rather see it as Defender of Faith, not *the* Faith, because it means just one particular interpretation of Faith, which I think is sometimes something that causes a [great] deal of a problem.... [We're] all actually aiming for the

1. Dimbleby, *The Prince of Wales,* pp. 526-528, 530-533.
2. For more information, see the discussion on the red dragon in Chapter 7, "The Heraldic Symbols in the Arms and their Interpretations."
3. Junor, p. 85.

same ultimate goal, I think. So I would much rather it was seen as defending faith itself."[1] As discussed here and in the later section titled, "Ties to the New Age Movement, the occult, and false religions," the prince has, perhaps more than any other contemporary figure, sought to ingratiate himself to the world's many "faith traditions."

It has been well-documented by others, and is beyond *knowledgeable* dispute, that *at their highest degrees and levels,* Freemasonry and its plethora of cult and occult branches, which include Mormonism, Theosophy, the New Age Movement, and even Anton LaVey's "Church of Satan," not only openly deride Christ and His work, but explicitly advocate the worship and adoration of Lucifer (Satan) as a means to achieve individual "godhood" and world "peace." Illuminist Freemasonry, which itself originated with the Rosicrucians and the Temple Knights, and from there Gnosticism,[2] Cabalism,[3] and the ancient mystery religions, especially Zoroastrianism, has long conspired to infiltrate, subvert, and co-opt, the major oligarchic, religious, military, financial, economic, political, governmental, educational, informational, and medical bodies and institutions of the world, including the Church, at their upper echelons, so as to eventually foist a full-fledged, Luciferic New World Order consisting of a "democratic" world government and a unified world religion upon mankind. Italy (Rome), France (Paris), England (London), Germany (Berlin, Hamburg), Russia (Moscow), and the United States (Washington and especially New York City) are among the major international bases of operation for this massive conspiracy (England being the most prominent currently), which is working heavily through the United Nations, the World Constitution and Parliament Association, and many other organizations and institutions to achieve its insidious aims.[4]

1. "How Hal muddied the holy waters for Charles," *Independent on Sunday,* No. 231 (London), 3 July 1994, p. 16. Also see Dimbleby, *The Prince of Wales,* p. 528.
2. Gnosticism is an occult view and explanation of the New Testament, and is largely predicated upon the Cabala.
3. Cabalism is essentially an occult view and explanation of the Old Testament, having much in common with the ancient mystery religions.
4. Kah, *En Route to Global Occupation,* pp. 9, 13-14, 16, 20-21, 30-40, 46, 48-65, 76-79, 83-85, 88-119, 133-136, 139-140, 164-168, 175-176, 182, 192-210. Regarding the Church,

233

Jesus stated, "No servant can serve two masters....
You cannot serve God and mammon [riches]" (Luke 16:13;
cf. Matt 6:24). Much of Freemasonry's control over governments and nations has been achieved financially,
through the establishment of national and international
banks and monetary institutions. As Joan Veon points out,
according to Dr. Carroll Quigley (whom President Clinton
admires), "the powers of financial capitalism had another
far-reaching aim, nothing less than to create a world system of financial control in private hands able to dominate
the political system of each country and the economy of
the world as a whole.... The apex of the system was to be
the Bank for International Settlements in Basle,
Switzerland, a private bank owned and controlled by the
world's central banks which were themselves private corporations.... The B.I.S. is generally regarded as the apex
of the structure of financial capitalism whose remote origins go back to the creation of the Bank of England in
1694 and the Bank of France in 1803.... It was set up
rather to remedy the decline in London as the world's
financial center by providing a mechanism by which a
world with three chief financial centers in London, New
York, and Paris could still operate as one [from
London]."[1] London's financial district remains "Europe's
pre-eminent center of financial services."[2]

Kah observes, "Another organization collaborating with [Philip] Isely's World Constitution
and Parliament Association is the World Council of Churches.... This organization has come
to represent the leadership of most of the mainline Protestant church denominations in
America and has privately been pushing for unification with the Church of Rome. But it
appears that the WCC is only trying to 'unite' Christianity in order to bring it into the New
World Order. [The council actively promotes] interfaithism—the merging of all the world's
religions under one umbrella" (*En Route to Global Occupation*, p. 84). James Shaw, a former American thirty-third degree Mason, adds, "I knew of many ministers and preachers
who were Masons, particularly those associated with the National Council of Churches"
(Kah, *En Route to Global Occupation*, p. 138). Besides a few individual churches, collaborating "Christian" organizations also include Christian Youth Fellowship in Nigeria, the Federa-
tion of Christian Churches in Pakistan, the National and International Councils of Christian
Churches as well as Gospel Faith Mission in the Ivory Coast, and Save the Children in Austria
(Kah, *En Route to Global Occupation*, pp. 186-187). (Note that Princess Anne is Patroness
for Save the Children.) For a cogent history of this international conspiracy and an outline of
its recent progress, see Kah's *En Route to Global Occupation*.

1. Carroll Quigley, *Tragedy and Hope* (Macmillan, 1965), p. 324. For more information, see
   Joan Veon, "Economic Globalization, Glass Steagall and the DOW" (Veon Financial Services,
   Inc.; P.O. Box 1323; Olney, MD 20830-1323), Dec. 1996, Vol. 10, No. 4, pp. 2-3.
2. Fred Barbash, The Washington Post, "Europe begins move toward common currency," *The*

Albert Pike, who wrote Freemasonry's preeminent work *Morals and Dogma,* in which he referred to The Triune God as "the Demons," had this to say in his blasphemous "Instructions" to Masonry's Supreme Councils:

If Lucifer were not God, would Adonay (The God of the Christians) whose deeds prove his cruelty, perfidy, and hatred of man, barbarism and repulsion for science, would Adonay and his priests calumniate him? Yes, Lucifer is God, and unfortunately Adonay is also God. For the eternal law is that there is not light without shade, no beauty without ugliness, no white without black, for the absolute can only exist as two Gods....the divine dualism.... That is why the intelligent disciples of Zoroaster, as well as, after them, the Gnostics, the Manicheans, and the Templars have admitted, as the only logical metaphysical conception, the system of the two divine principles fighting eternally, and one cannot believe the one inferior in power to the other. Thus, the doctrine of Satanism is a heresy; and the true and pure philosophic religion is the belief in Lucifer, the equal of Adonay; but Lucifer, God of Light and God of Good, is struggling for humanity against Adonay, the God of Darkness and Evil.[1]

Freemasonry, as a Luciferic religion of "good works" arising from the ancient mysteries, against which The LORD warned Israel, saying, "Woe to those who call evil good, and good evil; who put darkness for light, and light for darkness; who put bitter [poisonous] for sweet, and sweet for bitter" (Isa 5:20; cf. 5:18-21), advocates the same kind of ecumenism sought by Prince Charles. It finds its foundation in Satan's ancient lie, which denies the existence of absolute, unchanging, eternal truth. On pages 37, 226, and 525 of *Morals and Dogma,* for example, Pike asserted,

[A]ll truths are *"Truths of Period,"* and not truths for eternity.... Masonry, around whose altars the Christian, the Hebrew, the Moslem, the Brahmin, the followers of Confucius and Zoroaster, can assemble as brethren and unite in prayer to the one God who

---

Denver Post, 13 Feb. 1997, p. 36A.

1. Kah, *En Route to Global Occupation,* pp. 124-125; see also pp. 113-116. Although the names of many false gods are routinely invoked in Freemasonry, one is forbidden to publicly pray in the name of Jesus. In the York Rite's Royal Arch degree, the god of Masonry is revealed as a blasphemous combination of *Yah* (The God of Israel), Baal, and Osiris, called JAH-BUL-ON or J.B.O. (Kah, *En Route to Global Occupation,* pp. 134-135, 140).

is above *all* the Baalim, must needs leave it to each of its Initiates to look for the foundation of his faith and hope to the written scriptures of his own religion.... It reverences all the great reformers. It sees in Moses, the Lawgiver of the Jews, in Confucius and Zoroaster, in Jesus of Nazareth, and in the Arabian Iconoclast, Great Teachers of Morality, and Eminent Reformers, if no more: and allows every brother of the Order to assign to each such higher and even Divine Character as his Creed and Truth require.[1]

Lance Gay notes that "history shows that high-living hedonism and amorous escapades are embedded firmly in the British monarchy. Extramarital affairs and royal liscentiousness are more the rule than the exception."[2] (Even though the Church of England has condemned Freemasonry as "blasphemous" and "positively evil,"[3] it too, as graphically illustrated in the monarchy's bloody "Jack the Ripper" murders,[4] has been firmly embedded.) From Prince Charles' unrepentant promiscuous and adulterous lifestyle before[5] and after[6] his marriage to Diana, his avid "pursuit of the occult and New Age medicine,"[7] and his "openness" to, willing participation in, and overt defense of, false spiritualities and religions, it is evident that his Anglican confirmation never was representative of a genuine belief in The God of the Bible. The antichristian acting role he chose at the age of seventeen, less than a year after his confirmation, was therefore revealing: "[For] the school play at Christmas 1965, Prince Charles undertook the role of Shakespeare's Macbeth.... Charles' satanic thane...raised an impromptu buzz in the audience only when the three witches cried: 'All hail, Macbeth, that shalt be king

1. Kah, *En Route to Global Occupation,* pp. 125-127.
2. Scripps Howard News Service, "Antics normal for British royalty," *Rocky Mountain News,* 10 Dec. 1992, p. 58.
3. Kah, *En Route to Global Occupation,* pp. 134-135.
4. Coleman notes, "The Committee of 300 is for the most part under the control of the British monarch.... Queen Victoria is believed to have been quite paranoid about keeping it secret and went to great lengths to cover up MASONIC writings left at the scene of 'Jack the Ripper' murders, which alluded to the Committee's connections with 'experiments' carried out by a family member who was also a highly-placed member of the Scottish Rite of Freemasonry" (*The Committee of 300,* pp. 239-240).
5. Holden, *PRINCE CHARLES,* p. 223.
6. Nigel Dempster and Peter Evans, "Mayhem in the monarchy, Royal scandals crack foundation of the House of Windsor," *The Denver Post,* 6 June 1993, pp. 1A, 8-9A.
7. Hunt, *GLOBAL PEACE AND THE RISE OF ANTICHRIST,* p. 275.

hereafter!'"[1]

Marriage, ascension, and politics. Although Prince
Charles is often strongly contrasted with his father, Prince
Philip, particularly where personalities are concerned,[2] the
younger prince is, as we shall see in the following pages,
very much the activist in his father's mold: "Prince Philip's
public life is, at first sight, amazingly varied and exciting.
If the ambition of most aspiring beauty queens is 'to
travel', he out-travels them all, averaging something like
75,000 miles a year. He also delivers sixty to eighty major
speeches and gives an even larger number of shorter
talks.... The number of hands shaken...and crowds gratified make up a programme that is as exhausting and daunt-
ing as that of any American presidential candidate on the
stump.... Not only is he another pair of eyes and ears for
the Queen, but he believes he has a creative mission as
well: to present the monarchy as a dynamic, involved and
responsive institution.... This means being seen to react to
certain situations, to produce alternative proposals, to
exhort, advise, warn, and sometimes to rebuke."[3]

Prince Charles' 1981 marriage to Diana took place
before an estimated worldwide television audience of
seven-hundred and fifty million,[4] with a total combined
audience of nearly two billion in 141 countries,[5] making it
by far the most widely viewed event in history—that is,
until the untimely death and burial of Diana in August-
September of 1997, during which the prince also received
substantial coverage. The princess' death and burial were
followed by as many as two-and-one-half billion, covering

1. Holden, *PRINCE CHARLES,* pp. 142-143.
2. Prince Philip has rightly been called "bluff, outspoken, hearty, tough and something of a
   bully." Prince Charles' great desire for power and influence may derive in part from the fact
   that Prince Philip "has spent a lifetime criticizing him and quietly undermining his self-
   esteem" (Junor, p. 13).
3. Judd, *Prince Charles,* p. 214.
4. The London Bureau of People, "Once upon a Time...," *People Weekly,* 22 July 1991, p. 28.
   Michelle Green, Lydia Denworth, Terry Smith, and Margaret Wright, "PRINCE-LESS DIANA,"
   People Weekly, 11 Mar. 1996, p. 80.
5. Hoey, *Charles & Diana: The Tenth Anniversary,* p. 60. With the advent of global television,
   "Nearly 2 billion people saw her make those wedding vows, and most of them continued to
   pay attention as she and Prince Charles went about breaking them" (Martin Walker, "Can
   Charles grasp Diana's legacy?," *USA Today,* 2 Sept. 1997, p. 13A).

at least 44 languages (discussed later).[1] (Recall that the third most widely viewed event was the prince's 1969 investiture as Prince of Wales.) Upon her marriage to the prince, and for that sole reason initially, Diana became "the world's most famous woman," having to "cope with the unbearable attention and lack of privacy."[2] Subsequently, it was said, "The Princess of Wales has done more to popularize the concept of monarchy throughout the world than any other member of the Royal Family.... She has not only become perhaps the most famous and most frequently photographed woman in the world, but she has helped to bring the institution of monarchy to a new peak of popularity and boosted the image of Britain worldwide."[3] "When Prince Charles was single, he was considered to be the most eligible bachelor in the world.... However, nothing he had experienced in previous years compared with the mass adulation and widespread fascination he and his wife attracted at and after their wedding.... Together they were...the most sought-after couple on earth, and within a short period the Princess of Wales became the most photographed woman in the world, eclipsing every other member of the Royal Family.... Throughout the world, presidents and prime ministers vied with each other in their efforts to persuade the royal couple to visit them. Politicians of every hue wanted to be photographed in their presence.... [Due to the princess,] London has all but eclipsed Paris and Rome as the fashion centre of the world."[4] *TIME* magazine stated, "Charles and Diana are arguably the most famous, the most glamorous couple in the world."[5]

In more recent years, goaded by the media, the public became increasingly disillusioned with the obviously troubled marriage between Prince Charles and Princess

1. George Jahn, The Associated Press, "Billions worldwide take time to tune in," *The Denver Post,* 7 Sept. 1997, p. 17A. Pre-funeral estimates ranged from one-billion up to "several billion," which exceeds the limits even of possibility. The day before the funeral, William D. Montalbano of the *Los Angeles Times* asserted that the ceremony was "expected to draw...more than 2 billion television watchers around the globe" ("Ceremony symbol of change in stoic Britain," *The Denver Post,* 5 Sept. 1997, p. 11A).
2. *Charles & Diana: A Royal Family Album,* p. 11.
3. *Charles & Diana: A Royal Family Album,* pp. 58, 94.
4. Hoey, *Charles & Diana: The Tenth Anniversary,* pp. 10-11, 92-94.
5. *Charles & Diana: A Royal Family Album,* p. 72.

Diana—now ended in divorce and death—and the prince's seemingly bizarre activities. Of course, Prince Charles' rhetorical statement, "whatever 'love' is," made about Diana and marriage in a televised pre-ceremony interview, should have given the public some early apprehension. The prince is in fact "a serious-minded man who regards duty as a sacred trust to be preserved above all other emotions—including love."[1] Springmeier notes, "According to one informant, the reason that the British royals have been going through divorces—as fantastic as it may sound—is so that they will serve as role models to help break-up the family unit, which is an important Illuminati goal."[2]

Due to the highly publicized marital woes and infidelities of both the Prince and Princess of Wales, there have been frequent rumors asserting that Queen Elizabeth II might one day abdicate the British throne, or that she might consider bypassing Prince Charles in the royal succession. Such statements, however, appear to be unfounded. In fact, it seems doubtful that Prince Charles will become King of England, as opposed perhaps to Prince or King of the European Union, any time soon. If the prince is the AntiChrist, he will soon attain worldwide authority in the most elite of Earth's occupations, and then be utterly crushed by the King of kings and LORD of lords in a fiery judgment (see Rev 13:1-4, 13:18, 19:11-20; cf. 1 Sam 17:4, 17:7, 17:34-54; 2 Sam 21:19-20; Isa 9:6-7; Zech 12:1-10). Appealing to the chain of succession as a "divine right of kings," Holden points out that those who encourage abdication "fail to understand the nature of the British monarchy's popular appeal."[3] Nicholas Davies, for example, has speculated,

> The state of Charles' and Diana's marriage was one of the prime reasons the queen clearly indicated in her Christmas broadcast of 1991 that she intended to continue as monarch until her death....
> ....[If there were a formal separation or divorce], Charles

1. Hoey, *Charles & Diana: The Tenth Anniversary*, p. 16.
2. Written correspondence, quoted by permission, from Springmeier.
3. Holden, *PRINCE CHARLES*, pp. 312-313.

would find it all but impossible to take the [current] religious vows at his coronation as king and head of the Church....

If those events did indeed unfold, then the throne would pass directly to young Prince William.... And if the queen should die before William reached the age of 21, then Prince Charles would act as regent, ruling in the name of his son....[1]

"The prince, who [formally] separated from Princess Diana in December [1992], has pursued his interests more intently—'no longer walking in the shadow of his estranged wife,' said one of his aides."[2] Before the royal divorce, the British public generally considered Diana, who had obscenely denounced Charles before the queen and Prince Philip,[3] and who was herself guilty of adultery,[4] to be an ideal choice for a future queen. There are, and have been for some time, however, those who question the prince's suitability as a future king:

> [In 1993]..., Charles began courting the press—albeit in a stately way. Eager to establish himself as a player on the world stage, he made high-profile visits to [Western Europe,] Poland, Mexico and the Persian Gulf....
>
> ....Few [though] who read the transcript of Charles's 1989 phone conversation with Camilla [Parker Bowles] will ever forget his adolescent crudeness.[5]

> In truth, one year after the Waleses' separation, the Palace seems bent on removing Diana from the spotlight—and in pushing her estranged husband onto the stage....
>
> [A *Mail on Sunday* poll]...found that 31 percent of Britons believe that Prince William should succeed the Queen. That blow was followed by an attack by George Austin, the Archdeacon of York, who questioned whether Charles's affair with Camilla Parker Bowles renders him unfit to become Defender of the Faith....
>
> ....Still,...[the prince] and his handlers are said to be determined to make 1994 the Year of Charles....[6]

1. "Charles' wrecked marriage forces queen to make a fateful decision," *Rocky Mountain News,* 7 July 1992, p. 18.
2. Nicholas Davies, "More dirty linen? It's environmental," *The Denver Post,* 22 May 1993, p. 2A.
3. Nicholas Davies, "Shooting becomes a bone of contention," *Rocky Mountain News,* 8 July 1992, p. 23.
4. Michelle Green and Terry Smith, "Diss and Tell," *People Weekly,* 17 Oct. 1994, pp. 38-45.
5. Michelle Green, Terry Smith, and Margaret Wright, "The Outsider," *People Weekly,* 6 Dec. 1993, pp. 111-112, 114.
6. Michelle Green and Terry Smith, "Di Drops Out," *People Weekly,* 20 Dec. 1993, pp. 39-40.

...Just as his great-uncle Edward [VIII] had given up his throne for the woman he loved, Prince Charles, 45, was said to have given up his love for the throne he covets.... "After months of heart searching," reported [Nigel] Dempster, Charles had vowed to "remove any obstacle to his succession" by breaking off his [24-year] relationship with Camilla Parker Bowles....

Royal watchers quickly smelled a scam....

While the ploy [to "remain morally eligible for the throne"][1] seemed to work in some quarters—the Archdeacon of York, who had characterized Charles as morally unfit to be king, praised his apparent repentance—it may yet backfire.[2]

...[George] Austin seemed to change his mind..., declaring that if the affair was over, "I don't think there is a problem for the future. All Christians make mistakes...."

But the Rev. Tony Highton, a leading member of the General Synod, disagreed...: "From what I understand, there does not appear to be any hint of penitence.... I, therefore, do not think he is fit to become Defender of the Faith and Supreme Governor of the Church of England."

"I also think he is going to be in trouble over his remarks of wanting to be 'defender of all faiths,'" Highton added.[3]

Prince Charles is seeing his popularity **soar** in Britain since his TV admission that he wasn't faithful to Princess Diana after their marriage "irretrievably broke down."...

At the palace, "switchboards have been jammed with people ringing in to say nice things"..., says press secretary Richard Aylard. "People are saying that they appreciated the opportunity to see what the prince is really like."[4]

[The] Archbishop of Canterbury [is now]...supporting the future head of the Church of England in his desire to be not just the defender of the Anglican faith, but of all the others that are now a part of the multicultural society over which Charles will eventually reign. And...the opinion polls showed that most of the British public thought that he...would make a good king![5]

Suddenly, **the world**—and what it thought of **its future King**—had been stood on its head as poll after poll showed that these future subjects, who had been told for two years that he was *not* fit to be King....felt that the television programme had

1. "Charles ends relationship?," *The Denver Post,* 30 Jan. 1994, p. 20A.
2. "Age of Chivalry," *People Weekly,* 14 Feb. 1994, p. 56.
3. William Tuohy, "Charles' adultery admission, church stance raise firestorm," *The Denver Post,* 29 June 1994, p. 16A.
4. "Mea culpas a coup for the prince," *The Denver Post,* 6 July 1994, p. 2A.
5. "Royalty Today," *Royalty,* 1994, Vol. 13, No. 2, p. 4.

improved his image and that he was fit to be King—and would probably turn out to be a very good King.[1]

> ...Charles...shocked the nation by confirming rumors that he had committed adultery, but that was only the beginning. In Dimbleby's...biography,...the prince is portrayed as an emotionally deprived pawn abandoned by his mother, bullied by his father and tortured by a paranoid wife whom he may never have loved....
>
> ....Neither the constitution nor the Church of England forbids a divorcé from becoming monarch, though remarriage is not normally allowed by the church....
>
> ....Charles's partisans assert that he is determined to become King....[2]

The British press has gone so far as to suggest that Prince Charles might stoop to self-removal from the royal succession.[3] It seems far more likely, however, should the circumstances ever require it, that his mother would choose to bypass him, placing her grandson in the succession instead. Either way, if Prince Charles is removed, or the British constitution is altered or bypassed, or his mother continues into the next century as queen, it could result in a substantial *expansion* of his role as a social crusader—and perhaps actually clear the way for him to rise to world prominence:

> The possibility that Charles even would remove himself from the succession—an abdication of sorts—was floated in [1991].... [This]...would free Charles to carry on as a social critic.... ...Charles's stepping aside could be put forward as a noble sacrifice to allow him to complete his lifelong mission as an activist in a way that would not be possible if he were King [of England (as opposed to Europe)].[4]

"The prince has great popularity in the country," one of Prime Minister John Major's men told me sourly. "His views are taken seriously...."

"The Prince of Wales feels very clearly that Walter Bagehot's

1. *Royalty,* 1994, Vol. 13, No. 2, p. 44.
2. Michelle Green, Margaret Wright, Lydia Denworth, and Elizabeth Terry, "Prince of Pique," *People Weekly,* 31 Oct. 1994, pp. 47, 56.
3. For the order of succession to the British throne, see Lacey, *Majesty,* p. 309. For details of the royal household in addition to the succession, see James and Russell, *At Home with the Royal Family,* pp. 192-213, 216-217.
4. The London Bureau of People, pp. 34-35.

out the window, and that he can participate, if he wishes, in making his country a better place," says Harold Brooks-Baker, editorial director of Burke's Peerage. "The right to be consulted, the right to encourage, the right to warn" is Bagehot's endlessly quoted dictum for royals. But **Charles is not king yet and, technically, says Brooks-Baker, he can do whatever he wants.**[1]

[Charles] does not react kindly to anyone who threatens his position. Diana became a threat because she became a rival for the public's attention.... Separation or even divorce would not in any way stand in the path of his becoming King.... There is, as yet, not the slightest indication that he has fallen from public favour, in spite of what look suspiciously like attempts to blacken his name with his wife's approval. He still enjoys enormous goodwill, because he is still perceived as an essentially good man.... [He] should be aware that attempts to besmirch his character, and to upstage him, have singularly failed so far to turn his future subjects against him.[2]

The idea of abdication is of course a nonstarter. The Queen accepts her role as a sacred trust to which she is committed for life and, when she was anointed with holy oil at her coronation..., the religious aspect of the ceremony was real to her in every sense. There is no question of her 'opting out' in favour of her son.... He...wants nothing more than that his mother should reign until the twenty-first century.[3]

British Prime Minister John Major said this week that he is eager to help find real work for Prince Charles, who has been hanging around for years waiting for his mother to step down from the throne.... [The]...45-year-old prince will meet with a trade minister to discuss stepping up his role as a roving cultural and commercial ambassador for Britain.[4]

Princess Anne, eighth in line to the British throne, is being groomed by her mother, Queen Elizabeth II, to become a surrogate queen consort to the wifeless Prince Charles, said reports published in the London Daily Express yesterday. ...."The queen wants Princess Anne to be elevated to such a rank that when Prince Charles becomes king, she can be first lady of the land."[5]

1. Adam Platt, "What's it all about, Charlie?," *Esquire,* June 1992, pp. 114, 116.
2. "A Sense of Duty," *Majesty,* Nov. 1992, Vol. 13, No. 11, pp. 14-17.
3. Hoey, *Charles & Diana: The Tenth Anniversary,* pp. 97-98.
4. "Britain seeks real job for prince," *The Denver Post,* 25 Nov. 1993, p. 2A. As Prince Charles himself puts it, "I'm just a roving ambassador for Britain" (*Charles & Diana: A Royal Family Album,* p. 56).
5. "Princess readied for new status?," *The Denver Post,* 14 June 1994, p. 2A. With Diana's divorce from the prince, she was forced to give up any hope of becoming queen.

243

[In] 1981 [it] captivated Britain and the world as a once-in-a-century storybook romance. But...the fairy tale has been replaced by a reality in which the union appears to have been loveless, passionless and hollow from the first post-nuptial kiss.... The only remaining question would be whether a divorced person could be the monarch and the answer...is expected to be "yes."[1]

Ultimately...the biggest beneficiary of the split...may be Charles. "It was very clever that it was the Queen who seemed to run the divorce.... Charles is being portrayed as a Mr. Nice Guy."... As for the royal family, the task now at hand is to rehabilitate its soiled image....[2]

Death of a princess. The death of Princess Diana on August 31, 1997, was attended by unparalleled media coverage. Much of that coverage, however, was superficial and incomplete. Strange circumstances, hinting at a possible conspiracy, surrounded the princess' death. Further, it seems clear that the British monarchy had come to see Diana as an increasing, rather than decreasing, public rival and threat. Regarding Prince Charles, Junor comments, "He was being eclipsed by her, and...the frustration was unbearable.... The wife who had at first given him so much confidence and pride now appeared to have emasculated him. The more obsessive the media grew, the more Diana became obsessed with reading what they had to say about her. She was elated by being a superstar, she loved the adulation, delighted in the stir she caused, and revelled in being the most famous, most photographed, most sought after woman in the country, if not the world. But it was too much, too soon, and she began to believe her own publicity and enjoy the power of her position."[3] As Diana saw it, "Everybody always said when we were in the car, 'Oh, we're [on] the wrong side, we want to see *her,* we don't want to see him.' Obviously he wasn't used to that, and nor was I. He took it out on me. He was jealous."[4] The following information should aid the public discourse concerning the princess' death.

Strange circumstances. Henry Paul, driver of the

1. Louis J. Salome, "Pressure grows for royal divorce," *The Denver Post,* 19 Oct. 1994, p. 6A.
2. "The Big Kiss-Off," *People Weekly,* 29 July 1996, pp. 42-43.
3. Junor, pp. 221-222.
4. "The Diana Tapes," *People* weekly, 20 Oct. 1997, p. 104.

Mercedes S-280, was, we are told, quite drunk (over three times beyond the legal limit) as well as drugged with an "antidepressant" (possibly Prozac), yet he was apparently not detected as such by Dodi al-Fayed or Diana. At the same time, the drunken and drugged Paul was forced to drive rapidly (between 90 and 121 m.p.h.) in an effort to flee a gang of "paparazzi" in hot-pursuit on motorcycles: "If driver Henri Paul, 41, the deputy head of security at the luxurious Hotel Ritz, was legally drunk—his blood reportedly contained nearly four times the legal limit of alcohol concentration—how did he negotiate the seven sweeping turns before finally losing control of the car? Was he distracted by the photographers on motorcycles who had followed him, also at high speed, from the moment he picked up his passengers?" Not only did a witness describe the Mercedes as "surrounded by so many motorcyclists that he believed it was an official cortege," but "France 2 TV reported that a witness saw one photographer zigzag in front of the car before it crashed." The Mercedes then impacted a second vehicle, reportedly a black Fiat Uno, just before it hit a support pillar in the tunnel under *Place de l'Alma* in Paris.[1] The Fiat fled from the scene, suggesting that the Mercedes may have been run off the road. The motorcyclist and the Fiat weaved "in front of the Mercedes moments before it went out of control." CNN aired an early telephone call from a "witness" who claimed that Dodi was walking around looking dazed after the crash; the call was later said to be a "prank." Mohamed al-Fayed, Dodi's father, contended "that their deaths were caused not by the recklessness of a drunken driver employed by the Ritz, but by the paparazzi who pursued them." Following the crash, the paparazzi continued to hound the dying princess with incessant photographs, rather than offering assistance, even as the princess told them to leave her alone: "All around her, there were photographers who were machine-gunning (taking rapid-fire photographs). They were only a few centimeters from her face, taking her picture from every angle." Indeed, "within 30 seconds of the crash, photographers were taking pictures and tried to

1. According to Fritz Springmeier, *Place de l'Alma* is "an important Merovingian ritual site."

245

push rescuers and police away." "Le Monde reported...that, within 30 seconds of the crash, some photographers were taking pictures of the bleeding victims. Citing at least a dozen unnamed witnesses, it said some photographers actually pushed away rescuers and two policemen who arrived on the scene, saying they were ruining their pictures.... Her head was twisted to one side, and the photographers were taking pictures from just a few inches away." Several of the photographers are "under formal investigation for involuntary homicide and failing to come to the aid of the victims or impeding rescue efforts.... [Romuald] Rat had been one of the first to arrive on the accident scene and had interfered with rescue attempts. But Rat told the authorities that he had taken Diana's pulse to determine whether she was still alive." (Or, perhaps, whether she had yet died!)

A *six-mile* trip to *La Pitie-Salpetriere* Hospital in Paris by ambulance "took <u>an hour</u> to get from the crash site," so long that "waiting officials feared it was lost." Doctors attempted heart-massages on Dodi at the crash scene, and on Diana at the hospital. During the trip to the hospital, the "ambulance had to halt suddenly when the princess's heart stopped beating so she could be given a massive dose of adrenaline." At the hospital, Diana's heart again stopped, when the doctors discovered a broken pulmonary vein that resulted in "almost a gallon and a half of blood spilled into her rib cage area." However, instead of placing the princess on a heart-lung bypass machine to pump her blood and provide oxygen to it while attempting to repair the vein, doctors continued with heart massage "for two hours, long after the critical period had passed." According to "Robert Shesser, chairman of emergency medicine at George Washington University Medical Center in Washington, D.C.," "doctors could have tried something else: placing Diana on the heart-lung bypass machine that stands in for those organs during heart surgery. 'That would give you time to repair what was broken, and hopefully get the heart started.'" (Removal of the heart is a part of masonic ritual murder.) Finally, Rees-Jones, the sole survivor of the accident, was given such large doses of anesthesia that his memory was affected, having "told investigators that he does not remember the crash."[1]

The case for a conspiracy. A possible marriage between Diana and a non-Anglican Protestant, particularly the Muslim Dodi al-Fayed, would have been construed as a potential threat to the royal succession due to Diana's influence over princes William and Harry. Prince William had suggested that Diana "leave Britain to escape the paparazzi," whereas the princess' brother, Charles, the Earl of Spencer, had even earlier asserted that the paparazzi would one day bring about the princess' death. Following her death, the earl affirmed: "I would say that I have always believed the press would kill her in the end." (Was it a scenario just waiting to be exploited by the monarchy?) Indeed, according to Egyptian sources, "Diana was already pregnant with [Dodi] Fayed's baby."

Several Muslim news sources have suggested that the British monarchy had Diana assassinated to prevent a marriage to Dodi, who had helped to bring down the Conservative government of John Major in an apparent act of revenge for his not having been granted British citizenship. "Al-Fayed has been denied citizenship ever since he took over Harrods, and the wags guessed that he was taking his revenge on British society by having his son woo the mother of the future King William." "The ultimate revenge against the establishment would have been a marriage between Diana and Dodi. That would have made the Fayeds step-parents and grandparents to a likely future King of England—Diana's son, William. Before their untimely

1. "Charles publicly discusses how sons dealing with loss," *The Denver Post,* 20 Sept. 1997, p. 16A. John-Thor Dahlburg, Los Angeles Times, "Diana's last moments," *The Denver Post,* 11 Sept. 1997, p. 2A. Fred Coleman and Jack Kelley, "Report: He taunted the photographers," *USA Today,* 2 Sept. 1997, p. 1A. Marco R. della Cava and Maria Puente, "Alcohol, pursuit, speed are factors in probe," *USA Today,* 2 Sept. 1997, p. 3A. Craig R. Whitney, "Princess's driver drunk, speeding," *Rocky Mountain News,* 2 Sept. 1997, p. 3A. Craig R. Whitney, The New York Times, "Diana's car apparently collided with Fiat, then hit pillar," *The Denver Post,* 3 Oct. 1997, p. 2A. Steve Sternberg, "Questions raised over injuries, care at scene," *USA Today,* 2 Sept. 1997, p. 16A. Christopher P. Winner, USA Today, "Many questions still unanswered after accident," *The Denver Post,* 7 Sept. 1997, p. 24A. Anne Swardson, The Washington Post, "Fayed family denies driver drunk," *The Denver Post,* 7 Sept. 1997. Craig R. Whitney, The New York Times, "Ruling begins probe of paparazzi," *The Denver Post,* 3 Sept. 1997, p. 1A. Jocelyn Noveck, The Associated Press, "Di's chauffeur legally drunk," *The Denver Post,* 2 Sept. 1997, pp. 1A, 7A.

death, British newspaper commentators had written acidly of the Fayeds' seduction of Diana and compared Dodi to a 'toad' kissed by a princess. Some observers believe revenge was partly a motive on both sides for the sudden romance, with Diana seeking to annoy the royal establishment that rejected her." "No other celebrity courted and manipulated the media with as much savvy and charm.... Only six hours before she died, Diana called her favorite royal correspondent [from the Ritz].... Maybe she would marry her new love, Dodi Fayed. Then again, maybe not." Supposedly, "she planned to give up her role in public life." "Arab news media raised the theory that her life was ended instead by a conspiracy.... [From] the Persian Gulf to Libya, the theme was the same: Diana's affair with Dodi Fayed, an Arab and Muslim, went against the prejudices of the British establishment. Columnist Anis Mansour...put it directly in the Cairo daily Al-Ahram: 'She was killed by British intelligence to save the monarchy.... Nobody since Cromwell, who called for a republic in the 17th century, has been able to shake the royal family as Princess Diana did.'... Libya's official JANA news agency....accused Britain of 'setting up the accident' and France of carrying it out."

Although Diana was supposed to fade from the royal limelight with the divorce, she maintained her popularity through "good works," continuing to upstage Prince Charles and the monarchy generally: "She learned to use her fame to do good works—and also to punish the royal family she felt had abused and abandoned her." According to Diana, "I'm much closer to the people at the bottom than the people at the top, and the latter won't forgive me for it." However, "Whenever public attention shifted to Charles, Diana upstaged him with a photo-op.... Charles was toast. Diana was so skillful at manipulating media coverage that she fell into a common trap of great celebrity: She thought she could turn it off when she chose." Diana had actually embarked on a "campaign to paint Charles as unsuitable for the throne," "doing serious damage to the institution of England's royal family." "Others hint at unspeakable motives—such as race, class, and Royalist fervor—in blaming Britain's MI5 or others for Diana's death." (Of course, MI-5, like MI-6, reports to the monarchy.) While Diana would steal the limelight in death as well, at least it would be a temporary and transitory event. Of course, the monarchy would receive substantial press as well: "This is a funeral that has mobilized an entire people, even the people of the whole world," said one observer. Indeed, it also served the prince's ecumenist goals; for example, "A hastily arranged service at St. Paul's Cathedral, where Charles and Diana married in 1981, drew 2,000 mourners from all faiths." Moreover, it may free the prince to "marry again, in the eyes of the Anglican Church, of which he will be the titular head if he becomes king." A columnist had this to say, "Unless I want to get thrown out of the Global Media Conspiracy of Pundits, Commentators & Sundry Scurrilous Knaves, I must write about the death of Diana, Princess of Wales.... [If I were editing a mass-market magazine,]...I'd be among those waving big money at photographers, which leads to stakeouts and pursuits, and, perhaps, a gruesome auto accident." To avoid any implication of impropriety, the monarchy, at Prince Charles' behest, treated the princess' corpse royally in death, even draping her casket with the royal standard. Moreover, Queen Elizabeth II protested that "the initial shock of Diana's death was followed by 'disbelief, incomprehension, anger and concern for those who remain," adding, "I want to pay tribute to Diana myself. She was an exceptional and gifted human being.... I admired and respected her for her energy and her commitment to others, and especially for her devotion to her two boys." Really? Oddly, princes William and Harry, attending "regular Sunday church services in Scotland" with Prince Charles, amazed their vicar "at how dry-eyed and controlled they were." One reporter had earlier observed, "national mourning was punctuated by sharp criticism of the British royal family as cold, remote and unfeeling. Amid perhaps the greatest outpouring of public grief in British history, anti-royal anger echoed across newspapers.... 'Not one word has come from a royal lip, not one tear has been shed in public from a royal eye. It is as if no one in the royal family has a soul,' said Britain's largest newspaper, The Sun, in an editorial. 'From the outside looking in, the House of Windsor seems a cold, compassion-free zone where duty and protocol push emotions into a dark corner,' the popular tabloid said."[1]

Diana's death stands in stark contrast to the subsequent decommissioning of the royal yacht Britannia: "It was one of the most powerful public displays of emotion by the Royal Family in recent years. Stiff upper lips were forgotten as the Queen and even Prince Philip were reduced to tears.... Just three months ago, the Royal Family stood accused of not showing enough emotion in public ahead of Princess Diana's funeral. For the Royal Yacht Britannia, it was a Royal Family transformed. On the rain-swept dockside the Queen choked back tears as she paid an emotional tribute to the vessel and the sailors who had looked after her for the past 44 years. Then, when the Royal Standard was lowered for the last time, the tears flowed—an amazing finale...."[2]

Political   affiliations,   aspirations,   and   privileges.

1. Larry Kaplow, Cox News Service, "Diana's death a 'conspiracy,'" *The Denver Post,* 18 Oct. 1997, p. 31A. "Aggressive intrusion," *The Denver Post,* 1 Sept. 1997, p. 11B. "Diana's advice: 'Lead from the heart,'" *USA Today,* 2 Sept. 1997, p. 2A. Barbara Slavin, "Diana, Dodi shared sense of not belonging," *USA Today,* 2 Sept. 1997, p. 18A. Marco R. della Cava, "Reassigned a royal status stripped away in her life," *USA Today,* 2 Sept. 1997, p. 2A. Trey Graham, "Flood of conspiracy theories surges through on-line world," *USA Today,* 2 Sept. 1997, p. 18A. George Jahn, The Associated Press, "Billions worldwide to take time to tune in," *The Denver Post,* 7 Sept. 1997, p. 17A. Ed Quillen, "Sometimes lightning strikes," *The Denver Post,* 7 Sept. 1997, p. 2F. Alessandra Stanley, The New York Times, "Struggle for happiness touched women deeply," *The Denver Post,* 7 Sept. 1997, p. 22A. Roxanne Roberts, The Washington Post, "In death, Diana the victor in media war against royals," *The Denver Post,* 7 Sept. 1997, pp. 22A-23A. "Interview believed to have been Diana's last," *The Denver Post,* 7 Sept. 1997, p. 25A. Swardson, "Fayed family denies driver drunk." "Charles, young princes move among mourners," *The Denver Post,* 7 Sept. 1997. Ray Moseley, Chicago Tribune, "What's next for Charles?," *The Denver Post,* 1 Sept. 1997, p. 7A. "Britons mourn loss of 'people's princess,'" *The Denver Post,* 1 Sept. 1997, p. 13A. "Diana emulated, never duplicated," *The Denver Post,* 1 Sept. 1997, p. 14A. David Von Drehle, The Washington Post, "World dazzled by soap opera of icon's life," *The Denver Post,* 1 Sept. 1997, p. 18A. The Associated Press, "Arab media sense plot in Diana's death," *The Denver Post,* 3 Sept. 1997, p. 19A. Dean E. Murphy, Los Angeles Times, "Stiff upper lip prevails," *The Denver Post,* 2 Sept. 1997, p. 4A. William D. Montalbano, Los Angeles Times, "Royals bow to public, expand funeral access," *The Denver Post,* 4 Sept. 1997, p. 1A.
2. Robert Jobson and Sean Rayment, "For Britannia, tears that the Royals couldn't hide," *International Express,* U.S. Ed., 16 Dec. 1997, p. 7.

Elizabeth II is the queen not just of the United Kingdom, but also of Canada, Australia, and New Zealand (though the monarchy's affiliation with Australia has recently been weakened). By virtue of his relationship to the queen, Prince Charles enjoys some degree of authority over those nations, not to mention the British Commonwealth as a whole. Brian Hoey, before Diana's death, stated,

> ....Almost every day...a large number of people have been 'received by the Prince and Princess of Wales'. These people could range from the commanding officers of service units associated with Their Royal Highnesses, who arrive to be formally presented..., to leaders of Commonwealth countries who personally brief the Prince on matters concerning their particular country. Others who are summoned to the royal presence include businessmen, social workers, artists and politicians, all with one purpose in mind: to keep the Prince and Princess fully informed on the widest variety of issues. Each visitor has his or her own place in the royal scheme of things and, when the day comes that Prince Charles ascends the throne, he and his wife will surely be the most widely informed couple the British monarchy has ever known. This is in part what has given rise to the claims that there is a separate court, but the Queen is fully aware of what is taking place in St James's Palace and she has gladly given her approval....
>
> Even Margaret Thatcher found that there is no such thing as a free lunch where the Prince and Princess are concerned. When Prime Minister, she was frequently a guest only to find that her influence was needed.... However, no one seems to object to being manipulated in this way....
>
> ....Many Asians have become very successful and extremely rich businessmen and the Prince of Wales has not been slow in involving them in his pet projects.... They knew when they accepted the royal invitation that there was going to be a price to pay—and they were delighted to be associated with a project headed by the future king.[1]

Speaking of "the ordinary man in the street," Junor comments, "He cares about them and tries to improve their lot.... He goes to the trouble spots to...ask people...what they think.... Then he gathers together architects, builders, youth unemployment officers—anyone whose services he thinks he can manipulate to good effect—and tells them what he thinks should be done. Prince Charles

1. Hoey, *Charles & Diana: The Tenth Anniversary,* pp. 102-104, 108.

entertains widely, but as the many top businessmen, media executives and corporation bosses flattered by an invitation from His Royal Highness have soon realized, there is no such thing as a free lunch, not even at Kensington Palace. The Prince dispenses with formalities early on in the meal, and gets straight down to what he would like his guest to do or provide.... His sheer presence turns a mundane event into a major celebration, swamps a factory with orders, ensures that a charity gets a sudden flush of donations." In Prince Charles' own words, "I can go to all the dinners and banquets on earth, but it's not going to make any difference to the world. What I want to do is be a part of something that does."[1] In fact, the prince, who is "more than capable of carrying off the ritual diplomacy required of him," has traveled worldwide as a "seasoned ambassador" (of sorts) for the United Kingdom.[2] Holden adds,

> Elizabeth II...has encouraged her son from his earliest adulthood to take an active part in the constitutional process; he reads cabinet papers, and **since becoming a privy councillor in 1977 meets politicians of all hues on an intimate and confidential footing**....
> ...Prince Charles is constantly exploring new routes toward a more positive role.[3]

> He is the first Prince of Wales to have grown up in the era of mass communications, and he has taken pains to master its dominant medium. With a growing list of credits behind him, he is quite at ease in front of the cameras.... Prince Charles likes using television to promote his own multifarious activities and enjoys watching himself on the video cassettes he keeps of all his appearances.[4]

The *International Express* comments, "The Prince's views certainly have a contemporary ring to them. He may not have his heart in defending the faith. [Yet] it appears he would have no trouble at all defending political correctness."[5] Adam Platt adds, "On issues close to his

---

1. Junor, pp. 12-13, 247, 249.
2. Holden, *PRINCE CHARLES*, p. 268.
3. Holden, *PRINCE CHARLES*, p. 38.
4. Holden, *PRINCE CHARLES*, p. 241.
5. "Keeping faith," *International Express*, U.S. Ed. No. 132, 29 June - 5 July 1994, p. 8.

heart," Prince Charles, who "meets regularly with members of the cabinet," has been known to "barrage government ministers with unsolicited advice," giving them "memos and position papers."[1] The prince, according to Junor, "detests bureaucracy and red tape above practically everything else."[2] In July 1970, one year after his formal investiture as Prince of Wales, he met with then President Richard Nixon at the White House in Washington. Mr. Nixon recorded this account:

> From news accounts in the British and American press I expected to meet a rather callow, superficial youth with no particular interest in or understanding of world affairs. His conduct completely dispelled that image.
>
> He was serious without being dull, dignified without being pompous, respectful without being deferential. We discussed the whole range of East-West relations, NATO, the Third World countries, and the attitude of young people toward government in the US and Britain.
>
> His perception and knowledge with regard to developments in the Commonwealth nations was greater than that of many State Department professionals. Without crossing the line of interfering in British governmental policies, he expressed agreement with my long-held conviction that Britain must continue to play a role on the world stage—particularly in NATO and in those nations in Africa and Asia where the legacy of the British parliamentary system and the common law is so essential if ordered freedom is to survive.
>
> I told Mrs. Nixon after our meeting that the British and American media greatly underestimated him as a student of world affairs and as a man....[3]

Prince Charles is the most accomplished Prince of Wales, and perhaps one of the most accomplished men, in history. The prince "has had a far broader education than any of his predecessors, attending school and university and mixing with a large number of ordinary people."[4] In fact, few men could ever hope to rival the sheer magnitude and diversity of what Prince Charles has already accomplished. In this regard, he again takes after Prince Philip,

1. Platt, pp. 113, 116.
2. Junor, p. 117.
3. Holden, *PRINCE CHARLES*, pp. 262-263, 327.
4. "A Sense of Duty," *Majesty*, Nov. 1992, Vol. 13, No. 11, p. 14.

who, despite his lack of a university education, is himself remarkably accomplished, having a list of "various presidencies, decorations, patronages, foreign honours, membership of a host of clubs and associations, university honours, and so on," that "is a staggering, even awesome, testimony to his involvement in hundreds of organisations."[1] To call Prince Charles a "renaissance man" almost seems like a punishable understatement. As a royal ambassador, public speaker, university graduate, naval commander and ship's captain, frogman and commando, colonel-in-chief of *ten* army regiments, air force wing commander, pilot of military fighter jets and helicopters, as well as civilian aircraft, parachutist, race-car driver, international polo-player and national team's captain, jockey, steeplechaser, skier, hunter, painter, would-be actor, dancer, singer, and musician, not to mention knight and "Doctor of Laws," "the Prince of Wales has won the respect of the world."[2] Hoey remarks, "Prince Charles is also one of the world's great communicators, being able to converse easily with youngsters from deprived inner-city ghettos or with farm labourers..., and making them feel that what they have to say is worth listening to."[3] Junor comments, "His ideas are sound, his heart is in the right place, and he has a remarkable gift for communicating with the man in the street and understanding his needs. Furthermore, he cares about those needs, and has the clout among businessmen and politicians to make mountains move."[4] Holden adds,

> He is Earl of Chester, Duke of Cornwall, Duke of Rothesay, Earl of Carrick and Baron of Renfrew, Lord of the Isles and Great Steward of Scotland, Knight of the Most Noble Order of the Garter, Knight of the Most Ancient and Most Noble Order of the Thistle, Great Master and Principal Knight Grand Cross of the Most Honorable Order of the Bath. He is personal aide-de-camp to Queen Elizabeth II; commander, Royal Navy; wing commander, Royal Air Force; colonel-in-chief of ten regiments; member of a

1. Judd, *Prince Philip*, p. 248. For an amazing yet abridged list of Prince Philip's titles, patronages, presidencies, honorary citizenships, foreign honors, honorary degrees, and publications, see pages 248-252 of the same work.
2. Spink, p. 24. Hoey, *Charles & Diana: The Tenth Anniversary*, p. 43. Junor, p. 65.
3. Hoey, *Charles & Diana: The Tenth Anniversary*, p. 116.
4. Junor, p. 16. *Charles & Diana: A Royal Family Album*, p. 54.

dozen international orders of chivalry; president, patron, or member of some two hundred clubs, charities, committees, and learned organizations.

A thousand years of history merge in this...desperately well-meaning man.... He has a quick wit, a talent for mimicry, a sharp tongue.... He is a countryman at heart, but would rather like to have been an actor. He is proud, ambitious, romantic, and anxious to carve himself a place in history.

....He expects the deference due to his office, takes its pomp and circumstance very seriously, [and] enjoys the archaic rituals of royal ceremonial....

....His birthright provides incomparable material comfort and international respect, adulation, even awe. Government departments look after various aspects of his business.... On his birthday flags fly, guns sound, and judges don their scarlet robes....

....Every word he speaks is remembered or written down. His presence unnerves people..., they lose the power of speech..., they fight to touch him as if he were divine.[1]

Indeed, according to Burnet, there are those who expect Prince Charles to "walk on water."[2] (Will recovery from a fatal wound suffice?) Brown, in her biography on Prince Charles, adds, "Whenever Prince Charles is photographed or filmed, he is almost invariably surrounded by people. He meets as many new people every week as most of us meet in a year, and he must rate as one of the most widely recognized men in the world today."[3]

Accustomed to receiving red-carpet treatment,[4] Prince Charles and his family are also quite wealthy:

By FORTUNE's calculation, the Queen is the richest woman in the world and No. 4 overall, behind only the Sultan of Brunei ($25 billion), Saudi Arabia's King Fahd and his family ($18 billion) and America's Mars candy-bar clan ($12.5 billion). FORTUNE estimates Elizabeth's worth at $11.7 billion, but other appraisers believe it to be much higher, given such personal assets as her race-horses, stamp collection and art acquisitions. Charles, meanwhile, is believed to be worth about $536 million, which would still place him among Britain's 40 wealthiest people.[5]

1. Holden, *PRINCE CHARLES*, pp. xxv-xxvii.
2. Burnet, *In Private—In Public, THE PRINCE AND PRINCESS OF WALES*, p. 84.
3. Brown, *PRINCE CHARLES*, p. 155.
4. *People Weekly*, Extra: Summer 1988, p. 46.
5. Richard Lacayo and Jonathan Cooper, "Are These Folks Loaded, or What?," *People Weekly*, Extra: Fall 1990, p. 118.

255

> As one of the richest men in the world, Prince Charles can afford anything he or his family wants, and they do not stint themselves. Their homes...contain every conceivable luxury, and everything that they eat, drink, wear or otherwise use is the very best that money can buy.[1]
>
> ....Elizabeth II is reputed to be the world's richest woman. But royalty has its privileges.... Consider that...Prince Charles, voluntarily pays 25 percent of his estimated $5 million annual income in tax.
>
> Also, that queenly $11 billion net-worth figure is misleading. Some $10.5 billion of it, including the $4.5 billion royal art collection and $500 million in crown jewels, is controlled by the state and therefore belongs to the queen in name only. Her five official residences too are owned by the government....
>
> Some royal watchers argue that the [queen's] portfolio's true value is nearer $700 million.[2]

According to Lacey, "It is quite possible—probable indeed—that Queen Elizabeth II has private investments now worth tens of millions of dollars whose precise nature and size is known to a very small group of people indeed, and whose identity, shrouded in a complex pattern of nominees and holding companies, is effectively beyond the reach of any outside enquiry through existing legal—or even illegal—channels without her cooperation."[3] Actually, these estimates are so *grossly* low, that they may not even begin to convey the true nature and scope of the wealth, amassed over several centuries through succeeding generations of royals, available to the British monarchy, which Lyndon H. LaRouche Jr.'s *Executive Intelligence Review* has placed somewhere in the vicinity of nine-*trillion* dollars! That is, the British monarchy may have vastly more wealth at its disposal through its "complex pattern of nominees and holding companies" than the combined wealth of *all* of *Fortune* magazine's listed billionaires.

The power of the British monarchy goes well beyond influence, fame, and wealth. Although it heads the most elite of international orders, the Order of the Garter, it also

1. Hoey, *Charles & Diana: The Tenth Anniversary*, pp. 20-23.
2. John Sims, *Money Magazine*, "Queen's 1993 tax bill no small matter," *The Denver Post*, 7 Feb. 1993, p. 4G.
3. Lacey, *Majesty*, p. 279.

plays significant behind-the-scenes roles in several other pagan and occult orders. Prince Philip, as a typical example, holds the following foreign honors:

> Order of the Superior Sun, Afghanistan; Grand Cross of the Order of San Martin, Argentina; Grand Cross of Honour, Austria; Grand Cordon of the Order of Leopold, Belgium; Hon. Member of the Most Esteemed Family Order, Brunei; Medal of the Order of Dogwood, Canada; Knight of the Order of the Elephant, Denmark; Chain of the Most Exalted Order of the Queen of Sheba, Ethiopia; Grand Cross of the Order of the White Rose, Finland; Grand Cross of the Order of George I, Greece; Grand Cordon of the Supreme Order of the Chrysanthemum, Japan; Chevalier-Grand-Croix, Order of the Golden Lion, Luxembourg; Commander of the Order of the Golden Ark, Netherlands; Grand Cross of the Order of St Olaf, Norway; Grand Collar of the Order of Prince Henry the Navigator, Portugal; Member of the Distinguished Order of Izzuddin, Republic of Maldives; Hon. Member, Darjah Utama Temasek, Singapore; Member of the Order of the Seraphim, Sweden; Grand Cross, Yugoslav Star; Grand Cordon, National Order of the Leopard, Zaire; 1st Class Order of the Brilliant Star, Zanzibar.[1]

Ties to the New Age Movement, the occult, and false religions. Is it reasonable, given what we know so far, to think that the unbelieving world might one day hail Prince Charles as the "cosmic Christ" of the "New Age," having succeeded to a "second coming" as defined by Merovingian cabalists? At least one small group of Melanesian villagers, the Iounhanan tribe in the New Hebrides, has already succumbed to a similar case of "mistaken identity" where Prince Philip is concerned: "A group of villagers in the New Hebrides islands in the Pacific Ocean believe that the Duke of Edinburgh is their Messiah and that he will soon return to them to cure all sickness and to make the old young once more. The two hundred followers of the cult expect the Duke to restore paradise on earth, and to resume his rightful place as a Melanesian.... The villagers also believe that Prince Philip runs the Commonwealth and has deliberately kept his true identity a secret from the Queen. They are convinced that when the royal yacht *Britannia* passed close to their island in 1974, the Duke confessed to his wife that 'he was really a Melanesian Messiah

1. Judd, *Prince Philip*, p. 252.

257

and that the marriage could not last'. There has even been an authenticated exchange of gifts between the worshippers and the object of their veneration.... On 19 November 1979 a Buckingham Palace spokesman admitted the exchange of gifts."[1]

As pointed out earlier, the AntiChrist and his antichristian denials are explicitly mentioned only four times in the Bible. Based upon the scriptures, whoever denies the unique divinity of The Father and The Son, who are eternally united as One, is antichristian (1 John 2:18-29). Further, any spirit or person who denies that Jesus has come—and indeed will return—in the flesh (i.e., in the physical body in which He was resurrected from the dead), is antichristian (1 John 4:1-6); for this is the "doctrine of The Christ [Messiah]" (2 John 6-11). All cultists (e.g., Freemasons, Mormons, Jehovah's Witnesses, New Agers, etc.), participants in false religions and counterfeit "Christianities" (e.g., those who adhere to rabbinic Judaism, Buddhists, Hindus, many or even most Roman Catholics, Muslims, Christian Scientists, Scientologists, Unitarians, etc.), agnostics, and atheists are antichristian *by definition*.

Besides his prominent roles in the Order of the Garter, the Illuminati, and the Committee of 300, rumors about Prince Charles' occult activities and his interest in various forms of eastern and New Age mysticism abound. Indeed, even Diana, who felt "centered" (e.g., through *tai chi*), was involved in occultism and New Age philosophies (e.g., acupuncture, aromatherapy, astrology, healing crystals, homeopathy, hypnotherapy, and shiatsu massage), and she was said to engage in "reflections on The Prophet by Kahlil Gibran," having herself supposedly "come to rival Shirley MacLaine."[2] In other words, she had "an obsessive interest in astrologers [(e.g., Penny Thornton)], mystics, and clairvoyants."[3] "The New Age Princess," that is, "was enmeshed in a shallow world of psychics, astrologers,

1. Judd, *Prince Philip,* p. 227. For a photograph of a member of the Iounhanan tribe holding a picture icon of Prince Philip, see ibid., no. 61, between pp. 224-225.
2. Robert Lacey, "Diana, What Happened and Why," *LIFE,* Aug. 1992, pp. 31-32; Susie Pearson, "Diana," *Ladies' Home Journal,* June 1991, p. 132; and "The Diana Tapes," *People* weekly, 20 Oct. 1997, pp. 106, 108. **Please note that although much is, not *all* acupuncture, aromatherapy, homeopathy, or hypnotherapy is occult.**
3. "Princess Di will rebound, new book says," *The Denver Post,* 8 Nov. 1994, p. 2A.

fashion, aromatherapy, colonic irrigation, bulimia, self-mutilation, adultery, TV confessions, tell-all books, tapped phones, international playboys and Furies swooping down on her with cameras;" she was "the fallen goddess."[1] Likewise, Prince Andrew and his ex-wife Fergie support "Fergie's alternative health guru Jack Temple....[who uses] energy inducing rocks and poison detecting pendulums."[2] Fergie has also enjoyed the services of "one Madame Vasso—a psychic who once performed 'healing sessions' for her client under a blue plastic pyramid," and Fergie's personal trainer, Josh Salzmann, likes to think that "her exercise sessions have helped her to center herself."[3]

In March 1977, Prince Charles visited Ghana, where "he sat on a throne while he was crowned *Charles Naba Nampasa*—which [is] translated as *Charles Who Helps Mankind*."[4] Then in July 1977, while on an official visit to Alberta, Canada, to "commemorate an 1877 treaty with Blackfoot Indians near Calgary,"[5] *a Red Indian tribe made Prince Charles an honorary chieftain.*[6] Brown comments, "As a non-smoker Charles must have been relieved when the traditional peace-pipe rather ominously refused to smoke. But he willingly agreed to don the traditional costume of a tribal chief for the second time in four months. On this occasion it was not 'Naba Charles Mampasa' who appeared but 'Chief Red Crow' of the Kainai tribe. Complete with buckskins, feathered head-dress and war-paint, the new chief joined in the tribal dances in honour of the Sun, the Moon, the Grass and, inexplicably, the Chicken."[7] Heald and Mayo Mohs add, "Charles as Chief evokes an eerie echo of another Prince of Wales, his great-uncle David (Edward VIII). When David visited Canada in 1919, he was acclaimed 'Chief Morning Star'" (cf. Rev

1. Maureen Dowd, "Princess a prisoner of New Age," *The Denver Post*, 4 Sept. 1997, p. 11B.
2. Janice Min, "ROYAL WATCH: Navy Blues", *People Weekly*, 5 Aug. 1996, p. 66.
3. Michelle Green and Simon Perry, "Rue, Britannia", *People Weekly*, 25 Nov. 1996, pp. 52-55. For more information, see *Fergie: The Very Private Life of the Duchess of York* by Madame Vasso.
4. Dale, pp. 9, 12.
5. Tim Heald and Mayo Mohs, *The Man Who Will Be King, H.R.H.* (New York: Arbor House, 1979), n. pag.
6. Holden, *PRINCE CHARLES*, p. 329.
7. Brown, *PRINCE CHARLES*, p. 138. Actually, inasmuch as chickens lay eggs, the chicken here represented the *giver of life*.

22:16).[1]

In August 1984, "Prince Charles visited Papua New Guinea...to open the new Parliament building and was made 'supreme chief' on the island of Manus."[2] During his installation as the new "supreme chief," the prince wore a headband and necklace composed of wild-boars' teeth, while holding forth a carved chieftain's spear in his right hand. Besides wild-boars' teeth, the headband had a central cross.[3] Charbonneau-Lassay wrote, "In all the ancient literature the wild boar appears as typical of ferocity, independence, and fearless brutality.... But the Middle Ages recognized only the wild boar of David, who ravaged the Lord's vineyard [(Ps 80:13; see 80:8-19)]. It was regarded as the 'evil beast' of the Apocalypse, the Antichrist."[4] Previously, in 1966, the prince had visited Papua and New Guinea, "so that the native tribesmen might see 'the Great Son of the Queen.'" While there, "he shook thousands of hands, hiked through the jungle, waded rivers not immune from leeches and crocodiles, downed mysterious liquid concoctions at native feasts and was then rightly decked with necklaces of dogs' teeth as a symbol of courage.... One festive evening he watched dancers, as he noted, 'in magnificent head-dresses of bird of paradise feathers, cassowary feathers, hornbill beaks and chicken feathers' and then joined in, with his party."[5] Like boars, dogs are not favored in the scriptures (Ex 11:7; Ps 22:16, 22:20, 59:5-7, 59:14-15; Prov 26:11; Isa 56:9-11; Jer 15:3; Phil 3:2; Rev 22:15). Jesus said, "Give not that which is holy unto the dogs, neither cast ye your pearls before swine, lest they trample them under their feet, and turn again and rend you" (Matt 7:6; cf. 2 Pet 2:19-22). Prince Charles, it appears, revels in being associated with both swine and dogs.

In 1985, after asking the prince about his interest in spiritualism and mysticism, Burnet gave this account of his

---

1. Heald and Mohs, n. pag.
2. Burnet, *In Person, THE PRINCE AND PRINCESS OF WALES*, p. 20.
3. For a color photograph of this event, see *Charles & Diana: A Royal Family Album*, p. 48; or see Junor, between pp. 150-151.
4. Charbonneau-Lassay, pp. 143, 145.
5. Cathcart, pp. 64-65.

response:

> '....I've seen articles shown to me saying that I play with Ouija boards. I don't even know what they are. I've never seen one.
> 'I spend my entire time, apparently, trying to get in touch with Lord Mountbatten, and all sorts of other things. The answer is I don't, nor would I necessarily want to.
> 'I might as well say it, I might as well emphasize it, because I'm fed up with getting letters from people all the time saying "Don't touch the Ouija boards".'
> The Prince believes the reports about him on this began as a result of his admiration for the late Arthur Koestler, the author who was greatly interested in parapsychology [(the study of demonic powers)] and left a bequest for a professional chair for its study in a British university....
> Told that no British university might take up the offer, the Prince, as Chancellor of the University of Wales, wrote to the Vice-Chancellor saying it would be a great pity to lose the bequest.... The Prince thinks that the publicity began with just that scientific proposal.
> 'What I find so annoying is that it should be reduced to this level of absurdity.
> 'I'm not interested in the occult, or dabbling in black magic or any of these kinds of things or, for that matter, strange forms of mysticism. I'm purely interested in being open-minded.[1]

Regarding false prophets, Jesus said, "You will know them by their fruits." Prince Charles' fruits are clearly not those of a Christian, but of a pagan who is "open-minded" to the world's false religions and cults. During a five-day stopover in Japan in 1970, for example, the prince "dined with Emperor Hirohito—forging one of the many links of statecraft that culminated in the Queen and Prince Philip's 1975 state visit to Japan—and was ready [the] next day for...a round of temples, castles and palaces in the ancient Imperial capital.... The abbot who showed him around the temple of the great bronze Buddha [in Kyoto] was equally impressed by his intelligent questions on Shinto philosophy. 'I found that what the old man was saying I had believed, without realising it, all my life,' Prince

---

1. Burnet, *In Person, THE PRINCE AND PRINCESS OF WALES*, p. 45. Also see Dale, pp. 225, 227-229. Junor, rather ignorantly, states, "Stories appeared saying that he had become a vegetarian, that he had given up shooting, that he was dabbling in spiritualism and had been attempting to reach Lord Mountbatten with a ouija board.... It was all fantasy" (p. 221).

Charles said afterwards, encouraging words...not inexplicable to a younger generation who seek the common truths of religion rather than the differences.... ...four years later the Prince opened a new Sony factory in [Welsh] Glamorgan."[1] In November 1980, as yet another example, the prince toured India and Nepal, where "he undertook a three-day trek in the Himalayas...and also visited the Golden Temple at Amristar," at which he did homage.[2] In 1988, Prince Charles and Princess Diana "visited the Temple of the Emerald Buddha," and "in 1989, Prince Charles reached to touch a special statue of Buddha in the world's oldest Buddhist temple."[3] More recently, on the evening of February 28, 1996, the prince visited "a Hindu temple in North London," happily taking a red mark on the center of his forehead![4]

John Dale, an authority on the occult beliefs, practices, and activities of Britain's Royal Family, and Prince Charles in particular, has written a relatively thorough book titled, *The Prince and the Paranormal: The Psychic Bloodline of the Royal Family*. The following several pages of information are quoted from his book:

> On March 6, 1977, one of the world's best-known amateur aviators bounced the tyres of his trusty Andover down onto the overheated runway of [Kenya's] Nairobi Airport....
>
> For this was no ordinary safari. It was something much more than that—an exploration into Africa's soul and, simultaneously, into the soul of the Prince of Wales.
>
> So, on March 16, it was a handsome, bronzed and fit Charles who emerged from nine days in the wilderness, reassured, rejuvenated and spiritually refreshed....[5]

1. Cathcart, pp. 112-113. Dale notes the same experience, adding that the prince "told an interviewer that 'he felt he'd come home' at last" (pp. 200-201).
2. Burnet, *In Person, THE PRINCE AND PRINCESS OF WALES*, p. 45.
3. Hoey, *Charles & Diana: The Tenth Anniversary*, pp. 108-109.
4. Green, Denworth, Smith, and Wright, "PRINCE-LESS DIANA," *People Weekly*, 11 Mar. 1996, pp. 76-78. For a picture of the prince walking barefoot in a Hindu temple in India, see *Charles & Diana: A Royal Family Album*, p. 48.
5. John Dale, *The Prince and the Paranormal: The Psychic Bloodline of the Royal Family* (London: W.H. Allen & Co. Plc, 1986), pp. 9, 11. Neither the London-based publisher nor the Australian author of *The Prince and the Paranormal* could be contacted to obtain permission to quote the work's material, despite several calls to the United Kingdom and Australia. Dale's book has been officially **banned** in the UK by Prince Charles' mother, Queen Elizabeth II, and the publisher apparently is no longer in business. However, due to the important nature of the material for this work, it was deemed a necessary risk nonetheless to quote it.

Thus a new Prince was born, with a drive to challenge long-respected orthodoxy and to become the torch-bearer of radical, revolutionary ideas about how every one of us should live....

....For, there is evidence that deep inside himself, the Prince has become a super-ecumenist—somebody who believes that each of the world's religions—including Christianity—contains a relative truth, rather than an absolute one.

For some time members of the Royal Family, especially his parents, had been growing anxious about the way he was making this clear to those who could read the signs and recognize the codewords. At first, for more than two years, the Prince seemed oblivious of the very real dangers that were awaiting him. Then, late in 1985, the menace to his own position and potentially to the Crown was brought home to him. As the truth dawned, he belatedly began a damage-limitation exercise and tried to play the matter down.

He resorted to ridicule. 'It really is quite extraordinary,' he said. 'As far as I can make out, I'm about to become a Buddhist monk, or live halfway up a mountain or only eat grass. I'm not quite as bad as that.'

He employed flat denials. 'I'm not interested in the occult, or dabbling in black magic or any of these kind of things or, for that matter, strange forms of mysticism,' he replied to the 'approved' questions of Sir Alastair Burnet in a television interview.

But the truth is that the Prince has come to hold beliefs that many of his future subjects will find strange and questionable. They allow him to put aside rationalism, for instance, and to surrender to psychic influences. In a word, he has become absorbed in the *paranormal*—that is, phenomena which cannot be explained by modern science.

Here are some of the beliefs that this book will show he holds:

Coincidences are *signposts*—when he encounters one, he analyses it to see which path it is directing him along.

Dreams can foretell the future—for this purpose, he has tried keeping a dream diary and pen at his bedside.

Modern medicine must incorporate the psychic, spiritual and the paranormal.

Much can be learned from ancient prophecy systems

The author apologizes if having done so results in any copyright infringement or hardship to Mr. Dale, and he wishes to thank Mr. Dale in advance for his gracious support in this endeavor. Although the work is officially banned in the UK, the reader may nonetheless attempt to obtain a copy by writing to Bury House Christian Books; Clows Top; Kidderminster, Worcs; DY149HX; England; *or* Christian Truth in Victory Publications; 9088 Country Rd., 11 NW; Alexandria, MN 56308; United States of America. Copies may also be available at a local library, or through an inter-library loan.

such as I-Ching, astrology, and divination by pendulum.

All religions are ultimately one.

In addition the Prince appears to believe himself to be psychic.

It was in 1982 that the Prince first hinted publicly at such unusual spiritual beliefs. Then followed a period in which he attempted to discuss them as openly as possible. He saw himself as a sort of missionary, lending his prestige to a neglected but very worthy cause. The outcome, however, left him disappointed and even a little bitter....

The plain truth was that his intellectual and spiritual concepts were way above the heads of his audience, with the result that instead of being greeted as a 'pointer'—his word for someone who guides mankind onto the right path—he was treated as a crank. The tabloid press looked upon him as a freak and his personal reputation was put at risk....

....After all, this was not a joke to the Prince. It was religion—and on that subject, as always, he was deadly serious....

'It was the most extraordinary thing,' he [(Prince Charles)] told the writer Anne de Courcy. 'I was sitting at my desk at the time and I happened to look at my bookshelf and my eyes suddenly settled on a book about Paracelsus.' (Paracelsus was a sixteenth century physician who believed in an occult cosmic unity and, like the Prince, considered that all religions were part of a greater whole.) 'So I took the book down and read it and as a result I tried to make a speech around Paracelsus and perhaps a re-look at what he was saying and the ideas he propounded—wasn't it time to think again about the relationship between mind and body, or body and spirit?'...

....It is a long sentence but, because of its half-hidden meanings, an important one. 'Perhaps,' he said, 'we just have to accept it is *God's will* that the unorthodox individual is doomed to years of frustration, ridicule and failure in order to act out his role in the scheme of things until his day arrives and mankind is ready to receive his message—a message which he probably finds hard to explain himself, but which he knows comes from *a far deeper source than conscious thought*.' (Author's italics.) The irony is that the Prince could easily have been talking about himself.

....At one stage Prince Charles, although committed to Christianity, was also somewhat unsure about certain aspects of such matters, feeling there was a lack of positive evidence. Then, beginning in 1977, he began to climb off the fence and to line up with the mixed bag of visionaries, intellectuals, cranks and lunatics who say there are other planes of existence tangled inside and around the one which we inhabit.

The person who helped convince him was a writer and explorer, and a former political adviser to the Prince's favourite uncle, Lord Mountbatten. He is Renaissance Man reborn, a benign intellectual and the major single influence in the Prince's stage by stage spiritual development over the last ten years. His name: Laurens van der Post....[1]

Through all his rich and sometimes perilous experience, van der Post had never lost touch with what he considered to be the African side of his mind. He continued to cling to his belief that dreams contained, in effect, messages. He was sceptical of the way Western people placed too much reliance upon reasoning. He considered that intuition could sometimes offer much more valuable guidance than rational thought. He also believed that coincidences should not be ignored but warranted careful interpretation.

....[He] was introduced by his wife Ingaret to a man whose ideas would come to dominate much of the remainder of his life and, through him, radicalize the mind of the future King of England. That man was Carl Gustav Jung....[2]

What was it [that] van der Post believed?

First,...he...believed that dreams offered guidance as to future decisions. They were incapable of falsehood and were the true source of mythology, religion, legend and art.

Second, he considered coincidences to be equally meaningful, that they should not be ignored and that they indicated man's relationship with the cosmos.

Third, he thought that psychic intuition—listening with his 'inner ear'—was sometimes a better basis for decision-making than reasoning. He considered that Western man had come to rely too heavily upon rationalism.

Fourth, he believed in a world of spirit gods, able to aid or hinder ordinary mortals, sometimes even threatening their lives. Evidence for this latter conviction—that such benign and malign spirits existed—was displayed before him while he was in the Kalahari Desert in southern Africa in the 1950s making a documentary about the native Bushmen living there.

Van der Post witnessed how his filming party became jinxed because one of its members shot dead a steenbuck, thereby breaking a promise not to spill blood on sacred territory. After that, they were viciously attacked twice by huge swarms of

---

1. Dale, pp. 13-19.
2. Dale, p. 25. Junor too notes "the important part that intuition played in his life" (p. 2). According to Junor, van der Post "knew more about the African people and their spiritual heritage not only than any European alive, but more than most Africans themselves. He spoke several native dialects and loved Africa." Prince Charles was captivated by "the wise thoughts on man and nature that spilled forth from the elderly man." The prince was taken by van der Post's "fascination with the inner self," as well as his "inordinate interest in dreams" and Jungian interpretation. Van der Post's grandfather had taught him about Joseph's deliverance of Egypt and Israel through "his dreaming." Van der Post therefore "encouraged Charles to trust his intuition, to listen to his dreams and to pay attention to coincidence" (Junor, pp. 110-112, 220).

stinging bees which he sincerely came to suspect were dispatched by angry spirit gods. Then perfectly reliable equipment began to fail for no reason whatsoever. And evidently their Bushman guide, Samutchoso, was tossed over backwards by an unseen force when he knelt to pray. Finally, van der Post feared that even their Land-rovers might be cursed and they would be stranded in the desert to die.

He described how he watched Samutchoso go into a trance. The Bushman apparently contacted the spirit gods who conveyed the message that they were offended by the lack of respect shown by the party.

In all seriousness, van der Post decided to try to make amends. Before leaving, he wrote a letter to the spirits—a letter which, even to those accompanying him, seemed rather strange.

The letter began by begging for the pardon of spirits for any unintended display of disrespect. Van der Post flattered and praised them, saying how a cave painting of an eland—the Bushmen's most important religious symbol—showed the spirits could make flesh and blood create beyond their own physical constraints. Then, virtually as a penitent, he offered them his profound contrition and asked for forgiveness. Finally, he hoped that others who followed in his party's footsteps might not make their mistakes and would show the spirits the respect they deserved....

From that moment, noted van der Post later, his feeling of frustration lifted as he seemed to break through into another dimension of life.

On other occasions with the Bushmen, van der Post encountered additional paranormal phenomena, these seemingly connected with telepathic powers....

These then were some of the stories that Prince Charles learned about van der Post during the period when the two men spent many hours sitting together at Buckingham Palace....

And yet they were not the most astonishing stories in the Afrikaner's repertoire, the stories that must have seized the attention of Prince Charles.

These were the ones concerning Jung....[1]

....Over many years Jung had analysed 67,000 dreams. In addition to living with the Elgonyi in Kenya, he had spent much time interviewing Red Indians and Negroes in the United States. He toured the world in order to study mythology and religious development, particularly of the Chinese, Tibetans, Indians, Greeks and Babylonians.

From all this work he deduced that the minds of people completely separated by space, time and culture still contained much material in common. He said that some of this material came from outside the personal experience of those who possessed it. If it was not part of the *personal* unconscious, he asked, then

1. Dale, pp. 28-30.

where was it from? To his own question, Jung answered that it must come from somewhere else, from a force equally influencing all mankind—a force which he labelled the Collective Unconscious.

In a letter to van der Post, Jung told him that although he could not say what God was, his work proved empirically that the pattern of God existed throughout all mankind.

Jung became positive that the Collective Unconscious contained all the fundamental religious symbols and was the repository of all religious aspirations....

Van der Post's encounter with Jung ended the feeling of spiritual isolation that the Afrikaner had suffered all his life. At long last, he was able to share the inner core of his being with another person.

Even before going to Kenya in 1925, both men, independently of each other, had already learnt through personal experience the importance of dreams. Then both, in their separate explorations of Africa became further convinced of the existence of psychic forces and the paranormal....

Thirty years later, van der Post tried repeatedly to persuade the ageing Jung to return with him to Africa.... But Jung always refused. He told him that witchcraft also existed in Zurich and in the Swiss mountains—and until he had understood that, he had no right to go back to Africa....

Van der Post was also led into other realms of the paranormal by Jung. He came to share with Jung a belief in the I-Ching, a book of Chinese philosophy arguing that mankind and his cosmic and earthly environments made up an interacting unity. In this it is believed that the universe is composed of two equal and complementary forces, yin and yang. Yang is light and positive, and yin is dark and negative. Through the use of the I-Ching, a person can determine a course of action and consult a high form of moral guidance from, in effect, the cosmos....

So, to sum up, what does all this establish?

We know that in March, 1977, Prince Charles paid a secret visit to Africa, inspired by the ideas of Laurens van der Post.

The Prince chose to disappear into a wilderness that was a particularly meaningful part of Africa for both van der Post and Carl Gustav Jung. He would have found himself near, and probably among, the Elgonyi whose dreams and witchcraft had so influenced Jung. These were the very dreams and witchcraft which convinced Jung of the truth of religious relativism, an essential component of his theory of the Collective Unconscious. It helped him understand coincidence, dreams and intuition....

So when Prince Charles went there in 1977, it was not a randomly chosen destination. It was an area which possessed a deeply spiritual association for van der Post.... It had played a crucial role in the development of the Afrikaner's own spiritual views....

It was during this period that I believe the Prince underwent a spiritual transformation.

After Charles's return van der Post was quoted in *Harpers and Queen* magazine as saying that the Prince had had some sort of profound religious experience in Kenya, though he has since categorically denied making this statement.

If this were really so, then the Kenyan expedition represented Prince Charles's own 'road to Damascus and blinding flash'—an intense religious experience of the kind which van der Post certainly believes can happen. On that basis, it would truly amount to a turning point in his life....[1]

In 1981, Laurens van der Post read a book called *Something is Happening*, written by one of his good friends, Dr Winifred Rushforth, then aged 97. She was a Jungian analyst practising in Edinburgh....

Through this work, which she considered her true vocation, she met Jung himself and also van der Post and, of course, became a firm believer in the existence and influence of the Collective Unconscious. Her own gift was for interpreting the dreams through which the unconscious expressed itself and she set up numerous dream therapy groups. She argued strongly that dreams could be a guide to the future.

All this she explained in her book which was read by Prince Charles. For instance, in 1979, she had had a 'big dream'—a Jungian term for a dream which is prophetic. This one dealt with the unity between psychology and religion....

She also described her belief in telepathy.

These then were some of the ideas which so impressed Prince Charles as he read the pages of *Something is Happening* from start to finish. It left a profound mark upon him and he wrote to Dr Rushforth about it. As a specialist in the interpretation of dreams, she would have recommended that he keep a dream diary. This he did—later admitting he was 'remembering and recording dreams'. He added: 'I think one can probably learn a considerable amount from them.'...

The correspondence with Dr Rushforth was private and the Prince's letters came to rest safely in the hands of her daughter, Dr Diana Bates, who had properly maintained their complete confidentiality. But the Prince was sufficiently impressed by the answers to make a private visit to Dr Rushforth in 1983, accompanied by Princess Diana....[2]

One crucial question remains: to what extent did van der Post and Rushforth—these two followers of Jung—come to influence the Prince? Did they persuade him to believe in the radical

1. Dale, pp. 33-37.
2. Dale, pp. 39-42.

religious concept of the Collective Unconscious? In my view the only answer is *yes*....

[In]...quotes which he formally approved—the Prince...openly [declared]...his trust in intuition, dreams and coincidences.

[In]...mid-1985, the Prince was asked about Jung in another interview and said: 'I think [Jung] makes a great deal of sense in many, many areas, and particularly what is written in the Bible and Indian religions, and in Islam, and many others...definitely a pattern develops, I think, where we are all ultimately trying to explore, to go along the same path, to answer the same questions. We all approach it from different paths but ultimately, the paths meet somewhere in infinity, and that's the important thing.'

These were dangerous words from a future head of the Church of England. The Prince was taking the Jungian view that all religions are of equal value.

[The]...Prince selected Laurens van der Post as godfather to Prince William. It is a fact that van der Post believes all religions—Christianity, Islam, Animism or whatever—are components of the same force....

It seems highly likely that the Prince knew this was van der Post's religious position. Yet he still selected him for an important role in a Church of England ceremony for a child who might one day head that church. It is surely a proper question to be asked, whether Prince Charles fully agrees with van der Post. If so, then Charles, the future head of the Church of England, may be a super-ecumenist. It would cause tremendous trouble in almost every country in the world....

Taken as a whole, I believe the evidence proves beyond reasonable doubt that Prince Charles accepts the concept of the Collective Unconscious and is a follower of Carl Jung. More than that, it shows that his interest is not merely academic: it has already had tangible repercussions. It reveals that on occasions he is even willing to let the Collective Unconscious take over the decision-making process for him—through intuition, dreams and coincidences—in preference to rational thinking....[1]

Whatever the Royal Family discuss behind closed doors about the paranormal, they maintain the highest standards of discretion in public. But occasionally, by complete accident, they let something slip that gives the rest of us an insight.

One such slip that occurred in March, 1980, can be attributed to Prince Charles, a full two years before he began to express himself publicly on such matters....

The occasion was a visit he was making to an orphanage in south-west London. Among the assembled spectators was a group of people wearing lapel badges that announced: 'Healing is a Gift of the Spirit.'

1. Dale, pp. 45-47.

As the Prince went through his usual handshaking routine, one such badge caught his eye. 'Are you a Spiritualist [(i.e., spiritist)]?' he asked its wearer, Mr Derek Robinson.

'Yes,' replied Mr Robinson.

'How lovely,' said the Prince. 'Do you know Mr Fricker? I am reading his book. It is amazing.'

He then turned to Jean Bassett, a Spiritualist medium, also in the group. 'There's a lot of you about,' he joked.

Quite spontaneously and accidentally, the Prince had revealed several very personal features about himself. Firstly, by his immediate recognition of the lapel badge, he had showed himself familiar with Spiritualism, the religion which claims direct communication with the dead via the séance room. Secondly, he believed that being a Spiritualist, like Mr Robinson, was 'lovely'. Thirdly, he disclosed that at that very moment he was reading a book about Spiritualism, one of the most astounding ever written.

Ted Fricker, the author of the book the Prince found 'amazing', was a well-known Spiritual healer practising in London. He claimed to have once been a little boy in the Holy Land at the time of Christ. He had later been trained in Heaven before being sent back to earth, via Tottenham, to conduct his healing mission.

'It's not the first time I've been here,' Fricker told an interviewer. 'I used to run after Jesus, touching his clothing because I loved him so much. That's why God sent me back to earth as a miracle worker, just like Christ.'

In his book—*God Is My Witness*—Fricker explained more:

> Every night after I've gone to bed I'm surrounded by spirit peo- ple who come to talk to me, not only the doctors who advise me but many others who help me to solve the various problems which my patients bring to me....

Among his early patients was a businessman named M.H. Tester....

'Fricker is a gifted healer,' he wrote in a review, 'but as a spiritual philosopher I think he is naive and does himself injustice by the facile way he attempts to explain his gift.'

Tester added: 'The image of the boy walking in the wake of Jesus, the golden ring with the cross lit and a wreath of thorns burned into his inner face by a lightning bolt, the thinly-veiled comparison with Moses, and the general sugges- tion that he is one of the spiritual elite—about all this I'm sceptical.'

Tester was not alone in his scepticism. His was the wide- spread judgement in the Spiritualist world. Anyone who treated Fricker's claims seriously was thought naive. Yet here

was Prince Charles, with all the other demands upon his time, sitting down and reading this book and raising the subject matter in an impromptu street conversation. Why was he even interested in it?...[1]

Why would Prince Charles spend his time reading a particularly bizarre Spiritualist book which was dismissed by most Spiritualists as outrageous rubbish, and by most Christians as offensive? Was he interested in the healing career of Edward Fricker? Did he think it possible that Fricker had once been a boy on the Holy Land following in the wake of Jesus, or that he entertained the spirits of the dead at night in his bedroom?

To the outsider, the Prince's behaviour might appear inexplicable. But to the insider, to someone with knowledge of the Royal Family, these questions come as no surprise. There is evidence that by the time the Prince began to read Fricker's book, he was not only familiar with the religious concepts of Jung, but he may already have been initiated into the secrets of Spiritualism.

But equally important was that the Prince came from a family with profound, if concealed, interest in several aspects of the paranormal. It went back six generations and was part of the bloodline. It was something which the royals kept very much within their own circle....

The strong likelihood is that Prince Charles received his introduction to Spiritualism in the early 1950s, when he was at the impressionable age of about seven. It appears that he was introduced to the Spiritualist faith by his mildly eccentric great-great-aunt, Princess Marie Louise, then in her eighties. She was a grand-daughter of Queen Victoria.

There can be no doubt that she was very much involved in Spiritualist practices. She was a very regular patient of Harry Edwards, probably the most celebrated of all spiritual healers. The list of clients journeying into the North Downs to receive Edwards's healing touch included even more of the rich, famous and powerful than attended Fricker's clinic. Of course, many of these did not appreciate that Edwards believed his powers came from the dead....

How did this sweet old lady introduce Prince Charles to Spiritualism? The answer is that she almost certainly gave him a book on the subject, entitled *Spirit Stories for Children*. Edwards was a Spiritualist medium, able to go into trance and contact the Other Side. He believed his healing power came from the spirits of two dead medical pioneers....

'One day she purchased a copy of Mrs Burton's book,' wrote Edwards later. 'Some time afterwards she asked for another copy for, as she said, "a little boy you know very well".'

As far as Edwards was aware, there was only one possible candidate for this role....

1. Dale, pp. 49-50, 52.

'She did not specifically say it was for his Royal Highness Prince Charles,' he added, 'but the imputation was there.' What would the book have told the infant Prince?...

In the book's introduction, Mrs Burton, a medium herself, explains to the child readers that she has written down the stories as related to her by a spirit personality with whom she has been in contact. To that extent, she denies authorship.

'For each of you, there is someone in the spirit world or "Heaven" who tries to look after you, to help you do the right thing,' she says....

From the book, one's first impression is that the contents came through Mrs Burton's own mediumship. But this was not the case. The real source was Harry Edwards himself and one of his spirit guides, Reuben....[1]

As the Prince began to forge his radical spiritual views, he recognized that the process held some danger for him. The problem was that one day, when he succeeded to the throne, he would also become head of the Church of England. Some church leaders would undoubtedly welcome his enlightened opinions. But there would be many others, both in the pulpits and the pews, who would not.

They would find it difficult to accept that all the world's religions were one, that Christianity was neither more nor less important than the spirits of African witchcraft. As for Spiritualism itself, it had already split the Anglican church.

In 1937, the Church of England had mounted a systematic inquiry in which the investigators sat in séances with mediums. It had then suppressed the majority report. This was eventually leaked and found to be quite favourable to the Spiritualists.

Although the report was signed by seven of the ten committee members, the then Archbishop of Canterbury Dr Cosmo Lang was on the side of the minority. 'Spiritualism and spiritualistic services,' he said, 'are not countenanced or encouraged in the Church of England.'...

During the war years, the Scottish medium Helen Duncan was arrested during a séance in Portsmouth, tried at the Old Bailey and jailed for an allegedly fraudulent spirit materialization. It was the movement's *cause célèbre*. This caused Spiritualists to live in fear of the Witchcraft Act, the instrument of law employed....

As Spiritualism frequently involved the very practices which outsiders argued must be fraudulent—such as materialization of the dead—Spiritualists understandably felt they were a persecuted minority. However, in 1951 their persistent campaigning was rewarded when the Witchcraft Act was repealed—a move that would open the floodgate to Britain becoming the occult capital of the Western world by the 1980s....

In the circumstances, it is not surprising that the Prince

1.   Dale, pp. 53-56, 58.

realized that his views could propel him into a head-on collision with some Church of England leaders and many of its members.

He had a very wide choice of clerics to consult but the one he most favoured happened to be the most unorthodox: Dr Mervyn Stockwood, the Bishop of Southwark, and a man as interested in the paranormal as he was.

'If you were to cut out psychic occurrences from the Bible,' declared Stockwood, 'you would have to cut out a great deal. It is irritating when people dismiss the whole thing as black magic and roguery.'

Stockwood was the most senior Church of England cleric to have openly supported Spiritualism....

Now, in his adulthood, the Prince turned to Dr Mervyn Stockwood seeking answers to matters of faith—important to him, the Church and, ultimately, the nation....

Thus, if Prince Charles had suffered doubts and anxieties over the direction of his beliefs, they would have been alleviated by his discussions with the Spiritualist Bishop....[1]

In 1976 the now defunct weekly newspaper *Reveille* discovered that an unregistered medical practitioner had been visited separately by the Queen, Princess Margaret and Princess Alexandra. At once a cover-up was mounted to conceal the actual nature of the treatment.

The stress was laid upon the fact that the treatment, although unorthodox, was purely mechanical. this was the substance of the items published in the press. *It was untrue*.

The person visited was Kay Kiernan who runs the Bluestone Clinic in Harley House, near Harley Street, London. She offers several kinds of therapies—some physical, and others psychic and Spiritualist. She is a medium able to go into a trance.

The Queen went to see her because of recurring pain she suffered in a shoulder which she had sprained while chopping wood on one of her country estates. It was slow in healing. What Miss Kiernan offered were sessions on an American machine called a Diapulse, which transmitted pulses of high frequency electromagnetic waves through the body....

The truth is different. The interesting fact about the Diapulse is that in the hands of Miss Kiernan, it is more than merely mechanical. When it is switched on, Miss Kiernan tunes into it with her mind and uses it as a channel for her psychic and Spiritual powers. She admitted as much in an article later, saying she believed she was 'spirit-guided' to buy the machine while on holiday in New York.

Then she explained how her healing worked. 'I believe it is the perfect instrument to be used with psychic power,' she added....

The combination of royalty and horses brings us to Mrs

1. Dale, pp. 61-65, 67.

273

Lavender Dower.... She has two roles.

Second only to Prince Charles, she is the most important figure in the rapid transformation of alternative medicine from the marginally disreputable to the reasonably respectable. Since 1962, when she was way ahead of her time, she has been the driving force in trying to unite the many different therapies in order that they should become self-policing. She did this by founding the Institute for Complementary Medicine.... With her in the chair, it has established strong links with Prince Charles and other intimate members of the royal circle....[1]

As the driving force behind the Institute..., she has met Prince Charles. 'He's a great support,' she said.

The Institute is the most important body in making alternative medicine acceptable to the public....

Mrs Dower stressed that Prince Charles was not directly involved in supporting the Institute financially although he had expressed strong sympathy with its aims. But what is surprising—and quite unexplained—is the heavy involvement by members of the royal circle.[2] Its patrons, for instance, include:

Angus Ogilvy, husband of Princess Alexandra.

Major John Wills, whose wife Jean is a cousin of the Queen and one of her ladies-in-waiting.

Dr Charles Elliott, homoeopathic doctor to the Queen.

Lord Oaksey, racing friend of the Queen and the Queen Mother.

Sir Antony Acland, Permanent Under-secretary at the Foreign and Commonwealth Office and head of the Diplomatic Service—the man responsible for all executive-level royal staff.

Also involved is Dr Alec Forbes who, through the public endorsement by Prince Charles, has become Britain's best-known practitioner of alternative medicine....

He [(Anthony Baird, the Institute's administrator)] added: 'We have had letters from America saying we can hardly realize the effect Prince Charles's speeches have caused. It's reverberated throughout the Western world....'[3]

1. Dale, pp. 69, 71, 73.
2. In 1992, Princess Anne "visited two Tibetan refugee camps." While doing so, the "personal representative of the Dalai Lama...welcomed the Princess and showed her the feeding centres, clinic and school and, most interesting of all, the Tibetan medical centre. The centre uses herbal remedies—a great favourite with all the Royal Family, including the Princess—and works hand in hand with the Save the Children [Fund's] doctors and local hospitals" ("The Top of The World," *Majesty,* Nov. 1992, Vol. 13, No. 11, p. 8). **Please note that herbal remedies, when they work and are provided by non-occultists, are, even in the author's opinion, to be preferred to modern drugs, inasmuch as they are a natural provision from God.**
3. Dale, pp. 76-77. In one such speech, as a typical example, the prince observed, "More working days are lost because of back pain than for any other reason. It is a chronic problem.... Surely we should be investigating every method that might reduce that number, and there

I believe that Canon W.H. Elliott, who served as chaplain to George V, George VI and the present Queen was effectively a Spiritualist medium. He attended séances with the result that he came firmly to believe in communication with the dead. However, he recognized Spiritualism to be a major source of dispute within the Church of England and, bearing in mind his position, he scrupulously avoided supporting the movement as such—while taking little care to conceal his views.

'Why should anybody think it uncanny and wrong that a "sensitive", such as I am, can hear voices from the Other Side? I will not renounce my experience,' he said....

Was the royal chaplain a Spiritualist?

The answer is that although he never openly supported the Spiritualist movement as far as we know, he espoused the Spiritualist cause in a way which challenged Anglican orthodoxy head-on.

He believed that 'sensitives'—that is, mediums—such as himself could communicate with the dead. He spoke of the Other World being all around us, interpenetrating the world we see. He thought that the dead could come to the aid of the living.

This is Spiritualism, not Anglicanism....

So, what was Elliot's influence upon the Royal Family during the 31 years in which he served them?

First, I believe that they must have been aware of his views because they were made public in broadcasts and in print. The fact that they were tolerated, at the very least, says something about the sympathies of George V, George VI, and the Queen.

Second, in my opinion, he would not have opposed members of the Royal Family turning to clairvoyance, spiritual healing and the comfort of the séance room. Indeed, it seems likely he would have encouraged it—in the way he tried to encourage a deeper sense of spiritual awareness in the public at large.[1]

In the late 1950s, a well-known but ailing medium named Lilian Bailey told an astonishing story to her family.

In 1953, at her home in Wembley, North London, she had received a telephone call from a stranger, asking her for her services. He wished to hold a séance. He arranged with Mrs Bailey for her to visit an address in Kensington at a set time. She agreed....

She arrived at the location as planned, was led inside and was carefully blindfolded. Then she was taken to another house. There, she sat on a chair ready to begin the séance, hearing the rustle of skirts as the sitters took their places around her.

---

are two forms of alternative treatment, chiropractics and osteopathy, which have proved to be successful in a great many cases of back pain. Even doctors consult them. So what is there to lose by giving them a try?" (Junor, p. 259).

1. Dale, pp. 79-82.

Despite the difficult setting, she quickly went into a trance and made contact with her spirit guide....

Eventually Mrs Bailey emerged from her trance, the lights were raised and her blindfold removed. Then she saw who her sitters were—the Queen Mother, the Queen, Prince Philip, the Duchess of Kent and the latter's daughter Princess Alexandra....

Was Lilian Bailey bolstering her own importance by telling a tall story? The evidence suggests: *no*....

After the first séance, according to Morrow: 'There were several private sessions with the medium for the Queen Mother....'[1]

Another medium has also claimed to have served the Royal Family at this time. She was Bertha Harris....

'What I can tell you,' she said in 1976, 'is that the Royal Family have always had a deep interest in Spiritualism—but it would not do for them to admit it.'

She claimed she was summoned by George VI in the late 1930s. In an interview she agreed she had visited him 'many times' but refused to disclose details of their exchanges. 'That would be breaking faith,' she said. 'Their secrets are safe with me. I can only tell you he came to me about lots of things.'...

In fact, other reasons exist for believing Spiritualism is very familiar to the Queen Mother. Her devoted Extra-Woman-of-the-Bedchamber, Lady Elizabeth Basset, who has served her many years, is deeply interested in communication between the living and the dead.

She shows this in an anthology she compiled, *The Bridge of Love*, in which she quotes approvingly from Spiritualists....

Equally revealing are her lengthy quotations from Sir George Trevelyan, often called the high priest of the British psychic movement and a man much admired by Prince Charles....

And, in 1980, another well-known British clairvoyant Robin Stevens was quoted as saying: 'One has to keep some secrets but on occasions I have been called to Windsor Castle.'...

Nowadays, the Queen Mother is careful to avoid controversy, preferring her public image to be that of the 'nation's favourite grandmother', a role she plays to perfection. She leaves the contentious issues to various offspring, especially to the thoughtful and willing Prince Charles.[2]

As far as Prince Charles is concerned, royal fascination with the paranormal and Spiritualism is not confined to his mother's side of the family. It also comes from his father's side through the Greek Connection....

According to his biographer Philip Ziegler, [Prince Charles's favourite 'uncle', Lord] Mountbatten was open-minded about the Theosophical Society—which is spiritualist and occultist....

Ziegler adds: 'Mountbatten was fascinated by the theory of

1. Dale, pp. 91-92.
2. Dale, pp. 96-100.

reincarnation....'....

This is not surprising. Mountbatten was a secret member of the Ghost Club which, despite its frivolous-sounding name, is a serious organization, founded in 1862, for the pursuit of psychical research. [He]...would have met many of the most distinguished Spiritualists and occultists of the last half century....[1]

So what effect did this Greek fascination with the paranormal have on the young Philip Mountbatten, one day to step from relative obscurity to be Consort to the Queen of England? His mother was deeply committed to the Spiritual world and his two cousins, George and Paul, were practising Spiritualists. His Uncle Dickie believed in flying saucers, and another close Greek relative, the Duchess of Kent was also apparently turning towards the séance room....

It would have been unsurprising if Philip, too, [who does believe in flying saucers and the essential divinity of nature,] had become intrigued with the subject....

As we have seen, Prince Charles is deeply religious and firmly committed to a belief in spiritual forces that affect daily life....

....To Prince Charles, a student of Jung, the mind is in contact with the Collective Unconscious....[2]

Accepting Prince Philip to be the exception that proves the rule,[3] the fact is that whichever other part of the Royal Family one scrutinizes, there is evidence of unusual interest in the paranormal....

....It is part of the bloodline. It runs like a secret thread through the House of Windsor. It was the backcloth against which Prince Charles's mind was made receptive to the ideas of Laurens van der Post.

The only difference in his case was that he insisted upon being true to himself, stepping out of the royal confines and telling the world about it, whether that world was prepared or not.

---

1. Dale, pp. 113-114.
2. Dale, pp. 120-122.
3. At a National Press Club speech, Prince Philip proclaimed, "It is now apparent that the ecological pragmatism of the so-called pagan religions such as that of the American Indians, Polynesians, [and] Australian Aborigines, was a great deal more realistic in terms of conservation ethics than the more intellectual monotheistic philosophies of the revealed religions" (Hunt, *GLOBAL PEACE AND THE RISE OF ANTICHRIST*, p. 168). According to the prince, who is now the International President of the World Wide Fund for Nature, "If God is in nature, nature itself becomes divine" ("A Wing and a Prayer," *Majesty* magazine, June 1994, Vol. 15, No. 6, p. 29). While the Committee of 300 continues to plot the deaths of much of the world's population, so that "nature" may survive and thrive, Prince Philip, one of the inner-circle members of the committee, plays the hypocrite as well as anyone: "since he was appointed 1951's president of the British Association for the Advancement of Science, he has hammered at the themes...that commercial laboratories pursuing profitable ends in secret are starvers of the national good; the need to maintain humane priorities in science since 'we can either set the world free from drudgery, fear, hunger and pestilence, or obliterate life itself'; and the importance of preserving the world's wildlife" (Lacey, *Majesty*, p. 253).

If he is criticized for honestly held beliefs, then he must also be congratulated for displaying the guts to speak out where others have remained silent....

In speaking out, Prince Charles must have known that he was embracing six generations, reaching back to his great-great-great grandmother, Queen Victoria. For it was Victoria herself who set her descendants firmly upon this path, as she did for other European royalties of which she was also effectively grandmother....[1]

If there is one unusual enthusiasm for which the Royal Family is known, then that enthusiasm is homoeopathy. It is used regularly by the present generation of Royalty, particularly the Queen. And the royal bloodline reaches right back to the discipline's founder, Samuel Hahnemann....

This is where it differs completely from orthodox medicine.... [Homoeopaths] say that their remedies rely upon a *spiritual* force, not a material one. In this way, homoeopathy is unquestionably paranormal....

....Edward VIII, George VI and the Duke of Gloucester—all appointed a homoeopathic doctor.

The man who won this honour for homoeopathy was Dr John Weir. For this achievement alone, which many believe saved homoeopathy from virtual extinction, Weir is probably the discipline's most important figure since Hahnemann....

How much did the Royal Family use homoeopathic remedies? On the day of George V's funeral, Weir loved to recall, he wrote prescriptions for three kings and four queens. And in 1946 George VI, in a letter to his brother the Duke of Gloucester, wrote revealingly: 'I've been suffering from an awful reaction to the strain of war... Medicine, not even Weir's, is of any use as I really want a rest...'....

The present Queen carries a small box of homoeopathic remedies with her on her travels; belladonna for her sinusitis, and arsenic to prevent her sneezing in mid-speech. And more recently Prince Charles has been following closely the experimental use of homoeopathic remedies on pigs and cattle at the Elm Farm Research Centre, near Newbury....[2]

1. Dale, pp. 123-124. James and Russell note, "Recent evidence reveals the possibility that John Brown was in fact a medium, his clairvoyant powers keeping [Queen] Victoria in touch with her 'beloved Albert' beyond the grave" (*At Home with the Royal Family*, p. 50).

2. Dale, pp. 169-173. Lacey similarly observes, "Her faith in homeopathy was another token of her preference for the traditional and unsophisticated. Sir John Weir had introduced the royal family to its folk remedies in the 1920s, and after his retirement as Elizabeth II's personal physician he was succeeded by another homeopath, Margerie Blackie.... The homeopathic remedy for sinus trouble, Elizabeth II's one recurring problem in a remarkably healthy life, involves arsenic, to prevent sneezing, onions, to deal with a running nose, and deadly nightshade, for the sore throat" (*Majesty*, p. 240). James and Russell add, "she has her own homeopathic remedies: pills made from deadly nightshade for a sore throat, arsenic for cold symptoms, and half an onion (inhaled) to clear the nasal passages. The Queen has her own homeopathic physician to prepare the remedies" (*At Home with the Royal Family*, p. 114). Junor remarks, "[Prince] Charles had grown up with complementary medicine, particularly

By their selection of Dr John Weir as royal homoeopath, the Royal Family allied themselves with a particular wing of the homoeopathic discipline; Kentian homoeopathy.

Named after an American homoeopath, James Tyler Kent (1849-1916), it is the most extreme metaphysical form, a kind which is even further removed from orthodox medicine than standard homoeopathy.

'In 1950, the British Homoeopathic Society became the Faculty of Homoeopathy, established by Act of Parliament. This remarkable degree of official recognition makes Britain unique in the world....

Kent had been one of the first to paint word pictures, indicating the kind of personality which matched a particular medicine. These word pictures now became central to homoeopathy. Through links with a form of Spiritualism called Swedenborgianism, they showed that its practitioners believed homoeopathy to be divinely revealed.

It is in this form that the discipline has been accused of being a religious cult.

On one level, it seems to have descended from the 'doctrine of signatures', as endorsed by Paracelsus—the very figure whose principles were recommended to BMA doctors by Prince Charles in December, 1982....

'Since renouncing homoeopathy as occult, I have found my relationship with Jesus much more real and effective,' he [(Dr Douglas Calcott)] wrote in 1983. 'I am seeing Him heal as I pray against sickness in His name, something I had come to accept I could never experience. Homoeopathy, though producing results, had robbed me of faith in the highest source of healing, Jesus Christ the Son of God. Although the truth may offend some, I trust that for many it will be the truth that sets them free. Satan is desperate to deceive us on this issue and has raised up many counterfeit physicians and methods of treatment.'[1]

Before her death Dr Blackie—niece of one of the most famous homoeopaths, Dr James Compton-Burnett—paid tribute to the Queen in her book *The Patient, Not the Cure.* 'Our homoeopathic cause has the enormous privilege of having the Queen as patron of the Royal London Homoeopathic Hospital. May I, on behalf of homoeopathic doctors and patients, pay tribute to our Royal Family who for three generations have given their encouragement and support to homoeopathy.'....

---

homeopathic cures, which both the Queen and Queen Mother have been using for years. One of the oldest of the healing arts, it involves treating the person as a whole, looking at his or her medical history to find the cause of the specific illness, then administering [often toxic] remedies that are so dilute as to be scientifically indiscernible" (Junor, p. 214). **Again, please note that not *all* alternative medicine is occult or witchcraft; for example, taking belladonna for sinusitis is reasonable.**

1. Dale, pp. 175-178.

The current royal homoeopath, appointed in 1980, is Dr Charles Elliott, who is more reticent in print about his beliefs. Because of his royal connection, he has also stopped giving interviews. However, he is very much an admirer of Dr Blackie, to the extent of being the joint editor of her written estate. [He is]...a follower of the Kentian tradition.[1]

[In]...1971, Prince Charles made his first public gesture towards a psychic healer. He sent a message of good will to Paul Daws who had just completed a 240 mile 'healing hike' through Wales....

One day, more than a decade later, the Prince would reveal: 'Ever since I was a child, I've been interested in medical matters and in the business of healing—I've always wished that I could heal...'

Then came March, 1977, and his private expedition into the Kenyan wilderness inspired by Laurens van der Post.

But the Prince kept quiet about it.

That is, until June 30, 1978, when he was addressing the Salvation Army.

'What we should be worried about now,' he said, 'is whether people are going to become atheists...whether they are going to be given an idea of right or wrong...whether they are going to be given an awareness of the things of the spirit and the meaning of the infinite beauty of nature...'

This was hardly sensational but the liberal theology of other parts of the speech, condemning doctrinal bickering, created a furore.

And the reference to 'things of the spirit' was open to more than one interpretation.

The chance was seized by Maurice Barbanell, the respected founder and editor of *Psychic News*. One has to remember that for more than 20 years he had sat dumbly upon what he believed to be the greatest secret of Spiritualism: that medium Lilian Bailey had held séances for the Queen Mother, the Queen and others. Now, prompted by Prince Charles, he had to blurt out something.

In his diary notes of the issue of July 15, 1978, he ran the following headline: PRINCE CHARLES KNOWS...

The following text read, 'One phrase used by Prince Charles in his address on the futility of orthodox religious dogma was virtually unnoticed by those who have joined in the furore.

'The Prince of Wales said that to him it was more important that instead of arguing about theological dogmas, people should be given an awareness "of the things of the spirit and of the meaning and infinite beauty of nature".

'This suggests that he has some inkling of psychic matters. *The suggestion, as I know, is founded upon fact, but I cannot tell you why I make this statement. What I can say is that he, like*

1. Dale, pp. 182-184.

many members of our Royal Family, has an acquaintanceship with mediumship and its implications' (author's italics).[1]

As far as the public were concerned, the main task facing Prince Charles in the late 1970s was the one of choosing a bride.... They were well pleased when his eye stopped roving and settled upon the radiantly pretty Lady Diana Spencer.

The press and television insisted on treating their courtship like some modern-day fairy-tale.... The couple's wedding in St Paul's in 1981...was the world's biggest-ever media spectacular.

In the gush of money-spinning verbiage, no one stopped to ask what, if anything might be going on behind the Prince's smiling mask.

Eighteen months passed before he gave the first clue—a clue that most observers failed to appreciate. It happened on his installation as President of the British Medical Association, the doctor's 'trade union'.

To understand the background, we need to refer briefly to the first Medical Act of 1858.

The conventional view has been that it was this Act that elevated medical science, separated it from superstition and quackery, and enabled it to 'blitz' many illnesses and disorders almost out of existence. Belief in this interpretation was the rock on which the BMA was built.... Yet with the installation of Prince Charles, this edifice began to fall apart....

As we now know, Prince Charles was already taking a great interest in Jungian psychology, particularly the Collective Unconscious. His mentor was probably Laurens van der Post who had been Jung's close friend. And he had just encountered the book *Something Is Happening* by the Edinburgh Jungian analyst Winifred Rushforth. In this she dealt with the way that coincidences could also be *signposts* from that spirit world.

While in his library, wondering what to speak about to the BMA, the Prince's eye alighted upon a book by Paracelsus, the sixteenth-century German physician who, like Jung, believed in an occult cosmic unity.

As we have seen, the Prince interpreted this as his *signpost*.

....The result was the biggest jolt the BMA had ever received....

These were the most challenging words that the BMA had ever heard from a President.

'Perhaps,' continued the Prince, 'we just have to accept it is God's will that the unorthodox individual is doomed to years of frustration, ridicule and failure in order to act out his role in the scheme of things, until his day arrives and mankind is ready to receive his message; *a message which he probably finds hard to explain himself, but which he knows comes from a far deeper source than conscious thought'* (author's italics).

1. Dale, pp. 200-202.

Not only was he espousing the cause of the unscientific, he was implying, in my view, that unorthodoxy might be divinely inspired, that the things opposed by the medical establishment might possibly be messages from the Collective Unconscious....

'Through the centuries,' said the Prince, 'healing has been practised by folk healers who are guided by traditional wisdom that sees illness as a disorder of the whole person, involving not only the patient's body, but his mind, his self-image, his dependence on the physical and social environment, *as well as his relation to the cosmos*... I would suggest that the whole imposing edifice of modern medicine, for all its breath-taking successes is, like the Tower of Pisa, slightly off balance.'

That speech—delivered on December 14, 1982—can be seen today as the turning point for what is now promoted and marketed as alternative medicine.[1] It was reported worldwide. Its impact was not restricted to the doctors it attacked. The meaning was absorbed by a public not just in Britain but throughout the West.

If that had been the Prince's last word on the subject, he would still have achieved more than anyone else. But it was not his last word, far from it.

'Don't over-estimate the sophisticated approach to medicine,' he told an increasingly rattled BMA the following summer. He lectured them on taking note of 'what lies beneath the surface of the visible world...and those ancient, unconscious forces which still shape the psychological attitudes of modern man.'[2]

The weight of postal deliveries to Buckingham Palace following his challenges to the British Medical Association soon convinced the Prince that his *signpost* had been right. He found himself receiving a great deal of public support.

'It was unbelievable,' he said. 'I have *never—ever*—had so many letters.'

He added: 'I was riveted by this. While I was pretty sure I was going to stir up a hornet's nest—which I did, I think—I also realized there was a great deal more interest in and awareness of this aspect than I'd imagined, particularly among lay

1. Junor, in quoting the prince's speech, oddly omits his most "controversial" statements with no indication of having done so. Nevertheless, she quotes the prince as having remarked, "what is taken for today's unorthodoxy is probably going to be tomorrow's convention.... [Paracelsus] maintained that there were four pillars on which the whole art of healing rested. The first was philosophy; the second astronomy (or what we might now call psychology); the third alchemy (or biochemistry) and the fourth virtue (in other words the professional skill of the doctor). Paracelsus believed that the good doctor's therapeutic success largely depends on his ability to inspire the patient with confidence and to mobilize his will to health.... It is frightening how dependent upon drugs we are all becoming and how easy it is for doctors to prescribe them as the universal panacea for our ills. Wonderful as many of them are it should still be more widely stressed by doctors that the health of human beings is so often determined by their behaviour, their food and the nature of their environment" (Junor, pp. 213-214).

2. Dale, pp. 203-206.

people—although many doctors, especially the younger ones, also seemed to feel the same way.'

In the face of a seething medical establishment, he needed to be borne along by this sense of purpose, that **here was a mission for which he had been chosen by the very forces for which he was now a spokesman**....

Among the letters was one that particularly caught the Prince's attention and which came from a man who asked a favour of the Prince: would he open the new...centre which he was helping to set up.

The Prince knew that to lend his authority to such an enterprise would be the greatest gift he could give. He had no hesitation in accepting the invitation.

That is how on July 15, 1983, he came to be sharing the platform at the Bristol Cancer Help Centre with Dr Alec Forbes, the centre's unpaid medical director....

Then the Prince referred to the methods of treatment. 'It may be described as psychotherapy, or religion, or the power of prayer, or whatever,' he said, 'but it represents that invisible aspect of the universe which although unprovable in terms of orthodox science, as man has devised it, nevertheless cries out for us to keep our minds as open as possible and not to dismiss it as mere hocus-pocus.'...

[It]...is surprising that so few have stopped to discover the beliefs that Forbes really holds, especially considering the amount of publicity the Prince has generated for him:

> SPIRITUAL HEALING: Forbes says there are two kinds of beings in the spirit world. One group are unpleasant and untrustworthy; the others possess great understanding. Healers use the latter benign spirits to balance the emotional and mental energies of the sick.
>
> It is a rare gift unconnected with religious faith....
>
> PSYCHIC SURGERY:....
>
> ANTHROPOSOPHICAL MEDICINE:.... It involves maintaining harmony between four fields of force [which are affected by the Earth, Sun, Moon, Mercury, Venus, Mars, Jupiter, and Saturn, and which can be treated through the use of those bodies's respective metals—gold, silver, mercury, copper, iron, tin, and lead]....
>
> HOMOEOPATHY:....
>
> BACH FLOWER REMEDIES:.... [These] remedies consist of the dew precipitated on the leaves of plants. Different plants...impart different curative powers, though these are not bio-chemical....
>
> RADIONICS (WITH PSIONICS): Here the practitioner holds a pendulum over a hair or blood sample of the patient—who is not present—and 'dowses' for the

diagnosis. Then the remedy is 'transmitted' to the patient over any distance...by using psychically 'tuned' instruments....

OUT OF THE BODY EXPERIENCES: Forbes says that the healer's mind may leave his body and travel any distance to heal an ill person....

COLOUR AND GEM THERAPY: Here colour is said to represent chemical potencies in 'higher octaves of vibration'. Forbes...seems to agree that water can be charged by leaving it in sunlight in suitably coloured containers. It can then be drunk as medicine. Similarly, small gems can be left in alcohol, thereby conferring their curative imprint....

ORGONE THERAPY:....

[This employs]...the fundamental life force of the Universe—Orgone—which is everywhere and in everything....

VITA FLORUM: This is an ointment produced from water in which certain live flowers have been held in sunlight, until their curative power is believed to have passed into the fluid....

ASTROLOGY:....

REINCARNATION: He [(Forbes)] says that perhaps one third of all illness is Karmic—that is, inherited from a previous life....

There is no evidence, however, that any of these healing methods have ever been used at the Bristol Cancer Help Centre, other than the fact that the Centre states in its brochure that 'healing by touch, sometimes called spiritual healing, is available.'[1]

....Never before had the Prince provoked such a response. But his post also included criticism, especially from those who said he was dabbling with the occult.

'The establishment of the Bristol Cancer Help Centre is an extraordinary milestone in the progress of alternative medicine,' declared evangelist Roy Livesey.

He then took a sharp prod at the Prince. 'This range of therapies—and the support received from *so many places*,' he said, 'is

---

1. Dale, pp. 207-212. Junor, observing that the "Bristol Centre treats cancer patients not by drugs but by a combination of diet, positive attitudes and support from everyone around," once again offers a sterilized version of the prince's "controversial" remarks: "What they claim is that you have to put a great deal of effort as a patient into attacking your own disease, and that those who have the willpower, who are able to adopt the very strict diets...who are able to learn the relaxation and imagery techniques and who perhaps have a natural inclination to fight, are likely to do better." On another occasion, while attending a Royal Society of Medicine seminar on the subject of alternative medicine, the prince stated, "Many, many people in this country are predisposed towards various types of complimentary medicine.... Increasingly, I think, they are not getting all they want from orthodox medicine" (p. 215).

a measure of the longing on everybody's part to find some right answers. Nothing should be taken away from their sincerity, commitment, care and willingness. My plea is for the discernment of the spirits.'

Livesey quotes in full Prince Charles's support for Paracelsus. Then he adds: 'No Paracelsian philosophy, no royal or clerical approval, no measure of care or concern, can counter the great and inevitable dangers in store for those who fall for the wiles of Satan.'...

But by then, it was already too late, for **the Prince, in a bout of enthusiasm for the new health boom, had given the most unusual interview of his life....**

He used crucial expressions and described revealing behaviour which were highly significant to anyone well versed in the works of Carl Jung, especially those dealing with the Collective Unconscious. But to the relief of the Royal Family, it so happened that his interviewer, the highly respected journalist Anne de Courcy, was not particularly prepared for a discussion in this esoteric field of psychology...; neither were the references understood by the various editors who published her article all over the world....

'To me, it is very interesting to see how primitive societies—though I think "primitive" is a complete misnomer anyway—are the whole time *subconsciously* far more aware of their instinctive relationship with the things and people round them than we are in the so-called civilized world.'

Without naming them, he went on to agree with Jung and van der Post in supporting the African side of the mind, in saying in effect that man should use the Collective Unconscious in making decisions. Of this subconscious awareness he said:

'It's still there but buried under a mountain of...what?—anxieties, fears, worries, a feeling that it's something we should be ashamed of as though *rational* thinking is the only acceptable process. Yet I believe instinct, sensitivity, call it what you will, is enormously important.'

He told Anne de Courcy that, as a result of this, **he was trying to teach himself to become more aware by 'listening with his inner ear'....**

'Today,' said the Prince, 'the knowledge that Man is capable of harnessing nature to his own ends—that he even has the capability to destroy the whole planet—has given the feeling that *we* are masters of our fate; which is so far from the truth it makes one cry sometimes.'

With this statement he raised, but did not answer, the obvious question. Who, or what, did he believe was in charge of the planet?

He also spoke of modern societies need for

'pointers'—that is, figures who could teach a new under-standing of morality and metaphysics. [A pointer is] '...some-one to lead us, to show us the way... Once you have been pointed in a direction, you can follow it if it is a philosophy or way of thinking that suits you,' he said. 'But I don't think we have that many people who are "pointers". That's one prob-lem. Another is a lack of awareness....'

It was at this time that the Prince made another move that confirmed his interest in the paranormal.

His attention was caught by reports of a large bequest left by the author and psychic researcher Arthur Koestler for the estab-lishment of a chair of parapsychology at a British university.

Like the Prince, Koestler was fascinated by Jung's theory of the Collective Unconscious and particularly by the meaning of coincidence.... He certainly believed in the power of psychic forces and, apparently, in a spirit world. The Prince admired him very much indeed.

When he heard of the bequest, the Prince wrote to the Uni-versity of Wales, of which he was Chancellor, and asked the Prin-cipal: 'Why don't we have a go at taking up this scheme?'...[1]

Since the first hints of the Prince's spiritual predilections, sev-eral stories [about Windsor Castle] have appeared in the popular press which are unverifiable. Normally, they would not warrant serious scrutiny. But because of the Prince's interest in the para-normal, they become more credible....

Why should Windsor be the scene of so much supernatu-ral activity? The reason may be that the Long Walk lies upon an ancient ley line—a route that was established in pre-Christian days for astronomical and mystical purposes.

In fact, according to some researchers, Windsor Castle stands at the very centre of such a network, making the adja-cent area particularly susceptible to paranormal activity.

The well-known writer Colin Wilson says: 'It seems likely that the whole Windsor Park area is a site of the ancient relig-ion associated with the horned god of the witches and with Diana. Since the area is associated with the kings of England, it is even conceivable that the park was *the* centre of the old religion.'...[2]

1. Dale, pp. 213-217.
2. Siân Ellis remarks, "The longer history of the Buckingham Palace site is even more fascinating, conjuring up unusual ghosts where guards parade today. In medieval times a witch, Margarie Gourdemaine, lived in a hut where the present courtyard stands. She was burned at the stake, accused of sorcery against King Henry VI. When the guards change at the palace they are probably marching upon the very spot where the witch's hut once stood" ("Secret City," *Realm* magazine, Sept./Oct. 1997, No. 76, pp. 31-32). James and Rus-sell comment, "Most Guards prefer sentry duty at Windsor Castle..., despite the tales of George III's ghost which is said to appear periodically. From where the Guards stand they can count twelve statues but, strangely, sometimes there appear to be thirteen. Sentries have also heard the sound of someone tapping on a window, and on looking up they have

[Tom Johanson, secretary of the Spiritualist Association of Great Britain,] who has given regular healing displays in Trafalgar Square, promoted the phrase, 'Prince of Psychics'—a label which the Prince detests. He also quoted a friend of the Prince as saying: 'Charles is very definitely creating a problem in the family by insisting on the infallibility of working things out by psychic methods.'

And—implying he was on surprisingly intimate terms with royalty—Johanson wrote: '....**The fact is that the Prince is such an avid researcher in all aspects of the psychic field and is speaking so openly about it that many within his group of close friends refer to him as the "Prince of Psychics".**'...

It was after Johanson published the ouija board story that it was taken up by the tabloid press, both in Britain and abroad. It was this one item that most infuriated the Prince and provoked him to speak out. By safely attacking it as untrue, he attempted to cast doubt upon the credibility of all other allegations concerning himself and the paranormal. In his interview with ITN, he went so far as to say: 'I'm not interested in the occult, or dabbling in black magic of any of these kinds of things or, for that matter, strange forms of mysticism.'

This was rather over the top, a blanket denial which probably revealed more about his own anxieties than about the facts of the matter. His mother was reported to have been against the interview in principle, afraid that he would say something which could later be pulled to pieces. In this instance, her fears appear to have been fully justified. Indeed, in the very same broadcast, he also described how he had campaigned for the Arthur Koestler chair of parapsychology to be adopted by the University of Wales. As parapsychology is the study of the paranormal—from Uri Geller's spoon-bending to the mechanics of the occult and black magic—then the Prince must therefore be interested in such matters, no matter how vehement his denials. This is in addition to all the other evidence [thus far] revealed....

Such is also the view of people who have talked to him on the subject.[1]

Royal patronage has helped turn Britain into the occult capital of the Western world. Paranormal practices which are illegal in other countries can be promoted without hindrance. Seemingly inexplicable treatments such as radionics or orgone therapy—which were chased out of the United States, for instance—can be structured into professional bodies, advertised openly and awarded a scale of fees. British Spiritualists are probably the most celebrated on earth as they tour the globe,

---

seen the ghostly King's wild eyes staring blankly out at them, as if imploring to be let out of his prison" (*At Home with the Royal Family*, p. 128). Recall that George III was a Mason.

1. Dale, pp. 225, 227-229.

applying their healing powers. London possesses the finest facilities for homoeopathy, a discipline which was virtually saved from extinction by royal support. The National Health Service experiments with alternative medicine. And the British Government fends off Common Market regulations which would inhibit some paranormal therapists.

This all constitutes a wonderful tribute to British freedom. There is no other developed nation so tolerant of occult and paranormal practices when they are being performed seriously, for money, sometimes in life-and-death circumstances....

The evidence shows that Prince Charles believes firmly in the existence and power of paranormal forces governing our health and welfare. In doing so, he has hitched his reputation—and that of the Royal Family—to the credibility of the phenomena he has so carefully endorsed.

If, at some time, the occult and the unscientific are shown to be worthwhile and of benefit, then the Prince will be vindicated and hailed as a prophet. He will be seen as a man who was ahead of his time, a natural leader...perhaps, even, what he calls a *pointer*.

If, on the other hand, they are deemed wasteful, ineffective, harmful and demonic, the result for the Prince will be the gravest crisis of his public life. From one side he will be labelled a crank and from the other an occultist....

....[Having]...**drawn his conclusions, the Prince is equipped to defend them forcefully.**

During 1983 and 1984, this is what he tried to do, feeling that there was a general benefit to be spread by open discussion of such matters. He saw it as part of his leadership role to introduce these ideas at large, to act as one of society's 'pointers'.

But by the middle of 1985 his optimism had been replaced by disillusionment as he witnessed himself being turned into an object of ridicule, at least by some. At that point, both surprised and hurt by the cruelty of the attacks, he changed his position quite dramatically. Urged on by family and advisers, he adopted a wholly defensive posture and began to say he had been misunderstood—that he had only ever advocated an 'open' mind, nothing more radical than that.

Overnight he forgot all about his support for the unproven and how he had said he was trying to interpret dreams and coincidences. No longer did he refer to Winifred Rushforth or Carl Jung or his challenges to the British Medical Association. Suddenly, from having supported the unscientific, he wished to pose as an objective investigator.

Increasingly impatient with criticism, he categorically denies any interest whatsoever in the occult or strange forms of mysticism.

His claim was, however, inconsistent with the facts. At best, it might be said the Prince was confused; at worst, that his nerve had [at least temporarily] snapped. If '83 and '84 had been the years of the public transformation, '85 was the year of the public turnaround and recantation.

But there is one thing worth remembering: at no time did the Prince flatly contradict or deny the detail of his earlier statements in support of psychic and paranormal matters. From this fact alone it may be assumed that he still held such views but, for personal reasons, was no longer espousing them. The cause—family pressure and public relations....

It is the Prince's eternal misfortune that his religious faith can never be a private matter.... What he believes is of proper concern to all Anglicans worldwide, as well as to most British subjects, for whom, as monarch, he would also serve as spiritual leader. And this is bound to create problems.

Firstly, many church-goers, of all denominations, will find the Prince's apparent super-ecumenism unacceptable. He apparently considers all religions—Christianity, Islam, African spirit worship—to be parts of the same whole. More than that, there is the specific difficulty of reconciling his opinions with those of the Church of England, of which the monarch is head. Anglicanism is noted for its ability to accommodate many different interpretations of the gospels. But if the Prince were unable to reach such an accommodation—one in which both sides felt their integrity to be protected—then a real obstacle would block his path to the Succession....

It may be weakness which prompts some people to be drawn towards unusual spiritual beliefs....

But there are other individuals, often deeply impressive ones, who take up a spiritual quest not out of inadequacy, but in order to seek the ultimate religious truth, feeling such a mission is the sole cause able to instill their life with purpose.

In my opinion, it is into this latter category that Prince Charles falls; it is from a sense of mission, perhaps of destiny, that he has been driven to explore the mysteries of the spirit.

He is idealistic and compassionate. **He concerns himself with the state of the world. He obviously frets over what he sees as its physical and spiritual deterioration. Whereas many might surrender to the inertia of despair, he seeks an understanding of what is wrong in order that he might help find a cure and better serve mankind.**

That sense of vocation has led him to his present beliefs....

'Today's unorthodoxy is tomorrow's convention,' Prince Charles will no doubt repeat in his own defence.

And, in my opinion, he will be left with a choice, one that will decide his future and, perhaps, that of the [British] nation—to disguise his views, live a lie and preserve the constitutional peace, or be true to himself, his Church and his subjects, and face the consequences.[1]

Despite occasional public denials, whether or not he cares to admit it ("thou doth protest too much"), Prince Charles, who would like to have been an actor, is a dedicated New Age adherent and spiritist. Further, as we shall see, he may be loosely associated with Peter LeMesurier's *The Armageddon Script*. Holden writes,

[The]...face before you is a contemporary icon. You have seen it not just on a thousand news-stands, but on stamps and coins, T-shirts and dishcloths....

....Charles has become a disciple of Jung, who believed, among other things, in a "collective unconscious," the premise that diverse cultures share basic myths and symbols. Earlier this year, the prince took a trek into Africa's Kalahari Desert with his Jungian guru, Sir Laurens van der Post, who holds that the life and values of the "lost tribes" of the African desert have much to teach the civilized world.

....[He] has shown an interest in the occult, participating in primitive rituals, dancing beneath the stars with dusky African beauties and summoning up the spirits of the dead.... ...Charles believes the world is on a downhill slope and thinks it only logical to explore alternative solutions.

....Visitors...hear little but the long catalogue of his concerns: unemployment, housing, race [relations], drugs, the decay of the inner city, the environment and family life....

There is an unworldliness...about his otherwise admirable yearning to tackle the problems of Britain and the Third World....

....[Having studied world-history, archaeology, and anthropology, as well as pursued amateur theatrics, he] is an honors graduate of [Trinity College at] Cambridge....[2] The books he reads...are weighty ones about modern problems....

While Diana's presence can make a room glow, his tends to breed stiffness and formality....

....[When] puttering about his country estate, Highgrove in Gloucestershire [Scotland,]...he talks to his plants....[3]

Brad Darrach adds,

1. Dale, pp. 231-238.
2. Fry, *The Kings & Queens of England & Scotland*, p. 216.
3. Anthony Holden, "Man in a Gilded Cage," *LIFE*, Sept. 1987, pp. 32, 34-35.

[Prince Charles]...has a record of achievement unmatched by any other Prince of Wales....ruddy good health, scorching charm, lively wit, ever-ready virility and a flair for the arts....

....Charles has championed scholarships for the poor, raised financing for start-up businesses and launched a nationwide campaign to protect the environment.... "I want to be involved in something that makes a difference."...

....As the world has learned,...he has advocated alternative medicine and blithely admitted that he talks to plants to make them grow. He has even found a guru....Sir Laurens van der Post..., who plunged Charles into the archetypal world of psychologist Carl Jung, where for several years the prince has been paddling like a metaphysical fly in symbol soup.... But often Charles transcribes the night's dreams on a bedside notepad and in the morning telephones van der Post to discuss his collective unconscious.

....[He is] affable, sincere, generous, devoted to his people. But he can also play the arrogant aristocrat....[1]

Junor states, "[Prince Charles] has a magnetism about him which sets him apart, and such a talent for listening that even the toughest kids...cheer him when he leaves. His charm is extraordinary.... He is straightforward, direct and sincere.... Inefficiency and bureaucracy make him angry, as does the popular press sometimes.... His entire being is subjugated to duty." Although the prince "is hugely caring and concerned for everyone," displaying "genuine humility, humor and sheer vulnerability," he "can be selfish and spoilt."[2] Cathcart comments,

Prince Charles is...the first prince in history ever to have undertaken a systematic academic study of his craft, of the primitive roots of awe and the deep human need of tribal leadership that upholds the prestige of princes and the majesty of kings. These elements of his profession all arose in his year of social anthropology, 'from the origins of man through Stonehenge to Julius Caesar'....

His studies involved the folk mysteries of Frazer's *Golden Bough*[3] as well as modern theories of social behaviour. As he

1. Brad Darrach, "Prince Charles: A Dangerous Age," *People Weekly*, 31 Oct. 1988, pp. 97-98, 100.
2. Junor, pp. 3-4, 78.
3. James George Frazer's *Golden Bough* is a significant work for Prince Charles to have studied. In 1914, Frazer was knighted for his work, and in 1920, he became a Fellow of the Royal Society. Then, in 1925, he received the Order of Merit. Frazer's work is a famous study in paganism and witchcraft, which centers largely on the "slain god" of various pagan

worked it out, 'if more people can be assisted to appreciate and understand their own social behaviour, the better and more healthy our society will be... We should have a shrewd idea why we react to various situations and stimuli in the way we do.'... For Charles, anthropology...explained something of his own role in the world.... 'But I think it helps to illustrate the useful application of anthropology to modern existence.'...

....[He] stayed at a hotel in Les Eyzies, sallying forth to see the reindeer paintings in the local honeycomb of caves, and the primitive carvings.... [He also] made a point of visiting the tombs of his Plantagenet ancestors at the Abbey of Fontrevault and, in Brittany, he examined the mysterious avenues and circles that are equated with Stonehenge....

....At an R.A.I. [(Royal Anthropological Institute)] dinner, Prince Charles had eloquently spoken of the need to popularise anthropology as a source of knowledge of the motivations of mankind. The sequel was, of course, a race of television companies to secure him for their cameras, and his agreement to take part in a series to feature himself and others giving a personal view of 'the values of Man'....[1]

Prince Charles' enthusiasm for archaeology and anthropology is evidenced by the possibility that had he continued those studies, "instead of changing in his second year to history, he might even have come away with a first." Nevertheless, the prince recognized history as being "of

mythologies. Frazer, not surprisingly, relates virtually all pagan customs back to *Tammuz* in Babylon (*Adonis* in Greek). What is significant from the perspective of this work, however, is that according to Frazer, Christianity derives from the ancient pagan mythologies, rather than the mythologies themselves deriving from early pagan corruptions of the Zodiac. (In reality, before its ancient perversion, the Zodiac represented the complete Gospel message in a symbolic form.) Any reader who accepts Frazer at face value will come away with an historically twisted and completely perverted understanding of true Christianity—one that ties in well with the occult beliefs of the Merovingian dynasty. Frazer's accepting reader will see Christianity as merely a more sterile version of the ancient pagan mythologies. Mary Douglas, editor of *The Illustrated Golden Bough,* comments, "Frazer believed in a process of social evolution that had by now passed an irreversible judgment against all ritual slaying, whether the victim be animal or human being, or the god himself slain [only] to be offered to himself on behalf of his people. The full ambition of *The Golden Bough* is to place the sacrificial doctrines of Christianity, together with the doctrines of the Incarnation and of the Virgin Birth and of the Resurrection into the same perspective as totemic [(nature)] worship, together with the lusty antics of the Greek pantheon and with the burnt or bleeding carcasses on ancient altars of the Israelites. Whatever the stories were, they would be regarded as partial, imperfect versions.... But for the enlightened scholarship the task ahead...would be the adducing of more and more evidence for that worldwide evolution towards a purer spirituality.... Yet for all this, Frazer cannot escape the charge of superficiality. He chose to deal with reflections on life and death, humanity and animality, divinity and immortality" (Frazer, pp. 9, 11, 13). Prince Charles, no doubt, considers himself to be a part of "the enlightened scholarship."

1. Cathcart, pp. 74-75, 81, 170.

paramount importance and relevance to us all:" "I honestly believe that the only real way one can hope to understand and cope with the present, is by knowing and being able to interpret what happened in the past.... I don't think that's true of modern politicians."[1] Consider also these excerpts from Peter Davis' "real-life fiction" which explores the "fact and fantasy" of Prince Charles' life:

How indeed prepare a king? Let him know history....science...culture..., enough religion to know that he, like God, exists only if people believe he does....

....He sees a "dark side to man's psyche" and urges people to study psychology. He walks the Kalahari desert in Africa, meditating with his latest octogenarian guru.... He writes a children's book, *The Old Man of Lochnagar,* about a magical old man living in a cave on the Balmoral estate, where he can turn plants and animals into his friends and make himself vanish when he feels threatened by civilization.... PC....goes to vegetables and talks to flowers....

....Methodically, usefully, he writes down his dreams.

....PC ponders [the meaning of a dream].... On an archetypal level, one strives to reunite with some dynamic harmony in nature as represented by the trees, plants, and deer, perhaps some unconscious wish to be them, mirrored by their own collective wish to be oneself....

In a dream his grandfather's gold watch appears to PC. Instead of ticking, it talks to PC about healing an army of the disabled so that, cured, they can arise from their wheelchairs....

....His books are by the Greek philosophers, John Ruskin, Carl Jung, Alexander Solzenitsyn....

....When PC starts to walk off, a young black reaches out to touch him, saying, "You are the man, you are the man."...

Nature has inspired PC.... "I feel that deep in the mirror of mankind is a reflection of the beauty and harmony of the universe. Through the outer manifestation of that reflection we can attain the kind of peace for which we yearn...."[2]

The "Highlands" of Balmoral Castle in Scotland are perhaps Prince Charles' favorite place on Earth, and Lochnagar is his favorite place at Balmoral. Lochnagar means "Goat Lake." Perhaps it should not surprise us then that it was at Balmoral (cf. *Baal*-moral) "where in solitude he would

1. Junor, pp. 90-91.
2. Peter Davis, "Prince Charles Narrowly Escapes Beheading," *Esquire,* Apr. 1988, pp. 98, 100, 103, 106, 108, 111.

lose himself entirely, entering into...intimacy with nature."[1] Recall, therefore, the earlier discussion concerning the tail of the dexter (left-hand) supporter, as well as other lion beasts, in Prince Charles' coat of arms. There we learned that the lions of mythology have magic in their tails and that by waving them across their bodies, they are able to vanish. Such lions also have the power to resurrect their dead cubs.[2] With this in mind, the "magical old man" in the prince's book appears, at first glance, to be a veiled allusion not just to the Goat or *Satan,* but to the prince himself (e.g., when possessed), and his presence indicates that the prince has at least some familiarity with the mythological meanings of the various symbols in his arms. (Note as well the popular occult series of movies and films about a "highlander" from Scotland who has a bloody mission as the "chosen one" to save the world. These movies enjoyed great success in Western Europe.) "As a small boy he had imagined himself running away, escaping to the mountain of Lochnagar that loomed over the Balmoral estate and hiding in a secret cavern.... Contemplating the notion of the 'Wise Old Man', an archetypal figure representing that 'superior insight' which Jung discovered within himself, the Prince was encouraged by van der Post to believe that this 'guru' was, in his case, represented by the Old Man of Lochnagar—the mythical figure created by the Prince who inhabited the mountains at Balmoral and who was the subject of the children's book which he had written for his younger brothers when he was twenty."[3] Given this description, one has to wonder whether the "Wise Old Man" is not also an allusion to Merlin, the ancient "guru" of King Arthur's Round Table; for Merlin likewise could be viewed as Satan. The prince's full name is, of course, Charles Philip *Arthur* George.

Before continuing, we must look briefly at northern Scotland's Findhorn Foundation. As a "prototype New Age

---

1. Dimbleby, *The Prince of Wales*, p. 30. Junor, between pp. 150-151. As Colonel-in-Chief of the 2nd King Edward VII Own Goorkhas, Prince Charles wears, as part of that unit's insignia, what appears to be a goat's-head symbol (*Charles & Diana: A Royal Family Album*, p. 87).
2. For more information, see Chapter 7's sections titled, "The top of the arms" and "The dexter (left-hand) supporter."
3. Dimbleby, *The Prince of Wales*, pp. 89, 252.

community...that offers an ongoing educational program in the principles of New Age spirituality and world service," this foundation "emphasizes the sacredness of everyday living."[1] Elliot Miller calls Findhorn "an almost legendary New Age community."[2] However, as with other New Age organizations, the spirituality of Findhorn (cf. "find the little horn") is a form of Satanism. David Spangler, a well-known New Ager who co-founded and once led the Findhorn Foundation, makes the following statements concerning Lucifer in *Reflections on the Christ:*

> The true light of Lucifer cannot be seen through sorrow, through darkness, through rejection. The true light of this great being can only be recognized when one's own eyes can see with the light of Christ, the light of the inner sun. Lucifer works within each of us to bring us to wholeness and as we move into a new age, which is the age of man's wholeness, each of us in some way is brought to that point which I term the Luciferic initiation, the particular doorway through which the individual must pass if he is to come fully into the presence of his light and wholeness....
>
> Lucifer comes to give to us the final gift of wholeness. If we accept it then he is free and we are free. That is the Luciferic initiation. It is one that many people now, and in the days ahead, will be facing, for it is an initiation into the New Age.[3]

Larson states, "New Age proponents like the Findhorn Foundation...communicate with plants, believing them to be inhabited by elemental spirits called *devas.* Plant communicators seek wisdom and guidance from the spirits, whom they believe possess feelings and intelligence."[4] Miller adds, "The former luminaries of Scotland's famed Findhorn community...have channeled everything from nature spirits, to fairies, to elves, to the Greek god 'Pan,' to angels, to 'God.'"[5] As mentioned, Prince Charles frequently travels to Scotland, where he talks to plants. Also, he has traveled to the Kalahari desert with Sir Laurens van der Post, a personal friend of the late Jung,

1. Walter Martin, *The New Age Cult* (Minnesota: Bethany House Publishers, 1989), p. 116.
2. Elliot Miller, *A Crash Course on the New Age Movement* (Michigan: Baker Book House, 1989), p. 32.
3. David Spangler, *Reflections on the Christ* (Moray, Scotland: Findhorn Publications, 1981), pp. 44-45. Also see Michaelsen, p. 323.
4. Larson, p. 328.
5. Miller, p. 157.

to learn the "values of the 'lost tribes' of the African desert." Among these "values," which Sir Laurens himself adheres to, is doing homage to demonic spirits.[1]   It appears, therefore, that a connection may exist between Prince Charles, who is a disciple of the teachings of Carl Jung, and Scotland's Findhorn Foundation.

What makes this possibility most intriguing is the fact that Peter LeMesurier, author of *The Armageddon Script,* has, as Cumbey notes, a "publishing relationship with the Findhorn Foundation in Northern Scotland" (see below). LeMesurier's script is based upon "Jungian archetypes," so-called after psychiatrist Carl Jung, whose occultist ideas have heavily influenced the New Age Movement (not to mention modern psychiatry and certain heretical elements in the "Christian" Church). As Hunt points out, in the ecumenism of so-called "Christian" psychology, "Christ becomes the partner of Freud, Jung, Rogers, Maslow, and a host of other anti-Christians.... Such false 'Christianity' no longer holds truth to be important and thus can be embraced by the followers of all religions...."[2]   With T.A. McMahon, he adds,

> ....Psychiatrist C.G. Jung, whom Morton T. Kelsey raised to the level of a Christian leader and saint, believed that images originating within the mind were as real as those coming from external objects. Heavily involved in the occult, including seances for communicating with the dead, Jung explained the "ghosts" he saw on more than one occasion as "exteriorizations" of archetypal images within his mind originating in the deep psyche of the human race. Refusing to believe in a real spirit world of demons or angels, psychologists play mind-games with visual images....
>
> Miraculous cures, ecstatic experiences of universal love and personal transformation have been effected not only through visualizing "Jesus," but also by visualizing spirits of the dead, the great saints, ascended masters, and religious leaders from the past such as assorted ancient Hindu gurus or Buddha. What is the difference? Jung would say there is none; and this seems to be the teaching not only of Kelsey but of a number of other Christian leaders....
>
> If it doesn't matter whether we visualize Jesus or Buddha,

---

1. Laurens van der Post and David Coulson, *The Lost World of the Kalahari* (New York: William Morrow and Company, Inc., 1988), pp. 167-170; Dale, pp. 29-30.
2. Hunt, *GLOBAL PEACE AND THE RISE OF ANTICHRIST,* p. 158.

then it must not matter whether we *believe* in Jesus or Buddha....
Although it may be denied by some who practice it, that is the
only premise upon which inner healing can be said to rest. *Imagination* is the Creator of a whole new past, present, and future;
and is somehow confused with *revelation* from God.[1]

One writer comments,

The late occult Swiss psychiatrist Carl Jung....is the modern-
day father of symbology and also of visualization and inner healing. Jung admitted to possession by various spirits (demons), and
one of his books was written through his hands by a demonic
author. Jung believed that man could create reality with his
thoughts. *Therefore, man can use thought-power to give life to
symbols.*

Jung based his beliefs on his study of ancient Eastern religions such as Hinduism and on gnosticism. New Agers practically
worship Carl Jung, and they....are convinced that through visualization and meditation they can make symbols [and images] come
alive and that these symbols will ever after have life, living on in
the Collective Unconscious of the universe....

Scores of Catholic priests would agree with...Jung.[2]

In an article on dreams, New Age enthusiast Cate Ter-williger states,

Chuck Specht, a deacon and pastoral administrator in St.
Francis Parish, is a Christian Jungian dream worker[3] who occasionally uses his expertise in spiritual counseling....

Jung believed in archetypes—universal patterns in the unconscious that emerge in dreams, art, legends and myths. A snake in
a dream, for example, represents man's deepest awareness of the
life energy of nature. A mandala (a combination of a four-sided
figure and a circle) represents the self, or what Christians would
think of as the Christ within, Specht says.[4]

Concerning *The Armageddon Script,* and the staging of a counterfeit "Christ," Cumbey writes,

*"Their script is now written, subject only to last minute editing
and stage-directions. The stage itself, albeit as yet in darkness,*

1. Dave Hunt and T.A. McMahon, *The Seduction of Christianity* (Oregon: Harvest House Publishers, 1985), pp. 135, 177.
2. Marrs, *Mystery Mark of the New Age,* pp. 133-135.
3. Did you catch the oxymoron (i.e., "Christian Jungian")?
4. Cate Terwilliger, "Dreams," *Gazette Telegraph* (Colo. Springs, CO), 20 Oct. 1987, p. F3.

is almost ready. Down in the pit, the subterranean orchestra is already tuning up. The last-minute, walk-on parts are even now being filled. Most of the main actors, one suspects, have already taken up their roles. Soon it will be time for them to come on stage, ready for the curtain to rise...."....

....The above quote is the summation of *The Armageddon Script* by Peter LeMesurier a noted pyramidologist/occultist. It is a how-to manual for New Agers and intellectuals interested in staging a simulated second coming of Christ. The script they write, if successfully staged, could deceive "even the very elect."

It is logical and proper to question why one might expect the average person of intelligence to support such a scheme. To the contrary, it is precisely the intellectual whose support is being courted *and won* for this undertaking....

LeMesurier is a man with strong New Age connections, including a publishing relationship with the Findhorn Foundation in Northern Scotland. His books are widely promoted and sold in New Age bookstores. They show that he strongly supports and promotes the New Age philosophies....

....Crombie was **a dedicated patron of the Findhorn Foundation. He thought he frequently communed with "nature spirits."**...

Analogies of an actor on the stage are common among occult initiates.... As a matter of fact, the 1914 issue of *The Theosophist* carried a similar analogy. In 1914 the Theosophical Society was, as are the occultists of today, engaged in preparing the world to receive their New Age "Christ."... An article appearing in that magazine entitled "Why the World Does Not Understand" made it clear that what Theosophy was really all about was preparing the world to receive a myth—that the underlying actor was always the same....

....LeMesurier also says in effect that visualization is necessary for the manifestation of the Kingdom—for the kingdom of their deliberately staged false Christ!

"In the meantime the new world-leader must prepare himself for his role. He must study the scriptures and the Dead Sea Scrolls, immerse himself in current Jewish messianic expectations, thoroughly survey the general locality and familiar-ize himself with all the major prophecies and the best in New Age religious thought. *In short he must create in his own mind a crystal-clear idea of the vision which he has to fulfill. For only in this way can that vision be guaranteed to come into manifestation.*"[1]

In effect, *The Armageddon Script* and other, related

---

1. Cumbey, *A Planned Deception*, pp. 7-8, 116-117, 180.

New Age writings, advocate the introduction of a major world figure—one who is familiar with the significant prophecies and other teachings of the major religions—upon the world stage, so that, at the proper time, he could step forward to seemingly "fulfill" those prophecies. In other words, this individual, through a grandiose bit of acting, is to fool the bulk of the world's populace into thinking that he is their man, their "divinely" preordained leader who will finally usher in a spiritual new age of peace, security, and prosperity on Earth. When that time comes, in an effort to unite all mankind and ultimately eliminate religiously and ethnically motivated warfare, he is to claim to be the 'Coming One' for all the world's religions. Does such a scheme sound outlandish? Inasmuch as Britain's monarchy "has long enjoyed an association with entertainers and actors," and Prince Charles is a personal acquaintance of actor Peter Ustinov,[1] consider this article:

> Groups led by Academy Award-winning actor Peter Ustinov and former presidential candidate John Anderson are plotting world government—a goal they say is not far-fetched. Ustinov is president of the World Federalist Movement, an international group that wants to transform the United Nations into a powerful federation able to protect the environment, end war and curtail international terrorism. "If all goes well, it's a logical ending to a long road of intolerance and battle and all sorts of wretched things in the past," said Ustinov, who is British. He met at Wellesley College in Massachusetts with other members of the group and its sister organization in the United States, the World Federalist Association, headed by Anderson.[2]

Burnet recalls a speech given by the prince at a White House gala dinner in Washington in 1985:

> The Prince decided to take on the critics. In a speech at the dinner he hit back: 'What I want to know is what actually is wrong with being elite, for God's sake?' And 'how on earth do they expect us to get anything done without money?'
>
> He went on: '**How are we to have any hope of balanced**

1. Ross Benson, "Stars in Their Eyes," *Majesty* magazine, July 1995, Vol. 16, No. 7, pp. 19-20.
2. Associated Press and Reuter, "Actor plots world government," *Rocky Mountain News*, 14 June 1992, p. 150.

and civilized leadership in the future unless there are some people who have learned about service to others, about compassion, about understanding, as far as is humanly possible, **the other man's religion, the other man's customs**, and his history, about courage to stand up for things that are noble, and for things that are true?

'After all, there's so much to be done in this world—so much famine exists, so much disease, so much poverty, so much conflict, bigotry and prejudice, and there are so many people who are crying out for help, for their own simple dreams to come true.'[1]

Overtures to Muslims. The prince, of course, goes well beyond trying to understand the other man's religion and customs. Note, for example, the following excerpts from a recent article captioned, "Prince Charles calls for millennium money to be spent on mosques and temples to bridge some of the divisions in society":

> ...Prince Charles, writing in The Guardian...says that ideas [in Britain] to mark the millennium have 'not focused on its spiritual importance and the potential it holds for personal and national renewal'....
>
> Now our 20th-century Prince...wishes to ensure that this Christian celebration is made 'relevant' to other faiths....
>
> Of course the Heir to the Throne has been here before when, in a statement of equal eccentricity, he talked of his unconstitutional hope to be 'defender of all the faiths'....
>
> ...Charles talks about renewing Christian landmarks, for which I suppose we should be grateful even if it does mean, in his words, turning abandoned churches into 'health and healing centres which link together body and spirit in a complementary approach to healing'.
>
> But the man who will one day head the Church of England goes on to say that the millennium can be harnessed by 'those of all faiths and creeds'...and says the millennium funds should be used to build non-Christian places of worship....
>
> [This]...is a complete contradiction of the true spirit and meaning of the millennium, not a reaffirmation of it....
>
> What Britain should be doing, as a [supposed] Christian nation, is concentrating on how to spend the money to reinforce and celebrate our Christian heritage. ....what better way to 'make people's lives better in a way which will have real meaning for them', as the Prince put it.[2]

1. Burnet, *In Private—In Public, THE PRINCE AND PRINCESS OF WALES,* pp. 88-90.
2. Simon Heffer, "God save us from politically correct Princes," *Daily Mail,* 26 Jan. 1996.

The prince's advocacy of building mosques and temples is fascinating enough. Yet his overtures toward the world's one-billion-plus Muslims have become far more extreme. According to a few Muslim sources on the Internet, the prince has undergone the ceremonies necessary to "become a Muslim by the name of 'Abdus-Salem Hafidh ad-Deen,'" which means "The Guardian of faith." Perhaps due to the fact that Islam's top Muslim clerics are referred to as "guardians," or due to its similarity to the title "Defender of the Faith" held by Queen Elizabeth II as the "head" of the Church of England, *this title has prompted speculation among Muslims that Prince Charles intends to "become the leader of the Muslims."*[1] Note that as a schoolboy, the prince, like Prince Philip before him,[2] was given the similar Platonic title of "Guardian" as *head boy* at Gordonstoun,[3] an Illuminati-run school that practices a form of what we now know as "outcome-based education" (OBE). At Gordonstoun, the "Guardian" had ten "helpers," just as the AntiChrist shall command ten world leaders.[4] In fact, Gordonstoun is situated on a satanic site.[5]

1. Othman The Italian, *Is Prince Charles a Muslim?*, p. 1. The author possesses an HTML copy of this *formerly on-line* Muslim book (www.sinet.it/Islam/dwnload/charles.zip), which addresses Prince Charles, Prince Philip, and Freemasonry. Also, see the October 15, 1996, Internet article from *Londoner's Diary*, titled "Charles 'is a Secret Islam Convert,'" at "http://www.best.com/%7Einforme/mateen/Sufi/Prince/Prince_Convert.html": "The man making the claim is a respected religious leader—the Grand Mufti of Cyprus, Shaykh Nazim Adel, leader of Turkish Northern Cyprus' Muslims. He says Charles converted during a trip to Turkey. The Mufti is quoted in *The Riddle and the Knight: In search of Sir John Mandeville*, by Giles Milton.... 'Did you know,' the Mufti is reported as saying, 'that Prince Charles has converted to Islam. Yes, yes. He is a Muslim.' Milton, naturally, expressed astonishment. 'I can't say more,' responded the Mufti. 'But it happened in Turkey. Oh yes, he's converted all right. When you get home, check up on how often he travels to Turkey,' Milton says. 'He certainly wasn't joking.'"
2. Judd, *Prince Philip*, p. 77.
3. Dimbleby, *The Prince of Wales*, pp. 43 and 61, 89. "Charles had passed through this selection process stage by stage until the post of Guardian became a definitive recognition of merit imposed directly by his school fellows" (Cathcart, p. 69).
4. For more information, see Chapter 11's section titled, "The United World Colleges."
5. "In 1638..., Sir Robert Gordon, 1st Baron of Gordonstoun, bought the estate.... The next significant building work was carried out by the 3rd Baronet, known as Sir Robert the Wizard, who constructed...the [non-traditional] Round Square. According to legend...the reason for its odd shape arose from the fact that Sir Robert had struck a bargain with the Devil while a student in Padua. The Devil agreed to teach him 'the hidden secrets of the universe that the King of Heaven has denied to men' in return for his soul.... As the years passed Sir Robert brooded on the awful fate that approached. He finally hit on the idea of constructing a circle of magical proportions, a mathematical sanctuary in which the Devil would never be able to catch him.... The Round Square now houses the library, several classrooms, teachers' accomodation[s] and a few sleeping quarters, and it is said that the ghost of Sir Robert can

Prince Charles is said to take "regular advice on Islamic issues from a group of 12 religious leaders and academics." This is in harmony with other instances in which royals and their secret societies form groups of *thirteen* individuals, and likely parodies, in a satanic or Luciferic way, Jesus' calling of the twelve apostles. As the result of studied speeches made in October 1993 and December 1996 concerning Islam and the West, *the prince has become perhaps the most popular Westerner in the Muslim world today.*[1] Excerpts from his highly compelling and manipulative speeches,[2] made before hand-picked audiences including some of the world's most prominent Muslim clerics, follow:

> ....Unlike many of you, I am not an expert on Islam—though I am delighted...to be a Vice Patron of the Oxford Centre for Islamic Studies. The Centre has the potential to be an important and exciting vehicle for promoting and improving understanding of the Islamic world..., like the Oriental Institute and the Middle East Centre....
>
> ....I believe wholeheartedly that the links between these two worlds matter more today than ever before, because the degree of misunderstanding between the Islamic and Western worlds remains dangerously high, and because the need for the two to live and work together in our increasingly interdependent world

be seen to this day" (Junor, pp. 39-40). Note, therefore, that when Prince Charles was made Guardian at Gordonstoun, "he moved out of Windmill Lodge and into a room in Bob Waddell's flat in the Round Square" (ibid., pp. 64-65). Also, recall that the prince was invested as Prince of Wales on a circular platform of Welsh slate, at the center of which Satan was represented by the Welsh dragon. This, no doubt, was intended to emphasize the fact that Satan has also gained Prince Charles' soul.

1. For links to the full text of Prince Charles' speeches in defense of Islam, etc., to the West, as well as more information regarding his apparent acceptance of Islam and his Mideast travels and activities, see "Prince Charles and Islam" at "/Sufi/Prince/Prince.html" of the Internet page "http://www.best.com/%7Einforme/mateen".

   The full text of the prince's October 27, 1993, speech, made at Oxford's Sheldonian Theatre on a visit to the Oxford Centre for Islamic Studies, and titled "Islam and the West," may be found at "/pr_charles_speech.html" of the page "http://www.best.com/%7Einforme/mateen". *Key points* of that speech from the prince may be found at "/pr_charles_keypoints.html" of the same page. A response to it from *The Times*, titled "The Prince and Islam," may be found at "/Islam/Charles.html" of the same page. The full text of the prince's more recent speech, made on December 13, 1996, before a private audience of 70 religious leaders, academics, and businessmen at Wilton Park, Sussex, a Foreign Office conference center, may be found at "/Sufi/Prince/Prince_Speech.html", with a response from Ruth Gledhill of *The Times* at "/Sufi/Prince/Prince_Speech2.html", also of the same page.

2. Cathcart notes, "Like his father, he takes pains with his speeches, drafting and revising, memorising and often seeming to speak extempore, though a copy lies to hand" (p. 168).

has never been greater....

....There are one billion Muslims worldwide. Many millions of them live in countries of the Commonwealth. Ten million or more live in the West, and around one million in Britain. Our own Islamic community has been growing and flourishing for decades. There are nearly 500 mosques in Britain. Popular interest in Islamic culture in Britain is growing fast. Many of you will recall—and I think some of you took part in—the wonderful Festival of Islam which Her Majesty The Queen opened in 1976. Islam is all around us. And yet distrust, even fear, persist In the post-Cold War world of the 1990s, the prospects for peace should be greater than at any time in this century. **In the Middle East, the remarkable and encouraging events of recent weeks [with the signing of the Oslo peace accord] have created new hope for an end to an issue which has divided the world and been so dramatic a source of violence and hatred.** But the dangers have not disappeared. In the Muslim world, we are seeing the unique way of life of the Marsh Arabs of Southern Iraq, thousands of years old, being systematically devastated and destroyed. I confess that for a whole year I have wanted to find a suitable opportunity to express my despair and outrage at the unmentionable horrors being perpetrated in Southern Iraq. To me, the supreme and tragic irony of what has been happening to the Shia population of Iraq—especially in the ancient city and holy shrine of Kerbala—is that after the Western allies took immense care to avoid bombing such holy places (and I remember begging General Schwarzkopf when I met him in Riyadh in December 1990 to do his best to protect such shrines during any conflict) it was Saddam Hussein himself, and his terrifying regime, who caused the destruction of some of Islam's holiest sites. And now we have had to witness the deliberate draining of the marshes and the near total destruction of a unique habitat, together with an entire population that has depended upon it since the dawn of human civilization. The international community has been told the draining of the marshes is for agricultural purposes. How many more obscene lies do we have to be told before action is taken? Even at the eleventh hour it is still not too late to prevent a total cataclysm. I pray that this might at least be a cause in which Islam and the West could join forces for the sake of our common humanity.... Elsewhere, the violence and hatred are more intractable and deep-seated, as we go on seeing every day to our horror in the wretched suffering of peoples across the world—in the former Yugoslavia, in Somalia, Angola, Sudan, in so many of the former Soviet Republics. In Yugoslavia the terrible sufferings of the Bosnian Muslims, alongside that of other communities in that cruel war, help keep alive many of the fears and prejudices which our two worlds retain of each other. Conflict, of course, comes about because of the misuse of power and the clash of ideals, not to mention the inflammatory activities of unscrupulous and bigoted leaders. But it also arises, tragically, from an inability to understand, and from the powerful emotions which out of misunderstanding lead to distrust and fear. Ladies and gentlemen, we must not slide into a new era of danger and division because governments and peoples, communities and religions, cannot live together in peace in a shrinking world.

It is odd, in many ways, that misunderstandings between Islam and the West should persist. For that which binds our two worlds together is so much more powerful than that which divides us. **Muslims, Christians—and Jews—are all 'peoples of the Book'.** Islam and Christianity share a common monotheistic vision: a belief in one divine God, in the transience of our earthly life, in our accountability for our actions, and in the assurance of life to come. We share many key values in common: respect for knowledge, for justice, compassion towards the poor and underprivileged, the importance of family life, respect for parents. 'Honour thy father and thy mother' is a Quranic precept too. Our history has been closely bound up together. There, however, is one root of the problem. For much of that history has been one of conflict: fourteen centuries too often marked by mutual hostility. That has given rise to an enduring tradition of fear and distrust, because our two worlds have so often seen that past in contradictory ways. To Western school children, the two hundred years of Crusades are traditionally seen as a series of heroic, chivalrous exploits in which the kings, knights, princes—and children—of Europe tried to wrest Jerusalem from the wicked Muslim infidel. To Muslims, the Crusades were an episode of great cruelty and terrible plunder, of Western infidel soldiers of fortune and horrific atrocities, perhaps exemplified best by the massacres committed by the Crusaders when, in 1099, they took back Jerusalem,[1] the third holiest city in Islam.... The point, I think, is not that one or other picture is more true, or has a monopoly of truth. It is that misunderstandings arise when we fail to appreciate how others look at the world, its history, and our respective roles in it.

The corollary of how we in the West see our history has so often been to regard Islam as a threat—in medieval times as a military conqueror, and in more modern times as a source of intolerance, extremism and terrorism.... With the fall of the Ottoman Empire, Europe's triumph over Islam seemed complete. Those days of conquest are over. But even now our common attitude to Islam suffers because the way we understand it has been hijacked by the extreme and the superficial. To many of us in the West, Islam is seen in terms of the tragic civil war in Lebanon, the

---

1. Note Prince Charles' veiled reference to Godfroi de Bouillon. For more information, see Chapter 4, "Prince of this World—a *Diverse* Lineage."

killings and bombings perpetrated by extremist groups in the Middle East, and by what is commonly referred to as 'Islamic fundamentalism'. Our judgment of Islam has been grossly distorted by taking the extremes to be the norm. That, ladies and gentlemen, is a serious mistake....

For example, people in this country frequently argue that the Sharia law of the Islamic world is cruel, barbaric and unjust.... The truth is, of course, different and always more complex. My own understanding is that extremes, like the cutting off of hands, are rarely practised. The guiding principle and spirit of Islamic law, taken straight from the Qur'an, should be those of equity and compassion. We need to study its actual application before we make judgements. We must distinguish between systems of justice administered with integrity, and systems of justice as we may see them practised which have been deformed for political reasons into something no longer Islamic.... Women are not automatically second-class citizens because they live in Islamic countries. We cannot judge the position of women in Islam aright if we take the most conservative Islamic states as representative of the whole....

We in the West need also to understand the Islamic world's view of us. There is nothing to be gained, and much harm to be done, by refusing to comprehend the extent to which many people in the Islamic world genuinely fear our own Western materialism and mass culture as a deadly challenge to their Islamic culture and way of life.... The fact is that our form of materialism can be offensive to devout Muslims—and I do not just mean the extremists among them. We must understand that reaction, just as the West's attitude to some of the more rigorous aspects of Islamic life needs to be understood in the Islamic world. This, I believe, would help us understand **what we have commonly come to see as the threat of Islamic fundamentalism**. We need to be careful of that emotive label, 'fundamentalism', and distinguish, as Muslims do, between revivalists, who choose to take the practice of their religion most devoutly, and fanatics or extremists who use this devotion for political ends. Among the many religious, social and political causes of what we might more accurately call the Islamic revival is **a powerful feeling of disenchantment**, of the realisation that Western technology and material things are insufficient, and that a deeper meaning to life lies elsewhere in the essence of Islamic belief.

At the same time, we must not be tempted to believe that extremism is in some way the hallmark and essence of the Muslim. **Extremism is no more the monopoly of Islam than it is the monopoly of other religions, including Christianity.** The vast majority of Muslims, though personally pious, are moderate in their politics. Theirs is the 'religion of the middle way'. The

Prophet himself always disliked and feared extremism. Perhaps the fear of Islamic revivalism which coloured the 1980's is now beginning to give way in the West to an understanding of the genuine spiritual forces behind this groundswell. But if we are to understand this important movement, we must learn to distinguish clearly between what the vast majority of Muslims believe and the terrible violence of a small minority among them which civilized people everywhere must condemn.

Ladies and gentlemen, if there is much misunderstanding in the West about the nature of Islam, there is also much ignorance about the debt our own culture and civilisation owe to the Islamic world.... The mediaeval Islamic world, from Central Asia to the shores of the Atlantic, was a world where scholars and men of learning flourished.... The contribution of Muslim Spain to the preservation of classical learning during the Dark Ages, and to the first flowerings of the Renaissance, has long been recognised.... Not only did Muslim Spain gather and preserve the intellectual content of ancient Greek and Roman civilisation, it also interpreted and expanded upon that civilisation, and made a vital contribution of its own in so many fields of human endeavour—in science, astronomy, mathematics, algebra (itself an Arabic word), law, history, medicine, pharmacology, optics, agriculture, theology, music....

Islam nurtured and preserved the quest for learning.... Cordoba in the 10th century was by far the most civilised city of Europe.... That was made possible because the Muslim world acquired from China the skill of making paper more than four hundred years before the rest of non-Muslim Europe. Many of the traits on which modern Europe prides itself came to it from Muslim Spain. Diplomacy, free trade, open borders, the techniques of academic research, of anthropology, etiquette, fashion, alternative medicine, hospitals, all came from this great city of cities. **Mediaeval Islam was a religion of remarkable tolerance for its time, allowing Jews and Christians the right to practise their inherited beliefs, and setting an example which was not, unfortunately, copied for many centuries in the West.** The surprise, ladies and gentlemen, is the extent to which Islam has been a part of Europe for so long, first in Spain, then in the Balkans, and the extent to which it has contributed so much towards the civilisation which we all too often think of, wrongly, as entirely Western. Islam is part of our past and present, in all fields of human endeavour. It has helped to create modern Europe. It is part of our own inheritance, not a thing apart.

More than this, **Islam can teach us today a way of understanding and living in the world which Christianity itself is poorer for having lost. At the heart of Islam is its preservation of an integral view of the Universe. Islam—like**

Buddhism and Hinduism—refuses to separate man and nature, religion and science, mind and matter, and has preserved a metaphysical and unified view of ourselves and the world around us. At the core of Christianity there still lies an integral view of the sanctity of the world, and a clear sense of the trusteeship and responsibility given to us for our natural surroundings....

But the West gradually lost this integrated vision of the world with Copernicus and Descartes and the coming of the scientific revolution. A comprehensive philosophy of nature is no longer part of our everyday beliefs. I cannot help feeling that, if we could now only rediscover that earlier, all-embracing approach to the world around us, to see and understand its deeper meaning, we could begin to get away from the increasing tendency in the West to live on the surface of our surroundings, where we study our world in order to manipulate and dominate it, turning harmony and beauty into disequilibrium and chaos. It is a sad fact, I believe, that in so many ways **the external world we have created in the last few hundred years has come to reflect our own divided and confused inner state**. Western civilisation has become increasingly acquisitive and exploitive in defiance of our environmental responsibilities. **This crucial sense of oneness and trusteeship of the vital sacramental and spiritual character of the world about us is surely something important we can relearn from Islam....   ...I am appealing for...a wider, deeper, more careful understanding of our world: for a metaphysical as well as material dimension to our lives, in order to recover the balance we have abandoned, the absence of which, I believe, will prove disastrous in the long term. If the ways of thought in Islam and other religions can help us in that search, then there are things for us to learn in this system of belief which I suggest we ignore at our peril.**

Ladies, and gentlemen, **we live today in one world, forged by instant communications, by television, by the exchange of information on a scale undreamed of by our grandparents. The world economy functions as an inter-dependant entity. Problems of society, the quality of life and the environment, are global in their causes and effects, and none of us any longer has the luxury of being able to solve them on our own.** The Islamic and Western worlds share problems common to us all: how we adapt to change in our societies, how we help young people who feel alienated from their parents or society's values, how we deal with **Aids, drugs, and the disintegration of the family.** Of course, these problems vary in nature and intensity between societies. But the similarity of human experience is considerable. **The international trade in hard drugs is one example, the damage we are collectively doing to our environment** is another. We have to solve these threats to our communities and our lives together.... [We] have to learn to understand each other, and to educate our children...so that they understand too. We have to show trust, mutual respect and tolerance.... The Islamic and Western world can no longer afford to stand apart from a common effort to solve their common problems.... We have to...understand and tolerate, and build on the positive principles our cultures have in common.... Each of us needs to understand the importance of conciliation....

If this need for tolerance and exchange is true internationally, it applies with special force within Britain itself. **Britain is a multi-racial and multi-cultural society.... Where there are failings of understanding and tolerance, we have a need...for greater reconciliation among our own citizens.** I can only admire, and applaud, those men and women of so many denominations who work tirelessly...to promote good community relations. **The Centre for the Study of Islam and Christian-Muslim Relations in Birmingham is one especially notable and successful example.** We should be grateful for the dedication and example of all those who have devoted themselves to the cause of promoting understanding.

....These two worlds, the Islamic and the Western, are at something of a crossroads in their relations. We must not let them stand apart. I do not accept the argument that they are on a course to clash in a new era of antagonism. I am utterly convinced that our two worlds have much to offer each other. We have much to do together.... The further down that road we can travel, the better the world that we shall create for our children and for future generations.

I start from the belief that **Islamic civilisation at its best, like many of the religions of the East—Judaism, Hinduism, Jainism and Buddhism—has an important message for the West** in the way it has retained an integrated and integral view of **the sanctity of the world around us**. I feel that we in the West could be helped to rediscover the roots of our own understanding by an appreciation of the Islamic tradition's deep respect for **the timeless traditions of the natural order.**

I believe that process could help in the task of bringing our two faiths closer together. It could also help us in the West to rethink, and for the better, our practical stewardship of man and his environment—in fields such as health-care, the natural environment and agriculture, as well as in architecture and urban planning.

Modern materialism is unbalanced and increasingly damaging in its long-term consequences. **Yet nearly all the great** religions of the world have held an integral view of the sanctity of the world. **The Christian message with, for example, its deeply mystical and symbolic doctrine of the Incarnation, has been traditionally a message of the unity of the worlds of spirit and matter, and of God's manifestation in this world and in mankind.**

....Science has tried to assume a monopoly—even a tyranny—over our understanding. Religion and science have become separated.... Science has attempted to take over the natural world from God; it has fragmented the cosmos and relegated the sacred to a separate and secondary compartment of our understanding, divorced from practical, day to day existence.

We are only now beginning to gauge the disastrous results. We in the Western world seem to have lost **a sense of the *wholeness* of our environment, and of our immense and inalienable responsibility to the whole of creation.** This has led to an increasing failure to appreciate or understand tradition and the wisdom of our forebears....

In my view, a more holistic approach is needed now. Science has done the inestimable service of showing us a world much more complex than we ever imagined. But in its modern, materialist, one-dimensional form, it cannot explain everything. God is not merely the ultimate Newtonian mathematician or the mechanistic clockmaker. As science and technology have become increasingly separated from ethical, moral and sacred considerations, so the implications of such a separation have become more sombre and horrifying—as we see in genetic manipulation....

I have always felt that **tradition is not a man-made element in our lives, but a God-given intuition of natural rhythms, of the fundamental harmony that emerges from the union of the paradoxical opposites that exist in every aspect of nature. Tradition reflects the timeless order of the cosmos, and anchors us into an awareness of the great mysteries of the universe,** so that, as Blake put it, we can see the whole universe in an atom and eternity in a moment. That is why I believe Man is so much more than just a biological phenomenon....

....I nevertheless believe that the survival of civilised values, as we have inherited them from our ancestors, depends on the corresponding survival in our hearts of that profound sense of the sacred and the spiritual.

Traditional religions, with their integral view of the universe, can help us to rediscover the importance of the integration of the secular and the sacred. The danger of ignoring this essential aspect of our existence is not just spiritual or intellectual. It also lies at the heart of that great divide between the Islamic and Western worlds over the place of materialism in our lives. In those instances where Islam chooses to reject Western materialism, this is not, in my view, a political affectation or the result of envy or a sense of inferiority. Quite the opposite. And the danger that the gulf between the worlds of Islam and the other Eastern religions on the one hand and the West on the other will grow ever wider and more unbridgeable is real, **unless we can explore together practical ways of integrating the sacred and the secular in both our cultures in order to provide a true inspiration for the next century**.

Islamic culture in its traditional form has striven to preserve this integrated, spiritual view of the world in a way we have not seen fit to do in recent generations in the West. There is much we can learn from that Islamic world view in this respect.

There are many ways in which mutual understanding and appreciation can be built. Perhaps, for instance, we could begin by having more Muslim teachers in British schools, or by encouraging exchanges of teachers. **Everywhere in the world people want to learn English. But in the West, in turn, we need to be taught by Islamic teachers how to learn with our hearts, as well as our heads. The approaching millennium may be the ideal catalyst for helping to explore and stimulate these links, and I hope we shall not ignore the opportunity this gives us to rediscover the spiritual underpinning of our entire existence.**

Prince Charles is making a definite impact not just among Muslims, but also in the West. Major themes of his speeches concerning Islam and the West are now being echoed in the popular press:

> ....With the demise of communism, Islam has emerged as one of the world's most powerful ideologies, a religion that embraces more than 1 billion adherents who make up a majority in about 45 countries.
>
> Yet, as a new century dawns, Islam is undergoing change potentially more important than any time since the death of the Prophet Mohammed.... That change—a quest to determine its role in a modern world—poses a challenge to the West and to Islam itself.
>
> Its impact is vast, with implications for the flow of oil, trade, nuclear proliferation, even war. While Muslim countries account for just 4 percent of the world's economy, they make up one-fifth of its population—a potentially explosive mix.
>
> Already the revival has witnessed terrorism in Algeria, a battle over women's rights in Afghanistan, militancy in Iran. Its flip side has been grassroots work that has bettered the lives of millions.
>
> For the West, the renewal may mean confrontation or

co-existence with Islam, depending on attitudes on both sides at their many points of contact.[1]

In 1996, following the Muslim "holy month" of Ramadan, Prince Charles visited a London mosque where, dressed "in traditional Islamic cap and shawl," "he met with the Muslim worshippers including followers of Mawlana Shaykh Mohammed Nazim Adil al-Haqqani, Grand Mufti of Cyprus and world leader of the Most Distinguished Naqshbandi Order of Sufis."[2] On November 12, 1996, while in Uzbekistan, the prince wore an Islamic wedding gown given to him as a gift by "the country's religious leader, the Mufti Mukhtar Abdullaev," which, according to *The Times,* "ended up looking like a marriage between East and West." From there, after "meeting with the Mufti at the nearby Baraka-Khan Madrassah, a 16th-century Islamic seminary,....[in] a small, white-washed room," the prince went "to see the Osman Koran, said to be the world's oldest Islamic holy book," in which he "showed great interest," stating 'I'm so thrilled at having a chance to see this great Koran.'" While in Uzbekistan, typifying Prince Charles' ecumenism, the prince also met the Patriarch of Russia, who "told him of a 'very considerable' revival in the Russian Orthodox Church."[3]

Many New Agers are not currently looking for a "Coming One." Yet some New Age organizations *are,* and they have stated that he lives *in London,* where he has supposedly resided since 1977. Calling him "Maitreya Buddha," "The World Teacher," "the Avatar for the Age, the Representative of God, the Messiah of the Jews, the Imam Mahdi of the Muslims, Krishna returned," Benjamin Creme announced on May 14, 1982, "He is in England and has been in England for all these years since July 1977. The large town is London.... The community is the Pakistani-Indian community of South London.... The christ comes

---

1. "Islam evolves, seeks to define role in modern world," *The Denver Post,* 23 Jan. 1997, p. 20A.
2. See "HRHPrince_Charles.html" at "http://www.best.com/%7Einforme/mateen/".
3. At "http://www.best.com/%7Einforme/mateen/Sufi/Prince/", see "Prince_Uzbekistan.html" and "Prince_Quran.html". Other interesting articles on the prince's spiritual beliefs, as well as public reactions to them, may be found at this same Internet site.

not really to save—he comes to teach."[1] Ernest Ramsey, a New Ager who has written about the approaching *"Reappearance of the Christ and his Executives, the Masters of Wisdom,"* traveled "to London to try and see 'The Christ.'"[2] According to Dale, it was in 1977 that Prince Charles "began to climb off the fence and to line up with the mixed bag of visionaries, intellectuals, cranks and lunatics who say there are other planes of existence tangled inside and around the one which we inhabit," and "[it] was in 1982 that the Prince first hinted publicly at such unusual spiritual beliefs.... He saw himself as a sort of missionary...." Indeed, Dale credits a highly publicized speech that the prince delivered on December 14, 1982, "as the turning point for what is now promoted and marketed as alternative medicine."[3] With these things in mind, consider the following comments:

> ....Light-years ahead of anyone else on earth, he will teach marvelous new revelations and bring peace and prosperity. He will come as a savior, arriving just as the world is sliding into chaos and destruction to lead man into a bright, shining, glorious New Age.
>
> ....The New Age "Christ" is a blasphemous imitation of the true Christ of the Bible....
>
> Lola Davis identifies the New Age "Christ" as "the One for whom all religions wait, called Lord Maitreya by some in the East, Krishna, Messiah, Bodhisattva, Christ, Immam Mahdi." She promises, he "will bring new revelations and further guidance for establishing the World Religion."
>
> Currently, Davis explains, the New Age "Christ" resides on a different plane of consciousness from that which we experience. There he directs the Masters, "a group of advanced souls, most of them discarnate...known variously as the White Brotherhood, The Great White Lodge, the Masters of Wisdom, the Hierarchy, and the Angels around the Throne."...
>
> Alice Bailey, head of both the Arcane School and the Lucis Trust, has written a number of books which detail The Plan.... Bailey's *The Externalization of the Hierarchy* predicts that the New Age will be in full bloom soon after a global crisis occurs and in desperation the world turns to the "Christ" for leadership. This New Age "Christ" will affirm the essential divine nature of

1. Church, pp. 258, 261-262.
2. Cumbey, *A Planned Deception*, p. 171.
3. Dale, pp. 9, 13-19, 33-37, 175-178, 200-206.

312

humanity, says Bailey, and a New World Religion will come about.... Christianity will be eclipsed by the new religion....

The New Age holds that the term Christ can be applied to any person who reaches an elevated state of consciousness and thereby achieves divine status. It is said that we are all simply Christs-in-the-making. Nevertheless, historically only a few souls have found enough favor with the spiritual hierarchy of reincarnated ancient Masters to be chosen to return to earth as an *avatar*.

The concept of the avatar is derived from the Hindu religion, which teaches that avatars are reincarnations-in-the-flesh of the god Vishnu, messengers sent to the living from the "gods."... This corresponds to the New Age belief in the hierarchy of reincarnated ancient Masters.

....In the New Age scheme of things Jesus is not the Son of God, but just another enlightened, reincarnated spirit.

New Age disciples claim that in the near future we can expect an avatar to come who is far greater than either Jesus, Buddha, Krishna, Mohammed, or Gandhi. Rather than just *another* "Christ," this is to be the "Christ." He will be god realized, god incarnate.

Lord Maitreya, avatar and world teacher, is now claimed to be living in London, preparing himself for his eventual reign at the world's helm....

"Lord Maitreya" is identified by most New Age groups as their coming "Christ." However, to deflect criticism, many refrain from naming him. Instead, such general titles as "the enlightened one to come," the "Cosmic Christ," the "Universal One," or the "New Age World Teacher" are used.[1]

New Age leaders can't imitate Jesus' mind-boggling coming in the clouds with all power and glory, so they claim that their "Christ," the Lord Maitreya, *has already appeared* on Planet Earth. Benjamin Creme says that the New Age "Christ" is now in London living in a Pakistani community, though he has not as yet revealed his identity to everyone.[2]

On the basis of God's inspired Word, we can be certain that the Tribulation Period and the events preceding it will not unfold in precisely the manner foretold by the false prophets and prophetesses of the New Age Movement. Nevertheless, it is noteworthy that Buckingham Palace is near London's Southall, where a number of Pakistani and Indian families live. Therefore, some statements from New

---

1. Texe Marrs, *Dark Secrets of the New Age* (Illinois: Good News Publishers, 1987), pp. 56-59.
2. Marrs, *Mystery Mark of the New Age*, p. 247.

Age circles (e.g., that their so-called "Christ" lives in London) definitely do bear consideration.

As shown, Prince Charles openly airs his concerns about various social ills: "the Prince and Princess have shown great social concern, involving themselves in the problems of the underprivileged in a way that few others of their generation and class have done."[1] According to the prince, "The first function of any monarchy is the human concern for people."[2] It is interesting, therefore, that the very issues which Prince Charles has addressed publicly with the most zeal and repetition are the same ones that the mentioned New Age organizations claim as the primary concerns of their coming "Christ." Not only that, but they are also among the pressing reasons offered by today's one-worlders for the need to establish a global government.[3] Consider, for example, these statements from a full-page Tara Center advertisement in the January 12, 1987 edition of *USA Today*:

> *Drugs... A.I.D.S.... poverty... rampant crime... mass starvation... nuclear threat... terrorism.... Is there a solution? In answer to our urgent need...THE CHRIST IS IN THE WORLD. A great World Teacher for people of every religion and no religion. A practical man with solutions to our problems. He loves ALL humanity... Christ is here, my friends. Your Brother walks among you.*[4]

Is it mere coincidence that Prince Charles is making his views regarding these and other, related issues known? Subjects not mentioned in this Tara Center advertisement, in which Prince Charles likes to involve himself, include architecture[5] and the environment:

> ....Prince Charles pursues his ambitions to improve architecture, the state of the English language and the environment through his public speeches and the making of films for television....

1. Hoey, *Charles & Diana: The Tenth Anniversary,* p. 155.
2. *Charles & Diana: A Royal Family Album,* p. 55.
3. For more information, see Chapter 9, "Signs of the Times and the Rise of 'Global Governance.'"
4. Marrs, *Dark Secrets of the New Age,* p. 66.
5. For insight on the prince's seemingly disconsonant and overbearing interest in architecture, see Chapter 12, "Prince Charles, the Middle East Peace Talks, and Global Security."

....Charles...has become the voice of the people in his stand against pollution; pollution of the old values, represented by the falling standards of spoken English and modern architecture and by inner-city decay, as well as the pollution, in real terms, of the very air we breathe, the food we eat and the items we use in our everyday lives. The 'greening' of the Royal Family owes much to Prince Charles. He grows his own vegetables organically and refuses to allow any aerosol containers to be used in any of his homes. In other words, he practises what he preaches.[1]

....The prime requisite for a good architect [according to the prince] should be 'to be concerned about the way people live—about the environment they inhabit and the kind of community that is created by that environment.'...

....'Those who recall it [London before he was born] say that the affinity between the buildings and the earth, in spite of the city's great size, was so close and organic that the houses looked almost as though they had grown out of the earth, and not been imposed upon it—grown, moreover, in such a way that as few trees as possible were thrust out of the way.'

He faintly sugared the pill by praising some of the work that had been done in designing for the disabled,[2] but the burden of his speech [to the Royal Institute of British Architects] was damning....

The Prince was not so very out of step, however, as he discovered from the letters of support that poured in. Indeed he had put his finger most succinctly upon precisely what a great many people felt.... The issue of community architecture was based on more than just instinct; it was soundly based on what he had learned from talking to people who had to live in the buildings and environments that planners had created for them. Charles is a great listener....

Community architecture was not a new concept—enlightened architects had been practising it from time immemorial....

---

1. Hoey, *Charles & Diana: The Tenth Anniversary,* pp. 110, 150-151.
2. Prince Charles takes his concern for the disabled seriously. In 1981, for example, the prince served as Patron of the International Year of Disabled People. According to Junor, "Prince Charles had been eager to make a contribution [to the disabled] himself.... [He] had been camping and canoeing with them—and had come to appreciate the problems of living in a world designed for the able-bodied.... [So] it was suggested that Prince Charles should set up an advisory group which would not duplicate the good work already being done by other organizations in the field, but rather support them, pinpoint areas of weakness and act as a catalyst in getting things done.... [Consequently,] the Prince of Wales's Advisory Group on Disability had been formed.... [The advisors] have highlighted the five major areas of neglect: access, housing, employment, independent living and prevention, and are system- atically working through them" (pp. 219, 230). In the booklet *Living Options,* Prince Charles states, "Recognize that those who are affected by disability are people first and disabled sec- ond, and have individual attitudes, likes, aspirations, fears and abilities. Understand that although there may be special areas of need, people with disabilities wish to have the oppor- tunity to live in the same way as other people" (ibid., p. 232).

315

The Prince...had simply discovered that one of the biggest difficulties for people living in the inner cities was that their housing was unsuitable for their needs....

The result was that people became despondent. If they didn't like their surroundings they didn't look after them.... [They then]...reached rock bottom and hit out at society.... If people are happy in their homes and their environment they will become involved in looking after it and take a pride in what they are doing; this in turn will restore their own self-confidence and alter their entire outlook on life. This surely was the solution, and with this in mind Charles sought out architects who were already working in the field.[1]

Prince Charles attacked modern British architecture again...with a television documentary....

The heir apparent...wrote his own script [in which he spoke of the "Great Fire of 1666"].... He narrated it with grace, humor, and occasionally self-deprecating wit....

The queen, as monarch, is constitutionally forbidden from publicly expressing political views and does not give interviews, let alone make documentaries, but the prince is emerging as a public spokesman in his own right....[2]

In the television program, his main message was deeply serious.

"Man is more, much more, than a mere mechanical object whose sole aim is to produce money," he said. "Above all he has a soul, and the soul is irrational, unfathomable, mysterious. Throughout history our ancestors have derived their inspiration from the infinite richness of the natural world."[3]

Prince Charles, who banned aerosol sprays from his household out of concern for the ozone layer, is to write and present a TV documentary on environmental threats, the British Broadcasting Corp. said....

The 60-minute program is still being written, but the heir to the throne is expected to focus on global issues such as the destruction of the rain forests and the ozone layer....

The program is to be broadcast...as part of a project called One World, in which European stations are collaborating on a week of programs about world problems.[4]

---

1. Junor, pp. 216-218.
2. Recently, there have been rumors that within the coming decade, the British Constitution may be altered to permit changes to the monarchical system. One such change could involve the expression of political views. If so, Prince Charles could conceivably become the King of England and yet, so long as he is still called by a name and title that calculates to 666 (e.g., "Prince Charles of Wales"), fulfill the role of the AntiChrist.
3. The New York Times, "Prince Charles thrashes recent British architecture," *The Denver Post,* 30 Oct. 1988, p. 13A.
4. "Prince Charles promotes environment," *The Denver Post,* 24 Oct. 1989, p. 14A.

Prince Charles announced...in London the establishment of an international task force to promote self-help projects in the developing world.... The Business Leaders Forum, a charity the Prince sponsored in 1990, will oversee the project. The group will promote projects in communities to help them overcome hunger, poverty, homelessness and environmental degradation.[1]

Prince Charles urged Saudi and British oil merchants...to address the threat of global warming at once.
"This is an issue which we have to address now, not in 10 or 20 years' time," he said in a speech in Saudi Arabia's oil-producing Eastern Province.
"The penalty for failure will affect our children and grandchildren dramatically, not just here in the Gulf region, but in the world at large."[2]

Recall that Prince Charles has traveled to Africa's Kalahari desert with a man who openly pays homage to demonic spirits. With this, and the preceding information in mind, consider these excerpts from another full-page Tara Center advertisement printed on April 25, 1982, in various newspapers around the world:

THE WORLD HAS HAD *enough*...OF HUNGER, INJUSTICE, WAR. IN ANSWER TO OUR CALL FOR HELP, AS WORLD TEACHER FOR ALL HUMANITY, THE CHRIST IS NOW HERE.

HOW WILL WE RECOGNIZE HIM?

Look for a modern man concerned with modern problems—political, economic, and social. Since July, 1977, the Christ has been emerging as a spokesman for a group or community in a well-known modern country. He is not a religious leader, but an educator in the broadest sense of the word—pointing the way out of our present crisis. We will recognize Him by His extraordinary spiritual potency, the universality of His viewpoint, and His love for all humanity. **He comes not to judge, but to aid and inspire.**

WHO IS THE CHRIST?

Throughout history, humanity's evolution has been guided by a group of enlightened men, the Masters of Wisdom. They have remained largely in the remote desert and mountain places of earth, working mainly through their disciples who

1. "Prince Charles announces international aid project," *Rocky Mountain News,* 11 July 1992, p. 102.
2. "Prince urges action on global warming," *The Denver Post,* 9 Nov. 1993, p. 9A.

live openly in the world. This message of the Christ's reappearance has been given primarily by such a disciple trained for his task for over 20 years. At the center of this "Spiritual Hierarchy" stands the World Teacher, *Lord Maitreya* known by Christians as the *Christ*. And as Christians await the Second Coming, so the Jews await the *Messiah*, the Buddhists the fifth *Buddha*, the Moslims the *Iman Mahdi*, and the Hindus await *Krishna*. These are all names for one individual. **His presence in the world guarantees there will be no third World War.**[1]

---

1. Constance Cumbey, *The Hidden Dangers of the Rainbow* (Louisiana: Huntington House, Inc., 1983), p. 13 and the back cover.

11

Power Plays

Some of what follows is merely outlined. Because the points have significant import, however, they are nevertheless mentioned.[1]

The Order of the Garter, the Committee of 300, the Illuminati, and Freemasonry. As shown earlier, the British monarch and the Prince of Wales are the two highest ranking knights in the Order of the Garter. As such, both head the Committee of 300, and both have authority over the Illuminati and Freemasonry worldwide.[2]

The United World Colleges. Prince Charles is President of the United World Colleges (UWC), having taken over this role upon the death of his uncle, Louis Mountbatten. Following Mountbatten's death, the prince, thinking of the "UWC's great aims" and "ordinary people," "realized he had to keep going for their sake, to carry on where his great-uncle had left off, to work towards democracy and justice in the world and to strive towards peace through knowledge and understanding. 'The United World Colleges movement,' he said in his address at the memorial service, 'was a particular passion of his in the final years because he saw within the scheme a means of bringing peace and international understanding through students from many countries to a world that he had seen pull itself to pieces twice in twenty-five years....'"[3]

The elitist UWC exist "to promote international understanding through education; and to provide a pattern of

---

1. Lord willing and time permitting, these points and others will be presented in fully-documented detail in a second edition to this work. Should the reader desire such documentation in the meantime, the author would refer him to *The Prince of Wales* by Jonathan Dimbleby, besides other biographies on the prince and the Internet.
2. For more information, see the discussion on the Garter in Chapter 7, "The Heraldic Symbols in the Arms and their Interpretations."
3. Junor, pp. 148-149.

education adapted to meet the special needs of our time."
According to the prince, "My acceptance of the Presidency
was based really on a deep and personal conviction of the
intrinsic merits of the UWC concept, which I think in many
ways is close to the Gordonstoun ideal which essentially is
the belief in the importance of human relationships in world
affairs.... And last but not least the Presidency does provide me, in particular, with an ideal topic of discussion
with Heads of State and so on, throughout the world."
Prince Charles has used his position as such to promote
globalism and multiculturalism, emphasizing the importance
of "meeting people from all over the world and thus forming a more comprehensive picture of the things that unite
us all, rather than those which divide us." As a Finnish
student put it, "You start to see the truth from other people's points of view. That is how you change the world."[1]

Where globalist "experimental learning" is concerned,
we should point out that Prince Charles himself, like Prince
Philip before him (see below), was subjected to a form of
"outcome-based education" (OBE): "The Gordonstoun
authorities were just then preparing their 'Final Report to
Parents', an unorthodox document providing comment not
only on the standard reached in a pupil's studies but also
giving judgment on his public spirit and sense of justice; his
ability to follow the right course in the face of discomfort,
boredom, scepticism or impulses of the moment; his ability
to plan and organise, to deal with the unexpected, and on
his imagination and fighting spirit."[2] Gordonstoun, under
the strong German influence of Kurt Hahn, a Jewish Illuminist who was indirectly and ironically instrumental in Hitler's rise to power,[3] was closely associated with Salem in
Germany, where Prince Philip experienced "the most

1. Junor, pp. 133-135, 137-138.
2. Cathcart, pp. 69-70.
3. Kurt Hahn was the personal secretary and advisor to Max von Baden, Germany's last Imperial
Chancellor. As such, the German case at the Versailles peace negotiations "owed a good
deal of it substance to Hahn, a brilliant scholar." As a Rhodes Scholar at Christ Church of
Oxford when World War I began, Hahn returned to Germany to serve as an intelligence
expert on Britain and as a Liaison Officer with the Imperial army. Hahn later authored
"Brockdorff-Rantzau's impassioned speech repudiating Germany's 'war guilt.'" Consequently, "Hahn helped to coin the explosive slogan...which was to lead to the [German]
clamour for revenge, rearmament, the Nazi regime and, finally, the Second World War"
(Judd, *Prince Philip,* p. 68; also, see Junor, p. 35).

320

formative educational experience of his life." Having been described as "the man who made Philip," Hahn's educational ideas were "partly based on one of Hahn's principal inspirations, Plato, and his distinctly élitist philosophy,[1] and partly on the principals of Sparta, the austere soldier state of Greek antiquity." The German Salem, founded in 1918 by Prince Max of Baden with Hahn, "was on one of the family's estates," residing in part of Prince Max's castle at Salem. The school offered "an excellent, liberal German education." Earlier, Prince Philip had been educated at Cheam in England, a "progressive" school that Winston Churchill had also attended. The prince "hardly excelled, except in French, which he spoke as well as English and German and better than Greek." Since 1953, Prince Philip, in the experimental learning vein, has become Patron of the Outward Bound Trust in Britain, Canada, and Australia.[2] Speaking of Salem, Judd comments,

> Achievement through struggle, an aristocracy of accomplishment, it is not surprising that Hahn, who disliked socialism, believed in a form of leadership not unlike the Nazi *Führer* principle; indeed, he once called his system a kind of non-Jew-baiting Nazism. He denounced Hitler for "making good things look bad", and was horrified by Nazi violence, yet, predictably, Nazi influences permeated his school....

1. Having read Plato's *Republic* as a young man, Hahn fell in love with the Platonic philosophy that "any nation is a slovenly guardian of its own interests if it does not do all it can to make the individual citizen discover his own powers; and further, that the individual becomes a cripple from his or her own point of view if he is not qualified by education to serve the community." In other words, "Ask not what your country can do for you, but what you can do for your country." Based upon this same philosophy, Prince Charles has strongly advocated a kind of *compulsory* voluntary service to the community, or involuntary volunteerism (an oxymoron for forced servitude or slavery), for the youth of society. The Clintons' Americorps "volunteer" program, which Bill and Hillary would like to make compulsory for U.S. youth, is likewise in this vein. Junor, observing that Socrates, in Plato's *Republic*, "asserts that his citizens, if they are to be guardians of the state, must be 'spirited, swift and strong' and yet, at the same time, gentle and swayed by 'beauty and truth,'" ignorantly states, "The fundamental divergence from Plato's philosophy, however, was in religion. Gordonstoun was a Christian school, whereas Plato's *Republic* was a pagan slave state. Hahn, who was himself Jewish, simply took the best from Plato" (Junor, pp. 35-36). In fact, Hahn, the British monarchy, and the Clintons advocate "a pagan slave state," one trained for service, not an enlightened Christian state. Moreover, it is this philosophy which is to form the glue, so to speak, between East and West in the New World Order. The *Platonic ideal* will enable the elite to merge what *they* have determined are the "best" aspects of Communism-Socialism and Capitalism-Fascism into a global system made "partly of iron and partly of clay" (cf. Dan 2:41-43). For more information, see Chapter 7's section titled, "The Garter," as well as this chapter's later section titled, "The United Nations and public-private partnerships."

2. Judd, *Prince Philip,* pp. 65, 67, 69, 250. Also, see Junor, p. 35.

....The New regime could not appreciate that the children at Salem were being brought up in a fiercely patriotic spirit; nor could it understand how implicitly Hahn believed in the greatness of Germany, and even thought that "Hitler's cause could be good or made good". To the Nazis the most significant fact about Hahn was that he was a Jew....[1]

By a curious twist of fate, as Hahn was bound for Britain, the young Philip of Greece was on his way to Salem.... The official family line was that after his French and English schools, Philip would benefit from a spell of liberal German education....

"Prince Philip of Greece", as a foreigner, was exempt from the Hitler Youth activities....

The Duke of Edinburgh remembers the Nazis of Salem with distaste....

Ironically, while Philip's brother-in-law Berthold von Baden was battling against the Nazis at Salem, another brother-in-law, Prince Christopher of Hesse, was serving the Nazi regime as an S.A. officer.... An ideal alternative now existed, and, less than a year after entering Salem, Prince Philip returned to Britain.

His destination was Kurt Hahn's new school at Gordonstoun in Scotland, which opened in 1934. [Hahn had already]...assembled a board of governors of extraordinary distinction and authority. The board included William Temple, Archbishop of York, and later Archbishop of Canterbury, Claude Elliot, the Headmaster of Eton,[2] John Buchan...who [being pro-apartheid]...was subsequently to become Governor-General of Canada.... ...Hahn's ideas were a strange amalgam of the revolutionary and the reactionary.

....What did emerge at Gordonstoun was a system of education which blended the expected with the unconventional, while containing a good deal that was downright quirky.

....A heavy emphasis in fact on life-saving of all sorts which...was an intrinsic part of Hahn's philosophy....[3]

....According to Gordonstoun school reports to parents, pupils were expected to develop the ability "to state facts precisely", "to take the right course in the face of Discomforts, Hardships, Danger, Mockery, Boredom, Scepticism, Impulses of the

1. Hitler imprisoned Hahn and took over Salem's chancellorship. By that time, the school had become so famous and important to the elite that Britain's Prime Minister, Ramsay MacDonald, intervened directly to gain Hahn's release, at which point Hahn fled to Britain to establish Gordounstoun, "a school in the mould of Salem" (Junor, p. 36).

2. Like Gordonstoun, Eton has "a similarly self-elected hierarchy, which gives the school a limited form of self-government" (Junor, p. 36).

3. According to the antichristian Hahn, "He who drills and labours and encounters dangers and difficulties all to be ready to save his brother in peril," "he experiences God's purpose in his inner life." Much like the counterfeit Christianity of psychologists who push "self-esteem," Hahn preached "the good in man, and in particular the capacity of the young to produce their best when confronted by the challenge of responsibility for others." "It was this belief in the good in man and the means by which it could be drawn out that Prince Charles took away with him from Gordonstoun" (Junor, pp. 66-67).

Moment", and "to plan, organise, and deal with the unexpected".... Gordonstoun also demanded "Mental Concentration", "Conscientiousness" and "Manners"....

But, as Hahn's critics never tired of pointing out, studies in English, ancient languages, modern languages, history, natural science and mathematics, came rather low on the list of requirements, only just above practical work, art work..., fighting spirit and endurance....

....He has remained solidly loyal to Hahn and his methods, once remarking..., "For some reason it is perfectly respectable to teach history and mathematics, electronics and engineering. But any attempt to develop character, and the whole man, tends to be viewed with the utmost suspicion."...[1]

He had graduated in the quasi-military hierarchy of Gordonstoun from Room Leader to Captain to Colour Bearer to Helper (one of the ten boys in charge of particular activities...) and now, in his last year, he was elected Guardian or head boy, a distinction conferred on the school's most responsible and authoritative young man. Impatience and intolerance were his chief faults, and...they remain so."[2]

Speaking of the UWC, Hahn, and Prince Charles, Junor comments,

....Prince Charles was and is a truly international man; and he subscribed to Hahn's vision, shared by Earl Mountbatten, of a harmonious world where nations are so educated that they understand, and so tolerate, one another.

The belief that national barriers could be reduced and international cooperation fostered by education had been the principle behind an organization first called Atlantic College, and subsequently the United World Colleges, which Hahn cofounded in 1962.... Situated at Donat's Castle[3] in South Wales it was a

---

1. Gordonstoun strongly emphasizes self-improvement, as is implied in the school's motto, *Plus est en vous,* which is translated, "There is more in you" (Junor, p. 37). Hahn, "saw the young exposed to a series of decays: 'The decay of fitness, the decay of self-discipline, the decay of enterprise and adventure, the decay of skill and care that goes to make the crafts- man, and, most shattering of all, the decay of compassion.' He attributed these decays to defective education, concerned 'too exclusively with the transmission of knowledge...than with the development of character which is basic and fundamental'. The sacred purpose of education was to 'arrest these decays, to restore, to defend, to develop human strength in the young'" (ibid., p. 66). Prince Charles has praised "Hahn's principles" and "an education which tried to balance the physical and mental with the emphasis on self-reliance to develop a rounded human being." According to the prince, who credits Gordonstoun with having developed his "will-power and self-control," "giving shape and form and tidiness to your life...is the most important thing your education can do" (ibid., p. 65). That is, as in a mili- tary academy, education should regiment students.
2. Judd, *Prince Philip,* pp. 70-75, 77, 83.
3. Junor observes, "The round tower, with a sumptuous room at the top where Prince Charles

sixth form college which now has [over] three hundred international students, most of whom are on scholarships, combining two years of academic study with physically demanding activities and service to the community. The idea is that by living, studying and putting their lives in the hands of fellow students of every race, colour and creed under the sun, they will take the message of racial harmony home to their own countries, and bit by bit mankind will learn.... The students...study for an international school-leaving examination, the International Baccalaureate now recognized by most universities in the world, including Oxford and Cambridge.

Lord Mountbatten had become chairman of the College in 1968, and one of his first acts had been to change its name to United World Colleges.... After ten years...not only had the College got well and truly off the ground in Wales, but new colleges had been set up in Canada and Singapore....

Of all the colleges, the Prince of Wales is probably particularly proud of the Venezuelan one.... At the Simon Bolivar United World College of Agriculture in Venezuela, however, they have broken away from the traditional curriculum. They are teaching young people agricultural skills specially designed for the developing countries of the world; trying to tackle the problems of poverty, [under-productivity,] famine and disease; providing a practical training at [the] grassroots level to meet a fundamental need....

....[Colleges] had been opened in Singapore—the UWC South East Asia—and in Canada—the Lester B. Pearson UWC of the Pacific on Vancouver Island—but there was nothing in the pipeline for America. Prince Charles took up the search and in 1980 tentatively approached Dr [Armand] Hammer, [chairman and chief executive of the giant multinational Occidental Petroleum Corporation, and] a noted philanthropist. He told him about the movement..., and less than two years later a magnificent new college opened in Montezuma, New Mexico, aptly named the Armand Hammer UWC.... [It]...had opened the doors to 102 students from forty-six nations....

Another college opened in 1982. Waterford Kamhlaba in Swaziland which joined in 1981, the College of the Adriatic in Italy. With the Venezuelan college that opened in 1986, and the original Atlantic College in Wales, the total is now seven....[1]

---

stays if he needs a room overnight, overlooks the jousting field to one side and to the other the Beast Garden, where no matter in which part of the garden you stand one of the mythological stone creatures has its eye on you" (p. 137).

1. Junor, pp. 131-132, 136, 202-203. Armand Hammer has worked closely with both Prince Charles and Al Gore. Hammer's father was a founding member of the Communist Party in the United States.

In 1992, the *Jerusalem Post* reported, "Leaders of the United World College[s] (UWC), an institution dedicated to promoting world peace and international brotherhood, are planning to set up a branch in the Negev, which would concentrate on desert ecology, according to Batya Gershoni, a graduate of a branch of UWC abroad. She said that the institution, which has seven branches throughout the world, is headed by Britain's Prince Charles."[1] Junor elaborates,

> [Prince Charles]...believes that change in emerging countries must come from the villages and not from well-educated leaders....
>
> ...Prince Charles is still keen to try to get something going in India, convinced that UWC can contribute to the problem of food production and agricultural development in the Third World. 'I believe most strongly,' he said while visiting the Canadian college in 1980, 'that better food production and the development of the rural economy in may of the developing countries is vital tot he future of the whole world.'
>
> During his various tours of Commonwealth countries, the Prince had become increasingly preoccupied by the problems of the Third World. [He]...is concerned for the people there no less than for the people of the United Kingdom. He had read around the subject extensively, and had been particularly impressed by a book called *Small is Beautiful,* written by the late economist and philosopher E. F. Schumacher, who to propound his views had founded in the 1960s...the Intermediate Technology Development Group. Although Charles was always the guest of the President or Head of State when he traveled to developing countries, and was therefore restricted in what he saw, he was well aware of poverty, sickness and the devastating results of drought and mismanagement. His sister [Anne] had been able to tell him even more from her visits on behalf of the Save the Children Fund. He was convinced that the problem was not a local but a global one, for which we should all share responsibility. Integrating students in United World Colleges was one way....
>
> ....What was needed [according to Schumacher]...was technology appropriate to the people for whom it was intended: not giant machines that needed specialist knowledge to operate, but simple tools that anyone could use. When Schumacher first set up the group it was dismissed as the eccentric brainchild of an over-idealistic visionary, but since his death...quite a number of the mainstream charities such as Oxfam, Christian Aid and the

1. Itim, "New desert ecology college planned for the Negev," *The Jerusalem Post,* daily, 8 Dec. 1992, p. 3; accession no. 920001175 on the *Jerusalem Post* CD-ROM.

325

Save the Children Fund now turn to Intermediate Technology for advice.[1]

In his speech to the 1985 UWC International Council Meeting, Prince Charles stated, "If the world could see that, in addition to our more conventional educational efforts, we were playing a significant part in educating young people from across the globe to tackle some of the huge survival problems facing the developing world, e.g. hunger, poverty, conservation of our resources and health, we would surely the more easily and quickly attract the global attention and awareness which are two of our most obvious deficiencies.... [There is a] level of support from Governments which we need to achieve." The prince, of course, Is succeeding. Junor opines, "They are truly integrated. You cannot fail to go there and talk to the students without coming away convinced that there is hope for the world."[2]

In a remarkably poignant and sublimely manipulative speech, delivered in 1986 at the Harvard 350th Commemoration Ceremony, "the real Prince of Wales, stripped bare," touched upon a number of themes, even defining motives, which have since proved to be central to his globalist agenda and international prominence:

> Perhaps, too, as parents you may be wondering, like I do on frequent occasions, whether the educational system you are confronted with is the right one to produce the kind of balanced, tolerant, civilized citizens we all hope our children can become?...
>
> I cannot help feeling that one of the problems which is gradually dawning on the western, Christian world is that we have for too long, and too dangerously, ignored and rejected the best and most fundamental traditions of our Greek, Roman and Jewish inheritance. I would suggest that we have been gradually losing sight of the Greek philosophers' ideal, which was to produce a balance between the several subjects that catered for a boy's moral, intellectual, emotional and physical needs. While we have been right to demand the kind of technical education relevant to the needs of the twentieth century it would appear that we may have forgotten that when all is said and done a good man, as the Greeks would say, is a nobler worker than a good

1. Junor, pp. 136, 203-205.
2. Junor, pp. 136-137.

technologist. We should never lose sight of the fact that to avert disaster we have not only to teach men to make things, but also to produce people who have complete moral control over the things they make.... [The] emphasis has been too one-sided and has concentrated on the development of the intellect to the detriment of the spirit....

....All the best thought in Greece, Rome and Judea emphasized the interdependence of moral and intellectual training if we are to escape from the leadership of clever and unscrupulous men. There is no doubt in my mind that the education of the whole man needs to be based on a sure foundation [of faith and psychology].... That of course does not mean we have to deny the validity of other men's traditions. We should indeed look for those elements that unite us rather than concentrate on the things which make us different.... [It] is perhaps possible to learn to equate human rights with human obligations. It is possible then to see a relationship between moral values and the uses of science.... Surely it is important that in the headlong rush of mankind to conquer space, to compete with Nature to harness the fragile environment, we do not let our children slip away into a world dominated entirely by sophisticated technology, but rather teach them that to live in this world is not an easy matter without standards to live by.

And yet, at the same time, how do we guard against bigotry; against the insufferable prejudice and suspicion of other men's religions and beliefs which have so often led to unspeakable horrors throughout human history and which still do? How do we teach people to recognize that there is a dark side too to man's psyche [besides the "Zoroastrian" light side] and that its destructive power is immense if we are not aware of it?... There is in existence a proved and tested natural science dedicated to the study of the soul of man and the meaning of his creation. As in the past religious teaching was an essential part of the curriculum, perhaps there is now a need in universities for some introductions to the natural science of [Jungian] psychology? We are, to all intents and purposes, embarked on a perilous journey. The potential destruction of our natural earth; the despoliation of the great rain forests (with all the untold consequences of such a disaster); the exploration of space; greater power than we have ever had or our nature can perhaps handle—all confronts us for what could be a final settlement. But if we could start again to re-educate ourselves the result need not be so frightening. Over Apollo's great temple was the sign 'Man know thyself'. This natural science of psychology could perhaps help to lead us to a greater knowledge of ourselves; knowledge enough to teach us the dangers of the power we have acquired and the responsibilities as well as the opportunities it gives us. Could man, at last, begin to learn to know himself?[1]

In passing, we should note that Prince Charles has created and spurred other projects that have similar globalist aims to the UWC. One such project, Operation Drake, resulted in the creation of the Drake Fellowship. Taking youth who had "hit rock bottom," the fellowship thrust them "into team work, survival training, community service and the sort of outdoor activities that they had never even dreamt about." "At the end of six or eight months broken up into a series of short courses, between 70 and 80 per cent found jobs. The Fellowship now handles about 4500 young people a year."[2] Operation Drake subsequently gave rise to Operation Raleigh, the "most ambitious international expedition ever mounted:" "Operation Raleigh was very similar to the previous expedition, but on a far bigger scale than Drake, as Charles had wanted. It was still fully international, but instead of taking four hundred applicants there were to be four thousand, each spending up to three months in the field; in addition the whole venture was to last not two years, as before, but four. The expeditions comprised the same blend of scientific and community projects and adventure, designed to give the participants the 'challenges of war in peacetime', and to bring out the latent potential for leadership in people who came from all sorts of backgrounds, including the inner cities."[3]

Based upon Plato's philosophy, or the "Platonic ideal," as *noted* earlier in this section, Prince Charles has strongly advocated a kind of *compulsory* voluntary service to the community, or involuntary volunteerism (an oxymoron for forced servitude or slavery), for society's youth:

> Soon after Operation Raleigh was on its way, the Prince of Wales had another idea—a dream that he wanted to put into practice, an opportunity for young people to give service to their country.... Why was Britain the only country in Europe that did not have some form of [compulsory] national service? There must be a way [thought the prince]....
> ....Discussions were held with...industry, the employers and

1. Junor, pp. 270-273.
2. Junor, p. 207.
3. Junor, pp. 225-226.

the unions, the voluntary organizations, the government and the local councils....

It was called the Prince of Wales Community Venture, and the literature and application forms briefly explained his philosophy: 'I believe that we should all have the opportunity at one stage in our lives to make a [required] contribution to our community. It is also vital that we find ways in which people from all walks of life and backgrounds can operate together for a limited period in their lives. Ours is one of the very few countries where this does not happen.'

....Unlike Operations Drake and Raleigh this scheme was not looking simply for potential leaders....

....["Volunteers"] are paid [to]...do a mixture of community service and adventure activity, with a strong accent on teamwork.... On day one they go off on an outward bound type of course with the Drake Fellowship, which involves camping and hiking.... The next two weeks are spent visiting community centres like old people's homes, the Salvation Army, spastics' schools, and fire and police stations—all places where they will be seconded later in the year for an eight-week stint. They are shipped off to Atlantic College in Wales for a week's course in first aid, coastguard and lifeboat service, and cliff rescue. They work with the fire brigade for a month; they clean up and improve some derelict site within the city; work in some branch of the local health authority; and for two months go away again to work in a distant community, such as Pembrokeshire in South Wales, where the first team did conservation work like fencing, scrub clearing and tree planting. Three-quarters of the year is taken up with community service, but the remainder is adventure and enterprise....

The original idea was that the venturers would be interviewed by a personnel manager at the beginning and end of the year.... They now have one manager looking after every three volunteers; he introduces them to the world of business, gives them a visit to the works, teaches them how to fill in job application forms and how to present themselves in interviews....

So far the scheme has been a resounding success: it has been described as the finest project [of its kind] in the country.... Nobody could have been more delighted than the Prince of Wales, not just that another group of young people had been taught to care about others and to taste some adventure in their lives, but because he has been proved right to all those bureaucrats and negative thinkers [whose attitude he hates] who at the outset said it would never work.[1]

Alternative medicine. Prince Charles is credited by

1. Junor, pp. 226-230.

various biographers with having personally brought about the rise in popularity of alternative forms of medicine, some of which are overtly occult while others are truly beneficial and needed, in the United Kingdom—and from there, throughout the western world.[1]

Environmentalism, the Rio Earth Summit, and the Kyoto Protocol. As Henry Lamb has pointed out, the whole environmental movement for the past two centuries can be traced back to Britain, beginning with the British Fauna and Flora Protection Society. From this society came the International Union for the Conservation of Nature (IUCN), which has now been renamed the World Conservation Union (still IUCN). The World Conservation Union or IUCN is the most influential of all environmental organizations. In 1961, the IUCN created the World Wildlife Fund (WWF) and designated Prince Philip as its head.[2] Russel Train, President of the WWF USA, created the World Resources Institute (WRI). The WWF manages many environmental and other projects on behalf of the United Nations. These three organizations—the IUCN, the WWF, and the WRI—provide the impetus for the world environmental movement. Naturally, Prince Charles has also played a major role in these organizations, having been personally introduced to them by his father, Prince Philip, as well as by others.

In 1968, while his investiture as Prince of Wales was being planned, Prince Charles "was asked to chair the Welsh steering committee for European Conservation Year, designated for 1970."[3] In February 1970, Prince Philip took Prince Charles "to Strasbourg to attend a conservation conference under the auspices of the Council of

1. For more information, see the previous chapter's section titled, "Ties to the New Age Movement, the occult, and false religions."
2. In 1961, Prince Philip was designated President and "International Trustee of the World Wildlife Fund." The prince is also Patron of the Norfolk Island Flora and Fauna Society, and President of the Royal Agricultural Society of the Commonwealth. Due to his participation in blood sports, something that Prince Charles likewise avidly enjoys, Prince Philip has been accused of hypocrisy. The prince's publications include *Wildlife Crisis, Dilemmas in Conservation,* and *The Environmental Revolution: Speeches on Conservation* (Judd, *Prince Philip,* pp. 13-14, 250-252, and picture no. 44 between pp. 192-193).
3. Junor, p. 162.

Europe, initiating his son into a sphere of wider international statesmanship."[1] At the Conservation in 1970 Conference, the brash young prince, as chairman of the Countryside in 1970 Committee for Wales, "touched prophetically on 'the horrifying effects of pollution in all its cancerous forms,'" insisting that we "must be prepared" to "discipline ourselves to [environmental] restrictions and regulations that we feel we ought to impose for our own good." At the same time, Prince Charles "announced the Prince of Wales's Countryside Award for individual enterprise in protecting the environment."[2] Connecting the modern Prince of Wales to the modern Lady Salisbury, whose ancestor was used to create the Order of the Garter, as well as to the English Rothschilds, Junor elaborates,

> ....In this case he sought the advice of a family friend, Lady Salisbury, who had designed several gardens....
> What Lady Salisbury...does not know about plants is probably not worth knowing. She...has gardened without the use of chemicals all her life....
> ....Side by side,...he and Lady Salisbury made the garden; and in those early weeks and months Charles discovered a new passion in life. He began to read gardening books rapaciously, and....in a short time has become very knowledgeable....
> One of the organizations that was pleased to find the Prince of Wales taking an interest in conservation [in 1970] was the Society for the Promotion of Nature Conservation (now the Royal Society for Nature Conservation), founded in 1912 by Nathaniel Charles Rothschild....
> ....[Miriam Rothschild, having inherited her father's passion,] does not conduct her campaign just for the aesthetic value of the result.... A vast range of plants are used in medical preparations, and as research continues new species are found to have beneficial properties. If a species is allowed to become extinct, however insignificant it may have appeared to be, that is one potential medication lost to mankind for ever.
> Prince Charles,...when he acquired Highgrove...asked Miriam Rothschild if she would come and plant some wild flowers there. She too had known him since he was a child—she was an old friend of Lady Salisbury's—and so...she descended on the garden....
> ....Wearing his other hat, as Patron of the Royal Society for Nature Conservation, [Prince Charles]...is a passionate

1. Cathcart, p. 107.
2. Dimbleby, *The Prince of Wales,* pp. 421-422. Junor, p. 162.

conservationist, angered by the way man has plundered the natural habitat of plants and animals all over the world and caused the extinction of so many species as a result, and dismayed by the rape of the land due to the excessive use of chemicals and the fashion for tearing out hedgerows.[1]

In 1982, Prince Charles sent this message to the Royal Agricultural College's first organic food conference:

> For some years now modern farming has made tremendous demands on the finite sources of energy which exist on earth. Maximum production has been the slogan to which we have all adhered. In the last few years there has been an increasing realisation that many modern production methods are not only very wasteful but probably also unnecessary.
>
> The supporters of organic farming, bio-agriculture, alternative agriculture and optimum production are beginning to make themselves heard, and not before time.
>
> I am convinced that any steps that can be taken to explore methods of production which make better and more effective use of renewable resources are extremely important. Even if it may be some time before they are commercially acceptable, pioneer work is essential if our planet is to feed the teeming millions of people who will live on it by the twenty-first century. I hope that you will seek solutions which can have practical and economically viable results within a comparatively short space of time. I shall be watching the practical results with interest to see what might be applicable to our work in the Duchy of Cornwall....[2]

Not only has Prince Charles played *the* pivotal role in popularizing environmentalism—including organic farming, which is generally *good*—in Britain and Western Europe since making his seminal 1970 remarks, but *he has been personally credited for the success of the more recent Earth Summit in Rio de Janeiro* (see below). This summit is considered by many environmentalists and others worldwide to have been a *watershed* event in the modern thrust for global government, which often takes the form of rabid environmentalism.[3] According to Lamb, two very important documents to emerge from the Rio Earth Summit, which

1. Junor, pp. 160-163, 237.
2. Junor, pp. 237-238. Junor comments, "Thus the Prince of Wales's decision to experiment with an eighty-acre block at Broadfield Farm [which the Duchy purchased] was a massive boost to the organic movement [in Britain]" (ibid., pp. 241-242).
3. For more information, see *Cloak of Green* by Elaine Dewar.

are related to Agenda 21 (the U.N. global environmental agenda), are the Framework Convention on Climate Change and the Convention on Biological Diversity. Additionally, the Rio Earth Summit produced the U.N. Commission on Sustainable Development, with which the Prince of Wales Business Leaders Forum (PWBLF or BLF) now works through its core participation in Business as Partners in Development.[1] Regarding Prince Charles and the Rio Earth Summit, Dimbleby observes,

> By 1991, the momentum generated by the Prince's speeches on the environment had secured him an international reputation. In the run-up to the Rio summit which was planned for 1992, the Prince was determined to have his own input by bringing together key international figures in an attempt to achieve a degree of harmony between the conflicting attitudes of Europe, the United States and the developing nations, led by Brazil.[2] He alighted on the idea of using the royal yacht as the base for a two-day international seminar at the end of an official tour of Brazil in April 1991. Among others, he invited [then] Senator Albert Gore; senior officials from the World Bank; chief executives from companies such as Shell and BP; the principal non-governmental organizations [(NGOs)]; European politicians...; and...President Fernando Collor of Brazil.
>
> ....At the last moment, the Brazilian President threatened to cut short his appearance.... The Prince wrote to him...:

1. For more information, see this chapter's later section titled, "The United Nations and public-private partnerships."

2. "Brazil, the world's fifth-largest nation in area, is the most biologically diverse country, with more species of plants, insects, freshwater fish, monkeys and amphibians than anywhere else. Altogether it has 20 percent of the world's plant species and 30 percent of the planet's tropical rain forest.... In second place is Indonesia, a small country but the world's fifth most populous, with the greatest marine life diversity on Earth and large numbers of unique animals and plants.... Altogether, Latin American countries—Brazil, Mexico, Columbia, Peru, Venezuela and Ecuador—hold the planet's greatest diversity, with Asian nations—Indonesia, China, Malaysia and the Philippines—close behind, the data show. The United States also makes the list, one of only two developed countries, the other being Australia. Three African nations—South Africa, Madagascar and the Democratic Republic of the Congo—are included, as well as Papua New Guinea and India. The 17 countries, which cover just 25 percent of the planet's land surface, contain 80 percent of the world's endangered species. 'These countries play a fundamental role in efforts to conserve life on Earth,' said Russell Mittermeier, the president of Conservation International.... Environmental organizations, including Conservation International, have tried to preach the benefits of biodiversity, from eco-tourism to biological prospecting for medicines, to countries such as Brazil and Indonesia for years. So far progress has been slow.... Madagascar, for instance,...has over the past decade attracted large amounts of international funding for sustainable development it would not have gotten if not for its biodiversity, he said (Laurie Goering, Chicago Tribune, "Study takes stock of biodiversity," *The Denver Post,* 12 Dec. 1997, p. 60A).

> ...I was so keen to arrange this seminar, following our first meeting just before your inauguration as President...to reconcile conservation requirements with development pressure. [A]...great deal of time and effort has been expended...to attract the most influential and effective participants....
>
> I, personally, would be disappointed and disheartened by your absence because...many people...are looking towards the importance of the 1992 United Nations Conference....

Written in longhand, it was a characteristic letter with a characteristic effect: the President yielded to the Prince.

According to some of those present, the *Britannia* seminar played a crucial role in preparing North and South for the accommodation in their positions which would be needed if the Rio summit were not to be a diplomatic fiasco. [The]...participants...moved towards a much closer understanding of the predicament facing them all.[1]

On a recent Prophecy Club radio broadcast, Rod Lewis asserted, mistakenly, that Al Gore "has been commissioned as the next world leader."[2] In fact, Al Gore and the "Clintonites" practically work for the British monarchy, whether or not they care to admit it. Before the Rio Earth Summit, for example, the prince made a television documentary titled *The Earth in the Balance,* "in which he warned against the accelerating depredation inflicted on the planet by human greed and folly," having been "deeply engaged in a struggle to develop his own 'model' village on the outskirts of Dorchester" and having recently pleaded "for the rainforests."[3] The documentary was aired in May 1990, well before the publication of Al Gore's similarly titled book, *Earth in Balance.* Moreover, Prince Charles was working on a "village" concept long before Hillary Clinton. Not only does it appear that Al Gore, a New Age satanist and top member of the Illuminati, took the title for his popular antichristian book from the prince, but Hillary too has jumped on the bandwagon. It is worth mentioning that following the prince's 1969 investiture, "Charles and Anne held a dinner party for the younger set aboard the royal yacht anchored at Holyhead. Percys and Pagets, the Ormsby-<u>Gores</u>, the Nevill cousins, Kerrs and Soames's

1. Dimbleby, *The Prince of Wales,* pp. 497-498.
2. The Prophecy Club, 31 July 1997, multiple times on multiple A.M. radio stations.
3. Dimbleby, *The Prince of Wales,* p. 404.

were there, among other close personal friends."[1]

Prior to the royal yacht's 1997 decommissioning,[2] the prince regularly used it "to host seminars or conferences, or to entertain the rich and powerful." Having previously argued unsuccessfully against its abandonment, the prince remarked, "I believe the aim should be to...keep the Yacht in service until the year 2000—and whatever happens next is in the lap of the Gods...."[3]

In December 1997, the same month that the royal yacht was decommissioned, another item of great international interest came out of the Rio Earth Summit—the *Kyoto Protocol:*

> KYOTO, Japan — Negotiators from around the world agreed today on a package of measures that for the first time would legally obligate industrial countries to cut emissions of waste industrial gases that [a few elitist and globalist] scientists say are warming Earth's atmosphere....
>
> The agreement reached by delegates from more than 150 nations creates a landmark environmental policy to deal with global warming....
>
> The nations would have a year to ratify the treaty, starting in March [1998]. Talks on "trading" of emissions are expected take place in November 1998.
>
> Despite the uncertainties, some environmentalists hailed the agreement as a remarkable political and economic innovation, in that it would establish a global system for dealing with what many scientists believe [(this is an outright lie designed to seduce the public—see below)] is the overarching environmental concern.
>
> Opponents of the treaty condemned it as economically ruinous.
>
> The accord—known as the Kyoto Protocol—would require the industrial nations to reduce their emissions of carbon dioxide and five other heat-trapping greenhouse gases to 5.2 percent below those of 1990....
>
> Some countries may be allowed to increase emissions, but globally, emissions are to be reduced by 30 percent from the levels currently projected for 2010.
>
> After an all-night session..., the protocol was approved by representatives of more than 150 countries.
>
> The countries were modifying an agreement, negotiated in Rio de Janeiro in 1992, that called for voluntary efforts to limit

1. Cathcart, p. 97.
2. A new royal yacht is in the works.
3. Dimbleby, *The Prince of Wales*, pp. 511-513.

emission of greenhouse gases.[1] [Such efforts will now be compulsory.] The burning of fossil fuels like coal and oil is responsible for most emissions of carbon dioxide [(another lie—see below)], the most important greenhouse gas.[2]

The treaty, though, contains at least two worrisome flaws.

Most significantly, it doesn't impose restrictions on rapidly developing countries like China, India, Brazil and Mexico....

Moreover, it's not certain how the emission trading credits will be implemented.[3]

....Like the little boy who cried "wolf," environmental alarmists and scaremongers have exhausted their credibility.

Add the Great Global Warming Scare of 1997 to the list. This is more than a dispassionate debate over a questionable theory. To the greenies, global warming dissenters are heretics, challenging their religion. This is a blasphemy on Gaia, the goddess of the earth. It's like saying trees are not our equals.

Global warming hysteria is a convenient vehicle for the radical enviro political agenda. Energy use and economic growth are inherently "bad," as are their byproducts: suburban development, cars, RVs, SUVs, power boats, snowmobiles, materialism in general, and its handmaiden, capitalism. We must simplify our lives and return to nature. If that's the goal, then a false crisis, like global warming, is better than no crisis at all.

How can you help but be skeptical when the global warmers have quotes like these on their record:

✓ Stephen Schneider, Stanford University atmospheric scientist: "We have to offer up scary scenarios, make simplified, dramatic statements.... Each of us has to decide what is the right balance between being effective and being honest."

✓ Tim Wirth, outgoing Undersecretary of State for Global Affairs: "We've got to ride the global warming issue. Even if the theory of global warming is wrong, we will be doing the right thing in terms of economic policy and environmental policy."

✓ Vice President Al Gore: "Minor shifts in policy, marginal adjustments in ongoing programs, moderate improvements in laws and regulations and rhetoric offered in lieu of genuine change...are all forms of appeasement, designed to satisfy the public's desire to believe that sacrifice, struggle and a wrenching transformation of society will not be necessary."

....I choose to believe that, as we've demonstrated

1. The six gases are carbon dioxide, methane, nitrous oxide, and three halocarbons. Carbon dioxide, of course, is essential to plant life, as oxygen is to us. The likely result of increased carbon dioxide emissions would actually be lusher and more plant life, which in turn would churn out more oxygen into the Earth's atmosphere—a healthy and commonsense prospect.

2. William K. Stevens, New York Times, "Global emission accord gets nod," *The Denver Post,* 11 Dec. 1997, pp. 1A, 29A.

3. "A treaty to warm to," *The Denver Post,* 12 Dec. 1997, p. 7B.

throughout our history, we can solve tomorrow's problems with tomorrow's technology. And that we can do so without sacrificing our economic well-being....

In any event, 96 percent of all greenhouse gas emissions occur naturally; only 4 percent are attributable to human industrial influence. Solar activity alone, dwarfing human influence, could account for all of the recent global warming—which, incidentally, in moderate doses can be of net benefit to the planet.

Contrary to the assertions of the greenies, there is no scientific consensus on the exaggerated claims of global warmers. When members of the Meteorological Society and the American Geophysical Society were asked in a Gallup poll whether they thought human actions are causing global warming, only 17 percent agreed. Greenpeace likes to brandish the names of scientists who believe that current patterns of energy use will cause catastrophic climate change in the future. What they don't tell you is that their doomsayers represent only a small fraction of those surveyed.[1]

Christianity, Judaism, Islam, etc., and a unified world religion. As previously discussed, Prince Charles has a very wide range of religious and spiritual activities; there seems to be almost nothing in which he will not participate. He clearly is seeking to ingratiate himself to the world's major religious communities. More than that, however, it appears that the prince is trying to position himself to head apostate Christianity, apostate Israel, *and* the Muslim world.[2] In this vein, we may note that Prince Philip is currently in charge of the "Sacred Literature Trust," a United Nations project which seeks to distill and document the common tenets of the world's various religious systems and to revive what Al Gore refers to as the *Gaia* principle—"Mother Earth" worship. This project's findings are to serve as the basis for a new, unified world religion. Springmeier adds, "An example of how Gentile and Jewish Satanists collaborate together could be seen when Prince Philip of England's representative Martin Palmer and Rabbi Arthur Hertzberg jointly announced their plans at the United Nations in 1989 for the Sacred Literature Trust, which is a major project to revive Mother Earth

1. Mike Rosen, "Global warming is hot air," *The Denver Post*, 12 Dec. 1997, p. 7B.
2. For documentation, see the previous chapter's sections titled "A so-called 'Christian' heritage" and "Ties to the New Age Movement, the occult, and false religions." Also, see the next chapter, "Prince Charles, the Middle East Peace Talks, and Global Security."

worship. Moreover, Palmer has written on Gnostic and pagan themes which have been published by Lucis Trust, and in 1986, Rabbi Hertzberg, an aide to Jewish Illuminatus Edgar Bronfman, publicly advocated revival of Cabalism at Assisi, Italy."[1]

The European Union. The prince's activities, as described throughout this book, have served to help him make great inroads among the elite of the European Union. Not only does he have a strong Merovingian lineage, but he has all the other qualifications that the E.U. would seek in a future leader or monarch. As things currently stand, the prince appears to be awaiting a reply to his request to be the King of Europe.[2]

Race (ethnic) relations. In 1984, Prince Charles called a conference "on race and deployment, known as the Windsor Conference." Junor comments, "Gathered under one roof were the chairmen of sixty major companies in Britain and a crowd of bright, articulate members of the black community. For two working days and a night they mixed.... That conference is widely regarded as one of the most significant advances in race relations ever made [in Britain], and is still talked about today. The black community...had no idea that there were people in the white hierarchy who were seriously interested in their unemployment problems; and the white establishment, on the whole, admitted they had never realized there were intelligent members of the black community. Without the Prince of Wales such a confrontation would almost certainly never have taken place." It was this event that led to Prince Charles' initial 1985 presidency of Business in the Community (BiC). As BiC's new president, "Charles wanted to see what good had come out of the conference in Windsor.... So a special unit called the Black Economic Development Secretariat was set up at the BiC offices in City Road, to report back to the Prince every six months on progress; and progress was noticeable.... Prince Charles

1. Written correspondence, quoted by permission, from Springmeier.
2. For more information, see Chapter 2, "A Man for Our Times."

was [also] eager to have a black face on his staff.... [The prince] has an affinity for black people."[1]

The world of business and finance. Over the past two decades, Prince Charles has become one of the most influential men, if not *the* most influential man, in the global business world. His primary vehicle is the Prince of Wales Business Leaders Forum (PWBLF or BLF), an organization that he created and over which he presides as President. The PWBLF is very well-connected with multinational and other companies around the world:

> By the end of the eighties, the Prince had become ambitious to take BITC's [(Business In The Community's)] message to other countries. Enthused by the thought of inspiring **the world's most powerful multinational companies** to share his perspective, he and his team decided to hold an international forum in the American town of Charleston, South Carolina. They invited **more than a hundred senior executives** from the United States, Britain, Europe, Japan and Australia for a two-day meeting at which they talked freely about the responsibilities of international industry to the environment and to the community. Led by the Prince,....they broke up into small groups for intense debate about the issues raised by the Prince through BITC in Britain. The event was a success. Within a few months, [in 1990,]...what soon became know[n] as the Business Leaders Forum (BLF) was in operation. Over the next few years, [BITC executive Robert] Davies was to organise seventeen similar international meetings [(as of early 1994)], timed where possible to coincide with the Prince's official tours abroad, involving more than 4,000 [top] business leaders in North America, Latin America, Europe and Asia.
>
> ....With the opening of Eastern Europe,...the BLF was to form partnerships with more than ninety businesses working in Russia, Poland, the Czech Republic and Slovakia, setting up a range of [education,] training and environmental projects, forming a task force to help regenerate the cultural [and economic] life of St Petersburg, and transforming the Red Army Barracks outside Budapest into a series of units for small businesses.[2]
>
> In a separate initiative, more than 7,000 international hoteliers, responsible for more than two million rooms, have been mobilised to set new environmental targets for their industry worldwide. In the autumn of 1994, as president of the BLF, the Prince is due to launch a new project called 'Inter-City Action',

1. Junor, pp. 248, 251.
2. Dimbleby, *The Prince of Wales*, pp. 372-373, 569-570.

linking community leaders in the United States and other western countries to their counterparts in the developing world to tackle jointly their shared problems of youth unemployment, ethnic minority conflicts, shortages of housing and skills, and environmental degradation.[1]

Although it sounds breathtaking in scope, the above outline merely scratches the surface of a host of successful related initiatives by Prince Charles in Britain and the British Commonwealth that have led to the ultimate formation of the PWBLF. *Books* could literally be written on these initiatives alone.[2] As of early 1994, the PWBLF involved as many as one-hundred of the world's top multinational corporations. Consider, therefore, the following information from a recent study "written by Sarah Anderson and John Cavanagh using statistics largely drawn from charts published by Forbes" magazine and titled "The Top 200":

The global economic power of giant companies has grown to the point that they have become bigger than most of the countries where they do business.... In fact, more than half of the 100 biggest economies in the world are corporations.... Taken together, the world's 200 biggest companies control no less than 28 percent of the globe's economic activity. These companies are the powerhouses of [economic] globalization.... The multinational companies have the power to go anywhere to make or buy anything to be sold anywhere else in the world.... For most [small countries,]...the might of the big companies challenges their sovereignty.... The global firms...can wring concessions from governments eager to create jobs.... The 21 biggest economies in the world still are countries, with the United States at the top, Japan second, [and] Germany third...."[3]

With the above statistics in mind, one can only conclude that Prince Charles, through the highly influential PWBLF, has become a major, if not *the* major, behind-the-scenes economic "mover and shaker." Consider, for

1. Dimbleby, *The Prince of Wales,* p. 570.
2. For a current but brief summary, see Dimbleby, *The Prince of Wales,* pp. 567-574.
3. R.C. Longworth, Chicago Tribune, "Global companies control large part of world economy," *The Denver Post,* 13 Oct. 1996, p. 10A. Recall that Japan and Germany are among the small group of nations being considered as possible new permanent member-states of the U.N. Security Council (see Chapter 1, "The Footsteps of the AntiChrist").

example, these excerpts from a November 1996 article: "Arriving in Kiev at the start of a nine-day, five nation tour [including Ukraine and central Asia], the Prince was soon ensconced in a seminar of his Business Leaders Forum together with what he called the 'movers and shakers' of Ukraine's fledgling market economy. [The]...Prince listened to the aspirations of local executives as they spoke of the need for ethical business conduct and better business education. 'It is only too clear to all of us,' the Prince concluded, 'that the countries of the former Soviet Union are at an historic crossroads and urgently need the partnership of the West to tackle environmental problems and to alleviate the disillusionment of their young people.... If what we call free market systems are to be sustainable in the long run, international management must share its management skills.... For business to be actively involved in matters of social concern does help the reputation of business.' [At Mohlya Academy, a]...large crowd of students blocked the doorway brandishing photographs of the Prince and banners of greeting. 'Dear Prince Charles, You Are The Best Prince We Have Ever Seen,' said one."[1]

Junor, in a very brief summary of Prince Charles' youth-related activities, states, "He has not just put his name to other people's schemes, and taken on patronages. He has initiated projects, found the people to run them, provided the funds to get the ideas off the ground, and reaped the rewards. Some schemes have sent young people round the world, working as part of an international team in areas of need [(e.g., operations Drake and Raleigh)]. Others have taken them off the dole and given them a year's paid work, combining community service, teamwork and physical challenge. Yet others have given unemployed young people the chance to set up in business on their own by providing not just a grant to get them started, but professional guidance to help them over early problems."[2] *The Economist,* in a recent article on Prince Charles' Youth Business Trust, one of the initiatives

1. Robert Hardman, "Ukrainians need West's help, says Prince," *The Electronic Telegraph,* 5 Nov. 1996, No. 531, p. 1.
2. Junor, p. 12.

mentioned above, made these observations:

> AN AVERAGE annual compound growth rate of 25% over ten years; 30,000 businesses launched, 60% of which have survived at least three years: for any venture-capital fund, this would be a remarkable result. The brains behind this one is an unlikely financial whizz, a man with no job.... He is the Prince of Wales.
>
> The Prince's Youth Business Trust was launched a decade ago to help young people who have the motivation, but not the means, to start a business.... Alongside the cash, it provides the services of a business advisor for three years, or sometimes longer. It employs 300 people full-time and finances around 4,000 businesses a year.
>
> ....But, according to James Morton, in "Investing with the Grand Masters"..., the trust looks like a widely-diversified conglomerate.... "The return on capital employed," says Mr Morton, "is off the charts. It puts the professionals to shame."
>
> The trust is well managed and....benefits from an elaborate network of marketing, legal and financial advisers, some of whom are paid, some of whom are not.[1]

Governor of Hong Kong? In an effort to satisfy "the heir apparent's worldly vanity," former Prime Minister Margaret Thatcher, recalling Prince Charles' "frustrated ambition to become Governor-General of Australia," decided that he should become "Governor of Hong Kong for the last year of its life as a British dominion." It was "a chance for Charles to hold conspicuous, quasi-monarchical sway, while showing himself a man of his times." To the prince, "the remnants of what was his grandfather's empire, and will one day be his own global kingdom, are of paramount importance."[2] Although Chris Patten, not Prince Charles, became Governor of Hong Kong, the prince officiated for the queen and Britain at Hong Kong's turnover to bloody communist China at the start of July 1997, a highly publicized event. Somewhat reminiscent of the queen's "dotting the eye of a dragon," at which point it "is said to be

1. "Princely performance," *The Economist,* 23 Nov. 1996, p. 64. Speaking of Prince Charles' Youth Business Initiative (YBI), Junor offers similarly amazing statistics: "In contrast to the usual pattern of small businesses, which have a failure rate of 80 per cent, 85 per cent of the businesses funded by YBI are still trading; 20 per cent of those have employed other people; and of the 15 per cent that failed, half of those people who were unable to run a business of their own found jobs with employers soon afterwards. The type of businesses they have started could not be more diverse" (p. 210).
2. Holden, *King Charles III,* pp. 210-211.

alive and able to take part in a colourful procession," during her 1975 visit to Hong Kong,[1] the prince's handover of Hong Kong was attended by, among other things, dragon dances throughout the night.

We have already seen that Prince Charles was center-stage for the three most publicized events in the history of the world to date: 1) the untimely death and burial of Princess Diana, with an estimated total audience of up to two-and-one-half billion viewers and listeners; 2) the prince's 1981 marriage to Diana, with seven-hundred and fifty million viewers and a total audience of nearly two billion; and 3) the prince's 1969 investiture as Prince of Wales, with five-hundred million viewers.[2] Although the author has not seen any estimates as to the actual size of the viewing audience, it is highly likely that Prince Charles' handover of Hong Kong to communist China was among the top *four* most publicized and viewed events ever. Additionally, as noted much earlier, perhaps more biographies and other biographical material have been written on Prince Charles than *any other contemporary figure,* living or dead, and yet the prince has only *just begun* to make his mark in the annals of history.[3] Apart from the basic premise of this work, it is the author's opinion that this set of circumstances would seem to be *inexplicable.* Other than the two witnesses of Revelation 11, this incredible degree of publicity could reasonably be expected for just one person before Christ's return—the AntiChrist.

As we have seen throughout this book, where Prince Charles and the British monarchy in general are concerned, there is almost inevitably a story behind the story. More often than not, the hidden story is both shocking and sordid. In fact, the British monarchy's amazing duplicity and hypocrisy give new meaning to the term "spin doctor." The prince's involvement in Hong Kong is no different.

1. *Her Majesty The Queen,* p. 40.
2. For more information, see Chapter 8, "The Red Dragon and Prince Charles' Investiture as Prince of Wales," and Chapter 10's section titled, "Marriage, ascension, and politics." The recent wedding of Spain's Princess Cristina de Borbon to Inaki Urdangarin in Barcelona reportedly had a pre-ceremony estimated television audience of nine-hundred million ("Royal rites put spotlight on Barcelona," *The Denver Post,* 4 Oct. 1997, p. 2A). This, however, seems to have been a gross exaggeration of the true public interest.
3. For more information, see Chapter 2, "A Man for Our Times."

Holden, as quoted earlier regarding the prince, states, "Visitors...hear little but the long catalogue of his concerns: unemployment, housing, race, drugs, the decay of the inner city, the environment and family life." Prince Charles, in his own words, has remarked, "The Islamic and Western worlds share problems common to us all: ...how we deal with Aids, drugs, and the disintegration of the family.... The international trade in hard drugs is one example.... We have to solve these threats to our communities and our lives together."[1] However, as shown earlier, both the development and the continuance of the modern worldwide drug trade—to include opium, cocaine, heroin, tobacco, and pharmaceutical drugs—can in large measure be traced directly to the British monarchy![2] Britain is internationally known, for example, to have acquired Hong Kong and its surrounding territories as a direct result of its Opium Wars with China in the last century, wars that greatly enriched its monarchy's coffers. Little has

1. Prince Charles, "Islam and the West," 27 Oct. 1993. For the full text of this speech, made at Oxford's Sheldonian Theatre on a visit to the Oxford Centre for Islamic Studies, as well as Holden's statement in context, see Chapter 10's section titled, "Ties to the New Age Movement, the occult, and false religions."

2. To the extent that the British monarchy runs Great Britain, consider the following example from the tobacco industry: "SANTA CRUZ DO SUL, Brazil—Freakish tobacco plants that explode from the soil in the remote river valley grow huge leaves on stalks as thick as Louisville Sluggers. The growers here call it *fumo louco*. Crazy tobacco. Crazy not just because it grows so big and so fast. Crazy because it has been genetically altered by one of the world's largest tobacco companies to pack twice the nicotine of other commercial leaf. The farmers of Brazil's southernmost state are growing it by the ton for the world market.... *Fumo louco*—the farmers' generic term for several related strains of high-nicotine tobacco—is the offspring of a genetically altered plant created in U.S. laboratories for Brown & Williamson Tobacco Corp., the third largest U.S. cigarette maker.... *Fumo louco* blends give cigarette makers a new tool for adjusting nicotine levels in their products. They may also provide the U.S. Food and Drug Administration with a new argument for the assertion that the tobacco industry intentionally manipulates nicotine levels to 'hook' smokers.... 'It's weird stuff,' Neury de Oliveira said in his native Portuguese. The nicotine content is so high that 'just the crazy smell of it gets you dizzy. But, sir, it comes up like nothing you've ever seen.' The farmers said **they sell their high-nicotine tobacco to Souza Cruz, a Brazilian company owned by B.A.T. Industries, the same British conglomerate that controls Brown & Williamson....** The FDA learned in 1994 that Brown & Williamson had developed a nicotine-rich plant, code-named Y-1.... Y-1 cultivation began in Brazil in 1983, according to former Souza Cruz agronomists.... Souza Cruz, according to its own figures, shipped nearly 8 million pounds of Y-1 to the United States for Brown & Williamson between 1990 and 1994.... Grower David Moraes led a reporter to his sorting barn.... Bitter air buffeted the senses. A queasiness spread from the pit of the stomach up through the chest. 'That,' said Moraes, 'is the bite of *fumo louco*'" (Todd Lewan, The Associated Press, "'Crazy tobacco' packs a punch in world market," *Rocky Mountain News*, 21 Dec. 1997, p. 56A). Of course, the tobacco story runs much deeper. Notice, for example, that most cigarette brands bear the British monarch's heraldic achievement on their packaging!

changed. The monarchy, and Prince Charles in particular, retain strong "business" ties to Hong Kong, ties which continue to involve the worldwide drug trade. Perhaps the monarchy's direct participation in Hong Kong's handover, therefore, constituted more than just the next major international media-blitz for the prince since his extravagant wedding to Diana.[1] We have little choice, it seems, but to conclude that the prince's litany of supposed "concerns" is really just one more clever oligarchical ploy to manipulate the world's thinking toward a perceived need for "global governance"—under the very purveyors of the world's greatest decadence themselves. As Prince Charles has himself stated, "I don't want to be a figurehead, but one can reasonably hope to influence people to do what you think is good and useful."[2]

The United Nations and public-private partnerships. Prince Charles has already "partnered" with the United Nations. The PWBLF, for example, has collaborated with the World Bank and the United Nations Development Programme to form **Business as Partners in Development**, an organization which has already had an *enormous* impact on business, government, and education around world (see below).[3] Indeed, Business as Partners in Development is now *leading* the world into a new form of governance based upon the "Platonic ideal," as modeled in public-private (government-business) partnerships that employ elitist concepts of sustainable development. Such partnerships, which were first floated years ago in Pittsburgh,

1. For more information, see the discussion on the Committee of 300 in Chapter 7's section titled, "The Garter."
2. Cathcart, p. 92.
3. For more information, see the PWBLF's publication titled "Business as Partners in Development." This publication may be obtained by contacting **1)** The Prince of Wales Business Leaders Forum (15-16 Cornwall Terrace, Regent's Park, London NW1 4QP) *or* Jane Nelson (Tel: 44-171-467-3600, Fax: 44-171-467-3610, E-mail: jnelson@pwblf.org.uk, Internet: http://www.oneworld.org/pwblf/); **2)** The World Bank Group (1818 H. Street N.W., Washington DC 20433) *or* Amy Horng of Finanace and Private Sector Development (Tel: 202-473-1598, Fax: 202-676-9245, E-mail: ahorng@worldbank.org) *or* Douglas Maguire of MIGA (Tel: 202-473-6733, Fax: 202-522-2650, E-mail: dmaguire@worldbank.org) *or* Debra Sequeira of IFC (Tel: 202-458-7406, Fax: 202-676-9495, E-mail: dsequeira@worldbank.org); or **3)** The United Nations Development Programme (Division for the Private Sector in Development; One United Nations Plaza; New York, NY 10017) *or* Hank Jackelen or John Tucker (Tel: 212-697-9692, Fax: 212-697-5058, E-mail: henryjackelen@undp.org or johntucker@undp.org).

combine what the *elite* have now determined are the "best" and most useful aspects of Communism-Socialism and Capitalism-Fascism. They are to constitute a new global system made "partly of iron and partly of clay" (cf. Dan 2:41-43).[1] Through such public-private partnerships, power is literally shifting away from national, state, and local governments—at all levels—and toward Business as Partners in Development. In other words, the Prince of Wales *is* steadily and quietly taking control.

In a related effort, the prince, through his own PWBLF homepage,[2] also uses the Internet to "get his message out." As a *OneWorld Online* "partner," Prince Charles' homepage, like that of other British royals, has been incorporated into the more extensive OneWorld Online homepage[3] of One World Broadcasting Trust, a British "charity."[4] As of May 1996, the prince's "Millennium Agenda" message, offered in the form of a brief electronic video showing the prince in front of a background displaying his badge as heir-apparent, stated, "It seems to me, however, that the next challenge for *all international business leaders* is to develop a *new world vision,* a form of business ethic which sees this international commitment to good corporate citizenship as a natural part of business practice."[5]

Jane Nelson, speaking for the PWBLF, states, "Business as Partners in Development offers a global perspective on the evolving role of business in a complex and rapidly changing world.... This debate is likely to be one of the defining themes of the 21st Century, as both nation-states and corporations struggle to adapt to a world in which greater efficiency and effectiveness must be combined with more responsible and accountable governance; and in which economic competitiveness must be combined with social cohesion and environmental sustainability."[6] As

1. See the discussion on the "Platonic ideal" in this chapter's earlier section titled, "The United World Colleges," as well as Chapter 7's section titled, "The Garter."
2. http://www.oneworld.org/pwblf/
3. http://carryon.oneworld.org/
4. For other miscellaneous information, see "http://www.royalnetwork.com/".
5. Tokyo, Nov. 1990.
6. Jane Nelson, *Business as Partners in Development: Executive Summary* (United Kingdom: The Prince of Wales Business Leaders Forum, 1996; ISBN: 1 899159 94 0), p. 1.

this introduction to "the first stage in a series of consultations and case studies which The Prince of Wales Business Leaders Forum will be conducting in collaboration with the World Bank and UNDP" would imply, Business as Partners in Development is a major player in the push for global governance. "The next stages in the PWBLF- World Bank-UNDP programme will be focused on...the impacts of about 20 major multinational companies in selected countries; interviewing some 150 stakeholders...; and carrying out a series of roundtables and consultations in different countries around the world."[1] The organization seeks to "develop new types of consultation and partnership[, having social objectives,] between companies and their secondary stakeholders—communities, governments, non-governmental organisations and the general public."[2] It wishes to encourage "multi-stakeholder partnerships between multinational companies and international NGOs; between business and multilateral and bilateral development agencies; and between groups of companies."[3]

Nelson asserts that there is "a growing recognition...of the crucial linkages between economic growth, human development, social cohesion and environmental sustainability....[as] summed up in the concept of sustainable development," and that "these challenges can no longer be tackled by yesterday's rules of governance." "Fundamental to this is the growing importance of the private sector, ranging from large multinational corporations to millions of small and micro-enterprises; and of civil society, ranging from international and professionally managed non-governmental organisations, to grassroots community-based organisations and individual citizens." Moreover, in "most cases, the debate is no longer about extreme alternatives—about communism versus capitalism, the free market versus state control, democracy versus dictatorship—but about finding common ground. It is about developing co-operative, integrated and inclusive solutions...both within nations and between them. It is

1. Nelson, *Business as Partners in Development: Executive Summary*, p. 12.
2. Nelson, *Business as Partners in Development: Executive Summary*, pp. 4, 7.
3. Nelson, *Business as Partners in Development: Executive Summary*, p. 1.

about finding a balance."[1]

The organization's seal mentions environmental sustainability, human development, social cohesion, economic growth and participation, education, training, health, nutrition, soil, atmosphere, water, wetlands, cultivated natural assets, physical infrastructure, goods and services, finance, technology, and formal and informal associations (e.g., NGOs). The seal also portrays national wealth as a combination of natural or environmental capital, human capital, social capital, and man-made or economic capital between companies, communities, and countries.[2] A brief overview of related first-stage key-ideas, phrases, and words would include the following: *the environment (atmosphere, soil, water, wetlands, and natural assets)*—environmental protection, improvement, and accountability, not just sustainability, in the face of current degradation; maintaining biodiversity; *human development*—setting and spreading international ethics standards and business practices; enforcing laws, and tackling crime and corruption; promoting youth and community development, with volunteerism (e.g., utilizing university students for community work); *social cohesion, health, and nutrition*—increasing participation in child-care and health-care; addressing the problems of world poverty and its alleviation, unemployment, economic insecurity, rising inequality, child labor, and social dislocation and disintegration; supporting and strengthening humanitarian efforts for emergency and disaster relief and rehabilitation after natural and man-made disasters, including earthquakes, famine, and war; *global economic growth and participation, education, and training (goods and services, finance, technology)*—economic globalization, regionalization, and development; national wealth creation; promoting good governance and competitiveness; political transition and geo-political transformation; technological transformation, and the current transition from an industrial to a knowledge-based society (e.g., through the Internet); and *physical infrastructure*—urban renewal and rural

1. Nelson, *Business as Partners in Development: Executive Summary*, p. 2.
2. Nelson, *Business as Partners in Development: Executive Summary*, p. 3.

development.

Examples of "good" corporate action cited, to name just a few, include several in which Prince Charles has had either a direct or indirect hand: the Prince's Youth Business Trust (PYBT) in the United Kingdom, India, and South Africa; the prince's International Youth Foundation; the prince's International Hotels Environment Initiative (IHEI); the PWBLF in Poland and the PWBLF's St. Petersburg Partnership; the prince's Business in the Community (BiC), which led to the PWBLF, in the U.K.;[1] the U.K.'s Investors in People programme; the U.K. government's Advisory Council on Business and the Environment; Aim High in the U.K.; Groundwork in the U.K.; the Mega-Cities project; the World Business Council for Sustainable Development; the World Environment Centre; the World Wildlife Fund (WWF); Conservation International; President Clinton's Principles of Corporate Citizenship, and his Council on Sustainable Development; and Goals 2000 in the United States.[2]

Could it be that Prince Charles is not just influencing, but actually setting the U.S. government's agenda? A number of the Clinton administration's pet projects, only three of which have we noted, fall directly into the categories listed above. As just another example, in a significant strategy reversal,[3] the Clintons now suggest that "a large-scale federal program" is *not* the answer to the administration's socialist child-care agenda: "Instead, they explored solutions that relied more on public-private partnerships and efforts by businesses to help make child care more available to their workers. In addition to the scholarship program, the president...announced the formation of a group of business leaders to spur private investment in

---

1. Business in the Community (BiC) was initially modeled after similar successful initiatives already underway in the United States (e.g., see Junor, pp. 249-250).
2. Nelson, *Business as Partners in Development: Executive Summary,* pp. 7, 10-11.
3. Linda Chavez, for example, had commented, "if Clinton has her way, Thursday's White House conference on child care will usher in a new era in which Uncle Sam takes on primary responsibility for minding the nation's children.... For years, Hillary Rodham Clinton has worked for greater government involvement in the lives of children. From her early law-review articles arguing that courts should recognize the full legal rights of minor children (including the right to sue their parents) to her work on the board of the Children's Defense Fund,...Clinton has championed a greater government role in dictating how families function" ("Family feminism puts Uncle Sam in charge of our kids," *The Denver Post,* 22 Oct. 1997, p. 7B).

child care and said volunteers in the Corporation for National Service would help improve after-school care programs."[1]

Nelson concludes, "The purpose of Business as Partners in Development is to profile good practice; to emphasize the positive and the possible.... There is no time for complacency when more than a billion people still live in absolute poverty. When millions of others are out of work and when inequality and social exclusion are increasing in many countries. There is no time for complacency when climate change, environmental degradation, loss of biodiversity and declining food and water supplies threaten the ecological carrying capacity of our planet. And there is no time for complacency when crime and corruption are still growing.... The core issue is about changing attitudes and approach. It is about thinking and acting in non-traditional ways. It is about a new way of [global] governance—at both a societal and corporate level."[2] To this end, the organization sees the "need to activate a sense of common purpose on behalf of all sectors of society," which may be accomplished through "communications campaigns to inform, educate, motivate and in some cases mobilise the general public around specific...issues."[3]

The *Executive Summary* of Business as Partners in Development "recommends that corporate leaders and their counterparts in international NGOs and development agencies work more closely together" to 1) "encourage national governments to develop...partnership between the public and private sector," 2) "undertake joint awareness-raising and educational campaigns," 3) "identify and/or establish joint 'demonstration projects,'" 4) "support joint education and capacity-building exercises, based on experimental learning," 5) "invest in joint efforts to educate some of tomorrow's leaders by working with schools, universities and student organisations and developing teaching materials, mentoring programmes and other opportunities for

---

1. Barbara Vobjeda, The Washington Post, "Clinton unveils child-care plan," *The Denver Post*, 24 Oct. 1997, p. 2A.
2. Nelson, *Business as Partners in Development: Executive Summary*, p. 12.
3. Nelson, *Business as Partners in Development: Executive Summary*, p. 6.

today's decision-makers to inspire and inform tomorrow's."[1] "In this new world, the private sector has become the principal motor of development and its growth the test of economic strength.... [The] private sector can, and in numerous cases already is, playing a leadership role in moves towards sustainable development.... The growing strategic commitment to this new partnership approach by leaders in business, government and international institutions, and the growing...support from communities and NGOs, is a strong indication that we are witnessing the beginning of a new way of doing business. This way...needs to be understood and strongly encouraged by governments and international institutions at all levels."[2]

With all this in mind, it should not surprise us to learn that Prince Charles was chosen to provide the opening message at the June 4, 1996, award ceremony of Habitat II, the U.N. Conference on Human Settlements. Awards, sponsored by the Tokyo Metropolitan Government and the Dubai Municipality, were presented for "best practices," which "represent solutions to pressing social, economic and environmental problems," as well as "a different approach to defining problems and finding solutions in true partnership between civil society, public and private enterprise." "Conferees said that the partnerships should include State and non-State actors—local authorities, the private sector, parliamentarians and non-governmental, community-based and international organizations," noting "the need to develop broad partnerships to tackle the growing problems of urban centres." The 'Best Practices' Initiative "was officially launched at the first substantive session of the Habitat II Preparatory Committee in Geneva in April 1944." According to Boutros Boutros-Ghali, recipients "demonstrate that positive change and sustainable human settlement development are indeed possible."[3]

Global Governance, the Global Security Programme, and a possible "Economic Security Council." As Britain's

1. Nelson, *Business as Partners in Development: Executive Summary,* p. 12.
2. Nelson, *Business as Partners in Development: Executive Summary,* back cover.
3. "Twelve Awards Presented for 'Best Practices' by Secretary-General" (Habitat II - 2 - Press Release HAB/IST/8 4th Meeting), pp. 1-2.

future "Head of the Armed Forces," Prince Charles believes that "we delude ourselves if we think that humanity is becoming ever more civilised, ever more sophisticated and ever more reasonable;" rather, "There will always be dangerous, evil people, and people who will seek to take advantage of others in a weaker condition.... You only have to look at the way the world is now. It's becoming a far more dangerous place.... [The] one certainty is that we have to face the unexpected. Look at the [recent Persian] Gulf War." To the prince, military forces constitute an "insurance policy." Of even greater interest, however, is the fact that Prince Charles envisions the need for a permanent, standing United Nations army—*with himself as its head:* "the Prince was tempted to argue for British troops to play a permanent role within the United Nations as a standing army, financed by member states. 'I foresee that we will have to play a policeman's role all over the world.'... [The] Prince became the first public figure to suggest openly but tentatively that Britain might be 'paid' to provide its military services overseas. Knowing that to advocate openly a 'mercenary' role for the British armed forces was to court the charge that he was ready to see British soldiers die on foreign battlefields for alien causes, he countered that..., in any case, to play a leading part in a permanent United Nations force was an entirely honourable prospect. 'It wouldn't be an entirely mercenary army,' he insisted.... As head of the armed forces, the Prince of Wales would inherit the Queen's role as a focus for their loyalty and unity.... The Prince...as King...would be quite at ease in the role."[1]

Given the above, it should perhaps not surprise us to learn that Prince Charles is said to have *personally* initiated the United Nations' **Global Security Programme**, which came out of Cambridge University, through Maurice Strong and others.[2] This program involves three agendas, one of

1. Dimbleby, *The Prince of Wales*, pp. 524-526. Prince Charles holds top positions in each of the United Kingdom's armed services, and he wears all their various military uniforms. Moreover, he is often seen wearing his Garter Star on them (e.g., see Hoey, *Charles & Diana: The Tenth Anniversary*, pp. 74-75).
2. For more information, see *Our Global Neighbourhood*, a two-volume U.N. book published by the Oxford University Press. This report is on-line: "http://www.cgg.ch/home.htm". Also, see "http://www.cgg.ch/members.htm".

which is a global neighborhood watch using the Internet. While one might be tempted to dismiss the prince's idea of mercenary U.N. forces, it is nevertheless in harmony with what the Gorbachev Foundation advocated in its 1994 "Global Security Programme" (non-American English) report, which was delivered by Gorbachev himself "to 300 distinguished members of the New York Council on Foreign Relations:" "Effective measures are essential for restricting transfers, stockpiling and production of conventional arms through the establishment of an international authority and the imposition of a tax on their production and sale. The proceeds of the tax should go to the UN and, where appropriate, to regional security organizations for their peacekeeping operations."[1]

In June 1995, Sir Shridath Ramphal, co-chairman of the Commission on Global Governance, which is based at the University of Cambridge,[2] *stated that Prince Charles personally inaugurated the Global Security Programme's lecture series established by his commission in 1993,* when he (Ramphal) delivered the second "Global Security Lecture," entitled "Security in the Global Neighbourhood." More than that, however, Ramphal stressed the fact that both the commission and the programme are "at one with...the Prince of Wales—in taking a broad, inclusive view of security." At the same time, Ramphal recommended the establishment of "an Economic Security Council as an apex global economic body within the UN system but reaching beyond governments in its functioning," or "a global forum that can provide leadership in economic and social fields." From the preceding section, it appears that such a forum already exists, and it belongs to Prince Charles. Other commission members include Maurice Strong, who is "a member of the Queen's Privy Council of Canada," as well as Barber Conable, Jacques Delors, Adele Simmons, and Brian Urquhart, all of whom, like Ramphal,[3] have direct or indirect associations with the

1. "Mikhail Gorbachev unveils new *Global Security Programme*," Gorbachev Foundation USA, as reproduced by Gary Kah in *Hope for the World Update,* Fall 1995, pp. 3-4.
2. Recall that Prince Charles is an honors graduate of Trinity College at Cambridge, where he studied world-history.
3. Ramphal has an impressive *monarchy-centered* background: "Shridath Ramphal, Guyana

British monarchy.[1] According to Ramphal,

> Nation states are not about to disappear, or the nation state system to lose its centrality.

Yet something has happened on the way to the 21st century.... It is a transition to a new order and, as in all transitions, there is contention between old habits and perceptions and new realities and needs. All I say in this Lecture about security in our global neighbourhood is conditioned by this awareness....

But I run ahead of myself. I must start truly by expressing my warm appreciation to the University [of Cambridge] and to the Global Security Programme for providing me this very special opportunity to speak to the theme of global governance. I thank particularly the Vice-Chancellor, Professor David Williams, and the Director of the Programme, Dr Prins. To be asked to give the Second Global Security Lecture is a great honour. I look on it as recognition of the work undertaken by the Commission on Global Governance, which I have had the privilege of serving as co-chairman together with Ingvar Carlsson, the Prime Minister of Sweden. **To give such a lecture is under any circumstance a challenge, but to have to follow His Royal Highness the Prince of Wales, who inaugurated this series of lectures two years ago,[2] both enlarges the honour and heightens the**

Secretary-General of the Commonwealth from 1975 to 1990, and Minister of Foreign Affairs and Justice of Guyana from 1972 to 1975. Currently the Chairman of the International Steering Committee of LEAD International-the international Leadership in Environment and Development Program; Chairman, Advisory Committee, Future Generations Alliance Foundation; and the Chancellor of the University of the West Indies and of the University of Warwick in Britain. Member of each of the five independent international commissions of the 1980s, and chairman of the West Indian Commission, which issued its report in 1992. President of the World Conservation Union-IUCN from 1991 to 1993, and author of *Our Country, The Planet,* written for the Earth Summit" ("http://www.cgg.ch/members.htm").

1. See "http://www.cgg.ch/members.htm" for this information: **"Maurice Strong,**....Chairman of the Earth Council. **Has received the Order of Canada and is a member of the Queen's Privy Council of Canada.** Secretary General of the 1992 UN Conference on Environment and Development in Rio, and of the 1972 Stockholm Conference on the Human Environment. Member of the World Commission on Environment and Development." **"Barber Conable,** United States President of the World Bank from 1986 to 1991.... Has served on the boards of multinational corporations...." **"Jacques Delors**, France President of the European Commission from 1985 to January 1995.... Member of the European Parliament and President of its Committee on Economic and Monetary Affairs (1979-81)." **"Adele Simmons,**....an elected member of...the Council on Foreign Relations. In 1993, appointed by the Secretary General of the UN to the High Level Advisory Board on Sustainable Development. From 1977 to 1989,...she developed new programmes in population and health and in peace and international security. From 1978 to 1980, served on President Carter's Commission on World Hunger and from 1991 to 1992, on President Bush's Commission on Environmental Quality." **"Brian Urquhart**, United Kingdom.... Involved in the formation of the United Nations...and served as Under Secretary General for Special Political Affairs from 1972 to 1986."

2. Charles Gunawardena, speaking for the Commission on Global Governance, states, "The Prince of Wales inaugurated the Global Security Lecture series, established by the Cambridge Global Security Programme, in 1993" (written response to inquiry from the publisher).

challenge....

The central theme of Global Security Studies, the quintessence of the Global Security Programme is 'survival' .It is on this note that I should like to start, because all too often the very notion of 'survival' with its connotations of apocalypse invites disbelief and dismissal as hyperbole. And yet those who framed this Programme did in my judgement dare to face up to the most vital issue of our time—humanity's most clear and present danger, and the prospects for those who should follow us....

The most inviolable of human rights is the right to life....[1]

We have already so depreciated our stock of ecological capital that we cannot deliver the planet to our heirs in pristine condition. That is the magnitude of our offence....

....Certainly, a new generation understands better than we ever did that the world is more than an assortment of sovereign states and separate peoples; that there is a human society beyond frontiers; that each of us does belong to two countries, our own and the planet....

The Commission on Global Governance was established in September 1992 [just months before the Prince of Wales inaugurated its Global Security Programme lecture series], but the seeds were planted a few years earlier, in fact about the same time that the Global Security Programme was being set up in Cambridge. It was in 1989 that Willy Brandt, reflecting on the changing, post-Cold War landscape of international relations, began to give thought to the possibilities of arrangements to advance cooperation in a world freed of superpower tensions. Discussions at a meeting he convened in Konigswinter in January 1990 and at a somewhat broader gathering in Stockholm in April 1991 paved the way for the constitution of the Commission, with 28 members from almost as many countries....

We published our report in January—at the start of the UN 50th anniversary—calling it *Our Global Neighbourhood*: a signal we thought, of the kind of world that globalisation and technological change were creating....

Security was high on our agenda of concerns as we viewed the state of the world and its people. But from the outset the Commission was at one with the Global Security Programme—and with the Prince of Wales—in taking a broad, inclusive view of security. We were concerned with security in its conventional sense, of course, with **peace and security** and related issues such as disarmament and nuclear weapons on the one side and with such matters as peacekeeping on the other. We were also concerned about security in its economic and environmental dimensions, because our starting point was the security of people. But, beyond this, we were concerned with survival. 'Unprecedented increases in human activity and human numbers',

1. Ramphal is referring not to the unborn here, but to the born.

we said, 'have reached the point where their impacts are imping-ing on the basic conditions on which life depends'.

....What the end of the post war era both allowed and required was work on 'how' we were going to manage human affairs so that in these and other fields of global endeavour we could answer the challenge of 'survival' .Our central task was to suggest how world governance could be developed and improved to enlarge the probabilities of success.

The present framework of global governance is essentially what was put in place around the end of World War II: at Dum-barton Oaks, at Bretton Woods and finally at San Francisco.... The architecture of the global system is of the mid-1940s....

Consistent with the world of embattled states that shaped their ends at San Francisco, the UN's founders saw future dangers to peace and security arising essentially from conflict between nation states. It was the scourge of war between countries against which the United Nations would stand guard. Iraq's bid to grab Kuwait and its war against Iran are warnings that wars between states are not becoming extinct. But is it just the secu-rity of states and the integrity of frontiers that must concern us, when the higher probability today is that threats to the security of people will arise instead from situations within countries? Liberia, Rwanda, Somalia, the former Yugoslavia are all contemporary examples. There are others in the making. Is this not the very crux of our transition from a world of states to a world of people?...

....We must insist that, save only for self-defence, the use of force against countries is permissible only under the authority and control of the United Nations acting for our global community. That must be the basic norm of global security....

....The Commission on Global Governance has attached criti-cal importance to the reform of the Security Council; we have proposed...to enlarge the Council in respect of both long- and short-term (or rotating) members to make it more representative of UN members without making it unwieldy....

We...are strongly in favour of strengthening the UN's peace-keeping and peace-making role and, as I have said, of forming a UN Volunteer Force to enable the UN to respond more promptly in emergency situations....

But we have gone further in our Report and called for con-certed action to diminish accumulation and dispersal of conven-tional arms through treaty agreement to restrict arm sales and to prohibit the manufacture of a particularly insidious weapon that (as last week's conference in Cambodia highlighted) has brought death and suffering to hundreds of thousands of innocent people, namely landmines. And we call for a Demilitarization Fund to assist countries towards further demilitarization of the global neighbourhood....

....There is little moral difference between the legitimized sale of weapons of mass destruction to impoverished countries and the illegitimate sale by impoverished countries of addictive drugs in the market places of the rich. Our global neighbourhood would be a better one, and global security more realisable, without each of these evil traffickings....

....The global neighbourhood is not a mirage. Like all other neighbourhoods, it has to be good for all its people if in the longer term it is to be good for any....

The time has come, the Commission believes, to establish an Economic Security Council as an apex global economic body within the UN system but reaching beyond governments in its functioning. It is palpable that the world needs a global forum that can provide leadership in economic and social fields....

We envisage that the essential function for an Economic Security Council would be to continuously assess the overall state of the world economy and the interaction between major policy areas; provide a long-term strategic policy framework in order to promote stable, balanced and sustainable development; and secure consistency between the policy goals of the major international economic organizations, particularly the Bretton Woods bodies and the World Trade Organization....[1]

The Group of 7 might claim to be such an apex body. However, the G7 a self-constituted club of the nominally richest countries created to look after their own rather than global interests. But there are other reasons which go to the heart of the G7's inadequacies as a world economic directorate. ...China is the third largest economy after the United States and Japan; India is the fifth, ahead of France, Italy and Britain, with Brazil, Russia, Mexico and Indonesia in the first twelve, ahead of Canada.... The rich have yet to come to terms with the reality of economic multipolarity. An Economic Security Council will both reflect that reality and respond to its new challenges, which are at heart the challenges of globalisation. The Economic Security Council, we believe, has now become an essential part of the structure of global governance.

In the ultimate analysis global security, the security of people, of countries and of civilisation itself rests on planetary security.... Global security at its most basic level is now about survival on an endangered planet. The cumulative consequences of global warming, ozone shield depletion, rising consumption, population explosion, and other emerging critical stresses could lead to human extinction....

1. One would likely be hard-pressed to better describe the Prince of Wales Business Leaders Forum. Moreover, there is every reason to believe that the PWBLF is the forum intended.

....More apposite is the analogy of a tree dying from acid rain. For humanity, it is the tree of life that is endangered. Whether it dies altogether, or withers but clings to life, or loses its leaves and branches yet survives to bloom again, depends on our responses to the blight that afflicts it in the form of the crisis of environment and development—the crisis of global security.

As with other forms of global security there is a governance dimension to planetary security, and we have begun to acknowledge this. **Ever since** the UN's Stockholm Conference on the Human Environment in 1972, and with sharpened intensity since the Brundtland Commission's Report *Our Common Future* in 1987 and **the Earth Summit in Rio** five years later, **we have been addressing some of these governance issues.**[1] But, as the recent Conference in Berlin on the Climate Change Convention shamefully demonstrated, we have done so invariably in half measure, wanting to both have our planet and devour it. We espouse sustainable development as a virtue, but find it too demanding a creed to live by....

The Commission on Global Governance calls for a new level of response. We propose that the Trusteeship Council created in 1945 to administer territories in transition to independence be given a new mandate—to be trustees of the global commons and of the planet's life support systems....

We see the Trusteeship Council in its new role becoming the principal world forum for environmental matters, with its functions including the administration of environmental treaties in such fields as climate change, biodiversity, outer space and the oceans. There is no higher trusteeship than that of planetary security. Our systems of governance must reflect this primacy and provide authority for fulfilling it.

....The rule of law has been a critical civilising force in every free society. It is what distinguishes an authoritarian from a democratic society, what secures liberty and justice against oppression, what elevates equality above dominion....

....When the founders of the United Nations drew up the Charter they genuflected at the altar of the rule of law....

....The development of international law could have been a major chapter of the post-war era; it was to be a mere footnote. The era was characterised instead by the rule of military power and economic strength.... We must strive to ensure that the global neighbourhood of the future is characterised by law not lawlessness; by rules which all must respect; by the reality that all, even the weakest, are equal under the law; that none, even the most powerful, is above the law. We made proposals to that end.

For 45 years the Cold War held humanity in thrall threatening

1. Recall that Prince Charles is personally credited for the success of the Rio Earth Summit. For more information, see this chapter's earlier section titled, "Environmentalism, the Rio Earth Summit, and the Kyoto Protocol."

'mutual assured destruction'—our 'double-speak' for human survival.... [The] threat itself arose out of human failure to devise
saner approaches to global security.

And now, released from the compulsions of the nuclear arms
race and the larger tensions of the Cold War, we are failing to
capture the 'peace dividend' .Five years after the end of the Cold
War, the world is more tense, more fragile, more unstable, and its
people more fearful and uncertain. Humanity remains an endangered species.... On the eve of a new century and a new millennium, we probably have less reason for assurance than our ancestors had...that we are passing on to future generations the right
to life....

That we urgently need a new universal ethic of survival and a
reordering of global priorities appears no longer to be in doubt.
That ethic of survival will require us to recognize how we have
ravaged the planet and endangered its life forms, including our
species. It will require us to acknowledge that we could nullify all
of humanity's incomparable achievements unless we change
course. It will require us to consider how we stand poised
between a new globalism, heralding a more civilized society gov-
erned by the rule of enforceable law worldwide, and a return to
old instincts of power, arbitrariness, and selfcentred nationalism.

Does it matter if we fail to rise to the challenge of survival?
In cosmic terms, perhaps not. Whatever the manner of our
going, Earth will heal her wounds, however grievous; our planet's
flora and fauna, however transfigured, will have a better chance
to survive and flourish because we have gone....

But surely that cannot be our conclusion. What of our duty
to humanity itself, to our own worthiest qualities and the highest
purposes of human existence; what of our trust to the generations that should succeed us? Homo sapiens has a duty to sustain
life that transcends our capacity to destroy it.... As the Cambridge Global Security Programme, as your Global Security Studies
dictate, it is time we 'begin to find ourselves'.[1]

Architecture. Through much maneuvering, Prince Charles has become perhaps the most influential man in Britain
on the subject of architecture, having even authored a
book on the subject and started his own Institute of
Architecture.[2] Despite appearances, there is method to the
prince's "madness." As will be discussed in the next chapter, the prince's activities in this area have significantly

1. Sir Shridath Ramphal, "Security in the Global Neighbourhood: The Second Global Security
   Lecture," June 1995. For the full text of this lecture, visit "http://www.cgg.ch/cambrge.htm".
2. For more information, see the previous chapter's section titled, "Ties to the New Age Movement, the occult, and false religions."

contributed to the city of London's renewed international prominence.

12

Prince Charles,
the Middle East Peace Talks,
and
Global Security

Besides telling us that the AntiChrist is of Roman lineage, Daniel 9:26-27 indicates that he will accept personal responsibility to "strengthen," meaning either to confirm *or* to enforce (Heb., **גביר**), "a covenant with many [*rabim*]—one 'seven'" (Heb., **ברית לרבים שבוע אחד**). This covenant is generally understood as a treaty between Israel and her several adversaries. Central to it, will be the theme of "peace and security," for both apostate Israel and the unbelieving world (1 Th 5:3, Gk.). We must not overlook, therefore, the fact that U.N. Resolutions 242 and 338, to which this theme is central, have served as the basis for *all* peace negotiations and treaties with modern Israel since the nation regained sovereignty—for the first time in nearly 2,600 years—over the old city of Jerusalem, otherwise known as East Jerusalem, in 1967's Six Day War.[1] In fact, literally *thousands* of articles—if anything, this is an understatement—have been written over the past decade alone using the exact phrases "peace and security"

---

1. *U.N. Resolution 242* (passed on the November 22, 1967, following the war), emphasizes "the inadmissibility of the acquisition of territory by war and the need to work for a just and lasting peace in which every State in the area can live in security...." It also affirms that "the fulfillment of [U.N.] Charter principles requires the establishment of a just and lasting peace in the Middle East...." According to the resolution, this should include the withdrawal of "Israeli armed forces from territories occupied in the recent conflict" as well as "respect for and acknowledgment of the sovereignty, territorial integrity and political independence of every State in the area and their right to live in peace within secure and recognized boundaries free from threats or acts of force." Additionally, it affirms the "necessity" for "guaranteeing the territorial inviolability and political independence of every State in the area, through measures including the establishment of demilitarized zones" and for "achieving a just settlement of the [Palestinian] refugee problem" (Leonard J. Davis, *MYTHS AND FACTS 1989, A Concise Record of the Arab-Israeli Conflict*, ed. Eric Rozenman and Jeff Rubin {Washington, D.C.: Near East Research, Inc., 1988}, p. 294). Resolution 338 is essentially a reaffirmation of 242.

and "security and peace," as well as variants of them, in relation to Israel and the Mideast peace process.[1]

Before proceeding, some significant points must be made concerning the Hebrew text of Daniel 9:27. *First,* it speaks of a covenant "with many," which is literally rendered "with *rabim* [Rabin]." Note, therefore, that Yitzhak *Rabin,* whose name appears to derive from the Hebrew *rabim,* signed the Oslo II accord (or treaty) with Yasser Arafat,[2] as well as a related, but less significant, treaty with Jordan's King Hussein, on apostate Israel's behalf.[3] Had Rabin not been assassinated for his great *ignominy* before God, he would likely have remained on track to also sign a final Oslo III accord. *Second,* Daniel 9:27 speaks of "*a* covenant." That is, the word for "covenant" is not preceded by a definite article. This leaves open the possibility that the covenant in view could be one in a *series* of covenants, such as the second of two or the third of three consecutive accords. Rabin, as mentioned, signed the second of three planned consecutive accords, as well as an intermediate agreement with Jordan. *Third,* the phrase for "one 'seven'" lacks a preposition. In other words, the

1. This figure does not include the many additional articles employing the same phrases in relation to various United Nations and NATO operations, activities, and agendas. We should remember that the United Nations, and before it the League of Nations, is literally chartered to maintain international "peace and security."

2. Contrary to later press reports, Rabin and Arafat did *not* sign Oslo I, otherwise known as the "Declaration of Principles." Instead, while U.S. Secretary of State Warren Christopher and Russian Foreign Minister Andrei Kozyrev served as official witnesses, Shimon Peres and Mahmoud Abbas signed Oslo I, while countersigning letters of recognition that Rabin and Arafat had signed the previous week (Michal Yudelman and David Makovsky, "A Prospect of Peace," *The Jerusalem Post,* Int. Ed., 25 Sept. 1993, p. 1). Oslo II was a much more significant agreement, requiring far greater sacrifices on Israel's part, than Oslo I.

3. Just as the 1995 Oslo II accord or treaty derived from the 1993 "Declaration of Principles" signed with the PLO, which came to be called "Oslo I," so the 1994 Israeli-Jordanian peace treaty derived from a corresponding 1993 "Declaration of Principles" signed with Jordan the day after Oslo I was signed with the PLO in Washington. Of the four signed agreements, two were "Declarations of Principles," or frameworks and agendas for negotiating peace, and two were actual treaties. It was the two treaties that Rabin signed, not the declarations. Speaking of Oslo I, for example, Uri Dan and Dennis Eisenberg comment, "Weizman appears to have forgotten that the Oslo accords signed in Washington in September 1993 were only a declaration of principles, not a peace agreement." Moshe Kohn likewise has pointed out that the "Declaration of Principles" is "not [a] 'peace accord,' as people call it" ("Our local quislings," *The Jerusalem Post,* daily, 29 Aug. 1996, p. 6; "Back where we came from," *The Jerusalem Post,* daily, 7 Jan. 1994, p. 5; accession nos. 960006030 and 940020125 on the *Jerusalem Post* CD-ROM). That the 1995 treaty with the Palestinian Authority (PA), or the Oslo II accord, is considered to be more significant than the 1994 Israeli-Jordanian peace treaty is evidenced from, among other factors, the far greater media attention paid to it. These points are important in the context of the timing of Daniel 9:27.

Hebrew text of Daniel 9:27, which states "he shall strengthen a covenant with *rabim*—one 'seven,'" may be alternately rendered as "he shall strengthen a covenant...*for* one 'seven'" or "he shall strengthen a covenant...*that lasts* one 'seven.'" If we accept the former rendering, then the prophecy indicates that the Anti-Christ will strengthen the particular covenant for a seven-year period. If we accept the latter rendering, however, the prophecy's meaning may be quite different; it would then indicate that while the covenant itself lasts for seven years, the AntiChrist could at some *later* point, *after* the covenant's initiation, begin to confirm and ultimately enforce it. The former rendering requires the AntiChrist's direct involvement, whether behind-the-scenes or in the open, for the full seven-year duration of the covenant, or throughout the Tribulation Period. The latter rendering *allows* for his involvement to begin at some *indefinite* point following the start of the covenant's seven-year duration, or after the Tribulation Period has begun. In either case, it appears that the AntiChrist will serve as an international confirmer and eventual guarantor of Mideast peace through the prophesied covenant. *Finally,* notice that Daniel 9:27 is *silent* on the issue of whether the AntiChrist will actually sign the covenant or not. Although many have taught that he will do so, it is a presumption.

London's centrality to Mideast peace initiatives. For at least the past decade, the city of London has been undergoing a modern environmental and architectural "renaissance," another seemingly disconsonant event that Prince Charles, through continual active prodding of the architectural community and government of England concerning a myriad of his own environmental and architectural concerns, personally set in motion. This renaissance is now being recognized in fascinating ways. In the words of one writer, "As the 21st century approaches, their denizens boast that London can lay claim to being the world's most exciting city. 'There has been a culture change here in mind-set and environment. This is a new way to make a city,' said Camilla Cavendish, who heads a consortium of businesses and residents recasting[, under a wide-scale program initiated and overseen by Prince Charles,] a once-shabby neighborhood south of the Thames that now houses Europe's largest cultural center. 'This is a good time to be in London. It's become a magnet for creative people. Other European cities don't seem to have the critical mass or the flexible attitude.'... London is a fine place for architects."[1] This, however, just scratches the surface of the prince's hand in London's renewed prominence.

The Committee of 300 and the London-based Royal Institute for International Affairs (RIIA),[2] taking advantage of the friendly relationship between the United States and Israel, made heavy use of the U.S. Council on Foreign Relations — the RIIA's devoted step-child — and the office of the President, who serves the U.S. CFR, to oversee the covert Israel-PLO dialogue, and consequently the entire *Oslo* peace process, *from day one.* Indeed, according to Ron Pundak, an arab ombudsman and negotiator for the Oslo I accord, the U.S. State Department was fully informed from the start, being apprised by him personally at the conclusion of each negotiating session. Hussein too has admitted as much, stating that Clinton "was involved from the start."[3] Under the direction of the RIIA, which in turn reports to the Committee of 300, the U.S. CFR worked closely with its Israeli counterpart, the Israeli CFR. Rabin, for example, who was a member of the Israeli CFR, used a Washington D.C. lawyer, Yoel Zinger, to write the Oslo I accord. As we shall see, the following historical account makes all of this painfully clear. As documented earlier in this book, the British monarchy heads the Committee of 300 and the RIIA, both of which control the U.S. and Israeli CFRs. In other words, Queen Elizabeth II and Prince Charles sit at the real top of the entire Mideast peace process. Although *Inside Israel*'s Barry Chamish and others have largely missed this connection, it has always been the case. In the past, for example, the RIIA directed former

1. William D. Montalbano, Los Angeles Times, "New London a millennium high, City is celebrating renaissance," *The Denver Post,* 6 Nov. 1996, p. 31A.
2. For more information, see the note on this institute later in this chapter.
3. "A sudden chill," *The Jerusalem Post,* Int. Ed., 18 Oct. 1997, p. 9.

President Jimmy Carter and then Secretary of State Zbigniew Brzezinski (both of the U.S. CFR) to use Moshe Dayan (of the Israeli CFR) to keep Israel off-guard for the Yom Kippur War, and to subsequently persuade Menachem Begin to accept the Camp David Accords.[1] Moreover, it appears that Mideast peace talks have orbited London for at least thirty years.[2]

Prince Charles and the London Agreement of 1987. In November 1986, while touring the Persian Gulf states, Prince Charles and Steven Day, then head of the Middle East department of Britain's Foreign Office, "discussed ways in which the Prince could put his status to more effective use in a region where the desert rulers have long presumed a special affinity with the British royal family," agreeing that the prince should "establish a more effective and methodical framework for maintaining links with that region, and indeed with the Middle East more generally." Although favored by the Foreign Office, to "Mrs Thatcher it seemed as though the Prince was in the throes of setting up a Foreign Office in miniature, which would formulate policy and conduct relations with the Gulf quite independently of the proper machinery of government." The prince's plan was then "dropped."[3] At least, that's the "official" line. Even before 1986, Prince Charles had kept abreast of Mideast developments: "When all this trouble in the Lebanon flared up the last time, I asked the Foreign Office if they had any books on the subject that would give

1. Chamish, *Traitors and Carpetbaggers in the Promised Land,* pp. 13, 17, 25, 27, 29, 33-34, 41, 43-44, 51, 55, 80, 103-104, 106, 110-111, 176, 179, 181. The Royal Institute for International Affairs (RIIA), which functions as the foreign policy executive arm of the British monarchy and "was one of the earliest foreign policy executors of the Committee of 300" (Coleman, *The Committee of 300,* p. 188), is the London-based predecessor and counterpart to the Untied States Council on Foreign Relations (CFR) and its Israeli component, as well as to the Canadian Institute of International Affairs. Rabin and Peres are both known to have had close ties to the RIIA and the U.S. Council on Foreign Relations, and Peres was a member of the Socialist International, another Committee of 300 organization (ibid., p. 217). For more information, see Chapter 7's section titled, "The Garter."
2. In 1967, "THREE weeks after the Six Day War, Doctor Ya'acov Herzog met King Hussein in London. 'Is Your Highness ready to sign a peace treaty with Israel?' asked Premier Eshkol's special emissary. The king's reply was: 'Yes, I am ready. But give me time. I must go forward together with the rest of the Arab world'" (Moshe Zak, "Hussein: 'I am ready,'" *The Jerusalem Post,* daily, 18 Oct. 1994, p. 6; accession no. 940004212 on the *Jerusalem Post* CD-ROM).
3. Dimbleby, *The Prince of Wales,* pp. 401-402.

me some historical background to the friction and they came up with an excellent one, written by Sir Ian Gilmour's son which I read."[1]

In October 1987, then Israeli Foreign Minister Shimon Peres traveled to London, England, to meet King Hussein of Jordan. As an attorney for, and special representative of, Hussein,[2] one Lord Victor Mishcon—who has apparently also worked for Britain's royal family and specifically Prince Charles in the past, not to mention the RIIA—hosted the meeting: "Foreign Minister Shimon Peres's eight-hour marathon session with the king in 1987 was arranged by ardent Zionist, politician, eminent jurist and British peer Lord Victor Mishcon, who has close ties with dignitaries on both sides of the Jordan River."[3] Actually, this particular

1. Junor, p. 91.
2. For more information, see Chamish, *Traitors and Carpetbaggers in the Promised Land*, pp. 121, 156. Chamish asserts that a reference to a later meeting between the PLO and a group of Israeli settler leaders in London, which reads "outside Oxford at the home of a Jew who arranges and pays for these kinds of talks," is most likely speaking of Mishcon.
3. Greer-Fay-Cashman, "Private parleys: Shamir keeps mum on his talks," *The Jerusalem Post*, daily, 5 Aug. 1994, p. 8; accession no. 940008129 on the *Jerusalem Post* CD-ROM. Mishcon's name has been variously spelled "Mishcon," "Mishkon," and "Mischon" in Israeli newspapers. Mishcon, who is a Jewish peer and lord (i.e., aristocracy) of the British Labor Party, has given his London home "for secret Israeli-Jordanian meetings over the last 20 years": "The Americans also played a key part in the Jordan breakthrough.... However, the most interesting player was an Israeli named "Ephraim" who stepped in from the cold.... Foreign reports say he is the deputy director of the Mossad. By all accounts, including public remarks by Rabin, he mediated the deal, reportedly culminating a 25-year personal friendship with Hussein.... 'When the king saw List B, he said this means that Jordan will now be out of the picture in the territories,' a Jordanian official told an Israeli interlocutor. Israel-Jordan talks went into high gear. On May 19, Ephraim set up a Hussein-Rabin meeting at the home that Peres would later describe as the venue of Jordanian-Israeli meetings for years—the London home of <u>Lord Victor Mishkon</u>, an old Jewish Laborite. Hussein was joined by Hassan, while the prime minister was accompanied by Ephraim, Elyakim Rubinstein (the chief negotiator with Jordan), and Maj.-Gen. Danny Yatom. As the king recalled, he was stung by charges that he was not genuinely interested in moving forward. He asked: 'How am I not serious?' Rabin said the Israel-PLO agreement made it vital that Israel-Jordan ties become more concrete. The king responded, 'Fine, let's get on with it.' At that meeting and another, two weeks later, between the king and Rabin at the same place, compromises were made. Jordan agreed to move the peace talks to Jordanian and Israeli soil and to announce the move at the end of an upcoming trilateral meeting on economics, thereby breaking the de-facto Syrian veto. In return, Rabin agreed to discuss borders and water" (David Makovsky, "Hussein steps into light to avoid being eclipsed," *The Jerusalem Post*, daily, 5 Aug. 1994, p. 2; accession no. 940008166 on the *Jerusalem Post* CD-ROM; also see accession no. 900012343). Subsequently, on August 27, 1995, Hussein sent "a royal-crested plane to Ben-Gurion Airport to transport Foreign Minister Shimon Peres, Economics Minister Yossi Beilin, Israel's ambassador to Jordan Shimon Shamir and Peres's bureau chief Avi Gil to Aqaba to celebrate the 80th birthday of <u>Lord Mishcon</u>, who facilitated many of the clandestine meetings between the monarch and Israeli dignitaries" (*The Jerusalem Post*, daily, 1 Sept. 1995, p. 16; accession no. 950006093 on the *Jerusalem Post* CD-ROM). "Peres held talks with Jordan's King Hussein...at the monarch's mansion in Akaba.... The official reason

encounter is said to have been arranged by *Prince Charles* through Mishcon; the prince counts both Hussein and Peres as close friends. Together, Hussein and Peres made a preliminary agreement to call for an international conference involving the five permanent member-states of the U.N. Security Council (i.e., the United States, the then Soviet Union, Britain, France, and China). Under this "London Agreement," which was later secretly negotiated in Jordan in 1988,[1] the conference was to have as its goal direct negotiations between the various parties to the Middle East conflict.

Although Israel's subsequent Likud government under Prime Minister Yitzhak Shamir shelved the London Agreement,[2] clearly hoping to permanently kill it, Peres vowed that if he were ever elected Prime Minister, he would seek to revive it. When Yitzhak Rabin later took the position of Labor Party chief from Peres and accepted Peres as his running mate against Shamir, so that the two of them then came to power, Rabin conceded to Peres and the London Agreement was revived.[3] According to Knesset member Benny Begin, Peres actually met secretly with the Palestinian Liberation Organization (PLO) as early as 1984. The Palestinian (i.e., Philistine and Edomite) *Intifada,* therefore, arose directly from the early failure of the 1987 London Agreement.

In January 1990, Ezer Weizman, the nephew of former Committee of 300 member Chaim Weizman, met secretly with PLO officials in London, where he first proposed the "Gaza-Jericho first" tactic. Peres, who was both excited

---

given for the meeting in Akaba was a celebration of the 80th birthday of <u>Lord Victor Mishcon</u>, who has given his home for secret Israeli-Jordanian meetings over the last 20 years. Hussein sent a special plane to bring Peres and Economics Minister Yossi Beilin to his residence last night" (David Makovsky, *The Jerusalem Post,* daily, 28 Aug. 1995, p. 2; accession no. 950006345 on the *Jerusalem Post* CD-ROM).

1. Some sources appear to erroneously give 1988 as the year of the London Agreement.
2. Chamish adds, "According to Yossi Beilin, Yitzhak Shamir sent a personal envoy, Mossad agent Efraim HaLevy to co-sign a tentative peace agreement arranged by Shimon Peres and King Hussein in London and brokered by the U.S. in April 1987" (*Traitors and Carpetbaggers in the Promised Land,* p. 108).
3. In the 1980's, before the London Agreement was negotiated, Shimon Peres stayed as a guest of Prince Charles in London on numerous occasions. During these trips, Peres enthusiastically invited the prince to visit Jerusalem. In fact, standing invitations remain. To date, however, such visits, other than at Rabin's funeral, have been kept strictly private and have usually involved only Israel's highest national leadership.

by Weizman's report and still committed to the earlier London Agreement, yet knowing that Shamir would not countenance the idea, decided to move forward by treachery. Consequently, Peres plotted to keep the PLO track alive through Adi Tamir and Nimrod Novick (an appropriate namesake) while toppling the Israeli government with help from his deputy, Yossi Beilin, and the U.S. Secretary of State, James Baker (a U.S. CFR member).[1] That same year, then Foreign Minister Benjamin Netanyahu charged that U.S. policy toward Israel under Baker and Dennis Ross was "built upon a foundation of distortion and lies."[2]

The Madrid Peace Conference. Four years after the London Agreement, in October 1991, under the joint sponsorship of the United States and the Soviet Union (now Russia), formal peace talks began at the Royal Palace in Madrid, Spain, between Israel and her Arab and Palestinian adversaries. *Contrary to what most people think, therefore, the Madrid peace talks, hosted by King Juan Carlos, did not begin in Spain, but in London!* The London Agreement of 1987 was in fact a precursor not just to the Madrid Peace Conference, but to the Oslo process itself.

The King of Spain clearly is not the AntiChrist, yet the royal setting for the initial round of Madrid talks may have set an important precedent for future rounds. After the Madrid Peace Conference, Israel emphatically stated its preference to hold continuing negotiations in the Middle East, but until more recently most of her adversaries have accepted only European or American settings, usually with United States' mediators and observers present. Besides Spain, talks are known to have been held in Norway and Milan, Italy. Israel, however, may not accept this intransigence, if peace talks are to proceed beyond Oslo II, indefinitely. Eventually, the international hosts of the negotiations may have to find a location for the talks that is more relevant and suitable to all the parties involved. *If the Middle East continues to be unacceptable to Israel's*

---

1. Chamish, *Traitors and Carpetbaggers in the Promised Land,* pp. 29-30, 121.
2. David Makovsky, "The candidate becomes the leader," *The Jerusalem Post,* Int. Ed., 15 June 1996, p. 8.

enemies, then what location, may we speculate, might Israel and her Muslim adversaries more readily accept?

London, Prince Charles, and the gestation of the Oslo peace process. In the first decades of this century, Great Britain controlled much of the Middle East's territory, including not only the land that comprises modern Israel, but also the lands of a number of Israel's Muslim adversaries—Jordan, Iraq, Kuwait, Egypt, Saudi Arabia, Syria, Lebanon, and, to a lesser degree, Persia (now Iran). The dispute between Israel and her enemies, contrary to the biblical reality, is generally claimed to be about territory. Therefore, what better place could there be to host the talks than Great Britain or, for that matter, near or in her Royal Palace in London? As late as 1996, this author had subsequently remarked, "If this, or a comparable circumstance should arise, such that Prince Charles becomes clearly associated with the peace negotiations, it would tend to confirm, along with all the other evidence presented herein, that he is in fact the AntiChrist." Now, however, it has come to light that the once-secret "Oslo negotiations," so-called for their Norwegian location, were, like the Madrid talks, first plotted in *London.* Moreover, the media have reported that other secret Mideast negotiations, such as those concerning Syria, were likewise arranged there. That is not all, however. Apart from the earlier London Agreement, which resulted in the Madrid Peace Conference, it appears, as shown below, that *Prince Charles may have personally initiated the London plotting for Oslo.* To add icing on the cake, Israel was recently approached regarding a possibility of joining the British Commonwealth, which she is said to be actively considering (see below).

In 1992, Mishcon hosted a meeting, ostensibly held for masonic purposes,[1] between Rabin and Hussein in London:

---

1. Various Mideast rulers and leaders—both Arab and Israeli—are Freemasons, including those behind the Oslo peace process. As such, they share many of Prince Charles' occult beliefs and goals. Yitzhak Rabin was an active Mason. He joined the order just before traveling to Washington D.C. as Israel's new ambassador in 1968. In 1976, Rabin was caught on film presiding over a large international masonic convention in Jerusalem. Various newspapers have likewise observed that Jordan's King Hussein is a high-ranking and proud Mason who frequently—"several times a year"—travels to London to participate in masonic ceremonies

"When Peres and King Hussein conversed in Washington last month [(i.e., in July 1994)], the Jordanian monarch asked him if he had 'spoken to Victor [Mishcon]' about the positive developments in the peace process."[1] The product of the 1992 encounter, which also presumably was arranged by Prince Charles through Mishcon,[2] is believed to have been a subsequent secret meeting in London (see below), and then a series of secret negotiations in Oslo between key Israeli and Palestinian negotiators. On the Israeli side, these Oslo negotiators included Peres and Beilin. On the Palestinian side, they included Abu Mazen (Beilin's counterpart). Also, Yair Hirshfeld (a Jew) and Pundak (an arab) served as ombudsman. The January-February 1996 edition of *Inside Israel,* edited by Chamish, not only asserts "Yair Hirshfeld and Ron Pundak...negotiated the first Oslo Accord," but adds details concerning what transpired following the London meeting between Rabin and Hussein:

---

and other functions. In November 1994, at the signing of a formal peace treaty between Jordan and Israel, Rabin and Hussein were photographed exchanging a masonic handshake as Clinton applauded. The shot was published two days later by "the president of the Israel Order of Masons" in full-page Israeli newspaper advertisements headlined "MASONS OF PEACE." Following Rabin's assassination, the grand master of the Grand Lodge of Israel, Ephraim Fuchs, published advertisements "mourning the passing of 'a brother.'" Netanyahu too is reported to be a Mason, supposedly having been recruited while serving as Israel's ambassador to the United Nations in New York in the early 1980s. Also, Teddy Kollek, the current Mayor of Jerusalem, is said to be a Mason. In May 1996, Tel Aviv police raided an apartment reportedly "used for ceremonies by the Freemasons, an organization whose membership boasts cabinet ministers and high ranking army officers;" the apartment's "walls were covered in Latin script, skulls and bones graced the shelves, and crossed swords were mounted above and beside an altar." Fuchs, providing some interesting disinformation, later "claimed that the apartment was rented by a cult called the Illuminati, which had nothing to do with Freemasonry." Ha! According to Chamish, "The Masonic plan for the region is a well-kept secret, but Jerusalem is known to be especially important for the organization, as it traces its origins to the mythical Hiram [Abiff], the mason wrongly believed to have been the planner of Solomon's Temple" (*Traitors and Carpetbaggers in the Promised Land,* pp. 60, 103-105, 167-170). Kah observes that Syria's Hafez Assad, like Jordan's Hussein, is reputed to be a Mason. He adds, "For at least several centuries, Jordan has been a bastion for the secret societies in the Middle East and has much more influence in the region's behind-the-scenes politics than most people realize" (*En Route to Global Occupation,* n. on p. 145). For more information, see the investigative newsletter titled *Inside Israel,* ed. Barry Chamish (P.O. Box 389; BEIT SHEMESH, Israel; Phone-fax: +972-2-991-4936), July-August 1996, pp. 4-6. For subscriptions to *Inside Israel,* write to AB&C, P.O. Box 579, Swindon, Wiltshire SN4 OTL, England, UK (E-mail: merkava@tcp.co.uk).

1. Greer-Fay-Cashman, "Private parleys: Shamir keeps mum on his talks," *The Jerusalem Post,* daily, 5 Aug. 1994, p. 8; accession no. 940008129 on the *Jerusalem Post* CD-ROM.
2. Mishcon is *rumored* to have served more recently as a divorce attorney for Princess Diana.

Hirshfeld's influential position is hardly accidental. In the 1970s he was a chief aide to Austrian President Bruno Kreisky who was head of the Socialist International at the time....

While Kreisky was sworn to initiate the fall of [Prime Minister Menachem] Begin, he coordinated his activities with another member of the Socialist International, then-Israeli Labour Party chief Shimon Peres. Hirshfeld was sent to Israel to promote the agenda of the European branch of the movement to create a One World Government and quickly found a teaching position at Tel Aviv University. His leftist politics made him a friend of Palestinian and Israeli leftist leaders, especially Yossi Beilin and Palestinian leader Hanan Ashrawi. In November 1992, he was sent to **a London hotel** to meet PLO economics "minister" Abu Allah and when the meeting ended who just happened to be in the lobby "accidentally" but Beilin?

Hirshfeld just as "accidentally" reported on his meeting with Abu Allah. Beilin liked what he heard, told Rabin and thus was born the current peace process.[1]

The 1992 Labor victory of Rabin with Peres over the Likud was actually made possible through illegal agreements with the PLO, which resulted in a just passable 61-59 split. In a scheme devised by Peres and Baker, Peres conspired with Arafat beginning in June 1991. At a meeting between Yossi Beilin and the PLO's Said Kamal and Mahmoud Abbas at the King Hotel in Cairo, Beilin sought, under instructions from Peres, to obtain the arab vote in Israel in exchange for, among other things, freezing Israeli settlements in the "occupied territories," a land-for-peace policy, and cancellation of the Israeli law prohibiting meetings between Israelis and PLO members. Subsequently, on January 19, 1992, Beilin met with the PLO's Nabil Shaat at the Ramses Hilton Hotel in Cairo, where Peres upped the ante: a Labor government, in exchange for the arab vote, would support a PLO-led "independent autonomous entity," or a future Palestinian state in all but name. Peres and Beilin got what they wanted when Israeli arabs unanimously voted for Labor Party candidates, effectively changing Israel's government.

Although Rabin was willing to promote a settlement

1. "The Oslo Architects Target Jerusalem," *Inside Israel,* Vol. IV, Issue 1, January-February 1996, pp. 5-6. For a reprint of this article, see Chamish, *Traitors and Carpetbaggers in the Promised Land,* pp. 149-150.

freeze for the sake of ongoing talks with the Palestinians, he initially refused to honor Peres' secret agreements with the PLO, concerning which he at first claimed ignorance. Ultimately, however, Rabin succumbed to the combined pressure, arranged by Peres' deputy Beilin, of Bush (discussed later) and Mubarak, who, having already recovered the Sinai Peninsula, threatened to renege on the Camp David Accords. (Note that Bush, who was initiated into the Illuminist Skull and Bones society during his days at Yale University, is not just a member of both the Committee of 300 and the U.S. CFR, but is also a knight of the British monarchy.) In October 1992, Israel and Jordan drafted a joint "Declaration of Principles" for negotiating an Israeli-Jordanian peace treaty.[1] In November 1992, a series of meetings were held in London under the auspices of the U.S. CFR. During one such meeting, Yair Herschfeld, a left-wing academic, met Abu Allah in a hotel room. Upon leaving the room, Herschfeld "coincidentally" encountered Yossi Beilin in the lobby, where he reported the PLO's willingness to negotiate. Beilin then informed Rabin, and probably Peres also, that he had Norwegian contacts who would agree to host clandestine Israel-PLO talks.

By February 1993, Israeli settlements had been frozen and the law banning contacts with the PLO had been revoked. When Rabin, working through U.S. Secretary of State Warren Christopher (a member and former head of the U.S. CFR), then wanted to remove the PLO from the peace talks in favor of Syria, the PLO, resorting to its "old ways," planned to bomb the World Trade Center in New York. With Arafat's approval, it proceeded to do so. Rabin, this time along with the Clinton administration, which would apparently do *anything*—including covering for the perpetrators of the WTC bombing—for the sake of a well-publicized treaty between Israel and the PLO, again

---

1. "Israel and Jordan have forsworn the use of force against each other in a landmark document, hammered out between the two countries during the peace talks in Washington last week. Senior Israeli officials are hailing the move as a declaration of principles preceding a bilateral peace treaty" (David Makovsky, "Israel, Jordan pledge to use force no more," *The Jerusalem Post*, daily, 1 Nov. 1992, p. 1; accession no. 920003408 on the *Jerusalem Post* CD-ROM).

succumbed. The Rabin government too was showing its true colors. A campaign to brainwash the Israeli public into accepting an agreement leading to a Palestinian "entity" went into high gear. Using his contacts, Rabin virtually shut down Israel's television news and its free press. To stay in business, the television news and the free press had to "sell peace" by primarily reflecting the Labor Party's line. By September 1994, a majority of Israel's independent (non-state owned) publications simply "disappeared."

The Oslo I Declaration of Principles. In September 1993, with Labor's majority waning and no national referendum having been held, Rabin—bowing to "severe pressure" from the Clinton administration—and Arafat rushed to Washington, where Shimon Peres and Mahmoud Abbas signed a "Declaration of Principles," or what is now known as the "Oslo I accord" (i.e., a framework and agenda for negotiating a later treaty), on behalf of Israel and the PLO. The next day, Jordan signed its own "Declaration of Principles" with Israel, in which Israel not only promised, should an Israeli-Jordanian peace treaty be reached, to cede roughly one-third of all the agricultural land in the rift between the Dead Sea and the Red Sea, but to defend the Hashemite kingdom militarily in the event a third party, such as Iraq or Syria, attacked it.

According to Yair Hirshfeld, four days *before* the Oslo I signing, on September 9, 1993, a forum devised by Beilin and Mayor of Jerusalem Teddy Kollek (a reputed Mason), possibly under the direction of David Rockefeller (discussed later),[1] approved a preliminary plan to divide Jerusalem. Called "Metropolitan Jerusalem," the plan would give Jerusalem a Jewish mayor and an Arab deputy, with East Jerusalem, or the Old City, being divided into three separate municipal districts, one each for Jews, Muslims, and Christians. Also in September 1993, Israel's Foreign Ministry reportedly received a message from the Israeli Embassy in Rome stating, "According to the Peres plan, <u>the Old City will be under the control of the Holy See</u>. This will permit

---

1. Nelson Rockefeller had ties to the Nazis during and after World War II (Chamish, *Traitors and Carpetbaggers in the Promised Land*, p. 97).

Israel to strengthen ties to the Catholic world" (see below). In October 1993, Peres, presumably affirming the Metropolitan Jerusalem plan, sent a letter to Norway's foreign minister "committing Israel to respect PLO governing institutions in Jerusalem." If carried out, the plan, which is contrary to every public statement made by the Rabin government concerning Jerusalem's future, would lead to a Palestinian state with Jerusalem as its capital. Vying for a somewhat different scenario, Beilin authored or authorized a policy paper titled, "The Illegitimacy of Israeli Sovereignty Over Jerusalem." The paper calls for the division of Jerusalem into districts with U.N.-controlled border posts, essentially retaining West Jerusalem, or the modern additions to the Old City, for Israel, while giving East Jerusalem entirely to the "arabs." Travel between the two halves of the city would be restricted. As an active Mason, King Hussein would prefer to have an international council comprised of prominent Muslim, Christian, and Jewish religious leaders oversee the Temple Mount area.

Recall that in October 1993, Prince Charles, speaking before a distinguished hand-picked audience including some of the world's most prominent Muslim clerics, remarked, "In the post-Cold War world of the 1990s, the prospects for peace should be greater than at any time in this century. In the Middle East, the remarkable and encouraging events of recent weeks [with the signing of the Oslo peace accord] have created new hope for an end to an issue which has divided the world and been so dramatic a source of violence and hatred. But the dangers have not disappeared."[1]

Like the Clinton administration before it, the Rabin government had become willing to cover-up atrocities to keep the peace process alive. On April 23, 1994, Christopher met Jordan's King Hussein in London. The purpose of their meeting was to address *Hussein's* recent sponsorship of Palestinian terrorist bombings in Israel that had resulted in the deaths of over a dozen Israelis, mostly children. With Hussein back on board, Jordan's responsibility for the

---

1. See Prince Charles' speeches concerning Islam and the West in Chapter 10's section titled, "Ties to the New Age Movement, the occult, and false religions."

bombings was essentially ignored. In May 1994, Rabin and Hussein met again in London. Beilin, who has "quiet but close ties to the British," also was in London. Less than a month later, on June 2, Peres flew to London, where he caught another plane to meet Hussein at an undisclosed location. By mid-June, Hussein showed-up in Washington D.C., where he and the Clinton administration arranged a summit between Jordan and Israel in Aqaba. Chamish observes, "The role London is playing in the peace process has been decidedly downplayed."

The Vatican connection. The Vatican, having involved itself in the Mideast peace process since at least the start of the Madrid talks in October 1991, made its own agreements with Peres through Beilin, not wanting its property in Jerusalem to come under PLO control. In exchange for a mere "recognition accord" with Israel, Beilin agreed to give the Vatican the right to build on Mount Zion in Jerusalem, and to make all the Vatican's properties throughout Israel tax-exempt. Moreover, according to Shmuel Meir, the Deputy Mayor of Jerusalem, "properties promised to the Vatican in Jerusalem would be granted extraterritorial status." Besides its political motivations to establish formal diplomatic ties with Israel, the Vatican also has a religious motivation—not that it accepts Israel's God-given right to the scripturally delineated Land of Israel or that God still has a unique purpose for Israel as a nation. What is that motivation? As reported in July 1992, Pope John Paul II has a "dream of visiting the Holy Land to pray there together with Muslims and Jews for Middle East peace."[1] According to the pope, "Rigorous respect for the right to religious freedom is a major source and foundation of peaceful coexistence"—as if to say that faith in The God of Israel has little or no relevance.[2]

In "September 1993, Peres signed a secret deal with the Pope promising the Vatican hegemony over Jerusalem's Old City by the year 2000." In May 1994, Peres sent a letter to Pope John Paul II by the hand of Mark

---

1. Reuter, "Vatican and Israel vow to forge ties," *Rocky Mountain News,* 30 July 1992, p. 37.
2. Alan Cowell, The New York Times, "Sudan's Christians suffer like Jesus, pope says," *The Denver Post,* 11 Feb. 1993, p. 10A.

Halter, a close French friend. As Halter tells the story, "Peres offered to hand over sovereignty of Jerusalem's Old City to the Vatican.... The city will stay the capital of Israel but will be administered by the Vatican. The city will have an Israeli mayor and a Palestinian mayor, both under orders from the Holy See. The program was originally submitted to the Vatican by Peres two years ago, just before the Oslo talks began." According to Chamish, "Just before the signing of the [Oslo I] Declaration of Principles, Arafat agreed not to oppose the plan.... The Peres plan calls for the extraterritoriality of the Old City and the airport at Atarot, which will become an international meeting center.... Further details of the plan call for Jerusalem to become the second Vatican of the world, with all three major religions having some degree of autonomy but under the authority of the Vatican. A Palestinian state will emerge in confederation with Jordan with its religious capital being Jerusalem.... The IDF is actively changing its defense positions around the capital, literally returning to the 1948 lines.... Border patrol units are presently repositioning themselves in a circle around Jerusalem whose circumference is formed by the towns of Tzur Hadassah, Bet Guvrin, and Kibbutz Maale Khamisha, or the pre-1967 deployment." Peres agreed to give the Al Aqsa mosque "independence" from Israel, and to share sovereignty over Jerusalem with the PLO. Moreover, he accepted Arafat's demand that a "right of return" to "all currently disputed areas" be extended to the millions of Palestinians living outside Israel. Upset with the Peres' promises to the Vatican, the Russian Orthodox Church also made demands. In May 1995, Beilin responded by giving the Russian church control of disputed land in the midst of West Jerusalem. Chamish also notes a Gentile writer who was deported from Israel for having "described a Vatican-German plot to take over the Temple Mount in the Old City."

Arafat, criminal kingpin for the elite. Why would the elite choose to deal with Arafat? Could it have something to do with the fact that he is reputed to be "one of the world's leading Mafia godfathers who has personally amassed $12 billion selling arms and drugs," having "turned the autonomous regions into an international center for illegal trafficking of arms and narcotics"? Perhaps it also has to do with the fact that the British government created the earlier Supreme Moslem Council, from which the PLO and now the Palestinian Authority (PA) evolved. In 1921, in violation of the 1917 Balfour Declaration, "the British chose to create a Supreme Moslem Council to exercise a variety of powers over the Arab population of Palestine. As the grand judge or mufti of this precursor to the PA, they appointed Amin el-Husseini, whom historian Paul Johnson describes as 'a dedicated killer who devoted his entire adult life to race murder.' The mufti's greatest legacy, however, was not a great body count of Jewish settlers, nor even the fact that he organized a 'Moslem-SS legion' that fought on Hitler's side. Rather, it was, in Johnson's words, 'the systematic destruction of Arab moderates.... By the end of the 1930s Arab moderate opinion had ceased to exist.'"[1]

Following a June 1994 meeting between Peres and Kissinger in New York, Israel's Foreign Ministry turned down an offer from Bolivia to move its embassy to Jerusalem, stating, "Within two years the issue of Jerusalem will be settled and all the embassies will move there anyway." (Kissinger is a prominent Committee of 300 member, as well as the head of the U.S. CFR.)

"Peace" with Jordan. In July 1994, Netanyahu too traveled to London, where he was "persuaded" to support the upcoming Jordanian treaty despite the severe sacrifices of fresh water and land—some 300 square kilometers of the Negev Desert—that it would require from Israel. Two weeks before the completion of a formal peace treaty with Jordan, and three weeks before it was signed, Netanyahu again met King Hussein in London. Netanyahu subsequently refused to lead a Likud debate on the treaty, apparently accepting even "its secret clauses on Jerusalem." Chamish elaborates, "As even the Grand Master of Israel's

---

1. Angelo Codevilla, "Monsters vs. moderates," *The Jerusalem Post,* Int. Ed., 2 Aug. 1997, p. 13.

Grand Lodge subtly suggested, the treaty between Jordan and Israel was organized by the Masons."

On October 17, 1994, the very day he initialed the treaty, Rabin flew to London to meet with Prime Minister John Major. Just over a week later, on October 26, with no national debate (but with strong Knesset approval), Rabin signed the treaty, in which Israel would cede "at least 100 million cubic meters of water from the Sea of Galilee, some 10 percent of its annual supply, to Jordan in perpetuity."[1] As Clinton applauded, Rabin and King Hussein sealed the treaty with a *masonic* handshake. Netanyahu subsequently visited Amman, and then held "at least two more secret meetings with the Jordanian leadership in London." Also in November 1994, Kollek received David Rockefeller in Jerusalem on a rare visit. Kollek then traveled to Cairo, where he presented the semi-secret Jerusalem Forum's Metropolitan Jerusalem plan to Egypt's Foreign Minister, Omar Moussa, seeking his government's approval.[2] (David Rockefeller also is a prominent Committee of 300 member, and is viewed as the "guardian" of the U.S. CFR.)

1. On October 26, 1994, Prime Ministers Rabin and Abdul Salam Majali signed the peace treaty with Jordan (which they had previously initialed on October 17), with Clinton signing as a witness, while King Hussein, Crown Prince Hassan, Peres, and President Ezer Weizman observed. Never missing an opportunity for ecumenism, before "an estimated 5,000 guests, including close to a dozen foreign ministers and Arab officials from North Africa and the Persian Gulf," Clinton remarked, "Here in this region, which is the home of not only both your faiths, but mine, I say: 'Blessed are the peacemakers, for they will inherit the earth.'" In the same vein, verses were recited from the Koran and the Torah. The ceremony was attended by "dignitaries from 15 countries, including the US, Jordan, Egypt, Russia,...Europe, Japan, and China," with a total of "about 7,000 people" expected in "what one Israeli official [then] called the largest ceremony of the highest rank to ever to take place in the Middle East" (Alon Pinkas, "Israel, Jordan sign treaty. Peace sealed in gala Arava ceremony," *The Jerusalem Post*, daily, 27 Oct. 1994, p. 1; David Makovsky, "Israel, Jordan sign peace treaty today," *The Jerusalem Post*, daily, 26 Oct. 1994, p. 1; "Bleachers up for peace treaty signing," *The Jerusalem Post*, daily, 23 Oct. 1994, p. 2; "Israel, Jordan initial peace treaty," *The Jerusalem Post*, daily, 18 Oct. 1994, p. 1; accession nos. 940003589, 940003655, 940003895, and 940004168, on the *Jerusalem Post* CD-ROM). Subsequently, on November 8, Weizman also signed the treaty (Haim Shapiro and Itim, "Hussein to make 1st visit after tomorrow's border ceremony," *The Jerusalem Post*, daily, 9 Nov. 1994, p. 1; "Ties with Oman possibly in January," *The Jerusalem Post*, daily, 9 Nov. 1994, p. 2; accession nos. 940002813 and 940002823 on the *Jerusalem Post* CD-ROM). For the text of the Israeli-Jordanian peace treaty, see "Text of peace treaty between Jordan and Israel," *The Jerusalem Post*, daily, 26 Oct. 1994, page 4 (accession no. 940003697 on the *Jerusalem Post* CD-ROM).
2. Chamish, *Traitors and Carpetbaggers in the Promised Land*, pp. 11, 24-28, 30-32, 34, 38-39, 40-42, 46-48, 50, 58-59, 65-66, 72, 75-79, 86, 93-95, 97, 103-107, 111-112, 115, 124, 146-149, 166-167, 169-170, 179-180.

Rivalry between Rabin and Peres. Before Rabin's death, he and Peres were frequent rivals; neither one was particularly hesitant to stab the other in the back. According to the June 1992 coalition agreement, Peres was not to involve himself in the ongoing "Madrid" peace talks. Of course, inasmuch as those talks actually derived from the earlier London Agreement, Peres could not refrain. Peres, due to his background in the Socialist International and his close relationship with Prince Charles, favored a combination of French and English channels in the Oslo process. Rabin, on the other hand, generally favored American channels, even though they were themselves finally subservient to the English. Talks between the PLO and the Israeli government were held "in a number of European capitals, including London and Paris." At Peres' instigation, for example, regional peace talks were held on September 10, 1992, in Paris. Using the French Foreign Office, Peres persuaded Rabin to hypothetically offer to return the Golan Heights to Syria in exchange for certain security arrangements and a formal peace agreement; the Rabin government then temporarily embarked on a "Syria first" policy. In November 1992, meetings in London, between Herschfeld and Abu Allah, resulted in an agreement for French experts to help the PLO establish its own police force in a future autonomy arrangement with Israel. Later, Rabin, using Mordechai Nesiyahu, the programming director of the Labor Party's publishing house, tried to steal some of Peres' thunder by taking personal credit for the London-based meetings (even though Pundak also claims that Peres was not initially aware of them). Rabin broke his campaign promises not to negotiate on to Golan nor with the PLO. On November 12, 1993, following the signing of Oslo I, Peres attempted to revive the Syria-first approach through the French Juppe. However, Rabin and the U.S. Administration conspired to thwart Peres, rejecting French interference; at the same time, in opposition to both Rabin and Ariel Sharon, Clinton ordered the State Department to find a way to revive the Syria-first approach under U.S. auspices. In May 1994, Peres implored French

President Francois Mitterand, a Committee of 300 member, to open Syrian channels for him, asserting that the Clinton administration was losing interest. Peres even sought the intervention of "international businessmen." In the meantime, Beilin was spearheading Israeli talks with the U.S. State Department aimed at "the immediate breakup of settlements in the Golan and the territories, to be followed by the handing over of the emptied lands to the Syrians and Palestinians."

Tossing Israel to the wolves. Subsequently, in 1994, as the Clinton administration had earlier done for Arafat in the WTO bombing and as the Rabin government had done for Jordan's King Hussein in a terrorist spree, the Rabin government chose to overlook Syria's bombing in Buenos Aires which killed over one-hundred people (ninety-five of them Israelites), "just as it did twenty-eight months previously when a blast at the Israeli Embassy left twenty-nine dead." Assad wished to express his disapproval of the separate negotiations between Israel and Jordan, whereas Rabin and Peres, desiring "peace" at any price—even with Syria—would not admit the ugly truth. Syria was again pardoned when twenty-three people died following the October 1994 Tel Aviv bus bombing. This particular bombing was Syria's response to a proposal Peres made in Paris for a confederation between Israel and Jordan that would effectively merge the two countries.

Clinton, of course, also would not give up. In November 1994, following the signing of the Israel-Jordan peace treaty, Clinton flew from Israel to Syria, where he promptly threw Israel's future security to the wind in an attempt to bribe Assad. Clintion, while keeping silent concerning Syria's active preparation of a massive chemical weapons capability for use against Israel, promised Assad that 1) Israel would completely withdraw from the Golan Heights, 2) his administration, with Rabin's approval, would provide Syria with the very best weapons, including loaded F-16s, 3) Israel would significantly downsize its ground forces (something Rabin had told the Knesset before Clinton's visit), and **4)** the U.S. and Israel would let Syria completely control Lebanon, without interference.[1] This is the same Clinton whose administration opposes recognition of Jerusalem as Israel's capital, instructed its ambassador to Israel to boycott the Jerusalem 3000 celebrations, and worked with Rabin and Peres to whitewash the PLO's failure to amend its covenant calling for Israel's destruction. In exchange for "minimal security arrangements on the Golan Heights and normalization of relations with Israel," the Rabin government was prepared to "give Syria the whole Golan, control of Israel's water sources on the Heights and part of the Kinneret, and...withdrawal...from Lebanon."[2]

To further illustrate the depths of treachery of Israel's government under Rabin and Peres, we should note that the Oslo I accord was apparently accompanied by some particularly disturbing covert side agreements. Authored by Beilin, the "Palestine Interim Self-Government Agreement" or PISGA, for example, actually calls for the terrorist-murder of local Israeli settlement leaders, even as settlers are being disarmed by the Israeli government, in an effort to instill panic among residents. These same residents were to be portrayed as religious fanatics in the press to dehumanize and delegitimize them in the eyes of the Israeli public, with the goal being to break their will to remain in the territories which are to be handed over to the PLO. According to Chamish, "The main points are that the ultimate aims of the peace process are to roll back Israel's territory to the 1949 borders; to create a Palestinian "entity" which, after an interim period, will be granted statehood; to accede to this state exclusive rights to underground water resources geologically shared by both states [even though these resources currently supply 30 percent of Israel's water needs]; and to permit the right of return for any Palestinian to the new nation. The PISGA purportedly describes a plan to disarm settlers and force them to evacuate the West Bank and Gaza Strip, after which no Jews will be permitted to reside in the areas....

1. Chamish, *Traitors and Carpetbaggers in the Promised Land,* pp. 14, 17, 32, 40-41, 43-44, 58-60, 75, 80, 84-86, 101-102, 106-107, 109-110.
2. "Change policy on Syria," *The Jerusalem Post,* Int. Ed., 15 June 1996, p. 10.

Stage one calls for the disarming of the settlers.... Once the settlers become less able to defend themselves, [the] army presence on the roads leading to their homes will be greatly diminished, leading to heavy terrorist casualties.... This will cause the more passive residents to panic, sell their homes, and flee.... Beilin believes that Jewish retaliatory actions will be stopped cold if the perpetrators are sent to the Palestinian entity for trial and possible execution.... Many settlers and their supporters believe they are the victims of a planned program of executions. Some contend that their government was behind an initiative to destroy the settler movement.... [Knesset member] Ron Nachman...claims to have documents proving that violent attacks have increased substantially as a result of the troop reduction [ordered by General Ilan Biran] and that the IDF have stopped reporting the incidents."

Subjugating Israel to the United Nations and the New World Order. Unfortunately, the above example just scratches the surface of the Rabin government's contempt for Israel and her God. As part of the Oslo process, Beilin also worked to internationalize the Israel Defense Forces (IDF) under the United Nations. According to his book *Forty Plus,* Beilin would like to make the IDF a U.N. mercenary force, to be used in multinational peacekeeping operations around the world. Under Beilin, the IDF has already participated in U.N. missions in Somalia, Rwanda, Zanzibar, and Haiti. Indeed, the day before Kissinger awarded the UNESCO Peace Prize to Rabin and Peres, Beilin and U.N. Secretary-General Boutros-Boutros Ghali "reached a rather surprising preliminary agreement to move both the offices of the United Nations Relief Works Agency (UNRWA) and UNESCO from Europe to the Gaza Strip." On July 15, 1996, a decision was made to move the UNRWA headquarters to Gaza from Vienna. Speaking of Peres' "New Middle East," Chamish notes, "Peres has been the driving force behind a two-part plan to create a untied Middle East defense committee which will then join the Security Committee of the European Union." According to Pundak,

Beilin too believes "that national borders are the cause of all conflicts and doesn't view Israel's boundaries as sacred." Even Israel's economy is being manipulated to conform to "World Bank practices."[1] Perhaps we should not be all that surprised. After all, Peres and Beilin appear to be working toward fulfillment of David *ben* Gurion's twisted 1962 predictions that "countries will become united in a world alliance, at whose disposal will be an international police force. All armies will be abolished, and there will be no more wars. In Jerusalem, the United Nations will build a shrine to the Prophets to serve the federated union on all continents, as prophesied by Isaiah." (David *ben* Gurion was a Committee of 300 member.)[2]

A conspiracy of death. Chamish points to a number of "mysterious demises," including Israel's Deputy Defense Minister Motta Gur, who was, among other things, the "last and only link" of the settlers to the Rabin government, as well as Jorgan Holst, Norway's former foreign minister and its primary Oslo arbitrator, whose death "is commonly blamed on knowing too much about what was agreed to at Oslo." Ultimately, Rabin himself was assassinated in a conspiracy involving not just the Israeli General Security Service, or *Shabak,* but the very highest levels of the Israeli government, which directed the Shamgar Commission's *sham* conclusions. According to Chamish, those conclusions "merely reinforced the manufactured media image in the Israeli public's mind that radical Jewish extremism was responsible for the murder. The cover-up was as insidious as the crime."

Rabin's assassination took place at a rally financed and organized by Peres' confidant Jean Friedman, a French media magnate. From Rabin's standpoint, as Chamish paints it, "The Theme of the gathering on the fateful night was, 'No to Violence.' [Undercover Shabak agent Yigal] Amir was to have shot Rabin with blanks [(which he actually did)], Rabin was to have miraculously escaped an

1. Chamish, *Traitors and Carpetbaggers in the Promised Land,* pp. 49-54, 62, 83-84, 88-89, 100, 105, 109, 111, 113, 181.
2. For more information, see the discussion on the Committee of 300 in Chapter 7's section titled, "The Garter."

assassination attempt [(which he did not]), and then climbed back on the stage with a stirring speech written by his close aide, Eitan Haber. The public would react with revulsion against the attempted assassination by an extremist right-winger, and the government could justify a crackdown against opponents of the peace process." (Doesn't this sound just a bit like the Clinton administration's machinations at Waco, with the Weaver family, and in Oklahoma?) Interestingly, just as the more recent ambulance carrying the severely injured Princess Diana to a French hospital took an inordinate and inexplicable amount of time to reach its destination, hinting at foul play, Rabin's *700-meter* trip to an Israeli hospital, instead of taking just a minute, took "over eight minutes to complete." Menachem Damti, while driving Rabin to the hospital, even took time out to pick up Pinchas Terem, a policeman. Moreover, the hospital, which received *no* prior notification, was "totally unprepared to treat Rabin." The prime minister was apparently bludgeoned in the forehead and then executed with real bullets, at point-blank range (much closer than the distance from which Amir fired), during the grossly delayed trip to Ichilov Hospital inside his car. A policeman assigned to protect Rabin during the gathering, Yoav Kuriel, who had "yelled the bullets are blanks," was found similarly dead within a week, and left without his internal organs. (This, of course, sounds like a masonic murder.) Although Peres', Haber's, and Terem's direct involvement in the assassination is uncertain, whereas Damti's and Yoram Rubin's (see below) is not, it seems clear that both Peres and Haber, like Damti and Rubin, subsequently participated in a wide-ranging cover-up of the true circumstances behind Rabin's murder. As Chamish elaborates, "Three seconds before Rabin entered his car, the back passenger door (Rabin entered the car through the rear driver's side, followed by Rubin) closes. Someone was already in the car waiting for Rabin and as the prime minister entered, grabbed the car door and shut it from the inside.... None of the security or police personnel [who witnessed the event] detected any sign that Rabin was hurt, a quite inexplicable fact when one considers that he was not merely hurt but supposedly shot in the lung and spleen by two hollowpoint 9mm bullets.... The *Maariv* article reported that the assassination film shot by Ronni Kempler pointed out that three seconds before Rabin entered his car, the opposite side passenger door is slammed shut.... What many people find haunting is Shimon Peres' behavior on the film. After greeting the crowd, he walks to Rabin's car with four Shabak agents, stops, looks inside and points to Amir seated nine feet away. At this point there is a cut in the film and we now see Peres conversing with Rabin's driver, Menachem Damti. Peres [then] enters his car and Rabin descends the steps. The camera captures the [Shabak] agents at Rabin's rear stopping and allowing Amir a clear shot at Rabin.... Running the murder frame by frame, Rabin has supposedly taken a hollowpoint 9mm bullet in his lung, yet he doesn't wince or flinch. He is not even pushed forward by the impact, nor does his suit show signs of tearing. Instead, he continues walking forward and [quickly] turns his head behind him in the direction of the noise.... Rubin lied [repeatedly]. The police [report] proved conclusively that Rabin was shot point-blank. Amir never shot point-blank at Rabin."

Peres, in all likelihood, knows who really shot Rabin, and Damti and Rubin almost certainly know. Chamish concludes, "Rabin was unhurt by Amir's blank bullets and was shot inside the car. Rubin took a harmless arm wound [from a different weapon] to cover his role in the event and Damti picked up a policeman as a witness in case of future disbelief.... The event captured on the film that is the centerpiece of doubt is the issue of the door of Rabin's vehicle.... To almost everyone who watches that door close, it is certain that someone, likely the murderer, was waiting in the Cadillac for Rabin. This is in direct contradiction to the Shamgar Commission's conclusion that Rabin entered an empty car followed by his bodyguard, Yoram Rubin, and his driver, Menachem Damti."

That is not all. There may also be a Netanyahu connection. In 1994, around the same time that he was secretly negotiating with Hussein in London, Netanyahu was simultaneously pursing negotiations with Syria's Assad. Subsequently, Assad himself "publicly stated that he can get a better deal from Netanyahu than Rabin."[1] By the time of Rabin's assassination, both he and Peres had virtually lost credibility with the Israeli public; Rabin was loudly booed nearly everywhere he appeared in public. According to Itamar Rabinovich, Assad's disappointing response toward Peres' willingness to progress after Rabin's assassination was a major factor in Peres' decision to hold national elections.[2] We must ask, therefore, "Did the Mideast power brokers decide to reshuffle the Israeli government in an effort to sustain the Oslo peace process?" One must wonder.

The real international power brokers. While Chamish offers a tremendous amount of interesting information concerning the Oslo peace process, he has somehow managed to largely miss its higher-level Committee of 300 and RIIA connections, which ultimately point to the British monarchy. Chamish has instead focused on the U.S. and Israeli CFRs, as well as to a degree on the Trilateral Commission, which Brzezinski, Carter's former National Security Advisor, now directs.

Although he briefly notices Prince Charles, perhaps Chamish comes closest to recognizing the true reach of the peace-process conspiracy when he looks to the Kissinger machinations. In speaking of the owner of the *Jerusalem Post,* Conrad Black, who is also the CEO of the Hollinger Corporation, Chamish points out that the Hollinger Corporation is "one of the most prominent clients of Kissinger Associates, the high-powered consulting firm established by the former secretary of state." That Black is "a longstanding member of two of the world's leading 'globalist' organizations, the Council on Foreign Relations and the Trilateral Commission" is not lost on Chamish. Nevertheless, he fails to observe that like Bush and possibly Ezer

1. Chamish, *Traitors and Carpetbaggers in the Promised Land,* pp. 72, 96, 118-120. 124, 126, 132-141. For detailed information on Rabin's assassination, see ibid., pp. 125-141.
2. Jay Bushinsky, "Rabin murder dashed peace with Syria," *The Jerusalem Post,* Int. Ed., 5 July 1997, p. 32.

Weizman, Kissinger is a Committee of 300 member, and as such he is on the British monarchy's leash. Chamish continues, "Kissinger set the precedent for diplomatic pressure on Israel to secede lands won in war and is assumed to have had a decisive influence on Prime Minister Yitzhak Rabin's original accession to power. Last month it was Kissinger who presented Rabin and Foreign Minister Peres with the UNESCO Peace Prize in Paris.... Much has been written about Rabin's ties to Kissinger, the State Department, and ultimately the [U.S.] Council on Foreign Relations. While Rabin was ambassador to Washington from 1968-72, he fell under Kissinger's spell. Just prior to the outbreak of the Yom Kippur War, Rabin wrote a highly influential article declaring that war in the near future was out of the question. His words effectively created a feeling of apathy within military circles. During the early days of the Yom Kippur War in 1973, Dr. Kissinger withheld arms from Israel for nine days [until Israel's situation was desperate]. According to numerous Arab sources, one of the conditions for rearmament [in an American arms airlift] was that after the war Golda Meir resign as prime minister in favor of Rabin.... [After the war, Meir appointed Rabin minister of labor and...backed his candidacy for party leadership.] Rabin began and remained a Kissinger plant in the Israeli government." Chamish also shows that Kissinger, Rabin, King Hussein, and Assad conspired together to ignite and manipulate the 1974 Lebanese Civil War. Chamish points out that Edgar Bronfman, a Kissinger "protégé" and member of the U.S. CFR, used his influence to help Rabin get elected in 1992. Rabin met Kissinger at least three times before his assassination in 1995. Kissinger also exercises significant influence over Peres, who, in June 1994, "took a 5000-mile detour" to meet Kissinger in New York for a full six hours. According to an Israeli radio journalist, Yehoshua Meiri, Rabin had accepted a Kissinger plan for a New Middle East, to which Peres subsequently paid lip service. From Chamish's perspective, "Kissinger has an enormous and unexplainable influence on Israeli foreign policy." Maybe it isn't really so unexplainable.

Bush too exercised power over Rabin. In fact, according to Rabin himself, Bush forced him to allow for the possibility of a Golan Heights withdrawal. Chamish states, "Bush and his State Department had been responsible for putting Rabin in power and now he was calling in his chips. He wanted Israel out of the Golan Heights and the Administered Territories, and quickly. Rabin was given an ultimatum to prepare the Israeli public for a 'painful' Golan withdrawal in exchange for peace with Syria, and was ordered to start talking to the PLO. This was the true beginning of the Oslo Accords." (Chamish seems perpetually confused on the "true beginning" of the Oslo process, which, as the author has clearly shown, was much earlier.)

Peres, by the time of Rabin's funeral, was already being forced to toe the line. He was compelled by Clinton, Bush, and Christopher to advance Ehud Barak, "the most incompetent chief-of-staff in IDF history," whom Rabin under the direction of Christopher had been grooming to be his successor, to the position of Foreign Minister. At Rabin's behest, Barak had conducted secret negotiations with Syria, met Bronfman, and spent time with Kissinger. Peres was used, in other words, to "maintain the influence of the [U.S.] Council on Foreign Relations on Israeli diplomacy."[1]

The phased "peace and security" structure of the Oslo process. Prince Charles' likely pivotal behind-the-scenes contribution to the gestation of the Oslo peace process—through various Committee of 300 members, the RIIA and its U.S. and Israeli CFRs, as well as Mishcon, Hussein, and Peres—is significant. According to no less an authority than Peres himself, the Oslo negotiations were divided from the very start into *three phases* (I, II, and III) and *two stages*—security negotiations and peace negotiations (cf. 1 Th 5:3). The first stage, which centered upon *security* negotiations, was to span the first two of the three phases (i.e., the Oslo I and II accords). These two

---

1. Chamish, *Traitors and Carpetbaggers in the Promised Land,* pp. 87-88, 97-98, 112, 121-123, 142-146, 151, 154, 168. Chamish, "Peres' Inexplicable Cabinet Appointments," *Inside Israel,* Vol. IV, Issue 1, p. 4.

phases, now completed, led to apostate Israel's October 1995 Oslo II accord (an actual treaty) with the Palestinians (see below), and her October 26, 1994, intermediate peace treaty with Jordan, both of which Rabin signed as plausibly prophesied in the original Hebrew text of Daniel 9:27. The second stage, which is to center on *peace* negotiations and is to lead to the final, all-encompassing accord, or Oslo III, began shortly before Rabin's death. Oslo III, as Peres has envisioned it, is to include the formation of a regional security system with the possibility of external enforcement; for example, participating Mideast countries would routinely receive superpower spy satellite data concerning the region.[1] Briefly summarizing Peres' agenda while hinting at some of the problems with it, the Jerusalem Post commented, "In this kind of neighborhood, it is an exercise in futility to dream of Israel as a member of the Arab League, a participant in a Middle Eastern NATO-like alliance with Arab armies, a catalyst for a regional Marshall Plan financed by the G-7 industrial nations, and a partner in a Benelux-like union consisting of Israel, Jordan and a Palestinian entity.... But these are precisely the suggestions Peres has made in recent years.... Yasser Arafat still calls for jihad.... Concomitantly, he assures Arab audiences that the Oslo agreement is but a first step in the PLO's 'phased plan' of 1974, a blueprint for Israel's destruction in stages.... And the Palestinian army, still euphemistically called 'police,' has grown to such an extent that it must be taken into account as a serious, well-equipped, and well-trained fighting force numbering well over 35,000 troops."[2]

In fact, during the Oslo I and II security negotiations, the Clinton administration advocated placing U.S. forces and armor on the Golan Heights—a proposal repeatedly rejected by Rabin and Peres. When Peres subsequently sought a defense treaty with the United States, the Clinton administration called the request "premature." Peres' seeming desperation and mistrust of the United States is evidenced by the other parties he invited to place troops on

1. Shimon Peres, *The New Middle East* (New York: Henry Holt and Company, Inc., 1993).
2. "Wanted: Realism," *The Jerusalem Post,* Int. Ed., 8 June 1996, p. 10.

the Golan. Chamish comments, "In an odd and unpleasant twist of history, Shimon Peres actually invited German chancellor Helmut Kohl to place his country's soldiers on the Heights. In the same week as the Peres request to Kohl, Japan announced that it was considering putting its troops on the Golan. Peres' request to Kohl was part of a very strange deal with Germany. In exchange for Israel recruiting the American Jewish Congress to lobby for Germany's [permanent] inclusion in the U.N. Security Council, Germany agreed to push Israel as an associate member of the European Community.... Peres told the German media during an August [1994] visit to Bonn that Israel would support German entry into the Security Council.... Both France and Britain dropped previous objections to Israel being a partner in the European Community's research and development programs." In a meeting between Noel Dempsey, Ireland's deputy minister, and Beilin, Peres' deputy, "discussions purportedly concentrated on Ireland's participation in the as of yet unofficial U.N. force for 'keeping peace' in the Middle East."[1] Since Rabin's assassination and Peres' election-loss, Israel's new Prime Minister, Benjamin Netanyahu, all the more wary of Israel's security, has placed even greater emphasis on the need to find a suitable international guarantor. For the moment at least, the United States is not it. Currently, about "1000 peacekeepers from Austria, Canada, Japan and Poland are based on the Golan Heights."[2] Unlike the ever-scheming Arafat,[3] Netanyahu has rejected even a strategically minor offer of "an international military force, including U.S. troops, in Hebron."[4]

Is the Church already in Daniel's seventieth "week"?
With all this in mind, can we escape the conclusion that Oslo III, if and when it is completed and put into effect, will be the covenant spoken of in Daniel 9:27, a covenant unlike any other in Israel's long history? Or, if Oslo III fails

1. Chamish, *Traitors and Carpetbaggers in the Promised Land*, pp. 91, 105.
2. "Austria peacekeeper slain on Golan patrol," *The Denver Post,* 31 May 1997, p. 11A.
3. Barbara Slavin, "King Hussein's visit makes statement," *USA Today,* 16 Oct. 1996, p. 12A.
4. Rebecca Trounson, Los Angeles Times, "A dramatic return to West Bank," *The Denver Post,* 16 Oct. 1996, p. 13A.

to materialize, will we be forced to conclude that Oslo II, Rabin's final legacy of apostasy, is really it? Recall that the theme of "peace and security" is to be central to the covenant. Having asked these last questions, however, the author must point out that there are those who believe that either Oslo I or Oslo II is the prophesied covenant, and that the Church is therefore *already* in the seven-year Tribulation Period (see below). Some are even proclaiming it ardently.

Based upon the author's comprehensive biblical chronology in *Messiah, History, and the Tribulation Period,* not only will the *completion* of the seven-year Tribulation Period coincide with the end of the scriptural year 6000, but we can *possibly* expect the start of the Tribulation Period to occur either *around* September 2 of 1995 (if Jesus' crucifixion took place on April 25 of A.D. 31), in which case we would now be in it, or *around* August 1 of 1998 (if the crucifixion was on March 24 of A.D. 34).[1] As it turns out, Oslo II was initialed on September 24, 1995, immediately before the start of Rosh Hashana, and then signed on September 28 at Washington D.C.'s White House. In other words, Oslo II is, and Oslo III would be, well within the optimum chronological boundaries for the covenant. Oslo I, on the other hand, not only seems premature according to the above chronology, but we may now state that it is a scriptural impossiblity (see below).

The vote for Oslo I. Those who favor *Oslo I* note that it was not only the first agreement signed by Rabin—when in fact it was Peres, not Rabin, who signed it—but that its signing in Washington D.C., on September 13, 1993, was staged in the presence of the largest number of White House guests ever—about 3,000 foreign dignitaries and heads of state—as well as before a worldwide television audience. These "many" guests were all present to lend their support to, or "confirm," the accord. Additionally, in

1. Because specific months and days are in most instances not recorded with periods of years in the scriptures, the author's biblical chronology may have a maximum error of up to seventeen years, although one has to be *extreme* with the possibilities to obtain this. The author has attempted to mitigate against this error through careful harmonization of biblical events. Nevertheless, one-hundred percent accuracy may not be humanly possible. Therefore, the author's specified dates for the possible start of the Tribulation Period are at best close approximations, and at worst off by as much as seventeen years.

"September 1993, Peres signed a secret deal with the Pope promising the Vatican hegemony over Jerusalem's Old City by the year 2000."[1] This promise encompasses a seven-year period—1993 to the end of 1999.

These events are thought to spiritually match John's description of the opening of the Apocalypse's first seal, when he states that a rider of a white horse, who carries a bow, shall receive a *stephanos,* or crown of victory, and go forth conquering and to conquer (see Rev 6:1-2). Although the particular application is incorrect, we could surmise that white is the symbol of peace, a bow represents the ability to shoot arrows (or missiles) for defensive or offensive purposes, and a *stephanos* indicates a victory in some form of battle or competition, which Oslo I adherents might apply to the 1994 Nobel Peace Prize awarded jointly to Rabin and his partners in infamy. Fulfillment of the Apocalypse's second seal is less clear following this scenario, and will not, therefore, be addressed (see Rev 6:3-4). Regarding the *third seal,* they point out that from September 1995 to September 1996, various grain harvests failed worldwide, and that as a result, the world is now facing massive famines and starvation in the near future (cf. Rev 6:5-6). Finally, regarding the *fourth seal,* Oslo I adherents note that toward the end of September 1996, at the start of the fourth year since Oslo I was signed, the peace process between Israel and the Palestinians collapsed into great violence and bloodshed—the worst open warfare, in fact, since the 1967 Six Day War. Moreover, since these events occurred, there has been continual talk in the Mideast of a possible total collapse of the Oslo peace process leading to an all-out Arab-Israeli conflict (cf. Rev 6:7-8). Indeed, Syria and Israel appear to be poised for war over the Golan Heights, and indications are that Egypt and Jordan are about ready to abandon their peace treaties with Israel. Others, such as Marvin Byers, reported that on March 13, 1997, the Israeli government banned the Temple Faithful, who hope to one day rebuild the Temple, from offering morning and evening *prayers* on the Temple Mount

---

1. "Peres's First Acts," *Inside Israel,* Vol. IV, Issue 1, January-February 1996, p. 5. For a reprint of this article, see Chamish, *Traitors and Carpetbaggers in the Promised Land,* pp. 146-149.

(cf. Dan 9:27).

The vote for Oslo II. Those who prefer *Oslo II,* on the other hand, observe that it was the final and most signifi- cant treaty or agreement to be signed by Rabin (also at a White House ceremony), and that Rabin, having been assassinated soon thereafter, will clearly not sign Oslo III. Moreover, it was Peres, not Rabin, who signed Oslo I (cf. *rabim* in Dan 9:27). Regarding the *first seal,* they would note one of two possibilities. Under the first, they would make similar points on behalf of Oslo II's signing as are made on behalf of Oslo I's. That is, they would point to Oslo II's internationally observed signing at the White House, as well as to the large number of foreign dignitaries present to confirm it at Rabin's funeral. The second possi- bility would be Netanyahu's election victory over Peres on a platform of "peace with security" (as opposed to Peres' "security with peace") combined with his efforts to ensure Israel's sovereignty over East Jerusalem and prevent the actual formation of an independent Palestinian state (cf. Rev 6:1-2). Regarding the *second seal,* they would note that at the start of the second year since Oslo II was signed (i.e., in September 1996), Arafat incited the Pales- tinians, including a number of his armed "police," to take peace from Israel. Also, they would point to Netanyahu's shaky (on and off) cancellation of further territorial conces- sions to the PA due to continued Palestinian terrorism, a cancellation that has been called the "death" of the entire Oslo peace process (cf. Rev 6:3-4). (These are fourth-seal events according to Oslo I adherents.) Consider, for exam- ple, these October 1996 statements:

> ...Peres said..."the next year is the most essential one as far as the peace process is concerned."
> If we shall lose the trust we developed in the Arab world, it will be very hard to regain it, and this is what is happening.... To lose it would be catastrophic."...
> Israel...does not have the luxury of returning to "the old Mid- dle East"...because next time "the old Middle East shall be equipped with new weapons."
> Peres, and Rabin before him, always regarded Israel as engaged in a kind of race: Could it reach peace with all its

important Arab neighbors before the further spread of Islamic fundamentalist regimes and the proliferation of nuclear weapons among them?

Netanyahu, according to Peres, has stopped running that race, but **"the other horses—war, terror, fundamentalism—they are galloping."**[1]

All this, of course, is pure speculation. It seems far more likely that only time will make clear the actual fulfillments of the first four apocalyptic seals.

According to the White House Social Office, Prince Charles is *not* known to have been a guest at the signing and corresponding international "confirmation" of either Oslo I or Oslo II. Since Rabin's funeral, however, he *is* known to have sought to strengthen the Oslo peace process (see below). Where Oslo I is concerned, and possibly Oslo II, this circumstance would require us to accept the alternate interpretation of Daniel 9:27 that allows for the AntiChrist's confirmation and ultimate enforcement of the covenant to begin sometime following the start of the Tribulation Period.

Identifying the covenant of Daniel 9:27. Let's be honest. These *are* compelling arguments. Nevertheless, in looking toward either Oslo II or III, the author would make the following points. *First,* at least in the author's opinion, there must be *clear* possible fulfillments of the Apocalypse's first three seals (Rev 6:1-6), aspects of which combine in the fourth seal (Rev 6:7-8) and lead to the Great Tribulation, or the latter-half of the seven-year Tribulation Period. Scripturally speaking, these four seals summarize the events of the first four years of the Tribulation Period. Although the author has noted possible fulfillments for the seals in the differing chronological contexts of the Oslo I and II accords, he does not view his current knowledge of them as completely satisfactory. Moreover, as stated earlier, Oslo I can be ruled out altogether (see below).

Second, certain events *must* scripturally precede or coincide with the start of the Great Tribulation. While

---

1. Barton Gellman, *The Washington Post*, "Peres reflects on a life in politics," *The Denver Post*, 27 Oct. 1996, p. 15A.

these events, which are largely midtribulational, could transpire in quick succession, they cannot happen overnight. They include **1)** the implied construction of a Holy Place and presumably a Holy of Holies, with an altar and an outer court for the Gentiles (cf. Rev 11:1-3);[1] **2)** the start of *animal* sacrifice upon this altar, so that it may subsequently be stopped (cf. Dan 9:27; Isa 1:9-21, 66:1-4); **3)** the loss of half of Jerusalem—meaning *East Jerusalem*—to the Gentiles in war, so that its Israelite population, being surrounded by armies (a second fulfillment of Luke 21:20), shall go into captivity (see Luke 21:24; cf. Mic 4:9-11, 5:3), even as West Jerusalem's population remains free (see Zech 14:1-2; cf. Zech 12:2-3*a*); **4)** the halting (cessation) of animal sacrifice at the altar (Dan 9:27); **5)** the wounding "to the death" of the AntiChrist,[2] who, being Prince Charles of Wales (e.g., Rev 13:1-2, 13:18), shall then appear to miraculously recover (Rev 13:3; cf. 2 Th 2:9-12; Rev 13:12-14); **6)** an occurrence of the abomination that causes desolation (Dan 9:27, 12:11; cf. 11:31), when **a)** *Christians* (i.e., "you") shall "see[3] the abomination of desolation"—an image erected to the AntiChrist (Rev 13:14-15)—"standing in the Holy Place" (see Matt 24:15; Mark 13:14; Luke 21:21; cf. Dan 9:27), and **b)** the AntiChrist will enter the Temple or Holy Place, proclaim his own deity (see 2 Th 2:3-4), and generally exalt himself against God;[4] and **7)** the flight of believers from Judaea, *some of whom have already been warned concerning Prince Charles,* to the mountains of the wilderness (see Matt 24:16-21; Mark 13:14-19; Luke 21:21-23; Rev 12:6, 12:14-16); **8)** the AntiChrist's meteoric rise to the

1. The Greek word translated as "Temple" in 2 Thessalonians 2:4 as well as throughout the Apocalypse, Strong's number 3485, speaks not of the entire Temple compound, but specifically of its inner Holy Place and the Holy of Holies (e.g., see Thayer, 3485, p. 422), which officiating Levitical priests alone were permitted to enter.
2. The Apocalypse is literally rendered "as *though he* had been slain to death" (13:3, Gk.) and "wound of the death of him [it]" (13:12, Gk.).
3. This Greek word, Strong's number 1492, is equivalent to the Latin word *video* (Thayer, 1492, p. 172). This may suggest the possibility of a videotaped or filmed event.
4. Tuvia Saguy, an Israeli architect from Tel Aviv, claims to have located the ancient Holy of Holies in the midst of a new mosque being constructed by the *Wakf* beneath the Temple Mount in Solomon's Stables. These stables, along with their crusader additions made by the Knights of Malta and the Temple Knights, are "a pilgrimage destination for Freemasons" (Chamish, *Traitors and Carpetbaggers in the Promised Land*, p. 187). Will we one day see Prince Charles stand in the midst of this new mosque?

top of a world government (Rev 13:3-6), which must first be constituted with ten kings or world leaders;[1] and **9)** the establishment of international control, which shall last for 42 months or 1,260 days (i.e., three-and-one-half years), over the captive half of Jerusalem (Rev 11:2-3).[2]

Finally, Oslo III was planned while Rabin was still alive, and it is to be built upon the Oslo I and II accords; without Rabin's prior involvement, it could not come about.

Since the events just outlined were not fulfilled by early 1997, and consequently the Great Tribulation has not yet commenced, Oslo I cannot be the covenant of Daniel 9:27. Likewise, *if* they remain unfulfilled by the end of March 1999, Oslo II cannot be that covenant. Under such circumstances, those who currently favor Oslo II would have to reconsider, just as those who have favored Oslo I must reconsider. The author currently *hopes* that an Oslo III agreement will materialize, but should the outlined events occur between now and early 1999, he would, of course, have to abandon that prospect. We must also recognize that should that be the case, it will thoroughly discredit the historically recent theological arguments for either a pre- or midtribulational rapture.

Oslo II, Rabin's funeral, and Prince Charles. Although the author currently "favors" Oslo III, there is more to be said on behalf of Oslo II. In September 1996, Netanyahu confirmed that in September 1994, Rabin had reached an informal understanding with Syria's Hafez Assad on conditions for a full Israeli withdrawal from the Golan Heights.[3] One year later, Rabin's corpse lay in a coffin

---

1. For more information, see Chapter 1, "The Footsteps of the AntiChrist."
2. The presented sequence for these events is based upon the systematic Harmony of Weeks in *Messiah, History, and the Tribulation Period,* in which the author demonstrates that every significant aspect of the Crucifixion Week is not only to be found in the Week of History and the Tribulation Week (among other biblical weeks), but in precisely the same sequence. That is, it shows that the crucifixion and resurrection of Jesus Christ, and that week's surrounding events, which God ordained before time began, set forth the pattern, sequence, and timing of corresponding events in the seven-millennium Week of History and the seven-year Tribulation Week (cf. Rev 19:10), with national Israel serving in a "messianic" capacity outside the Crucifixion Week. Among other things, this provides the first comprehensive and testable theological explanation for the numerous biblical parallels between national Israel and The Messiah. For more information, see *Messiah, History, and the Tribulation Period.*
3. According to Netanyahu, "Newspaper reports that the late prime minister, Yitzhak Rabin, indirectly agreed to withdraw from the Golan Heights, to the June 4, 1967, lines (if) a num-

before the largest group of Mideast leaders and dignitaries, not to mention those from outside the Middle East, ever assembled in Israel. Among those present, seated and standing along the front row before Rabin's body, were Britain's John Major and Prince Charles, the prince having attended as part of the RIIA.[1] The prince, unlike the other foreigners around him, wore a Jewish head covering.[2] Others on the front row included the French Prime Minister, Spain's King Juan Carlos (next to Prince Charles), Germany's Helmut Kohl and Roman Herzog, the United Nations' Secretary General Boutros Boutros-Ghali, Egypt's Hosni Mubarak, Jordan's King Hussein, the United States' President and Hillary Clinton, the Netherlands' Prime Minister Kim Kok and Queen Beatrix, and Peres—all of whom, except for Prince Charles, spoke in support of the Oslo I and II accords.[3] (Notice the prominence afforded *England*

ber of conditions were met by the Syrians, and that this agreement has been conveyed to the United States, are true." These "revelations" supposedly have "shocked many Israelis." Peres concurs: "I didn't see a written commitment, but it was made clear to the Syrians that Israel was willing to withdraw for full peace" (The Associated Press, "Rabin gave tacit nod to withdrawal," *The Denver Post,* 13 Sept. 1996, p. 10A). Before Rabin's assassination, Chamish reported, "According to well-informed security sources, Rabin is prepared to trade all of the Golan Heights for an agreement with Syria and throw in Israel's nuclear option to boot.... This year Syria purchased a 27-MW nuclear reactor from China [through North Korea] capable of producing its own atomic weaponry" (*Traitors and Carpetbaggers in the Promised Land,* pp. 92-93).

1. As a committed globalist, Prince Charles frequently uses the "non-political" cover of *Non-Governmental Organizations* (NGOs) recognized by the U.N., such as the Royal Institute for International Affairs, for his otherwise constitutionally questionable participation in, and occasionally outright instigation of, politically-charged events and activities around the world. On the occasion of Rabin's funeral, Prince Charles, risking exposure of the British monarchy's central involvement in the Mideast peace process, "kept a low profile and refused to be interviewed" (Batsheva Tsur, "Royalty, presidents, and premiers pay their respects," *The Jerusalem Post,* daily, 7 Nov. 1995, p. 2; accession no. 950002788 on the *Jerusalem Post* CD-ROM).

2. For a photograph, see Chamish, *Traitors and Carpetbaggers in the Promised Land,* p. 147.

3. Rabin's funeral served as the rallying occasion for one of the most high-powered international gatherings ever. Highlighting the guest list, David Makovsky and Hillel Kuttler wrote, "Representatives from at least 86 countries will be among those bidding Rabin a final farewell. Among them will be US President Bill Clinton, former presidents George Bush and Jimmy Carter, Jordan's King Hussein and Prime Minister Zid Bin Shaker, Egyptian President Hosni Mubarak, Moroccan Prime Minister Abdul Afif Filali, Russian Prime Minister Viktor Chernomyrdin, UN Secretary-General Boutros Boutros-Ghali, Prince Charles of Wales, British Prime Minister John Major, French President Jacques Chirac, German President Roman Herzog and Chancellor Helmut Kohl, and Turkish Prime Minister Tancu Ciller." ("Yitzhak Rabin to be buried today," *The Jerusalem Post,* daily, 6 Nov. 1995, p. 1; accession no. 950002831 on the *Jerusalem Post* CD-ROM). As Batsheva Tsur put it, "Royals, presidents, prime ministers past and present from almost 80 countries gathered at Beit Hanassi throughout the morning to convey their condolences.... They came in force: heads of state, accompanied by ministers

and parliamentary leaders,...and often also journalists who would cover the story which has captured the headlines worldwide.... Many of the visitors had recently been here—Queen Beatrix of the Netherlands, British Prime Minister John Major,...and others.... There were numerous visitors for the photographers to immortalize, including Britain's Prince Charles.... There were also heads of international organizations, such as UN Secretary-General Boutros Boutros-Ghali and the head of the World Bank. But it was clearly the ministers from Arab countries—such as Mauritania, Qatar, Oman, and Morocco—openly visiting the Israeli capital for the first time, who generated the most excitement. 'We are all deeply shocked and came to express solidarity with the people and government of Israel,' said the foreign minister of Oman. 'We continue to support the peace process for which Mr Rabin sacrificed his life...'... Hussein stressed that 'we have to continue Rabin's legacy—to bring peace for generations to come.' Hosni Mubarak, who had not visited Israel since assuming the presidency of Egypt, also stressed the importance of continuing the peace process" ("Royalty, presidents, and premiers pay their respects," p. 2). Makovsky offers a more complete list: "THE world leaders who will be attending today's funeral of Yitzhak Rabin, include 22 presidents, 25 prime ministers, 15 foreign ministers, one king, one chancellor, and the heir apparent to the throne of England. Below is the list of those expected to attend: United States: President Bill Clinton; former presidents George Bush and Jimmy Carter; Secretary of State Warren Christopher;...former secretaries of state Henry Kissinger, James Baker and George Shultz;...and other top leaders. Russia: Prime Minister Viktor Chernomyrdin; Foreign Minister Andrei Kozyrev. Egypt: President Hosni Mubarak; Foreign Minister Amr Moussa. Jordan: King Hussein; Crown Prince Hassan.... United Nations: Secretary-General Boutros Boutros-Ghali. Albania: President Sali Berisha. Armenia: President Levon Ter-Petrosyan. Australia: Prime Minister Paul Keating. Austria: President Franz Vranitsky. Azerbaijan: President Heydar Aliyev. Belarus: Foreign Minister Vladimir Senko. Belgium: Prime Minister Jean-Luc Dehaene. Britain: Prince Charles of Wales; Prime Minister John Major; Foreign Minister Malcolm Rifkind; Labor Party leader Tony Blair; and Social Democratic leader Paddy Ashdown. Bulgaria: President Zhelyu Mitev Zhelev. Canada: Prime Minister Jean Chretien. Colombia: Vice President Humberto de la Calla Lombana. Costa Rica: Foreign Minister Fernando Narajo Villalobos. Czech Republic: Prime Minister Vaclav Klaus. Denmark: Prime Minister Poul Nyrup Rasmussen. Estonia: President Lennart Meri. Ethiopia: President Zenawi Meles; Vice President Layne Tamirat. European Commission: President Jean Santer. Finland: President Martti Ahtisaari, Prime Minister Paavo Lipponen. France: President Jacques Chirac. Georgia: President Eduard Shevardnadze. Germany: Chancellor Helmut Kohl; Foreign Minister Klaus Kinkel; President Roman Herzog. Ghana: President Jerry Rawlings. Greece: Foreign Minister Karolos Papolias. Hungary: Prime Minister Gyula Horn. Iceland: Prime Minister David Oddsson. India: Finance Minister Manmohan Singh. Ireland: Prime Minister John Bruton. Italy: Prime Minister Lumberto Dini; Foreign Minister Susanna Agnelli. (President Luigi Scalfaro was in the country yesterday to pay respects, but could not remain for the funeral.) Japan: Foreign Minister Yohei Kono. Kenya: Vice President George Saitoti. Khazakistan: Foreign Minister Kasymzhumart Tokayev. Latvia: President Guntis Ulmanis. Lithuania: Prime Minister Adolfas Slezevicius. Luxembourg: Prime Minister Jean-Claude Juncker. Malta: Prime Minister Eddie Fenech Adami. Mexico: Foreign Minister Jose Angel Gurria Trevino. Moldova: President Mircea Snegur. Morocco: Prime Minister Abdul Afif Filali, and top aide to King Hassan, Andrei Azulay. Netherlands: Queen Beatrix; Prime Minister Wim Kok. Norway: Prime Minister Gro Harlem Brundtland, Foreign Minister Tore Godal. Oman: Foreign Minister Yusuf Bin-Alawi Portugal: President Mario Soares. Romania: President Ion Iliescu; Prime Minister Nicolae Vacaroio. Singapore: Vice President Lee Hsien Loong. Slovakia: Prime Minister Vladimir Meciar. Slovenia: President Milan Kucan. Socialist International: Chairman Pierre Mauroy. South Africa: Executive Deputy President Thabo Mbeki. South Korea: Prime Minister Yi Hong-ku. Spain: Prime Minister Felippe Gonzalez, who also holds the rotating leadership of the European Community. Sweden: Prime Minister Ingvar Carlsson. Switzerland: President Kaspar Villager. Turkey: Prime Minister Tancu Ciller; Foreign Minister Erdal Inonu. Ukraine: President Leonid Kuchma. Also attending will be a minister from Qatar and an unnamed representative from China" ("22 presidents, 25 prime ministers here for funeral," *The Jerusalem Post,* daily, 6 Nov. 1995, p. 12; accession no. 950002867 on the *Jerusalem*

(Britain), France, and Germany, apart from the United States and Mideast leaders and dignitaries.)[1] It can be stated without reservation that Prince Charles and the British monarchy enjoy significant influence over nearly every dignitary and royal personage just mentioned. Major serves the British monarchy; the French and German leaders are influenced as members of the European Union and through the Committee of 300; the Secretary General of the United Nations owes the very creation of his job to the RIIA, which the British monarchy heads; Juan Carlos, Hussein, and Peres are all close personal friends of the prince; President Clinton, who has British royal ancestry, serves the U.S. Council on Foreign Relations (CFR), which in turn exists to serve the RIIA; and Queen Beatrix is a member of the Committee of 300, which Queen Elizabeth II heads.[2] Prince Charles descends from the royal houses of England, France, Germany, Spain, Jordan (through Mohammed, inasmuch as Hussein is a Hashemite), and the Netherlands—*all* the royal houses of the nations just mentioned![3]

Immediately following the funeral, at which the Oslo peace process was repeatedly reaffirmed and hyped—*confirmed*—by world leaders and other dignitaries, Prince Charles and Major met privately with Peres. Although the prince had not spoken publicly, he and Major together insisted that Peres go to the Palestinians' Orient House in East Jerusalem "to make peace with Syria." According to the January-February 1996 edition of *Inside Israel,* "Just hours after Yitzhak Rabin was safely buried, the race for the Golan Heights began. Arriving for the funeral were Prince Charles Windsor of the Royal Institute for International Affairs, who never publicly met Rabin, and his Prime Minister John Major. They insisted Peres come to Orient House to make peace with Syria. Peres turned the Brits down [on a visit to Orient House] but....promised Clinton

---

Post CD-ROM).

1. Recall the earlier scenario in which these three nations—*England, France, and Germany*—just happen to be the ones that a European Union monarch could use to gain "democratic" control of an expanded U.N. Security Council and a world government arising from it.
2. For more information, see Chapter 7's section titled, "The Garter."
3. For more information, see Chapter 4, "Prince of this World—a *Diverse* Lineage."

that Syria could take over control of the South Lebanon Security Zone as part of the peace package. In effect,....[the] promise...opens a possible Syrian war front on the northern border, thus returning Israel completely to its 1948 lines."[1] In other words, *Prince Charles not only affirmed the Oslo II accord, but since at least the time of Rabin's funeral, he has directly involved himself in the Mideast peace negotiations, and in this case, the Oslo III process* (peace negotiations).

The prince, it appears, had been briefed on the secret status of the talks between the Rabin government and Syria. Martin Indyk, former U.S. ambassador to Israel, has asserted that "there was a real chance of peace between Israel and Syria on the eve of prime minister Yitzhak Rabin's assassination, but it was dashed immediately." According to Indyk, "Israel was willing to pay the price [and]...there was a clear commitment by Assad to reach [a] peace agreement with Israel."[2]

Chamish, who has only a partial, surface understanding of the New World Order, states, "The Syrian-Iranian axis is allied to the French-German branch of the NWO whose major components are the Socialist International, old money, and the Vatican.... Until the assassination of Yitzhak Rabin, this was the NWO branch which controlled Shimon Peres. But after Rabin's murder, George Bush, Jimmy Carter, Prince Charles, and Bill Clinton made it very clear to Peres that they would not tolerate any change to Rabin's Anglo-Saxon NWO alliance. To strengthen their hold on the Israeli government, Peres was forced to take Rabin's protégés, Ehud Barak and Haim Ramon, into his cabinet." In January 1996, Peres embarked on secret talks "with Hamas bigshots in London," and in February 1996, he "received his first strong messages." Chamish elaborates, "After London talks between Israelis and Hamas sponsored by the Royal Institute for International Affairs reached a deadlock, five suicide bombers [operating out of Hebron with finances from Jordan] killed fifty-nine people in

1. "Peres's First Acts," *Inside Israel*, Vol. IV, Issue 1, January-February 1996, p. 5. For a reprint of this article, see Chamish, *Traitors and Carpetbaggers in the Promised Land*, pp. 146-149.
2. Jay Bushinsky, "Rabin murder dashed peace with Syria," *The Jerusalem Post*, Int. Ed., 5 July 1997, p. 32.

Jerusalem, Tel Aviv, and Askelon. In the wake of the carnage Barak, Ramon, and Yossi Beilin...met to discuss a *putsch*. Peres was to be replaced by Barak as defense minister and Beilin was supposed to take over as foreign minister. With Ramon already interior minister, the Anglo-Saxon triumvirate would have had effective control over Israel. Peres understood the threat and agreed to switch his allegiances."[1] (Netanyahu has since scuttled Rabin's understanding with Assad and Peres' efforts.)

Continued treachery over Jerusalem. In November 1995, Moshe Shachal, Israel's Internal Security Minister, disallowed "a Palestinian Authority meeting at the Vatican's Notre Dame Hospice in Jerusalem," asserting that "the Palestinians were planning to 'use the Vatican to circumvent the Oslo Accords.'" Nevertheless, in harmony with Peres' earlier promises to the Vatican, its Secretary of State for Foreign Affairs then visited Jerusalem, where he addressed the Israeli CFR. At the same time, the pope promised Uri Baram, Israel's Tourism Minister, that "he will visit Jerusalem in the year 2000," while Ehud Olmert, Jerusalem's mayor, "expressed his...wishes that the trip would be sooner."[2] In early 1996, apparently following Beilin's earlier policy paper, Hirshfeld and Pundak, with Likud Knesset member Ronnie Milo's blessing, conducted secret meetings with Faisal el-Husseini—the Palestinian "Minister for Jerusalem Affairs" and Amin el-Husseini's successor—in a further effort to cantonize Jerusalem. Once again, Beilin's earlier betrayal of Israeli settlers was not lost on the Palestinians. In January 1996, Arafat reached an agreement with Hamas in Cairo "that gave the latter terror group free reign to kill as many Israelis as it wants, just so long as it operates from outside the boundaries of the Palestinian Authority." The *Jerusalem Post* noted this same PLO-Hamas agreement, stating, "the Hamas can operate against Israel as long as it does not do so from PA-controlled territory."[3] (This, of course, enables

1. Chamish, *Traitors and Carpetbaggers in the Promised Land,* pp. 154-156.
2. "Peres' First Acts," *Inside Israel,* Vol. IV, Issue 1, January-February 1996, p. 5. For a reprint of this article, see Chamish, *Traitors and Carpetbaggers in the Promised Land,* pp. 146-149.
3. "Wanted: Realism," *The Jerusalem Post,* Int. Ed., 8 June 1996, p. 10.

Arafat to claim that the PA is not responsible and should not be penalized when terrorist attacks occur, as he has done repeatedly in the face of a small wave of bombings in 1997.) Between April and September 1996, Likud's Olmert secretly joined Peres' forces in plotting to divide Jerusalem. Olmert approved a variation, developed by the Jerusalem Center for Israeli Studies, of Beilin's and Kollek's Metropolitan Jerusalem scheme. The variation, which has been blessed by Beilin and Kollek, would divide Jerusalem "into Jewish secular, Jewish religious, and Arab sectors," with the Arab sector becoming "the capital of a Palestinian state." Following Peres' 1996 election loss to Netanyahu, the Israeli media widely speculated that between the forced appointments of Barak and Haim Ramon, Peres threw the election. The media claimed that Peres "simply froze" as Barak and Ramon "sabotaged" his chances, whereas Peres held that "outside forces, especially Iran," were to blame.

On May 21, 1996, just eight days before Netanyahu's victory, the *Jerusalem Post* revealed that Faisal el-Husseini had made it clear on more than one occasion that in the final-status negotiations, the PLO would "demand Palestinian sovereignty not only in eastern Jerusalem but also in the western part of the city." The *Jerusalem Post* observed, "What Arab sources say about negotiations between Israel and the Palestinians has often proved more reliable than Israel's [government-supplied] information. When the initial Oslo talks were at an advanced stage, Yasser Arafat announced that negotiations were being conducted with Israel on the highest level. The government flatly denied it...as late as three weeks before the agreement was announced, on August 16, 1993.... Similarly, when Arafat announced that he had a letter from Peres committing Israel to the continued operation of Palestinian institutions such as [the illegal] Orient House in Jerusalem, Peres flatly denied it. But in fact such a letter did exist. That is why it may be useful to heed what Arafat says concerning Jerusalem. He....told Arab ambassadors in Stockholm: 'Peres and Beilin have already promised me half of Jerusalem, but ultimately we'll have it all.'" The agreement with the PLO "included the redeployment of Israeli forces in the Sheikh Jarah area, Azariya, Shu'afat, Beit Hanina—all of which are situated northeast of Jerusalem—and outside the Old City."[1] Had Peres won, according to both Hirshfeld and Beilin, there "would have been a Palestinian state with a suburb of Jerusalem as its capital and a total withdrawal from the Jordan valley."[2]

Benjamin Netanyahu—an unpredictable pawn in the grip of the New World Order. Netanyahu is similarly influenced by the Committee of 300, which, it would appear, has attempted to groom him as a political Trojan horse. Although Netanyahu's rise to power is telling, he is not playing the game according to the rules of the elite; rather, he has genuine concern for Israel.

Originally planning to study architecture, Netanyahu instead obtained a degree in business administration from the Massachusetts Institute of Technology. He then worked for the Boston Consulting Group under Ira Magaziner, who was later a key figure in the Clinton administration's attempt to socialize health care in the United States. In 1979, Netanyahu returned to Israel to organize a conference on terrorism, to which then CIA-director Bush, U.S. Secretary of State George Shultz, and Reagan-administration arms negotiator Richard Perle were invited. (Like Bush, Shultz is a member of the Committee of 300, and all three—Bush, Shultz, and Perle—are members of the U.S. CFR.) In 1982, impressed with Netanyahu's earlier performance and fluent English, Moshe Arens, Israel's ambassador to the United States, invited Netanyahu to serve as his deputy. In 1984, Peres (of the *Labor* Party), going contrary to Shamir, appointed Netanyahu Israel's ambassador to the United Nations. According to Arens, Netanyahu "was the best ambassador to the UN we've had." During his ambassadorship to the U.N., Netanyahu authored *Terror: How The West Can Win.* The book greatly impressed Reagan and Shultz, who had not only

1. "Jerusalem again," *The Jerusalem Post,* Int. Ed., 1 June 1996, p. 10.
2. Chamish, *Traitors and Carpetbaggers in the Promised Land,* pp. 149, 156, 171-173, 176-178.

made the fight against terrorism a top administration priority, but subsequently visited Netanyahu often in New York. At the same time, then Vice-President Bush "was appointed to head a front for illegal covert activities called the Anti-Terror Task Force." The media too latched onto Netanyahu, who received much positive press, both before and during the 1991 war against Iraq, in the *Washington Post,* the *New York Times,* and *Newsweek,* as well as on CNN—all of which, interestingly enough, are controlled by the U.S. CFR. (Ted Turner, owner of CNN, is now also a member of the Committee of 300.) Chamish comments, "Once in New York in 1984, CFR-affiliated media such as CNN, the *New York Times, Washington Post, Newsweek,* and CFR members [Ted] Koppel and [Larry] King turned Netanyahu into a major political figure; so much so that George Shultz became a close friend." Netanyahu's prestige and publicity further increased when he then organized a second conference on terrorism in Washington D.C., which Shultz chaired.

Bush likewise had a stake, as is possibly evidenced, Chamish notes, in Netanyahu's mysterious ties to Systematics: "In short, the allegations are that the National Security Agency had handed Systematics stolen software called PROMIS that opened a trap door to the world's secret banking transactions. About 250 Americans, mostly politicians, had their illegal foreign accounts emptied of over $3.5 billion in the operation. It is claimed that Colin Powell dropped out of the presidential race [against Clinton] after his account electronically vanished. Leading figures in the operation included George Bush, Caspar Weinberger, and two Arkansas attorneys, Vince Foster Jr. and Hillary Rodham Clinton on behalf of Clinton financier Jackson Stephens. The research invariably concludes that Foster was murdered because he knew too much."

In Israel, although his rise to power began with the Labor Party, Netanyahu became a Likud darling. With the help of his Committee of 300 and U.S. CFR allies, he won the 1993 Likud Party primaries.[1] Netanyahu "brought

---

1. Chamish, *Traitors and Carpetbaggers in the Promised Land,* pp. 157-164. For some of this and additional information, see Liat Collins, "From A to Bibi: A guide to Netanyahu," *The*

about an ideological revolution that made the Likud adopt a less hawkish line, while transforming it from a populist party into a liberal-capitalistic one," striving to "establish an American-style Republican party in Israel."[1]

According to Chamish, in August 1994, Beilin set up a meeting between the future Prime Minister and two shady financiers: Marc Rich and Pinchas Green. They agreed to help Netanyahu with the understanding that he would uphold the Olso I and II accords if elected. Chamish comments, "As one source in the Foreign Ministry says, 'Netanyahu spent five years as the Israeli ambassador to the United Nations. The ties he made there are stronger than his loyalty to the ideals of the Likud.'"

From 1994 to 1996, Netanyahu participated in at least six secret meetings with Jordan's King Hussein and Crown Prince Hassan, along with Mishcon, in London. These meetings—arranged by Dore Gold, who was a Netanyahu delegate to the Madrid Peace Conference—began at least a year before Netanyahu was elected Prime Minister.[2] Even as Rabin and Arafat signed the Oslo II accord, Netanyahu refused a Likud pledge to cancel it; that is, at the same time that Netanyahu was denouncing the accords publicly and in the Likud, he was also recognizing them as legitimate. When, in 1995, Netanyahu tried to persuade Kissinger to proclaim that U.S. troops should *not* be placed on the Golan Heights, Rabin and Kissinger just laughed. Contrasting Netanyahu with Rabin before the 1996 Israeli elections, Chamish commented, "Netanyahu's outside ties are no less noteworthy. In the past few months, he has conducted meetings with German chancellor Helmut Kohl, French president Jacques Chirac, British prime minister John Major, and naturally, American president Bill Clinton.... His actions have assured that the Rabin peace process passes safely through the Knesset, and according to reliable sources he has promised...that if the government changes next year, the 'peace' process will go on as unhindered as he can arrange." We may note that

Jerusalem Post, Int. Ed., 15 June 1996, pp. 7, 14.
1. Sever Plocker, "Bibi: The New Israeli," *The Jerusalem Post,* Int. Ed., 15 June 1996, p. 29.
2. Makovsky, "The candidate becomes the leader," p. 8.

Hussein, unlike Mubarak and Arafat, was reluctant to assume the worst concerning Netanyahu when he first came to power. The *Jerusalem Post* aptly commented, "What is most striking about the Arab reaction to Netanyahu's election is the incessant threats of violence and war.... The 'peace process' means only one thing to these regimes: complete Israeli withdrawal to the June 4, 1967 lines and the establishment of a Palestinian state with at least part of Jerusalem as its capital. (In fact, the constitution now being prepared for the Palestinian state is likely to define its borders as those of the 1947 UN partition plan.) Anything less, they warn, means war.... The three years of 'final-status' negotiations were presumed to be a period necessary for the preparation of the Israeli public opinion for these egregious concessions. Even a plan for the gradual division of Jerusalem was being prepared.... But now that Netanyahu has indicated that the final-status talks are not a pro-forma charade, but real negotiations on the future of the country, Arab threats have been pouring in with growing intensity and frequency."[1] "The government's plans have included allowing the establishment of a Palestinian state in Judea, Samaria and Gaza, the division of Jerusalem (the blueprints for which have been developed by Labor's '100-day team'), and a complete evacuation of the Golan. Such steps would have been a sure prescription for war. Netanyahu's challenge is to convince the West that hope for peace lies in transforming the region's regimes into democracies, not in appeasing its tyrants."[2]

Actually, Hussein made his preference for Netanyahu clear when he publicly refused to support Peres during the campaign, even while the Clinton administration openly interfered in Israel's election process by characterizing "a vote for Netanyahu as a vote against peace." Chamish speculates that Netanyahu promised the king future "Jordanian hegemony over the Temple Mount." Of Netanyahu's victory, Hussein remarked, "I don't think there is any change...whatsoever regarding the issue of peace."

1. "Negotiating under threat," *The Jerusalem Post,* Int. Ed., 15 June 1996, p. 10.
2. "Netanyahu's challenge," *The Jerusalem Post,* Int. Ed., 8 June 1996, p. 10.

David Makovsky of the *Jerusalem Post* added, "Hussein is...privately relieved that the Golan deal will fall through under Netanyahu, as he fears such a peace deal could strengthen Damascus as a regional power at his expense."[1] Not only did Netanyahu win, but he is Israel's first Prime Minister to have received "a direct popular mandate and outright [Jewish] majority," leading Peres "by more than 11% in the Jewish population."[2]

Since his election, Netanyahu has kept Oslo I and II alive, albeit so haltingly that he has on several occasions drawn the public fury of Hussein, who simply "can't understand" the Israeli Prime Minister's actions. Netanyahu has also "refused to support investigations" of the current Likud or previous Labor governments.

In March 1996, Chamish reports, Beilin and Abu Mazen "concluded a final treaty between Israel and the Palestinian Authority. The main points were that a Palestinian state would emerge with its capital being the Jerusalem suburb of Abu Dis. There would be a corridor linking Abu Dis with the Temple Mount which would be under PLO control. ...Israel would give up large chunks of land in the Negev Desert to expand the Gaza Strip. Israel would also give up control of the Jordan Valley." In May 1996, *Inside Israel* revealed that at a meeting of the Israeli CFR, Netanyahu retreated from his campaign pledges by saying that he would agree to meet Arafat after all. Chamish adds, "Since taking office [following his May 29 victory], Netanyahu has fueled fears of international control by his actions.... [The] CFR is still running the latest prime minister." He cites Netanyahu's decision to appoint Yaacov Frenkel, who worked for the World Bank from 1971 to 1990, to head Israel's economy. Frenkel supported World Bank loans totaling ten-billion dollars to Israel, with U.S. guarantees. Subsequently, the Bush administration used these loans as leverage against the Shamir government in an effort to force Israel into line. In the end, Frenkel lost out to Dan Meridor, but a *Maariv* headline revealed "Meridor Will Act, Frenkel Will Lead." Frenkel, who suggests

1. Makovsky, "The candidate becomes the leader," p. 8.
2. "Netanyahu's challenge," p. 10.

"closer association with Europe's monetary union" for Israel in the light of a world that "is going to be organized in a much sharper, multi-polar way," now serves as the Governor of the Bank of Israel.[1]

In July 1996, Kissinger arranged a conference in Amman, Jordan, "aimed at determining the future of the Middle East after the year 2000." Among the globalist guests were Lord Rothschild of London (various Rothschilds are members of the Committee of 300 and most are masons), Frenkel, Milo, Meir Shamgar (who "whitewashed the Rabin assassination and Hebron massacre of 1994"), Beilin, and Netanyahu's political advisor, Dore Gold. Following the conference, Kissinger flew in Black's jet to Jerusalem, where he intimidated Netanyahu in a private meeting. Kissinger asserted, "The new prime minister must be made to realize that the peace process is good for Israel." Subsequently, Gold adopted a "new approach" to the Syrian track, which he "conceived...based on Kissinger's Helsinki model for Europe during the 1970s." Chamish comments, "Gold's plan calls for renewing discussions [between Israel and Syria] at the Wye Plantation, a facility owned by the Council on Foreign Relations' (CFR) sister organization, the Aspen Institute [founded by Les Aspen].... The committees will be chaired alternatively between the U.S. and France and members will be all the nations of the Middle East. In effect, a regional bloc will be formed in the same manner as the Helsinki Convention which helped disintegrate the Soviet Union." (This plan is reminiscent of Peres' "New Middle East.") "To further the plan, Dr. Gold flew to Paris and met secretly with Senator Arlen Spector of the CFR who, afterward flew to Damascus with a message to Assad from Gold." Spector, of course, whitewashed the Kennedy assassination, and, like Kissinger, Ross, and Martin Indyk, is a betrayer of Israel's true national interests. Like Beilin and Barak, Gold enjoyed a tenure at the Washington Center for Near East Studies. According to Chamish, "His mentor at the time was Martin Indyk, who was conducting secret negotiations with Ambassador

1. "New world calling," *The Jerusalem Post,* Int. Ed., 18 Oct. 1997, p. 29.

Itamar Rabinovich to arrange an Israeli withdrawal from the Golan Heights. Gold returned to Israel and heaped praise on Kissinger."

In September 1996, David Levy, Netanyahu's Foreign Minister, flew to Rome, apparently to prevent a meeting between the pope and Arafat. Subsequently, he flew to Ireland. At the same time, the Vatican and the World Council of Churches held a conference in Greece concerning the future of Jerusalem, in which they demanded that Israel "liberalize its hold on the city."[1]

On a number of occasions since Netanyahu came to power the possibility of a unity government between the Likud and Labor parties has been floated. In May 1996, immediately following Netanyahu's election victory, Peres rejected an offer by Netanyahu to form a coalition "because 'Netanyahu insisted on appointing Ehud Barak as his foreign minister.'" How odd. Kissinger has pushed his own idea of a unity government through Sharon, who "has met Dr. Kissinger every time he's flown to America over the past twenty-five years." On October 17, 1996, Kissinger and Sharon met to discuss the future of the Mideast peace process. Chamish comments, "Sharon and Peres are busy plotting the latter's return to power within the Netanyahu government." Also in October 1996, former Oslo opponent Michael Eitan, now working with Labor Party Knesset members Beilin, Ephraim Sneh, Ramon, Shlomo Ben Ami, Uzi Baram, and Avraham Shohat, came out in support of the March 1996 Beilin-Mazen final settlement plan, announcing, "The time has come for a national unity government." That same month, the Clinton administration nearly ignited a war between Israel and Syria in its efforts to push the peace process forward. As a result, "Assad decided that he could no longer trust Washington as a go-between." Regarding U.S. interference, Chamish quotes journalist Nahum Barnea as stating, "During Begin's time, they groomed Dayan, [Chaim] Weizman, and Aharon Barak. The fruits of the effort were the Camp David Accords. In Shamir's time they groomed Meridor, Olmert,

---

1. Chamish, *Traitors and Carpetbaggers in the Promised Land*, pp. 107-108, 120-125, 157, 164-166, 173-177, 185.

[David] Levy, and Milo. The result was the Madrid Conference. Currently, they are busy grooming Levy, President [Ezer] Weizman, and Defense Minister Yitzhak Mordechai."[1] (Like David *ben* Gurion, Chaim Weizman was a Committee of 300 member.)

Netanyahu—forced to play the "peace process" game.
Shortly following a major outbreak of violence and bloodshed between Israeli soldiers and Palestinian "police" and civilians at the start of Israel's Feast of Tabernacles celebrations in 1996, Netanyahu "called on Syria to renew peace talks on the basis of UN Security Council resolutions 242 and 338" while "speaking [in <u>London</u>] outside the Downing Street residence of British Prime Minister John Major on the first leg of a three-nation European visit that also took him to <u>France and Germany</u>."[2] As a consequence of these events, Arafat, for example, remarked, "We have no alternative but to continue in our efforts <u>to strengthen and protect</u> the [Oslo] peace process for our children."[3]

Buckingham Palace lowers its guard. Ezer Weizman, Chaim Weizman's nephew (and a possible Committee of 300 member), is now taking a more active role in the Oslo process, having even visited *Buckingham Palace* in 1997: "President Ezer Weizman and his wife, Reuma, will pay a three-day state visit to the United Kingdom on February 25. They will be the guests of Queen Elizabeth II and Prince Philip, and will stay at Buckingham Palace. Following meetings with members of the royal family, the prime minister, and leader of the opposition in London, Weizman will go to Cambridge University."[4] While in London,

1. Chamish, *Traitors and Carpetbaggers in the Promised Land,* pp. 178, 184-186, 189-190.
2. Douglas Davis and David Rudge, "Netanyahu calls on Syria to resume talks," *The Jerusalem Post,* Int. Ed., 5 Oct. 1996, p. 32.
3. Nicholas Goldberg, Newsday, "Israeli president, Arafat discuss peace process," *The Denver Post,* 9 Oct. 1996, p. 9A. Arafat, who remains a dedicated liar and would-be terrorist bent on Israel's destruction, knows only too well that these events have brought out the great fragility of Israel's peace with Egypt, and to a slightly lesser extent Jordan, not to mention her rocky relations with other nations around the world. They have literally brought the Oslo peace process to the brink of collapse, if not right over the cliff.
4. Batsheva Tsur, "Weizmans to Britain," *The Jerusalem Post,* Int. Ed., 15 Feb. 1997, p. 4. Recall that Cambridge University is the seat of the Commission on Global Governance and the Global Security Programme for the United Nations, and that Prince Charles not only personally inaugurated the latter's lecture series, but is said to have initiated the program itself at the United Nations through Maurice Strong and others. For more information, see Chapter

"Weizman went to the reciprocal banquet traditionally given by visiting heads of state for their host, Queen Elizabeth II, in Spencer House.... The queen was to host a banquet at Buckingham Palace in Weizman's honor..., but since the Israeli Embassy is not large enough to have held Weizman's return affair, Jacob Rothschild generously stepped in to lend Israel the grand and glittering Spencer House for the function, which was to be attended by the leading lights of British society and Anglo-Jewry."[1]

Also in February 1997, Netanyahu and his wife, Sara, traveled to the Vatican, where, dressed in black, they met with the pope, who was, of course, dressed in white (another Zoroastrian contrast). During the meeting, Netanyahu invited the pontiff to visit Jerusalem in the year 2000; however, the pope, according to Netanyahu, "said he wanted to come before that time." The ecumenist pope told the Prime Minister that "he hopes the Holy Land could be a place where 'Jews, Christians, Moslems, Israelis and Arabs, believers and non-believers can create and consolidate a concrete peace in respect of everyone's rights and dignity.'" According to the same *Jerusalem Post* article, "Last year, the pope accepted an invitation from Palestinian Authority leader Yasser Arafat to visit for the year 2000.... The Vatican wants international guarantees protecting Jerusalem as sacred to Christians, Moslems, and Jews."[2] Another *Jerusalem Post* article reports, "Netanyahu stressed, as has every Israeli leader, Israel's commitment to freedom of religion and preservation of all holy places. The Vatican insists that it is not concerned with the political status of Jerusalem, only in the interests of religious freedom and of peace. Yet the Vatican, like the United States and most other countries, refuses to recognize Jerusalem as Israel's capital. The Vatican would very much like to have a role in the final status talks...regarding

---

11's section titled, "Global Governance, the Global Security Programme, and a possible 'Economic Security Council.'"

1. Tom Gross, "Weizman to host queen in Diana's old home," *The Jerusalem Post,* Int. Ed., 1 Mar. 1997, p. 2.

2. Jerusalem Post Staff and news agencies, "Pope wants visit before 2000," *The Jerusalem Post,* Int. Ed., 15 Feb. 1997, p. 4.

the city of Jerusalem."[1]

In May 1997, Weizman, who "has tried in the past to smooth relations between Israel and the PA that have been rocky since Netanyahu took office," planned to meet with Arafat "in a bid to get the stalled peace process back on track." Around the same time, Netanyahu stated, "the Middle East is not about to go up in flames, but there are dangers.... The peace process can move forward if leaders want to, and I want to.... [However, the Palestinian] dream of the return to the 1967 borders, the redivision of Jerusalem, and the massive return of refugees will not happen." Exasperated, Arafat responded, "There is no way of getting out of this crisis without international intervention."[2] Weizman then urged the Netanyahu government "to rethink the situation in Lebanon and to return to the negotiating table with Syria," asserting, "We have to raise questions with the Syrians that are very painful.... We can plan new battle tactics — or we can sit down and talk peace."[3]

A Commonwealth gambit. In August 1997, the Secretary General of the British Commonwealth approached Israel, seeking her *membership*. Previously, the PA, which evolved from the earlier British-created Supreme Moslem Council, had asked about the possibility of its own future "associate" membership:

> Israel is actively considering joining the British Commonwealth, following an "unofficial approach" to its ambassador in London from the secretary-general of the 53-member organization. The approach was made earlier this month in a meeting between Ambassador Moshe Raviv and the Commonwealth's secretary-general, Chief Emeka Anyaoku. The move is being seen as especially significant at a time when Israeli ties with the European Union and other international bodies have been strained over the stalled Middle East peace process. A spokesman for the Commonwealth confirmed that a meeting had taken place between Chief Anyaoku and Mr. Raviv, but declined to provide further

1. "A welcome papal visit," *The Jerusalem Post,* Int. Ed., 15 Feb. 1997, p. 10.
2. Hillel Kuttler and Michal Yudelman, "Arafat, Weizman to meet," *The Jerusalem Post,* Int. Ed., 10 May 1997, pp. 1-2.
3. Batsheva Tsur and David Rudge, "Weizman: We must negotiate with Syria," *The Jerusalem Post,* Int. Ed., 31 May 1997, p. 32.

details. The approach came in the wake of a visit to London earlier this month by Yasser Arafat, during which the Palestinian Authority chief asked Commonwealth officials whether a future Palestinian state could have associate membership of the organization.[1]

The big picture. It seems only fair to ask at this point, "Could the prophetic picture be any clearer?" That is, are those prophecy teachers, "scholars," and "authorities" who fail to recognize the significance of the Oslo peace process to the covenant of Daniel 9:27 missing the boat? *The world will soon know.*

The European Union—through England, France, and Germany—is now looking to play a major role in the Mideast peace process. France's approach has been especially obnoxious and offensive: "French Foreign Minister Herve de Charette said it was crucial for Europe to have a role in the region.... France has a long history of influence in the Middle East, especially in Lebanon and Iraq.... French President Jacques Chirac last week tried to play the power broker in the region. In a visit to Israel, he shouted at protective Israeli security guards and became the first Western leader to address the Palestinian parliament.... ...Germany thinks 'Europe should not overestimate its role.' And British Foreign Secretary Malcolm Rifkind could not resist a dig at Chirac.... 'Our involvement could be slightly less romantic, slightly less colored, slightly less dramatic than that of other countries, but it could be in fact more effective,' he said.... Charette shot back, calling Rifkind's remarks 'misplaced...based, no doubt, on some old Franco-British rivalry.'"[2] "President Jacques Chirac has boldly gambled..., hoping for a payoff in power, prestige and, eventually, lucrative [Arab] defense contracts.... The specter of French meddling in the delicate peace talks discomfited European Union partners such as Britain, as well as the United States.... Israel issued a flat 'no' to Chirac's push for greater involvement.... Defying Western wisdom, Chirac lauded Syrian President Hafez Assad, called Iraq a 'great country' and snubbed Israel with his failure to

1. MED, "Israel could join British Commonwealth," *Weekend News Today,* 25 Aug. 1997.
2. Elizabeth Wise, "Europe seeks niche in Middle East," *USA Today,* 29 Oct. 1996, p. 4A.

address the Knesset. The address would have balanced his speech before the Palestinian Legislative Council—the first by a Western leader. He also called for a Palestinian state and the return of the Golan Heights to Syria."[1] We may note that despite recent attempts to unite France and Britain through such machinations as the amazing underwater "Chunnel," which runs between the French city Coquelles and the British city Folkestone, the simmering Mideast diplomatic row between the two countries demonstrates that the centuries-old Merovingian struggle for supremacy, between the British monarchy—using the Order of the Garter and its control of Illuminist Freemasonry—and the French leadership, continues unabated. French government officials, for example, worry that "the Internet could overwhelm the French language," noting that some "85 percent of Internet sites are in English, while about 2 percent are in French."[2] It appears that the British monarchy will win the struggle.

Chamish adds these insightful, though somewhat misguided, observations: "The real war being fought over Jerusalem centers on the year 2000. The foreign participants in the battle, including the Vatican, the Russian Orthodox church, and the Masons, are staking their claims.... It is essential for the credibility of all three that their tenets and prophecies are achieved and Israel be caught in an Armageddon situation. If the year 2000 passes without judgment in Israel, believers will abandon the churches by the droves, while the Masonic program for chaos followed by a one-world government will have to be put on ice." Clearly not all of the Rabin government's conflicting commitments can be honored. This realization has led the PLO to assert that there is an "Armageddon Plan" afoot. A London-based Palestinian journalist commented, "Do you think Hussein would ever have signed the treaty if Israel didn't secretly give him future control of the Moslem holy sites in Jerusalem? Palestinians are opposed to the agreement because we know we lost out. And if Hussein

1. Elaine Ganley, The Associated Press, "France adopts a risky role as Middle East negotiator," *The Denver Post,* 27 Oct. 1996, p. 9A.
2. Los Angeles Times, "Integrity of language an issue," *The Denver Post,* 7 Feb. 1997, p. 33A.

did get control, then the Masons got their foothold on the Temple Mount." The same journalist elaborated, "Hussein's Masonic ties are well known to Arab reporters, and we believe Hussein is being used to give his friends in London a foothold in the city by the year 2000."[1] Of course, *true* Christians—who are neither Roman Catholic, Russian Orthodox, nor Masons, and who at best are only looking to the vicinity of the year 2000 for the fulfillment of prophecies related to Christ's return—will not abandon the *real* Church. *True* Christians know that God's Word will be literally fulfilled to the very last stroke.

If the Israeli government is to attempt to fulfill the promises made by Peres and Rabin, it would appear that the Vatican and the Masons—or, loosely speaking, the French and English sides of the peace-process conspiracy—must ultimately partner with one another. Such a scenario, in which the final Roman pontiff joins forces with the head of the masonic hierarchy, or *Prince Charles,*[2] is precisely what the Apocalypse seems to indicate; that is, the false prophet and the AntiChrist shall work together to deceive and dominate mankind. Moreover, it perfectly agrees with the overtures of Prince Charles, who is slated to one day head the apostate Anglican Protestant Church, toward Pope John Paul II and the Roman Catholic Church.[3] It would be more than just a return to "the old European order, in which the pope rules the spiritual realm and the emperor the secular."[4] Such an alliance would also represent a significant coming home, in both an historical and religious context, for the Temple

1. Chamish, *Traitors and Carpetbaggers in the Promised Land,* pp. 115-117, 169. Arafat, enraged by the "special status" that the Israeli-Jordanian treaty grants to Jordan as custodian of Jerusalem's Muslim "holy shrines," openly threatened Hussein, declaring "in Gaza to Hamas and Islamic Jihad supporters that anyone who didn't agree that Jerusalem is Palestinian and that the custodianship of the holy places should be in the hands of Palestinians could go and drink Gaza sea water." As Hussein sees it, "Jerusalem remains a trust with the Hashemites, who are resolute on its patronage and reconstruction and on the supervision of its holy sites.... We will never relinquish our religious responsibilities toward the holy sites under all circumstances" (Alon Pinkas, Associated Press, "Hussein: Our religious role in Jerusalem is everlasting," *The Jerusalem Post,* daily, 23 Oct. 1994, p. 1; Moshe-Zak, "Hussein and Arafat in Conflict," *The Jerusalem Post,* daily, 28 Oct. 1997, p. 6; accession nos. 940003526 and 940003890 on the *Jerusalem Post* CD-ROM).

2. For more information, see Chapter 7's section titled, "The Garter."

3. See Chapter 10's section titled, "A so-called 'Christian' heritage."

4. Hilton, *The Principality and Power of Europe,* p. 16.

Knights and the Rosicrucians, who originally split off from Roman Catholicism, only to give rise to Freemasonry and the vast British Empire and Commonwealth. It would perhaps also surprise many true Christians, who have been taught that the AntiChrist would arise not from a Protestant denomination, but from the Roman Catholic Church. As mentioned earlier, Committee of 300 members are usually chosen from among apostate Anglican Protestants. Just as being a "Christian" became essential for advancement in the still-pagan Roman Empire of Constantine, who mixed the holy and the profane to give the world Roman Catholicism, so an ecumenist "Christianity" is perhaps the major means by which the British monarchy, down through the centuries, has deceived the world.

Prince Charles—Islam's choice ambassador from the West, and Israel's counterfeit Davidic prince. During Prince Charles' honeymoon in 1981, "The royal couple also paid a courtesy call on President Sadat of Egypt. Less than two months later, Prince Charles would return to Cairo to walk in the funeral procession of the assassinated Egyptian president."[1] Later, in 1989, while on a "six-day visit to Kuwait and the United Arab Emirates," the prince enjoyed a relatively quiet "desert picnic at an oasis in Abu Dhabi."[2] Much, as we have seen, has happened since then. Prince Charles, whom *Majesty* magazine more recently called the "Prince of Peace" (cf. Isa 9:6-7),[3] has already played a somewhat visible Mideast role: "Eager to establish himself as a player on the world stage, he made high-profile visits to [Western Europe,] Poland, Mexico and the Persian Gulf [in 1993], and he delivered a hard-hitting speech at Oxford in which he decried the 'unmentionable horrors' perpetrated by Saddam Hussein."[4] After denouncing Saddam Hussein and calling for "greater understanding between Christians and Muslims" in his Oxford speech, the prince found himself greatly esteemed in the eyes of the

1. Hoey, *Charles & Diana: The Tenth Anniversary*, p. 69.
2. *Charles & Diana: A Royal Family Album*, p. 56. Hoey, *Charles & Diana: The Tenth Anniversary*, pp. 30-31, 70-71, 154-155.
3. Alan Hamilton, "Prince of Peace," *Majesty* magazine, July 1995, Vol. 16, No. 7, p. 14.
4. Green, Smith, and Wright, "The Outsider," *People Weekly*, 6 Dec. 1993, p. 111.

Middle East's more moderate Sunni Muslims. During his six-day, 1993 tour of the region, he enjoyed the lavish hospitality of Saudi Arabia, Kuwait, the United Arab Emirates, and Jordan, and he repeated his verbal attack on Saddam Hussein, likening the Iraqi leader to a lunatic. Prince Charles' statements, combined with Great Britain's part in the 1990 war against Iraq, have given him "immense popularity in the region."[1] In April 1993, the prince, who "pontificates on how to save the world," also gave "an earnest speech about global security."[2] Kah, remarking on Mideast peace and the AntiChrist's rise to power, observes,

> The Gulf War...was only the latest tactic used by [globalist] insiders [such as President Bush and his cabinet][3] to accomplish their goal.... [It] would unite the nations of the world against a common enemy—which was necessary to take humanity the final step into a one-world system. [Saddam] Hussein played the [unwitting] role of the perfect villain....
>
> The war would also...[show] other countries what they would encounter if they opposed the emerging world system. It would make true patriots who opposed the concept of a New World Order appear to be unpatriotic, while making globalists who supported the U.N. appear as patriots....
>
> The recent war with Iraq might have been only a dress rehearsal for something much larger yet to come. The fact that Saddam Hussein is still in power [as made possible by Bush]...seems to be an indicator of more trouble ahead. If there is another Middle East conflict, it could result from, or start out very similar to, the recent crisis; only this time, the chances of it escalating into a regional, or even a global conflict would be much greater....
>
> Two world wars have already been fought.... In each case, an aggressive power was used [as a pawn by one-worlders] to ignite a crisis that drew in the rest of the world.... After each war, a supranational organization was established for the alleged purpose of promoting world peace [and security], first the League of Nations, then the United Nations....
>
> The United Nations today is the closest thing to world government that humanity has ever known.... The U.N. [currently] lacks only the power to implement and enforce its strategies....
>
> ....The mere threat of a major world conflict could be enough

1. Alan Hamilton, "Prince Charles visits the Gulf," *Majesty* magazine, January 1994, Vol. 15, No. 1, pp. 13-17.
2. Leslie Shepherd, The Associated Press, "Diana most likely to succeed with press," *The Denver Post*, 1 May 1993, p. 22A.
3. Kah, *En Route to Global Occupation*, pp. 51-55.

to scare the public into accepting such a change....

At some point, the beast, or one of his representatives, will step forth with what will appear to be a brilliant plan for Mideast peace.... The agreement would probably guarantee Israel's security and would allow the Jews to rebuild their long-anticipated [third] temple.... The beast will succeed where others before him have failed.

His appearance will most likely be as a democratic leader,...appearing as a genuine man of peace.[1]

On a 1995 trip to Egypt and Morocco, Prince Charles, who continues to be "held in high esteem in the Arab world," was met by several high-ranking Muslim and Greek Orthodox dignitaries, including Egypt's Hosni Mubarak. Indeed, a "large portrait of the royal guest was lifted aloft by balloons alongside another of President Mubarak, the signal for mass cheering all around." The prince not only visited several mosques, the great pyramid of Cheops, the Sphinx, and "the dark, scented labyrinths of Fez, the greatest medieval city in the Arab world," but also received a clipping from what is said to be the ancient bush from which God spoke to Moses at the base of Mount Sinai. When asked, "How would you like to be Pharaoh?," the prince replied, "I don't know. I haven't been anything else." As yet another indication that "Prince Charles is rapidly becoming Britain's most accomplished ambassador to the Arab world," "the Moroccan Crown Prince...heaped further praise on his Islamic initiative."[2] Perhaps in a similar vein to his receipt of the "burning-bush" clipping, the prince once drove "through the trick parting of the Red Sea at Universal" Studio, Hollywood.[3]

The prince is also very popular among today's unregenerate Israelis, and, as mentioned in the earlier discussion on his lineage, Israel's Channel 2 television noted in May 1996 that he is connected to Israel by his supposed Davidic descent. *If Israel joins the British Commonwealth, as proposed, Prince Charles will literally be acknowledged as her Davidic prince.* This brings us to another interesting point. Not only was David Israel's king, but he also

1. Kah, *En Route to Global Occupation*, pp. 64-65, 141-143, 147.
2. Robert Hardman, "Desert Prince," *Majesty* magazine, May 1995, Vol. 16, No. 5, pp. 41-42.
3. Cathcart, p. 146.

functioned as a prophet and high priest.[1] Unlike the *cohenim* (priests) currently being trained for the resumption of Levitical duties at a rebuilt Temple in Israel, Prince Charles has the scripturally required documentation, spurious or not, to make the necessary claims. A priesthood without a registered genealogy is considered unclean; for this reason, many Israelites will not accept Temple worship until The Messiah comes. Regarding the issue of Temple worship, we should also note that the Priory of Zion, which is looking for the "Prince of Lorraine" (i.e., Prince Charles), claims to possess "the lost treasure of the Temple of Jerusalem," which it says will be "returned to Israel when the time is right."[2] Will the Anti-Messiah, Lucifer's counterfeit Davidic king, prophet, and priest, fool Israel?

1. As stated in *Messiah, History, and the Tribulation Period,* "David was not only the King of Israel, as well as a prophet of God, but at times he also exercised certain responsibilities of the high priest (e.g., see 1 Sam 23:6, 23:9-12, 30:7-8; 2 Sam 6:13, 6:17-18; 1 Chr 15:11-12, 16:1-4), while wearing the high priest's garments (e.g., see 2 Sam 6:14; 1 Chr 15:27; cf. Ex 28:2-15, 28:25-31, 29:4-5; Lev 8:6-7; 1 Sam 2:18, 2:28, 14:3, 22:18...)."
2. Baigent, Leigh, and Lincoln, *Holy Blood, Holy Grail,* p. 225. For more information, see Chapter 4, "Prince of this World—a *Diverse* Lineage."

13

Potential for a Fatal Wound

And I stood upon the sand of the sea. And I saw a beast rise up out of the sea.... I saw one of its heads as *though he* had been slain to death, and the wound of his death was healed. And all the world marveled after the beast. So they worshiped the dragon who gave authority to the beast; and they worshiped [revered, honored, did homage to, deferred to] the beast, saying, "Who *is* like the beast? Who is able to make war with it?" And it was given a mouth speaking great things and blasphemies, and he was given authority to continue for forty-two months.... And it was granted to it [him] to make war with the saints and to overcome them. And authority was given to it [him] over every tribe and tongue and nation. And all those dwelling on the Earth—whose names have not been written in the Book of Life of the Lamb slain from the foundation of the world—will worship it [him].... Then I saw another beast rise up from the Earth, and it [he] had two horns like a lamb and spoke as if a dragon. And it [he] produces [brings about] all the authority of the first beast in its sight, and causes the Earth and those dwelling therein *to think* that they should worship the first beast, whose deadly wound was healed. And it [he] produces great signs, so that it [he] even makes fire come down out of the heaven [sky, atmosphere] onto the Earth in the sight of men. And it [he] deceives those dwelling on the Earth by the signs which it [he] was granted to do in the presence of the beast, saying to those dwelling on the Earth to make an image to the beast who had the wound of the sword and lived. (Rev 13:1, 13:3-5, 13:7-8, 13:11-14, Gk.)

Since 1979, both Pope John Paul II and former President Ronald Reagan have received nearly fatal wounds, and each has recovered. In April 1985, Prince Charles and Princess Diana had a "private audience with Pope John Paul II at the Vatican."[1] Also, in November 1985, the prince met with President Reagan at the White House and Vice-President Bush at the British Embassy,[2] and later, in February 1990, with then President Bush. In 1991, Prince Charles' son William sustained a fractured skull when he

1. Burnet, *In Person, THE PRINCE AND PRINCESS OF WALES*, p. 8.
2. *Charles & Diana: A Royal Family Album*, pp. 50-51.

was "accidentally struck with a golf club," an injury that might have been, if not for modern surgical procedures, a deadly wound.[1]

What about Prince Charles? In May 1969, shortly after his arrival in Aberystwyth, Wales, for a two-month term that was to conclude with his formal investiture as Prince of Wales, "Gelignite was found in disused chimneys, hastily dumped machine-guns were retrieved from a lake dredged by the police, a time-bomb blew up at an R.A.F. radio post, and a fanatical plan for an armed uprising ran far beyond the scope of student japes.... On the final day of his visit [to Wales] a booby-trap bomb exploded in Caernarvon and gravely injured a young schoolboy playing with a football close by; he had to have a leg amputated."[2] Two men also died while attempting to plant a bomb on a railway line the prince was to use the morning of the investiture. In all, "There were fifteen bomb attacks before the investiture was over, the last one on the morning of 1 July itself, which was to have repercussions for years to come."[3] One week after a 1973 diplomatic stopover at Bermuda, during which Prince Charles conferred with Sir. Richard Sharples regarding the "forthcoming independence of the neighbouring Bahamas," Governor Sharples and an aide were "shot dead."[4]

There has been speculation that the prince might one day be "targeted by IRA assassins," and "Di has confided to friends her belief that Charles 'has a death wish.'"[5] In fact, an IRA "killer-turned-informer" has disclosed that "he was involved in an aborted plot to kill Prince Charles and Princess Diana" in which "the Irish Republican Army asked him to kill the couple at a rock concert at London's Dominion Theater on July 20, 1983."[6] Recalling the IRA's successful assassination of Mountbatten, Prince Charles decried the death, "through the agency of some of the

1. The London Bureau of People, p. 34. Prince William's injury required a seventy-minute operation to fix a depressed fracture on his skull.
2. Cathcart, pp. 87, 98.
3. Junor, pp. 80, 86.
4. Cathcart, p. 138.
5. The London Bureau of People, p. 35.
6. The Associated Press, "IRA member tells of plot in '83 to kill royal couple," *The Denver Post*, 29 Nov. 1992, p. 3A.

most cowardly minds imaginable," of "a man who was desperately trying to sow the seeds of peace for future generations." To the prince, Mountbatten became "a lifeless reminder of that dark, inexplicable side of man's nature, which brings death and misery to countless people all over the world."[1]

On January 26, 1994, a crowd of several thousand watched as a university student in Australia interrupted an outdoor ceremony at which the prince was about to speak. Apparently lacking concern for his own safety, the prince hardly reacted when the student "ran out of a crowd, lunged at him and fired two blank shots from a starter's pistol...."[2] "Noted the Daily Mirror: 'Ice-cool Prince Charles shrugged off the attack that could have cost him his life.' Independent Television News said the incident 'may have done more for the prince's reputation than a legion of public relations staff.'"[3] Then, on February 8, 1994, a New Zealander sprayed air-freshener at the prince as he "chatted with well-wishers...in Auckland, the country's largest city."[4] As the guarantor of Israel's security, or in some other internationally prominent capacity, the prince would be an even more enticing target. (Consider, for example, the Muslim terrorist attempts on the life of the then Secretary General of the United Nations, Boutros Boutros-Ghali.)

After his 1981 wedding to Diana, Prince Charles took some precautions. What was the couple's Highgrove home has "a steel-lined room for use in the event of an attack by terrorists. This is on the first floor, and measures twenty feet square; the staff at Highgrove call it the 'iron room'—though it is made entirely of steel. The room has been constructed in such a fashion that, if necessary, the whole room can fall intact onto the ground floor, even if the rest of the house is destroyed. Inside are medical supplies, long-lasting food and drinks, radio transmitters, air purifiers and special lavatories, all of which would enable the occupants to survive inside the 'iron room' for several months." It was at Highgrove that the prince held

1. Junor, pp. 145-146.
2. "Charles shows his princely cool under attack," *The Denver Post,* 27 Jan. 1994, p. 8A.
3. "Attack gives career boost to Charles," *The Denver Post,* 28 Jan. 1994, p. 2A.
4. "Anti-royalist charged in attack on Charles," *The Denver Post,* 8 Feb. 1994, p. 6A.

his "board meetings," where "the directors of what is known (behind his back) as 'Prince Charles Limited'" gathered.[1]

The author would perhaps be remiss if he failed to mention at least some of the potentially fatal accidents experienced and witnessed by the prince to date. Indeed, Prince Charles is known to be a bit of a "daredevil." In 1972, although he "had been driving fast sports cars since the age of nineteen, and was good at it," the prince, at "the invitation of world champion racing driver Graham Hill to have a spin," "nearly killed himself in a Formula II racing car," having ignorantly run dry tires on a wet track.[2] More recently, Prince Charles witnessed the death of a close friend and the severe injury of that friend's wife in an avalanche—one that the prince very narrowly escaped—during an off-course skiing adventure. Finally, recall that in 1990, the prince nearly shattered his right arm in a polo fall.

We should keep in mind that what would have been construed as a fatal wound at the time of John's apocalyptic vision is often survivable today with prompt and proper medical care. Even so, however, the Apocalypse states clearly that the AntiChrist will be wounded "to death" (Rev 13:3, Gk.); at a minimum, his fatal wound will result in an actual appearance of death. It seems plausible, therefore, that the world shall view his subsequent recovery as a resurrection. We have already seen that Prince Charles and the royal family, besides supporting good forms of alternative medicine, also favor various forms of demonic healing.

---

1. Hoey, *Charles & Diana: The Tenth Anniversary,* pp. 136, 143.
2. Junor, pp. 119-120.

14

The Image and Mark of the Beast

Then I saw another beast rise up from the Earth, and it [he] had two horns like a lamb and spoke as if a dragon. And it [he] produces [brings about] all the authority of the first beast in its sight, and causes the Earth and those dwelling therein *to think* that they should worship [revere, honor, do homage to, defer to] the first beast, whose deadly wound was healed. And it [he] produces great signs, so that it [he] even makes fire come down out of heaven [the atmosphere] onto the Earth in the sight of men. And it [he] deceives those dwelling on the Earth by the signs which it [he] was granted to do in the presence of the beast, saying to those dwelling on the Earth to make an image to the beast who had the wound of the sword and lived. And it [he] was granted to give a vibration of air[1] to the image of the beast, that the image of the beast might *both* utter sound [speak] and cause as many as would not worship the image of the beast to be killed. And it [he] makes [compels] all, both small and great, rich and poor, free and slave, so that it[2] might give to them a mark [stamp] on their right hand or on their foreheads, and that no one *should* be able to buy or sell except one who has the mark, or the name of the beast, or the number of his name. Here is wisdom: Let him who has understanding calculate the number of the beast; for it is the number of a man, and his number *is* 666....

Then a third angel followed them, saying with a loud voice, "If anyone worships the beast and its [his] image, and receives *its [his]* mark on his forehead or on his hand, even he shall also drink of the wine of the fury [indignation, wrath] of God, having been mixed without dilution in the cup of His wrath. And *he* shall be tormented in fire and brimstone in the presence of the holy angels and in the presence of The Lamb; and the smoke of their torment ascends forever and ever. And those worshiping the beast and its [his] image, even if anyone receives the mark of its [his] name, *shall* have no rest day or night." Here is *the* patience [endurance] of the saints; here *are* those who keep the commandments of God and the faith of Jesus. (Rev 13:11-18, 14:9-12, Gk.)

1. Compare "a vibration of air" with today's electronic speakers and speech synthesis. Interestingly, the two most popular commercial speech-recognition software packages bear the satanic titles "Dragon NaturallySpeaking" and "DragonDictate." From Dragon Systems, both have a red dragon logo. *PC World* wrote, "The accuracy of the program was almost scary."
2. This may refer to the image of the beast.

How will we recognize the coming image and mark of the beast for what they truly are? What is already known about the image of the beast? *First,* it will represent the AntiChrist in some manner. As shown, Prince Charles' coat of arms is a literal depiction of the first beast. *Second,* the image will speak, though not necessarily understand speech. *Third,* unregenerate men will worship it. Biblically, worship can include prostration before (lying face down on the ground), kneeling before, stretching forth a hand toward, kissing a hand (e.g., as is done to the pope), or bowing of the forehead. *Fourth,* the image will be associated with buying and selling, and with a mark or stamp (e.g., a tattoo). The Greek text *might* also allow for the possibility of an implantable electronic bio-chip, which, in the fashion of integrated circuits generally, is made through a technological process involving a series of photo-graphic plates or "stamps."

What do we know about the mark itself? *First,* it will be placed upon or *maybe* in the right hands or foreheads of eternally lost, divinely condemned men and women. *Second,* those who do not receive it, may not be permitted to buy or sell. *Third,* it may contain either "the name of the beast, or <u>the number of his name</u>" (cf. Rev 13:17); for the saints shall "overcome the beast, his image, and <u>his mark, of the number of his name</u>" (Rev 15:2, Gk.; cf. 12:10-11, 20:4). The "number of his name," or the "number of the beast," is six hundred and sixty-six (Rev 13:18), which could conceivably take the form of three sixes.

Already, much of the industrialized world uses electronic cash registers to scan bar-codes—a kind of mark or stamp—on groceries and other items when they are purchased, inventoried, and sold. Many of these registers have voice-synthesis capability. In other words, they speak. Further, the infrared scanners attached to them are capable of reading certain types of permanent, invisible ink. As this author first observed in *1987,* if the world's major governments move to eliminate their respective currencies, opting instead to do all monetary transactions electronically, it would be relatively easy for them to require each of their citizens to obtain an *invisible, permanent bar-code tattoo* on the right hand or forehead. Under such circumstances, developing nations might feel compelled to follow suit, eventually resulting in a worldwide system of monetary subjugation.

In addition to incorporating the increasingly popular number of the beast (666), his name, or his superscription (cf. Matt 22:17-21),[1] such a mark could, for example, consist of some form of international social security number. This would facilitate access to an individual's personal information, including bank accounts. To purchase or sell an item, a person with such a mark would necessarily stretch forth his or her right hand (cf. Ps 44:20-21), or bow his or her forehead, toward a scanner.

Does such a scheme sound far-fetched? What if a cash register had an image of the beast upon it (e.g., a copy of Prince Charles' coat of arms), or an image of the AntiChrist himself? What if it had a recorded message from the AntiChrist which it delivered audibly, by voice synthesis, when used?

In fact, several governments around the world are now moving toward cashless systems, thinking that they will not only be more efficient, but also less susceptible to certain kinds of crime—electronic excepted, of course. As Kah points out, a surprising number of countries have already issued, and others plan to issue, new national currencies that would eventually share a common *international* holographic image. Due to rapid technological advances, however, it now appears that the world community may further conspire to go directly to an invisible, bar-code based, monetary system and currency.[2] Various governments and corporations have already experimented with similar marks, not to mention integrated-circuit (bio-chip) implants (e.g., in animals and human test-subjects, including some military personnel, in the United States and Europe). In early March 1996, Cable News Network (CNN) aired the story that *Prince Charles and his two sons,*

1. Note that Queen Elizabeth II currently has her image and superscription as the so-called "Defender of the Faith" on British coinage, and the two-pence is imprinted with Prince Charles' badge as the heir-apparent to the British throne.
2. Kah, *En Route to Global Occupation*, pp. 9-11, 201-204.

princes William and Harry, are among the first human beings to have voluntarily received such implants.[1] Diana, on the other hand, is rumored to have refused it, despite the fact that its purpose is ostensibly to permit tracking, including by satellite, of the whereabouts of certain members of the royal family.

Mondex International Limited corporation. Once again, there is a story behind the story. From the following information, largely provided by a trustworthy Canadian source who wishes to remain anonymous, it appears that the British monarchy may ultimately control the development and implementation of at least some of the key cashless technologies. An excellent example is the Mondex International corporation. Mondex International came out of Prince Charles' bank, the NATWEST Group, which, like most if not all the British banks, is controlled by masons. Mondex, which uses a three-ring masonic device as part of its heraldic achievement, is supplying technology that could perhaps one day facilitate the implementation of the mark of the beast. In fact, *Mondex itself* has *directly* associated its electronic chip, which is packaged as a button-sized device called an "iButton" and pronounced "eye-button," with the "all-seeing eye" of Lucifer in the capstone of the seal of the Illuminati.[2] Mondex is showing, in other words, that it is an Illuminati technology. Being "fully auditable," with no true privacy, it not only stores "cash," but also transactions[3] (e.g., purchases) and other personal information. That is, it is much more than just a replacement for "cash." Although MasterCard now owns 51% of Mondex, the NATWEST Group nevertheless controls the company, which is attempting to work with hundreds of the world's

1. Texe Marrs, in *Project Lucid,* mentions Prince William's implant.
2. For blatant examples of "being blatant," as the author's Canadian friend would put it, visit "Wallet/index.html" and "Crypto/index.html" at "http://www.ibutton.com/" to see Mondex's "Electronic Wallet" and "Cryptographic iButton" on the Internet.
3. According to Janet Crane, President and CEO of *Mondex International,* who spoke to reporter Nial McKay on March 12, 1997, in Los Angeles, "The Mondex card system is fully auditable. There is an electronic record of the time, date, amount, and participants of each transaction" (see "http://insight.mcmaster.ca/org/efc/pages/mondex/"). Other Mondex International employees have attempted to contradict this claim. However, based upon who it is that stated the technology *is* "fully auditable," we may presume this to be the case.

major banks and corporations to become *the* global electronic currency standard. Besides MasterCard, shareholders include the Royal Bank of Canada—which intends to implant prisoners, parolees, and others (e.g., residents of *Guelph* Ontario,[1] where the technology is now in use)—as well as the Canadian Imperial Bank of Commerce (CIBC), British Telecom, etc.[2] Consider this article:

> SAN FRANCISCO — Mondex International, the electronic cash vendor, is leading a double life.
>
> While Mondex International promotes its electronic cash scheme as private to users, it also admits that it is auditable to government organizations, such as the tax authorities.
>
> In an internal memo[3] the company advised its Canadian licensees of the "significant risk" to the electronic cash system's creditability if privacy campaigners discover that the system is auditable.
>
> With Mondex, electronic credits are downloaded from a bank to a microprocessor on a user's smart card. Users can then buy goods or services with these credits by transferring them to a merchant's card at a store. The merchant then cashes these credits at a bank.
>
> The strength of the system is that it transfers electronic credits from the user's microprocessor to the merchant's microprocessor, and unlike credit card systems, it is not run by a central computer program. Therefore, as with cash, each transaction is not stored, allowing Mondex to offer a modicum of privacy, company officials **say**.
>
> However privacy organizations in both in the U.K. and Canada, where Mondex has run extensive trials, are disturbed by the company's claims to privacy because users' cards store the last 10 transactions, and merchant cards store the last 300 transactions.
>
> When each card comes in contact with the issuing bank's computer systems, it downloads the customer number, date, and amount of each transaction. These records can then be compared with each other.
>
> Privacy campaigners argue that the company's choice of 10

1. Recall that Queen Elizabeth II and Prince Charles are of the House of Guelph, descending from *Godfroi de Bouillon* through Henry the Black of the Guelph Line. This is the most prominent strand of the Merovingian lineage, which is the most prominent lineage within the Illuminati. Testing the Mondex system within a city by that name, therefore, appears to directly implicate the British monarchy and the Order of the Garter, not just the Illuminati. For more information, see Chapter 4, "Prince of this World—a *Diverse* Lineage."

2. For Mondex International's own information, visit "http://www.mondex.com/" (Mondex International), "http://www.mondexusa.com/" (Mondex USA), and "http://www.mondex.ca/" (Mondex Canada).

3. See "http://insight.mcmaster.ca/org/efc/pages/mondex/cibc-memo.30jan97.html".

transactions for a user's card and 300 transactions for a merchant's card will give Mondex a record of about 90 per cent of all transactions.

"Think about it — how many times do you use cash between trips to the [Automated Banking Machine]. I have studied this and most people say that they would carry out less than 10 transactions. That means that Mondex is not cash-like[1] and does not offer much privacy", said David Jones, president of the Electronic Frontier Canada and an assistant professor of computer science at McMaster University in Hamilton.

Analysts agree that once records are kept, the information can be used and analyzed by the bank or sold to a third party, if not now, then in the future....

Mondex has carried out pilot studies in both Swindon in the United Kingdom and the university town of **Guelph**, Ont.

"There has been a well-orchestrated deception worldwide about the privacy of Mondex", said Simon Davies, visiting fellow at the computer security research center of The London School of Economics in England and director of Privacy International in Washington D.C. "The statement that only a cardholder will have access to the entries on their card is an outright lie. Mondex keeps an audit trail of transactions."

At Mondex, different divisions have made conflicting statements about the auditability of the electronic cash system.

"We do not keep a record of every transaction, but there is a way to track payments", said Cynthia Bengier, vice-president of product management and marketing for Mondex USA in an interview with the IDG News Service. "Mondex is auditable."

Meanwhile Mondex officials in Canada say that it is impossible to keep track of all transactions because they all happen off-line. "There is no way that we can keep a full audit trail", said Tim McNaughton, manager of the pilot and implementation at the Mondex division of the Royal Bank of Canada in Toronto. "Everything happens off-line. It's not fully auditable."...

"If anybody could really establish a record of the public's cash spending patterns, then that information would be very valuable indeed", said Zona's Ryder. "My fear is that Mondex is not testing the technology in **Guelph**", said P.J. Lilly, a researcher and rights activist based in **Guelph**. "After all, the technology has not changed since the Swindon trial. What they are really testing is the public's acceptance of the scheme."

However Mondex USA's Bengier maintains that this is not on the Mondex agenda. "Mondex international is currently in the process of establishing a code of practice[2] to ensure privacy", she

---

1. See "http://insight.mcmaster.ca/org/efc/pages/mondex/".
2. Of course, a "code of practice" is only as legitimate as its practitioner, and governments and their financial agencies are known these days for their abuse of such information.

said.[1]

Mondex International franchises its system for whole countries or regions. The Royal Bank of Canada and CIBC are the franchisees for Canada, whereas Paz Oil and Discount Investment Corporation (DIC) are being used to implement (strong-arm really) the Mondex system in Israel. Paz Oil, formerly called Shell Company of Palestine, is a member of Shell Trading and Transport, which the House of Windsor controls. On July 21, 1997, the Mondex International Newsroom released the following information:

> Discount Investment Corporation (DIC), part of the IDB Holding Group and Paz Oil Co. today announced that they have purchased the Mondex electronic cash franchise rights for Israel....
>
> DIC is one of Israel's largest investment companies with holdings in many corporations that are cash oriented and are natural targets for electronic cash....
>
> Paz Oil Company Ltd. is Israel's largest supplier of refined petroleum products. Together with some 20 subsidiaries, affiliates and a nationwide marketing network, Paz is a highly integrated concern involved in every aspect of the country's petroleum industry....
>
> Mondex is a new payment smartcard which brings together the advantages of paying by cash with the convenience of paying by card. **Mondex is being introduced by leading banks and retailers throughout the world.** This is because Mondex utilises smartcard technology, which works off-line, and provides an extremely cost-effective solution for low value payments both in the real and the virtual world.
>
> In contrast to previous Mondex franchise operators, DIC and Paz have taken the decision to develop Mondex with a coalition of partners from banking, industry and the merchant community to ensure that there is immediate widespread acceptance. The group plans to introduce Mondex in the first quarter of 1998 utilising the new MULTOS operating system for smartcards.
>
> MULTOS enables card issuers to put Mondex electronic cash securely alongside a wide range of smartcard based business services including loyalty, [membership,] transportation and healthcare....[2]

1. Niall McKay, Infoworld Canada, "Mondex's double life: E-Cash both 'private' and 'fully auditable'—Officials tell different stories on privacy and security," *IDG News Service, International Data Group, Inc.,* 7 May 1997. This same article, with links, may be visited at "http://insight.mcmaster.ca/org/efc/pages/media/infoworld.07may97.html". E-mail McKay at "niall_mckay@idg.com".
2. This sounds like a replacement for other forms of identification, not just cash.

Michael Keegan, CEO of Mondex International, said, "Mondex is rapidly becoming the dominant electronic cash system in the world, offering a truly global product, but with the flexibility to adapt to local market needs. In the fast paced economy of Israel, Mondex provides a **future-proofed technology**[1] which will deliver real benefits to consumers, merchants and businesses for many years to come."

Mondex is considered the most 'cash-like' of the various electronic smartcard products in use or being tested in pilots around the world. Mondex International Limited is an independent payments company that is majority owned by MasterCard International in addition to twenty-seven other major organisations across Europe, North America, Asia and Australasia. **Headquartered in London**, Mondex International is responsible for managing the global development of the Mondex technology which supports MasterCard's global chip platform.[2]

It has been suggested that "Mondex" is an anagram for "Demon X," meaning *ten demons*. Another source, however, whom the author has not met, asserts that "Mondex" represents a combination of "monetary" for *money* and "dexter" for *right-hand,* or *money for the right hand.* Further, he states, "MONDEX International, the premiere cashless smartcard system, is set for rapid global implementation. Founded in 1993 by NATWEST ([a] personal bank of the royal family), and 51% owned by MASTERCARD, it is now the decided victor of the electronic cash systems. The first countries [slated] to employ MONDEX nationwide by 1998 are the UK, Canada, Australia, New Zealand, Israel, Hong Kong, China, Indonesia, Macau, Malaysia, [the] Philippines, Singapore, Thailand, India, Taiwan and Sri Lanka.... 'This is the final stage in becoming a global reality,' said Robin O'Kelly of Mondex International. 'With MasterCard's backing, there's nothing to stop Mondex now from becoming the global standard.'"[3]

1. A "future-proofed" technology is one that is Year-2000 (Y2K) compliant. In other words, when commercial financial institutions begin to fall like dominoes between 1999 and 2001 due to unsolvable system conflicts and crashes caused by the inability to distinguish the year 2000 from the year 1900, so that the world's industrial economies are thrown into chaos, Mondex will be there to help. Should we already be in the Tribulation Period, the AntiChrist could perhaps proclaim, "Mondex to the rescue!," or something similar. It's scary, isn't it?
2. Mondex International Newsroom, "Discount Investment Corporation and Paz Oil," 21 July 1997. Please note that this information was provided through e-mail to the author, and that there is a possibility that it represents two articles rather than one. This is currently unclear.
3. Ken Crouch.

Lucifer's seal or mark is on its way. Kah comments, "The technology for such a worldwide electronic system is already in place.... In the not too distant future, products on our grocery store shelves may become labeled with an invisible bar code. The Universal Product Code (UPC), which many have complained is an eye sore on product packaging, will still be there. However, only the [laser] scanner will be able to read it. Once this transition to an invisible code begins to take place, it will only be a matter of time before humans are tattooed with a similar mark."[1] Steven C. Wright quotes Dr. Kirk E. Koch, "a professor who has lectured at over 100 universities in 65 countries on the New World Order under the United Nations," as stating, "each person will have a registered number, without which he will not be allowed to buy or sell, and there will be one universal world church. Anyone who refuses to take part in this universal system will have no right to exist."[2] The appearance of the AntiChrist, as well as the institution of his mark, could be very near.

1. Kah, *En Route to Global Occupation,* pp. 12, 150.
2. Wright, "Environmental Warfare" video.

15

Conclusion

Is Prince Charles of Wales *the* AntiChrist? When John the Baptizer, having "heard...the works of Christ," sent disciples to ask Jesus, "Are you the Coming One, or do we expect another?," do you not suppose that John should have already known the answer? Indeed, The LORD replied, "relate to John the things which you hear and see: blind *ones* see and lame *ones* walk about; lepers are cleansed and deaf *ones* hear; dead *ones* are raised and poor ones are evangelized [hear the Gospel]. And blessed is he who is not offended in Me" (Matt 11:2-5, Gk.; cf. 9:1-8, 9:18, 9:24-33). Was Jesus The Messiah, the Coming One? When asked, he did not respond by saying "yes," but instead pointed to those signs that scripturally, as well as according to rabbinic tradition, The Messiah *alone* could perform (e.g., see Isa 29:18-19, 35:5-7; Luke 4:18-21 {cf. Isa 61:1-2*a*}; John 5:36, 10:25-27, 10:36-38; cf. John 3:1-2, 9:30-33, 20:30-31). In other words, Jesus did not ask John to "leap before he looked." Although Jesus had yet to accomplish His primary mission as Messiah the Son of Joseph, not having suffered the great tribulation of the cross for our sins and risen bodily from the grave to impart to us eternal life, his credentials were unequivocal. If John knew and *believed* the scriptures—even though Jesus' actions were not to that point what he, nor the rest of Israel for that matter, had anticipated—he could arrive at only one conclusion. John had two choices. He could disbelieve, or he could set aside his predispositions and face the scriptural facts; for John, like Israel in general, had looked not just for Messiah the Son of Joseph, who would suffer, die, and rise from the dead as The Lamb of God who takes away the sins of the world, but for Messiah the Son of David, who would gloriously conquer and reign. If John had concluded that Jesus might not be The Messiah because he had not yet seen Him accomplish His primary mission, let alone throw off Rome's oppressive yoke, John would not just have been wrong, but he would have demonstrated a distinct lack of faith in both the written and living Word of God. Friend, consider this matter.

Let us ask once again, "Is Prince Charles *the* AntiChrist?" His name (and title), "Prince Charles of Wales," calculates to exactly 666, and it does so in both English and Hebrew! The prince is not only of Roman lineage, as the AntiChrist must be, but he also claims descent from royalty worldwide, including Israel's King David! He may actually be a descendant of Israel's Danites, from whom, according to some early Christian theologians, the AntiChrist was to come, and he supposedly descends from Islam's Mohammed. The prince also appears to have a stronger occult Merovingian lineage, which is said to derive from Jesus and Mary Magdalene, than King Juan Carlos of Spain. His ancestors include not only the Habsburgs, but also Godfroi de Bouillon, giving him a greater claim, should he choose to make it, to the crusader title "King of Jerusalem." With such a diverse lineage, Prince Charles will, if he is the AntiChrist, attain prominence in international affairs—especially where Jerusalem, the City of David, is concerned; for Judaism, Roman Catholicism, and Islam are the three major religions that have historically vied for Jerusalem.

Prince Charles' historically unique heraldic coat of arms is a literal, graphic representation of the beast described in Daniel and in the Apocalypse; it represents and typifies the AntiChrist and his eventual dominion. Its major symbols include the red dragon, which was central to his investiture as the Prince of Wales, the lion-leopard-bear first beast, and a unicorn with eyes like those of a man. Where the pagan religions and peoples of the world are concerned, the prince, merely by virtue of the satanic symbols on his arms, is sure to be warmly received.

Highly respected worldwide, Prince Charles is *extremely* well-connected—royally, religiously, environmentally, politically, militarily, financially, and otherwise—having personally met most of the world's top leaders and visited their respective nations. The prince is also very wealthy, and looking for a major role to play in mankind's future. Indeed, not only has Prince Charles already requested to become the King of Europe, but it appears that he may be personally responsible for bringing about the entire Mideast peace process since the London Agreement of 1987.

While many view him as a "Christian," the prince—like other New Agers—is thoroughly antichristian, coming from a family with a long history of involvement in Satanism and the occult. As the supposed "Prince of Psychics," who has a great interest in solving the world's major problems, Prince Charles would like to introduce mankind to a new age of cosmic consciousness. He not only advocates rapprochement between Protestant Christianity and Roman Catholicism, but as an ecumenist, he is not opposed to unification of the world's religions. In fact, as one of the most influential and powerful members of the Illuminati ever, he has publicly proclaimed that when he becomes king, he would like to be known as the "Defender of Faith," meaning *of all religious beliefs,* as opposed to "the Faith," or just Protestant Christianity. The prince has shown himself to be an enthusiast when it comes to participating in the various occult rituals of pagan cultures that he has visited around the world. As just one example, the prince has now apparently undergone the ceremonies necessary to become a Muslim, taking an Arabic title meaning "The Guardian of faith," something which has prompted speculation among Muslims that Prince Charles intends to become the leader of the Muslim world.

With the exception of Prince Charles, no human being in the past twenty-five hundred years, not even in contemporary history, has met more than half of the biblical requirements to be *the* AntiChrist. Yet Prince Charles not only is "fully qualified," but he also meets or exceeds all reasonable, extra-biblical expectations.

Get Involved

Now that you have read this book, perhaps you realize its *immense* significance to this generation, as well as to future theologians and historians. It is the author's and the publisher's strong conviction that *every Christian alive today* needs to hear the vital information contained in *The AntiChrist and a Cup of Tea*. Although called and chosen by God, neither the publisher nor the author can possibly accomplish such an enormous task alone. Given the apparent hour in the current countdown to the Great Tribulation and The LORD's return, this task *demands* the involvement of informed Christians everywhere. Fellow laborer in Christ, *you* can help, *you* can make a difference. To start, you can tell your Christian brothers and sisters that this material *exists*. Next, you can give the order forms at the back of this book to others who need to read it. Finally, you can become a distributor of this book. If you are a Christian pastor or part of a Christian ministry, or you are a Christian host of a radio or television program, God has given you the power to alert the body of Christ, the true Church, to this material. (Remember Mordechai's warning to Esther.) If you have the means to help place this work into the hands of other Christians, *use them*. Know that the very fact that God has allowed this material to be released at this juncture in history evidences that the clock is rapidly winding down. Finally, realize that due to its amazing contents, *this book constitutes one of the greatest evangelistic tools given to this generation*. Exploit it! Win the lost while you still can, and be faithful to Christ!

To facilitate and encourage wide distribution, this book may be purchased at full retail or at volume discounts. For more information, visit the Prophecy House web site at "http://www.prophecyhouse.com". If you are interested, but do not have Internet access, you may also write to Prophecy House, Inc., at the address on the title page.

Message of Salvation. Friend, if you have yet to meet

the one and only true God, there is *no better time* than now to do so:

> In the beginning was The Word, and The Word was with God, and The Word was God. This One was in the beginning with God. All things came into being by Him, and apart from Him nothing came into being that has come into being. In Him was Life, and The Life was The Light of men. And The Light shines in the darkness, and the darkness did not comprehend nor overwhelm Him.... He was in the world, and the world was made through Him, and the world did not know Him. He came to Israel, His inheritance, and those who were His own did not receive Him. But as many as received Him, to them He gave authority to become the children of God, to those who believe in His name, who were born, not of bloods, nor of the will of the flesh, nor of the will of man, but of God. AND THE WORD BECAME *A MAN MADE OF* FLESH AND DWELT AMONG US; and we beheld His glory, glory as of the only begotten from The Father, full of grace and truth.... And of His fullness we all have received, and grace for grace. For the Torah [Law] was given through Moses, *but* the grace and the truth were realized through Yeshua The Messiah [Jesus The Christ]. (John 1:1-17, Gk.; see Deut 18:15-22)

> For there are three who bear witness in heaven: The Father, The Word, and The Holy Spirit; and these three are *united as* One (Echad). And there are three that bear witness on earth: The Spirit, the water, and the blood; and these three are in agreement. (I John 5:7-8, Gk.; see Deut 6:4 in Heb.)

If you do not know Messiah Yeshua (Christ Jesus), The great God and Savior of Israel, as your personal God and Savior, then please consider these truths. We are all sinners (Rom 3:23), and the penalty for sin in God's Torah is eternal death (Rom 6:23) and separation from God our Creator (2 Th 1:5-10). We are *all* condemned to eternal death by the Torah (Law) of God for our sins, yet Yeshua came to save those who would believe in Him, who know that He is The Lamb of God (John 1:29) who made atonement for our sins with His own blood (Rom 3:24-26; Eph 2:1-10). As the only sinless man to ever live, who *alone* is both God and man, Yeshua had power to never transgress the Torah of God (1 John 3:4-9, AKJV; see Gal 3:10). As a sinless man, voluntarily subjected to the Divine Law, Yeshua as our High Priest offered Himself up once, as The Lamb of God, to be slain for *our* sins (Heb 7:22-27, 9:1 to 10:18; see Rom 6:8-10). Yeshua, in His great love for us, freely offered His own blood, His *life,* upon an altar made in the form of a wooden cross, to atone for us: "For the life of the flesh *is* in the blood, and I have given it to you upon the altar to make atonement for your souls; for it *is* the blood *due to the life that* makes atonement for the soul" (Lev 17:11, Heb.; see Heb 7 to 10).

Though He had never sinned, Yeshua took the sins of all who would believe in Him as Lord and Savior—past, present, and future—upon Himself. He paid the ultimate penalties of death and Sheol (Hades or Hell) in full for all who believe (John 19:30; see Ps 16:10; Isa 53; Heb 2:9-28). Yeshua said, "Most assuredly, I say to you, if anyone obeys My word, he shall never see death" (John 8:51). Those who will not believe, however, must pay these penalties for themselves—for all eternity. As the scripture says, "it is appointed to men to die <u>once</u>, but after this judgment" (Heb 9:27, Gk.). And what will be the outcome of the judgment? As it is written,

> He who believes in Him is not condemned; but he who does not believe is condemned already, because he has not believed in the name of the only begotten Son of God. And this is the condemnation, that Light has come into the world, and men loved darkness rather than Light, because their deeds were evil. For everyone who does evil hates The Light and does not come to The Light, lest his deeds should be exposed. But everyone who does what is **true** comes to The Light, so that all may see that his actions are accomplished through God. He who believes in The Son has everlasting life; and he who does not believe The Son will not see life, but the wrath of God abides upon him. (John 3:18-21, 3:36)

> Beware lest anyone take you captive through philosophy and empty deceit, according to the tradition of men, according to the basic principles of the world, and not according to The Messiah. (Col 2:8; see Prov 14:12)

> Do you not know that the unrighteous will not inherit the kingdom of God? Do not be deceived. Neither fornicators, nor idolaters, nor adulterers, nor homosexuals, nor sodomites, nor thieves,

nor covetous, nor drunkards, nor revilers, nor extortioners will inherit the kingdom of God. (1 Cor 6:9-10)

There shall not be found among you anyone who makes his son or his daughter pass through the fire, or one who practices witch-craft, or a soothsayer, or one who interprets omens, or a sorcerer, or one who conjures spells, or a medium, or a spiritist, or one who calls up the dead. For all who do these things are an abomi-nation to The LORD.... You shall be blameless before The LORD your God. For these nations which you shall dispossess listened to soothsayers and diviners; but as for you, the LORD your God has not suffered you to do so. (Deut 18:10-14)

Being sinless, Yeshua cleansed us from our sins by tak-ing them upon Himself (2 Cor 5:18-21; Gal 3:10-14). Yeshua said, "I am The Way, and The Truth, and The Life: no one comes to The Father, but through Me" (John 14:6; see 1 Tim 2:5). Because He took our sins upon Himself, and, spiritually speaking, became sin in our place (2 Cor 5:21), His righteousness required that He pay the price which is written in His own Torah, the Law of God, and that price was death. However, because He is God, it was not possible for death or the grave, which He Himself created for sinners, to hold Him. Yeshua, who had power to both lay down His Life and take it up again, rose three days and three nights later (Matt 12:40). God will save all who repent, who forsake their sins for Him, by receiving Yeshua as LORD and Savior of their lives (2 Peter 3:9; see John 15:13-14 and 1 Cor 1:18).

SALVATION IS A *FREE GIFT* FROM GOD; our "good" works can *never* justify us before Him. Where God is con-cerned, *all* of the "righteousnesses" of man are like filthy garments (Isa 64:6). No sinful human being can enter the Kingdom of Heaven based upon his own merits: "For by grace you have been saved through faith, and that not of yourselves; it is the gift of God, not of works, lest anyone should boast. For we are His workmanship, created in Messiah Yeshua for good works, which God prepared beforehand that we should walk in them" (Eph 2:8-10). Yeshua lives forevermore as Lord and Savior of all who believe in His name, who obey His commandments by the

power of The Holy Spirit which He has given to them
(Acts 2:1-40; see 1 John 3:10-24). Yeshua said,

> If you love Me, keep My commandments. And I will pray to The
> Father, and He will give you another Helper, that He may abide
> with you forever, even The Spirit of Truth, whom the world can-
> not receive, because it neither sees Him nor knows Him; but you
> know Him, for He dwells with you and will be in you. I will not
> leave you orphans; I will come to you. A little while longer and
> the world will see Me no more, but you will see Me. Because I
> live, you will live also. At that day, you will know that I am in My
> Father, and you in Me, and I in you. He who has My command-
> ments and obeys them, it is he who loves Me. And he who loves
> Me will be loved by My Father, and I will love him and reveal
> Myself to him.... If anyone loves Me, he will keep My word; and
> My Father will love him, and We will come to him and make Our
> home with him. He who does not love Me does not keep My
> words; and the word which you hear is not Mine but the Father's
> who sent Me. These things I have spoken to you while being pre-
> sent with you. But The Helper, The Holy Spirit, whom The Father
> will send in My name, He will teach you all things, and bring to
> your remembrance all things that I said to you.
> (John 14:15-21,23-26)

> For I am not ashamed of the good news of Messiah, for it is the
> power of God to salvation for everyone who believes, TO THE JEW
> FIRST and also to the Greek. For in it the righteousness of God is
> revealed from faith to faith; as it is written, "But the JUST [RIGHT-
> EOUS] BY FAITH shall live." (Rom 1:16-17, Gk.; see Acts 15:7-9,
> Rom 3:21 to 5:21, 7, 10)

> But what does it say? "The Word is near you, in your mouth and
> in your heart"—that is, The Word of faith which [whom] we
> preach, that if you confess with your mouth The Lord Yeshua, and
> believe in your heart that God raised Him from the dead, you shall
> be saved; for with the heart *one* believes to righteousness, and
> with *the* mouth *one* confesses to Salvation. For the scripture says,
> "Whoever believes in Him will not be put to shame." For there is
> no distinction between Jew and Greek; for the same Lord over all
> is rich to all who call upon Him. For "whoever calls upon the
> name of The Lord shall be saved." (Rom 10:8-13, Gk.)

> And this is the message that we have heard from Him and we
> announce to you, that God is Light, and no darkness is in
> Him—none. If we say that we have fellowship with Him and we
> walk in the darkness, we lie and do not practice the truth. But if
> we walk in The Light, as He is in The Light, we have fellowship

with one another, and the blood of Messiah Yeshua His Son cleanses us from all sin. If we say that we have no sin, we deceive ourselves, and The Truth is not in us. If we confess our sins, He is faithful and righteous to forgive us our sins and to cleanse us from all unrighteousness. If we say that we have not sinned, we make Him *out to be* a liar, and His Word is not in us. (1 John 1:5-10, Gk.; see James 5:13-16)

But even if our good news is veiled, it is veiled to those who are perishing, in whom the god of this age [(Satan or Lucifer)] has blinded the minds of those who do not believe, lest The Light of the good news of the glory of the Messiah, who is the image of God, should shine on them.... Therefore, if anyone is in Messiah, he is a new creation; old things have passed away; behold, all things have become new. (2 Cor 4:3-4, 5:17, Gk.)

The Spirit Himself bears witness with our spirit that we are children of God. (Rom 8:16, Gk.)

For the message [Word] of the cross is foolishness to those who are truly perishing, but to us who are being saved *it is the* power of God. For it is written, "I will destroy the wisdom of the wise, and I will set aside the understanding of the prudent." Where is the wise? Where is the scribe? Where is the disputer of this age? Has not God made foolish the wisdom of this world? For since, in the wisdom of God, the world by *its* wisdom did not know God, it pleased God by the foolishness of preaching, to save those who believe. And since Judaeans [Jews] request a sign, and Greeks seek *worldly* wisdom, we thus preach Messiah crucified...the power of God and the wisdom of God. Because the foolishness of God is wiser than men, and the weakness of God is stronger than men.... But we speak the wisdom of God in a mystery, even the hidden wisdom which God ordained [predetermined] before the ages for our glory.... But the natural man does not receive the things of The Spirit of God, for they are foolishness to him; nor can he know *them,* because they are spiritually discerned. (1 Cor 1:18-25, 2:7, 2:14)

Friend, if you *have* received Jesus, read the Word of God, so that you may be instructed in the truth and the knowledge of God. Finally, seek regular fellowship with other Christians, "and so much the more as you see the Day [of Christ] approaching" (Heb 10:22-25). Shalom.

Product	Price	Quantity	Total	Discount*	SHIP TO:
THE ANTICHRIST *and a Cup of Tea*	$19.95			–	Name and address
A&CT book + Lineage Chart	$26.95			–	
1-hr A&CT VHS Presentation	$19.95			–	
1-hr A&CT VHS Interview	$19.95			–	
3-hr A&CT Audio Overview	$15.95			–	
Messiah, History, and the Tribulation Period	Send note to *Prophecy House* for availability notification.				Phone:

Sum total(s) and discount(s) above as SUBTOTAL

Non-retailers and non-501c3 customers, add 3.8% in CO or 6.25% in OH ☞ **TAX**

See chart at bottom for SHIPPING

U.S. dollars TOTAL

Satisfaction Guaranteed! Orders enjoy a 30-day money-back guarantee. All returns must be in salable condition and include original proof of purchase. Shipping charges will *not* be reimbursed.

Quantity	Shipping
Single item, U.S.A.	$5.00
Single item, *non-U.S.A.*	$10.00
Additional items, U.S.A.	$2.00 each
Additional items, *non-U.S.A.*	$5.00 each

It's Easy To Order—Pick Your Method*

☐ Check or money order enclosed
☐ MasterCard ☐ VISA
☐ AMEX ☐ Discover

Card number:

Expiration date:

Name on card:

Signature:

Signature required on all credit card purchases.

Make payment to: Prophecy House, Inc.

*To pay by **credit card**, call 800-247-6553 or 888-32BOOKS, or fax this form to 419-281-6883. *Outside the U.S.A.*, call 419-281-1802. If the above is obsolete, *and only then*, sign and mail this form or fax 303-693-8093. You may also order on-line at "www.prophecyhouse.com/order". To use a **check** or **money order**, mail it with this form to **Prophecy House, Inc. • P.O. Box 461104 • Aurora, CO 80046-1104 • U.S.A.** *For volume discounts, call us or visit our web site.*

Product	Price	Quantity	Total	Discount*
THE ANTICHRIST *and a Cup of Tea*	$19.95			–
A&CT book + Lineage Chart	$26.95			–
1-hr A&CT VHS Presentation	$19.95			–
1-hr A&CT VHS Interview	$19.95			–
3-hr A&CT Audio Overview	$15.95			–
Messiah, History, and the Tribulation Period	Send note to *Prophecy House* for availability notification.			–
Sum total(s) and discount(s) above as SUBTOTAL				
Non-retailers and non-501c3 customers, add 3.8% in CO or 6.25% in OH ☞ **TAX**				
See chart at bottom for SHIPPING				
U.S. dollars TOTAL				

Satisfaction Guaranteed! Orders enjoy a 30-day money-back guarantee. All returns must be in salable condition and include original proof of purchase. Shipping charges will *not* be reimbursed.

Quantity	Shipping
Single item, U.S.A.	$5.00
Single item, *non-U.S.A.*	$10.00
Additional items, U.S.A.	$2.00 each
Additional items, *non-U.S.A.*	$5.00 each

SHIP TO:

Name and address

Phone:

It's Easy To Order—Pick Your Method*

☐ Check or money order enclosed
☐ MasterCard ☐ VISA
☐ AMEX ☐ Discover

Card number:

Expiration date:

Name on card:

Signature:

Signature required on all credit card purchases.

Make payment to: Prophecy House, Inc.

*To pay by **credit card**, call 800-247-6553 or 888-32BOOKS, or fax this form to 419-281-6883. *Outside the U.S.A.,* call 419-281-1802. If the above is obsolete, *and only then,* sign and mail this form or fax 303-693-8093. You may also order on-line at "www.prophecyhouse.com/order". To use a **check** or **money order**, mail it with this form to **Prophecy House, Inc. • P.O. Box 461104 • Aurora, CO 80046-1104 • U.S.A.** *For volume discounts, call us or visit our web site.*